AUTHORS, ILLUSTRATORS, AND REPRESENTATIVE BOOKS

1989   ED YOUNG
Lon Po Po:
A Red Riding Hood
Story from China

1988   PAUL FLEISCHMAN
Joyful Noise:
Poems for Two Voices
ILLUS. ERIC BEDDOWS

1988   ELOISE GREENFIELD
Nathaniel Talking
ILLUS. JAN SPIVEY GILCHRIST

1988   VIRGINIA HAMILTON
Anthony Burns:
The Defeat and Triumph
of a Fugitive Slave

1987   RUSSELL FREEDMAN
Lincoln: A Photobiography

1987   JOHN STEPTOE
Mufaro's Beautiful
Daughters:
An African Tale

1987   JANE YOLEN
Owl Moon
ILLUS. JOHN SCHOENHERR

1986   NICHOLASA MOHR
Going Home

1985   PATRICIA MACLACHLAN
Sarah, Plain and Tall

1985   CHRIS VAN ALLSBURG
The Polar Express

1982   TOSHI MARUKI
Hiroshima No Pika

1981   YOSHIKO UCHIDA
Jar of Dreams

1970s

1978   PAUL GOBLE
The Girl Who
Loved Wild Horses

1977   KATHERINE PATERSON
Bridge to Terabithia

1977   DAVID MCCORD
One at a Time

1976   JEAN FRITZ
What's the Big Idea,
Ben Franklin?
ILLUS. MARGOT TOMES

1976   BYRD BAYLOR
Hawk, I'm Your Brother
ILLUS. PETER PARNALL

1976   MILDRED TAYLOR
Roll of Thunder,
Hear My Cry

1975   TOMIE DEPAOLA
Strega Nona

1975   NATALIE BABBITT
Tuck Everlasting

1975   SHARON MATHIS
The Hundred Penny Box
ILLUS. LEO & DIANE DILLON

1975   LAURENCE YEP
Dragonwings

1974   VIRGINIA HAMILTON
M. C. Higgins, the Great

1973   SUSAN COOPER
The Dark Is Rising

1972   ARNOLD LOBEL
Frog and Toad Together

1971   MISKA MILES
Annie and the Old One
ILLUS. PETER PARNALL

1971   MURIEL FEELINGS
Moja Means One:
Swahili Counting Book
ILLUS. TOM FEELINGS

1970   BETSY BYARS
Summer of the Swans

1960s

1969   JOHN STEPTOE
Stevie

1968   DON FREEMAN
Corduroy

1968   URSULA K. LE GUIN
Wizard of Earthsea

1967   VIRGINIA HAMILTON
Zeely
ILLUS. SYMEON SHIMIN

1964   MAURICE SENDAK
Where the Wild Things Are

1964   LLOYD ALEXANDER
The Book of Three

1962   MADELEINE L'ENGLE
A Wrinkle in Time

1962   EZRA JACK KEATS
The Snowy Day

Lee Galda

Bernice E. Cullinan

Sixth Edition

Literature and the Child

CD-ROM CONTAINS VIDEO AND ON-LINE TITLE SEARCH ENGINE

☆ *Updated booklists*

☆ *Integrated discussion of all facets of diversity*

☆ *An improved and enhanced CD-ROM*

Explore children's literature with the Sixth Edition of Galda and Cullinan's highly esteemed guide

Reflecting the tone and feel of children's books, Galda and Cullinan's beautifully written and illustrated *Literature and the Child* offers your students a survey of the major genres of children's literature and discusses the numerous ways they can bring literature into their classrooms.

In this Sixth Edition, you'll find Galda and Cullinan's distinguished coverage of classic and contemporary children's literature highlighted with new examples of the latest titles, extensively updated booklists that students can consult throughout their teaching careers, and a broader discussion of books that reflect the diversity of today's society.

Throughout the book, Galda and Cullinan continue to include many teaching tips and resources that will aid future educators in their selection of literature for the children and adolescents they instruct. They also provide suggested articles from the prestigious publication, *The Horn Book Magazine* (accessible through students' free four-month subscription to InfoTrac® College Edition—see page 8 for details on this powerful online resource).

Additionally, a fully updated CD-ROM that includes a new video component, an improved title search engine, and a collection of materials designed for use by classroom teachers accompanies new copies of the Sixth Edition. This text and CD-ROM pairing ensures that your students have a strong selection of resources at their disposal.

Turn the page to begin your Preview of the Sixth Edition

preview

1

The thoroughly updated and enhanced CD-ROM—filled with valuable resources

On the CD-ROM that accompanies every new copy of *Literature and the Child,* Sixth Edition, your students will find a rich selection of tools and materials they can use in your course and in their own classrooms.

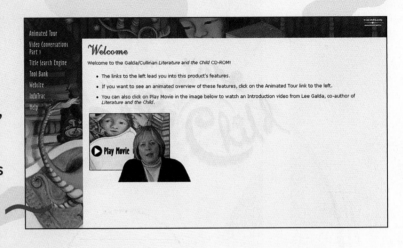

Video interviews

Video interviews with Mary Casanova, James Ransome, Debra Frasier, Lindsay Lee Johnson, Kate DiCamillo, Bonnie Graves, Avi, Lisa Westberg Peters, Lauren Stringer, and Jane Kurtz— filmed exclusively for this CD-ROM—expose your students to authors' and illustrators' creative processes and enhance their appreciation of children's literature in general.

Reflection questions prompt students to think about how the ideas presented in the videos relate to their teaching and their own understanding of children's books.

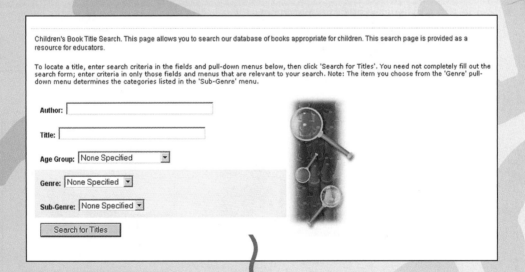

Tool Bank

The Tool Bank provides additional materials that your students can use as they share literature with children and adolescents. These materials include numerous activities, as well as tools that can help teachers and their students keep track of their work and assess their progress over time. Because the materials are created in Microsoft® Word, your students can alter them to suit their needs, thus ensuring that this resource remains a dynamic and customizable tool they can use throughout their teaching careers.

Online Title Search Engine

The CD-ROM's improved Online Title Search Engine gives your students access to an extensive database that features a comprehensive booklist that is updated yearly by the authors.

Coverage of literature that reflects the diversity of children's experience

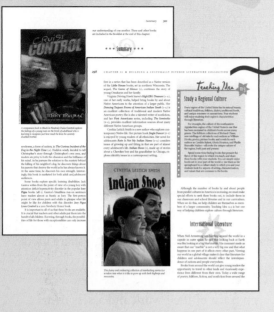

The authors reference and discuss books that explore and examine differences in culture, exceptionality, and sexual orientation, thus extending the scope of the book's diversity coverage.

Chapter 11, "Building a Culturally Diverse Literature Collection," now appears in Part II of the text, to emphasize that multiculturalism is not a "genre" unto itself, but a means of introducing young readers to a broader range of experiences, attitudes, beliefs, and customs.

Chapter 5, "Folklore," now offers more balanced coverage between European and non-European stories.

preview 4

Comprehensive, thoroughly updated booklists with hundreds of appropriate titles

As you and your students scan this edition's extensively updated and more inclusive **booklists,** you will find numerous examples of books published as recently as 2004, as well as many more books that represent multiple cultures and points of view.

Added information on literature for older children and adolescents

Enhanced coverage of young adult literature appears throughout this edition, in recognition of growing interest in this topic.

• • • COMING-OF-AGE • • •

Not surprisingly, some of the most popular books for children and adolescents are about growing up. Because our society has few formalized rites of passage, the way to adulthood is less clear for our children; they must mark their own paths. Books that portray a character struggling toward adulthood allow readers to see themselves reflected, and provide a rehearsal for real life. There are numerous picture storybooks for primary-grade readers that depict realistic characters trying to cope with growing up. Many of these books deal with children's increasing independence from adults, and with the fear and delight that accompany that independence. We discuss these in Chapter 3.

Older readers continue to struggle for independence, often confronting conflicting feelings, difficult moral choices, and personal challenges along the way. Young people are engaged in a process of trying to find out who they are, what they like and do not like, and what they will and will not do. They are passionately preoccupied with themselves and may look to literature for solutions to or escape from their

Expanded discussion of picture book content in Chapter 3 includes further information on intermediate and advanced picture books.

Features that focus on exemplary works of children's literature and their creators

A Close Look At features offer in-depth discussion of books that exemplify the genre addressed in that chapter. Such literary elements as characterization, plot, setting, and theme often serve as headings to organize the discussion.

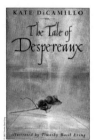

Profile

Profile

Avi

W*riting is hard. And writing very well is very hard. Never believe any writer who suggests otherwise. Scratch the surface of any successful author. Just below—in fetal position, sucking a thumb—is an insecure writer. For all of us writing well is always a struggle.*
(from Avi's Newbery Medal acceptance speech, Toronto, June 22, 2003)

Avi knows what it means to write well. Since 1975 he has engaged in the struggle to create award-

Kate DiCamillo

K*ate DiCamillo's writing career began with a childhood lie. Not exactly a lie, she was quick to explain in a speech she delivered at the University of Minnesota. A misunderstanding, really. Having found a story in a children's magazine that she particularly liked, a young Kate transcribed the words in her own

Profile boxes in Chapters 2 through 10 introduce readers to such prominent authors and illustrators as James Ransome, Kate DiCamillo, Avi, Lauren Stringer, and NCTE award-winning poets. The Profiles, which are often connected to the books presented in the "A Close Look At" features, provide biographical and bibliographical information, and also describe the authors' and illustrators' personal experiences, their training and development, and their artistic process—all of which offer insight into the works that they create.

preview

6

Ideas your students can implement in their own classrooms

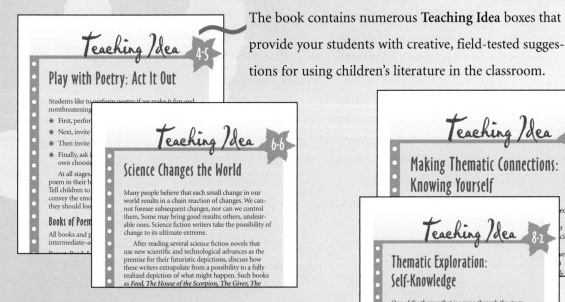

The book contains numerous **Teaching Idea** boxes that provide your students with creative, field-tested suggestions for using children's literature in the classroom.

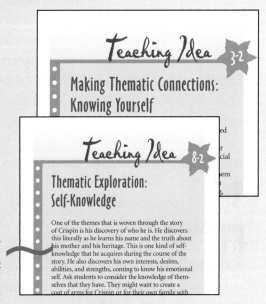

Several new "thematic" Teaching Idea boxes, which span multiple chapters, help students think about the specific theme of self knowledge as it applies to different genres.

Helpful guidelines for selecting, evaluating, and using children's literature

Chapter 1 includes a section titled "The Challenge of Selecting and Using Literature for Children and Adolescents," which provides overarching principles for choosing appropriate children's books. Additionally, each genre chapter lists specific criteria for selecting books of that genre.

The Challenge of Selecting and Using Literature for Children and

Books can play a significant role the extent to which they will d surrounding them. Books an Velcro; they don't stick to each from significant others, inclu teachers, librarians, communi others who come into contact w sible for determining a child's l and presenting nursery rhymes poetry, great novels, and rivetin process is neither easy nor with erature is important. Knowing equally important.

Criteria for Evaluating Poetry

Poetry for children and adolescents refers to things children and adolescents know. We treasure poems that have stood the test of time, ones that have won significant awards, and ones that have received positive reviews from literary critics. The final test, however, is the level of understanding of the child. Although some poetry from the past still speaks to today's children, some does not. A wealth of excellent poetry has been written in the last decade.

In 1977 the National Council of Teachers of English (NCTE) established an award to honor poets who write for children. The award, established in memory of Bee Cullinan's son Jonathan (born 1969, died 1975), recognizes the outstanding contribution of a poet who writes expressly for children. Charlotte S. Huck (president of NCTE from 1975 to 1976), Alvina Burrows (colleague at New York University), John Donovan (director of the Children's Book Council), and Sister Rosemary Winkeljohann (director of the ele-

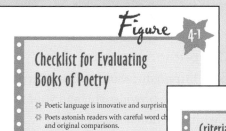

Accompanying figures summarize these guidelines for evaluation in checklist format.

Teaching and learning resources

Instructor's Manual
0-495-00253-4

The Instructor's Manual contains resources designed to streamline and maximize the effectiveness of your course preparation. It contains chapter outlines and summaries, key terms and definition lists, activity ideas (including suggestions for using articles from *The Horn Book Magazine* found in InfoTrac® College Edition), instructions for using the new video clips, and reflection questions for these video clips (which will also be included on the CD-ROM itself).

Video: Literature and the Child

0-495-00246-1
Available to qualifying adopters, this unique resource enhances your classroom lecture presentations using in-depth video interviews with leading children's book authors and illustrators.

CD-ROM

The thoroughly updated and revised CD-ROM includes an all-new video component featuring in-depth interviews with leading children's book authors and illustrators, an improved children's literature search engine (with a booklist updated yearly by the authors), an online Tool Bank feature with collections of materials (such as forms and checklists) designed for use by classroom teachers, and video reflection questions that students can answer and email to you. See pages 2 and 3 of this Preview for additional details.

Print Version of Tool Bank

You may opt to package a printed version of the Tool Bank with this text for a nominal price. To do so, use ISBN 0-495-07074-2 when placing your textbook order.

InfoTrac® College Edition with InfoMarks®

NOT SOLD SEPARATELY. Now FREE four-month access to InfoTrac College Edition's online database of more than 18 million reliable, full-length articles from 5000 academic journals and periodicals (including *The Horn Book Magazine*) includes access to InfoMarks®—stable URLs that can be linked to articles, journals, and searches. InfoMarks allow you to use a simple "copy and paste" technique to create instant and continually updated online readers, content services, bibliographies, electronic "reserve" readings, and current topic sites. And, incorporating InfoTrac College Edition into your course is easy—references to this virtual library are built into many of our texts in margins, exercises, etc. In addition, ask about other InfoTrac College Edition resources available, including InfoMarks print and Online Readers with readings, activities, and exercises hand-selected to work with the text. And to help students use the research they gather, their free four-month subscription to InfoTrac College Edition includes access to InfoWrite, a complete set of online critical thinking and paper writing tools. To take a quick tour of InfoTrac College Edition, visit **http://www.infotrac-college.com** and select the "User Demo." *(Journals subject to change. Certain restrictions may apply. For additional information, please consult your local Thomson representative.)*

Book Companion Website

Accessible at **http://education.wadsworth.com**
This interactive site provides you and your students with additional teaching and learning resources.

resources
8

Literature and the Child

SIXTH EDITION

Lee Galda
UNIVERSITY OF MINNESOTA

Bernice E. Cullinan
NEW YORK UNIVERSITY

WADSWORTH

★

THOMSON LEARNING™

Australia • Brazil • Canada • Mexico • Singapore • Spain • United Kingdom • United States

WADSWORTH
THOMSON LEARNING

Literature and the Child, Sixth Edition
Lee Galda, Bernice E. Cullinan

Publisher: Vicki Knight
Education Editor: Dan Alpert
Development Editor: Tangelique Williams
Assistant Editor: Dan Moneypenny
Editorial Assistant: Larkin Page-Jacobs
Technology Project Manager: Barry Connolly
Marketing Manager: Terra Schultz
Marketing Assistant: Rebecca Weisman
Marketing Communications Manager: Tami Strang
Project Manager, Editorial Production: Paul Wells
Art Director: Maria Epes

Print Buyer: Barbara Britton
Permissions Editor: Kiely Sisk
Production Service: Joan Keyes, Dovetail Publishing Services
Text Designer: Marsha Cohen
Photo Researcher: Linda Sykes
Copy Editor: Michele Jones
Cover Designer: Marsha Cohen
Cover Illustration: Lauren Stringer
Compositor: Lachina Publishing Services
Printer: Transcontinental Interglobe

Printed in Canada

1 2 3 4 5 6 7 09 08 07 06 05

For more information about our products, contact us at:
Thomson Learning Academic Resource Center
1-800-423-0563

For permission to use material from this text or product, submit a request online at **http://www.thomsonrights.com**. Any additional questions about permissions can be submitted by email to **thomsonrights@thomson.com**.

Library of Congress Control Number: 2005924773

ISBN 0-534-55544-6

Thomson Higher Education
10 Davis Drive
Belmont, CA 94002-3098
USA

Asia (including India)
Thomson Learning
5 Shenton Way
#01-01 UIC Building
Singapore 068808

Australia/New Zealand
Thomson Learning Australia
102 Dodds Street
Southbank, Victoria 3006
Australia

Canada
Thomson Nelson
1120 Birchmount Road
Toronto, Ontario M1K 5G4
Canada

UK/Europe/Middle East/Africa
Thomson Learning
High Holborn House
50–51 Bedford Row
London WC1R 4LR
United Kingdom

Latin America
Thomson Learning
Seneca, 53
Colonia Polanco
11560 Mexico
D.F. Mexico

Spain (including Portugal)
Thomson Paraninfo
Calle Magallanes, 25
28015 Madrid, Spain

FOR

Haydn Charles Ellinger

A NEW READER

AND

FOR

Dan Alpert

A SUPERB EDITOR

Brief Contents

Contents

Chapter 3

Content of Picture Books   55

Chapter 4

Poetry and Verse   85

Chapter 5

Folklore   127

Chapter 6

Fantasy and Science Fiction   161

Chapter 7

Contemporary Realistic Fiction   185

Chapter 8

Historical Fiction   209

Chapter 9

Biography   237

10
Nonfiction   259

PART TWO

Children and Books

11
Building a Culturally Diverse
Literature Collection   285

Chapter

12

Developing Responsive Readers   313

Chapter

13

Literature-Based Instruction in Preschool and Primary Grades   343

Chapter

14

Literature-Based Instruction in Intermediate Grades and Middle School   357

Preface

• • THE WORLD OF BOOKS • •

Books have shaped our lives. They are our tickets to adventure without leaving our living rooms, our window into the lives of others, our resource for discovering interesting things about our world, our means of thinking about what kind of people we are and what we value. It is because of our passionate attachment to books that this text is now in its sixth edition. Just about 25 years ago, the first edition was published. Our message today is the same as it was then: Give children books and books will shape their lives. That message remains constant, but the books do not. Although older books remain wonderful reading fare, new books bring fresh voices and visions to the field. As the field of children's and adolescent literature has continued to expand and change over the years, so has this text.

• • ABOUT THE • •
SIXTH EDITION

In this new edition, we have kept the features that our readers tell us they find useful. Thus you will find that Chapters 2 through 10 contain a section titled "A Close Look At," in which we discuss one particular book that is an excellent example of the focal genre. All but two of these books are new to this edition. We have included several recent award-winning books, such as Kate DiCamillo's *The Tale of Despereaux,* Nancy Farmer's *The House of the Scorpion,* Patricia Reilly Giff's *Pictures of Hollis Woods,* Avi's *Crispin: The Cross of Lead,* and James Cross Giblin's biography *The Life and Death of Adolf Hitler,* as well as other outstanding books both old and new.

We have also kept the extensive Booklists at the end of Chapters 1 through 12. We thought about making the lists shorter and including annotations, but decided that what works best is to point you in the right direction but let you discover the particular books you like. The books in the Booklists are all excellent examples of children's and adolescent literature, so there is not much possibility of a bad choice. We firmly believe that the opportunity to find and read some of the wonderful books that are available will turn everyone into an avid reader. The Booklists also appear on the text-specific website, which is accessed through the

CD that accompanies this book. We are committed to updating the Booklists every year for the life of this edition.

Because readers have responded so positively to them in the past, we have continued to include Teaching Ideas throughout the text. These Teaching Ideas provide both preservice and inservice teachers with ideas for using literature in the classroom. This book is not a methods text, but the Teaching Ideas offer a wide variety of examples of ways to bring literature and students together. Those who use this text who are not interested in teaching can easily skip over this feature (although you'll miss some good ideas!). The Teaching Ideas are either updated or new. New to this edition, most chapters include a Teaching Idea that relates to the theme of "knowing yourself," a theme that permeates many of the books that we focus on in this edition. These interrelated Teaching Ideas are meant to give readers an idea of the interesting and powerful possibilities for connecting multiple genres of books that share similar themes.

The internal design of most chapters in Part 1 remains the same—a vignette that illustrates a response to the focus book, a brief introduction to and definition of the genre, a discussion of how children respond to it, a close look at an exemplar book, and then a discussion of the books available. As always, the books that we discuss are a mix of old favorites and exciting new titles.

We have reorganized the book a bit. "Poetry" is now Chapter 4, with "The Art of Picture Books" as Chapter 2 and "The Content of Picture Books" as Chapter 3. Chapter 5, "Folklore," has been substantially revised, and Chapter 9, "Biography," is now organized around the special nature of the biographical subject as well as chronologically. Chapter 11, "Building a Culturally Diverse Literature Collection," has been expanded to include sexual orientation and exceptionalities, and has been moved to Part 2. We did this to highlight the fact that excellent, diverse books are available in all genres (and, indeed, appear in each chapter in Part 1) and that it is the presence of diverse literature in young readers' lives that is so crucial. We follow this chapter by an exploration of readers themselves and how students develop as responsive readers. The last two chapters focus on literature in use in classrooms. We describe real classrooms, real children, and real teachers to bring to life the range of choices that exist for materials, organization, and instruction when books are the basis of the curriculum. We end

Chapter 14 with a description of how the use of culturally diverse texts can transform a curriculum.

We so loved the lush paintings of Lauren Stringer and the bright and cheerful design of the fifth edition that the design of the sixth edition is very similar. We have used Lauren's beautiful art again, moving what was the Part 1 opener to the cover of this edition. We just couldn't bear to part with the art!

• • MEDIA RESOURCES • •

We have continued the **InfoTrac** feature, with ideas for further reading and discussion or writing suggestions at the end of each chapter. InfoTrac is an online database of articles from quality journals, including the respected *Horn Book Magazine.* We hope that connecting articles in *The Horn Book Magazine* to each chapter in this text will help you develop the habit of reading professional journals to continue to learn about literature for children and adolescents.

We have added a **Video** feature. Accompanying this text is a CD that contains 120 minutes of conversations between us and 10 different writers and illustrators. In these discussions, the writers and illustrators explore aspects of their craft that are specific to this text. For example, we feature James Ransome in Chapter 2, and in our discussion with him we ask him how he creates the art for his many picture books. This video is meant to inform our readers and serve as a tool to use to introduce young readers to some of the wonderful people who make books for children and adolescents. An expanded version of the video is also available to instructors in videocassette form.

Finally, the Booklists can be accessed electronically via a link on the CD-ROM that came with this book. This allows you to download yearly updated versions of the Booklists for the life of this edition.

• • ACKNOWLEDGMENTS • •

We are most grateful to Lauren Stringer, who once again interrupted her busy schedule as a children's book artist and mother to revise the Part 1 opener from the fifth edition so that it worked for the cover of this edition. Lauren also graciously allowed us to film her in her studio, and she talked about the process she went through as she illustrated Lisa Westberg Peters's *Our Family Tree: An Evolution Story.* Lisa invited us into her study, where she explained the origins of this book and how she wrote it. We also visited Debra Frasier, author of *The Incredible Water Show,* in her studio, where she regaled us with an explanation of how she makes the wonderful picture books that she both writes and illustrates. Illustrator James Ransome also discussed his creative process as he illustrates such books as *Bruh Rabbit and the Tar Baby Girl.* Lindsay Lee Johnson talked about her

book *Soul Moon Soup* and the power of poetry, and Kate DiCamillo talked about writing *The Tale of Despereaux* and the power of fantasy. Bonnie Graves discussed how she writes transitional chapter books of contemporary realism, such as *Taking Care of Trouble,* and Avi talked about the writing of historical fiction, especially *Crispin: The Cross of Lead.* Mary Casanova commented on the close ties among setting, characters, and plot in her novels, such as *Moose Tracks,* and Jane Kurtz explored how she draws on her own childhood experiences as she writes such books as *Jakarta Missing* for young readers. That they took the time to talk with us so that our readers could have the accompanying CD as a resource indicates the depth of their commitment to their art. Thank you all.

Rebecca Rapport, at the University of Minnesota, extensively revised Chapter 5, "Folklore." Her attention to detail, enthusiasm, and knowledge have made this edition a better book. She also is always willing to talk about books and children, and thus has influenced the text as a whole. Debbie Wooten, University of Tennessee, Knoxville, helped us update Chapter 3 and brought us the benefit of her knowledge of picture books for older readers. Sarah Hansen, a poet and a teacher with a passion for poetry, helped us revise Chapter 4 and contributed many wonderful ideas to that chapter. We are grateful that she was willing to share her busy life with us as we got this edition finalized. She and Tacardra Rountree have also helped us update the Booklists for the past three years. Jessie Dockter, a middle school English teacher and an M.A. student at the University of Minnesota, has organized our reference lists and made sure that nothing—or at least not much—was forgotten. Deb Kruse-Field contributed the extensive example of Book Club in Chapter 14. And Cathy Zemke, the most patient of support staff, cheerfully and patiently helped us with formatting problems that seemed insurmountable to us "book" people.

Thanks also go to Rabbi Eric Weiss, who responded thoughtfully to the vignette in Chapter 9. Energy and inspiration also came from Karen Nelson Hoyle, curator of the Kerlan Collection at the University of Minnesota, and from the many writers and illustrators who have spoken there. The children's literature communities in the Minneapolis/ St. Paul area and in New York City are rich and exciting places to work, and it would take pages to name all of those who have contributed to our enthusiasm for this literary life. The divas—Priscilla Specht, Greer Hawkins, Cathy Nelson, Becky Rapport, and Kate DiCamillo—are an inspiration, as are Martha Davis Beck of the Minnesota Humanities Commission and Wendy Woodfill of the Hennepin County Library System. Those who are at the heart of the Red Balloon Bookstore and the Wild Rumpus Bookstore, especially Liz Sandler and Liisa Schmitt, are always eager to discuss, and suggest, great books. Thank you all.

Many superb teachers and librarians have also inspired our writing, among them Terry Nestor, Karen Hankins, Karen Bliss, Betty Shockley Bisplinghoff, and especially Lisa

Stanzi, all living and working hard in Georgia. Rene Goepfrich and Susan Kalin at Kenwood Elementary School in Minneapolis are kind enough to share their students with Lee once a week. It was last year's fourth/fifth grade group that field-tested the teaching ideas in Chapter 4. Thanks, kids!

Taffy Raphael, University of Illinois at Chicago; Karen Jorgensen and Deborah Dillon, University of Minnesota; and Lauren Liang, University of Utah, have helped us understand more clearly how literature functions in children's and adolescents' literate lives. Lauren has an incisive critical sense and an extensive knowledge of reading and responding to literature, and she has written an excellent Instructor's Manual for this edition.

Nance Wilson, University of Illinois at Chicago; Charlotte Huck and Joan Irwin, American Educational Publishers; John Micklos and Alida Cutts, International Reading Association; Kent Williamson and Kathy Egawa, National Council of Teachers of English; and Kent L. Brown and Wendy Murray, Boyds Mills Press, have also provided help and encouragement.

We also acknowledge the many good ideas that our reviewers provided to us. It is always gratifying to have reviewers like the text, and it's really wonderful to have them not only like the text but add to it! Thank you to

Andrea N. Aguilar, Sierra College

Ann M. Neely, Vanderbilt University

Louise Stearns, Southern Illinois University at Carbondale

Mary Anna C. Dimitrakopoulos, Indiana University, South Bend

Matthew D. Zbaracki, University of Northern Colorado

Sandra Imdieke, Northern Michigan University

Susan Honeyman, University of Nebraska, Kearney

Denise H. Stuart, University of Akron

Andrea Maxworthy O'Brien, University of Wisconsin, Whitewater

Kathryn Patten, Middle Tennessee State University

Alison Black, SUNY Oneonta

Karen S. Donnelly, Louisiana State University

Kathleen C. Tice, University of Texas at Arlington

Joyce H. Swan, University of Tennessee at Martin

David Partenheimer, Truman State University

Frieda Domino-Armour, Dillard University

And last, but certainly not least, is the Wadsworth staff. You might have noticed that we dedicate this edition to our editor, Dan Alpert. He deserves it. He is unfailingly kind, has wonderful ideas, and always remembers that authors are people too. We are also grateful to our talented development editor, Tangelique Williams, who supported us throughout the revision process. Thank you Larkin Page-Jacobs, Barry Connolly, and Paul Wells for your invaluable assistance. Thank you Joan Keyes of Dovetail Publishing Services for taking on the monumental task of production management for a second time. We thank the video producer and staff: Becky Stovall, Ken Cargile, and Alex Motlagh. They were wonderful. To all, thank you.

Finally, the support of Lee's family—Tony, Adam, and Anna—once again allowed her to write longer than they wanted her to. Adam and Anna have both grown up with this book, and they have been amazingly tolerant of sharing their mother's time with a textbook. And they both love to read!

Lee Galda
Bernice E. Cullinan

About the Authors and Illustrator

Lee Galda

After teaching in elementary and middle school classrooms for a number of years, Lee Galda received her Ph.D. in English Education from New York University. A former professor at the University of Georgia, she is now a professor at the University of Minnesota where she teaches courses in children's literature and language arts. Lee is a member of the National Reading Conference, the National Council of Teachers of English, the International Reading Association, the American Library Association, and the United States Board on Books for Young People and sits on the review boards of many professional journals. She was the Children's Books Department editor for *The Reading Teacher* from 1989 to 1993 and a member of the 2003 Newbery Award selection committee. Author of numerous articles and book chapters about children's books, Lee co-authored a chapter on research in children's literature in the *Handbook of Reading Research, Volume III.* She lives in Minneapolis, Minnesota, with her husband and two children.

Bernice E. Cullinan

Bernice E. Cullinan is known both nationally and internationally for her work in children's literature. She has written over 30 books on literature for classroom teachers and librarians, including *Literature and the Child* (6th edition), *Poetry Lessons to Dazzle and Delight,* and *Three Voices: Invitation to Poetry across the Curriculum.* She has also written a book for parents, *Read to Me: Raising Kids Who Love to Read.* Bee is editor in chief of Wordsong, the poetry imprint of Boyds Mills Press, a Highlights for Children company, and has collected poems written by the recipients of the National Council of Teachers of English Award for Poetry in *A Jar of Tiny Stars.* She served as president of the International Reading Association, was inducted into the Reading Hall of Fame and The Ohio State University Hall of Fame, and was selected as the recipient of the Arbuthnot Award for Outstanding Teacher of Children's Literature. Bee lives in New York City, New York.

Lauren Stringer

Lauren Stringer was born in Great Falls, Montana. She received her Bachelor of Arts in Art and Art History from the University of California, Santa Cruz, in 1980, and continued her art education with the Whitney Museum of American Art until 1982. Lauren lived in New York for eight years, exhibiting her work in museums and galleries, as well as designing sets and costumes for theater and dance. In 1984, she was an artist-in-residence at both the Edward Albee Foundation and the Millay Colony for the Arts, where she began sculpting. In 1986, she was an artist-in-residence in the Dominican Republic at Altos de Chavon. Minnesota became her home in 1988, where she taught in schools as an artist-in-residence. In 1991, she received the McKnight Foundation Fellowship for sculpture. In 1994, she illustrated her first children's book, *Mud* by Mary Lyn Ray, which won the Minnesota Book Award for illustration, the IRA Children's Choice Award, and the Crayola Kids Best Book of the Year Award. Since *Mud,* Lauren has painted illustrations for *Scarecrow* by Cynthia Rylant; *Red Rubber Boot Day* by Mary Lyn Ray; *Castles, Caves, and Honeycombs* by Linda Ashman; *Our Family Tree* by Lisa Westberg Peters; and *Fold Me a Poem* by Kristine O'Connell George. Lauren is currently illustrating *Winter Is the Warmest Season,* authored by herself. She lives in a huge Victorian house in Minneapolis with her husband, two children, and three cats.

Children's and Adolescent Literature: Yesterday, Today, and Tomorrow

Lynnie had always thought crickets and even crows were good luck. Now and then I thought I heard Lynn's lively voice. The cricket sang, "Chirp! Chirp!" but I heard "Kira-kira!" The crows called "Caw! Caw!" and I heard "Kira-kira!" The wind whistled "Whoosh! Whoosh!" and I heard "Kira-kira!" My sister had taught me to look at the world that way, as a place that glitters, as a place where the calls of the crickets and the crows and the wind are everyday occurrences that also happen to be magic.

—CYNTHIA KADOHATA, *Kira-Kira*, pp. 243–244

ARLENE'S SIXTH-GRADE LANGUAGE ARTS STUDENTS HAD BEEN ATTENTIVE all through her reading of *Kira-Kira* (1), and now that she has just one more paragraph to read, she pauses. "Kira-kira," she says musingly. "What have I seen and heard today that seems ordinary, but is really kira-kira?" she wonders aloud. "Perhaps the pussy willows that have just begun to bloom even though there's snow on the ground. Or perhaps the chickadee who comes to my feeder every morning when I have my coffee. Those things are everyday, but they're kira-kira, too. They are something special, if I look at them that way."

She goes on to read the final paragraph, and the students are silent at the end. The book has given them a lot to think about—racism, family relationships, self-esteem, love, happiness, optimism—and they don't quite know where to begin. Wisely, Arlene sets them an individual task: to begin a free write about ordinary things in their lives that, when seen from a different point of view, could become "kira-kira," glittering with joy.

Good books like Cynthia Kadohata's 2005 Newbery Medal–winning *Kira-Kira* speak to their readers from the very first line, pulling them into the world between their covers. The lure of a good book is palpable. Whether you walk through the purple door at The Wild Rumpus, an independent children's bookstore in Minneapolis, or through the red door at The Red Balloon, an independent children's bookstore in St. Paul, inside you find books, and children, everywhere. Little ones come with their mothers for story hour; elementary school children appear after school, looking for the next good book to read; adolescents, trying not to show how much they enjoy the experience, browse the shelves, picking up a book, reading a bit, and then going on to another until they've found what they like. When authors and illustrators come to visit, there's barely enough room for everyone. This late January day, everyone is looking for the recently announced Newbery, Caldecott, Printz, Siebert, and King award–winning books.

The local public library is busy, too, with story hours in the morning for preschoolers, and schoolchildren hurrying in after school to check out new books. The crowd seems bigger in the late afternoon as patrons hurry to find what they need before the library closes at five, earlier than it used to, because of reduced funding. School libraries, too, do a bustling business, with some children even spending part of their lunch hour in the library, reading and talking.

Not too long ago, critics, educators, and politicians proclaimed the death of reading—and of books. "Kids don't read anymore" was a common observation, and many would add, "The book will be replaced by the computer." Fortunately, neither of these proclamations appears to be true. Children's books, and reading, are still alive and well, thriving in many ways. The amazing popularity of the **Series of Unfortunate Events** and **Harry Potter** series confirmed what those of us in the field knew all along, and changed the way many people thought about children's books and reading. The popularity of these books and others also demonstrated that children's literature can be financially successful.

Teachers, librarians, and parents continually seek to find the right book for any particular child. The **Harry Potter** books turned out to be the right books for millions of young readers, but it is usually not that easy to choose the perfect book. There are thousands more "right books" just waiting to be put into the hands of young readers. This text will help you learn how to do just that.

In this chapter we present some basic information about literature for children and adolescents, such as definitions of the major *genres,* a bit of the history of children's literature, a description of current trends and issues, basic criteria for evaluating books, and how to deal with censorship. The next nine chapters explore the major genres in children's and adolescent literature. In the second part of this book, Chapter 11 presents information about creating a diverse collection of books for use in the classroom or library. Chapter 12 offers information about the children and adolescents who read these books, and some basic ways of enhancing their reading experience through classroom activities. Chapters 13 and 14 portray teachers and children in action, from primary through middle school levels.

The Value of Literature

Literature entertains and informs. It enables young people to explore and understand their world. It enriches their lives and widens their horizons. They learn about people and places on the other side of the world as well as ones down the street. They travel back and forth in time to visit familiar places and people, to meet new friends, and to see new worlds. They can explore their own feelings, shape their own values, and imagine lives beyond the one they live.

Literature contributes to language growth and development. When children and adolescents read or hear stories read to them, they learn new vocabulary. They encounter a greater variety of words in books than they will ever hear in spoken conversation or on television. Each learner builds an individual storehouse of language possibilities and draws on that wealth in speaking, writing, listening, and reading. Young people who read literature have a broad range of experiences and language to put in their storehouse; they have greater resources on which to draw than do people who do not read. Literature develops readers' facility with language because it exposes them to carefully crafted poetry and prose.

Literature helps students become better readers. Engaging stories, poetry, and information appeal to readers and entice them to read. The more they read, the better they get. The better they read, the more they learn. The more they learn, the more curious they become. And the more curious they become, the more they read.

Literature helps students become better writers. When students read a lot, they notice what writers do. They see that writers choose from a variety of language possibilities in their writing. When readers write, they borrow the structures, patterns, and words from what they read.

Literature leads students to love reading. They seek out exciting stories, interesting information, and compelling poems. They turn to reading as a source of pleasure and entertainment.

Literature prompts students to explore their own feelings. They gain insight into human experience and begin to understand themselves better. When they explore their own feelings, they also understand why others react as they do.

Literature reflects the lives of millions of children and adolescents worldwide who are diverse in their ethnicity, religion, nationality, and social and economic status but united by commonalities of youth. Literature provides insights into the realities and dreams of young people and of the authors and illustrators who interpret those dreams and realities. It reflects life throughout the course of time and across national boundaries. Literature keeps people's dreams alive, presenting a vision of what is possible.

Books are a powerful force in the lives of children and adolescents; teachers and librarians can take advantage of the force and power of books by shaping and enriching curriculum around literature. Even in today's world of standards, accountability, and testing, books form the vital core of an education for the 21st century. The richness and diversity that typifies literature today means that teachers, librarians, parents, and young people have a wealth of books from which to select. The power of books to open new worlds, to cause readers to think in new ways—in short, to transform their ways of knowing—makes books the greatest single resource for educating our children to become contributing members of our society. How fortunate that we have so many good books to present to our young readers.

Genres of Literature for Children and Adolescents

What is children's and adolescent literature? A basic definition might state that it is books written for this particular audience; we might also add that it includes books that children and adolescents enjoy and have made their own. Figure 1.1 summarizes the genres of children's and adolescent literature discussed in this chapter.

There are many ways to categorize these books. One basic distinction can be made between narratives and other structures such as exposition, description, or argumentation. *Narratives* tell a story; they often have a *character* or characters who encounter some kind of problem and work to resolve it. The narrative is developed through the *plot*—the temporal events or actions that lead to the solution of the problem—which progresses to a *climax,* or solution to the problem, and ends with a *resolution,* or closure to the story. See Figure 1.2 for a summary of literary elements and how they function in narratives. Texts that are not narratives do

Figure 1-1

Genres in Children's and Adolescent Literature

Category	Brief Description
Poetry and Verse	Condensed language, imagery. Distilled, rhythmic expression of imaginative thoughts and perceptions.
Folklore	Literary heritage of humankind. Traditional stories, myths, legends, nursery rhymes, and songs from the past. Oral tradition; no known author.
Fantasy	Imaginative worlds, make-believe. Stories set in places that do not exist, about people and creatures that could not exist or events that could not happen.
Science Fiction	Based on extending physical laws and scientific principles to their logical outcomes. Stories about what might occur in the future.
Realistic Fiction	"What if" stories, illusion of reality. Events could happen in real world; characters seem real. Contemporary setting.
Historical Fiction	Set in the past; could have happened. Story reconstructs events of past age, things that did occur or could have occurred.
Biography	Plot and theme based on a person's life. An account of a person's life, or part of a life history; letters, memoirs, diaries, journals, autobiographies.
Nonfiction	Facts about the real world. Informational books that explain a subject or concept.
Picture Books*	Interdependent art and text. Story or concept presented through combination of text and illustration. Classification based on format, not content.

* All genres appear in picture books.

Figure 1-2

Literary Elements and How They Function in Narrative

Narratives contain certain literary elements that authors and illustrators work with to create memorable stories. They include setting, characterization, plot, theme, and style.

Setting

Setting is the time and place in which the story events occur. Most stories are set in an identifiable place, but in others the setting is almost irrelevant. Broad brush strokes paint a picture of real or fanciful, rural or urban, home or school, and details are not necessary. Picture books with vague settings offer artists the opportunity to create images that the text does not define, to present their own vision of the physical surroundings of the story. In other stories setting is very important; details about a particular city, a part of the country, an historical period, or a special place affect the development of the characters and the plot. Picture books supply information about the setting through illustrations, with art detailing the background the story demands.

Characterization

Characterization refers to the means by which an author establishes credibility of character. Characters are the personalities that populate literature. Like people, characters are multidimensional, with varied strengths and weaknesses, and over the course of time they grow and change. This change or development is most often due to the events that occur as the characters seek to resolve some kind of problem. Authors develop characters by describing how they appear, what they do, think, or say, what others say about them or to them, and what others do to them, and by what the narrator reveals. In picture storybooks, character is also interpreted by illustrators who reveal appearance, thoughts, and actions.

Plot

Plot refers to the sequence of story events. Most children want action in a story; they want something to happen, and happen fast. Most often, the plot is told in a straightforward chronology, but sometimes authors use a flashback, episodic, or alternating plot. Flashbacks provide background information about earlier events that led to the creation of the problem the character faces. Episodic plots highlight particular events in characters' lives, and alternating plots enable authors to tell stories from different points of view.

The plot usually revolves around a central conflict or conflicts. The most common conflicts are self against self, in which the main character engages in an internal struggle; self against other, in which the struggle is between the main character and one or more others; self against society, in which the main character combats societal pressures or norms; and self against nature, in which the main character struggles with the forces of nature.

Theme

A *theme* is a central, unifying idea. Often a theme is the reason authors write in the first place: a story allows them to say what they want to say. Many stories have several interwoven themes. Interpretation of themes varies among readers; each reader internalizes the theme in an individual way.

Style

Style is how an author writes—the vocabulary and the syntax that create the story. A tale is all in the telling, so style is an all-important criterion. The style needs to reflect the time, place, and characters in a way that is readable. Good dialogue sounds natural, and descriptions are vivid and fresh.

Point of view is part of style. Many stories are told through the voice of the central character, who reports events in a first-person narrative, solely from his or her point of view. This allows readers to understand thoroughly the thoughts of the central character and often provokes a strong identification with that character. Another point of view, third-person limited, limits the information that is conveyed to what the central character could logically know, but it does so in a more detached tone, using third-person rather than first-person pronouns. Omniscient narrators, ones who are all-knowing, can reveal the thoughts and inner feelings of several characters. They can move about in time and space to report events from an unbiased position. This point of view allows readers to know a great deal about what all the characters are thinking and doing. It also puts more distance between the reader and the main character, because the reader is viewing the protagonist through the narrator's eyes rather than viewing the story world through the protagonist's eyes.

Authors generally select one point of view and stick with it throughout the story, although some alternate between two or among several narrators. In a well-written story, the point of view provides a perspective that enriches the story.

Poets and authors who work with nonnarrative forms such as nonfiction also work with elements of style as they seek to illuminate the concept or idea that unifies their work. In the chapters that follow we discuss the unique qualities of the literary elements that define each genre.

not tell a story but rather present information. They may be argumentative, descriptive, expository, or persuasive; they may also be poetry, mood pieces, or nonfiction that presents concepts and information.

Another way to categorize literature is by *genre,* as we do in Figure 1.1. A genre is a category of composition that has such defining characteristics as type of characters, setting, action, and overall form or structure. The defining characteristics of each genre help us recognize the organization of the discipline of literature, provide a framework for talking about books, and help guide our selection. The major genres include picture books, poetry, folklore, fantasy, science fiction, realistic fiction, historical fiction, biography, and nonfiction. These genres are based on content, with the exception of picture books, which are based on format. Each genre is discussed in detail in Chapters 2 through 10, but we provide a brief overview here.

Distinguishing features help readers recognize genres. For example, *poetry* contains short lines, imagery, and elements of sound, such as rhythm and rhyme. Ancient stories that were told by word of mouth are known as *folklore;* stories focusing on events that could happen in the real world today are works of *realistic fiction;* realistic stories set in the past are called *historical fiction; fantasy* stories could not happen in the real world; *science fiction* might happen in the future; and stories that tell the tale of a person's life are *biography.* Books that present information are called *nonfiction.* In the case of *picture books,* the content might be any of the aforementioned genres; the distinguishing feature is the importance of the art in how the book conveys meaning.

Books may be narrative or nonnarrative, fiction or nonfiction, picture book or nonillustrated book. Fiction may be historical or contemporary, realistic or fantasy or science fiction. This textbook shows you how to recognize different genres; students will discover various types of books gradually, by reading them and by having them read to them. You will also learn to select books according to the grade level of students likely to enjoy reading them. In this text we indicate the appropriate age range with N = Nursery (birth to age 5), P = Primary (ages 5 to 8), I = Intermediate (ages 8 to 12), and A = Advanced (ages 12 and up).

• • PICTURE BOOKS • •

Picture books tell a story, present a poem, or develop an understanding of a concept through a unique combination of text and art. Unity between the text and the illustrations defines a high-quality picture book; together text and art create meaning greater than that conveyed by either art or words alone. The content of picture books may be realistic, historical, factual, or fanciful; the format defines this genre.

The artistic possibilities of picture books attract skilled artists to the field. For instance, David Diaz, Trina Schart Hyman, Allen Say, Maurice Sendak, Chris Van Allsburg, David Wisniewski, and Paul Zelinsky—talented artists who have won the Randolph Caldecott Medal—continue to produce beautiful books. Marcia Brown has received the Caldecott three times; she adapts her artistic style to extend the meaning of each story. Compare her art in the three Caldecott winners: Perrault's *Cinderella* (P), *Once a Mouse* (P–I), and Blaise Cendrars's *Shadow* (P–I). Notice that she uses ethereal misty blues and pinks with delicate line for the dreamlike sequence of *Cinderella,* stylized woodcuts in earth tones for *Once a Mouse,* and collage silhouettes arising from black shadows in *Shadow.* Sendak also adapts his

On the day you were born
a forest of tall trees
collected the Sun's light
in their leaves,
where, in silent mystery,
they made oxygen
for you to breathe…

Debra Frasier's **On the Day You Were Born,** *written for her own daughter, is loved by many parents and their children.*

art to the story. He creates cartoonlike drawings of impish children for Krauss's *A Very Special House* (N–P); he draws ferocious adoring beasts in *Where the Wild Things Are* (N–P); and he develops elaborate romantic richness with subtle undertones in *Outside over There* (I–A). Debra Frasier's stunning art and lyrical voice made *On the Day You Were Born* (N–P) so popular that it has been in print for over ten years.

Picture books for young children include small books made from cardboard that are just right for babies to grasp, look at, and chew. They also include pop-ups, cloth books, and alphabet books. Formerly, preschool and primary-grade children were the main audience for picture books, but today there are many picture books that are intended for older readers, including the increasingly popular *graphic novel* and *graphic picture book*. We explore the art of picture books in Chapter 2 and the content of picture books in Chapter 3.

• • **POETRY AND VERSE** • •

Poetry is the shorthand of beauty; its distilled language captures the essence of an idea or experience and encompasses the universe in its vision. Emerson suggests that poetry says the most important things in the simplest way. Lots of poetry is rhythmic and rhymed, appealing to the ear as well as to the mind and emotions, but many wonderful poems are free verse or concrete forms. The best poetry and verse—from nonsense rhymes and limericks through lyrical and narrative poetry—shape an experience or idea into thoughts extraordinary.

Paul Fleischman's Newbery Medal–winning *Joyful Noise: Poems for Two Voices* (I–A) has delighted countless teachers and young readers for more than 15 years with its witty word play and brilliant use of sound to evoke meaning. Kristine O'Connell George's *Fold Me a Poem,* stunningly illustrated by Lauren Stringer, and *Hummingbird Nest* (both P–I), with gorgeous watercolor paintings by Barry Moser, offer young readers the opportunity to savor both words and images.

Each year the number of published books of poetry for children is greater than the year before. The increase in quantity reflects an increase in interest over the past 15 years. Parents have discovered that poetry lulls children to sleep at night. Teachers have discovered that poetry teaches reading, expands oral language development, provides techniques for young writers to experiment with, and enriches experiences across the curriculum. Researchers have found that poetry learned by heart in childhood stays in the mind for a lifetime. First awarded in 1977, the Award for Poetry for Children, presented by the National Council of Teachers of English, calls attention to outstanding poets who write for

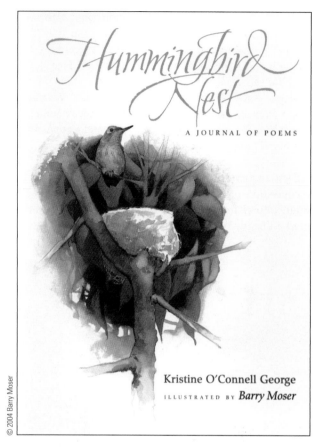

A JOURNAL OF POEMS

Kristine O'Connell George

ILLUSTRATED BY **Barry Moser**

© 2004 Barry Moser

Kris George observed a hummingbird in her family's backyard, keeping a journal of what she saw. She then created this lovely series of poems, beautifully illustrated by Barry Moser.

children. See Appendix A for a complete listing of the winners. Today, publishers who once published only one or two poetry books per year create entire divisions devoted to poetry. We explore poetry in Chapter 4.

• • **FOLKLORE** • •

Folklore is composed of stories that were passed down through generations by word of mouth before they were ever written down. As such, they have no known author. As people told the stories to one another, they changed and molded them to suit their fancy. Eventually Charles Perrault and the Brothers Grimm, folklore collectors, wrote the stories down. Over time, other retellers have continued to shape the stories, as Lise Lunge-Larsen does in *The Hidden Folk* (P–I–A). Folklore reflects the values of the culture in which it grew; it encompasses universal experience as shaped by individual cultures.

Folklore comes in many forms, including *nursery rhymes* from Mother Goose; *folktales* and *fairy tales* such as Cinderella or the Anansi stories; *tall tales* exaggerating the strength and riches of America, such as John Henry and Paul Bunyan; *fables*—simply told, highly condensed morality tales—such as "The Boy Who Cried Wolf"; *mythology,* which explains the origins of the earth and the relation between humans and gods; *hero tales, epics,* and *legends,* such as Robin Hood; *folksongs;* and *religious stories.*

Folklore comprises folktales from around the world and reflects an increasingly international view. Similarly, as the composition of North America has become increasingly multicultural, folklore for children has expanded beyond a predominantly Western European tradition to include folklore of many cultures. Virginia Hamilton's posthumously published retelling of a Gullah tale, ***Bruh Rabbit and the Tar Baby Girl,*** illustrated by James Ransome, and Hamilton's ***The People Could Fly: The Picture Book*** (both P–I), newly illustrated by Leo and Diane Dillon, are recent additions to a growing number of books that are retellings of African American tales. We discuss folklore in Chapter 5.

● ● FANTASY ● ●

Fantasy is imaginative literature distinguished by characters, places, or events that could not happen in the real world. Animals can talk, inanimate objects have feelings,

In ***Rapunzel,*** *Paul Zelinsky creates stunning oil paintings to reveal esoteric beauty, physical luxury, and an evil mother figure.*

time follows the author's rules, and humans accomplish superhuman feats. Fantasy ranges from talking animal stories for very young children to complex novels that explore universal truths. Although fantasy stories could not possibly happen in reality, their carefully constructed plots, well-developed characters, and vivid settings cause readers to suspend disbelief.

The fantasy genre continues to grow as modern fantasy writers create powerful stories redolent with the legacy of folklore and ancient tales. From E. B. White's well-loved *Charlotte's Web* (p–i) to the recent success of *Harry Potter and the Sorcerer's Stone* (i), the genre of fantasy is thriving. The final book in Philip Pullman's **His Dark Materials** trilogy, *The Amber Spyglass* (a), won Great Britain's prestigious Whitbread Book of the Year Award in 2001. In 2004 Kate DiCamillo won the Newbery Medal for her fantasy, *The Tale of Despereaux* (p–i). Nancy Farmer's *The Sea of Trolls* (i–a) is a funny, engaging adventure tale wrapped up in a quest story that keeps readers glued to the book. We explore fantasy in Chapter 6.

*Nancy Farmer's **The Sea of Trolls** is an exciting book for reading alone or out loud.*

© 2004 Tim O'Brien

• • SCIENCE FICTION • •

Science fiction is an imaginative extrapolation of fact and theory: stories project what could happen in the future through a logical extension of established theories and scientific principles. Science fiction describes worlds that are plausible and that could exist someday. Scientific advances cause writers to speculate about the consequences of those advances; science fiction is the result. For example, space travel led to stories of space colonies and intergalactic wars. Garbage pileups led to stories of people and places drowning in garbage. In John Christopher's recently reissued **White Mountains** (a) trilogy, a future world is reduced to a primitive society; in Madeleine L'Engle's *A Wrinkle in Time* (i–a), Meg releases her brother from the grasp of evil.

Nancy Farmer also writes science fiction, including *The House of the Scorpion* (a), winner of both a Printz Honor and a Newbery Honor. In this gripping story, she presents a future world in which cloning has become a way for the rich and powerful to prolong their own lives, and drug trafficking creates countries ruled by drug lords. Lois Lowry spells out a possible future world in *The Giver, Gathering Blue,* and *Messenger* (all a). *The Giver* is one of the most popular science fiction books with teachers and students alike. A discussion of science fiction appears in Chapter 6.

• • CONTEMPORARY • • REALISTIC FICTION

Realistic fiction (contemporary realism) is fiction set in modern times with events that could occur in the real world. Authors create characters, plots, and settings that stay within the realm of possibility. Many readers respond to these stories as if the characters were actual people.

Realistic fiction grapples with a wide range of human conditions and emotions. Writers address hunger, death, divorce, and homelessness as well as more traditional themes of growing up and making friends. Both picture books and novels address the joys and complications of living in today's world. Katherine Paterson's *Bridge to Terabithia* (i), Cynthia Rylant's *Missing May* (i), Cynthia Voigt's *Homecoming* (i–a), Sharon Creech's *Walk Two Moons* (i–a), and Avi's *Nothing But the Truth* (a) explore serious issues, such as death, abandonment, and freedom of speech. Patricia Reilly Giff examines the meaning of family in *Pictures of Hollis Woods* (i–a). There are also many humorous realistic books, such as Carl Hiassen's *Hoot* (i), and realistic books that are about sports, that are adventure stories and animal stories, mysteries and romances. Many of the series books that young readers devour are also realistic fiction.

Realistic fiction writers today write knowingly from many cultures and lifestyles. Many writers for the intermediate and advanced grades—Gary Soto, Walter Dean Myers, Joseph Bruchac, and Laurence Yep—produce books that reflect the true cultural diversity of America. We discuss realistic fiction in Chapter 7.

• • HISTORICAL FICTION • •

Historical fiction tells stories set in the past; it portrays events that actually occurred or possibly could have occurred. Authors create plot and character within an authentic historical setting. Today we are fortunate to have skilled authors writing from careful research and from various cultural perspectives. Historical fiction ranges from stories set in prehistoric times to those reflecting the issues and events of the 20th century. The stories are usually told through the perspective of a child or adolescent who is living life in a particular time and place. Taken all together, historical fic-

tion for children and young adults represents a broad range of voices and cultures.

Although much historical fiction is written for intermediate and advanced-grade readers, there also are many fine picture books—such as Joyce Carol Thomas's *I Have Heard of a Land* (P–I), illustrated by Floyd Cooper—that bring the past to life for younger readers. We discuss historical fiction in Chapter 8. Teaching Idea 1.1 presents ways to help young readers distinguish between fantasy, contemporary realistic fiction, and historical fiction using picture storybooks.

• • BIOGRAPHY • • AND MEMOIR

Biography tells about a real person's life. The subjects of biography are usually people who were famous, such as national leaders, artists, sports figures, writers, or explorers,

Teaching Idea 1-1

Distinguish among Fantasy, Contemporary Realism, and Historical Fiction

Choose three picture books (use the Booklists at the end of Chapters 3, 6, 7, and 8)—one fantasy, one contemporary realistic fiction, and one historical fiction. If you can find three with similar themes, your comparisons will be richer. Read the books aloud and compare them on relevant points, including genre, characters, plot, setting, theme, and any important details. Ask students to answer the following questions, using both the text and the illustrations to explain their answers:

✷ Which stories could really have happened? How do you know?

✷ Which story could not really have happened? How do you know?

✷ Which story is contemporary, set in today's world? How do you know?

✷ Which story is historical? How do you know?

✷ How are these stories alike?

✷ How are these stories different?

Then help your students generate some descriptors of each of the three genres.

© Brad Yeo

The Shadows of Ghadames, by Joëlle Stolz, won the 2005 Batchelder Award for Catherine Temerson's translation of this story of a young girl coming of age in 19th-century Libya.

but there are also many biographies and memoirs that are about "ordinary" people who do extraordinary things. These stories are told in picture books and in lengthy texts. In a book that contains biographies of several people (called a collective biography), author Judith St. George and illustrator David Small take a lighthearted look at 42 presidents in their Caldecott Medal–winning *So You Want to Be President?* (i–a). They point out some good things and some bad things about the job; they always take the humorous angle.

Every biography bears the imprint of its author; although the story of the person's life provides the basic facts, the writer selects, interprets, and shapes elements to create an aesthetic work. Russell Freedman casts a new light on three famous people in his award-winning photobiography, *Lincoln* (i–a), and in *Eleanor Roosevelt* (i–a) and *The Wright Brothers* (a), both of which were Newbery Honor books. James Cross Giblin explains his subject's accomplishments and failures in *The Amazing Life of Benjamin Franklin* (i). In *The Life and Death of Adolf Hitler* (a) he presents a chilling portrait of one of history's worst villains.

Like biographies, autobiographies and memoirs are stories of a person's life, but they are written by the subjects themselves. A number of current authors have written their memoirs. Tomie dePaola tells his own story in *26 Fairmount Avenue, Here We All Are, What a Year,* and *On My Way* (all p), slim chapter books that allow readers who have enjoyed hearing dePaola's picture books read aloud to read about his childhood. Chris Crutcher's *King of the Mild Frontier: An Ill-Advised Autobiography* and Walter Dean Myers's *Bad Boy* (both a) offer adolescent readers insight into how the lives of these authors shaped the books those readers enjoy. We discuss biographies and memoirs in Chapter 9.

• • NONFICTION • •

Nonfiction books are informational sources that explain a subject. Children are naturally curious about the world they inhabit. They observe and explore, question and hypothesize about how this world works. Nonfiction outnumbers fiction 12 to 1 in most children's libraries and is available for children from preschool through the advanced grades.

Nonfiction presents information in a variety of formats: as picture books and photoessays, as how-to manuals, or as descriptive or expository texts. Nonfiction covers diverse topics, ranging from dinosaurs to endangered species, cathedrals to igloos, triangles to probability, artistic design to book construction. Many nonfiction books are works of art as well as works of fact. For example, David Macaulay's *Mosque* (i–a) and Lisa Westberg Peters's *Our Family Tree: A Story of Evolution* (p), illustrated by Lauren Stringer, are beautiful as well as informational. Alphabet and counting books, once intended only for the very young, now have

sophisticated formats in which artists demonstrate their talents. Books designed to inform have evolved into books designed to inform and delight.

Informational books about any topic you might imagine appear on library shelves. Topics that become important in our lives appear in nonfiction for children; the environment, outer space, world hunger, and other natural science topics appear in children's books as rapidly as they appear in the daily newspaper. Social studies topics range from histories of particular periods or events, such as the Civil War, to books that explore social science concepts, such as Sylvia Johnson's intriguing *Mapping the World* (i). Johnson does not just present information about maps, but uses maps to explain how people's conceptual understanding of the world changed over time. We discuss nonfiction in Chapter 10.

These genres illustrate the breadth and depth of books available to children and young adults today, but this hasn't always been the case. The literature of yesterday looked quite different.

Children's and Adolescent Literature Yesterday

Literature written especially for children's pleasure is a recent development in history. In 1744 John Newbery (1713–1767) opened a bookstore in St. Paul's Churchyard, London, where he sold books for children. (He also published them.) Up until that time, children had been given chapbooks (crudely printed little books sold by peddlers or chapmen), battledores (folded sheets of cardboard covered with crude woodcuts of the alphabet or Bible verses), and hornbooks (small wooden paddles with lesson sheets tacked on with strips of brass and covered with a transparent sheet of cow's horn). These materials, like other books of their day, were intended for the instruction of children. One of Newbery's early books, *A Little Pretty Pocket-Book: Intended for the Instruction and Amusement of Little Master Tommy and Pretty Miss Polly,* contained the alphabet, proverbs, and rules of behavior. In 1765 Newbery published *The Renowned History of Little Goody Two Shoes,* a bittersweet story of orphan Marjorie Meanwell, who is overcome with gratitude when a clergyman and his wife buy her a pair of shoes. She cries out, "Two shoes, Madam, see my two shoes." Newbery's books were meant to teach children proper behavior but did not threaten them with the standard fire and brimstone if they did not behave. The most prestigious U.S. award in children's books today is named in honor of John Newbery.

The Industrial Revolution helped develop a middle class that had leisure time to read. Children, who had formed a large part of the workforce, were eventually released from the workplace and sent to school to learn to read and write. As child labor decreased, time to read increased, and children became literate; literature written especially for them came into being.

Most children's books came to the United States from England. At first they were intended for instruction, but it soon became clear that the books nurtured children's imagination. The greatest among the imaginative books written for pleasure, Lewis Carroll's *Alice's Adventures in Wonderland* (1865/1992), was soon reprinted in English-speaking countries all over the world. Other books from the same period, such as George MacDonald's *At the Back of the North Wind* (1871/1989) and Charles Kingsley's *The Water Babies* (1863/1995), which described a make-believe world alongside a real one, are still read today. The revolutionary quality of Lewis Carroll's two books, *Alice's Adventures in Wonderland* and *Through the Looking Glass* (1871/1977), derives from the fact that they were written purely to give pleasure to children. There is not a trace of a lesson or moral in the books. Their publication gave rise to a new class of literature in English-speaking countries worldwide.

Early Canadian literature had a "survival" theme, something that is evident in Canada's first children's novel, Catharine Parr Traill's *Canadian Crusoes: A Tale of the Rice Lake Plains* (1852/1985). In Australia, the novels of Ethel Turner reflected an artificial idea of childhood rather than the realization of it. Her first and most famous book was *Seven Little Australians* (1894/2004), which is still in print and is regarded as a classic. The best-known and best-loved talking animal (a koala) in Australian children's literature appears in Dorothy Wall's *Blinky Bill* (1933/1990) and its sequels, but the first creatures invented for the bush were May Gibbs's Gumnut Babies in *Snugglepot and Cuddlepie* (1918) and its successors. During the 1920s a favorable climate for children's literature began to develop in New Zealand. Early books with a New Zealand setting had been preoccupied with the indigenous Maori people and with the land itself.

Nathaniel Hawthorne is considered the author of the first American book written specifically for children, *A Wonder Book for Boys and Girls* (1851/1893). However, England was the first and steadiest source of books for American children. It continued as a major source of literature for North American children for generations, and led the way to global publishing. American children made no distinction among British and American books or those from other countries. They read Carlo Collodi's *Pinocchio* (1833/1993) from Italy, Johanna Spyri's *Heidi* (1881/1945) from Switzerland, Selma Lagerlof's *The Wonderful Adventures of Nils* (1906–1907/1991) from Sweden, and Antoine de Saint-Exupéry's *The Little Prince* (1943) from France with equal enthusiasm.

The first child labor laws, which were passed in 1907, freed children to go to school. As more children learned how to read and write due to universal first- through eighth-grade public schools, the quantity and the types of books published for them rapidly increased. At the same time, new technologies helped reduce publishing costs, and the public generosity of charitable individuals allowed public library systems to develop rapidly, putting books in the hands of vast numbers of children worldwide. Howard Pyle (1853–1911) was considered a notable writer at the turn of the 20th century. He published a story in *St. Nicholas* magazine and for many years continued to write fairy tales animated by the richness of the genuine folktale. Gradually he put more of his own thinking into the stories. His collection of fairy tales and verses, *Pepper and Salt* (1886/1913), was followed by *The Wonder Clock* (1888/2003).

Publishers began to establish departments of children's books. In 1919 the U.S. publishing house Macmillan launched a department devoted entirely to children's books. Louise Bechtel Seaman, who had worked as an editor of adult books and taught in a progressive school, was appointed department head. In 1922 Helen Dean Fish became the first children's book editor at Frederick A. Stokes and Company, and in 1923 May Massee took the leadership of the children's book department at Doubleday. In 1924, *The Horn Book Magazine* was published by the Bookshop for Boys and Girls in Boston under the guidance of Bertha Mahony and Elinor Whitney. In 1933 May Massee moved from Doubleday to open a children's book department at Viking. Soon other publishers began to open children's book departments, and children's literature blossomed into the 20th century. Modern picture books began to develop during the 1920s and 1930s; in the 1940s through the 1960s, children's and adolescent books became an increasingly important part of libraries, schools, homes, and publishing houses. Appendix E contains more details about the history of children's books, and Figure 1.3 lists some milestones in the history of literature for children and adolescents.

Children's and Adolescent Literature Today and Tomorrow

The spread of public libraries with rooms devoted to children's and teenagers' reading interests opened the floodgates, inviting an eager audience to read books and magazines and to listen to stories told aloud. Early publications sought to instill a community's values in the young, to socialize them, and to teach them. Over the past 150 years this approach has changed to reflect a broad spectrum of social values that come from many cultures and cross international boundaries. Teaching Idea 1.2 describes a way to help young readers compare old and new books so they can understand how children's books have changed over the years.

Today's literature for children and adolescents is marked by continued experimentation with innovative formats and

Milestones in Literature for Children and Adolescents

1865	Lewis Carroll, *Alice's Adventures in Wonderland*
1902	Walter de la Mare, *Songs of Childhood*
	Rudyard Kipling, *Just So Stories*
	E. Nesbit, *Five Children and It*
	Beatrix Potter, *The Tale of Peter Rabbit*
1904	J. M. Barrie, *Peter Pan*
1908	Kenneth Grahame, *The Wind in the Willows*
	L. M. Montgomery, *Anne of Green Gables*
1922	Margery Williams, *The Velveteen Rabbit*
1924	A. A. Milne, *When We Were Very Young*
1934	Jean de Brunhoff, *The Story of Babar*
	P. L. Travers, *Mary Poppins*
1936	Edward Ardizzone, *Little Tim and the Brave Sea Captain*
1938	Marjorie Kinnan Rawlings, *The Yearling*
1939	Ludwig Bemelmans, *Madeline*
	T. S. Eliot, *Old Possum's Book of Practical Cats*
1940	Maud Hart Lovelace, *Betsy-Tacy*
	Eric Knight, *Lassie Come-Home*
1941	Robert McCloskey, *Make Way for Ducklings*
	H. A. Rey, *Curious George*
1943	Esther Forbes, *Johnny Tremain*
1950	C. S. Lewis, *The Lion, the Witch, and the Wardrobe*
	Elizabeth Yates, *Amos Fortune: Free Man*
1952	Ben Lucien Burman, *High Water at Catfish Bend*
	Mary Norton, *The Borrowers*
	E. B. White, *Charlotte's Web*
1954	Lucy M. Boston, *The Children of Green Knowe*
	Rosemary Sutcliff, *The Eagle of the Ninth*
	J.R.R. Tolkien, *The Fellowship of the Ring*
1958	Philippa Pearce, *Tom's Midnight Garden*
1962	Joan Aiken, *The Wolves of Willoughby Chase*
	Ezra Jack Keats, *The Snowy Day*
	Madeleine L'Engle, *A Wrinkle in Time*

1963	Maurice Sendak, *Where the Wild Things Are*
1964	Lloyd Alexander, *The Book of Three*
	Roald Dahl, *Charlie and the Chocolate Factory*
	Louise Fitzhugh, *Harriet the Spy*
	Irene Hunt, *Across Five Aprils*
1968	Ursula Le Guin, *A Wizard of Earthsea*
	Paul Zindel, *The Pigman*
1971	Virginia Hamilton, *The Planet of Junior Brown*
	Robert C. O'Brien, *Mrs. Frisby and the Rats of NIMH*
1972	Richard Adams, *Watership Down*
1974	Robert Cormier, *The Chocolate War*
1976	Mildred Taylor, *Roll of Thunder, Hear My Cry*
1977	Katherine Paterson, *Bridge to Terabithia*
1978	Janet and Allan Ahlberg, *Each Peach Pear Plum*
1983	Anthony Browne, *Gorilla*
	Mem Fox, *Possum Magic*
1985	Patricia MacLachlan, *Sarah, Plain and Tall*
1988	Paul Fleischman, *Joyful Noise*
1993	Lois Lowry, *The Giver*
1997	Karen Hesse, *Out of the Dust*
1998	J. K. Rowling, *Harry Potter and the Sorcerer's Stone*
	Louis Sachar, *Holes*
1999	Walter Dean Myers, *Monster*
2000	Philip Pullman, *The Amber Spyglass*
2001	Marc Aronson, *Sir Walter Raleigh and the Quest for El Dorado*
2003	Kate DiCamillo, *The Tale of Despereaux*
2004	Russell Freedman, *The Voice That Challenged a Nation: Marian Anderson and the Struggle for Equal Rights*

literary techniques and with expanding the boundaries of genre. Literature for adolescents, collections of short stories, and books of fantasy and science fiction are becoming much more plentiful. The literature continues to reflect the concerns of society, as books about September 11, 2001, and books with a Middle Eastern setting or characters are now available. Technology and the marketplace still influence children's literature. Finally, today's literature reflects, at least in part, the diversity of our increasingly global society.

• • EXPERIMENTING WITH • • GENRE AND TECHNIQUE

The verse novel—a novel-length narrative written in verse— appeared on the adolescent literature scene with the publication of Virginia Euwer Wolff's *Make Lemonade* (A) in 1993. By 2004 there were about 30 titles, including Karen Hesse's Newbery Medal–winning *Out of the Dust* (A); *True Believer* (A), also by Wolff and winner of the National Book Award; and Angela Johnson's *The First Part Last* (A), winner of the

Teaching Idea 1-2

Compare Picture Books of Past and Present

Ask students to gather picture books of the past from parents, grandparents, relatives, neighbors, friends, librarians, antique book dealers, flea markets, or garage sales. Visit a museum or library collection of historical children's books to examine the books at close range. If you cannot locate early books, select reprinted classics, such as *The Tale of Peter Rabbit, John Gilpin's Ride,* or *Peter Parley.* Choose early Newbery (*The Story of Mankind,* 1922/1972) and Caldecott (*Animals of the Bible,* 1938) Medal winners. Also collect several recent picture books, preferably award winners, to compare with the old. Prepare a comparison chart as shown here.

	Old Title	New Title
Color		
Style of Art		
Relation to Story		
Quality of Art as Art		
Attractiveness		
Visual Appeal		
Portrayal of Children		

Questions to Ask About the Books

✳ Is the art coordinated with the text? What do you think about the art?

✳ What differences in the use of color, media, or other artistic elements do you notice?

✳ How are children portrayed in the early books? In later books?

After completing the chart, discuss the differences your students found.

Michael L. Printz Award in 2004. By the end of 2004 there were more than 45 (Campbell, 2004), some of which, such as Sharon Creech's *Love That Dog* (I), Lindsay Lee Johnson's *Soul Moon Soup* (I–A), and Jacqueline Woodson's *Locomotion* (I–A), a Boston Globe–Horn Book honor book, were appropriate for a somewhat younger audience. This innovative genre seems to be here to stay, and some of our best writers are experimenting with it.

Although not a new genre, the short story is appearing more frequently, especially in adolescent literature. Most of these are collections of stories from various writers, such as Michael Cart's edited *Necessary Noise: Stories about Our Families as They Really Are* (A), Gordon Snell's edited *Thicker than Water: Coming-of-Age Stories by Irish and Irish American Writers* (A), and Sharon Flake's *Who Am I without Him? Short Stories about Girls and the Boys in Their Lives* (A). Some of them, however, are interlocking stories that together form a well-crafted novel in which the story is told through different points of view. Examples of this approach include Paul Fleischman's *Seedfolks* (A) and Ellen

Wittlinger's *What's in a Name?* (A). Like Wittlinger's book, Walter Dean Myers's *145th Street Stories* (A) occurs over a considerable span of time and is told by multiple narrators.

Myers broke new ground with his 2000 Printz Award–winning novel, *Monster* (A), in which he combined the journals of a young man on trial for murder with the script for the film that the same young man was composing about his experience. Paul Fleischman's *Seek* (A) is told entirely in dialogue—from various supporting characters, radio broadcasts, and the protagonist. Innovative novels such as these build on earlier experimentation by authors such as Avi in *Nothing But the Truth* (A) and *Who Was That Masked Man Anyway?* (A).

More than just long, bound comic books, graphic novels have rapidly gained popularity, especially among adolescents. Today there is much more available than the **Tin-Tin** books. In Japan, graphic novels have been very popular for many decades, and the increasing globalization of children's and adolescent literature brought them to the attention of North American readers (Michaels, 2004). Older children

© Helen Robinson

Lindsay Lee Johnson's **Soul Moon Soup** *tells a painful story through beautiful language and evocative images.*

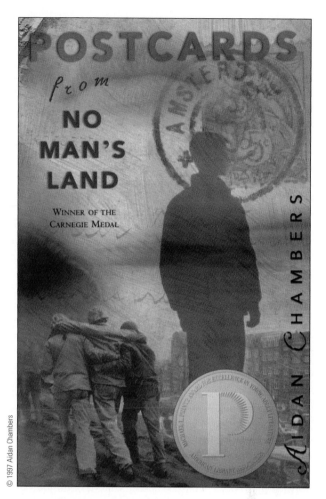

© 1997 Aidan Chambers

This powerful novel tells the stories of two sets of people separated by time but linked by love.

and adolescents responded with great delight. Although Art Spiegelman's **Maus** books were not intended for an adolescent audience, young readers quickly made them their own. Other popular adult authors, such as Neil Gaiman in his **Sandman** series, have produced graphic novels that enthrall young readers. From this interest on the part of both the readers and the creators has come an innovation in genre—the graphic picture book, which we discuss in Chapter 3.

Creative authors and illustrators ignore prior constraints and convention to expand genre, age-level appropriateness, and standard formats. Where does Louis Sachar's Newbery Medal–winning *Holes* (I) belong? Is it fantasy or realistic, historical or contemporary? Is it a spoof or a coming-of-age story? Is Aidan Chambers's *Postcards from No Man's Land* (A), winner of both the Carnegie Medal and the Printz Award, an historical fiction novel about World War II or a contemporary realistic novel about a young man's coming of age in Amsterdam? Even the Library of Congress cannot decide, describing it as "alternating stories" and giving it no less than six descriptors.

Innovative literary techniques developed in adult literature also appear in books for young readers. David Almond's *Skellig* (I–A), winner of the 2001 Printz Award, and some of his subsequent books contain magical realism, a literary device usually associated with adult authors from South America in which the boundary between realism and fantasy is blurred so as to make readers accept the fantastic as reality. Ann Cameron also experiments with magical realism in *Colibri* (A).

• • BLURRING AGE • • BOUNDARIES

Picture books are not just for small children anymore. Increasing numbers of picture books are being published for older readers, and many of them explore issues that are not appropriate for discussion by young children. Older children and adolescents who look at lots of television, computer screens, videos, and movies become visual learners, and many of today's picture books are geared to their sensibilities. Although some worry about the amount of TV, video, and computer viewing done by older readers and claim that today's students do not read as well as students of two decades ago, comparison studies show that they read equally as well as earlier generations (Kamil, Mosenthal, Pearson, & Barr, 2000).

Adolescent literature is enjoying an increase in both popularity and production. There are so many novels for adolescents published today that in 1999 the American Library Association (ALA) established the Michael L. Printz Award specifically for young adult fiction. With the resurgence of adolescent literature came the resurgence of what we call "crossover" books, books that are written for adolescents that adults read and books written for adults that adolescents adopt as their own. For example, Yann Martel's *The Life of Pi,* which won Great Britain's coveted Booker Prize, is delighting many young readers. Mark Haddon's *The Curious Incident of the Dog in the Night-Time* was published in two editions—one for adults and one for adolescents (Wynne-Jones, 2004). There are also several adaptations of popular adult books that reach a younger audience, such as *Revenge of the Whale: The True Story of the Whale-ship* **Essex** (I–A), by Nathaniel Philbrick, an adaptation of his National Book Award winner, *In the Heart of the Sea: The Tragedy of the Whaleship* **Essex.** Editor Michael Cart created a literary journal, *RUSH HOUЯ,* published twice a year, that appeals to older adolescents and adults in their early 20s. The stories, essays, art, poetry, and excerpts from forthcoming books published in each volume of the journal are thematically focused.

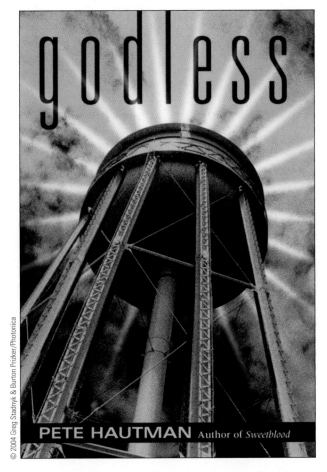

At first it seemed funny to worship a water tower, but then it became something much more serious in Pete Hautman's **Godless.**

• • TIMELY TOPICS • •

Along with the upsurge in the popularity of adolescent literature came a broadening of audience; now review journals such as *The Horn Book Magazine* distinguish between adolescent fiction for middle school readers and that for high school readers. Indeed, this distinction became necessary because of the edgier nature of books for older adolescents, such as the focus on sex and high school boys in Melvin Burgess's *Doing It* (A). Generally, the fiction for younger adolescents is less intense and graphic.

New ideas and topics always appear in literature, as literature itself reflects what is happening in our changing world. Today we have several excellent books about the September 11, 2001, tragedy. Michael Cart's edited volume, *911: The Book of Help* (A), is an anthology of essays, stories, and reflections by a variety of notable authors for children and adolescents. Wilborn Hampton's moving account of that day, *September 11, 2001: Attack on New York City* (A), narrates the stories of a diverse group of New Yorkers just prior to, during, and after the attack. He also describes what

Mohamed Atta did the night before. Maira Kalman's *Fireboat: The Heroic Adventures of the* **John J. Harvey** (P–I), winner of the Boston Globe–Horn Book Award, acknowledges the tragedy in a way that is manageable for younger readers, as does Jeanette Winter's *September Roses* (P).

Although there have been a number of excellent books set in the Middle East, such as Suzanne Fisher Staples's *Shabanu* and *Haveli* (both A), there has been a recent increase in books set in that region or about people who have fled from that region. *Running on Eggs* (I), a story of friendship between a Jewish girl and a Palestinian girl by Anna Levine, is a positive picture of possibilities for friendship and peace. Daniella Carmi's *Samir and Yonatan* (I–A) also explores Palestinian-Israeli friendship but is less hopeful. Naomi Shihab Nye, a Palestinian American writer, has given us *Sitti's Secrets* (P–I), a lovely picture book describing an Arab American girl's visit to her Palestinian relatives; her novel *Habibi* (I–A) is based on the same premise but graphically explores the political and social realities of living in Palestine. Her book of poetry, *19 Varieties of Gazelle* (I–A), is again focused on Palestine and offers older readers a glimpse of a culture that is on the brink of being shattered.

Beginning with *The Breadwinner* (I), Deborah Ellis sets three books in contemporary Afghanistan. Other authors have given us many new stories of children who are refugees from political oppression, the violence of war, or abject poverty. There are many new books that explore issues that are important in today's society, such as sexual orientation and religion. Pete Hautman's *Godless* (A), an exploration of the struggle of many adolescents as they reject their parents' religious beliefs, won the 2004 National Book Award. We discuss these books in several chapters in this text.

• • TECHNOLOGY • • AND COMMERCIALISM

Sparked by the spectacular sales of the recorded versions of the **Harry Potter** books, audiobooks for young readers are now a fast-growing market. Publishing houses, such as Random House and HarperCollins, are increasing their production of audiobooks, and parents, teachers, and librarians are thinking and talking about their place in the world of children's reading (Varley, 2002). Listening to a book is certainly not the same as reading it, but listening to a wonderful recording of a great book offers its own opportunities for engagement, literary appreciation, and comprehension. Listening to Listening Library's full-cast recording of Philip Pullman's **His Dark Materials** trilogy is as amazing an experience as reading the books. Filmmakers too have successfully adapted several popular books, such as J. K. Rowling's **Harry Potter** series and the Lemony Snicket **Series of Unfortunate Events,** Chris Van Allsburg's *The Polar Express,* and Kate DiCamillo's *Because of Winn-Dixie.*

Commercialism has become dominant. The end of the 20th century and the early years of the 21st century have been a time of dramatic change in the publishing world. We've seen mergers, buyouts, conglomerates, the establishment of new publishers, disagreements among writers and publishers vying for electronic rights, and a continuous search for that one "big book" that will sell millions of copies and ensure financial success. Economics drives business in bookstores and in publishing. Once upon a time, the person who owned the publishing company also ran the company, made the publishing decisions, and knew the authors personally. No more. Big business practices make warm and friendly personal relationships between publishers and authors less likely. The same kind of change is apparent in the bookselling industry as well. Many independent bookstores have vanished; big chains prevail.

Increasingly, there's more to a book than just words and pictures. Books come with finger puppets and a finger puppet theater, felt board pieces to stuff into the tummy of the old lady who swallowed a fly, dress-up outfits or animals to

Children extend their imaginative play by pretending that book characters come to life in stuffed animals and dolls.

cuddle with. Children's and adolescent literature now encompasses stories, poetry, and nonfiction in every medium. In addition to books, we have computers, film, videos, CD-ROM products, videodiscs, microcomputer software, audiocassettes, interactive games, and the Internet for a visually oriented audience. The ALA provides an annual list of notable children's videos and great websites for kids (go to www.ala.org/ala/alsc; follow the links).

In late fall 2002, the International Children's Digital Library (ICDL) was launched, a joint project of the Human-Computer Interaction Laboratory at the University of Maryland and the Internet Archive in San Francisco. By early 2004 there were almost 400 books online; almost 10,000 more will be added in the next five years (Cummins, 2004). Although the system is not yet perfect, the ICDL's goal of providing free access to children's books from around the world, to the children of the world, is magnificent.

• • INCREASING DIVERSITY • •

Through international cooperation among publishers and worthy projects like the ICDL, we now have a global literature. International coedition publishing ventures in which the same book is published simultaneously in several different countries are developed annually at the Bologna Book Fair, the Frankfurt Book Fair, the London Book Fair, and the Guadalajara Book Fair. International publishing poses special problems, as there are conflicting ideas about how different cultural practices should be presented in "imported" editions. Should certain cultural information be changed to make a book easier for a different audience to understand? The title of J. K. Rowling's first book was changed from *Harry Potter and the* **Philosopher's** *Stone* to

Harry Potter and the Sorcerer's *Stone* for the American edition, purportedly because publishers were unsure about American children's ability to relate to the word *philosopher.* Recently, however, publishers are realizing that keeping the flavor of the original language and customs is more important and that young readers can and do manage unusual words! If a book is culturally "sanitized," readers lose the opportunity to participate in another's world.

Organizations such as the International Board on Books for Young People and the International Reading Association, with members from around the world, also help sustain a global perspective.

North American literature for children and adolescents is also continuing to become more diverse, although the pace is still painfully slow. Publishers dedicated to multicultural literature, the increasing number of talented writers and illustrators of many backgrounds, and the demand of children, librarians, and teachers support this increasing diversity. The establishment of awards that specifically recognize achievement in literature by and about particular cultural groups also supports the development of diverse literature. Awards draw attention to books, and attention means better sales, which get the attention of the publishing business. For example, the Coretta Scott King Awards and the Pura Belpre Awards reflect the increasingly important presence of books by and about African Americans and Latinos.

• • BUILDING ON • • THE PAST, LOOKING TOWARD THE FUTURE

Predicting the future of children's books became easier when Roger Sutton, editor in chief of *The Horn Book Magazine,* devoted an entire issue (November/ December 2000) to the topic. He asked several literary critics to hypothesize just how children's literature might look in the new millennium. He also asked a number of writers to choose one book from the 20th century that he or she would most like to see survive into the 22nd. Among those selected were Robert McCloskey's *Make Way for Ducklings* (P), selected by Natalie Babbitt; Philippa Pearce's *Tom's Midnight Garden* (I), selected by Susan Cooper; Frances Hodgson Burnett's *The Secret Garden* (I), selected by Lois Lowry; T. H. White's *The Once and Future King* (A), selected by Jane Yolen; E. B. White's *Charlotte's Web* (I), selected by Katherine Paterson; and Natalie Babbitt's *Tuck Everlasting* (I), selected by Tim Wynne-Jones. Other professionals in the field of children's and adolescent books selected 100 books that shaped the 20th century. A selection from this list appears in the Booklist at the end of this chapter. Anita Silvey (2004), a former editor for Houghton Mifflin and of *The Horn Book Magazine,* has created her own list in *100 Best Books for Children,*

although she couldn't resist adding a few extra titles at the end! How fortunate we are that it is so difficult to select only 100.

Given the history and durability of children's and adolescent literature, the future will certainly be interesting. No doubt we will have more international literature; more culturally diverse writers and artists will present their culture more accurately; global economics will play a stronger role; readers will have ready access to interviews with authors and illustrators on the World Wide Web; and projects such as the IDCL will help bring literature to all children. The many talented writers and illustrators who fill our lives with wonderful books will continue to do so, and new talent and new permutations of genre will never cease to emerge. At the same time, attempts at censorship will increase, as will pressures on schools and libraries in the form of lack of funding, mandated high-stakes testing, and increasing numbers of children who need food, clothes, and stability as well as books. Our world is changing, and literature for children and adolescents will change with it. For now, we have wonderful books to offer our children.

The Challenge of Selecting and Using Literature for Children and Adolescents

Books can play a significant role in the life of the young, but the extent to which they will do so depends on the adults surrounding them. Books and children aren't made of Velcro; they don't stick to each other without a little help from significant others, including parents, grandparents, teachers, librarians, community leaders, volunteers, and others who come into contact with them. Adults are responsible for determining a child's literary heritage by selecting and presenting nursery rhymes, traditional tales, beautiful poetry, great novels, and riveting nonfiction. This selection process is neither easy nor without pitfalls. Knowing the literature is important. Knowing children and community is equally important.

• • JUDGING QUALITY • •

Never before have we had so many beautiful books and such high-quality books from which to choose, but we need informed judgment to select them. Once you become familiar with the various genres in contemporary children's and adolescent literature, and once you learn the types of books your students connect with, you will find many ways to use books in the classroom. Part Two of this text discusses the interaction of children with books—specifically, how carefully selected, culturally diverse literature enhances children's appreciation of their world, and how literature can be used effectively across the curriculum.

It is important to build a diverse collection, because culturally diverse books portray the uniqueness of people while demonstrating a common humanity that connects us all. Human needs, emotions, and desires are similar; books can help us appreciate the similarities as well as celebrate the uniqueness of cultural groups. North America, once considered a melting pot where cultural differences disappeared, is more like a patchwork quilt today—patches of varying colors, textures, shapes, and sizes, all held together by a common thread of humanity (Jackson, 1992).

Children's books offer opportunities for building background knowledge and understanding about the world. Picture books, poetry, folklore, realistic and historical fiction, biographies, and nonfiction that celebrate cultural diversity are available for a wide range of readers. Culturally diverse books help achieve the goal of cross-cultural understanding. We discuss building a culturally diverse collection in Chapter 11, and we describe how these books can be used in the classroom in Chapters 13 and 14.

Selecting books to use in classrooms is a multidimensional task. First, think of all the excellent pieces of literature you want your students to know about and, second, think of how literature can enrich your curriculum in every subject area. Because of the diversity and richness in children's literature today, your students' experiences with books can be infinitely varied. With so much to choose from, we as teachers can select high-quality literature: books that use interesting language in creative ways, develop important ideas, are potentially interesting to children, and (through picture books) contain artistically excellent illustrations. Criteria for selecting each genre are summarized in Figure 1.4. We elaborate on and apply these criteria in each genre chapter, and they form the basis for our discussion of building a culturally diverse collection in Chapter 11.

• • STANDARDS, • • MANDATES, AND TESTS

Although there are many joys in sharing books with young readers, there are also many challenges. Two of the biggest challenges are finding time in the school day and dealing with the censorship of books and other materials.

Figure **1-4**

Criteria for Good Books by Genre

Genre	Text	Illustration
Poetry	Rhythmic, sensory images.	Interprets beyond literal meaning.
Folklore	Patterned language, fast-paced plot. Sounds like spoken language.	Interpretive of the tale and cultural origins.
Fantasy	Believable, consistent, logical world. Clearly defined conflict. Strong characterization.	Extends fanciful elements; reflects characterization and events.
Science Fiction	Speculative extrapolation of fact. Hypotheses about life in untraveled worlds.	Visualizes imaginative worlds; reflects characterization and events.
Realistic Fiction	Story is possible, reasonable, plausible. Well-defined conflict; strong characterization.	Verisimilar; reflects mood, characterization and events accurately.
Historical Fiction	Setting affects plot; details and language in keeping with period.	Authentic images of the period.
Biography	Story of a person's complete life or an interesting part of the person's life.	Authentic images of life segments.
Nonfiction	Clarity; factual accuracy.	Clarifies and extends concepts.

In the past few years our schools have been under extreme scrutiny, and teachers under extreme pressure. We have standards in most states that describe what schoolchildren should be able to do at each grade level. This is a good thing, when the standards are sound, as we all should know the goals that we are trying to accomplish. National organizations, too, have set national standards. The International Reading Association and the National Council of Teachers of English worked together to create Standards for the English Language Arts, which can be found at the websites of those organizations (www.reading.org and www.ncte.org). If you examine these standards, you will find that many of them can best be met through the combination of children's literature and good teaching. The point is that children's literature can help you teach so that your students meet the standards.

Whereas standards can be beneficial and can serve to promote reading, too many national and state-mandated tests can work against the inclusion of children's literature in the curriculum. When a high-stakes test looms and both a teacher's job and the students' futures are on the line, time to read seems to evaporate. Yet reading a variety of texts for a variety of purposes does serve students well, even when they are taking tests. Generally, students who read the most are also among the best readers and the best test takers. Creative teachers, knowing that they have an obligation to prepare their students to do their best but not wanting to allow standardized tests to take over their curriculum, often teach their students how to take the tests—how to read and answer questions—much as they teach their students how to read and understand a genre of literature. Tests, like literary genres, have structures and formats that can be taught so that they are familiar to students. When treated in this manner, preparing for these tests becomes simply another unit.

It is vital that we do not let testing take over our teaching, for if time to read and savor books disappears, there will be fewer avid readers. Books are the secret ingredient that keep children doing the hard work of learning to read, learning to read fluently, and learning to read with comprehension. Much of the recent research on motivation indicates that children's literature plays a central role in engaging readers (Pressley et al., 2003). Reading engaging books, and thinking, writing, and talking about them with others also provide opportunities for students to develop the higher-order thinking skills that will enable them to be successful citizens of the 21st century. (See Strickland, Galda, & Cullinan, 2004, for a discussion of this topic.)

For these reasons, and others mentioned at the beginning of this chapter, it is important that we offer wonderful books to our students so that they view books as a vital part of their lives. We must be careful in what we choose. Even when we are, however, it is not unusual to have a book "challenged" by a parent, community member, or even administrator. Challenges to your students' right to read are called *censorship*.

✳ ✳ CENSORSHIP ✳ ✳ AND SELECTION

Books about virtually any topic or issue in the world are found in children's and especially adolescent literature. For example, Laurie Halse Anderson's main character in *Speak* (A) remains silent for most of the novel but finally reveals that she has been sexually abused and identifies her attacker. Walter Dean Myers's *Monster* involves the murder of a Korean storekeeper and the trial for murder of a teenage boy. The wide range of topics covered in children's and adolescent literature gives young people access to a comprehensive picture of their world; it also invites serious attempts to censor what they read. Many people feel that children should not face difficult issues; others believe that difficult issues should be presented in books that reflect the real world children face. Sometimes an author's realistic portrayal of language or customs disturbs adults, as in Kris Franklin's *The Grape Thief* (I–A), which caused some argument about whether the ethnic slurs present in the book—as used by the characters in the 1920s small-town setting—were too nasty or not nasty enough to be realistic.

Even books that seem quite harmless, such as Beatrix Potter's *The Tale of Peter Rabbit* (N–P), can cause some adults to want to keep it from children. In the case of Peter, many felt that it was sexist, because the girls were good and the boy got to have all the fun, and they wanted the book removed from nursery schools in London. The outpouring of challenges to the use of the **Harry Potter** books, and fantasy in general, occurred because many people believe that magic is not fantasy at all, but real, and as such is the work of evil. The point is that although we all have beliefs and preferences, we cannot prevent others from reading, viewing, or listening to the material they choose. That is what the First Amendment is all about. The ALA's Office for Intellectual Freedom publishes a list of frequently challenged books. *Hit List for Children 2* and *Hit List for Young Adults 2* provide resources for withstanding challenges to the targeted books.

Most professional organizations, such as the ALA, the International Reading Association (IRA), and the National Council of Teachers of English (NCTE), believe that parents have the right to decide what their own children read but not the right to tell other people's children what they should read. Sometimes books that teachers and librarians choose for school study provoke criticism from parents or community members. Often parents simply request that their child not read a particular book; it is easy to make provisions for that. Sometimes, however, an individual parent, school board member, or member of the larger community will request that no child be allowed to read a particular book; this is a bigger problem.

Suppressing reading material is *censorship,* a remedy that creates more problems than it solves. Choosing reading material that does not offend our taste, however, is *selection—not censorship.* Censorship is the attempt to deny others the right to read something the censor thinks is offensive. Selection is the process of choosing appropriate material for readers according to literary and educational judgments.

The NCTE (1983, p. 18) differentiates between selection and censorship in five dimensions: (1) Censorship *excludes* specific materials; selection *includes* specific material to give breadth to collections. (2) Censorship is *negative;* selection is *affirmative.* (3) Censorship intends to *control* the reading of others; selection intends to *advise* the reading of others. (4) Censorship seeks to *indoctrinate and limit access* to ideas and information, whereas selection seeks to *educate and increase access* to ideas and information. (5) Censorship looks at specific aspects and *parts of a work in isolation,* whereas selection examines the relationship of *parts to each other and to a work as a whole.*

The controversy surrounding many books is rooted in a blatant attempt to impose censorship, to limit student access to materials, and to impose the religious and political views of a small segment of society on those whose views may differ. The IRA (www.reading.org), the NCTE (www.ncte.org), the ALA (www.ala.org), and the National Coalition Against Censorship (www.ncac.org) condemn attempts by self-appointed censors to restrict students' access to quality reading materials. Professional associations and most school districts have established procedures for dealing with attempts at censorship. School media specialists or principals need to have a standard process to follow if a book is challenged.

All these organizations have wonderful websites that provide information and guidance about censorship. Go to those websites and familiarize yourself with their information. For example, the NCTE publishes *Guidelines for Selection of Materials in English Language Arts Programs,* in which they advocate for a clear, written policy that reflects local interests and issues for the selection of materials in any English language arts program. Because selection must be tied to community standards, there is no one set of guidelines, but rather general principles: material must have a clear connection to established educational objectives and must address the needs of the students.

NCTE's Anti-Censorship Center (www.ncte.org/about/issues/censorship) offers a wealth of information about what to do if a book is challenged. There is a site for reporting a censorship incident, and a listing of sites that contain news reports of censorship. A listing of helpful online resources includes instructions on how to obtain a series of written rationales for the most commonly challenged books, as well as the site for Students' Right to Read, which gives detailed procedures for responding to challenges, including a copy of the "Citizen's Request for Reconsideration of a Work." This form asks those who complain about a book for detailed information through questions that stress the sound educational reasons the book was selected by the teacher or school. This form is also available in the Tool Bank for this text.

If a book you have chosen is challenged, don't panic. Get the complaint in writing and take it to your media specialist, principal, or other appropriate school-based person. The most important thing to remember is to select wisely—know your resources for making good selections as well as your reasons for selection.

Resources for Selecting Literature

The voluminous body of high-quality children's and adolescent literature shows that the field attracts talented writers and illustrators. Creative people respond to and change their world; innovation is abundantly evident in the children's book world. The number of books published continues to grow, which makes selection even more difficult. Our job as teachers, librarians, and parents is to select the best from the vast array of books. The primary goal of this textbook is to help you recognize good literature and to develop your ability to select quality material. Resources that you will find useful are review journals, awards, and other material that calls attention to literature for children. As poet Walter de la Mare stated, "Only the rarest kind of best is good enough for children" (1942, p. 9).

• • REVIEW JOURNALS • •

Sources of information about new children's and adolescent literature include review resources: *Booklinks, Booklist, Bulletin of the Center for Children's Books (BCCB), The Horn Book Magazine,* the *Horn Book Guide, Publisher's Weekly,* and *School Library Journal.* Although not primarily review journals, *Language Arts, The Reading Teacher, Journal of Children's Literature,* and *Journal of Adolescent and Adult Literacy* contain useful book reviews as well. Descriptions of these and other resources are found in Appendix B.

• • BOOK AWARDS • •

Excitement in the children's and adolescent book world reaches fever pitch in January, when the Newbery, Caldecott, Printz, Siebert, King, and other awards from the ALA are announced. Separate selection committees, one for each award, read *all* the recommended books published during the year and meet for several days to decide which books will receive the prestigious awards. Waiting to hear who won is like waiting for the announcement of the Pulitzer Prize for Literature.

Why are these awards so important? Experts declare that the winners are the outstanding examples of children's literature for the year. The awards have significant educational, social, cultural, and financial impact. Books that receive the awards will be read by millions of children around the world. In the United States alone, every public and school library will purchase the appropriate award-winning books. Winning one of these awards, therefore, also guarantees considerable financial reward for the author, illustrator, and publisher. The awards receive widespread media attention, and winning authors and illustrators receive numerous speaking invitations. The winners of these and some of the many other awards, both national and international, appear in Appendix A.

• • ELECTRONIC • • DATABASES

Teachers and students can access an infinite amount of current information about children's books, authors, illustrators, professional publications, teaching ideas, library collections, conferences, and other activities through the World Wide Web. You need only access to the Internet, a search engine such as InfoTrac College Edition, and a few key terms: "children's literature," "adolescent literature," "young adult literature," "children's books," "children's authors," and "children's illustrators" should get you started. You will find numerous websites to help you find out about children's and adolescent literature. Many of them, such as the Children's Literature Network (www.childrensliteraturenetwork.org), will have live links to other sites, including authors' sites.

Many authors have a home page; typing an author's name into a search engine will usually get you there. At the home page you can initiate a conversation, ask questions, learn about the authors' new books, and find out about their speaking appearances. Many publishers have programs online that provide access to teaching ideas, books, and author information. Several publishers sponsor online interviews with authors, illustrators, librarians, teachers, book reviewers, and editors. See Figure 1.5 for some helpful Internet sites.

Figure 1-5

Electronic Databases for Children's and Adolescent Literature

www.acs.ucalgary.ca/~dkbrown/
A reliable source with a search function for literature resources. Located at the University of Calgary, Canada.

www.ala.org
Access the American Library Association and the awards they administer, as well as the annual lists of notable books, videos, and websites.

www.bookwire.com
Switch back and forth among *School Library Journal, Publisher's Weekly,* and *Library Journal.* Book reviews. You'll visit this website frequently.

www.britannica.com
Access the *Encyclopedia Britannica.* Full-text articles free of charge.

www.carolhurst.com
Carol Hurst is an informed book person. She posts lively discussions of books to use with suggested thematic units as well as other pertinent information.

www.cbcbooks.org
Maintained by the Children's Book Council, this site is full of information, including author and illustrator links.

www.childrensliteraturenetwork.org
Contains just about everything you would want in a children's literature website, including links to other good sites.

www.downhomebooks.com/authors.htm
Contains interviews with authors and other information.

www.education.wisc.edu/ccbc
The Cooperative Children's Book Center contains reviews of over 50,000 books. ccbc-net is an interesting discussion list.

www.lcweb.loc.gov
The Library of Congress is the place to find book titles by a specific author. Click on "Search Our Catalogs" and "Other Libraries' Catalogs." Conduct a simple search by last name of author, first name. Click on "Search."

www.nationalgeographic.com
National Geographic has several interactive activities, such as finding the hidden animals in a forest and learning about them.

www.ncte.org
Access the National Council of Teachers of English and the awards they administer.

www.reading.org
Access the International Reading Association and the awards they administer.

www.scils.rutgers.edu/special/kay/kayhp2.html
Information and ideas about children's and adolescent literature ranging from censorship and research to the history of children's literature.

••• Summary •••

The story of children's and adolescent literature is intertwined with the social, political, and economic history of the world. Children's and adolescents' books are shaped by prevailing views of what adults believe children should be taught, but also by the amount of time children have to explore books and by competing sources of entertainment available to children. Today we have a wealth of literature for children and adolescents. We have moved from crude hornbooks and religious tracts to books of artistic and literary excellence. Young readers are the beneficiaries of this wealth.

Exploring the field of literature for children and adolescents can seem overwhelming at first, but knowledge about books is addictive. The more you know, the more you want to know and to share with young readers. With each new day there is more to know. This textbook will help you begin to explore the wonderful world of books. Enjoy!

In "Storyselling: Are Publishers Changing the Way Children Read?" in the September/October 2002 issue of *The Horn Book Magazine,* Daniel Hade asks some very provocative questions about the role of big corporate publishing houses and their spin-off merchandising in promoting reading. Read his article and think about his points. Do you agree or disagree?

Look at the first segment of the video that accompanies this text, in which Mary Casanova talks about writing books for children. Note what she says about weaving stories from what she knows about and what she is curious enough to find out about, and how her settings and characters influence one another.

Booklist

Selections from One Hundred Books That Shaped the Century

Four librarian book experts (Karen Breen, Ellen Fader, Kathleen Odean, and Zena Sutherland) chose 100 books that shaped the 20th century ("One Hundred Books That Shaped the Century," 2000). An asterisk (*) indicates that the book was a unanimous first-round selection. A double asterisk (**) indicates that the *author* was a unanimous first-round selection but that there were differences of opinion over which works to include.

*Cormier, Robert, *The Chocolate War*
Cresswell, Helen, *Ordinary Jack*
Crews, Donald, *Freight Train*
Dahl, Roald, *Charlie and the Chocolate Factory*
dePaola, Tomie, *Strega Nona*
*Fitzhugh, Louise, *Harriet the Spy*
Fleischman, Paul, *Joyful Noise: Poems for Two Voices*
Fox, Paula, *The One-Eyed Cat*
*Frank, Anne, *The Diary of a Young Girl*
*Freedman, Russell, *Lincoln: A Photobiography*
**Fritz, Jean, *And Then What Happened, Paul Revere?*
Gag, Wanda, *Millions of Cats*
Garden, Nancy, *Annie on My Mind*
*George, Jean Craighead, *Julie of the Wolves*
Grahame, Kenneth, *The Wind in the Willows*
**Hamilton, Virginia, *M. C. Higgins, the Great*
**Hamilton, Virginia, *The People Could Fly: American Black Folktales*
Henkes, Kevin, *Chester's Way*
Hesse, Karen, *Out of the Dust*

Hinton, S. E., *The Outsiders*
Hoban, Tana, *Shapes and Things*
Holling, Holling C., *Paddle-to-the-Sea*
*Keats, Ezra Jack, *The Snowy Day*
Kerr, M. E., *Dinky Hocker Shoots Smack*
Kipling, Rudyard, *Just So Stories*
*Konigsburg, E. L., *From the Mixed-Up Files of Mrs. Basil E. Frankweiler*
Lauber, Patricia, *The Eruption and Healing of Mt. St. Helens*
Lawson, Robert, *Rabbit Hill*
Le Guin, Ursula, *A Wizard of Earthsea*
*L'Engle, Madeleine, *A Wrinkle in Time*
*Lewis, C. S., *The Lion, the Witch, and the Wardrobe*
Lindgren, Astrid, *Pippi Longstocking*
*Lobel, Arnold, *Frog and Toad Are Friends*
**Lowry, Lois, *Anastasia Krupnik*
**Lowry, Lois, *The Giver*
**Macaulay, David, *Cathedral*
**Macaulay, David, *The Way Things Work*
*MacLachlan, Patricia, *Sarah, Plain and Tall*
Marshall, James, *George and Martha*
Martin, Bill, Jr., and John Archambault, *Chicka Chicka Boom Boom*
**McCloskey, Robert, *Make Way for Ducklings*
McCord, David, *Far and Few*
McKinley, Robin, *The Hero and the Crown*
McKissack, Patricia, *Mirandy and Brother Wind*
Merrill, Jean, *The Pushcart War*
*Milne, A. A., *Winnie-the-Pooh*
Minarik, Else, *Little Bear*

Montgomery, L. M., *Anne of Green Gables*

Myers, Walter Dean, *Fallen Angels*

*O'Dell, Scott, *Island of the Blue Dolphins*

*Paterson, Katherine, *Bridge to Terabithia*

Paulsen, Gary, *Hatchet*

Pearce, Philippa, *Tom's Midnight Garden*

Piper, Watty, *The Little Engine That Could*

*Potter, Beatrix, *The Tale of Peter Rabbit*

Raschka, Chris, *Yo! Yes?*

Raskin, Ellen, *The Westing Game*

Rey, H. A., *Curious George*

Rowling, J. K., *Harry Potter and the Sorcerer's Stone*

Scieszka, Jon, *The Stinky Cheese Man and Other Fairly Stupid Tales*

*Sendak, Maurice, *Where the Wild Things Are*

*Seuss, Dr., *The Cat in the Hat*

Silverstein, Shel, *Where the Sidewalk Ends: Poems and Drawings*

Singer, Isaac Bashevis, *Zlateh the Goat*

Slepian, Jan, *The Alfred Summer*

Slobodkina, Esphyr, *Caps for Sale: A Tale of a Peddler, Some Monkeys and Their Monkey Business*

**Steig, William, *Sylvester and the Magic Pebble*

Steptoe, John, *Stevie*

Sutcliff, Rosemary, *The Lantern Bearers*

Taylor, Mildred, *Roll of Thunder, Hear My Cry*

Tolkien, J.R.R., *The Hobbit*

Travers, P. L., *Mary Poppins*

**Van Allsburg, Chris, *The Polar Express*

**Voigt, Cynthia, *Homecoming*

Wells, Rosemary, *Max's First Word*

*White, E. B., *Charlotte's Web*

*Wilder, Laura Ingalls, *Little House in the Big Woods*

Young, Ed, *Seven Blind Mice*

Zelinsky, Paul O., *Rumpelstiltskin*

Zindel, Paul, *The Pigman*

Zolotow, Charlotte, *William's Doll*

The Art of Picture Books

Watch out behind you, Bruh Wolf! Better look out for Bruh Rabbit when next the day leans over and night falls down.

—VIRGINIA HAMILTON, ***Bruh Rabbit and the Tar Baby Girl,*** illustrated by James Ransome, unpaged

D AN'S FIRST/SECOND GRADE CLASS IN MINNESOTA HAS JUST HEARD Virginia Hamilton's ***Bruh Rabbit and the Tar Baby Girl*** (P–I) read aloud. This tale from the South Carolina Sea Islands was just what they needed to warm them up on this cold January day. James Ransome's sun-washed illustrations add to the warmth as well as the humor of the tale, and everyone was giggling by the time Dan finished reading the story.

Dan chose this particular book to read aloud because it meets three of the goals he has set for the winter months. He is collaborating with the art teacher to help students learn how to recognize the work of different illustrators, one of whom is James Ransome. This book is a bit different from most of Ransome's work, as it is watercolor rather than oils and of animal rather than human characters, so it will expand their understanding of Ransome's art. Dan also is trying to encourage his students to pay close attention to the words they read and hear and then to use them in their own speaking and writing. Virginia Hamilton's use of Gullah words and phrases has delighted the students, and they will probably all go home tonight and tell their parents that dawn is really "dayclean" and evening is "daylean." Finally, Dan and his class are going to study trickster tales from around the world, and this is a great example of an African American trickster tale.

From just one 32-page picture storybook comes the opportunity to learn about art, language, and folklore from many cultures, as well as the occasion for a great deal of delight.

Defining Picture Books

Picture books, as we described in Chapter 1, are a unique genre in the world of children's and adolescent literature, as they are categorized by virtue of their format rather than their content. Picture books are those books in which the illustrations are as important as the text in the creation of meaning—sometimes even more important. Some picture books do not have text at all; we call them wordless books. These books tell stories or present information entirely through the illustrations. Most picture books, however, are a combination of text and illustration. When text and illustrations are masterfully combined, their interaction, often referred to as *unity,* creates a unique work of art—the picture book. Indeed, awards given for picture books can be based on either the text, as is the Charlotte Zolotow Award for outstanding writing in a picture book, or the illustrations, in the case of the Caldecott Medal. A complete list of Charlotte Zolotow Award winners appears in the Booklist at the end of this chapter; Appendix A includes a complete list of Caldecott Medal winners.

Writers and illustrators who create picture books are literary artists. The authors tell their stories, explain their concepts, or create their images with skillful and creative use of words, and the artists create images using line, shape, color, and other essential elements of art. Although most books are written by one person and illustrated by another, some picture-book creators, such as William Steig and Kevin Henkes, are equally skilled as writers and illustrators. In Henkes's Caldecott Medal–winning *Kitten's First Full Moon* (N–P), the language is simple yet engaging, and the emotional content is clearly relevant to younger readers. Kitten sees what she thinks is a bowl of milk in the sky—the moon—and tries to get it. Alas, she licks a bug, tumbles down the steps, climbs too high up a tree, and ends up in a pond, having pounced on the moon's reflection. Fortunately, she finds a real bowl of milk waiting for her at home. The illustrations are black and white, with thick black lines and soft shading defining Kitten's shape as well as her personality, and highlighting the full moon. Henkes's simple words and simple lines combine to form a story that is, simply, satisfying.

It is this combination of visual and verbal art in the format of a book that makes picture books different from other forms of art, such as painting or sculpture. In picture books, the visual art is judged not simply as a work of art but as a vital portion of a literary work.

In many picture books, illustrations verify the text, reflecting the same story that the words are telling. Contemporary artists, however, almost always extend the text in some way by adding visual information or meaning not presented in language. Barbara Cooney's illustrations in the Caldecott Medal–winning *Ox-Cart Man* (P–I) visually support and verify the text, while also supplying details about

It was Kitten's first full moon.
When she saw it, she thought,
There's a little bowl of milk in the sky.
And she wanted it.

*Kevin Henkes captures the brightness of the full moon with simple lines and a muted black and cream palette in **Kitten's First Full Moon**.*

time and place that author Donald Hall does not present in his spare language. Georg Hallensleben's vibrant paintings supply many of the details of a cat's overland journey home in Kate Banks's *The Cat Who Walked across France* (P). Philippe Goossens interprets and extends the emotions of a young child having a tantrum through oil paintings that illustrate Thierry Robberecht's *Angry Dragon* (N–P). Ken Robbins uses his photographic talent to illustrate *Seeds* (P), in which he uses the photographs to convey much more information than is conveyed by the text itself.

Mordicai Gerstein both wrote and illustrated the Caldecott Medal–winning *The Man Who Walked between the Towers* (P–I). As he tells in words the story of the young French aerialist, Philippe Petit, who in 1974 danced on a tightrope strung between the World Trade Center towers, he also tells it in pictures. With both words and pictures, he depicts Petit's determination and his joy in life, so that readers can understand why Petit performed such a daring, and illegal, feat. Gerstein goes well beyond mere visual reflection. The illustrations extend the text in such a way that readers feel what it might be like to be almost pulled over

As the rising sun lit up the towers, out he stepped onto the wire.

Through his clever use of perspective, Mordicai Gerstein helps readers feel what it might be like to be up high above New York. If you have vertigo, don't read **The Man Who Walked between the Towers***!*

the edge by a falling cable, just as they feel what it might be like to step out onto a cable five-eighths of an inch thick, 1,340 feet above the earth. Without the illustrations, neither the danger nor the thrill of walking between the towers would be as immediate or as powerful.

The picture-book version of Virginia Hamilton's *The People Could Fly* (P–I), stunningly illustrated by Leo and Diane Dillon, is a powerful example of an African American slavery tale. In this one, certain slaves were able to fly away to freedom, whereas others had to run. The illustrations extend the central image of flight by portraying clouds shaped as wings, people rising from the earth, groups of people floating upwards, and hands reaching out of slavery land into freedom. Each page is bordered with a thin line of color, brown at the bottom that gradually shades to other colors, depending on what is being depicted. In the bad times the border gets darker, turning black; as the people soar toward freedom, the brown shades to green and blue. This book received a Coretta Scott King Illustrator Honor.

The art in some books not only reflects and extends the text but also presents visual information that creates a story within a story. Marla Frazee does this brilliantly in *Roller Coaster* (P–I), in which she tells multiple side-stories through her illustrations. In the text, the book tells the story of a roller coaster ride, focusing on one young girl who has never ridden a roller coaster before: her initial trepidation, joyful ride with her big brother, and desire to do it over again. The illustrations tell several stories, all of them humorous. For example, behind the girl and her brother in line are three big men, bulging with muscles and, in one case, fat. The biggest one, in a muscle shirt with a tattoo on his arm, doesn't even make it onto the ride; he abandons his friends to sit and watch. The other two nonchalantly get on, arms casually draped on the sides of the car, sunglasses in place—until the first downhill, when they grab the seat in front of them (and one of them loses his cap). They hang on for dear life, close their eyes (and lose their sunglasses), and grimace until they get off, clutching their stomachs. In this case, the illustrations tell much, much more than the single story told by the text.

There are also multiple stories in the hand-colored etchings that accompany the spare text of Bonnie and Arthur Geisert's *Desert Town* (P–I), part of a series of books that describe life in small towns in varied geographic settings. The text is matter-of-fact and informative; the illustrations supply details and depict the dramas that occur "behind the scenes."

Wordless books, of course, tell stories or impart information without text. Vincent Gabrielle's *A Day a Dog* (I–A) is a thought-provoking wordless story for older readers; Pat Schories tells delightful stories about a young boy and his dog in *Breakfast for Jack* and *Jack and the Missing Piece* (both N–P); and Emily Arnold McCully's wordless books about a mouse family, *School, Picnic, New Baby,* and *First Snow* (all P), enchant young readers. These books offer opportunities for students to use their visual skills to create

If you look closely at the illustration, you can see who is afraid, who is having fun, and who is ready to be sick—small stories within a story told entirely through the illustrations in **Roller Coaster.**

both oral and written stories from the images, calling on their knowledge of story structure to do so.

An *illustrated book,* in contrast, consists of both text and illustrations; the text depicts the story or content, and the illustrations contribute significantly, but not equally, to the development, depth, and breadth of the story or content. Sharon Bell Mathis's ***The Hundred Penny Box*** (I–A) features accomplished illustrations by Leo and Diane Dillon and makes artful use of language to explore aging. Art in illustrated books may enhance, enrich, and extend the text, but these books are not true picture books.

Whether wordless or composed of text and illustration, picture books occupy a unique place in the world of children's literature. Because we classify picture books according to format rather than content, they actually span the other genres. We have picture books that are also folklore, fantasy or science fiction, contemporary realistic fiction, historical fiction, or nonfiction—including informational books, concept books, and biography—as well as poetry and song. Figure 2.1 summarizes the different genres found in picture book format, and Teaching Idea 2.1 offers ideas for exploring these genres with children.

Picture books not only span a number of genres; they also span a wide range of ages. They are available for the youngest readers as well as for adolescents. From board books that present simple concepts or tell simple stories to books that pose significant questions and explore complex issues, picture books have an important place in children's lives. Barbara Bader notes this when she defines picture books as "text, illustrations, total design; an item of manufacture and a commercial product; a social, cultural, historical document; and, foremost, an experience for a child" (1976, p. 1).

Picture-Book Genres

Fiction

Fiction includes folklore, fantasy and science fiction, realistic fiction, and historical fiction.

✳ Characters are dynamic and dimensional as well as fanciful (fantasy, science fiction); dynamic and dimensional as well as believable (realistic fiction, historical fiction); or flat, static, stock (folklore).

✳ The story is set in the real world of the past (historical fiction), the real world of present times (realistic fiction), an imagined world of the future (science fiction), or in a fanciful world (fantasy and folklore).

✳ The events of the story are plausible and logical in the real world of the present (realistic fiction), in the real world of the past (historical fiction), in a fanciful world (folklore, fantasy), or in a future world (science fiction).

Nonfiction

Nonfiction includes informational books, concept books, and biography.

✳ The book presents details about a concept (concept book), facts about a topic, or a realistic report about a person's life (biography).

✳ Content is verifiable.

Poetry or Song

✳ The language is verse, poetry, or song lyrics.

Teaching Idea   **2-1**

Using Picture Books to Help Students Learn about Literature

Because picture books span the range of genres and include examples of outstanding writing, they can be used to teach students—from kindergarten through high school—whatever you want them to learn about literature. If we read picture books aloud and talk about them without ever talking about their literary quality, we miss a wonderful opportunity to help students learn how literature works. Here are some things to think about in planning literature lessons using picture books:

✳ What do you want students to learn?

✳ What books do you have in your classroom library that will help you teach this concept?

✳ What kinds of activities can you do with students that will help them explore this concept?

✳ How can you build on initial understandings as you go on to read more books with your students?

If, for example, you are working with younger students and want to help them make the basic distinction between fact and fiction, then you will want to collect picture books about the same topic that are fiction, fact, or factual information embedded in fiction. For example, you could collect imaginative stories about dinosaurs, expository nonfiction about dinosaurs, and narrative nonfiction (information set within a story frame) about dinosaurs. Read the books with your students and talk about them, noting characteristics of each in a chart that allows you to list what is fictional and what is factual. If you are working with older students, they can take a more sophisticated look at this same idea, by talking about what is "true" and what is "plausible" in the historical fiction they read.

Or you might want to look at how authors and illustrators develop character and at how characters grow and change over the course of a story. If so, then you would select picture books with strong, engaging characters. You can help students learn to think about theme, or big ideas, by selecting picture storybooks and asking them to tell you the "most important word" in the story. After collecting their answers, you can lead them into a discussion of those words, which turns naturally into a discussion of theme. You can study metaphor, allusions, foreshadowing, parallel plots—whatever you care to study—using picture books. The possibilities are almost endless.

To help you get started, you might want to consult *Using Picture Storybooks to Teach Literary Devices,* by Susan Hall (Oryx Press, 1990), and *Looking through the Faraway End: Creating a Literature-Based Reading Curriculum with 2nd Graders,* by Lee Galda, Shane Rayburn, and Lisa Stanzi (International Reading Association, 2000), as well as the various genre chapters in this textbook.

Picture Books in Children's Lives

Picture books enrich children's lives; they tell stories, elaborate concepts, impart information, enchant with poetry and song—all things that learners need. Students of all ages read picture books. Preschoolers, as well as students in primary, intermediate, and advanced grades, read picture books appropriate to their interests. Infants and toddlers grasp sturdy cardboard or cloth books with bright pictures that capture their attention. Nursery and primary-grade children listen as picture books are read aloud. Captivated by stunning illustrations and lyrical texts, they eagerly anticipate what comes next and gradually memorize their favorite books. This is exactly what we want them to do. They participate in the act of reading, grow in their understanding of what books are for, and develop a lifelong love for reading. Older students turn to picture books to see vivid examples of literary techniques and the writer's craft, and to explore difficult concepts presented in a concise manner. Older students are also engaged by graphic novels, in which the pictures, often in the form of comic strips, tell the story with the support of speech and thought bubbles and brief narration.

In Chapter 3 we explore the varied content of picture books and how picture books relate to children's lives. Here we look closely at the art of picture books, beginning with the elements and styles of art that illustrators employ as they create meaning with pictures. We then go on to consider the language of picture books—how writers employ techniques of narrative fiction, nonfiction, and poetry to create meaning with words. Finally, we look at book design, or how picture books are put together, cover to cover. We then pose criteria for evaluating picture books and take a close look at one exemplary book, Virginia Hamilton's ***Bruh Rabbit and the Tar Baby Girl,*** illustrated by James Ransome. Finally, we briefly discuss learning about the art of picture books in the classroom.

Considering the Artistic Quality of Picture Books

Artists have many resources and techniques at their disposal. They can choose a medium, technique, and style that fit the text they are illustrating, or they can choose texts for which their unique style is suitable. When the right art is combined with a memorable text, the result is a superb book.

• • ELEMENTS OF ART • •

Art in children's picture books involves the entire range of media, techniques, and styles used in all art. The *medium*—the material used in the production of a work—may be watercolors, oils, acrylics, ink, pencil, charcoal, pastels, tissue paper, acetate sheets, fabric, or any other material that artists employ. The technique might be painting, etching, woodcut and linoleum block printing, airbrush, collage, photography, or many other means. The individual artist combines medium and technique in his or her own particular style to evoke setting, establish character, convey theme, display information, explain a concept, or create a mood.

When illustrating a picture book, artists decide what media and techniques they will use, and they make other aesthetic choices as well. They must decide about color, style, and composition in their illustrations. They must make choices about line, shape, placement on a page, the use of negative space, and texture. Artists work with the basic elements of art (line, shape, color, and texture) and with the principles of design (rhythm, balance, variety, emphasis, spatial order, and unity) to create a unified image that conveys meaning.

Line

Line is a mark on paper or a place where different colors meet. Each stroke starts with a dot that grows into a line that may be slow and rolling, sleek and fast, quiet or frenetic. Artists create lines that move in the direction in which they want to focus the viewer and that pull the eye in a particular direction. Lines can suggest delicacy (thin lines) or stability (thick lines). Artists use the angle, width, length, and motion of line to express the meaning they want to convey. David Diaz, Peter Sis, David Wiesner, Douglas Florian, and Brian Selznick all use line in different and effective ways.

Mo Willems uses line to create a memorable character in *Don't Let the Pigeon Drive the Bus!* (P). Soft black lines convey motion, and emotion, as the pigeon's dream is left unfulfilled but not forgotten. Willems won a Caldecott Medal

for this book. Eric Rohmann uses thick black lines to define his characters, depict movement, and propel readers from one page to another in his Caldecott Medal–winning book, *My Friend Rabbit* (N–P). David Wisniewski uses cut paper as black line in *The Warrior and the Wise Man* (P–I). Robert Sabuda in Marguerite Davot's *The Paper Dragon* (P–I) and Holly Meade in Minfong Ho's *Hush! A Thai Lullaby* (P) also use cut paper as line.

In *Zin! Zin! Zin! a Violin* (P), Marjorie Priceman uses wonderfully lyrical lines that complement the text. The charming story in verse by Lloyd Moss describes the humorous antics of assembling a chamber music group. Each element of Priceman's concert hall is drawn with a wiry, pulsating line, much like musical notations. Lines dance across the pages with increasing exuberance and syncopation, and the reader imagines the sound intensifying with the addition of each performer.

Molly Bang uses thick lines and color that become thicker and more brilliant when emotions are heightened in *When Sophie Gets Angry—Really, Really Angry . . .* (P). In this story, the little girl, Sophie, is initially outlined in a sunny yellow, but as she loses her temper the line registers her fury and gradually turns a flaming red. When Sophie actually has a screaming fit, multiple rich red pulsating lines surround her and create the impression that she is about to explode. As Sophie runs off into the woods, her anger gradually subsides, and she returns home her old self, with a sunny yellow outline.

© 1999 Molly Bang

Thick, pulsing lines of color help Molly Bang portray Sophie's emotions in **When Sophie Gets Angry—Really, Really Angry . . .**

Color

Artists like Molly Bang use color—or the lack of it—to express character, mood, and emotion. Color conveys warmth or coolness, personality traits, indifference, and feelings. Color can vary in *hue*—ranging across the rainbow of colors—and *intensity*. Subdued colors can express weariness, boredom, and serenity, whereas intense colors evoke feelings of energy, vibrancy, and excitement. Colors can also vary in *value*, or the amount of light and dark. A range of values creates drama or movement; an absence of contrast creates a quiet or solemn mood.

Lisbeth Zwerger limits her palette to rustic tones in Grimm's *Hansel and Gretel* (P). She conveys foreboding through somber clothing, dark lines on faces, and backgrounds of brown, ecru, and gray. In Malachy Doyle's *One, Two, Three O'Leary* (N), Will Hillenbrand uses bright colors against white backgrounds to add to the playful, cheerful tone of the text. In contrast, Jean Gralley uses muted colors to extend the dreamlike quality of her bedtime book, *The Moon Came Down on Milk Street* (N).

Although illustrating a story of the Holocaust, Wendy Watson uses muted colors and tones of gold that create a hopeful, positive feeling in her illustrations for Karen Hesse's *The Cats in Krasinski Square* (I). Jeanette Winter also uses subdued colors in *The Librarian of Basra: A True Story from Iraq* (P), but not to reflect the mood of her story. Instead, she contains the emotional impact of this war story by framing her illustrations in colors. A rich gold frames the first third, depicting the buildup to the war; a muted lavender frames the middle third, in which the books are saved as Basra burns; and a periwinkle blue frames the final third, in which the librarian waits for peace, guarding her books.

Shape

Shape is an area or form with a definite outline. It, along with line, directs the viewer's eye and suggests feelings and ideas. Shapes can be geometric (circles, triangles, squares), abstract (suggestive, less well-defined shapes, such as clouds), or realistic and representational. Shape can contribute to the volume or three-dimensional quality of an illustration. In some illustrations, shapes seem to jut out from the front, or plane, of the picture, coming toward the viewer. Artists make decisions about the placement of shapes (positive space) on the background (negative space).

Manuel Monroy extends Jorge Luján's spare, poetic text—in Spanish, with an English translation by Elisa Amado

The next day, soldiers come to Anis's restaurant.
"Why do you have a gun?" they ask.
"To protect my business," Anis replies.
The soldiers leave without searching inside.
*They do not know that the whole of the library
is in my restaurant,* thinks Anis.

At last, the beast of war moves on.
Alia knows that if the books are to be safe,
they must be moved again,
while the city is quiet.
So she hires a truck to bring all thirty thousand books
to her house and to the houses of friends.

*In **The Librarian of Basra,** Jeanette Winter contains the emotions of this story of war and courage by framing her illustrations in soft colors.*

*Manuel Monroy's use of color and shape is a poetic accompaniment to the lyric text of **Rooster/Gallo.***

below the Spanish, set in a smaller, different-colored font—in *Rooster/Gallo* (N–P), a mythic hymn to the dawn. The colors are dramatic, and the shapes of rooster, beak, and star are a rhythmic accompaniment to the lyrical text.

Lauren Stringer uses rounded shapes to project a womblike safety and comfort in her illustrations for Linda Ashman's *Castles, Caves, and Honeycombs* (P). Even the rabbit's ears and the woodpecker have a soft, rounded quality to them. In contrast, Debra Frasier uses angular shapes to convey exuberance and excitement in *On the Day You Were Born* (N–P). Lois Ehlert highlights geometric shapes in many of her books, including *Color Zoo* (N). Her books are marked by bright colors; clear, vivid lines; and shapes that seem to jump off the page. Shape is an essential element of Ellen Stoll Walsh's *Mouse Paint* (P), Ashley Bryan's *Beautiful Blackbird* (P), and Steve Jenkins's *Biggest, Strongest, Fastest* (P).

Chris Raschka combines the elements of simple line, shape, and color to depict music visually in *John Coltrane's Giant Steps* (P–I). Using the soft pastel colors of three

Chris Raschka uses shape, color, and strong line to visually portray a famous piece of music in **John Coltrane's Giant Steps.**

shapes—raindrops, snowflake, and box—superimposed on each other like notes of music, and a cat of thick black line for a melody, Raschka explores the energy of this piece of music with the energy of his art.

Texture

Some illustrations seem smooth, others rough. Some, like collage, do have a rough texture in the original art, whereas in others texture is entirely visual. Texture conveys a sense of reality; interesting visual contrasts or patterns suggest movement and action, roughness or delicacy.

Denise Fleming uses an unusual process to create illustrations for *Barnyard Banter* (N–P), *Lunch* (N–P), *In the Small, Small Pond* (N–P), *Where Once There Was a Wood* (P–I), and *The Everything Book* (N–P). She pours colored cotton pulp through hand-cut stencils, which results in handmade paper images. The art is satisfyingly textured and more softly edged than most cut-paper illustrations. The softness of the paper tempers the intense colors and active composition to make her art appealing to children and fascinating to adults.

In *Pie in the Sky* (N–P), Lois Ehlert creates texture through her use of paint, pencils, oil pastels, and crayons on hand-made paper, with the addition of wood, metal, wax paper, metal wire, and tree branches to create her vibrant, colorful art. Javaka Steptoe's collage illustrations for Karen English's *Hot Day on Abbott Avenue* (P) are textured with layers of paper on painted planks of wood. David Diaz's textured collages for Eve Bunting's story *Smoky Night* (I–A) convey the turmoil, fear, and anxiety caused by riots. Diaz uses material that reflects the events in the text: wooden matches texturize the illustration for fire; plastic bags and hangers symbolize the looting of the cleaners. Diaz won the Caldecott Medal for this book.

In the Caldecott Medal book *Snowflake Bentley* (P–I)—Jacqueline Briggs Martin's biography of William Bentley, a photographer of natural phenomena—Mary Azarian's hand-colored woodcuts have a folksy, down-home quality that is appropriate for this story, which takes place in the Vermont countryside at the end of the 19th century. As we look at the rustic woodcuts, we can almost feel the rough wood furnishings, the scratchy wool knits, and the coarse weave of the lumber jacket. We can see the diversity of textures of fields

Fall brought their first shearing.
Then as the days turned cold
their winter wool grew in.
It kept them warm right through the snow.

The wool of the sheep is so textured that it seems as though we could reach out and touch it, in George Ella Lyon's **Weaving the Rainbow,** *with watercolors by Stephanie Anderson.*

and flowers, and of course the beauty of the snowflakes that became Bentley's favorite subject matter.

Texture can be achieved by painters as well, as in Peter Sis's textured watercolors in *The Three Golden Keys* (P). Stephanie Anderson's watercolor illustrations for George Ella Lyon's *Weaving the Rainbow* (P) are smooth, beautiful landscapes and textured close-up images of the sheep, the weaver, her wool, and the beautiful cloth she weaves.

Design

Artists use the basic elements of art to create meaning and feeling; they manipulate the elements through principles of design to express their unique visions. Artists work to achieve unity, or a meaningful whole, through *composition* of their art. To achieve unity, artists make use of balance, repeated rhythms, variety, emphasis, and spatial order. Balance means giving equal weight to the lines, shapes, textures, and colors in a picture; without it the picture seems awkward (Greenberg & Jordan, 1991, 1993, 1995). *Repetition* in art helps achieve visual harmony and balance, whereas *variety* sets up a paradox or a progression that leads the eye from one point to another. Artists draw attention to a particular part of their piece by emphasizing size, placement, color, or line; these elements work together to force the viewer's eyes to focus on a particular place in an illustration.

In her book *Picture This: How Pictures Work* (2002), Molly Bang describes the formal principles of design; we have summarized them here:

- ⚫ Smooth, flat, horizontal shapes present a sense of stability and calm. (p. 42)

- ⚫ Vertical shapes are more exciting and active, implying energy and reaching. (p. 44)

- ⚫ Diagonal shapes are dynamic, implying motion or tension. (p. 46)

- ⚫ The upper half of a picture connotes freedom, happiness, triumph, spirituality. (p. 54)

- ⚫ The bottom half connotes threat, heaviness, sadness, constraint. (p. 56)

- ⚫ An object in the upper half carries "greater pictorial weight" or emphasis. (p. 56)

- ⚫ The center of the page is the point of "greatest attraction." (p. 62)

- ⚫ The edges and corners of the picture are the ends of the picture world. (p. 66)

- ⚫ White or light backgrounds feel safer than dark backgrounds. (p. 68)

- ⚫ Pointed shapes frighten; rounded shapes or curves comfort, feel safe. (p. 70)

- ⚫ The larger an object is, the stronger it feels. (p. 72)

- ⚫ We link the same or similar colors more readily than the same or similar shapes. (p. 76)

- ⚫ Contrasts enable us to see. (p. 80)

Artists such as Molly Bang work with these principles to compose their illustrations so that a reader's eye is guided by the art as the artist intends.

Margaret Chodos-Irvine's *Ella Sarah Gets Dressed* (N) is full of soft, bright colors and rounded shapes that help tell the happy story of a spunky little girl who knows exactly what she wants to wear, no matter what anyone else suggests. The focus is on Ella Sarah—we can't see all of the mother's, father's, or sister's figures, as they are out of the plane of the picture. In one double-page spread there are five images of her getting dressed: pants, dress, socks (two of them) and shoes, arranged in a curve across the expanse of white space, with text placed near the appropriate image. The next spread shows her putting on her big red hat, which actually breaks the plane of the top of the picture, signifying the triumph of this independent little girl.

In her retelling of Aesop's fables, *Unwitting Wisdom: An Anthology of Aesop's Fables* (P–I), Helen Ward uses a variety of fonts and sizes to emphasize words, some of which are incorporated in her oversized watercolor illustrations. In the opening of "The Hare and the Tortoise," the hare almost leaps off the page, ready to win that race. Lynne Rae Perkins's *Snow Music* (P) is a beautiful book in which text and pictures are so closely integrated that on some pages the text actually becomes a part of the illustration. Perkins uses shadows, tracks, fences, and branches as horizontal lines to push the eye across one page and on to the next.

Media and Technique

Artists make choices about the media and techniques they use. As mentioned earlier, *media* refers to the material used in the production of a work. *Technique* refers to the method artists use to create art with the chosen medium. Artists can work with virtually any medium—clay, wood, metal, watercolors, oils, fabric, acrylics, ink, pencil, charcoal, pastels—or with any combination of media. Artists may use the same medium for several books, but produce a very different effect by using different techniques.

Stephen T. Johnson uses pastels to create gentle, delicately colored drawings in Lenore Look's *Love as Strong as Ginger* (P–I); Jim LaMarche in Louise Erdrich's *Grandmother's Pigeon* (P–I) uses pastels to create highly luminous, richly hued painterly pictures. David Shannon uses acrylics in his humorous signature illustrations for *No, David!, David Goes to School,* and *David Gets in Trouble* (all N–P). Gregory Christie's use of acrylic with colored

Snow Music is so beautifully designed that the words of the text become part of the illustrations, here as the tracks of the deer.

pencil illustrations for Tonya Bolden's *The Champ: The Story of Muhammad Ali* (P–I) emphasize the head and hands of this boxer famous for his intellectual stance on war as well as for his boxing ability. Trina Schart Hyman achieves yet another effect with acrylics in her meticulously detailed, realistic illustrations for Katrin Tchana's *Sense Pass King: A Story from Cameroon* (I). The illustrations are also filled with the folk motifs and natural beauty of northwestern Cameroon.

Watercolor is a favorite medium of many artists. Peter Sis illustrates *The Train of States* (I–A) with line and watercolor paintings, and in a completely different palette, Phil Huling reflects the vibrancy of the Mexican setting in Eric Kimmel's *Cactus Soup* (P). Emily Arnold McCully's watercolors in *Squirrel and John Muir* (P) depict the beauty of Yosemite as well as the relationship between Muir and a young girl who learns from him how to observe nature. E. B. Lewis is known for his beautiful, realistic watercolor paintings, such as those that adorn Nikki Grimes's poetic biography, *Talkin' about Bessie: The Story of Aviator Elizabeth Coleman* (I).

Artists also use a variety of techniques in addition to painting, such as etching, linoleum block printing, airbrush, collage, stitching, computer art, and photography. Ken Robbins's hand-tinted photographs in *Bridges* (P–I) create an almost painterly, artistic effect that not only adds to the in-

formation about bridges but also conveys their romance; his photographs for *Seeds* (P) are informational. Those in Maya Ajmera and John Ivanko's *Be My Neighbor* (N–P) also are clear and focused on conveying information, as are Michael Doolittle's photographs for Susan Goodman's *Skyscraper: From the Ground Up* (P–I).

In Martin Waddell's *Tiny's Big Adventure* (N–P), John Lawrence's lush engravings in blues and golds extend the mood of the story, as do Barry Moser's more somber-colored wood engravings for Virginia Hamilton's *Wee Winnie Witch's Skinny: An Original African American Scare Tale* (I). Mary Azarian uses woodcuts to good effect in *Gardener's Alphabet* (N–P) and in Jacqueline Briggs Martin's *Snowflake Bentley* (P–I).

Many artists use collage materials but create different effects using a variety of techniques and materials. Holly Meade uses torn-paper collages in *Sleep, Sleep, Sleep: A Lullaby for Little Ones around the World* (N–P), by Nancy Van Laan. Ed Young uses crisply cut collage shapes in *Seven Blind Mice* (P–I). Artists may change the character of their collages by adding a variety of media, as Jeanne Baker does in her stunning books *Window* and *Home* (both P–I–A), in which she presents both environmental and social concerns through her richly textured collage art. Christopher Myers uses ink and gouache with cut and torn pieces of collage in *Harlem* (P–I), by Walter Dean Myers. Simms Taback

Trina Schart Hyman combines lush landscapes and folk designs in her acrylic illustrations for **Sense Pass King**.

uses mixed media—watercolor, gouache, pencil, ink, and photography—and collage on craft paper in *Joseph Had a Little Overcoat* (N–P–I). Susan Roth illustrates *Hard Hat Area* (P) with collage overlaid on a photomontage of the skyline of New York City, and Kyrsten Brooker combines oil paints and collage in Patricia McKissack and Onawumi Jean Moss's *Precious and the Boo Hag* (P).

As in other areas of 21st-century life, computers are making an impact. Although computer-generated art was initially considered inferior, enormous advances have been made in technology. Now, with proper training one can draw with a penlike stylus and approximate any medium, which then appears on a monitor; the images can be corrected, adjusted, and enhanced. Such artists as Janet Stevens and Mo Willems make use of the computer to great effect. In Mo Willems's Caldecott Honor–winning *Knuffle Bunny: A Cautionary Tale* (N–P), Willems digitally incorporates his brightly colored cartoon characters into sepia-toned photographs. Janet Stevens used the computer to enhance her original art in Anne Miranda's *To Market, to Market* (P), and the resulting illustrations are full of energy.

Figure 2.2 presents examples of the variety of media and techniques found in picture books.

• • STYLES OF ART • •

An artist's style is what makes his or her work recognizable as unique to that artist. Style refers to a configuration of artistic elements that together constitute a specific and identifiable manner of expression (Cianciolo, 1997). Style reflects the individuality and artistic strength of the artist; it is influenced by the content and mood of the text and by the intended audience (Cianciolo, 1976). Artistic styles available in books for children are many and varied. Here, we discuss some styles that are frequently found in picture books for children and adolescents.

Representational Art

Representational art consists of literal, realistic depictions of characters, objects, and events. Paul Zelinsky creates exquisite realistic oil paintings in the style of the French and Italian Renaissance painters to illustrate the Grimm's fairy tale *Rapunzel* (P–I). Beautifully rendered settings and emotionally evocative portraits of the leading characters add drama and dimension to the old tale. Bert Kitchen's animals, in

Media and Techniques Used in Picture Books

In the following list, we begin with the name of the illustrator, and include the author's name following the title if the author is someone other than the illustrator. We mention only one or two books for each illustrator, but their other books might include similar art. Also review the chapter text for other ideas. Some publishers now state the media, technique, and typography used in their books. Check the copyright page of each book for this information.

Acrylic

Christie, R. Gregory, *The Champ,* by Tonya Bolden

_____, *Yesterday I Had the Blues,* by Jeron Ashford Frame

Cooney, Barbara, *Miss Rumphius*

Oxenbury, Helen, *Big Momma Makes the World,* by Phyllis Root

Pilkey, Dav, *Paperboy*

Shannon, David, *No, David!*

_____, *When David Goes to School*

Stringer, Lauren, *Mud,* by Mary Lyn Ray

_____, *Scarecrow,* by Cynthia Rylant

Cut Paper and Collage

Baker, Jeanne, *Home*

Bryan, Ashley, *Beautiful Blackbird*

Carle, Eric, *The Very Hungry Caterpillar*

Ehlert, Lois, *Mole's Hill*

Fleming, Denise, *Barnyard Banter*

Frasier, Debra, *On the Day You Were Born*

Jenkins, Steve, *Biggest, Strongest, Fastest*

Keats, Ezra Jack, *The Snowy Day*

Lionni, Leo, *Frederick's Fables*

Meade, Holly, *Hush! A Thai Lullaby,* by Minfong Ho

Mullins, Patricia, *Hattie and the Fox,* by Mem Fox

Piven, Hanoch, *What Presidents Are Made Of*

Walsh, Ellen Stoll, *Mouse Paint*

Wisniewski, David, *Golem*

_____, *Rain Player*

Young, Ed, *Seven Blind Mice*

Computer-Generated or Computer-Augmented Art

Harley, Avis, *Fly with Poetry*

_____, *Leap into Poetry*

Isadora, Rachel, *ABC Pop!*

_____, *Listen to the City*

Pelletier, David, *The Graphic Alphabet*

Stevens, Janet, *To Market, to Market,* by Anne Miranda

_____, *Cook-a-Doodle-Doo!*

Willems, Mo, *Knuffle Bunny*

Gouache

Bang, Molly, *When Sophie Gets Angry—Really, Really, Angry . . .*

Cousins, Lucy, *Katy Cat and Beaky Boo*

Kalman, Maira, *Max in Hollywood, Baby*

Priceman, Marjorie, *Zin! Zin! Zin! a Violin,* by Lloyd Moss

Graphite/Pencil

Selznick, Brian, *Amelia and Eleanor Go for a Ride,* by Pam Muñoz Ryan

Mixed Media

Bunting, Eve, *Smoky Night,* illustrated by David Diaz

Chen, Chih-Yuan, *On My Way to Buy Eggs*

Johnson, Stephen T., *Alphabet City*

_____, *City by Numbers*

Doris Orgel's retellings in *The Bremen Town Musicians: And Other Animal Tales from Grimm* (P–I), are detailed and realistic, while also exhibiting a bit of personality. Jan Peng Wang's beautiful realistic paintings provide detail and elaborate character in Paul Yee's moving story, *A Song for Ba* (I). Ntozake Shange's poetic remembrance of some of the African American men who changed the world, *Ellington Was Not a Street* (P–I), is brought to life by Kadir Nel-

son's realistic oil paintings. Nelson's work received a Coretta Scott King Award.

Surrealistic Art

Surrealistic art contains "startling images and incongruities" that often suggest an "attitude or mockery about conventionalities" (Cianciolo, 1976, p. 40). Surreal pictures are

Mixed Media, continued

McDermott, Gerald, *Raven: A Trickster Story from the Northwest*

Myers, Christopher, *blues journey,* by Walter Dean Myers

_____, *Harlem,* by Walter Dean Myers

Pinkney, Brian, *Duke Ellington: The Piano Player and His Orchestra,* by Andrea Davis Pinkney

Pinkney, Jerry, *John Henry,* by Julius Lester

Schwartz, Amy, *What James Likes Best*

Sis, Peter, *Tibet: Through the Red Box*

Stevens, Janet, *Why Epossumondas Has No Hair on His Tail,* by Coleen Salley

_____, *Tops and Bottoms*

Taback, Simms, *There Was an Old Lady Who Swallowed a Fly*

_____, *Joseph Had a Little Overcoat*

Watson, Wendy, *The Cats in Krasinski Square,* by Karen Hesse

Oil

Ransome, James, *The Old Dog,* by Charlotte Zolotow

Zelinsky, Paul, *Rapunzel*

_____, *Rumpelstiltskin*

Pastels

LaMarche, Jim, *Grandmother's Pigeon,* by Louise Erdrich

Spengler, Margaret, *What's That AWFUL Smell?* by Heather Tekavec

Trivas, Irene, *One Lucky Girl,* by George Ella Lyon

Scratchboard/Engraving

Cooney, Barbara, *Chanticleer and the Fox*

Krommes, Beth, *The Hidden Folk,* by Lise Lunge-Larsen

Moser, Barry, *Wee Winnie Witch's Skinny,* by Virginia Hamilton

Pinkney, Brian, *The Faithful Friend,* by Robert D. San Souci

Watercolor

Bania, Michael, *Kumak's Fish: A Tall Tale from the Far North*

Dyer, Jane, *Cinderella's Dress,* by Nancy Willard

Henkes, Kevin, *Owen*

James, Simon, *Baby Brains*

McCloskey, Robert, *Time of Wonder*

Paschkis, Julie, *Bottle Houses: The Creative World of Grandma Prisbrey,* by Melissa Eskridge Slaymaker

Pinkney, Jerry, *The Ugly Duckling*

Polacco, Patricia, *Butterfly*

Ransome, James, *A Pride of African Tales,* by Donna Washington

Say, Allen, *Tea with Milk*

Shulevitz, Uri, *Snow*

Small, David, *The Garden,* by Sarah Stewart

Wallner, Alexandra, *Grandma Moses*

Wiesner, David, *Tuesday*

_____, *Sector 7*

Williams, Vera B., *A Chair for My Mother*

Woodcuts

Azarian, Mary, *Snowflake Bentley,* by Jacqueline Briggs Martin

Bowen, Betsy, *Anther, Bear, Canoe: A Northwoods Alphabet*

Brown, Marcia, *Once a Mouse*

Emberley, Ed, *Drummer Hoff*

Huneck, Stephen, *Sally Goes to the Beach*

often composed of the kinds of images experienced in dreams or nightmares or in a state of hallucination. Chris Van Allsburg's surrealistic paintings in *Jumanji* (I) extend the clever challenge of the text and are full of garishly funny details. Anthony Browne's surrealist paintings in his many books, such as *Willy and Hugh* (P) and *The Shape Game* (P), enhance the ideas he conveys in the texts. In David Wiesner's wordless books, such as *Tuesday* (P–I),

strange phenomena occur, and totally surreal events unfold in the skies.

Impressionistic Art

Impressionist artists emphasize light and color; they create an impression of reality. They may break an image into many small bits of color to mimic the way the eye perceives

*Kadir Nelson's realistic oil paintings underscore the power
of the African American men that Ntozake Shange presents
in Ellington Was Not a Street.*

She helped Grandmother grow chilies and coriander.
Mai searched for empty glass bottles. When she
put them upside down in the ground around her hut,
they sparkled.
This is how Mai lived for many years.

The texture of the pa'ndau, *a tapestry with traditional symbols and
images embroidered by Hmong women, creates beautiful illustrations
for* The Whispering Cloth.

and merges color to create images. Ed Young's *Lon Po Po*
(N–P–I) and Emily Arnold McCully's *Mirette on the High
Wire* (P) both won Caldecott Medals for their beautiful, impressionistic paintings. Jerome Lagarrigue's impressionistic
paintings in Janice Harrington's *Going North* (P–I) beautifully depict the experiences of a young African American
girl and her family in the 1960s as they drive from Alabama
to Nebraska, seeking a better life "up north."

Folk Art

Folk art is a broad designation for the style of artistic expression of a particular cultural group. Folk art may simplify,
exaggerate, or distort reality, but it does so in a way that is
characteristic of the traditional art of a culture, often through
the use of traditional motifs, symbols, and techniques.

There are as many folk art styles as there are folk cultures. Many artists illustrate folktales told in the style of a
particular culture using the characteristics, motifs, and symbols found in the art of that culture. Anita Riggio's illustrations for Pegi Dietz Shea's *The Whispering Cloth* (P–I) are
pa'ndaus, Hmong tapestries that contain traditional sym-

bols and images. Holly Berry relies on traditional Romanian
folk art designs to illustrate Sabina Rascol's retelling of the
classic Romanian tale *The Impudent Rooster* (P–I).

Naive Art

Naive art is technically unsophisticated but marked by an
artist's clear, intense emotions and visions. Artists may be
self-taught or may give the impression of ignoring traditional academic standards of art. There is almost always adherence to frontal posture or profile and a disregard for traditional representation of anatomy and perspective. Naive
art presents the essence of experiences and objects in a simplified fashion, using clearly recognizable forms for people
and places.

Ashley Bryan in *Sing to the Sun* (P–I) uses flat, frontal
depiction of people, a flattened perspective, and vivid colors. In Monica Gunning's *Not a Copper Penny in Me House*
(P–I), Frané Lessac creates brilliantly colored naive paintings that capture the charm and simplicity of life on the island of Jamaica. The vivid images conveyed in the words of
the poems are perfectly complemented by the richly detailed naive pictures.

Cartoon Art

Cartoon art emphasizes line, reduces features to simplified
shapes, and uses exaggeration in two dimensions to create

Frané Lessac's naive art is a perfect accompaniment to the sights, smells, and sounds of the Caribbean captured in Monica Gunning's poetry.

caricature (Cianciolo, 1976). The artist may employ such techniques as slapstick and may use ludicrous distortions of characteristics to depict absurdities and incongruities of situations so as to evoke laughter or at least a smile. Both adults and children are regularly exposed to cartoon art through comic strips, political cartoons, and, of course, animated films and videos. Because of its exaggerated expressive qualities, cartoon art communicates most directly and can often be understood without words.

There used to be a tendency to disparage cartoon art, perhaps because of its connection to comic books, comic strips, and animated films. Cartoon art has become more sophisticated, however, and is increasingly popular with artists and readers. Many of our greatest children's illustrators were clearly inspired by cartoon art, and they continue work in that style. Such brilliant author-illustrators as Maurice Sendak, creator of *Where the Wild Things Are* (N–P), William Steig, creator of *Sylvester and the Magic Pebble* (P–I), Tomi Ungerer, creator of *The Moon Man* (P–I), and James Marshall, creator of a comic version of *Goldilocks and the Three Bears* (P), all use their cartooning skills to create award-winning books. Rosemary Wells, author of *Max's Dragon Shirt* (N–P) and the many Max books, uses her cartoon humor to tell of the escapades of this mischievous boy bunny, Max.

Olivier Dunrea's cartoon ink and watercolor art in *Ollie* (P) is beautifully drawn and full of energy and the humor of surprise. In his **David** books, David Shannon uses full-color

David Shannon tells a funny story through succinct text and cartoon art in **No, David!**

Teaching Idea 2-2

Study the Art of Your Favorite Illustrator

Many artists develop a characteristic way of presenting ideas visually; some vary their style according to the text. Read aloud books by the illustrators discussed in this chapter or in Pat Cummings's *Talking with Artists,* vols. 1 and 2. Ask listeners to respond to the art. Later, see if they can recognize the artist's style when you cover up the names and titles. Play "Name That Illustrator": Hold up an illustration and ask, "Who is the illustrator?"

Collect several books by one illustrator and compare them. Is the art similar across books? Does the art represent a distinct approach? Ask students to describe each illustrator's work and to use examples of the work to illustrate their points.

The following are some illustrators you might want to consider:

Debra Frasier (cut paper, collage, mixed media)
Variety of moods, vibrant energy, total design
Patricia Polacco (watercolor, ink)
Warm, inviting, integrated with story

Peter Sis (watercolor, pen and ink)
Emotional, lots of detail, stories within art
Tomie dePaola (naive, folk art)
Strong outlines, sturdy people, hearts, birds
Chris Van Allsburg (surrealist)
Ranges from pencil to full color, bull terrier in every book
Jan Brett (representational)
Uses intricate borders
Eric Carle (collage)
Bold color, strong line
Ted Rand (representational)
Varies light and shadow throughout his books
Lauren Stringer (acrylics)
Rich colors and rounded shapes

Sources:

Cummings, P. (Ed.). (1992). *Talking with artists* (Vol. 1). New York: Bradbury.

Cummings, P. (Ed.). (1995). *Talking with artists* (Vol. 2). New York: Simon & Schuster.

---

cartoon art to create a portrait of a perfectly believable but impossible little boy. The cartoon art of Mo Willems's *Don't Let the Pigeon Drive the Bus!* winner of the Caldecott Medal, *The Pigeon Finds a Hot Dog!* and *Knuffle Bunny,* a Caldecott Honor book (all P), is a perfect accompaniment for his minimalist texts. Brock Cole is a master of cartoon art. His illustrations for *George Washington's Teeth* (P), by Deborah Chandra and Madeleine Comora, enhance their true but humorous tale. Another master, David Small, won the Caldecott Medal for his illustrations for Judith St. George's *So You Want to Be President?* (I–A). His many books with his wife, Sarah Stewart, such as *The Friend* (P), have helped bring cartooning into a new, sophisticated realm.

Recently there have been increasing numbers of graphic picture books or graphic novels, in which the story is told through a combination of cartoons with speech bubbles and, sometimes, a brief narrative text below each cartoon. Dav Pilkey's **Captain Underpants** (P–I) series is popular with younger readers, and adolescents are captivated by many graphic novels, such as Art Spiegelman's **Maus** (A) books, for example, *Maus: A Survivor's Tale. I: My Father Bleeds History.* Nicolas Debon uses this format to present his biography of artist Emily Carr in *Four Pictures by Emily Carr* (I–A), in which he tells his entire story through cartoon art and speech bubbles with handwritten text.

All these many styles of art—representational, surrealistic, impressionistic, folk, naive, and cartoon—are found in picture books. Teaching Idea 2.2 offers ideas for studying the style of a favorite illustrator.

Considering Text and Illustration in Picture Books

Except in wordless books, the art of the picture book is a combination of text and illustration. Here we consider text in picture storybooks, nonfiction picture books, and picture books of song and verse.

• • **PICTURE STORYBOOKS** • •

Many picture books are narratives—books that tell a story. The narratives may be folklore, fantasy, contemporary realistic fiction, or historical fiction. Whatever the type of narrative, we evaluate the text quality of the literary elements—setting, character, plot, theme, and style. The literary criteria may vary somewhat according to content, as we discuss in Chapter 1. The illustrations in picture storybooks provide visual representations, elaborations, or extensions of the setting, characters, and plot that are presented in the text. The illustrations also reflect the theme and the mood of the text.

Setting

Setting—the time and place of a story—is often presented succinctly in the text of picture books, as visual details about time and place can be portrayed clearly and economically through the illustrations. Good folklore settings reflect ethnic and cultural traditions associated with the origins of tales. Settings in contemporary or historical fiction reflect details appropriate to the time and place. In Michael Bania's *Kumak's Fish: A Tall Tale from the Far North* (P), the Arctic setting is clear in both text and pictures. Her light watercolor washes outlined in ink with plenty of white space highlight the icy setting, as do the details of place and the Inupiat people. Similarly, Belle Yang captures San Francisco's Chinatown in 1967 in both words and images in *Hannah Is My Name* (P), the story of a young girl who immigrates from Taiwan and hopes to make a home in her new world.

Characterization

Characterization—establishing characters—varies according to genre in picture storybooks. In folklore, characters are usually stereotypes—the good princess, the brave prince, the wicked stepmother. In well-written realistic or fantasy narratives, the characters are well-developed personalities that often show some evidence of growth and change over the course of the story. Many fantasy picture books contain talking animal characters with habits, behaviors, thoughts, and feelings that are human rather than animal. Realistic books, whether contemporary or historical, contain recognizably human characters. Whether animal or human, characters in picture storybooks are most often children or adolescents, depending on the intended audience. They reflect the actions, thoughts, and emotions of children and adolescents in the narration, the dialogue, and the art. Well-developed characters in picture storybooks are active rather than passive; they interact with their story worlds to solve their own problems.

Characters are realized through both the text and the art. As the text describes a personality trait, the art interprets that trait and presents a portrait of the character. As the story progresses, the art reflects characters' emotions and the growth and change that occurs. Jacqueline Woodson uses words to develop her characters, young Ada Ruth and her grandma, with whom Ada Ruth stays home when Mama goes north to Chicago to earn money during World War II. E. B. Lewis uses watercolor paintings to visually convey Ada Ruth's emotions, as well as the time and place. The combination of words and pictures creates the memorable story, *Coming on Home Soon* (P), a Caldecott Honor book.

Plot

In picture storybooks, plot—the sequence of events—is usually presented in a straightforward chronological order. Plot usually centers on a problem or conflict, generally a problem that children recognize and relate to. As the character works to solve the problem, the plot unfolds into an event or series of events that lead to a solution. The action of the story is apparent in both the text and the illustrations. As we discussed earlier, sometimes the illustrations offer a subplot that the text does not. Peggy Rathman's text in the Caldecott Medal–winning *Officer Buckle and Gloria* (P) tells only part of the story. The story behind the story, and the humor, is carried entirely by her illustrations.

Theme

Theme, a major overriding idea that ties the whole together, often reflects a child's or adolescent's world. Picture books for younger children are often organized around the theme of growing up—increasing independence and self-reliance, increasing ability, increasing understanding. Memorable themes are neither blatantly stated, as in an explicit moral to a story, nor so subtle that they elude young readers. The theme evolves naturally from plot and character, and permeates the illustrations. Peter Sis's *Madlenka's Dog* (P) is a tour de force, a beautifully rendered story about self-reliance and the power of the imagination.

Style

Style of language is essential to quality in a picture book; because words are limited, they must be carefully chosen. Most picture books for young readers contain rich language—well beyond the reading ability of the intended audience—because they are meant to be read aloud. Picture books are most often introduced to babies, toddlers, or preschool children by an adult reading *to* the child. The language in most picture books for younger children is language that adults can read and that children can understand. Most picture books are not meant for beginning reading material. Those that are should still contain language that is interesting, even if simple, and that is a pleasure to read aloud. For older readers, the text can be more complex. In any case, good picture storybooks have interesting words used in interesting ways, with language that builds excitement, creates images, and has an internal rhythm and melody. If it sounds natural when read aloud, it is probably well written. We discuss style further in Chapter 3.

The choice of words helps create the *mood* of the text. Books can be humorous or serious, lighthearted or thoughtful. The style of art must match the mood of the text. It might, for example, be inappropriate to illustrate books about a serious theme with bright, happy colors. Niki Daly's illustrations for Louise Borden's *The Greatest Skating Race: A World War II Story from the Netherlands* (I) are somber and serious, in shades of grays and browns with deep reds. The somber mood of the illustrations perfectly matches the somber story. Sometimes the unity of text and illustrations happens in unexpected ways. For example, the graphic novel series **Maus** (A) contains gripping stories of the Holocaust, yet is illustrated very effectively with cartoons that present animal characters.

• • NONFICTION • • PICTURE BOOKS

Nonfiction picture books include informational books designed to provide readers with knowledge about a particular topic, concept books that seek to present a particular concept in a way that young readers can understand, or biographies based on factual information about a subject. The text should be accurate, organized in a manner appropriate to both the information presented and the intended audience, designed in an attractive and appropriate fashion, and written and illustrated with verve and style.

Nonfiction picture books reach a broad range of students, enabling students at many different ability levels to access information. Producing picture books appropriate to a young reader's age or to a struggling older reader's ability creates a special challenge for nonfiction writers, who have to find ways to explain a subject simply enough to be understood and still be accurate. Nonfiction picture books for older, more advanced readers can present more complex, detailed information.

Nicola Davies's *Surprising Sharks* (P), intended for a primary-grade audience, presents many different sizes and shapes of sharks, pointing out some of the surprising results of adaptation as well as the commonalities of anatomy and behavior. The text is humorous and informative, and the bright colors and clever art of James Croft add to both the humor and the information. This book blends accuracy with fun, a perfect combination for the subject and the intended audience.

In his picture-book biographies, Don Brown displays his gift for conveying information about his subjects through a brief but straightforward text and carefully composed illustrations. In *Odd Boy Out: Young Albert Einstein* (P), Brown presents the genius as an introspective child who struggled in school, effectively selecting events and details

to narrate and most often illustrating Einstein alone, with closed or downcast eyes.

• • PICTURE BOOKS • • OF POETRY AND SONG

Some picture books present an artist's visual interpretation of a song, poem, or verse. In these books, the artist arranges the text across the pages, often with only one or two lines per page, and then illuminates each thought expressed by the text. The lyrical language of the text should be both interesting to and understandable by the intended audience. Brief, rhythmic verses, narrative verses, and children's and folk songs make excellent picture-book texts. Some books contain several separate texts; others present single poems or songs.

In beautifully designed picture books of poetry and song, the arrangement of the text across the pages reflects the natural breaks in the meaning and sound of the original. Illustrations depict both action and feeling, matching the mood established by the author, as interpreted by the artist. Lynne Rae Perkins's *Snow Music* (P), discussed earlier, is a perfect example of a beautifully designed picture book containing a single poem. In picture-book form, Karla Kuskin's humorous poem *Under My Hood I Have a Hat* (N–P) is clearly and colorfully interpreted by Fumi Kosaka's illustrations. Marla Frazee brings new life to a Woody Guthrie song with her clever and energetic illustrations for *New Baby Train* (P).

From Cover to Cover

In picture books, principles of design apply to the overall design of the book as well as to individual pictures, and reflect and enhance the content. The book's size and shape, cover design, text placement, typography, endpapers, illustrations, and use of space are all elements of the total design. Arrangement and sequencing of design elements lead the eye effectively through a book. Lane Smith uses every inch of available space to increase the feeling of delighted shock in Jon Scieszka's *The Stinky Cheese Man and Other Fairly Stupid Tales* (I). The cover, title page, dedication page, table of contents, and typeface are all manipulated to playfully violate conventions. The text consists of hilarious versions of familiar folktales; the surrealistic art heightens the mockery of folktale conventions. Beyond that, the text and illustrations play with the format of the picture book itself, achieving a remarkable unity of text and illustration.

Debra Frasier carefully considers every aspect of design as she crafts her books. Thinking of a picture book as theater, she likens opening the cover of a book to a curtain rising on stage. In *The Incredible Water Show* (P–I), she extends this metaphor by creating a play about water within the pages of her book. The setting is a stage, with each page turn resetting the stage for the next scene, and the text is contained entirely in speech bubbles as the characters talk to one another and their audience. From front cover to back, Frasier invites readers to enter her theater and watch her show. The fun begins on the cover, where two children frame the title, which looks like a poster advertising a performance. We open the cover and find the setting for the performance, a neighborhood park, detailed on the endpapers, and on the title page we see the performers putting up the curtain. After presenting the characters in a show bill on the copyright page, Frasier fills the rest of the book with art in bright primary colors, featuring a lot of blue and bubbles. She uses every speck of space to convey her information and her enthusiasm.

Brian Selznick is another master of design, as is evident in Barbara Kerley's *The Dinosaurs of Waterhouse Hawkins* and Pam Muñoz Ryan's *When Marian Sang* (both I). Selznick also thinks of the picture book as a stage, but the texts he illustrates are not plays themselves. Rather, he frames the texts of these books as if readers were watching a stage performance, with curtains going up as the book begins. He also uses every part of the book to convey his vision. Keen-eyed readers will notice how much time has passed in *The Dinosaurs of Waterhouse Hawkins* by looking closely at the illustrations on the last three pages of the book.

Paul Fleischman and Kevin Hawkes don't use curtains to frame their narrative, but the performance of *Sidewalk Circus* (P–I) begins on the cover, when the shadow of a worker stretching while yawning, handbill in hand, projects onto the brick wall behind him as a shadowy ringmaster. The only words in this book are in the illustrations on signs on the buildings and on the marquee of the theater across the street from the bus stop bench where a young girl sits, watching the performance. The full-color spreads give us a lot to look at and to think about.

James Rumford's *Sequoyah: The Cherokee Man Who Gave His People Writing* (I), which won a Siebert Honor, is another beautifully designed book. All aspects of this book work together to present information and explore a theme. The tall, rectangular size, the brown cover and green endpapers, the image of a Sequoia tree reaching up, disappearing at the top edge of the illustration on the dedication page but continuing to soar skyward in our mind's vision, the Cherokee text, the textured illustrations framed by black lines, and the elegant reproduction of the Cherokee script as Sequoyah developed it make this book a visual treat. The text is straightforward and full of information, and helps readers understand the significance of Sequoyah's accomplishment. This would be enough of an achievement, but

Debra Frasier uses every available inch of space to tell her story in **The Incredible Water Show.**

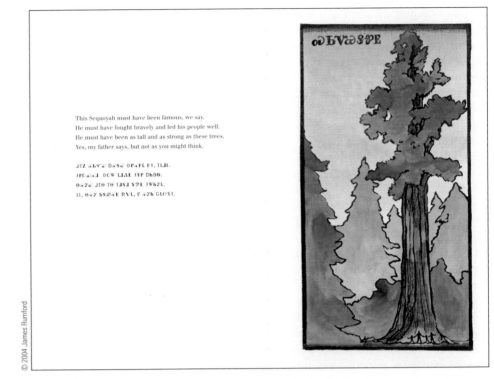

This Sequoyah must have been famous, we say.
He must have fought bravely and led his people well.
He must have been as tall and as strong as these trees.
Yes, my father says, but not as you might think.

ᎠᏥ ᎠᎥᏯᎥ ᏓᎥᏍᏫ ᎣᏆᎥᏞ ᎻᎢ, ᎢᏞᏂᎢ.
ᎢᏢᏌᏐᎠᏒ ᎣᏣᏫ ᏞᎵᎠᎡ ᎢᏱᏢ ᎠᎯᏃᎦ.
ᎦᎥᏯᎥ ᎠᎢᎦ ᎢᎦ ᎢᎯᏌᏯ ᏚᎨ ᎢᏪᎯᏯᎡ.
ᎢᎢ, ᎦᎥᏯ ᎮᏐᎦᏒᎡ ᏒᏃᎡ, ᎾᏥ ᎥᏯᎮ ᎬᎵᏬᎢᎢ.

© 2004 James Rumford

*This beautifully designed book uses strong vertical lines and heavy black print—
in both English and Cherokee—to present the story of Sequoyah.*

Rumford goes beyond, framing his informative text with another story, of a family looking at the giant Sequoia trees in California and wondering where the name came from. When the children comment that Sequoyah must have been famous, a brave fighter, and a tall, strong leader of his people, the father says, "Yes, but not as you might think." After presenting the story of Sequoyah, Rumford returns to the family, small black silhouettes under the trees taller than the top of the illustration, and returns to his theme as well, as the children have expanded their ideas about fame, courage, and leadership, and learned how the Cherokee people stood "tall and proud," like the giant Sequoia.

Books such as these represent the possibility that picture books hold—a unique combination of elegant words, brilliant illustrations, and inspired design.

Criteria for Evaluating Picture Books

There are many things to consider when evaluating the quality of a picture book: the quality of the text, if there is one; the quality of the art; and the quality of the overall design of the book. There are so many outstanding picture books from which to choose that it is never necessary to give an inferior book to a reader. We have already considered aspects of text, art, and overall design. In Figure 2.3, we offer some general guidelines pertaining to fiction, nonfiction, and poetry and song for you to think about as you select picture books. These guidelines will help you determine what you might want to talk about with your students as you help them learn about the art of the picture book.

In addition to the guidelines presented in Figure 2.3, consider the artfulness of the book as a whole. What is the relationship between the illustrations and the text? How do the illustrations support or extend the text? Are the medium, technique, and style appropriate to the text? How do the elements of design work to enhance the meaning, both in individual pictures and across the book as a whole? What makes the book special?

✳ ✳ ✳

A CLOSE LOOK AT

Bruh Rabbit and the Tar Baby Girl

The balance between text and illustration, James Ransome's brilliant artistic interpretation, and Virginia Hamilton's exciting text are what make **Bruh Rabbit and the Tar Baby Girl** (P–I) a special book. In it Hamilton retells the familiar trickster tale as it is told by the Gullah people of the South Carolina Sea Islands.

Figure 2-3

Checklist for Evaluating Picture Books

All Picture Books

✿ The language is rich, with interesting words used in interesting ways.

✿ Illustrations are artistically excellent.

Fiction

✿ Text and illustrations establish the mood, setting, characters, and theme of the story.

✿ Illustrations expand on the story appropriately.

✿ Layout and design are visually appealing.

Nonfiction

✿ Text and illustrations are accurate.

✿ Text and illustrations are organized in an appropriate manner.

✿ Text and illustrations are attractive, and show verve and style.

Poetry and Song

✿ The language is lyrical.

✿ Illustrations match the feeling established by the text.

Language

Hamilton's gift with language is evident from the opening of the story, with the words, "It was a far time ago." She tells her story with a perfect balance of distinctive Gullah dialect and standard written English. The Gullah constructions that she chooses to use are all understandable to young readers. Such words as *Bruh, tricky-some, nary, scarey-crow, daylean, croker sack,* and *dayclean* are understandable within the context of the story and in their relation to standard written English or their descriptive properties. Sentences such as "Guess me, somebody been into my peanuts," or "For true, somebody been here," convey the thoughts of the characters, the events of the story, and the flavor of the Gullah dialect. Indeed, the link between the written text and the orality of the original tale is a close one. You can hear the storyteller's voice in Hamilton's prose as the lazy rabbit "sneakity-sneaks" along until "WHOOM!" he sees the

James Ransome's bright, happy colors, carefully placed characters, and strong horizontal lines at the bottom of the page create an image that makes readers want to open the cover and enjoy the story.

© James Ransome

James Ransome

James Ransome is a man with a vision. That vision began during his childhood in rural North Carolina, when he drew pictures of hot rods, imitated the images of the comic books he read, and copied images from the Bible. As he read the Bible aloud to his grandmother, who raised him, visions filled his head as the words sparked his imagination. He drew those visions. Then he discovered *Mad* magazine and began creating stories about himself and his friends. There were no art classes in his local school, so he looked at library books about

drawing, watched television shows about artists, and even enrolled in a correspondence course. Finally, he moved to Bergenfield, New Jersey, to attend high school. There he took filmmaking and photography classes, and this training influenced the work he does today.

As Ransome tells it, "through photography, I discovered the power perspective, value, and cropping could have on a single image. Through filmmaking, I discovered the many ways to pace a story with the aid of camera angles and framing images." Finally, he took a drawing and painting class. From high school he went on to earn a bachelor of fine arts degree from Pratt Institute, where he met Jerry Pinkney, a prominent African American illustrator who became both a friend and a mentor.

Ransome has many books and many prizes to his credit. He received the Coretta Scott King Award for illustration and the IBBY Honor for *The Creation,* the Coretta Scott King Honor for *Uncle Jed's Barbershop,* also a feature on *Reading Rainbow,* as are *How Many Stars in the Sky?* and *Sweet Clara and the Freedom Quilt.* His watercolor illustra-

tions for Virginia Hamilton's *Bruh Rabbit and the Tar Baby Girl* are stunning examples of his talent. They also represent a departure for him; he worked almost exclusively in oils but is now experimenting with watercolors—and very successfully!

Ransome painted the cover and part openers for the third edition of *Literature and the Child,* and he has agreed to do the same for the seventh edition. Recently, he was named by the Children's Book Council as one of 75 authors and illustrators everyone should know. His talent and passion are evident in his work. He says, "What makes illustrating books so exciting is that because each book has a special voice, my approach toward each is different. Whether it be through my choice of palette, design or perspective, there is always a desire to experiment and explore what makes each book unique."

James and his wife, Lesa Kline-Ransome, live in upstate New York with their children, Jamie, Maya, Malcolm, and Leila.

Source: www.jamesransome.com

---

scarey-crow. The text simply begs to be read aloud, as a good retelling of an oral story should.

Illustrations

Ransome's watercolor with pen-and-ink illustrations are beautiful. Further, they not only reflect the events of the tale but create a detailed setting, develop the stock characters, and extend the humor.

We know this will be a light-hearted story just from the front cover, because of the way the title and the author's name curve around the huge sun that fills the center of the page, anchored by the brown wooden fence and green grass running horizontally across the bottom, and because of the predominance of yellow and gold. The two characters of the title—the rabbit and the tar baby girl—are centered on the page, directly in front of the sun. The fence, the briars that are visible behind it, and the size of the sun are the first hints of the setting.

Ransome continues to develop the setting in the endpapers. As we open the book we see, literally, a bird's-eye view of a countryside scene; the particular bird has a bonnet on her head. There's an old frame house, with a typical southern chimney and roof, a pond with ducks being watched by an alligator almost hidden in the bushes, and bluish mountains off in the distance. Everything is green, except where the grass has worn away to the orange-brown dirt. In this scene Ransome also begins to develop the characters. We see Bruh Wolf at work in his garden, while Bruh Rabbit is racing down the path from his burrow door toward the pond, fishing pole and bucket in hand. On the next page, opposite the title page, we see Bruh Rabbit throwing horseshoes, and on the dedication page he is fishing while Bruh Wolf pushes a wheelbarrow in the background. Before the story even begins, it is clear from the illustrations that Bruh Rabbit likes to have fun. The character development and the humor continue as we see Bruh Rabbit asleep in the first two pictures, and Bruh Wolf working hard on his scarey-crow.

The humor of this story is evident in the sight of Bruh Rabbit, with a sheepish look in his eye, perched on the back of the Tar Baby Girl.

The seamless integration of text and illustration make ***Bruh Rabbit and the Tar Baby Girl*** an outstanding example of a picture book. Ransome's touching dedication of the book to the late Virginia Hamilton and the endnote about the origins of the tale add to the impact of the book.

* * *

Learning about Picture-Book Art in the Classroom

Children learn how to think and talk about the art of picture books by reading and responding to outstanding picture books. If they are guided by teachers like Dan in the opening vignette, they will learn to notice the careful use of words; the way color, shape, texture, and line are used; and the varied styles, media, and techniques that artists choose.

Children who encounter excellent picture books learn how to read not only the words but also the pictures. They pay close attention to what they see, often discovering things in the illustrations that most adults would miss. Just as children notice the writer's craft, which we discuss more extensively in Chapter 3, they notice the artist's craft and

discuss it. In fact, a good question to ask students after reading a picture book is, "What do you notice?" Kiefer (1986) listened to students of all ages talk about what they noticed about elements of design in picture books. First graders discussed line, shape, texture, and color with ease; older students considered the expressive qualities of illustrations. In every case, teachers provided time for children to explore books, to discover and develop individual responses, and to share those responses with others. Teachers also provided a wide selection of books and gave children varied opportunities for response while sharing their knowledge of the elements of language and visual art, as well as their own critical aesthetic responses.

We often think of selecting books that contain similar themes, structures, or literary devices. We can also select books that demonstrate similarities and differences in visual art. Careful selection can lead students to compare the use of line and color, for example, or to note how different artists use texture, light, and space. A thoughtful selection of books that demonstrate particular qualities of visual art can educate students' eyes as well as their minds and hearts. Students can also explore art firsthand, by working with various media and techniques. Teaching Idea 2.3 presents ideas for exploring the media and techniques illustrators use.

Children come to school full of images and ideas, with the imagination to expand on them. By providing them with the opportunity to explore the thousands of wonderful

Teaching Idea 2-3

Exploring Art Media

Experiment with the media and techniques illustrators use. You can collect the following books as models, select from those listed in Figure 2.2, or use those that are favorites with you and your students.

Paper

Fox, Mem, *Hattie and the Fox* (tissue paper collage)

Frasier, Debra, *On the Day You Were Born* (cut paper)

Keats, Ezra Jack, *The Snowy Day, Peter's Chair* (cut textured paper)

Wisniewski, David, *Golem* (cut paper)

Use tissue paper, construction paper, magazines, newspaper, wallpaper, and gift wrap to make book illustrations, collages, mosaics, and paper sculptures.

Watercolors

Shulevitz, Uri, *Dawn*

McCloskey, Robert, *Time of Wonder*

McDermott, Gerald, *Arrow to the Sun*

Use watercolor paints, tempera, gouache, and water-base paint for book illustrations, landscapes, crayon-resist painting, seascapes, skyscapes, and backgrounds.

Crayons, Pastels, Scratchboard

Frasier, Debra, *The Incredible Water Show*

_____, *Miss Alaineus: A Vocabulary Disaster*

Lunge-Larsen, Lise, *The Hidden Folk,* illustrated by Beth Krommes

Pinkney, Andrea Davis, *Alvin Ailey,* illustrated by Brian Pinkney

Use crayons, Cray-Pas, pastels, water crayons, and markers; include crayon scratch drawings, crayon resist, chalk paintings, crayon texture drawings, and any other combination of media.

Printing Techniques

Bowen, Betsy, *Anther, Bear, Canoe: A Northwoods Alphabet*

Emberley, Barbara, *Drummer Hoff,* illustrated by Ed Emberley

Lionni, Leo, *Swimmy*

Martin, Jacqueline Briggs, *Snowflake Bentley,* illustrated by Mary Azarian

Use linoleum blocks, wood blocks, potato halves, Styrofoam, cardboard, sandpaper, and yarn. Create shapes to dip into paints and stamp onto paper. Make relief prints, etchings, cardboard cuts, and potato prints.

Cartoons and Comic Strips

Aliki, *How a Book Is Made*

Feiffer, Jules, *Bark, George*

Steig, William, *The Amazing Bone*

Write characters' dialogue in speech balloons. Illustrate the action.

Computer-Generated or Computer-Augmented Art

Isadora, Rachel, *1 2 3 Pop!*

_____, *ABC Pop!*

Harley, Avis, *Fly with Poetry*

Use a computer program to create art. Illustrate a picture book or a poetry book with it.

Photographs

Frasier, Debra, *Out of the Ocean*

Hoban, Tana, *Just Look*

Robbins, Ken, *Bridges*

Give children disposable cameras and have them take photographs to illustrate stories or informational pieces about their own life and neighborhood.

---

picture books that are available, we can feed their imaginations and encourage them to think about the symbol systems of language and art that we use to convey our ideas. A wonderful example of this is captured—not surprisingly—in a picture book. Rita Golden Gelman's *Doodler Doodling* (P–I), illustrated by Paul Zelinsky, begins with a young girl, sitting at her school desk, playing with words and images—doodling. As her imagination takes flight, her wordplay and her drawings become funnier and more complex. Perhaps this book is also a metaphor for the artistic process of the writers and artists who create wonderful picture books.

• • • • **Summary** • • • •

Picture books are artful books that hold a special place in the lives of children who read them. These books are the first exposure to fine art for many children. They can enrich children's worlds by providing opportunities for experiences through pictures and print. Illustrators use a full range of artistic elements and styles as they create picture books, seeking to interpret an author's words through their art. There are picture books in all genres, each of which poses particular constraints as well as possibilities. When we experience excellent picture books and share them with our students, we are educating imaginations.

In her article "Half the Story: Text and Illustration in Picture Books" in the January/February 2004 issue of *The Horn Book Magazine,* Anne Hoppe, herself an editor of picture books, describes the unique relationship between writer and artist, text and illustration. Read her article and then think about the picture books with which you are familiar, asking yourself how the illustrations reflect and extend the text. See also the March/April 1998 issue of *The Horn Book Magazine* that is devoted entirely to picture books.

In his conversation with us, James Ransome talks about his creative process, how he works with someone else's ideas and words to create illustrations to bring them to life and make them his own. In our visit to Debra Frasier's studio, she shows us how she develops her own ideas through words and pictures. Watch both of these interviews and think about how the process differs when an artist is interpreting the words of someone else as opposed to his or her own words. Discuss this, using books you have read as examples. If you have read the Anne Hoppe article, consider what she has to say as well.

The following list contains the titles of the winners, honor books, and commended books of the Charlotte Zolotow Award for outstanding writing in a picture book published in the United States.

2004

WINNER

Schwartz, Amy, *What James Likes Best*

HONOR BOOKS

Coy, John, *Two Old Potatoes and Me,* illustrated by Carolyn Fisher

O'Connell, Rebecca, *The Baby Goes Beep,* illustrated by Ken Wilson-Max

Paye, Won-Ldy, and Margaret Lippert, *Mrs. Chicken and the Hungry Crocodile,* illustrated by Julie Paschkis

Rumford, James, *Calabash Cat and His Amazing Journey*

Shannon, George, *Tippy-Toe Chick, Go!* illustrated by Laura Dronzek

HIGHLY COMMENDED

Banks, Kate, *Mama's Coming Home,* illustrated by Tomek Bogacki

Chandra, Deborah, and Madeleine Comora, *George Washington's Teeth,* illustrated by Brock Cole

Fleming, Denise, *Buster*

Frame, Jeron Ashford, *Yesterday I Had the Blues,* illustrated by R. Gregory Christie

Jenkins, Steven, and Robin Page, *What Do You Do with a Tail Like This?*

Nye, Naomi Shihab, *Baby Radar,* illustrated by Nancy Carlson

Perkins, Lynne Rae, *Snow Music*

U'Ren, Andrea, *Mary Smith*

Willems, Mo, *Don't Let the Pigeon Drive the Bus!*

2003

WINNER

Keller, Holly, *Farfallina and Marcel*

HONOR BOOK

Swanson, Susan Marie, *The First Thing My Mama Told Me,* illustrated by Christine Davenier

HIGHLY COMMENDED

Andrews-Goebel, Nancy, *The Pot That Juan Built,* illustrated by David Diaz

Banks, Kate, *Close Your Eyes,* illustrated by Georg Hallensleben

Henkes, Kevin, *Owen's Marshmallow Chick*

Herrera, Juan Felipe, *Grandma and Me at the Flea,* illustrated by Anita de Lucio-Brock

McMullan, Kate, and Jim McMullan, *I Stink!*

Okimoto, Jean Davies, and Elaine Aoki, *The White Swan Express: A Story about Adoption,* illustrated by Meilo So

Shannon, David, *Duck on a Bike*

Shertle, Alice, *All You Need for a Snowman,* illustrated by Barbara Lavallee

Wilson, Karma, *Bear Snores On,* illustrated by Jane Chapman

Wong, Janet, *Apple Pie Fourth of July,* illustrated by Margaret Chodos-Irvine

2002

WINNER

Willey, Margaret, *Clever Beatrice,* illustrated by Heather Solomon

HONOR BOOK

Jenkins, Emily, *Five Creatures*

HIGHLY COMMENDED

Look, Lenore, *Henry's First Moon Birthday,* illustrated by Yumi Heo

MacDonald, Margaret Read, *Mabela the Clever,* illustrated by Tim Coffey

Russo, Marisabina, *Come Back, Hannah*

Stock, Catherine, *Gugu's House*

Wong, Janet, *Grump,* illustrated by John Wallace

2001

WINNER

Banks, Kate, *The Night Worker,* illustrated by Georg Hallensleben

HONOR BOOK

Myers, Christopher, *Wings*

HIGHLY COMMENDED

Christian, Peggy, *If You Find a Rock,* illustrated by Barbara Hirsch Lember

Cronin, Doreen, *Click, Clack, Moo: Cows That Type,* illustrated by Betsy Lewin

Harjo, Joy, *The Good Luck Cat,* illustrated by Paul Lee

Kajikawa, Kimiko, *Yoshi's Feast,* illustrated by Yumi Heo

Pinkney, Sandra, *Shades of Black: A Celebration of Our Children,* photographs by Myles Pinkney

Van Laan, Nancy, *When Winter Comes,* illustrated by Susan Gaber

2000

WINNER

Bang, Molly, *When Sophie Gets Angry—Really, Really Angry . . .*

HONOR BOOKS

Best, Cari, *Three Cheers for Catherine the Great!* illustrated by Giselle Potter

Feiffer, Jules, *Bark, George*

HIGHLY COMMENDED

Diakite, Baba Wague, *The Hatseller and the Monkeys*

George, Kristine O'Connell, *Little Dog Poems,* illustrated by June Otani

Graham, Joan Bransfield, *Flicker Flash,* illustrated by Nancy Davis

Howard, Elizabeth Fitzgerald, *When Will Sarah Come?* illustrated by Nina Crews

Schwartz, Amy, *How to Catch an Elephant*

Thomas, Joyce Carol, *You Are My Perfect Baby,* illustrated by Nneka Bennett

Zimmerman, Andrea, and David Clemesha, *Trashy Town*

1999

WINNER

Shulevitz, Uri, *Snow*

HONOR BOOKS

Meade, Holly, *John Willy and Freddy McGee*

Steig, William, *Pete's a Pizza*

HIGHLY COMMENDED

Fleming, Denise, *Mama Cat Has Three Kittens*

Henkes, Kevin, *Circle Dogs,* illustrated by Dan Yaccarino

Jones, Bill T., and Susan Kuklin, *Dance,* photographs by Susan Kuklin

Reiser, Lynn, *Little Clam*

Stuve-Bodeen, Stephanie, *Elizabeti's Doll,* illustrated by Christy Hale

1998

WINNER

Williams, Vera B., *Lucky Song*

HONOR BOOK

Kasza, Keiko, *Don't Laugh, Joe!*

HIGHLY COMMENDED

Bauer, Marion Dane, *If You Were Born a Kitten,* illustrated by JoEllen McAllister Stammen

Cooper, Elisha, *Country Fair*

Fleming, Denise, *Time to Sleep*

McKissack, Patricia, *Ma Dear's Aprons,* illustrated by Floyd Cooper

Waber, Bernard, *Bearsie Bear and the Surprise Sleepover Party*

Wells, Rosemary, *Bunny Cakes*

Content of Picture Books

This chapter was updated with the assistance of Dr. Deborah Wooten.

They are redwood trees. They have been alive
for thousands of years. They are called the Giant Sequoia.
Where did the name come from?

—JAMES RUMFORD, *Sequoyah: The Cherokee Man*
Who Gave His People Writing, unpaged

DEBBIE'S THIRD GRADERS FOLLOW HER OVER TO THE READ-ALOUD SECTION in their classroom. She is clutching a picture book close to her chest, full of anticipation that her students will respond enthusiastically when she reads it aloud. She is sure they will be able to make connections to the story and that it will breathe life into their study of Native Americans. Debbie begins by showing the cover of the book to her students, telling them that it stands tall among her favorite picture books. Everyone laughs when she says that—a lot of books are among her favorites. Her students well know that she loves books.

Debbie has selected James Rumford's *Sequoyah* (I) not only because her students are learning about Native Americans but also because she wants her students to think about overcoming obstacles. Sequoyah had a physical disability, was raised by one parent, and was ridiculed for his dreams and beliefs, yet he took risks and did something amazing. After she finishes reading, Chris says that it makes him think about Louis Braille because he invented writing for the blind, and Sequoyah created writing for his people. Dawn observes that Louis Braille could not see and Sequoyah had a physical disability. That makes them wonder how he was injured, so Joe goes to the computer to find the answer, and a classmate joins him. Sarah says it reminds her of Wilma Rudolph in *Wilma Unlimited* (P–I) because Wilma had had polio as a child. Another student wonders if bad things only happen to famous people. They talk, they think, they talk some more. Joe has printed something and hands it to Debbie, who reads aloud that Sequoyah was injured in a hunting accident and that his disability caused him to have more time for contemplation and study. Aha! The faces of the children light up as they realize that, rather than being disabling, Sequoyah's hunting accident meant that he had time for his amazing invention, the Cherokee alphabet.

During this read-aloud time, Debbie has once again demonstrated her love for books. She has captured her students' interest in an important Native American figure, caused them to make connections to other people and books that they know about, and helped them begin to think about "disabilities" in a new way. And, above all, they have heard interesting language used in interesting ways and seen a visually beautiful book, complete with Cherokee writing. They will revisit this book repeatedly for the rest of the school year.

Picture Books for Developmental Stages

Picture books are a powerful force in children's language and literacy development. Books provide models of language usage; they demonstrate meaningful concepts and represent the world a child is coming to know. Books build a foundation for reading as a pleasurable activity; children learn that good stories come from books. Concept development, language development, and children's storehouses of experiences are strengthened through books. Considering children's voracious appetite for language, almost any book can become a source for learning. We have many books available, however, so we can be selective in those we choose. Only the best are good enough for children.

Picture books possess the unique ability to take a complicated or huge topic and break it down for a wide audience to enjoy and learn from. Picture books have pleased young children, their parents, and their teachers over many years. In the past 20 years we have seen the emergence of picture books written for older audiences as well. Thus older children and adolescents can find picture books that engage them with beautiful language and stunning illustrations.

• • PICTURE BOOKS • •
FOR VERY YOUNG CHILDREN

Board Books and Participation Books

Board books appeal to infants and toddlers up to three years of age; the books are often 6 to 12 pages long, made of sturdy cardboard. There are also cloth books, shape books, pudgy books, lift-the-flap books, toy books, and plastic bathtub books. Books of this type, appropriate for children in the picture identification stage, are also good for those in the earliest stages of reading. *Max's First Word* (N), by Rosemary Wells, is a favorite board book. Big sister Ruby tries time and again

to get Max to say a word. He responds only with "Bang." Just to surprise Ruby and show that he is no dummy, when she holds up an apple, Max says, "Delicious." Children point to pictures and label them, creating meaning from texts.

Donald Crews created *Inside Freight Train* (N), a sturdy board book with sliding doors that open on each railroad car. Children's fascination with trains starts early and continues for many years. This book is a treasure. Children also enjoy books about children and parents. *¿Me quieres, mamá?* (N) is a Spanish version of the very popular *Do You Love Me, Mama?* Other board books appear in the Booklist at the end of the chapter.

The words and pictures in both the English and the Spanish versions of the popular Do You Love Me, Mama? *portray loving reassurance.*

¿Cuánto?

Participation books provide concrete visual and tactile materials for children to explore: textures to touch, flaps to lift, flowers to smell, and pieces to manipulate. A classic by Dorothy Kunhardt, *Pat the Bunny* (N), asks children to look in a mirror, play peek-a-boo, and feel a scratchy beard; babies love touching this book. Eric Carle's *The Very Busy Spider* (N), reissued as a 24-page board book, has brightly colored collages and tactile renderings of the spider's growing web. Young children enjoy saying the repetitive phrases with the onomatopoeic sounds and feeling the spider web. These and other excellent participation books are included in the Booklist at the end of the chapter.

Storybooks and Poems

Whether in board book form or typical picture-book format, stories for the very young have a simple plot line, are about familiar childhood experiences, and contain clear illustrations. Toddlers who enjoy participation books also enjoy simple stories, Mother Goose rhymes, counting rhymes and alphabet jingles, and other rhythmic texts. Rebecca O'Connell's *The Baby Goes Beep* (N), illustrated by Ken Wilson-Max, invites young listeners to join in saying the rhythmic text. These same readers enjoy the rhythm and rhyme of Peggy Rathman's *The Day the Babies Crawled Away* (N–P), even as their eyes are glued to the dramatic black silhouette illustrations.

As toddlers turn pages and point to pictures in books, they develop concepts about books and how they work. Simple storybooks introduce children to stories and help them learn about narrative by capturing and holding their interest even if they have short attention spans; these books often are the ones children turn to again and again. Kevin Henkes's Caldecott Medal book, *Kitten's First Full Moon* (N), is a quiet, satisfying story of one kitten's adventure as she tries to drink the bowl of milk that she mistakenly thinks is waiting for her in the full moon. Expressive pictures and a brief, lyrical text hold the attention of young listeners.

Amy Schwartz captures the life of one young boy in *What James Likes Best* (N), which is not always what the adults in his life would think he would like. Schwartz presents four simple stories about everyday events, followed by the question "What did James like best?" and four possible answers, drawing young children into participating in the storytelling. Young children also enjoy the single-mindedness of Ella Sarah in Margaret Chodos-Irvine's *Ella Sarah Gets Dressed* (N), especially those who insist, as Ella Sarah does, on choosing their own clothes in the morning.

Mo Willems tells the classic tale of the "blankie" or "lovey" lost and found again in *Knuffle Bunny: A Cautionary Tale* (N–P), a Caldecott Honor book. Young listeners identify with the child who misplaced her bunny and uttered her very first words when it was finally found. Older children enjoy the humor too. There are many more simple storybooks and poems that appeal to children who are not yet

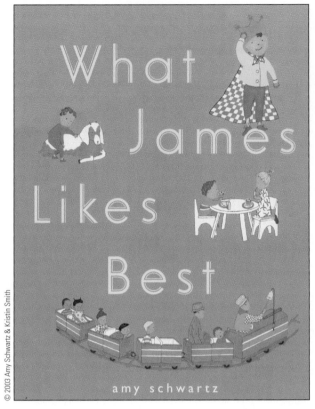

Any Schwartz captures the world of a small child and the interest of young readers in **What James Likes Best.**

ready for long stories. These books generally have a brief text and engaging illustrations. Examples of stories for very young children appear in the Booklist at the end of the chapter.

• • PICTURE BOOKS • • FOR CHILDREN

As children mature and their worlds expand, the number of books available to them also expands. Children in the preschool and primary grades have their choice of concept books, alphabet and counting books, books that support their early attempts at independent reading, and books that relate to every facet of their world.

Concept Books

Concept books, simple nonfiction books, appeal to a wide audience. Young children learn about the world through engaging concept books. Preschool and primary-grade children are developing their concept of time, and Geraldine McCaughrean's *My Grandmother's Clock* (N–P), illustrated by Stephen Lambert, will help them do that. This is a simple story, redolent with the affection between grandmother and granddaughter, that looks at time from a much larger perspective than minutes and hours.

Actual Size (P–I) is a book that Steve Jenkins created to help children understand the concept of size. His inspiration for this book originated when observing his son comparing his hand to a cast of a gorilla's hand during a visit to the San Diego Zoo. The book contains pictures of the eyeball of a giant squid and the head of an Alaskan brown bear, among other animals. Each page includes the height and weight of each animal; additional information about each animal is included in the back of the book.

Concept books contribute to a child's expanding knowledge and language by providing numerous examples of an idea. Some books present abstract ideas, such as shape, color, size, or sound, through many illustrations, as Tana Hoban does in *Cubes, Cones, Cylinders, and Spheres* (N–P). Hoban, a master of the art of concept books and a skilled photographer, uses no words in the book about shapes. Instead, she uses crystal-clear photographs of objects that children could find in their own environment. Children enjoy working with this book and often experiment with creating images using shapes and color on their own.

Some books tell stories that focus on specific concepts or involve the viewer by asking questions. Steve Jenkins and Robin Page challenge a broad range of readers to expand their knowledge about the function of body parts in *What*

Do You Do with a Tail Like This? (P–I). The authors include information about each animal in the back of the book.

Exploring the concept of kindergarten itself, Rosemary Wells put together a treasure when she collected hundreds of songs, activities, games, counting, alphabet songs, measuring, and science projects all in one book, *My Kindergarten* (P). This is an ideal book for kindergarten teachers, parents, grandparents, or anyone who has children in the first year of school. Other outstanding concept books appear in the Booklist at the end of the chapter.

Alphabet Books

Alphabet books serve many useful purposes, only one of which is related to learning the alphabet. Children ages two to four years old point to pictures and label objects on the page; five-year-olds may say the letter names and the words that start with each letter; six-year-olds may read the letters, words, or story to confirm their knowledge of letter-sound correspondence. However they are read, alphabet books help children develop an awareness of words on the page; they increase language learning and serve as a pleasurable activity for children.

We never need to settle for a mediocre alphabet book, because magnificent ones are available, such as Lisa Campbell Ernst's *The Turn-Around, Upside-Down Alphabet Book*

The huge **gorilla** and the **pygmy mouse lemur** both have hands a lot like ours.

gorilla: 5½ feet tall, 600 pounds   mouse lemur: 2½ inches tall, 1 ounce

© 2004 Steve Jenkins

Steve Jenkins's illustrations in **Actual Size** *help all readers put the concept of relative size into perspective.*

(N–P), Andy Rash's *Agent A to Agent Z* (P), *A Gardener's Alphabet* (P), by Mary Azarian, *ABC Pop!* (N–P), by Rachel Isadora, Steve Johnson's *Graphic Alphabet* (N–P), and Brian Floca's *The Racecar Alphabet* (N–P). Jon Agee's *Z Goes Home* (N–P) combines fun with bold graphics as it follows the journey of Z, heading home across a bridge, eating a doughnut, and so on until it arrives home, the Z in the City Zoo. Ross MacDonald treats the alphabet humorously in *Achoo! Bang! Crash! The Noisy Alphabet* (P).

In Helen Oxenbury's classic *ABC of Things* (N), the elongated shape and simple format appeal to young readers. Each double-page spread contains both uppercase and lowercase letters, one or more words beginning with the letters, and objects associated with the letters. Children enjoy the way the illustrations place the objects in humorous situations, such as a cat and a cow sitting on a chair while a crow carries in a cake full of candles.

Some authors use the ABCs to structure the information that they want to present. For example, Kristin Joy Pratt uses the alphabet for *A Walk in the Rain Forest* and *A Swim in the Sea* (both P). These books are organized by the alphabet, but don't really focus on the alphabet as such. Alphabet books for older readers are discussed later in this chapter, and other excellent alphabet books appear in the Booklist at the end of the chapter.

Counting Books

Some counting books help children learn numbers, numerical concepts, days of the week, months of the year, and the four seasons. Anita Lobel does all that and wraps it in an engaging story in *One Lighthouse, One Moon* (P–I). Many counting books are available for the nursery and primary grades, starting with those that use simple pictures to illustrate the progression from 1 to 10, such as Rachel Isadora's *1 2 3 Pop!* (P). Lynn Reiser's *Ten Puppies* (N) illustrates paired integers whose sum is ten with adorable puppies that make young readers want to look closely at the *nine* pink tongues and *one* blue tongue as they count. Reading Maurie Manning's *The Aunts Go Marching* (N), a very cheerful, engaging text with plenty of things to count, leads children into singing along, movement, and counting out loud.

Other counting books go far beyond 10 or count in sets, such as *Anno's Counting Book* (P–I), which moves from 0 to 12 and from January to December. Mitsumasa Anno begins his counting book with an empty landscape that becomes a small village with 12 houses, 12 adults, and 12 children who go to church at 12 P.M. and see 12 reindeer in the sky. Steve Johnson's *City by Numbers* (N–P) pulls young readers into visualizing the shapes of numbers with illustrations that demonstrate how to look to find number shapes in the world around us.

Philip Yates builds on children's interest in Egypt in *Ten Little Mummies: An Egyptian Counting Book* (P), in which

*The illustrations in Rachel Isadora's **1 2 3 Pop!** make it easy for young children to count objects.*

the 10 little mummies leave the tomb and go to play in the desert, where they disappear, one by one. Molly Bang's delightful *Ten, Nine, Eight* (N–P), recently reissued, also counts backwards; as a father helps his daughter at bedtime, they count down from 10 toes to 1 sleepy child all ready for bed. The illustrations depict bedtime activities that invite young readers to find the numbered objects and to enjoy the loving story. Counting books help children develop concepts of quantity and numerical order through fine visual portrayal of number concepts. The best illustrations for young children avoid distracting clutter so that the objects to be counted can be identified and counted without confusion. In books for older children the illustrations can be more complex. More counting books appear in the Booklist at the end of the chapter.

Books for Emerging Readers

As children mature, their taste for books matures; their cognitive and linguistic capabilities increase as well as their need for books. Learning to read and being able to unlock the secrets of a printed page mark an important step toward maturity. Many books are available for developing readers, including those we have already discussed. There are also special kinds of storybooks—wordless books, predictable books, and beginning-to-read books as well as illustrated easy chapter books—that support children's attempts at independent reading.

Wordless books are appropriate for children of all ages who are developing a sense of story and are learning language rapidly. Predictable books are ideal material for the child who is beginning to pay attention to print. Beginning-to-read books are perfect for children who have just become independent readers but still need the support of simple but interesting texts. Picture storybooks, books of poetry and song, and nonfiction continue to play an important role in a child's reading, as well.

WORDLESS BOOKS Wordless books tell a story through illustration alone. Young children who do not yet read can retell a story from looking at the pictures; beginning readers, through their developing concept of story, are able to narrate the story with character and narrator voices. Older, struggling readers can grasp the story elements in wordless books. All students can use wordless books as a springboard to writing and oral storytelling. Good wordless storybooks contain all the important elements found in all good storybooks—except for the dialogue and narration, which are supplied by the reader. Some good wordless books appear in the Booklist at the end of the chapter.

Wordless books provide an excellent opportunity to explore how stories work. Children produce narration for wordless books; their ideas can be written down by an adult or tape-recorded and used for reading instruction material. If young children are narrating a wordless book, they can watch their own words being written and learn intuitively the relation between print and sound. This means of teaching, called the language experience approach, provides a meaningful foundation for reading, especially when accom-panied by a strong read-aloud program based on good literature. Older students, too, benefit from using wordless books as a foundation for their own oral language or writing. The story they create from a wordless picture storybook is *their* story—they have composed it—and it is therefore easier for them to read.

Barbara Lehman's *The Red Book* (P–I), a Caldecott Honor winner, is, appropriately, bright red. The watercolor, gouache, and ink illustrations, with their straightforward, geometric shapes, present the story of a young girl who finds a red book in the snow on the city sidewalk, picks it up, and takes it to school. When she opens the book, she sees a map of islands. The illustrations then zoom into a close-up of the island on which a boy walks along the beach, and he finds a red book in the sand. When he opens it up he sees a city and, as the pictures zoom in again, the girl. They gaze at each other, entranced. The girl leaves school, buys many balloons, and sails off to meet the boy on the island, dropping the red book. They do meet, and end up in the pages of the dropped book, together. At least until a boy on a bike picks up the lost book. With its clever plot, expressive characters, and exploration of the power of books and the imagination, this wordless book is a treasure.

When a boy wanders into an abandoned theater, he begins a journey through time that lands him right in the middle of a Shakespeare play. Enraged, William Shakespeare chases him through Elizabethan London. Full of comic details, *The Boy, the Bear, the Baron, the Bard* (P–I), by Gregory Rogers, pictorially tells a very funny story.

In **The Red Book,** *Barbara Lehman portrays surprise, delight, and eager anticipation as boy and girl realize the magical possibilities in a book each happen upon.*

Another funny wordless book, *You Can't Take a Balloon into the National Gallery* (P–I–A), by Jacqueline Preiss Weitzman and Robin Preiss Glasser, gives readers several subplots, as well as a background activity, art, geography, maps, people, architecture, and humorous detail. Students of all ages can enjoy David Wiesner's book *Sector 7* (P–I) and Jeanne Baker's *Window* and *Home* (both P–I–A), each for different reasons. Charlotte Dematons gives children a lot to look at in *The Yellow Balloon* (N–P), as the illustrations, through a series of aerial views, present the world travels of an escaped balloon.

All students learn about story structure and form when they translate the pictures of a wordless storybook into language. The structure of the story, along with the character development, provides a good model for writers, and students can also explore the visual characterization, setting, and theme that wordless books provide.

PREDICTABLE OR PATTERNED BOOKS Predictable books have a strong rhythmic pattern in the language. This helps children anticipate what is going to happen next and predict the next word to come. Many four- and five-year-old children can make predictions and use their knowledge of phonics to read books on their own after hearing them read aloud once or twice. In *The Seals on the Bus* (N–P) Lenny Hort replicated the pattern of a familiar song, turning the wheels on the bus into the seals on the bus who go "errp, errp, errp" all around the town. In *Cold Little Duck, Duck, Duck* (N–P), Lisa Westberg Peters uses a similar pattern of repetition. A little duck comes to the pond only to find it still frozen. The text is written in large letters: "One miserable and frozen spring: brisk brisk brisk. A cold little duck flew in: Brr-ack Brr-ack Brr-ack. Her pond was stiff and white: creak creak creak." The interesting sounds Peters repeats make children want to read along.

Predictable books are structured using strong language patterns, such as repeated phrases, rhyme, and rhythm; cumulative story structures that add, or accumulate, information; and familiar concepts, songs, or sequences (like days of the week). Detailed illustrations reinforce the language patterns and provide a visual reproduction of the text. Dayle Ann Dodds's *Where's Pup?* (N–P) contains a very simple text consisting of two and three word sentences, rhyming words, and a limited vocabulary, yet manages to tell an engaging story that young children can actually read on their own. Pierre Pratt's colorful illustrations provide a context that both engages and supports young readers. Characteristics of predictable books are listed in Figure 3.1.

Reading involves sampling, predicting, and confirming (Goodman, 1985; Smith, 1978). Fluent readers build hypotheses about text meaning as they read. They predict a probable meaning based on the information sampled and then confirm it by checking to see if it makes sense, matches the letter-sound correspondence in the print, and sounds like real language. For beginning readers, patterned books are ideal fare, because they match expectations every step of the way. Poetry also meets the criteria. Through rhythm, repetition, and rhyme, Jane Yolen creates a story in *How Do Dinosaurs Say Goodnight?* (P) that uses dinosaurs to capture childlike behavior. Beginning readers chime in the second time through the book and soon can read it on their own. Other outstanding patterned books appear in the Booklist at the end of the chapter.

Patterned, predictable books help beginning readers confirm their knowledge of sound-letter correspondence. Often

© 2000 Sam Williams

With predictable books such as Lisa Westberg Peter's **Cold Little Duck, Duck, Duck,** *listeners join in to say repeated phrases. Gradually they become the readers.*

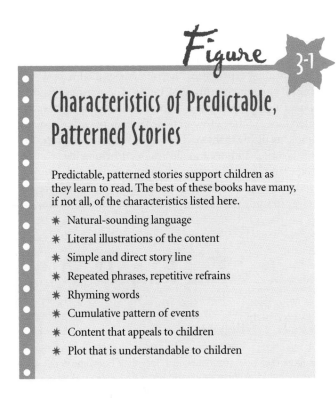

Characteristics of Predictable, Patterned Stories

Predictable, patterned stories support children as they learn to read. The best of these books have many, if not all, of the characteristics listed here.

* Natural-sounding language
* Literal illustrations of the content
* Simple and direct story line
* Repeated phrases, repetitive refrains
* Rhyming words
* Cumulative pattern of events
* Content that appeals to children
* Plot that is understandable to children

the books have an illustration followed by a single line of text. For example, Mem Fox's *Where Is the Green Sheep?* (N–P), illustrated by Judy Horacek, contains patterned, lilting, rhyming statements with art that precisely reflects the language until, toward the end of the story, readers are cautioned to turn the page quietly because the green sheep is fast asleep.

BEGINNING-TO-READ BOOKS Beginning-to-read books are ones that children who have just become independent readers can enjoy on their own; they combine controlled vocabulary with creative storytelling. Good beginning-to-read books have strong characterization, worthy themes, and engaging plots. The sentences are generally simple, with few embedded clauses, and the language is often direct dialogue. Lines of text are printed so that sentence breaks occur according to natural phrases; meaningful chunks of language are grouped together.

Illustrations depict the characters and action in ways that reflect and extend the text, which contains a limited number of different words and tells an interesting story. Arnold Lobel's classic series, including *Frog and Toad Are Friends* (N–P), is a favorite with newly independent readers. Frog and Toad, humanlike characters in animal form, solve understandable problems with naïveté and wit.

Cynthia Rylant, a wizard with words, creates **Henry and Mudge** (P), a warm and wonderful series of stories about a very large dog and the boy who loves him. Illustrations depict the action and provide emotional details about the characters. Rylant chooses words wisely; her stories are so well written that they are a pleasure to read. Denys Cazet's **Minnie and Moo** series has a loyal following of young readers. In *Minnie and Moo: Will You Be My Valentine?* (P) the humor is high and the text easy for young readers to decode.

Appealing to a slightly older audience, Pamela Duncan Edwards pares down two historical moments in *The Wright Brothers* and *Boston Tea Party* (both I). Pamela employs two mice in each book to add asides of humor and significant

But where is the green sheep?

Here is the car sheep, and here is the train sheep.

© 2004 Mem Fox & Judy Horacek

*The rhyming, rhythmic verse in **Where Is the Green Sheep?** supports new readers as they read all by themselves.*

facts to the overall stories. These and other good beginning-to-read books are suggested in the Booklist at the end of the chapter.

Highly illustrated chapter books, although they are not true picture books, are an important part of a young child's development as an independent reader. Cynthia Rylant's **Cobblestreet Kids** series, Paula Danziger's **Amber Brown** series, and many others discussed in Chapter 7 offer young readers the opportunity to read longer, more complex texts that are still supported by illustrations.

As children grow in their reading ability, they move beyond listening to picture books and working with easy-to-read materials to chapter books and then toward full-length texts. However, even though children outgrow reading about Frog and Toad and other characters from their early reading experiences, they remember their happy, successful encounters with these books. These strong, positive experiences propel them into more positive connections with literature. As they grow in their familiarity with the many books available to them, children will begin to develop a list of "favorite" authors and illustrators. Teaching Idea 3.1 uses the example of Chris Van Allsburg, a very popular author with primary, intermediate, and advanced readers, to present a way to study the body of an author or illustrator's work.

Teaching Idea 3-1

Study the Body of an Author's or Illustrator's Work

Any author or illustrator with five or more books is a candidate for an author or illustrator study. Here we show how a study of Chris Van Allsburg might look.

Collect Chris Van Allsburg's picture books. Pass them out to small groups of two or three students and then have the groups position themselves in chronological order according to the books' copyright dates. Students sit in a circle in this chronological order. Provide time for students to read and explore each book. Students introduce their book and comment about the illustrations and text. (You can record this information if desired.) Next, have students find connections among these books. How are the writing and art similar? How did Van Allsburg's work change over the years? Are there any thematic similarities? Where is the dog in each book? The possible questions are endless. A chart similar to the example here can help students keep track of their ideas.

Title	Publication Date	Illustration Style	Genre	Setting	Theme or Important Message	Point of View or Perspective	Spot the Dog
The Garden of Abdul Gasazi	1979						
Jumanji	1981						
Ben's Dream	1982						
The Wreck of the Zephyr	1983						
The Mysteries of Harris Burdick	1984						
The Polar Express	1985						
The Stranger	1986						
The Z Was Zapped	1987						
Two Bad Ants	1988						
Just a Dream	1990						
The Wretched Stone	1991						
The Widow's Broom	1992						
The Sweetest Fig	1993						
Bad Day at Riverbend	1995						
Zathura	2002						

✳ Students place a check in the column indicating that they have found the dog in each book, and note where.

Source: Deborah Wooten

Children in the preschool and primary grades continue to enjoy hearing well-written picture storybooks, books of poetry and song, and nonfiction books read aloud. Many of these books are discussed later in this chapter, when we talk about making connections between life and literature. Each year there is a crop of wonderful books just waiting to be placed in the hands, minds, and hearts of young children, and older ones as well.

• • PICTURE BOOKS • •
FOR OLDER CHILDREN
AND ADOLESCENTS

In the past, most picture books were published primarily for students in preschool and primary grades. Today, publishers offer a variety of picture books that appeal to older students, such as picture books for struggling readers, second-language bilingual books, graphic picture books and graphic novels, as well as nonfiction picture books. These books appeal to visually sophisticated students; they are also accessible to struggling readers who learn more easily using books with more pictures and sparser text. Students learning English also learn more easily using picture books and other illustrated texts.

Like counting books for younger readers, some books for older readers present information organized numerically. Peter Sis is a genius; he created *The Train of States* (I–A), which presents the 50 American states as train cars, in the order in which they became states. Every state is pictured as a train car where you find the capital, state flower, presidents, and lots of other information. *The Buck Stops Here: The Presidents of the United States* (I–A), by Alice Provensen, starts with, "First and Foremost, Washington, Our best beloved President One." This book presents the presidents numerically in rhyming style. The illustrations add historical information about each president.

Alphabet books are not exclusive to primary grades either. Avis Harley uses the alphabet to present poetic forms in *Fly with Poetry: An ABC of Poetry* (I–A). In alphabetical

Peter Sis provides a lot of visual and verbal information about the states in a format pleasing to a wide range of readers.

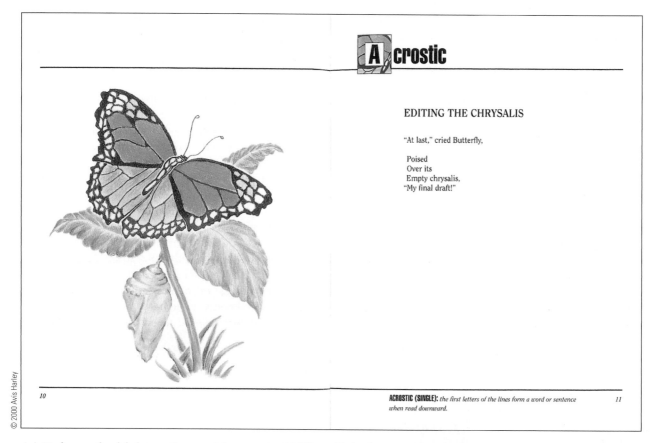

Avis Harley uses the alphabet as a framework for presenting 26 different kinds of poems, with explanatory notes on each, in Fly with Poetry: An ABC of Poetry.

order, she defines a poetic form and presents a poem in that form to explain exactly what she means. For example, she explains what an acrostic poem is and then presents a poem in that form.

Other authors use the alphabet as a structure for information. *The Queen's Progress: An Elizabethan Alphabet* (I–A) lures readers by providing alphabetical bite-size nuggets of information about the reign of Elizabeth I. Reflecting the Elizabethan Age, the illustrations complement the text. Another example is Arthur Yorink's *The Alphabet Atlas* (I–A). This alphabetical atlas transforms geography into stunning quilted artwork. Its beauty inspires students to want to write and illustrate their own alphabetical atlas.

Q Is for Quark: A Science Alphabet Book and *G Is for Googol: A Math Alphabet Book* (both I–A), written by David M. Schwartz, are directed to upper-grade students. Some teachers use these books to complement their math and science curricula by providing a "letter-a-day" read-aloud experience or by reinforcing a topic such as DNA for "D" when it connects to the subject students are studying. The two books make complicated topics friendly and fun. "D" for DNA, for example, employs plain, simple language and silly drawings that make DNA comical and intriguing

rather than boring and difficult to understand. Teaching students how to say "rhombicosidodecahedron" (the biggest polyhedron, with 240 faces) adds linguistic sparkle to a geometry lesson because it becomes a fun word to say and "show off" to others.

Just as there are counting and alphabet books for older readers, there are also pop-up books that appeal to a wide range of students. *Brooklyn Pops Up* (all ages) is an engineering tour de force that shows landmarks in Brooklyn, New York, including Coney Island, Grand Army Plaza, and the Brooklyn Museum of Art. Several artists and pop-up designers worked on the book, including Maurice Sendak and pop-up master Robert Sabuda. Sabuda's stunning *Alice's Adventures in Wonderland* (I) appeals to intermediate audiences. Christopher Bing seamlessly weaves history and art into a rare treasure in *The Midnight Ride of Paul Revere* (I). Bing's masterpiece goes well beyond the familiar narrative poem, and it takes several viewings to grasp even a portion of the information contained in the pictures.

Jon Scieszka wrote and Lane Smith illustrated books difficult to categorize but delightful to read: they had fun with *Math Curse* and recently have produced *Science Verse* (both I). Author and illustrator permeate the topics of math and science with humor; readers devour both books. *Science Verse* is a zany series of poems that parody the styles of Joyce Kilmer, Edgar Allan Poe, Lewis Carroll, Robert Frost, and many others. Each book comes with a CD featuring Scieszka and Smith reading aloud each piece.

In an integrated, literature-based curriculum, students explore topics in nonfiction picture books that convey relevant information geared to their interest level. The publishing trend has been to produce more reader-friendly books with increased illustration and less densely packed texts. Picture books for older students are longer, have more complex text and themes, and deal with topics that are more abstract and more intellectually demanding. We discuss nonfiction picture books in Chapters 9 and 10.

There are also many picture storybooks for older students, books that explore themes and events that are not suited for a younger audience. For example, in Patricia Polacco's *Pink and Say* (I–A), African American Pinkus saves Sheldon's life as they fight side by side on a Civil War battlefield. Pinkus takes his wounded white soldier friend to his own home, where his grandmother nurses Sheldon back to health. Despite his generous acts, Pinkus is hanged at

Andersonville jail soon after arriving there as a Confederate prisoner. Ann Turner's *Nettie's Trip South* (I–A) is another picture book for older readers that helps them emotionally engage with the implications of slavery. Tom Feelings's *Middle Passage* (A) needs no words to convey the horrors of the slave trade.

The late Virginia Hamilton published a collection of 24 American black folktales. One of those stories, *The People Could Fly* (I–A), is considered her finest. Fortunately, it is now published as a stand-alone book with all new illustrations by Leo and Diane Dillon. The combination of text and illustration is so convincing that readers almost believe the story to be true even while they understand the metaphorical meaning of flying. These and more picture storybooks that are appropriate for older readers are discussed in Chapters 5 through 8.

Graphic picture books and novels have become popular with upper elementary and adolescent readers. The visual nature of these books is especially appealing to many students. Marcia Williams created two graphic picture books: *Tales from Shakespeare* and *Bravo, Mr. William Shakespeare!* (both I–A). Each book contains seven of Shakespeare's most

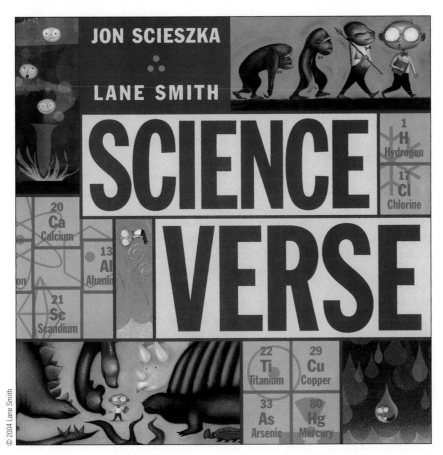

Zany humor, clever wordplay, and enticing illustrations make **Science Verse** *a favorite with students and teachers alike.*

popular plays. The first contains *Romeo and Juliet, A Winter's Tale, Macbeth, A Midsummer Night's Dream, Julius Caesar, Hamlet,* and *The Tempest.* The second contains *As You Like It, Richard III, Antony and Cleopatra, Much Ado about Nothing, Twelfth Night, King Lear,* and *The Merchant of Venice.*

Little Vampire Goes to School (I), by French author Joann Sfar, was a Children's Choices Award Winner in 2004. This book is an interesting mix of cartoon style and creepy content and is appealing to many readers, including reluctant ones. Avi's graphic picture book, **Silent Movie** (I–A), illustrated by C. B. Mordan, is, appropriately, black and white and told only through images and title cards. The rags-to-riches immigrant story, complete with villain, appealing young child and mother on their own, and happy ending is perfect fare for the silent movie and the audience. The melodrama is a wonderful stimulus for some extended dramatic writing.

Picture books have a special place in the lives of children and adolescents. Children and adolescents make connections between the books they read and the life they live because these books reflect every aspect of their expanding world.

Making Connections between Life and Literature

Children's language develops from birth onwards, and they grow as social beings as their world expands. They learn about themselves and their families, their friends, and others they might encounter. They also learn about the natural world and the aesthetic world of art, music, dance, and literature. This learning occurs in many places—home, community, school—and also in books. As children mature, their imagination feeds on new experiences with both life and literature. Picture books support and enrich children's spiraling, expanding development, offering experiences well beyond children's lives, as well as imaginative language experiences. When readers connect with books, they bring the world of the book into their lives and make it their own.

Engaged readers make connections to the books they read. They might connect a book to themselves, using a book to understand themselves and their lives, or using their own experiences to understand a book. When they do this they might remark that a particular story reminds them of themselves or their family or friends. They might note that they have had experiences or feelings similar to the experiences and feelings of the characters in the story. These connections can also help them understand the book, as they think about their own experiences and feelings in

order to make sense of what they are reading. Indeed, making connections between themselves and the books they are reading is an important component of reading with understanding and engagement.

Engaged readers also connect books to books. When students read a lot of books and talk about them, as we saw in the opening vignette in this chapter, they often seek to understand one book in relation to another they have read. These connections grow as they read more and more books. Sometimes students realize that they have read other books written or illustrated by the same author and discover ways in which the books are similar. For example, students have commented that **The Rough-Face Girl** (P–I) reminded them of **Encounter** (I–A) because the illustrations look the same (and are indeed by the same illustrator), only to realize later that the illustrations are only the beginning of the possible ways in which the books are similar.

Often the connections that readers make between books are thematic. That is, they will link books about the same idea. We talk more about connecting to books in Chapters 12 through 14. Here we present picture books in general thematic groupings. Reading a number of books from any single category will help readers make connections among books as well as between books and themselves. Teaching Idea 3.2 offers suggestions for helping students think about who they are and how they feel, comparing themselves to the characters they meet in books. In the remaining chapters in this book, this Teaching Idea is repeated with different books, across different genres and in different contexts.

• •   T H E   I N N E R   W O R L D   • •

In a supportive environment, children know that they are loved and unique; they are able to express themselves and to make choices. They understand that they are not the only people who have needs and feelings. They learn that others see the world differently from them, and they begin to develop self-esteem based on what others say to them. Many picture books address these important self-concepts.

Children in the preschool years are busy learning about themselves—who they are and what they can do—and about others. Their self-concept develops as a direct result of their interaction with the environment, including the reactions of others to their own actions. When children see that their actions meet with approval, they are encouraged to explore, to express their ideas, and to discover their world. Books mirror primary experiences that shape children's actions, reactions, and feelings; books can bring subtle issues to a conscious level, making it possible to discuss them. Books can play an important role for the child who is experiencing the conflicts of growing up; they enrich understanding when they can be related to real life. Issues such

Teaching Idea 3-2

Making Thematic Connections: Knowing Yourself

Gather several picture books, such as those suggested in the text and in the "Inner World" section of the Booklist for this chapter. Over a period of a week or so, read these books aloud to your class. It is beneficial for you to read them aloud so that all students will have the "same" reading experience, but do leave them in a place where your students can read them again if they desire. In discussions following each reading, pose questions that will help students explore the theme of "knowing yourself." You might want to ask them to describe the characters and to talk about how they "know" that the characters are this way. In many of these books, it is the characters themselves who realize their own inner strengths or weaknesses.

After discussing the characters, ask students to either write or talk about how they are like or unlike the main characters. To keep track of the insights your students are having, create a simple chart that they, or the class, can fill in for each book, with one column for a character, another for themselves, and space to write or draw. When all the books have been read and discussed, you can put everything together to create a chart comparing characters across books, leaving one column empty for each individual student to insert his or her own characteristics.

After you do this, students will be likely to notice character traits, compare new characters to those they have already met in books, and compare themselves to the characters they meet.

change the doll, taking her along with her on her outdoor adventures. The illustrations reflect the change in Dahlia as she gets muddy and torn, and her face softens into "a sweet, warm smile."

Children are discovering not only who they are but what they can do for themselves. Self-reliance, or resourcefulness, is a theme that appears in many picture books for nursery and primary-grade readers. In *Nino's Mask* (P), by Jeanette Winter, Nino wants to wear a mask to the village fiesta, but Mama and Papa, like parents everywhere in the world, tell him to wait until he is older. Determined, Nino watches the mask-maker at work and carves and paints his own mask. *Vera Rides a Bike* (P), by Vera Rosenberry, continues the series of stories about the indomitable Vera with an engaging tale of determination. Vera wants to ride her two-wheeler on her own, and she does, as long as she has someone to hold the bike when she gets on and to stop her when she wants to get off. When she finds herself on her bike, alone, she rides and rides until she comes up with a solution to her immediate problem—how to stop.

The protagonist of Michael Foreman's *Wonder Goal!* (P–I) is teased by the other players on his new soccer team until he fires off a perfect shot, upon which the action freezes and we are in the boy's bedroom, where he dreams of winning the World Cup with another wonder goal and fears that his overworked father will miss his big play. We return to the field, and the wonder goal is scored, dad present, in a World Cup final. Younger readers might need help with the action freeze, bedroom dreaming, and flash-forward action, but they won't need help recognizing the power of having a dream and realizing it.

Resourcefulness of another kind is apparent in Keiko Kasza's *My Lucky Day* (N–P). When Fox opens the door to a plump piglet, Fox is delighted. He was all set for roast pig for dinner anyway. Pig, however, isn't going to be anyone's tender meal, and he manages to trick Fox into giving him a hot bath, a massage, and a great meal. Fox is exhausted, and Pig is quite happy—just as planned!

Children often have fears, and Barbara Bottner tackles that issue head-on in *The Scaredy Cats* (P), cleverly illustrated by Victoria Chess. In a perfect reversal of the usual, Mr. and Mrs. Scaredy Cat are the fearful ones; they have the "what ifs," and badly. Only when Baby Scaredy Cat points out that all sorts of things can happen and that "what ifs" can be good as well as bad things do the parents relax a little. The illustrations provide a lot of the humor, especially the rendition of the large-eyed cats.

Sometimes the "what ifs" are realized in a devastating way, as is the case in Katherine Leiner's *Mama Does the Mambo* (P), with illustrations by Edel Rodriguez. Young Sofia has lost her father, and she has also lost the vision of her mother dancing the mamba with him. She worries that Mama will never dance again. This is a lyrical story of loss, acceptance, recovery, and remembering.

as sex-role stereotyping, childhood fears, and moral reasoning are some of the ideas that appear in picture storybooks for children.

Whether it's learning to be proud of your name and who you are, as in *Chrysanthemum* (N–P), or worrying about going to school, as in *Wemberly Worried* (N–P), both by Kevin Henkes, children have an inner life that picture storybooks mirror. The protagonist of Martin Waddell's *Hi, Harry!* (N), illustrated by Barbara Firth, knows he is slow, being a tortoise, but he is comfortable being slow, wishing only for a friend to play with. Appreciating the slow life is the thoughtful theme in this charming picture storybook. Young Charlotte, the protagonist of Barbara McClintock's *Dahlia* (P), also knows herself pretty well. She doesn't want a fussy, lacy doll like Dahlia, so she decides to

Around and around and around Vera went. Her legs were tired, and the air was chilly.

Finally, Vera said firmly, "I will just have to use the brakes and stop myself, or I will be here all night."

© 2004 Vera Rosenberry

*Vera finally decides that she is going to have to stop her bike herself in **Vera Rides a Bike.***

We learn to understand ourselves better through stories that feature characters who make mistakes as we do. In Debra Frasier's ***Miss Alaineus: A Vocabulary Disaster*** (P–I), Sage copies down the wrong vocabulary, leading to an embarrassing experience that her classmates and teacher find hysterical. This book reminds us of how easy it is to get confused and as a result to want to never return to school again. Sage redeems herself in a clever way at the end of the book. This book doesn't just tell a good story; it also encourages students to perform their own vocabulary dramas.

Picture books that support children's developing understandings and inner feelings about themselves appear in the Booklist at the end of the chapter.

• • THE FAMILY WORLD • •

Home is a child's first school; it has a lasting influence on a child's intellectual, personal, and social development. Children are affected by all the events and relationships that involve the family, including new babies, adoption, mothers who stay at home, mothers who work outside the home, preschool, day care, divorce, grandparents, stepparents, single parents, homelessness, death of a family member, and countless others. Books address these and many other issues that affect families. The best ones explore sensitive issues in family life and present a realistic picture of a variety of loving relationships.

The loving relationship depicted in Sarah Stewart's ***The Friend*** (P) is not that of parent and child, but rather one between child and housekeeper. Belle's parents are too busy to pay much attention to her, so good-hearted Bea, the housekeeper, allows Belle to "help" with chores and tag along on errands. They both enjoy going to the beach, hand in hand. When Belle goes alone and ends up almost drowning, it is Bea who rescues her. David Small's illustrations depict the friendship, highlighting Belle's small size against her huge home and Bea's solid presence.

Stephanie Stuve-Bodeen received the Ezra Jack Keats Award for ***Elizabeti's Doll*** (N–P), illustrated by Christy Hale. When her mother cares for Obedi, her new baby brother, Elizabeti finds a huggable rock she names Eva. She pretends Eva is her doll and imitates her mother's loving care. In the sequel, ***Mama Elizabeti*** (P), her mother has another new baby, and Elizabeti must assume care for Obedi; he is not as easy to care for as the rock.

Close relationships between parents, grandparents, and children are at the heart of many picture storybooks for nursery-, primary-, and intermediate-grade readers. Jacqueline Woodson's ***Coming on Home Soon*** (P), illustrated by

© 1998 Christy Hale

When Elizabeti did her chores, she also tied Eva onto her back with a kanga. Mama had to help a little.

A child in Tanzania learns about caring for younger siblings, even though her "baby" is a cold, hard rock, in Stephanie Stuve-Bodeen's Elizabeti's Doll.

E. B. Lewis, is set in the past—World War II—but the story is timeless. The palpable longing of Ada Ruth for her mother, and the calm and loving relationship between Ada Ruth and her grandmother shine through the words and the illustrations.

A close and loving relationship between Jonathan and his dad is the underlying theme of Nira Harel's *The Key to My Heart* (N). On the surface a story about lost keys, the dominant feeling here is the love between family members. The Israeli setting is noticeable in Yossi Abulafia's watercolor illustrations, but the story is universal.

Cari Best depicts a wonderful grandmother-granddaughter bond in *Three Cheers for Catherine the Great!* and *When Catherine the Great and I Were Eight!* (both P), illustrated by Giselle Potter. Sara and her spunky Russian grandmother, Catherine, learn from and with each other as they share Catherine's memories and Sara's childhood. Family memories, in the form of stories, are the centerpiece of Lynne Rae Perkins's *The Broken Cat* (P). As Andy and his mother, grandmother, and aunt sit at the veterinarian's office and wait with their injured cat, they tell family stories that help them cope with their worry. They each, of course, remember different versions of the stories and constantly correct one another, the way all families do. This might be a perfect book for eliciting some family stories from young readers, and Teaching Idea 3.3 presents ideas for exploring the fam-

Teaching Idea 3·3

Create a Book of Family Lore

Families in every culture have unique traditions, and celebrate holidays in their own special ways. They have special foods to prepare, clothes to wear, services to attend, and stories to tell. Ask students to write about their traditions to create a picture book about their family. Sections might include photographs of parents, grandparents, weddings, religious celebrations, favorite things to do, friends, favorite foods, favorite books, and family stories.

Family lore values the small details of life; realize that these details are important enough to write about. Read some of the following books to see what others have written about:

Ada, Alma Flor, *Under the Royal Palms: A Childhood in Cuba*

Brinkloe, Julie, *Fireflies*

Carrick, Carol, *Left Behind*

Cooney, Barbara, *Miss Rumphius*

dePaola, Tomie, *Here We All Are*

_____, *26 Fairmount Avenue*

Friedman, Ina, *How My Parents Learned to Eat*

Garza, Carmen Lomas, *Stories of My Family*

Hurwitz, Johanna, *A Dream Come True*

Keats, Ezra Jack, *Peter's Chair*

Khalsa, Dayal Kaur, *How Pizza Came to Queens*

McPhail, David, *Lost!*

Rabinovici, Schoschana, *Thanks to My Mother*, translated by James Skofield

Rylant, Cynthia, *Christmas in the Country*

_____, *When I Was Young in the Mountains*

Zolotow, Charlotte, *Someone New*

ily lore of children in your classroom. Other books that explore family life appear in the Booklist at the end of the chapter.

• • **THE SOCIAL WORLD** • •

Social development intersects all other areas of growth; it reflects and influences a child's total development. Friendships with others develop slowly; they may not be truly possible until children develop an identifiable self-concept.

By the time children enter school, they are beginning to know how to interact with others; they can identify with a peer group and slowly begin to sort out special friends within it.

The theme of friendship permeates two small books by Olivier Dunrea, *Gossie* and *Gossie and Gertie* (both N–P), perfect for preschoolers but also very readable by beginning readers. Gossie and Gertie, two engaging goslings, are brought together by their mutual love of brightly colored boots and then go on to do everything together. Other books for beginning readers, such as the **Frog and Toad** series, also focus on friendship.

School is the primary source of new friendships for most children, and there are many books set in classrooms. In Soyung Pak's *Sumi's First Day of School Ever* (N–P), illustrated by Joung Un Kim, the first-day jitters are even worse for Sumi, who also has new-language jitters—she's just learned her first English words that morning. The school is big, the classroom noisy; one of her classmates is mean, but her teacher is nice, and that, plus the opportunity to draw, helps her begin to feel at home in her strange new surroundings.

Friendship is a mixture of good and bad times; all friendships encounter some stumbling blocks. Oftentimes children experience internal and external conflicts as they try simultaneously to declare their independence as a person and to develop relationships with others. Best friends Renee and Kishi are angry at each other in *Hot Day on Abbott Avenue* (P), by Karen English, illustrated by Javaka Steptoe. Their anger is impervious to the blandishments of the neighbors, but the magic of double Dutch brings them back together, friends again. Sometime adults fight with other people just because they are different, and children do this, too. Bruce Edward Hall depicts the conflict between a group of children from Chinatown and a group from Little Italy in *Henry and the Kite Dragon* (P–I), illustrated by William Low and based on a true story of such a conflict in New York City in the 1920s. The Chinese kids don't understand why the Italian kids throw rocks at their kites, ruining them, until they come together to confront each other, only to realize that the Italian kids were worried about the kites' effect on their homing pigeons. The compromise they work out is perfect, and the model of conflict resolution is one that sparks good conversations. Other stories about children's social world appear in the Booklist at the end of the chapter.

• • THE NATURAL WORLD • •

Children learn about nature as they explore their ever-widening worlds. Firsthand experiences are primary, of course, but books can deepen and extend children's awareness of the natural world. Books can draw attention to nature in sensitive and thoughtful ways; many do not so much tell a story as establish a mood or celebrate natural beauty through both words and pictures. Many others present factual information in a beautiful, graceful manner. Books explore seasonal change, special habitats and ecosystems, natural phenomena, and animals. They offer children experiences with the natural world that they wouldn't otherwise have and confirm the knowledge of nature that they have gained from their own life experiences. D. B. Johnson praises the beauty of the natural world in *Henry Hikes to Fitchburg* (P), which is based on a passage from Thoreau's *Walden.* In the story, one friend chooses to earn money for a train ride to Fitchburg, but Henry chooses to walk the 30 miles in order to enjoy the beautiful landscape. The scenes suggest that the walker is the wiser person.

Beautiful paintings and photographs often offer children visions of natural life that they wouldn't otherwise notice, helping them understand and appreciate the complex beauty of the natural world. Many books about the natural world are discussed in Chapter 10, and others are suggested in the Booklist at the end of this chapter.

• • THE AESTHETIC WORLD • •

As children's interests broaden, the aesthetic environment—art, music, dance, and literature—can add immeasurably to their overall sense of well-being. Many children first encounter the cultural arts through books; there they can discover the aesthetic world at an early age. Early and continued exposure to the arts lays a firm foundation on which children build an ever-increasing appreciation for their aesthetic world.

Picture books about the arts may be storybooks that explore a problem or theme related to the arts, such as a child's desire to practice an art or a child's effort to become good at an art, or that relate a story in which the arts play an integral part in the main character's life. Nonfiction books about the arts often focus on explaining various aspects of a particular art form. Whether fiction or nonfiction, these picture books use both illustrations and text to create meaning. The illustrations may elaborate events and emotions, as in Emily Arnold McCully's *Mirette on the High Wire* (P–I), a story about a young girl who struggles to learn the art of tightrope walking and who seeks to restore her talented teacher's confidence in himself.

Music, of course, is an integral part of an aesthetic life. Almost from the time they hear their first lullaby, young children can hum or follow along with favorite melodies. Every culture is replete with songs of its people. Many books—whether they are single-edition picture books or part of a collection—offer lavish visual interpretations of those rhymes or songs, such as Chris Raschka's *John Coltrane's Giant Steps* (P–I), discussed in Chapter 2. Others, such as Walter Dean Myers's *Blues Journey* (I), explore a particular type of music. In this case the mood of Myers's poetic language and of the illustrations by Christopher Myers perfectly matches the mood of the blues.

Aliki's *Ah, Music* (I) is about the history of music, composers, instruments, and more. Its content is layered in an accessible style so that readers of all ages will want to refer to this book again and again for years to come. Other books about music explore musical instruments, musical groups, and musicians' lives. Alan Blackwood's book *Orchestra: An Introduction to the World of Classical Music* (I) gives a history of the orchestra. It introduces classical composers, conductors, and instruments and presents a day in the life of an orchestra.

Expressive movement is natural to children; they sway, tap their feet, and bounce, impelled by the pure joy of being and moving. Music, stories, and poems invite expressive participation on the part of children. Stories about dance and dancers often intrigue young readers. Andrea Davis Pinkney presents a dancer's life in *Alvin Ailey* (I), illustrated by Brian Pinkney.

Children are sensitive to the visual art that surrounds them; much of that art is contained in picture books. When children have the opportunity to read and savor many picture books, they begin to recognize individual artists' styles and develop a sense of taste. Books about art for children are generally either about a particular artist or about looking at selected art. Some books have readers looking at shapes or images or styles of art through the presentation of reproductions accompanied by explanatory text. Children who become interested in the lives of artists can find some fine biographies of both contemporary children's book artists and important artists of the past. James Warhola's *Uncle Andy's* (P) is such a biography. Warhola tells the story of one particular visit in 1962, right after Andy Warhol, his famous uncle, had made the transition from being an illustrator to being a "fine" artist. The pictures, fittingly, are full of details, the text is lively, and the portrait of this eccentric artist is fresh and engaging.

Anthony Browne takes his readers right into a museum, and not just any museum but the Tate gallery in London, in *The Shape Game* (P). As we visit the Tate with Browne's fictional family, we are drawn into considering in a new way the art that they see, actually connecting fine art to their (and our) real lives. Browne's surrealistic art is the key to making this book work.

· · THE IMAGINATIVE · · WORLD

Being able to visualize things and ideas that may not exist is important for higher-order thinking and reading. Imagination plays an important role throughout a child's life. Adults can sometimes catch a glimpse of that imaginative world by observing a child at play with an imaginary friend, a favorite toy that has been invested with life, or other children. During these play episodes, children create their own narratives. Parents and teachers can contribute to an environment that is conducive to children's imaginative play by discussing dreams, playing "let's pretend" games, and making up stories. They can also read imaginative stories. Peter Sis created two stories about a child with a vivid imagination. In *Madlenka* (P), a young girl discovers that she has a loose tooth and must tell all her friends. Her trip around the block is like a trip around the world as she announces her loose tooth to the French baker, the Indian news vendor, the Italian ice cream man, the German lady who sits by her window, the Latin American greengrocer, and the Asian shopkeeper. She makes the same journey in *Madlenka's Dog* (P), discussed in Chapter 2. The art in these beautiful books creates another level of imagination for readers.

Steve Johnson's almost wordless *As the City Sleeps* (P–I) presents images that, just like Van Allsburg's *The Mysteries of Harris Burdick* (I–A), are sure to provoke imaginative oral and written stories. You can pair these two with Guy Billout's *Something's Not Quite Right* (I), a collection of 29 full-page paintings, each of which contains an anomaly or an illusion and is capped by one carefully selected word that will challenge anyone's vocabulary.

Adults who fear that too much fantasy will affect a child's sense of reality need not worry; a lively imagination is a central part of the developmental process. Imaginative stories provide a source of pleasure as well as a focal point for children's developing imagination and sense of story. In fact, children who have been deprived of traditional tales and other fanciful stories will create their own (Chukovsky, 1963). Some of the most distinguished literature for children builds on the imaginative life of the central characters. In these stories stuffed animals come to life, creatures hide under beds, and imaginary friends are real. Books that explore imaginative worlds appear in the Booklist at the end of the chapter.

✳ ✳ ✳

A CLOSE LOOK AT
The Tale of Peter Rabbit

We are fortunate that Beatrix Potter let her imagination run wild, for that resulted in a series of wonderful picture books imagining a number of small animals in various situations. Some of her stories are among the most beloved by children today, such as *The Tale of Peter Rabbit* (N–P), originally published in 1902.

Synopsis

Peter is a young rabbit who lives with his mother and three sisters near Mr. McGregor's vegetable garden, a tempting

*Peter turns his back to his family and faces the viewer, suggesting that he may not be listening to his mother's instructions. (**The Tale of Peter Rabbit,** by Beatrix Potter)*

but dangerous place where Peter's father met an untimely death. When Mrs. Rabbit goes to the baker's, disobedient Peter immediately squeezes under the garden gate and gorges himself on the treasures in Mr. McGregor's garden. Mr. McGregor spots him and chases Peter through the garden and into a shed, where Peter eludes him. Peter finally finds his way out of the garden and back home, where he is put to bed to recuperate from his excesses.

Setting

As in many fantasy narratives for young children, the setting in **The Tale of Peter Rabbit** is briefly presented with words and is detailed in the illustrations. Potter introduces the story as follows:

> Once upon a time there were four little rabbits, and their names were—Flopsy, Mopsy, Cotton-tail, and Peter. They lived with their Mother in a sand-bank, underneath the root of a very big fir-tree. (p. 9)

This description is accompanied by a delicate, realistic watercolor illustration of the four rabbits and their mother

peering at the reader from their fir tree home. Ears and tree trunk stand straight up, pulling the viewer's eye upward; the colors are muted browns and greens. Mother rabbit is in the foreground, with her back to the viewer; her head is turned to look much as a real rabbit looks when startled by a person. Three small faces appear around the roots of the tree. One set of hind legs and a tail are visible under the left-hand root; we infer later that this is Peter.

Characters

The first three pages also establish the characters. Once readers get to know Peter, they guess that the tail in the first illustration must belong to him, as Peter is the naughty one. In this picture the rabbits appear to be realistic—that is, they look like wild rabbits. The very next illustration, however, shows the rabbits dressed in pink and blue human clothes, against a white background. The three girls are clustered around their mother, and Peter has his back to his family and is facing the viewer. His little blue jacket hides his front paws. Thus, by the second page of the book, the reader understands that this is a fantasy. Potter's fantasy, however, is special. Her animal characters may dress in human clothes and use language, but they act like animals. Everything Peter does is possible for a rabbit to do, but his personality is that of an irrepressible child.

In the second illustration Peter is obviously not listening to his mother's injunction to stay away from Mr. McGregor's garden, and in the third, Mrs. Rabbit is leaning down toward Peter, buttoning the top button of his jacket while Flopsy, Mopsy, and Cotton-tail are already going down the path. The text, "Now run along, and don't get into mischief" (p. 13) is obviously directed toward Peter, the only one close enough to Mrs. Rabbit to hear her. It is only by seeing the illustration and reading the text that the full implications of this double page can be understood.

Later in the book we see Peter, ears upright, squeezing under a gate, with the accompanying text telling us, "But Peter, who was very naughty, ran straight away to Mr. McGregor's garden and squeezed under the gate!" (p. 18). Thus a combination of text and art presents Peter as a naughty but endearing young rabbit who is recognizable as a human child—curious and apt to ignore a mother's restrictions in order to find out about the world. He not only goes into the garden but loses his clothes!

Plot

The sequence of action in **The Tale of Peter Rabbit** is straightforward, clear, and logical. Readers view the action as they read it, seeing Peter eating carrots, coming face-to-face with

*We are aware of Peter Rabbit's small size and vulnerability as we see him knocking over flowerpots when he tries to escape from Mr. McGregor's big foot. (**The Tale of Peter Rabbit**, by Beatrix Potter)*

Mr. McGregor, getting caught in the net, diving into the watering can, leaping out the window, and collapsing on the floor of the rabbit hole. After he has lost his jacket, he again looks like the wild rabbit he is. The excitement builds twice: once when he is chased by McGregor, and again as he finds his way out of the garden. The resolution is clear: he is home, he is safe, and he is exhausted.

As the adventure takes place, the illustrations heighten the sense of panic. Potter uses perspective to indicate how small Peter really is. When he is in the garden she is careful to place him with objects that make his small size apparent; we see him among plants and flowerpots, by a watering can, and near Mr. McGregor himself. Perhaps the most vivid image of his vulnerability is when he flees out a window, knocking over pots of geraniums, pursued by Mr. McGregor's hobnailed boot.

Theme

The theme, which is easily identified and understood by young readers, is established by the text and extended by the illustrations. The temptation to mischief, something that is very real to children, is exciting precisely because it is dangerous. Returning home to mother is reassuring. Both emotions are familiar ones to young readers, and these readers can see the excitement and the relief in the illustrations.

*Mother Rabbit makes sure that Peter hears her admonitions as she buttons the top button of his jacket: "Run along and don't get into mischief." (**The Tale of Peter Rabbit**, by Beatrix Potter)*

Illustrations

The illustrations are delicate, carefully wrought watercolors that, as we have seen, work in conjunction with the words to express the action, characterization, and theme. Potter was a keen observer of nature, and that is apparent in the detail that graces her illustrations. Peter consistently looks like a real rabbit, even when he is dressed in human clothes. The position of his ears, for example, is both realistic and indicative of his emotions. When Peter cries beside the locked door, he is standing like a sad child, one foot on top of the other, with a paw in his mouth; his ears, like those of a tired and scared rabbit, are back rather than straight up (as they are throughout most of the story).

Potter's accurately detailed, realistic style, her delicate lines, and her glowing watercolors are unsurpassed. Other illustrators have tried to illustrate Potter's story, but none can compare with the original. Those who hear the story without seeing Potter's pictures do not experience the full meaning of *The Tale of Peter Rabbit.*

*A tear leaks out of a remorseful Peter's eye. His ears droop; he puts one foot on top of another. He could easily be chewing on his paw while he reflects upon his misbehavior and adventure. (**The Tale of Peter Rabbit**, by Beatrix Potter)*

Language

Potter uses interesting words in imaginative ways and makes her story a delight to read aloud. *Mischief, naughty, dreadfully frightened,* and *exert* are but some of the interesting words and phrases Potter provides for her audience. The onomatopoetic words she uses—*kertyschoo* for a sneeze, *lippity* for a slow hop, *scr-r-ritch* for the sound of a hoe—all increase the vivid quality of the story. One sentence from the middle of the story, when Peter is caught in the gooseberry net, illustrates the complex and interesting quality of the language of this story: "Peter gave himself up for lost, and shed big tears; but his sobs were overheard by some friendly sparrows, who flew to him in great excitement, and implored him to exert himself" (p. 33). Children, delighting in these interesting words, will walk around chanting, "I implore you to exert yourself" after hearing the story.

Beatrix Potter's *The Tale of Peter Rabbit* exemplifies the criteria for excellent picture storybooks. Created through pictures and words, the story is captivating and understandable. The characters, seen through Potter's keen artistic eye, are vivid and engaging, and the theme is identifiable and memorable. The pictures and the words are strong and elegant and serve to unify story, characters, and theme. Books like this offer children wonderful experiences with literature.

✷　✷　✷

Using Picture Books in the Classroom

Picture books of all kinds are staples in primary-, intermediate-, and advanced-grade classrooms. Teachers and librarians have discovered that picture books have an important place on classroom and library shelves. Picture books offer a unique opportunity for children to experience outstanding visual art, well-crafted language, and intriguing content. They can support every area of the curriculum.

Excellent fiction, nonfiction, and poetry in picture-book format are essential to any reading-writing program. Students naturally use the books they read as models for their own thinking and writing; picture books are resources for students' language production. They serve as fine examples of the author's craft. Excellent nonfiction gives children models for their own expository writing just as excellent stories and poems provide models for other modes. Literary devices such as imagery, foreshadowing, parody, metaphor, simile, and analogy are all found in picture storybooks and poetry. Talking about these devices can become a natural part of discussing favorite books when children are writers as well as readers; they constantly notice the choices that authors and illustrators make. Hall (2001) provides a source list of picture-book titles that are good examples of a number of literary devices.

Picture books that support learning in social studies, science, art, music, and mathematics abound; many are discussed in Chapter 10. These books not only serve as fine models of writing in the various fields but also explain concepts more clearly than traditional textbooks and encyclopedias. They provide numerous pictures, make comparisons easily available, and encourage critical thinking.

Children respond enthusiastically in classrooms that are rich with books and that offer the opportunity to read and respond to the books. In a yearlong study of elementary schoolchildren responding to picture books in literature-rich classrooms, Kiefer (1986) discovered that a supportive, enriched classroom environment was an important factor in children's responses. Teachers can create lively classrooms of book-loving children almost anywhere, but it takes planning and work. Teachers create readers when they read aloud often, talk with children about books, and make frequent connections between books and to their own lives. Effective teachers discuss all aspects of books—dedication page, copyright page, title page—and use appropriate terminology to discuss the language and visual art.

Good teachers provide the time and the opportunity for children to explore their own responses to the books they read—how they feel, what they are thinking about. After teachers encourage children to clarify their understandings, reflect on what they like and dislike, and talk about feelings and personal connections, children are ready to "go back to the book" to discover artistry in the language and the illustrations. We discuss these ideas more in Chapters 12 and 13.

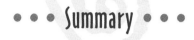

• • • Summary • • •

Picture books are artful books that hold a special place in the lives of the children who read them. They are often children's first experience with fine art. They can enrich and extend children's worlds and provide experiences (through picture and print) that allow children to confirm their own worth, learn about others, and learn about the world. They provide stunning examples of art and language, and they become resources from which children draw as they develop their own abilities to shape and reshape their world.

In the November/December 2004 issue of *The Horn Book Magazine,* Barbara Bader discusses the special relationship between words and art found only in picture books, and raises some interesting questions about the history and future of picture books. Read her article and, using the picture books that you have discovered, discuss the relationship between pictures and words, much as we have done in the close look at *The Tale of Peter Rabbit.*

For Very Young Children

PARTICIPATION BOOKS

Ahlberg, Allan, *The Bravest Ever Bear,* illustrated by Paul Howard

Ahlberg, Janet, and Allan Ahlberg, *Each Peach Pear Plum*

Carle, Eric, *The Very Busy Spider*

Cousins, Lucy, *Katy Cat and Beaky Boo*

Hill, Eric, *Spot Goes Splash!*

_____, *Where's Spot?*

Isadora, Rachel, *Babies*

Kunhardt, Dorothy, *Pat the Bunny*

Miller, Margaret, *Whose Hat?*

Pomerantz, Charlotte, *Flap Your Wings and Try,* illustrated by Nancy Tafuri

BOARD BOOKS

Alexander, Martha, *Willy's Boot*

Cousins, Lucy, *Farm Animals*

Greenaway, Elizabeth, *Cat Nap*

Hawkins, Colin, and Jacqui Hawkins, *Hey Diddle Diddle*

Hoban, Tana, *What Is It?*

Hudson, Cheryl Willis, *Good Night Baby,* illustrated by George Ford

Leslie, Amanda, *Play Kitten Play: Ten Animal Fingerwiggles*

MacDonald, Amy, *Let's Pretend*

Maris, Ron, *Ducks Quack*

Oxenbury, Helen, *I Hear*

_____, *I See*

_____, *I Touch*

Slier, Deborah, *Baby's Places*

Waddell, Martin, *Owl Babies,* illustrated by Patrick Benson

Wells, Rosemary, *Max's Bath*

_____, *Max's Birthday*

_____, *Max's Breakfast*

_____, *Max's First Word*

_____, *Max's New Suit*

_____, *Max's Ride*

SIMPLE STORYBOOKS AND CONCEPT BOOKS

Baer, Gene, *Thump, Thump, Rat-a-Tat-Tat,* illustrated by Lois Ehlert

Barton, Byron, *Bones, Bones, Dinosaur Bones*

_____, *I Want to Be an Astronaut*

Brown, Margaret Wise, *Goodnight Moon,* illustrated by Clement Hurd

_____, *Red Light, Green Light,* illustrated by Leonard Weisgard

Bynum, Janie, *Otis*

Crews, Donald, *School Bus*

_____, *Truck*

Ehlert, Lois, *Color Farm*

_____, *Color Zoo*

_____, *Red Leaf, Yellow Leaf*

Gibbons, Gail, *Trucks*

Godwin, Laura, *Central Park Serenade,* illustrated by Barry Root

Hest, Amy, *In the Rain with Baby Duck,* illustrated by Jill Barton

Hoban, Tana, *Exactly the Opposite*

_____, *Of Colors and Things*

Jonas, Ann, *Color Dance*

Keller, Holly, *That's Mine, Horace*

McMillan, Bruce, *Super Super Superwords*

Meddaugh, Susan, *Hog-Eye*

Noll, Sally, *Watch Where You Go*

Oxenbury, Helen, *Good Night, Good Morning*

_____, *The Important Visitor*

_____, *Mother's Helper*

Rathmann, Peggy, *Goodnight, Gorilla*

Rockwell, Harlow, *My Nursery School*

Serfozo, Mary, *Who Said Red?* illustrated by Keiko Narahashi

Tafuri, Nancy, *Spots, Feathers, and Curly Tails*

Uff, Caroline, *Lulu's Busy Day*

Wells, Rosemary, *Edward in Deep Water*

_____, *Edward's Overwhelming Overnight*

_____, *Edward Unready for School*

For Young Children

Selections in this section are appropriate for nursery–primary children unless otherwise noted.

ALPHABET, COUNTING, AND CONCEPT BOOKS

Agee, Jon, *Z Goes Home*

Aylesworth, Jim, *Old Black Fly,* illustrated by Stephen Gammell

Bowen, Betsy, *Antler, Bear, Canoe: A Northwoods Alphabet Year*

Ehlert, Lois, *Eating the Alphabet*

Fisher, Leonard Everett, *The ABC Exhibit*

Fleming, Denise, *Alphabet under Construction*

Floca, Brian, *The Racecar Alphabet*

Giganti, Paul, Jr., *How Many Snails? A Counting Book,* illustrated by Donald Crews

Girnis, Meg, *ABC for You and Me,* photos by Shirley Leamon Green

Grossman, Virginia, *Ten Little Rabbits,* illustrated by Sylvia Long

Hayes, Sarah, *Nine Ducks Nine*

Hughes, Shirley, *Lucy and Tom's 1 2 3*

Isadora, Rachel, *Listen to the City*

_____, *1 2 3 Pop!*

Johnson, Steve, *Alphabet City*

_____, *City by Numbers*

Katz, Michael Jay, *Ten Potatoes in a Pot and Other Counting Rhymes,* illustrated by June Otani

Kellogg, Steven, *Aster Aardvark's Alphabet Adventures*

Kitamura, Satoshi, *From Acorn to Zoo: And Everything in between in Alphabetical Order*

Lester, Mike, *A Is for Salad*

Lobel, Anita, *Alison's Zinnia*

_____, *One Lighthouse, One Moon*

Lobel, Arnold, *On Market Street*

MacCarthy, Patricia, *Ocean Parade: A Counting Book*

MacDonald, Ross, *Achoo! Bang! Crash! The Noisy Alphabet*

MacDonald, Suse, *Alphabatics*

_____, *Puzzlers,* illustrated by Bill Oakes

Martin, Bill, Jr., and John Archambault, *Chicka Chicka Boom Boom,* illustrated by Lois Ehlert

Martin, Bill, Jr., and Michael Sampson, *Chicka Chicka 1, 2, 3,* illustrated by Lois Ehlert

McKenzie, Ellen Kindt, *The Perfectly Orderly House,* illustrated by Megan Lloyd

Merriam, Eve, *Halloween ABC,* illustrated by Lane Smith

Owens, Mary Beth, *A Caribou Alphabet*

Paul, Ann Whitford, *Eight Hands Round: A Patchwork Alphabet,* illustrated by Jeannette Winter

Rankin, Laura, *The Handmade Alphabet*

Rash, Andy, *Agent A to Agent Z*

Rockwell, Anne, *Bear Child's Book of Hours*

Ryden, Hope, *Wild Animals of Africa ABC*

Scott, Ann Herbert, *One Good Horse: A Cowpuncher's Counting Book,* illustrated by Lynn Sweat

Seeger, Laura Vaccaro, *The Hidden Alphabet*

Shannon, George, *Tomorrow's Alphabet,* illustrated by Donald Crews

Sis, Peter, *Madlenka and Time*

_____, *Trucks, Trucks, Trucks*

Walsh, Ellen Stoll, *Mouse Count*

Wormell, Christopher, *An Alphabet of Animals*

Ziefert, Harriet, *Empty to Full, Full to Empty,* illustrated by Susan Baum

_____, *Mommies Are for Counting Stars,* illustrated by Susan Baum

_____, *Night Knight,* illustrated by Susan Baum

_____, *Toes Have Wiggles, Kids Have Giggles,* illustrated by Susan Baum

WORDLESS BOOKS

Baker, Jeannie, *Home* (P–I–A)

_____, *Window* (P–I–A)

Banyai, Istvan, *Zoom* (P–I–A)

_____, *Re-Zoom* (P–I–A)

dePaola, Tomie, *Pancakes for Breakfast*

Goodall, John, *Little Red Riding Hood*

Hoban, Tana, *Colors Everywhere*

Hutchins, Pat, *Changes, Changes*

Keats, Ezra Jack, *Pssst! Doggie*

Koren, Edward, *Behind the Wheel*

Jenkins, Steven, *Looking Down*

Lehman, Barbara, *The Red Book* (P–I)

Mayer, Mercer, *Frog Goes to Dinner*

McCully, Emily Arnold, *Picnic*

Ormerod, Jan, *Moonlight*

_____, *Sunshine*

Sis, Peter, *Dinosaur!*

Wiesner, David, *Free Fall* (P–I)

_____, *Sector 7* (P–I)

_____, *Tuesday* (P–I)

PATTERNED BOOKS

Cummings, Pat, *Angel Baby*

Ehlert, Lois, *Feathers for Lunch*

Fleming, Denise, *In the Tall, Tall Grass*

Fox, Mem, *Hattie and the Fox,* illustrated by Patricia Mullins

Gammell, Stephen, *Once upon MacDonald's Farm*

Guarino, Deborah, *Is Your Mama a Llama?* illustrated by Steven Kellogg

Hennessy, B. G., *Jake Baked the Cake,* illustrated by Mary Morgan

Hort, Lenny, *The Seals on the Bus,* illustrated by G. Brian Karas

Hutchins, Pat, *What Game Shall We Play?*

Katz, Michael Jay, *Ten Potatoes in a Pot and Other Counting Rhymes,* illustrated by June Otani

Kovalski, Maryann, *The Wheels on the Bus*

MacDonald, Amy, *Rachel Fister's Blister,* illustrated by Marjorie Priceman

Martin, Bill, Jr., *Brown Bear, Brown Bear, What Do You See?* illustrated by Eric Carle

_____, *Polar Bear, Polar Bear, What Do You Hear?* illustrated by Eric Carle

Martin, Bill, Jr., and John Archambault, *Chicka Chicka Boom Boom,* illustrated by Lois Ehlert

Marzollo, Jean, *Pretend You're a Cat,* illustrated by Jerry Pinkney

Neitzel, Shirley, *The Bag I'm Taking to Grandma's,* illustrated by Nancy Winslow Parker

_____, *The Jacket I Wear in the Snow,* illustrated by Nancy Winslow Parker

Peters, Lisa Westberg, *Cold Little Duck, Duck, Duck,* illustrated by Sam Williams

Robart, Rose, *The Cake That Mack Ate,* illustrated by Maryann Kovalski

Rosen, Michael, *We're Going on a Bear Hunt*

Schaefer, Lola M., *This Is the Sunflower*

Shaw, Nancy, *Sheep in a Shop,* illustrated by Margot Apple

Stojic, Manya, *Rain*

Stow, Jenny, *The House That Jack Built*

Suteyev, Vladimir, *Chick and the Duckling,* translated by Mirra Ginsburg, illustrated by Jose Aruego and Ariane Dewey

Swope, Sam, *Gotta Go! Gotta Go!* illustrated by Sue Riddle

Waber, Bernard, *Do You See a Mouse?*

Walsh, Ellen Stoll, *Mouse Paint*

Walsh, Melanie, *Do Donkeys Dance?*

_____, *Do Monkeys Tweet?*

_____, *Do Pigs Have Stripes?*

Zelinsky, Paul, *The Wheels on the Bus*

BEGINNING-TO-READ BOOKS

Ahlberg, Allan, *A Bit More Bert,* illustrated by Raymond Briggs

Baer, Gene, *Thump, Thump, Rat-a-Tat-Tat,* illustrated by Lois Ehlert

Brown, Marc, *Play Rhymes*

Browne, Anthony, *I Like Books*

_____, *Things I Like*

Byars, Betsy, *The Golly Sisters Go West*

Caple, Kathy, *The Friendship Tree*

Cushman, Doug, *Inspector Hopper*

Dodds, Dayle Ann, *Where's Pup?* illustrated by Pierre Pratt

Edwards, Pamela Duncan, *Boston Tea Party,* illustrated by Henry Cole (I)

_____, *The Wright Brothers,* illustrated by Henry Cole (I)

Fleming, Denise, *In the Tall, Tall Grass*

Fox, Mem, *Where Is the Green Sheep?* illustrated by Judy Horacek

Goennel, Heidi, *My Dog*

Hoberman, Mary Ann, *You Read to Me, I'll Read to You: Very Short Fairy Tales to Read Together,* illustrated by Michael Emberley

Lobel, Arnold, *Days with Frog and Toad*

_____, *Frog and Toad All Year*

_____, *Frog and Toad Are Friends*

_____, *Frog and Toad Together*

Mahy, Margaret, *The Horrendous Hullabaloo,* illustrated by Patricia MacCarthy

Marshall, James, *The Cut-Ups Crack Up*

Martin, Bill, Jr., and John Archambault, *Here Are My Hands,* illustrated by Ted Rand

Marzollo, Jean, *Pretend You're a Cat,* illustrated by Jerry Pinkney

Minarik, Else, *Father Bear Comes Home,* illustrated by Maurice Sendak

_____, *A Kiss for Little Bear,* illustrated by Maurice Sendak

Noll, Sally, *Watch Where You Go*

Parish, Peggy, *Scruffy,* illustrated by Kelly Oechsli

_____, *Teach Us, Amelia Bedelia,* illustrated by Lynn Sweat

Porte, Barbara Ann, *Harry in Trouble,* illustrated by Yossi Abolafia

Ransom, Candace F., *Danger at Sand Cave,* illustrated by Den Schofield

Rosen, Michael, *We're Going on a Bear Hunt,* illustrated by Helen Oxenbury

Rylant, Cynthia, *Henry and Mudge and Annie's Perfect Pet,* illustrated by Suçie Stevenson (P)

_____, *Henry and Mudge and the Bedtime Thumps,* illustrated by Suçie Stevenson (P)

_____, *Henry and Mudge: The First Book,* illustrated by Suçie Stevenson (P)

_____, *Henry and Mudge in Puddle Trouble,* illustrated by Suçie Stevenson (P)

_____, *Henry and Mudge in the Sparkle Days,* illustrated by Suçie Stevenson (P)

_____, *Henry and Mudge Take the Big Test,* illustrated by Suçie Stevenson (P)

Shaw, Nancy, *Sheep in a Shop,* illustrated by Margot Apple

Thomas, Shelley Moore, *Good Night, Good Knight,* illustrated by Jennifer Plecas

Van Leeuwen, Jean, *Oliver, Amanda, and Grandmother Pig,* illustrated by Ann Schweninger

_____, *Oliver Pig at School,* illustrated by Ann Schweninger

Ziefert, Harriet, *The Gingerbread Boy,* illustrated by Emily Bolam

For Older Children and Adolescents

Adler, David, *A Picture Book of Sojourner Truth*

_____, *Martin Luther King, Jr.: Free at Last*

Agee, Jon, *The Incredible Painting of Felix Clousseau*

Alexander, Sue, *Nadia the Willful,* illustrated by Lloyd Bloom

Aliki, *Ah, Music*

Anno, Mitsumasa, *Anno's Journey*

Base, Graeme, *Animalia*

Baylor, Byrd, *I'm in Charge of Celebrations,* illustrated by Peter Parnall

Bjork, Christina, *Linnea in Monet's Garden*

Browne, Anthony, *Piggybook*

_____, *The Tunnel*

Bruchac, Joseph, *Crazy Horse's Vision,* illustrated by S. D. Nelson

Bunting, Eve, *Fly Away Home,* illustrated by Ronald Himler

_____, *Smoky Night,* illustrated by David Diaz

_____, *The Wall,* illustrated by Ronald Himler

Chorao, Kay, *Pig and Crow*

Crew, Gary, and Steven Woolman, *Watertower*

dePaola, Tomie, *Bonjour, Mr. Satie*

Dragonwagon, Crescent, *Home Place,* illustrated by Jerry Pinkney

Feelings, Tom, *The Middle Passage*

_____, *Soul Looks Back in Wonder*

Foreman, Michael, *War Games*

Garland, Michael, *Dinner at Magritte's*

Goble, Paul, *The Death of the Iron Horse*

Goffstein, M. B., *A Writer*

Hendershot, Judith, *Up the Tracks to Grandma's,* illustrated by Thomas B. Allen

Hooks, William, *The Ballad of Belle Dorcas,* illustrated by Brian Pinkney

_____, *Freedom's Fruit,* illustrated by James Ransome

Hopkinson, Deborah, *Sweet Clara and the Freedom Quilt,* illustrated by James Ransome

Hunt, Jonathan, *Illuminations*

Innocenti, Robert, *Rose Blanche*

Lawrence, Jacob, *The Great Migration: An American Story*

Locker, Thomas, *The Boy Who Held Back the Sea*

_____, *Snow toward Evening*

_____, *Where the River Begins*

Macaulay, David, *Black and White*

Maruki, Toshi, *Hiroshima No Pika*

Medearis, Angela Shelf, *The Freedom Riddle,* illustrated by John Ward

Morimoto, Junko, *My Hiroshima*

Polacco, Patricia, *Pink and Say*

Say, Allen, *Grandfather's Journey*

Scieszka, Jon, *Math Curse,* illustrated by Lane Smith

_____, *Science Verse,* illustrated by Lane Smith

_____, *The Stinky Cheese Man,* illustrated by Lane Smith

Sendak, Maurice, *Outside over There*

Steig, William, *Caleb and Kate*

Van Allsburg, Chris, *Bad Day at River Bend*

_____, *The Wretched Stone*

Willard, Nancy, *The Voyage of the Ludgate Hill: Travels with Robert Louis Stevenson,* illustrated by Alice and Martin Provensen

Yolen, Jane, *All Those Secrets of the World,* illustrated by Leslie Baker

_____, *Encounter,* illustrated by David Shannon

Zee, Vander Ruth, and Roberto Innocenti, *Erika's Story*

The Inner World

Selections in this section are appropriate for nursery–primary–intermediate readers.

RESOURCEFULNESS

Battle-Lavert, Gwendolyn, *The Shaking Bag,* illustrated by Aminah Brenda Lynn Robinson

Falconer, Ian, *Olivia . . . and the Missing Toy*

Henkes, Kevin, *Chrysanthemum*

Holabird, Katharine, *Angelina and Alice,* illustrated by Helen Craig

Hooks, Bell, *Skin Again,* illustrated by Chris Raschka

Inns, Christopher, *Help!*

James, Simon, *Baby Brains*

Keiko, Kasza, *My Lucky Day*

Mathers, Petra, *A Cake for Herbie*

McCully, Emily Arnold, *Monk Camps Out*

McKissack, Patricia, *Flossie and the Fox,* illustrated by Rachel Isadora

McPhail, David, *Emma's Pet*

_____, *Emma's Vacation*

_____, *Fix-it*

_____, *Pig Pig Gets a Job*

Nimmo, Jenny, *Esmeralda and the Children Next Door,* illustrated by Paul Howard

Schwartz, Amy, *Annabelle Swift, Kindergartner*

Shannon, David, *David Gets in Trouble*

Steig, William, *Brave Irene*

FEARS

Bottner, Barbara, *The Scaredy Cats,* illustrated by Victoria Chess

Bunting, Eve, *Ghost's Hour, Spook's Hour,* illustrated by Donald Carrick

Carrick, Carol, *Left Behind,* illustrated by Donald Carrick

Grifalconi, Ann, *Darkness and the Butterfly*

Henkes, Kevin, *Sheila Rae, the Brave*

McPhail, David, *Lost!*

Spinelli, Eileen, *Wanda's Monster,* illustrated by Nancy Hayashi

Stolz, Mary Slattery, *Storm in the Night,* illustrated by Pat Cummings

HUMOR

Cronin, Doreen, *Click, Clack, Moo: Cows That Type,* illustrated by Betsy Lewin

Dumbleton, Mike, *Dial-a-Croc,* illustrated by Ann James

Fearnley, Jan, *Mr. Wolf's Pancakes*

Hale, Lucretia, *The Lady Who Put Salt in Her Coffee,* adapted and illustrated by Amy Schwartz

Kellogg, Steven, *Prehistoric Pinkerton*

Khalsa, Dayal Kaur, *How Pizza Came to Queens*

Kitamura, Satoshi, *Me and My Cat*

Macaulay, David, *Why the Chicken Crossed the Road*

Mahy, Margaret, *The Great White Man-Eating Shark: A Cautionary Tale,* illustrated by Jonathan Allen

Meddaugh, Susan, *Hog-Eye*

Noble, Trinka Hakes, *The Day Jimmy's Boa Ate the Wash,* illustrated by Steven Kellogg

Stevenson, James, *No Laughing, No Smiling, No Giggling*

The Family World

GRANDPARENTS

Selections in this section are appropriate for primary readers.

Ackerman, Karen, *Song and Dance Man,* illustrated by Stephen Gammell

Dorros, Arthur, *Abuela,* illustrated by Elisa Kleven

_____, *Isla,* illustrated by Eliza Kleven

Farber, Norma, *How Does It Feel to Be Old?* illustrated by Trina Schart Hyman

Flournoy, Valerie, *Patchwork Quilt,* illustrated by Jerry Pinkney

_____, *Tanya's Reunion,* illustrated by Jerry Pinkney

Fox, Mem, *Wilfrid Gordon McDonald Partridge,* illustrated by Julie Vivas

Griffith, Helen V., *Grandaddy's Place,* illustrated by James Stevenson

Howard, Elizabeth Fitzgerald, *Papa Tells Chita a Story,* illustrated by Floyd Cooper

Johnson, Angela, *When I Am Old with You,* illustrated by David Soman

Lyon, George Ella, *One Lucky Girl,* illustrated by Irene Trivas

McMullan, Kate, *Papa's Song,* illustrated by Jim McMullan

Skolsky, Mindy Warshaw, *Hannah and the Whistling Teakettle,* illustrated by Diane Palmisciano

Stevenson, James, *We Hate Rain!*

Williams, Barbara, *Kevin's Grandma,* illustrated by Kay Chorao

Woodson, Jacqueline, *Visiting Day,* illustrated by James E. Ransome

INTERGENERATIONAL BONDS

Selections in this section are appropriate for primary and/or intermediate readers.

Cooney, Barbara, *Hattie and the Wild Waves*

_____, *Island Boy*

_____, *Miss Rumphius*

Johnston, Tony, *Yonder,* illustrated by Lloyd Bloom

Houston, Gloria, *The Year of the Perfect Christmas Tree,* illustrated by Barbara Cooney

Martin, Jacqueline Briggs, *The Water Gift and the Pig of the Pig,* illustrated by Linda S. Wingerter

Polacco, Patricia, *The Keeping Quilt*

Pomerantz, Charlotte, *The Chalk Doll,* illustrated by Frané Lessac

Say, Allen, *Tree of Cranes*

SIBLINGS

Selections in this section are appropriate for primary readers.

Browne, Anthony, *The Tunnel*

Graham, Bob, *Has Anyone Here Seen William?*

Henkes, Kevin, *Julius, the Baby of the World*

Hutchins, Pat, *Very Worst Monster*

_____, *Where's the Baby?*

Polacco, Patricia, *My Rotten Redheaded Older Brother*

Williams, Vera B., *"More More More," Said the Baby*

_____, *Stringbean's Trip to the Shining Sea,* illustrated by Vera B. Williams and Jennifer Williams

PARENTS AND FAMILY AS A UNIT

Selections in this section are appropriate for primary readers.

Banks, Kate, *Mama's Coming Home,* illustrated by Tomek Bogacki

Fox, Mem, *Harriet, You'll Drive Me Wild!* illustrated by Marla Frazee

Gleeson, Libby, *Cuddle Time,* illustrated by Julie Vivas

Harel, Nira, *The Key to My Heart,* illustrated by Yossi Abulafia

Keller, Holly, *Horace*

Loh, Morag, *Tucking Mommy In,* illustrated by Donna Rawlins

McBratney, Sam, *You're All My Favorites,* illustrated by Anita Jeram

McPhail, David, *Emma's Vacation*

Montanari, Eva, *Tiff, Taff, and Lulu*

Steig, William, *Spinky Sulks*

Stuve-Bodeen, Stephanie, *Mama Elizabeti,* illustrated by Christy Hale

Weiss, Nicki, *On a Hot, Hot Day*

Willems, Mo, *Knuffle Bunny: A Cautionary Tale*

Woodson, Jacqueline, *Coming on Home Soon,* illustrated by E. B. Lewis

Yang, Belle, *Hannah Is My Name*

The Social World

Selections in this section are appropriate for primary and/or intermediate readers.

Belpre, Pura, *Santiago,* illustrated by Symeon Shimin

Cohen, Miriam, *Second Grade Friends,* illustrated by Lillian Hoban

_____, *Will I Have a Friend?* illustrated by Lillian Hoban

DeGroat, Diane, *Liar, Liar, Pants on Fire*

Fleischman, Sid, *Scarebird,* illustrated by Peter Sis

Frasier, Debra, *Miss Alaineus: A Vocabulary Disaster*

Fraustino, Lisa Rowe, *The Hickory Chair*

Howard, Elizabeth Fitzgerald, *Virgie Goes to School with Us Boys,* illustrated by E. B. Lewis

Keller, Holly, *What a Hat!*

Kellogg, Steven, *Best Friends*

Lacome, Julie, *Ruthie's Big Old Coat*

Mathers, Petra, *Sophie and Lou*

Tsutsui, Yoriko, *Anna's Secret Friend,* illustrated by Akiko Hayashi

Waber, Bernard, *Evie and Margie*

Wells, Rosemary, *Emily's First 100 Days of School*

The Natural World

Selections in this section are appropriate for primary, intermediate, and/or advanced readers.

Baker, Jeannie, *The Hidden Forest*

_____, *Window*

Baylor, Byrd, *The Desert Is Theirs,* illustrated by Peter Parnall

Bishop, Nic, *Digging for Bird-Dinosaurs: An Expedition to Madagascar*

Budiansky, Stephen, *The World according to Horses: How They Run, See, and Think*

Florian, Douglas, *Mammalabilia*

Ford, Miela, *Sunflower*

French, Vivian, *Growing Frogs,* illustrated by Alison Bartlett

George, Jean Craighead, *How to Talk to Your Cat,* illustrated by Paul Meisel

_____, *How to Talk to Your Dog,* illustrated by Sue Treasdell

Gibbons, Gail, *Farming*

Hadithi, Mwenye, *Crafty Chameleon,* illustrated by Adrienne Kennaway

Johnson, D. B., *Henry Hikes to Fitchburg*

Kurtz, Jane, *River Friendly, River Wild,* illustrated by Neil Brennan

Lewison, Wendy Cheyette, *Going to Sleep on the Farm,* illustrated by Juan Wijngaard

Lyon, George Ella, *Come a Tide,* illustrated by Stephen Gammell

McPhail, David, *Farm Boy's Year*

Perkins, Lynne Rae, *Snow Music*

Rumford, James, *Calabash Cat and His Amazing Journey*

Vestergaard, Hope, *Hello, Snow!* illustrated by Nadine Bernard Westcott

Wong, Herbert Yee, *Tracks in the Snow*

Yolen, Jane, *Owl Moon,* illustrated by John Schoenherr

The Aesthetic World

Selections in this section are appropriate for intermediate and/or advanced readers.

Agee, Jon, *The Incredible Painting of Felix Clousseau*

Blizzard, Gladys S., *Come Look with Me: Exploring Landscape Art with Children*

Briggs, Raymond, *Ug: Boy Genius of the Stone Age and His Search for Soft Trousers*

dePaola, Tomie, *The Art Lesson*

Dunrea, Olivier, *The Painter Who Loved Chickens*

Micklethwait, Lucy, *A Child's Book of Art*

Pinkney, Andrea Davis, *Alvin Ailey,* illustrated by Brian Pinkney

Raschka, Chris, *John Coltrane's Giant Steps*

Roaf, Peggy, *Looking at Paintings: Dancers*

The Imaginative World

Selections in this section are appropriate for primary and/or intermediate readers unless otherwise noted.

Cronin, Doreen, *Diary of a Worm,* illustrated by Harry Bliss

Dorros, Arthur, *Abuela,* illustrated by Elisa Kleven

Fox, Mem, *Possum Magic,* illustrated by Julie Vivas

Gauch, Patricia Lee, *Tanya and Emily in a Dance for Two,* illustrated by Satomi Ichikawa

Gordon, Gaelyn, *Duckat,* illustrated by Chris Gaskin

Hines, Anna Grossnickle, *It's Just Me, Emily*

Hoffman, Mary, *Amazing Grace,* illustrated by Caroline Binch

Johnson, Crockett, *The Carrot Seed* (N–P)

_____, *Harold and the Purple Crayon* (N–P)

Joyce, William, *Bently and Egg*

_____, *Dinosaur Bob and His Adventures with the Family Lazardo*

_____, *George Shrinks*

Kellogg, Steven, *Jack and the Beanstalk*

Martin, Rafe, *Will's Mammoth,* illustrated by Stephen Gammell

Pearce, Philippa, *Emily's Own Elephant,* illustrated by John Lawrence

Ringgold, Faith, *Tar Beach*

Root, Phyllis, *Big Momma Makes the World,* illustrated by Helen Oxenbury

Speed, Toby, *Brave Potatoes,* illustrated by Barry Root

Stanley, Diane, *Goldie and the Three Bears*

Van Allsburg, Chris, *Bad Day at Riverbend* (I–A)

_____, *The Garden of Abdul Gasazi* (I–A)

_____, *Jumanji* (I)

_____, *The Mysteries of Harris Burdick* (I–A)

Willems, Mo, *Don't Let the Pigeon Drive the Bus!*

_____, *The Pigeon Finds a Hot Dog!*

Poetry, Verse, and Song

Aliki, *Go Tell Aunt Rhody* (P)

Brown, Marc, *Play Rhymes* (P)

Brown, Margaret Wise, *Where Have You Been?* illustrated by Leo and Diane Dillon (P)

Field, Rachel, *General Store,* illustrated by Nancy Winslow Parker (P)

Godwin, Laura, *Barnyard Prayers,* illustrated by Brian Selnick (P)

Goldstein, Bobbye, *Mother Goose on the Loose* (P–I)

Greenfield, Eloise, *Night on Neighborhood Street,* illustrated by Jan Spivey Gilchrist (P–I)

_____, *Under the Sunday Tree,* illustrated by Amos Ferguson (P)

Griego, Margot C., Betsy L. Bucks, Sharon S. Gilbert, and Laurel H. Kimball, editors and translators, *Tortillitas para Mama and Other Nursery Rhymes, Spanish and English,* illustrated by Barbara Cooney (P)

Gunning, Monica, *Not a Copper Penny in Me House,* illustrated by Frané Lessac (P–I)

Harrison, David, *Somebody Catch My Homework,* illustrated by Betsy Lewin (I–A)

Hart, Jane, compiler, *Singing Bee! A Collection of Favorite Children's Songs,* illustrated by Anita Lobel (P)

Higginson, Vy, *This Is My Song! A Collection of Gospel Music for the Family,* illustrated by Brenda Joysmith (P)

Hudson, Wade, and Cheryl Hudson, *How Sweet the Sound: African American Songs for Children,* illustrated by Floyd Cooper (P)

Hughes, Langston, *The Book of Rhythms,* illustrated by Matt Wawiorka (P)

Krull, Kathleen, *Gonna Sing My Head Off!* illustrated by Allen Garns (I–A)

Longfellow, Henry Wadsworth, *Hiawatha,* illustrated by Susan Jeffers (I–A)

_____, *Hiawatha's Childhood,* illustrated by Errol Le Cain (I–A)

_____, *The Midnight Ride of Paul Revere,* illustrated by Christopher Bing (I–A)

_____, *Paul Revere's Ride,* illustrated by Ted Rand (I–A)

Schertle, Alice, *The Skeleton in the Closet,* illustrated by Curtis Jobling (P–I)

Siebert, Diane, *Mojave,* illustrated by Wendell Minor (I–A)

Smith, William Jay, *Around My Room,* illustrated by Erik Blegvad (P)

Spier, Peter, *The Fox Went Out on a Chilly Night* (I)

Zemach, Margot, *Hush, Little Baby* (P)

Poetry and Verse

This chapter was revised and updated with the assistance of Sarah E. Hansen.

CICADAS

Afternoon, mid-August	
Two cicadas singing	*Two cicadas singing*
	Air kiln-hot, lead-heavy
Five cicadas humming	*Five cicadas humming*
Thunderheads northwestward	
Twelve cicadas buzzing	*Twelve cicadas buzzing*
	Up and down the street
the mighty choir's	*the mighty choir's*
Assembling	*assembling*
Shrill cica-	
das	*Ci-*
droning	*cadas*
	droning
	in the elms
Three years	*Three years*
spent underground	
	among the roots
in darkness	*in darkness*
Now they're breaking ground	
	and climbing up
	the tree trunks
splitting skins	
and singing	*and singing*
	Jubilant
rejoicing	*cicadas*
	pouring out their
fervent praise	*fervent praise*
	for heat and light
their hymn	*their hymn*
sung to the sun	
Cicadas	*Cicadas*
	Whining
whin-	
ing	*ci-*
	cadas
	whirring
whir-	
ring	*ci-*
	cadas
	pulsing
pulsing	
chanting from the treetops	*chanting from the treetops*
sending	
forth their	*sending*
booming	*forth their*
boisterous	*booming*
joyful noise!	*Joyful noise!*

—PAUL FLEISCHMAN, from
Joyful Noise: Poems for Two Voices

The joyful noise singing from Caroline's classroom is not the humming of insects but the jubilant chanting of fourth-grade students responding to Paul Fleischman's "Cicadas" by reading in boisterous, booming voices. Caroline's students bring academically and culturally diverse voices to the poem; choral reading challenges them to harmonize their interpretations of poetic sound and meaning.

Reading from a version of the poem printed on large chart paper, students dissolve into laughter as they stumble over lines that call for two voices to read different phrases simultaneously. Caught up in the magic of sound, they persevere, working hard to synchronize their voices to interpret the cadence of Fleischman's cicadas. To help them understand how sound shapes a poem, Caroline invites her students to sit in a cluster in front of the chart. She draws an imaginary line down the center of the room, dividing the class into two groups. Each group represents one "voice" in the poem.

At first, each group reads its lines independently. The class listens carefully to the descriptive sound words in each line and discusses how to use their voices to interpret the meaning of the words. One fourth-grade boy, Ben, suggests that his group say "booming" with great force so as to emphasize the loudness of the cicada chorus. Sonia agrees and adds that her group might want to pause extra long in the middle of "pulsing" to give the word a heartbeat. Caroline records several of the students' suggestions on chart paper and then encourages them to share more sound ideas with their group members. Good ideas are contagious, and the room is suddenly filled with energetic talk. Caroline recognizes that the noise is purposeful; she knows that children's enjoyment of poetry increases when they can engage in enthusiastic conversations about the genre with each other. She circulates around the room, allowing her students and their enthusiasm for sound and meaning to be the center of their attention.

When the two groups bring their voices together, something poetic happens. Suddenly, the words begin to hum and chant. And when their voices sing different lines simultaneously or the same words chorally, there is an echo reminiscent of the rhythm of insects. Students' interpretations of sound have revealed meaning; the poem is a pulsing chorus of cicadas! Students are proud of their performance and are delighted by the joyful noise they have made through poetry.

Caroline has planned so well that her students are having a wonderful time exploring the relationship between sound and meaning in poetry. They are having fun, learning a great deal, and forging important connections between their own lives and the poetry they are reading in the classroom. This experience will help them build a strong foundation both for understanding how poetry works and for appreciating it.

Defining Poetry

Poetry is a poet's intuition of truth. Poetry combines rich meaning with sounds of language arranged in an interesting form. Poets select words and arrange them carefully to call attention to experiences we have not known or fully recognized. It is easier to say what poetry does than to describe what it is; poetry eludes precise definition. We know that poetry can make us chuckle or laugh out loud. It can startle us with insight or surprise us with its clarity. It can also bring a sense of peace and a feeling of repose. Some poems express feelings that we did not even know we had until we read them; then we say, "Yes, that's just the way it is." Poetry deals with the essence of life and experience. Poetry, says Gregory Corso (1983, p. 11), is "the opposite of hypocrisy."

Poets themselves are often the best source for a definition of poetry. Many poets write about poems and the act of creating them. Bobbye Goldstein collected several poems on poetry in *Inner Chimes* (P–I–A). In "Inside a Poem," from *It Doesn't Always Have to Rhyme* (P–I), Eve Merriam captures the essence of poetry and reveals some of its characteristics. She says poetry has a beat that repeats, words that chime, an inner chime, and images not imagined before. Eleanor Farjeon gives a more elusive definition in *Poems for Children* (P–I):

> What is Poetry? Who knows?
> Not the rose, but the scent of the rose;
> Not the sky, but the light in the sky;
> Not the fly, but the gleam of the fly;
> Not the sea, but the sound of the sea;
> Not myself, but what makes me
> See, hear, and feel something that prose
> Cannot: and what it is, who knows?
>
> ELEANOR FARJEON

Poetry in Children's Lives

Understanding poetry is a continual process that evolves through the experience of hearing, reading, discussing, and writing poetry. Children develop understanding as they internalize poetry. They profit little from verbal definitions and descriptions. It is their firsthand experience of listening to, reading, writing, and discussing poetry that contributes the most to fostering their love of it. Children who live with poetry in their homes and in their schools turn to poems again and again for pleasure.

• • POEMS MAKE US SMILE • •

We all like to laugh; poetry gives us a chance. Poems contain every kind of humor. It may come from wordplay, from descriptions of preposterous situations and events, from an unexpected angle on an everyday concern; but it is not malicious, sadistic, or hurtful. Humorous poems evoke laughter by taking delight in the absurd; they recognize the funny side of life. John Ciardi's "The Hairy-Nosed Preposterous," from his book *Someone Could Win a Polar Bear* (P), evokes belly laughs from primary-grade children who enjoy wordplay and exaggeration.

THE HAIRY-NOSED PREPOSTEROUS

The Hairy-Nosed Preposterous
Looks much like a Rhinosterous
But also something like a tank—
For which he has himself to thank.

His ears are the size of tennis shoes
His eyes the size of pins.
And when he lies down for a snooze
An orchestra begins.

It whistles, rattles, roars, and thumps
And the wind of it comes and goes
Through the storm-tossed hair that grows in clumps
On the end of his capable nose.

JOHN CIARDI

Douglas Florian creates humor by imitating the spelling of the word *aardvark* and creating laughable images in *Mammalabilia* (I). He says,

> *Aardvarks aare odd.*
> *Aardvarks aare staark.*
> *Aardvarks look better*
> *By faar in the daark.*
>
> DOUGLAS FLORIAN

Poems for readers of all ages can bring a chuckle or a loud shout of laughter. Truly funny poems are often a child's first happy experience with poetry. Rose Fyleman offers

© 2000 Douglas Florian

Florian's distinctive watercolor illustrations are as playful as his poems in **Mammalabilia.**

young readers humorous verse in *Mary Middling and Other Silly Folk: Nursery Rhymes and Nonsense Poems* (N–P). Jack Prelutsky also caters to primary-grade children with *The Frogs Wore Red Suspenders* (P) and *Scranimals* (P–I). *Exploding Gravy: Poems to Make You Laugh* (I), by X. J. Kennedy, and *Corn Chowder* (P–I), by James Stevenson, speak to students seeking funny poems in the intermediate grades. These and many other good collections of humorous poems are listed in the Booklist at the end of the chapter.

• • POEMS CREATE IMAGES • •

Many poems create sensory images. Poets craft words in such a way that readers almost see, smell, taste, touch, or hear what a poem describes. For example, in *Creatures of Earth, Sea, and Sky* (I) Georgia Heard describes an eagle in flight:

EAGLE FLIGHT

Eagle gliding in the sky
Circling, circling way up high—
Wind is whistling through your wings.
You're a graceful kite with no string.

GEORGIA HEARD

Heard's image of the eagle as a stringless kite is powerful; it allows readers to visualize precisely how the bird soars. Readers almost feel the imaginary tug connecting them to the eagle as it loops the sky on lifted wings. Strong images give readers vicarious experiences such as this; images put readers in the position of living moments through language that perhaps they have never before known. Good poetry uses imagery to help readers stretch their sensory encounters.

A master of imagery, Valerie Worth offers primary through intermediate readers 26 descriptively rich poems in *Peacock and Other Poems* (P–I). In *Toasting Marshmallows* (P–I), Kristine O'Connell George uses imagery to describe the sights and sounds of camping in the woods—a subject that appeals to many children. *Home to Me: Poems across America* (P–I), an anthology of works selected by Lee Bennett Hopkins, also contains poems with images appropriate for primary-grade children. *The World according to Dog: Poems and Teen Voices* (A), by Joyce Sidman, captures the essence of four-legged friends in images that empower advanced readers almost to reach out and pet the dogs featured in the anthology. Liz Rosenberg also speaks to advanced readers in *Roots and Flowers* (A). This specialized anthology features the work of many poets who use strong images to describe the bonds between family members. The Booklist at the end of the chapter lists additional books that contain sensory poems.

© 1992 Jennifer Owings Dewey

EAGLE FLIGHT

Eagle gliding in the sky,
circling, circling way up high—
wind is whistling through your wings.
You're a graceful kite with no string.

Georgia Heard creates memorable images in words that Jennifer Owings Dewey extends in art in Creatures of Earth, Sea, and Sky.

• • POEMS EXPRESS • • FEELINGS AND STIR EMOTIONS

Poetry expresses feelings in ways we have never thought about before. Good poetry is neither trite nor sentimental; it can help us understand ourselves and our emotions. Whether we are sad or lonely or happy, there are words to express our feelings, as Mary Ann Hoberman does in "My Father," from the book *Fathers, Mothers, Sisters, Brothers* (P):

MY FATHER

My father doesn't live with us.
It doesn't help to make a fuss,
But still I feel unhappy, plus
I miss him.

My father doesn't live with me.
He's got another family;
He moved away when I was three.
I miss him.

I'm always happy on the day
He visits and we talk and play;
But after he has gone away
I miss him.

MARY ANN HOBERMAN

Hoberman expresses feelings that have a solid ring of truth. Nikki Grimes is another poet who conveys strong emotions through language. Two of her anthologies, *Stepping Out with Grandma Mac* (P–I) and *My Man Blue* (I) are especially poignant for intermediate readers. Kristine O'Connell George also stirs the emotions of intermediate readers in *Swimming Upstream: Middle School Poems* (I–A). Patrice Vecchione gives advanced readers an opportunity to grapple with emotions in *Revenge and Forgiveness: An Anthology of Poems* (A). The Booklist at the end of this chapter includes other books of poems that express feelings.

• • P O E M S   P R O M O T E • •
S C H O O L   L E A R N I N G

Poetry does more than make children laugh or cry, or create images; it helps students remember academic content. Poetry pays off in the hard currency of school learning. Did you memorize a poem as a child? Most likely you can recite it today. When students memorize poems, they often remember them for a lifetime. If you want students to remember specific information, give it to them in poetry. Who will ever forget Longfellow's words: "Listen my children and you shall hear—The Midnight Ride of Paul Revere"?

Poetry can make history memorable. Marilyn Nelson helps advanced readers learn history through poetry in *Carver: A Life in Poems* (A). Through narrative verse, students hear the voices of people who shaped the life of George Washington Carver. The poetic rendering of this influential scientist's life and work empowers students to experience history in a way that is more intense than that provided by reading prose. Nelson does the same in *A Wreath for Emmett Till* (A), in which she uses the strict form of 15 interlinked sonnets to contain the sorrow and pain of the 1955 lynching of this young black man. The emotional intensity of the poems helps readers live the past and internalize historical experience.

Kevin Major, a talented contemporary poet, uses historical settings and events in *Ann and Seamus* (A). Seventeen-year-old Ann Harvey joins her father and brother when they go to rescue 163 stranded shipwreck survivors in 1828. One of the survivors is Seamus Ryan, a bold young Irishman who wants to get as far away from "the vile English" as he possibly can. Elegant pencil-and-wash illustrations evoke the bitter cold of Newfoundland and the tender love of the teenagers.

Poetry also makes science come alive for children. Jane Yolen combines beauty with information in *Fine Feathered Friends* (P–I), illustrated with magnificent photographs of birds taken by her son, Jason Stemple. Brief inserts of information about the birds appear in each subsection. The photographs and poetry are spectacular, the information

Photo courtesy Tuskegee University Archives/Design by Helen Robinson

*Marilyn Nelson helps history come alive in **Carver: A Life in Poems.***

accurate and engaging. Kristine O'Connell George's lyrical poems in *Hummingbird Nest: A Journal of Poems* (I) capture her experience of watching a hummingbird make a nest, lay eggs, and raise her babies. Barry Moser's delicate watercolors are visual complements to the images the words create.

Jon Scieszka and illustrator Lane Smith asked themselves what would rhyme with their popular *Math Curse* (I). They agreed on *Science Verse* (I), and created a book with a DVD in which everything becomes a science poem. J. Patrick Lewis, also a master at using poetry to promote school learning, created *Scien-Trickery: Riddles in Science* (I), a text in which the answers to his science riddles are hidden on the pages. Other poetry books that promote science and social studies learning include J. Patrick Lewis's *A World of Wonders: Geographic Travels in Verse and Rhyme* (I), Diane Ackerman's *Animal Sense* (P–I), and Constance Levy's *Splash! Poems of Our Watery World* (I).

Poetry draws students into listening. Students pay attention to poetry because it plays with the sounds of language; uses interesting, intriguing words; and deals with fascinating topics. Poetry increases students' vocabulary. We all learn the language we hear; if we hear ordinary conversational language, we will use ordinary conversational language when we speak. If we hear poetic language, we will use poetic language in our writing and speaking. Students recognize words in print more readily if they have heard those words spoken and read aloud. Because book language often differs from spoken language, we need to hear book language—especially poetic language—read aloud.

Poetry helps children learn how to read. Beginning readers can learn to decode print in verse more easily than in prose, because in poetry the lines are often short, words may rhyme, and the accent falls on meaningful words. These clues tell a reader what should come next in the text. When they hear Maurice Sendak's *Chicken Soup with Rice* (P), they can easily supply the final word in "Sipping once, sipping twice, sipping chicken soup with _____."

Poetry is excellent material for developing phonemic awareness, the ability to segment and manipulate speech sounds. Children learn to discriminate sounds, hear parts of words, and make connections between sounds they hear and letters they see. Because poetry and verse are often patterned, predictable, and repetitive, children know what a word should be and probably is going to be. When they recognize beginning consonants, they are likely to say the right word. Many poems have *alliteration* (words beginning with the same consonant sound) and rhyme (words ending with similar sounds). These features also help beginning readers decode print. Teaching Idea 4.1 suggests some poems that are appropriate for beginning readers.

Poetry helps students learn how to write by giving them a storehouse of words and language patterns to draw from in their own speaking and writing. Poetry also presents students with a pattern or framework for writing; they see that writers often use patterns when structuring paragraphs, stories, or expository manuscripts. The framework of poetry is visible because it is not hidden beneath layers of words; its skeleton shows.

Teaching Idea 4-1

Poems for Beginning Readers

Children learning to read need texts that support their early efforts to decode print. They need

* A small number of words on a line
* Predictable combinations of words said in a single phrase
* Words that are easily pronounced
* Predictable words that follow logically

These text characteristics describe poetry and stories in rhyme. Rhymed text helps children learn to read. The following books are good for beginning readers.

Easy-to-Read Poems and Stories in Rhyme

Agell, Charlotte, *Dancing Feet*

Ahlberg, Janet, and Allan Ahlberg, *Each Peach Pear Plum: An "I Spy" Story*

Appelt, Kathi, *Bayou Lullaby*

Asch, Frank, *Baby in the Box*

Baker, Keith, *Hide and Snake*

_____, *Who Is the Beast?*

Barracca, Debra, and Sal Barracca, *Adventures of Taxi Dog*

Bemelmans, Ludwig, *Madeline*

Brink, Carol Ryrie, *Goody O'Grumpity*

Bunting, Eve, *Flower Garden*

Cameron, Polly, *I Can't Said the Ant*

Cauley, Lorinda Bryan, *Clap Your Hands*

Christelow, Eileen, *Five Little Monkeys Sitting in a Tree*

Clifton, Lucille, *Everett Anderson's Christmas Coming*

Crews, Donald, *Ten Black Dots Revised*

Domanska, Janina, *If All the Seas Were One Sea*

Fleming, Denise, *Barnyard Banter*

Fox, Mem, *Where Is the Green Sheep?*

Guarino, Deborah, *Is Your Mama a Llama?*

Hennessy, B. G., *School Days*

Hopkins, Lee Bennett, *More Surprises*

_____, *Surprises*

Kuskin, Karla, *Roar and More*

Kraus, Robert, *Whose Mouse Are You?*

Martin, Bill, Jr., *Brown Bear, Brown Bear, What Do You See?*

_____, *Polar Bear, Polar Bear, What Do You Hear?*

Martin, Bill, Jr., and John Archambault, *Chicka Chicka Boom Boom*

Sendak, Maurice, *Chicken Soup with Rice: A Book of Months*

Seuss, Dr., *I Can Read with My Eyes Shut*

Williams, Sue, *I Went Walking*

Other Resources

Miles, Betty, *I'm Reading! A How-to-Read Book for Beginners*

Wells, Rosemary, *My Kindergarten*

Poetry helps students learn to think by showing them how to look at their world in a new way. It presents fresh perspectives on life and upends stereotyped ways of thinking. Poetry builds on paradox, ambiguity, and contradictions; it sets these features in stark relief so they become apparent to naive readers. Slender poetic texts do not cloud issues or bury them deep under a pile of verbiage. Poetry brushes away the clutter and helps ideas shine. These are good reasons to use poetry in the classroom.

Criteria for Evaluating Poetry

Poetry for children and adolescents refers to things children and adolescents know. We treasure poems that have stood the test of time, ones that have won significant awards, and ones that have received positive reviews from literary critics. The final test, however, is the level of understanding of the child. Although some poetry from the past still speaks to today's children, some does not. A wealth of excellent poetry has been written in the last decade.

In 1977 the National Council of Teachers of English (NCTE) established an award to honor poets who write for children. The award, established in memory of Bee Cullinan's son Jonathan (born 1969, died 1975), recognizes the outstanding contribution of a poet who writes expressly for children. Charlotte S. Huck (president of NCTE from 1975 to 1976), Alvina Burrows (colleague at New York University), John Donovan (director of the Children's Book Council), and Sister Rosemary Winkeljohann (director of the elementary section of the NCTE) helped define the criteria for excellence in poetry for children; they developed the procedures used to select the recipients of the award. The award is given for the entire body of a poet's work for children. For six years, the award was given annually. The committee realized they would soon run out of poets; in 1983 a new policy was instituted to present the award every three years. The combined works of the 13 poets who have received the award thus far form the foundation for poetry study in the field of children's literature. Miniprofiles of the NCTE award winners—David McCord, Aileen Fisher, Karla Kuskin, Myra Cohn Livingston, Eve Merriam, John Ciardi, Lilian Moore, Arnold Adoff, Valerie Worth, Barbara Juster Esbensen, Eloise Greenfield, X. J. Kennedy, and Mary Ann Hoberman—appear in this chapter.

After 10 poets had received the NCTE Award for Excellence in Poetry for Children, Cullinan conducted a national survey to discover children's favorite poems by each award recipient. Children's top five favorites for each poet appear in *A Jar of Tiny Stars*. All proceeds are used to support the NCTE poetry award.

The National Council of Teachers of English Award for Excellence in Poetry for Children, designed by Karla Kuskin, 1976. (Kuskin knew that Jonathan loved to climb trees and read books. She combined both interests in the medallion.)

© Andi McLeod & Charlotte Staub

Children's top five favorites from each NCTE award-winning poet appear in *A Jar of Tiny Stars*.

Individual poems can be judged on how well children understand them, on the emotions they elicit, on the images they create, on their rhythm and sounds, and on the appropriateness of their form. We can evaluate the overall quality of our classroom collections in terms of the multicultural diversity of content and in terms of the mood, language use, and variety of forms they contain. Books of poetry should present children with poems that play with language in surprising ways. They should contain poems that combine

Profile

Little, Brown and Company

Thomas V. Crowell

HarperCollins Publishers

David McCord, 1977

Poetry, like rain, should fall with elemental music, and poetry for children should catch the eye as well as the ear and the mind. It should delight; it really has to delight. Furthermore, poetry for children should keep reminding them, without any feeling on their part that they are being reminded, that the English language is a most marvelous and availing instrument.

David McCord is considered the dean of children's poets. His collected works appear in *One at a Time*. Other popular collections of his work appear in *Every Time I Climb a Tree* and *For Me to Say*. "Nature abounds in McCord's poetry," noted David A. Dillon (1978), "and the reader is treated to a sensual feast of sights, sounds, and touch, captured as a result of the poet's careful observation of common things which many of us fail to notice[:] colors, speeds, sizes, textures, shapes" (p. 379). David McCord was the first recipient of the NCTE Award for Excellence in Poetry for Children.

Aileen Fisher, 1978

Poetry is a rhythmical piece of writing that leaves the reader feeling that life is a little richer than before, a little more full of wonder, beauty, or just plain delight.

"Since the early 1930s," commented Lee Bennett Hopkins (1978), "Aileen Fisher . . . has reached and touched thousands upon thousands of children with her warm, wise and wonderful writing" (p. 868). A nature poet, Fisher lived as a child on 40 acres of land near the Iron Range on the Upper Peninsula of Michigan. She returned to the country as an adult to write full-time. Her popular books include *Sing of the Earth and Sky: Poems about Our Planet and the Wonders Beyond; Always Wondering; The House of a Mouse; Like Nothing at All; Out in the Dark and Daylight; Rabbits, Rabbits;* and *Anybody Home?*

Karla Kuskin, 1979

If there were a recipe for a poem, these would be the ingredients: word sounds, rhythm, description, feeling, memory, rhyme, and imagination. They can be put together a thousand different ways, a thousand, thousand . . . more.

An artist as well as a poet, Karla Kuskin designed the medallion for the NCTE poetry award; when she won the same award three years later, friends teased her about designing awards she would win. "Her pictures and her verse and poetry," noted Alvina Treut Burrows (1979), "are brimming over with the experiences of children growing up in a big city" (p. 935). Fittingly, Kuskin's poetry appears in New York subways as part of the Poetry in Motion program. Her most popular books include *Near the Window Tree; Dogs and Dragons, Trees and Dreams; The Upstairs Cat; The Sky Is Always in the Sky;* and *I Am Me.* Her anthology, *Moon, Have You Met My Mother?* is a collection of all her poems.

Sources:

Burrows, A. T. (1979). Profile: Karla Kuskin. *Language Arts, 56,* 934–939.

Dillon, D. A. (1978). Perspectives: David McCord. *Language Arts, 55,* 379–385.

Hopkins, L. B. (1978). Profile: Aileen Fisher. *Language Arts, 55,* 868–870.

The opening quotations for these profiles are from the poets' acceptance speeches for the NCTE poetry award. (The speech is given in November of the year the award is received.)

sounds in ways that make words sing. The structures of the poems students find in poetry books should be purposeful; form should convey meaning. Perhaps most important, poetry books should be evaluated on how well the content of their poems speaks to the interests of the individual children reading them. Figure 4.1 suggests some criteria to use as you evaluate books of poetry. Keep the criteria in mind as you search for excellent poetry books to delight your students.

LANGUAGE THAT SURPRISES

Outstanding poems arrest readers' attention with innovative word choice and comparisons. Nothing about poetic language is mundane or prosaic. Poets choose words carefully to describe objects, events, feelings, or fantasies in new and surprising ways. Although their words may be familiar ones, poets select and arrange them purposefully to capture our imagination. The experience conveyed in poetry may be commonplace, but it becomes extraordinary when seen through the poet's eye. As literary scholar Northrup Frye (1963, p. 63) says, "The poet's job is not to tell you what happened, but what happens; not what did take place, but the kind of thing that always takes place." The language of poetry startles us into seeing with wide-open eyes the extraordinariness of our everyday experiences.

Figure 4-1

Checklist for Evaluating Books of Poetry

- ✿ Poetic language is innovative and surprising.
- ✿ Poets astonish readers with careful word choices and original comparisons.
- ✿ Sounds are combined in ways that make words sing.
- ✿ Rhyme, rhythm, repetition, and other sound elements are used purposefully to convey meaning.
- ✿ Form helps readers understand more about the poetic subject or mood.
- ✿ Subjects speak to readers and are highly engaging.

SOUND THAT SINGS

Children like poems that sing to them. Sound combinations that emphasize the repetition of whole words, initial consonant sounds, or internal vowel sounds appeal to young ears. They give words a musical quality that can make the act of reading and listening to poetry alternatively soothing, invigorating, calming, or energizing, depending on how poets compose their sounds. Artful poets also use sound to convey meaning. When Barbara Esbensen repeats the "s" sound in her poem about a snake in *Words with Wrinkled Knees* (P–I), her work becomes more than a collection of words; the "s" sounds allow readers to hear the snake hiss. Sound used in musical and purposeful ways such as this makes poetry almost irresistible to children.

STRUCTURE THAT SUPPORTS MEANING

In well-constructed poems, the shape of words, lines, and stanzas says something about what the poems mean. Poets structure their poems to reveal more about their subjects than words alone can. Douglas Florian, for example, often uses form to convey meaning in his poems. When writing about a sawfish in his anthology *In the Swim* (I), he arranges his lines in a zigzag pattern to make his words "saw" down the page. His salmon poem hurtles diagonally upward across the page, reinforcing the fish's dramatic movement. Lee Bennett Hopkins's anthology, *Hoofbeats, Claws, and Rippled Fins: Creature Poems* (P–I), contains additional examples of how poets use form purposefully. Discovering how form supports meaning in individual poems is often a "Eureka!" moment for children. They take much pleasure in "divulging" how skillful poets use form in sophisticated ways to help readers understand their poems.

SUBJECTS THAT SPEAK TO US

Children like poems they can understand. They also enjoy poems that expand their understanding, those that need to be read and discussed in the company of peers and adults who are interested in exploring poetry. Children respond to carefully selected poems that are geared to their intellectual development and that speak of their experiences. Poetry can evoke laughter, create images, and express feelings when it is about subjects and experiences that interest children.

Children want to read poetry—it appeals to them. When students begin to explore poetry, they may like humorous poems with strong rhythm and rhyme more than they like

Profile

Marilyn Sanders

Bachrach

Houghton Mifflin Company

Myra Cohn Livingston, 1980

*T*rained as a traditionalist in poetry, I feel strongly about the importance of order imposed by fixed forms, meter, and rhyme when I write about some things; yet free verse seems more suitable for other subjects. It is the force of what I say that shapes the form.

Myra Cohn Livingston was highly respected for her "commitment to the need for higher standards for children's creative writing" (Porter, 1980, p. 901). She published around 80 books of poetry or writings about poetry. Her work includes such titles as *Riddle-Me Rhymes, Lots of Limericks, Call Down the Moon,* and *Poem-Making: Ways to Begin Writing Poetry.*

Eve Merriam, 1981

*T*here is a physical element in reading poetry out loud; it's like jumping rope or throwing a ball. If we can get teachers to read poetry, lots of it, out loud to children, we'll develop a generation of poetry readers; we may even have some poetry writers, but the main thing, we'll have language appreciators.

It is the physical thrill of poetry "that Eve Merriam want[ed] children to experience for themselves" (Sloan, 1981, p. 958). She felt that "children, like poets, are intrigued by the wonderful things that words can do: how their sounds mimic what is being described, how puns are possible, how language can be made . . . to 'natter, patter, chatter, and prate'" (p. 958). Merriam's poetry is widely anthologized. Some of her books include *It Doesn't Always Have to Rhyme, There Is No Rhyme for Silver, The Singing Green: New and Selected Poems for All Seasons,* and *Higgle Wiggle: Happy Rhymes.*

John Ciardi, 1982

*P*oetry and learning are both fun, and children are full of an enormous relish for both. My poetry is just a bubbling up of a natural foolishness, and the idea that maybe you can make language dance a bit.

"There is magic in the poetry John Ciardi has written for children," said Norine Odland (1982, p. 872). She felt that the "humor in his poems allows a child to reach for new ways to view ordinary things and places in the world" (p. 872). John Ciardi began writing poetry for his own children. His first book was *The Reason for the Pelican.* Other favorites include *You Read to Me, I'll Read to You; You Know Who; The Monster Den: or Look What Happened at My House—and to It; The Man Who Sang the Sillies;* and *I Met a Man.*

Sources:

Odland, N. (1982). Profile: John Ciardi. *Language Arts, 59,* 872–874.

Porter, E. J. (1980). Profile: Myra Cohn Livingston. *Language Arts, 57,* 901–903.

Sloan, G. (1981). Profile: Eve Merriam. *Language Arts, 58,* 957–962.

The opening quotations for these profiles are from the poets' acceptance speeches for the NCTE poetry award. (The speech is given in November of the year the award is received.)

free verse with abstract symbolism. They may enjoy narrative poetry because it is based on their natural love of story. Children's responses to poetry depend heavily on the way it is introduced to them. If initial encounters with poetry are happy ones, then a love for and understanding of poetry can grow. During the early childhood years, children hear jingles and readily commit them to memory. They sing songs as they play and will join in to sing refrains with delight. Happy experiences with sound, rhythm, rhyme, humor, and story shape children's preferences for poetry.

✳ ✳ ✳

A CLOSE LOOK AT

Joyful Noise: Poems for Two Voices

Paul Fleischman begins *Joyful Noise* (I–A) with a special note: "The following poems were written to be read aloud by two readers at once, one taking the left-hand part, the other taking the right-hand part. The poems should be read from top to bottom, the two parts meshing as in a musical duet. When both readers have lines at the same horizontal level, those lines are to be spoken simultaneously." In this anthology of insect poems, Fleischman leads readers to experience poetry out loud together and invites them to become interpreters of sound, form, and meaning. *Joyful Noise,* illustrated by Eric Beddows, does what good poetry must always do—it helps children make language sing.

Innovative Language

In Fleischman's poems, insects don't buzz; they drone, whine, whir, and rejoice. Fleischman's choice of words is surprising. Readers must pause to wrap their tongues and minds around delightful new ways of describing the humming sounds of insects. The best poetry for children and young adults uses language in innovative ways such as this to awaken readers to fresh ideas.

Several of Fleischman's innovations are captured in the comparisons he draws. In "Fireflies" he likens lightning bugs to calligraphers.

from FIREFLIES

Light	*Light*
	is the ink we use
Night	*Night*
is our parchment	

Fleischman surprises readers by reversing the associations people usually make between light and dark. The light in this case is not the white paper used for writing, but the ink. The dark sky, which might normally be associated with black ink, is instead the paper. Good poetry captivates us with original comparisons.

Intricate Sound

It is not by accident that Fleischman's mayflies swarm and swerve. He uses the repetition of initial consonant sounds, or alliteration, purposefully in "Mayflies" and in other poems in *Joyful Noise* to add depth of sound to his work. He also uses repetition of whole words and phrases to reconstruct in language the echoes of insect rhythms in nature. Fleischman's use of alliteration and repetition in "Whirligig Beetles" almost makes readers dizzy!

from WHIRLIGIG BEETLES

We're whirligig beetles	
we're swimming in circles	*We're whirligig beetles*
black backs by the hundred.	*we're swimming in circles,*
	black backs by the hundred.
	We're spinning and swerving
We're spinning and swerving	*as if we were on a*
as if we were on a	*mad merry-go-round.*
mad merry-go-round.	
We never get dizzy	
from whirling and weaving	*We never get dizzy*
and wheeling and swirling	*from whirling and weaving*
	and wheeling and swirling.

The swirl of "w" and "s" sounds, along with the "say" and "re-say" phrasing pattern, creates in sound the spinning motion of the whirligig beetles. In poetry that is thoughtful, sound helps convey meaning.

Purposeful Form

Fleischman's sprite grasshoppers jump from line to line in one or two words. His water striders, as their name suggests, tread in longer lines of two to six words. Just as Fleischman uses sound in "Whirligig Beetles" to convey the dizzying motion of the insects, he uses line breaks purposefully in "Grasshoppers" and "Water Striders" to show readers how these insects move differently. Further, the arrangement of each of the poems in the collection into parallel voices fulfills the overall purpose of the book: to bring readers together in the choral reading of poetry. In *Joyful Noise,* line breaks and stanzas are intentional; form supports meaning.

Engaging Content

The degree to which children find the content of poetry engaging depends on many factors, not the least important of which is their personal interest in the world around them. *Joyful Noise* speaks to readers' diverse interests. Fleischman's poems focus on insects and offer insight into their characteristics and habitats. But they are also whimsical. His Queen Bee is of two very different minds when it comes to evaluating the pros and cons of her important role in the hive. His moth is in love with a porch light. For those readers who appreciate humorous poems, Fleischman provides

© 1988 Eric Beddows

Eric Beddows's whimsical insects illustrate Paul Fleischman's Joyful Noise: Poems for Two Voices.

"Book Lice" and others. "Requiem" and "Chrysalis Diary" present more somber moods. *Joyful Noise* is valuable as a classroom anthology because it succeeds in examining a unified theme from a variety of angles. Children need choices. *Joyful Noise* gives developing readers the opportunity to select poems that please them.

* * *

Children's Poetry Preferences

Researchers have studied the kinds of poems children like, as well as the kinds of poems teachers read to them. For example, in two national surveys, Terry (1974) studied the poetry preferences of students in the upper elementary grades, and Fisher and Natarella (1982) replicated her study with primary-grade children. These researchers found that children in their studies liked

- Contemporary poems
- Poems they could understand
- Narrative poems
- Poems with rhyme, rhythm, and sound
- Poems that related to their personal experiences

They also found that children in their studies disliked poems that had a lot of figurative language and imagery because they did not understand it. They disliked highly abstract poems that did not make sense to them. Haiku was consistently disliked. Favorite poems were humorous ones about familiar experiences or animals. John Ciardi's poem "Mummy Slept Late and Daddy Fixed Breakfast" in *You Read to Me, I'll Read to You* and limericks of all sorts ranked high among the children's choices.

Although the research by Terry (1974) and Fisher and Natarella (1982) provided much-needed baseline information about the types of poems elementary students prefer, their studies did not systematically investigate how experiences of classroom poetry shape children's poetry preferences. What children prefer and what they can learn to appreciate in the company of others and an enthusiastic teacher are often very different.

McClure (1985) extended Terry's study (1974) and found that classroom experiences change children's responses to poetry. In supportive environments, children respond more positively to a wider variety of poetry, showing that teachers' attitudes and practices make a tremendous difference. In other words, what you do with poetry in the classroom determines how your students respond to poetry.

A case study focusing on the classroom poetry experiences of a fourth- and fifth-grade class in the Midwest also supports the idea that children may change their poetry preferences when their school experiences support their exploration of the genre (Hansen, 2004). Based on Terry's research (1974), the study began by asking students to rate poems selected for elements of sound, rhyme, form, voice, mood, and imagery and figurative language. After six months of classroom poetry experiences, during which students explored poetry with enthusiastic teachers, students rated and responded to similar poems in a follow-up survey. The results of the study suggested that students' appreciation for free verse and simile increased over the course of the study. Students also became more articulate about what they liked and disliked about specific poems after participating in the classroom poetry experiences.

Although the quantitative results of this study say much about the effect teaching has on children's poetry preferences, it is hearing students relate in their own words how their poetry preferences broadened as a result of their school experience that offers the most compelling reasons to bring poetry into the classroom. "I used to only like to read funny poems," Sam reflected during his last poetry session, "but now I like to read and write ALL poetry." Ty also felt changed by the classroom poetry sessions: "I used

Profile

HarperCollins Publishers

HarperCollins Publishers

© Temple Studios

Lilian Moore, 1985

Poetry should be like fireworks, packed carefully and artfully, ready to explode with unpredictable effects. When people asked Robert Frost—as they did by the hundreds—what he meant by "But I have promises to keep / And miles to go before I sleep / And miles to go before I sleep," he always turned the question aside with a joke. Maybe he couldn't answer it, and maybe he was glad that the lines exploded in so many different colors in so many people's minds.

Lilian Moore taught school in New York and worked in publishing for many years. Her work, characterized by "the truth of accurate observations, without sentimentality" (Glazer, 1985, p. 647), may be found in her collections of poetry, including *I Feel the Same Way, Something New Begins, Poems Have Roots,* and *Adam Mouse's Book of Poems.*

Arnold Adoff, 1988

I look for craft and control in making a form that is unique to the individual poem, that shapes it, holds it tight, creates an inner tension that makes a whole shape out of the words. (from Pauses [Hopkins, 1999, p. 219])

Many of Adoff's anthologies reflect the varied experiences of African American people and frequently celebrate racial pride and family strength. "Another unique feature of Adoff's work," commented Mary Lou White (1988, p. 586), "is his technique of creating a series of poems within a book that acts as a prose work yet is different from both a single narrative poem or a prose story. Read together, the individual poems tell a story." Some of Adoff's popular works include *I Am the Darker Brother, Black Out Loud, Black Is Brown Is Tan, All the Colors of the Race, My Black Me,* and *Make a Circle, Keep Us In.*

Valerie Worth, 1991

Never forget that the subject is as important as your feeling: The mud puddle itself is as important as your pleasure in looking at it or splashing through it. Never let the mud puddle get lost in the poetry—because in many ways, the mud puddle is the poetry.

Valerie Worth's small poems are crystal-clear images, luminous word jewels about the simplest things—coat hangers, pebbles, or marbles. Sharing these images with others was important to Worth; she commented that winning the NCTE Award for Excellence in Poetry for Children was "proof that poetry is not just a solitary pursuit, not just a rare flower blooming in isolation, but actually a very effective means of communication" (quoted in Hopkins, 1991, p. 501). A collection of her small poems and others can be found in *All the Small Poems and Fourteen More.*

Sources:

Glazer, J. I. (1985). Profile: Lilian Moore. *Language Arts, 62,* 647–651.

Hopkins, L. B. (1991). Profile: Valerie Worth. *Language Arts, 68,* 499–501.

Hopkins, L. B. (1999). *Pauses: Autobiographical reflections of 101 creators of children's books.* New York: HarperCollins.

White, M. L. (1988). Profile: Arnold Adoff. *Language Arts, 65,* 584–588.

Unless otherwise noted, the opening quotations for these profiles are from the poets' acceptance speeches for the NCTE poetry award. (The speech is given in November of the year the award is received.)

to hate poetry and now I know it's more than just . . . roses are red violets are blue." Many students shared Ty's feeling that learning about the different kinds of poetry helped them like the genre more. Jin felt that this understanding directly affected his attitude toward writing poetry: "I never liked poetry but now I have a lot more interest in it because I know that there are many different kinds of poetry and so there is a lot of choices to write a poem so you have a big selection." Pat also noted, "I've learned about the names of a specific style and onomatopoeia, alliteration and now I like it more." "What changed about poetry," said Angel, "was that I used to hate poems very much but now when you guys came I learned a lot and I started liking poetry."

Exploring poetry in the classroom gave many students in the study the confidence to read, discuss, and write poetry outside their academic setting. "I used to think poetry was kinda boring," commented Hilary, "but now I learned so much . . . and I really like poetry and I write poems in the car and at home not just at school." At a community poetry reading, held at an off-school location, 10 participants in the study volunteered to read poems they had found or composed. One student who regularly felt uncomfortable reading in front of large groups nonetheless attended the event and participated as an audience member. The poetry reading captured the contagious energy and enthusiasm that participants in the study generated for poetry over the course of six months. As one fifth-grade girl wrote, "I loved poetry when we started. Nothing changed. Well, except I love it a bagillion times more—literally!"

Poetry grows increasingly popular as more poetry is published in appealing formats. Since 1974, the International Reading Association (IRA) and Children's Book Council have annually conducted a national field test called Children's Choices; the results show that children consistently select poetry books as among their favorites. Preference for poetry prevails amid opportunities to choose from hundreds of other picture books, novels, and nonfiction. Children choose humorous poems about familiar things, poems that astonish them, and poems that help them to see the world in a new way.

We may not know why a particular poem appeals to children, but we do know that poems read aloud with enthusiasm are likely to become their favorites. Teachers' selections soon become children's choices. Results of the IRA Teachers' Choices project show that teachers frequently choose poetry as their favorite books for teaching. Teachers choose poems that reflect our multicultural heritage, poems with beautiful language, and poems that help them teach subject-area content. When teachers select poems they like, their enthusiasm is apparent to their students.

Poets Use Language in Interesting Ways

Poets manipulate the elements of sound, rhythm, and meaning to create an impact more powerful than any found in prose. Sound and rhythm are more pronounced in poetry than in prose, and meaning is more condensed. Poets use language in unique ways. The terms that are used to describe these language techniques are defined in this chapter and are listed in the Glossary. Students will not need to learn the meanings of all the terms, but teachers should be comfortable enough with them to answer questions and discuss techniques of favorite poets. If, for example, children comment on the repetition of initial consonant sounds, you might say, "That's called 'alliteration.' Let's look to see how it works in this poem." Teachers who are willing to explore poetry become role models for children, leading their students to explore poetry. Teaching Idea 4.2 lists several books on language and wordplay. Also see Harrison and Cullinan's *Easy Poetry Lessons That Dazzle and Delight* (2003) for accurate terminology.

• • WORDS AS SOUND • •

Of all the elements of poetry, sound offers the most pleasure to children. The choice and arrangement of sounds make poetry musical and reinforce meaning. Rhyme, alliteration, assonance, and onomatopoeia are among the language resources of sound.

Rhyme refers to words whose ending sounds are alike (despair/fair). Although poetry need not rhyme, children often relish the way rhyme clicks phrases together in melodic ways. Rhyme is not as fashionable with adults as it once was, but children still enjoy reciting it. It sticks better in the mind and lingers longer on the tongue. Generation after generation repeats the same jump rope jingles and rhyming street games.

An example of the familiar end rhyme, in which the rhyming words appear at the ends of lines, appears in Jane Yolen's "Sky Scrape/City Scape," in her book of the same title:

SKY SCRAPE/CITY SCAPE
Sky scrape
City scape
High stone
Steel bone
Cloud crown
Smog gown

Hurry up
Hurry down.

JANE YOLEN

Teaching Idea **4-2**

Wordplay and Poetry

Poets are wordsmiths who play with the infinite possibilities of language. They make us hear the repetition of similar sounds, they challenge us to probe double or triple meanings, they surprise us with unusual combinations of words and events. Poets savor language and pack their poems with multiple meanings, like firecrackers ready to explode. Poets craft their poems the way a potter shapes clay—turning, refining, polishing, smoothing until it satisfies. You can become sensitive to the nuances of words, too. Look at books about words. Discover what they offer. Here are some examples.

Agee, Jon, *Sit on a Potato Pan, Otis! More Palindromes*

_____, *Who Ordered the Jumbo Shrimp? and Other Oxymorons*

Cleary, Brian P., *Give Me Bach My Schubert*

Heller, Ruth, *Many Luscious Lollipops: A Book about Adjectives*

_____, *Up, Up and Away: A Book about Adverbs*

Hoban, Tana, *Exactly the Opposite*

McMillan, Bruce, *Play Day: A Book of Terse Verse*

_____, *Super, Super, Superwords*

Merriam, Eve, *Chortles: New and Selected Wordplay Poems*

_____, *A Poem for a Pickle: Funnybone Verses*

Terban, Marvin, *The Dove Dove*

_____, *Hey Hay*

_____, *It Figures! Fun Figures of Speech*

_____, *Superdupers! Really Funny Real Words*

_____, *Time to Rhyme: A Rhyming Dictionary*

Young, Sue, *Scholastic's Rhyming Dictionary*

Create word walls, word maps, word balloons, and sunbursts. Put one word in the middle of a page. Encircle it with all the other words that come to mind. Cluster the words that go together in some way. Play with the words. Rearrange them on the page to see if they suggest a poem or verse. Try different combinations to create a tone or mood.

When the last word of one line rhymes with the first word of the next line we call it runover rhyme. In *One at a Time* (P–I), David McCord gives us a beautiful example of this (together with end rhyme) in his "Runover Rhyme":

RUNOVER RHYME

*Down by the pool still fishing
Wishing for fish, I fail
Praying for birds not present
Pheasant or grouse or quail.*

*Up in the woods, his hammer
Stammering, I can't see
The woodpecker, find the cunning
Sunning old owl in the tree.*

*Over the field such raucous
Talk as the crows talk on!
Nothing around me slumbers;
Numbers of birds have gone.*

*Even the leaves hang listless
Lasting through days we lose
Empty of what is wanted
Haunted by what we choose.*

DAVID MCCORD

David Harrison extends David McCord's idea of runover rhyme by linking lines together in *link rhymes*. In *Easy Poetry Lessons That Dazzle and Delight,* he looks at the child he was and considers the person he will become:

THE FUTURE ME

*Looking back, I see
Me, unafraid
Eager, teasing
Pleasing, first grade.*

*Part on the right
Light cowlick hair
Lopsided grin
Thin, blue eyes, fair.*

*Who am I now?
How am I to be?
Looking behind
To find the future me.*

DAVID HARRISON

Children are willing explorers who will experiment with rhyme schemes when they are invited to the feast of poetry. They learn when to use rhyme to add to the meaning of a poem.

Sky Scrape/City Scape

Sky scrape,
City scape,
High stone,
Steel bone,
Cloud crown,
Smóg gown,

Hurry up,
Hurry down.

Jane Yolen

*Jane Yolen captures the pace and rhythm of the city, which Ken Condon echoes and enriches in the art of **Sky Scrape/ City Scape.***

Poets' ears are also tuned to the *repetition* of consonants, vowels, syllables, words, phrases, and lines, separately and in combination. Anything may be repeated to achieve effect. Repetition is like meeting an old friend again; children find it reassuring. Repetition underscores meaning, establishes a sound pattern, and is a source of humor in many rhymes, as in this chant by David McCord from the book *One at a Time:*

III

The pickety fence
The pickety fence
Give it a lick it's
The pickety fence
Give it a lick it's
A clickety fence
Give it a lick it's
A lickety fence
Give it a lick
Give it a lick
Give it a lick
With a rickety stick
Pickety
Pickety
Pickety
Pick

DAVID McCORD

Alliteration refers to the repetition of the initial consonant sounds of words at close intervals. Tongue twisters such as "rubber baby buggy bumpers" play with alliteration. Karla Kuskin starts with alliteration, adds end rhyme, and then jumps to an unexpected statement in "The Meal."

THE MEAL

Timothy Tompkins had turnips and tea.
The turnips were tiny.
He ate at least three.
And then, for dessert
He had onions and ice.
He liked that so much
That he ordered it twice.
He had two cups of ketchup
A prune, and a pickle.
"Delicious," said Timothy.
"Well worth a nickel."
He folded his napkin
And hastened to add
"It's one of the loveliest breakfasts I've had."

KARLA KUSKIN

Rhoda W. Bacmeister uses alliteration and *assonance,* the repetition of vowel sounds at close intervals, in "Galoshes":

GALOSHES

Susie's galoshes
Make splishes and sploshes
And slooshes and sloshes
As Susie steps slowly
Along in the slush.
They stamp and they tramp
On the ice and concrete
They get stuck in the muck and the mud;
But Susie likes much best to hear
The slippery slush
As it slooshes and sloshes
And splishes and sploshes
All around her galoshes!

RHODA BACMEISTER

She also makes use of *onomatopoeia,* or words created from natural sounds associated with the thing or action designated—for example, *slush, slooshes, sloshes, splishes,* and *sploshes.* Onomatopoeia, in combination with other sound resources, can achieve poetic effect to light up any child's eyes.

• • WORDS AS RHYTHM • •

Rhythm in language is created by the recurrence of specific beats of stressed and unstressed syllables. Human beings respond to regularity in the beat; this response may develop in the womb, when the fetus hears the mother's steady heartbeat. Rhythm is everywhere in life—in ocean waves, in the tick of a clock, in a horse's hoofbeats, in one's own pulse. In poetry, rhythm refers to the repeated use of syllables and accents, and to the rise and fall of words spoken or read. In "Inside a Poem" from *It Doesn't Always Have to Rhyme* (P–I), Eve Merriam calls "the repeat of a beat . . . an inner chime that makes you want to tap your feet or swerve in a curve." All good poetry is rhythmical, as are other forms of high art, from visual arts to dance, music, and even prose.

The rhythm in poetry is most often metrical. Meter is ordered rhythm, in which certain syllables are regularly stressed or accented in a more or less fixed pattern. *Meter* is defined as "measure," and metrical language in poetry can be measured. The meter in poetry can range from that of tightly structured verse patterns to loosely defined free verse. Whatever it is, rhythm helps create and then reinforce a poem's meaning. In *Circus* (N–P), Jack Prelutsky adjusts his rhythms to the subject:

Over and over the tumblers tumble
with never a fumble
with never a stumble
top over bottom and back over top
flop-flippy-floppity-flippity-flop.

The tumblers pass by, followed by the elephants, whose plodding walk echoes in the new rhythm:

Here come the elephants, ten feet high
elephants, elephants, heads in the sky.
Eleven great elephants intertwined
one little elephant close behind.

JACK PRELUTSKY

Prelutsky makes the rhythm in the elephant stanza plod along in the same lumbering way that elephants walk. He makes the sound echo the sense.

Word order contributes to the rhythm of poetry as well. Arranging words is central to creating a poem. Teachers and student writers should be aware of the ways poets manipulate syntax to make poetry distinctive from prose. One noticeable feature of poetic language is the way it varies from the straight declarative sentence. An example is Robert Louis Stevenson's "Where Go the Boats?" from *A Child's Garden of Verses* (P):

WHERE GO THE BOATS

Dark brown is the river
Golden is the sand.
It flows along forever
With trees on either hand.

ROBERT LOUIS STEVENSON

The literal meaning of the poem could be communicated in this way:

The river is dark brown
The sand is golden.
The river keeps on flowing forever
With trees on both sides.

Retaining Stevenson's words but rearranging them totally destroys the visual image. Poets manipulate syntax until they find an order and rhythm that is pleasing to them and that communicates more than the literal message. Inverted word order used for poetic effect may interfere with meaning; however, students grow in their ability to comprehend inverted sentences when they hear poetry read aloud.

• • WORDS AS MEANING • •

Poetry often carries several layers of meaning and, as is true of other literature, is subject to different interpretations. The meaning children create is directly related to what their experience prepares them to understand; our background knowledge determines what we can see.

Researcher Terry (1974) read William Jay Smith's "The Toaster" to children of varying levels of development and asked them to draw a picture of what the poem was about. The poem describes the toaster as "a silver-scaled dragon." Children in the primary grades believed that it was an actual dragon and drew fiery-mouthed dragons to show that they understood the poem at a literal, concrete level. Older children, above the fourth grade, drew pictures of toasters that resembled dragons, suggesting that they understood the figurative language Smith used in the poem.

Poetic devices used to convey meaning include *figurative language, imagery, denotation,* and *connotation.* Writers use poetic devices to suggest that the words mean more than meets the eye or ear. Something left unsaid is often as important as what is stated on the page, as in this poem from *Whistling the Morning In* (P–I), by Lillian Morrison:

DAILY VIOLENCE

Dawn cracked;
> *the sun stole through.*
Day broke;
> *the sun climbed over rooftops.*
Clouds chased the sun
> *then burst.*
Night fell.
The clock struck midnight.

LILLIAN MORRISON

Figurative language produces a meaning beyond the literal meaning of the words used. In poetry, figurative language is used frequently. Figurative language affects meaning dramatically; metaphor, simile, and personification make the language of poetry different from that of prose. As poets create vivid experiences, they use language metaphorically; they help us see or feel things in new ways. It is not enough just to have the idea; poets must also have the words. The special and particular words often involve figurative language, as in this poem from Eve Merriam's *It Doesn't Always Have to Rhyme:*

METAPHOR

Morning is
a new sheet of paper
for you to write on.

Whatever you want to say,
all day,
until night
folds it up
and files it away.

The bright words and the dark words
are gone
until dawn
and a new day
to write on.

EVE MERRIAM

Children need experience in using and understanding figurative language in order to fully appreciate poems that rely on it. How well they understand figurative language in a poem depends on their background knowledge and experience. Young children understand a comparison made on a physical plane but not on a psychological one. Snow-covered bushes that look like popcorn balls, and cars that look like big, fat raisins are more likely to make sense to young children than a prison guard's heart of stone. Young children interpret the prison guard's heart as being physically of stone.

As children become more sophisticated language users, they understand how figurative language contributes to meaning; poetry assumes a deeper dimension. Recognizing contrast, comparison, and exaggeration on a psychological level adds a richer interpretation. More complex comparisons can be made using the devices of metaphor and simile, which compare one thing to another or view something in terms of something else. The comparison in a simile is stated and uses the words *like* or *as* to draw the comparison. A comparison in a metaphor is inferred; something is stated as something else. Eve Merriam makes an unmistakable comparison by using the title "Metaphor" and by saying that morning is a new sheet of paper.

Personification refers to representing a thing or abstraction as a person. When we say "Fortune smiled on us" or "If the weather permits," we are giving human qualities to an idea—fortune—and to the weather. Poets often give human feelings or thoughts to plants and animals. In her poem "Crickets," Valerie Worth uses personification to make ideas more vivid or unusual. She says that crickets "talk" and dry grass "whispers." Langston Hughes uses personification in "April Rain Song" when he advises to let the rain "kiss" you and "sing you a lullaby." Lilian Moore uses personification in her poem "Construction," from *I Thought I Heard the City* and *Something New Begins* (both P–I).

CONSTRUCTION
The giant mouth
chews
rocks
spews them
and is back for
more.

The giant arm
swings up
with a girder
for
the fourteenth floor.

Down there,
a tiny man
is
telling them
where
to put a skyscraper.

LILIAN MOORE

Poets create imagery through the use of words in ways that arrest our senses; we can imagine that we almost see, taste, touch, smell, or hear what they describe. Little escapes the poet's vision; nothing limits the speculations upon what he or she sees. In a poem from ***All the Small Poems and Fourteen More*** (P–I), Valerie Worth creates imagery when she compares a dandelion with a cratered moon:

DANDELION

Out of
Green space,
A sun:
Bright for
A day, burning,
Away to
A husk, a
Cratered moon:

Burst
In a week
To dust:
Seeding
The infinite
Lawn with
Its starry
Smithereens.

VALERIE WORTH

Barbara Juster Esbensen creates imagery through word pictures in ***Words with Wrinkled Knees*** when she says a frog goes splat and lands wet and squat upon the page:

Touch it with your
pencil
Splat!   The word lands   wet
and squat
upon the page   F R O G

Feed it something light
With wings   Here's one!
Tongue flicks   bright
wing   caught!
Small poem
gone

BARBARA JUSTER ESBENSEN

Denotation refers to the literal meaning of a word or phrase. *Connotation* refers to the suggested meaning associated with the literal one, the overtones of meaning. Connotations can vary with the individual person. Water, for instance, may have connotations of refreshment, cooling, beauty, pleasure, or cleansing, depending on which of its many aspects you are thinking about and where you have enjoyed water the most. But it might also arouse feelings of terror for a person who has been in danger of drowning.

Poetry makes use of both denotative and connotative meaning, saying what it means but suggesting much more. Connotation enriches meaning. Sometimes the sounds of words combine with their connotations to make a very

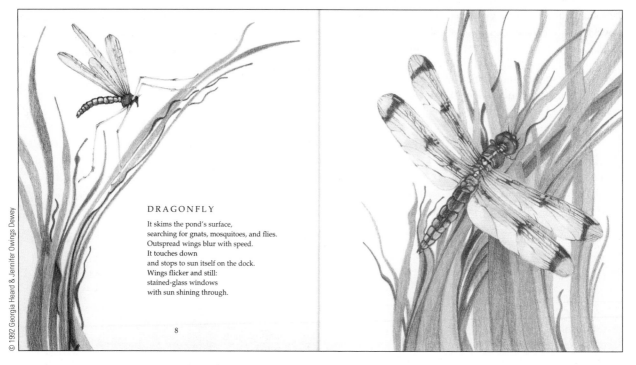

DRAGONFLY

It skims the pond's surface,
searching for gnats, mosquitoes, and flies.
Outspread wings blur with speed.
It touches down
and stops to sun itself on the dock.
Wings flicker and still:
stained-glass windows
with sun shining through.

8

*Jennifer Owings Dewey envisions the dragonfly's wings as stained glass windows with sun shining through in Georgia Heard's **Creatures of Earth, Sea, and Sky.***

pleasing pattern. Georgia Heard uses the connotations of stained glass windows to make us think about dragonflies in a new way in *Creatures of Earth, Sea, and Sky:*

DRAGONFLY

It skims the pond's surface
searching for gnats, mosquitoes, and flies.
Outspread wings blur with speed.
It touches down
and stops to sun itself on the dock.
Wings flicker and still:
stained-glass windows
with sun shining through.

GEORGIA HEARD

Good poets make use of poetic devices that help them best express what they are trying to say. Children who hear and read poetry that contains excellent examples of these poetic devices will gradually understand and appreciate the use of such devices as well as expand their language learning. Many will also use these tools in their own writing. Lee Bennett Hopkins has anthologized many works that make use of poetic devices. *A Song in Stone: City Poems* and *Small Talk: A Book of Short Poems* (both P–I) are two of his poetry books that serve as good resources for introducing primary-grade and intermediate students to figurative language. *Songs Are Thoughts: Poems of the Inuit* (P–I), edited by Philip Neil, and *Night Garden: Poems from the World of Dreams* (P–I–A), by Janet S. Wong, also contain figurative language for developing readers and writers to explore. Naomi Shihab Nye offers advanced readers examples of figurative language in *This Same Sky: A Collection of Poems from around the World* (A). Figure 4.2 lists the ways in which poetry promotes language learning.

Poetry Comes in a Variety of Forms

Poetry comes in many forms. Poems look different from prose writing; the visual form, which reflects the poetic form, affects the way we read and comprehend the meaning of a poem. Poetic forms are clearly defined, although poets alter conventional and traditional forms as often as they manipulate word meanings.

Poetry forms include narrative, lyric, free verse, haiku and cinquain, concrete, limerick, ballad, and sonnet. Poets continue to introduce variations: poems for two or more voices, rap, echo voices, and many others. Teachers wisely begin with narrative poetry or with brief, humorous verses, and gradually expose children to a broader range of forms. When teachers expand students' experiences with poetry, they increase children's potential for greater interest and understanding.

• • NARRATIVE POETRY • •

Narrative poetry tells a story. Think about stories from childhood that you first heard through poetry. Perhaps "The Pied Piper of Hamelin," "Casey at Bat," "Hiawatha," "Paul Revere's Ride," or another rhymed story comes to mind. Many children enjoy narrative verse, and this is not surprising—they enjoy and are familiar with stories of all kinds. A book-length narrative poem (one that is longer than a picture book) is called an epic, but most story poems for children are relatively short and relate one or more episodes.

Narrative poetry sets a story with characters, plot, and theme—like any other story—into a poetic framework, which can make even a humble story memorable. A. A. Milne, Henry Wadsworth Longfellow, and Rosemary and Stephen Vincent Benét are known for their narrative poems. Contemporary writers of narrative poems include Jack Prelutsky, Aileen Fisher, and Shel Silverstein.

When poetry is read aloud, the words can truly sing, and listeners may savor the musical quality of the verse. Oral presentations accentuate meaning in narrative poems. Listening to story poems helps children develop an appreciation for the charm of the spoken word and the melody of verse. They learn narrative poems by heart after hearing them a number of times.

Figure 4-2

Poetry Promotes Language Learning

Poetry promotes language learning because it
* Contains highly charged words
* Uses only a few words to say a great deal
* Is melodic; it sings as it says
* Contains rhythm, repetition, and rhyme
* Captures the essence of a concept
* Suggests more than it says
* Has layers of meaning
* Is the natural language of childhood

Profile

HarperCollins Publishers

Barbara Juster Esbensen, 1994

As a child growing up in Madison, Wisconsin, I read everything in sight, and drew pictures on anything that looked like it needed decoration. I wrote stories with my two best friends, and we all intended to be writers. When I was fourteen-and-a-half, my teacher looked at a poem I had written and told me I was "a writer." When she introduced me to poets like Amy Lowell, Stephen Vincent Benét, and Emily Dickinson, she literally changed my life. Until then, I had not known that it was possible to use words in such exciting ways.

What impressed the NCTE Poetry Award Committee about Barbara Juster Esbensen's work was "the clarity of [her] images, the differentness of [her] images" (Greenlaw, 1994, p. 544). When asked if her work as an artist influenced her poetic images, Esbensen said, "I'm sure that I'm looking all the time. I'm sure of that because I am an artist, and that's what I have really been doing all my life. I'm a looker! And I'm an exaggerator . . . I tell children you are allowed to say things that are absolutely off-the-wall in poetry" (p. 544). Esbensen's poetry anthologies for children include *Swing around the Sun, Cold Stars and Fireflies, Words with Wrinkled Knees,* and *Who Shrank My Grandmother's House?*

HarperCollins Publishers

Eloise Greenfield, 1997

There's a desperate need for more Black literature for children, for a large body of literature in which Black children can see themselves and their lives and history reflected. I want to do my share in building it.

Eloise Greenfield has played a significant role in contributing to African American literature in several genres; her poetry books are frequently cited by teachers and scholars. She received ALA Notable citations, the Coretta Scott King Award, and the Mary McLeod Bethune Award for her work, particularly for *Honey, I Love* and *Nathaniel Talking.* "[Greenfield's] poetry reflects or comments on the specific cultural experience of growing up African American in this society," noted Rudine Sims Bishop (1997, p. 632), "but the topics and themes—love, family, neighbors, dreams, the joy of living, the resilience of the human spirit— reach out to all children."

Poets experiment with the narrative form; several books, including Joyce Carol Thomas's *Gingerbread Days, Brown Honey in Broomwheat Tea,* and *I Have Heard of a Land* (all P–I), contain a series of short poems that, taken together, tell a story. Eloise Greenfield contributes narrative poetry in *Night on Neighborhood Street,* as does Nikki Grimes in *Come Sunday* (both P–I). Jack Prelutsky's *The Headless Horseman Rides Tonight* (P–I) is also a classic example of narrative poetry. *Amber Was Brave, Essie Was Smart,* by Vera B. Williams, and *Tales from Gizzard's Grill* (both P–I), by Jeanne Steig, offer additional poetry for children exploring the narrative form. Books like this, plus many beautifully illustrated single editions of narrative poems, are listed in the Booklist at the end of the chapter.

© Curtis Brown, Ltd.

© Helen Neafsey

Profile

X. J. Kennedy, 2000

R hyme and meter have been in the doghouse of adult poetry lately, and some have claimed that children, too, don't like such old-fangled devices. But children do. This makes me glad, for I have never been able to write what is termed free verse. I love the constant surprise one encounters in rhyming things, and the driving urge of a steady beat.

For years, X. J. Kennedy wrote poetry for children but kept it in the bottom drawer of his desk until

For years, X. J. Kennedy wrote poetry for children but kept it in the bottom drawer of his desk until Myra Cohn Livingston asked him to send some of it to her editor, Margaret McElderry. McElderry published his first book of poetry for children, *One Winter Night in August.* Since then, Kennedy has authored more than a dozen collections of verse for children. Daniel L. Darigan (2001) observed, "[Kennedy's] topics are timely and accessible, his use of the language sophisticated, and his humor leads children and adoring adults into a genre that often gets overlooked and ignored. Children who read his collections as well as his anthologies will receive a better understanding of what poetry is and the joys it holds for them" (p. 298).

Mary Ann Hoberman, 2003

V isual language . . . is for writers. So are word games and word play. Just think of what you can do with words . . . [E]ach time you discover the perfect word for your purpose, each time you shape a sentence, each time you awaken a reader's imagination, you will feel fulfilled. (quoted in Ernst & McClure, 2004)

Mary Ann Hoberman is a master of rhyme, rhythm, and wordplay. She began publishing for children in 1957 with *All My Shoes Come in Twos.* Since then, Hoberman has created lasting favorites, including *A House Is a House for Me; Fathers, Mothers, Sisters, Brothers: A Collection of Family Poems;* and *The Llama Who Had No Pajama: 100 Favorite Poems.*

Sources:

Bishop, R. S. (1997). Profile: Eloise Greenfield. *Language Arts, 78,* 630–634.

Darigan, D. L. (2001). NCTE poetry award recipient X. J. Kennedy. *Language Arts, 78,* 295–299.

Ernst, S. B., & McClure, A. A. (2004). A poem is a house for words: NCTE profiles Mary Ann Hoberman. *Language Arts, 81,* 254–259.

Greenlaw, M. J. (1994). Profile: Barbara Juster Esbensen. *Language Arts, 71,* 544–548.

Unless otherwise noted, the opening quotations for these profiles are from the poets' acceptance speeches for the NCTE poetry award. (The speech is given in November of the year the award is received.)

• • LYRIC POETRY • •

Lyric poetry is a statement of mood or feeling. It is probably the type of poetry most children read. It offers a direct and intense outpouring of thoughts and feelings. Any subjective, emotional poem can be called lyric, but most lyric poems are songlike and are expressive of a single mood. As its Greek name indicates, a lyric was originally sung to the accompaniment of a lyre. Lyric poems have a melodic quality to this day; they are songs, as is Eleanor Farjeon's "Morning Has Broken," from her book *The Children's Bells* (P–I):

MORNING HAS BROKEN

Morning has broken
*   like the first morning*
Blackbird has spoken
*   like the first bird.*
Praise for the singing!
*   Praise for the morning!*
Praise for them, springing
*   fresh from the Word!*
Sweet the rain's new fall
*   sunlit from heaven*

Like the first dew fall
*   on the first grass.*
Praise for the sweetness
*   of the wet garden*
Sprung in completeness
*   where His feet pass.*
Mine is the sunlight!
*   Mine is the morning*
Born of the one light
*   Eden saw play!*
Praise with elation
*   praise every morning*
God's re-creation
*   of the new day!*

ELEANOR FARJEON

Many children's poems are lyrical because of their sing-ing quality and their expression of personal feeling. Read and sing lyric poems many times over. Older students with a rich understanding of symbolism have a better apprecia-tion for lyric poetry. Poetry in the lyric mode requires that children trust their own feelings in response to a poem; there is no one right interpretation when it comes to poetry.

Songs are often the first lyric poems children hear. For *Hush Songs: African American Lullabies* (N–P–I), Joyce Carol Thomas collected traditional songs sung by cradling mothers and caring fathers to lull a child to sleep. A sooth-ing melody sung with comforting words works its magic on sleepy children:

ALL THE PRETTY
LITTLE HORSES

Hush-a-bye
Don't you cry
Go to sleep
My little baby

When you wake
You shall have
All the pretty little horses

TRADITIONAL LULLABY

Walter Dean Myers captures the feelings and emotions of Harlem residents during the 1940s in *Here in Harlem* (I–A), an excellent example of lyric poetry for advanced readers. Myers' descriptions of the pride, heartache, aspira-tion, determination, and elation felt by the people of Harlem resonate in the text; his words depict an emotional world in which the experiences of individuals shout—and sometimes whisper—across borders of time, speaking directly to modern readers' sensitivities. Eloise Greenfield offers primary-grade students lyric poetry in *Honey, I Love*

© 2004 Holiday House

Walter Dean Myers captures emotion in **Here in Harlem: Poems in Many Voices.**

and Other Love Poems (P–I). Additional collections of lyric poetry are listed in the Booklist at the end of this chapter.

• • FREE VERSE • •

Free verse is unrhymed verse with an irregular pattern or no visible metrical pattern. Elements that distinguish free verse include its arrangement on the page, the essence of its sub-ject, and the density of thought. Teachers who encourage children to write in free verse help them avoid some of the difficulties of trying to rhyme.

In *Fold Me a Poem* (P–I), Kristine O'Connell George composes a series of free verse poems about a clever young boy who creates origami animals. After creasing colorful sheets of square paper into a rooster, a buffalo, a camel, a robin, a green dog, a crow, a cheetah, and a lion, George's character wonders what creature will next appear:

POSSIBILITIES

Forty bright sheets
of colored paper,
a world of animals.
Who will be next?

KRISTINE O'CONNELL GEORGE

George's form is succinct and unfettered by meter; her free verse structure reflects the openness of the artistic boy's imagination. Readers soon learn that a frog jumps into the boy's mind:

POND

My lily pad
will not
need a
flower.

It has
a frog.

KRISTINE O'CONNELL GEORGE

With Lauren Stringer's expressive origami-animal illustrations that almost leap off the page, *Fold Me a Poem* demonstrates how stimulating free verse can be for young readers.

Arnold Adoff is another master of free verse. He offers several anthologies of original work for young readers, including *Black Is Brown Is Tan, Eats: Poems,* and *In for Winter, Out for Spring* (all P–I). Two collections by Gary Soto, *Fire in My Hands* and *Neighborhood Odes* (both A), also contain poems written in free verse. Although children may initially prefer rhymed, metered poetry, they learn to appreciate free verse when they see it, say it, hear it, and experiment with writing it. The Booklist at the end of the chapter cites additional examples of free verse, and Teaching Idea 4.3 offers suggestions for exploring line breaks in free verse with students.

• • HAIKU AND CINQUAIN • •

The word *haiku* means "beginning." Haiku frequently refers to nature, to a particular event happening at one moment, and to an attendant emotion or feeling, often of the most fragile and evanescent kind. This Japanese verse form consists of three lines and seventeen syllables: the first line contains five syllables; the second line, seven; and the third, five. A haiku usually focuses on an image that suggests a thought or emotion. Students experimenting with the form should not stress counting syllables; instead they should feel free to think about the meaning they want to convey. Paul Janeczko notes that haiku often features nature in rural areas, but he sought out haiku that shows the natural beauty of everyday city streets in his collection *Stone Bench*

*Origami animals seem to move across the pages of Kristine O'Connell George's **Fold Me a Poem,** illustrated by Lauren Stringer.*

Teaching Idea 4-3

Break It Up! Exploring Line Breaks in Free Verse Poetry

Line breaks in free verse poems are precise and purposeful; each break helps the reader understand something about the poem (Livingston, 1991; Heard, 1989). Help both primary and more advanced students explore how poets use line breaks to communicate meaning in free verse poems by giving them the opportunity to arrange (and rearrange) the words of a free verse poem in ways that make sense to them. The following steps are adaptations of excellent teaching ideas presented by Georgia Heard (1989) in *For the Good of the Earth and Sun: Teaching Poetry* and by Myra Cohn Livingston (1991) in *Poem-Making: Ways to Begin Writing Poems:*

Before the Lesson

✳ Select a free verse poem that describes an experience you can easily help students visualize.

✳ Record the poem on a piece of large chart paper.

✳ Record each word of the poem on an index card and number each of the cards. (For primary-grade students learning to decode print, you may want to cut around the outline of each word to highlight the prominent features of letters.)

During the Lesson

✳ Sit with students in a circle. (Younger students usually enjoy sitting on the floor; older students may prefer to gather their chairs in a circle.)

✳ Have students close their eyes as you lead them in visualizing the experience depicted in the poem (Heard, 1989). Be sure to use descriptive words that will help them see, hear, and touch the subject of the poem. It's important that students get a sense of the subject's mood, motion, sound, and so on.

✳ After they have visualized the experience described in the poem, tell students that a poet has used free verse to capture the experience.

✳ Lay out the index cards containing the words of the poem in a continuous line in the center of the circle. Challenge students to keep the words in sequential order while arranging them in a way that will capture their visualized experience. For example, if the poem is about a person feeling lonely, students may choose to put the word *lonely* by itself in a line to emphasize the meaning of the word and the mood of the poem.

✳ As students take turns arranging the index cards with line breaks, encourage them to be thoughtful about their choices; ask them to explain how their choices capture the meaning of the poem.

✳ Encourage students to think innovatively—get excited about their poetic decisions! Praise students when they "think like poets"; wink and tell them they must be "kindred spirits" with the poet when they make decisions that reflect the poem's published form. This will spark a surge of creativity in the room. Your circle will become more of a cluster as students find being close to the words irresistible!

✳ Participate, and model revision. Talk out loud as you consider and reconsider your own line break choices; rearrange "your" index cards to reflect more clearly what the class considers to be the essence of the poem's subject.

✳ After all the index cards have been arranged, read the poem and discuss how the line breaks convey in form what the poet describes in words.

✳ Ask students if they would like to see what line break decisions the poet made when composing the poem. Reveal (dramatically, if possible!) the poem as you printed it on the piece of large chart paper.

✳ Discuss how the poet made line break decisions that were both similar to and different from the decisions the class made. Talk about how both the poet and the class made their decisions based on how line breaks convey meaning in free verse poetry.

After the Lesson

✳ Encourage students to record the words of their own free verse poems on note cards.

✳ Provide students with time to practice using line breaks purposefully to help readers understand their poems.

Resources for Teaching about Line Breaks

Livingston, Myra Cohn, *Poem-Making: Ways to Begin Writing Poems*

Heard, Georgia, *For the Good of the Earth and Sun: Teaching Poetry in an Empty Park* (A). Selected poems include these by Jane Yolen and Anita Wintz:

> *Pigeons strut the rails*
> *Of the city reservoir*
> *Doing a rain dance.*

JANE YOLEN

> *from the tar papered*
>   *tenement roof, pigeons*
>   *hot-foot it into flight.*

ANITA WINTZ

These two haiku by David McCord appear in his collection *One at a Time:*

> *Take the butterfly:*
> *Nature works to produce him.*
> *Why doesn't he last?*

> *All these skyscrapers!*
> *What will man do about them*
> *When they have to go?*

DAVID MCCORD

Poets who master the haiku form sometimes stretch its boundaries by varying the five-seven-five syllable count while maintaining the essence of its meaning. Issa, a noted Japanese poet, demonstrates in *Don't Tell the Scarecrow* (I) the beauty of haiku in these two variations:

> *Where can he be going*
>   *In the rain,*
>   *This snail?*

> *Little knowing*
> *The tree will soon be cut down*
> *Birds are building their nests in it.*

ISSA

Striking black-and-white photos add their lyric perspective to city life in Paul Janeczko's book of selected haiku.

Although haiku is a favorite with teachers, Terry's study of children's preferences in poetry (1974) suggested that it was not always a favorite with students—a signal for teachers to handle it with care. Teachers who want to know the essence of haiku need to read ***Wind in My Hand: The Story of Issa, Japanese Haiku Poet*** (I), by Hanako Fukuda. Collections of haiku by Issa, cited in the Booklist at the end of this chapter, provide examples for students. Other poetry books that help young readers explore haiku include Sylvia Cassedy's ***Red Dragonfly on My Shoulder*** and Nikki Grimes's ***Pocketful of Poems*** (both P–I).

A cinquain consists of five unrhymed lines usually in the pattern of two, four, six, eight words, and two syllables in the fifth line. A simplified variation has five lines with one, two, three, four words, with the fifth line just one word that is a synonym for the title. The pattern is as follows:

Line 1: One word, the title, usually a noun

Line 2: Two words describing the title

Line 3: Three words that show action

Line 4: Four words that show feeling or emotion

Line 5: One word, a synonym for the title

The following cinquains are variations that nine-year-old students wrote after studying the form:

SNIFFLES AND SNEEZES

Coughing
Sneezing a lot
Missing school, missing friends
I would feel bad at home a lot
Feel bored

ROY STUDNESS

WHERE I LIVE

Port Washington
Sleepy village
Busy and growing
Nice place to be
Home

JASON REAM

Haiku and cinquain are probably the most abstract poetry that children will experience. Because the symbolism

*Chris Raschka's torn-paper illustrations add whimsy to Paul Janeczko's collection of concrete poems in **A Poke in the I.***

and imagery of haiku and cinquain are elusive for many children, students need to have wide exposure to other forms before they meet these. Even then, they need a lot of experience exploring the form.

• • CONCRETE POETRY • •

Concrete poetry uses the appearance of words on a page to suggest or illustrate the poem's meaning. Children call these poems *shape* (or picture) *poems.* The actual physical form of the words depicts the subject, so the work illustrates it-self, as shown in Maureen W. Joan Bransfield Graham's "Popsicle."

"Popsicle," along with many other examples of shape poems, appears in Paul Janeczko's indispensable *A Poke in the I: A Collection of Concrete Poems* (P–I). *Doodle Dandies: Poems That Take Shape,* by J. Patrick Lewis, and *Splish Splash,* by Joan Bransfield Graham (both P–I), are also must-have resources for young readers discovering concrete poems.

• • LIMERICKS • •

Limerick, a form of light verse, has five lines and a rhyme scheme of a-a-b-b-a. The first, second, and fifth lines (which rhyme) have three feet (in poetic meter), whereas the third and fourth (which rhyme) have two feet.

Limericks appeal to children because they poke fun and have a definite rhythm and rhyme. Edward Lear (1812–1888) is credited with making limericks popular, although he did not create the form. Limericks often make fun of people who take themselves too seriously. James Marshall's *Pocketful of Nonsense* (P–I) pokes fun through words and illustration:

> *There was an old man of Peru*
> *who dreamed he was eating his shoe.*
> *He woke in the night*
> *In a terrible fright*
> *and found it was perfectly true.*

JAMES MARSHALL

Students with a good sense of humor devour limericks. Some limericks have become folklore; their original author-ship is forgotten. One such is

> *A flea and a fly in a flue*
> *Were imprisoned, so what could they do?*
> *Said the fly, "Let us flee."*
> *Said the flea, "Let us fly."*
> *So they flew through a flaw in the flue.*

ANONYMOUS

In **Pocketful of Nonsense,** *James Marshall's art spoofs the ridiculous situation described in the limerick.*

Children laugh at the nonsense primarily because the verses play with the idiosyncrasies of language; limericks encapsulate a joyful absurdity. Many children enjoy Myra Cohn Livingston's *Lots of Limericks* and Arnold Lobel's *The Book of Pigericks* (both P–I). These and other collections of limericks are included in the Booklist at the end of the chapter.

• • BALLADS • •

A ballad is a story told in verse; it is often sung. Regular bal-lads, long ballads, and short ballads vary in pattern and rhyme scheme. A regular ballad has a four-line stanza in which lines one and three are iambic tetrameter (four sets of da DA) and lines two and four are iambic trimeter (three sets of da DA). The rhyme scheme is generally a-b-a-b (first and third lines end in a rhyme; second and fourth lines end in a rhyme) or a-b-c-b (only the second and fourth lines end in a rhyme). A long ballad is like a regular ballad except that every line has four feet (4, 4, 4, 4) instead of alternating (4, 3, 4, 3). Like the regular ballad, its rhymes may occur on the second and fourth lines (designated as a-b-c-b) and can rhyme on the first and third lines as well (a-b-a-b). Ballads are frequently written in couplets (a-a-b-b). Pat Lessie reinterprets Aesop's fables in *Fablesauce: Aesop Reinterpreted in Rhymed Couplets* (I). Christina Rossetti uses the short ballad form (the number of feet per line is 3, 3, 4, 3; the rhyme scheme is a-b-c-b) in "Who Has Seen the Wind?"

> Who has seen the wind?
> Neither I nor you;
> But when the leaves hang trembling
> The wind is passing thro'.
>
> Who has seen the wind?
> Neither you nor I
> But when the trees bow down their heads
> The wind is passing by.

CHRISTINA ROSSETTI

Ballads are lyrical and tell a story relating a single incident or thought. Some poets use dialogue to tell a story in repeated refrains. Myra Cohn Livingston's *Abraham Lincoln: A Man for All the People* (P–I) extols the trials and tribulations of Lincoln's life. Livingston's *Keep on Singing: A Ballad of Marion Anderson* (P–I) focuses on the triumphs of the great singer.

There are folk ballads and literary ballads. Folk ballads have no known author; they have become anonymous and are handed down in song. "John Henry" is a well-known folk ballad. Modern vocalists, such as Beth Orton, Tracy Chapman, Van Morrison, James Taylor, k.d. lang, and Paul Simon express themselves through ballads.

Generally, ballads sing of heroic deeds and of murder, unrequited love, and feuds. Carl Sandburg's *The American Songbag* (A) is a classic collection of the ballads of railroad builders, lumberjacks, and cowboys. Ernest Lawrence Thayer's *Casey at the Bat* (I) is a ballad young readers enjoy. It begins

> The outlook wasn't brilliant for the Mudville nine
>   that day:
> The score stood four to two, with but one inning more
>   to play,
> And then when Cooney died at first, and Barrows did
>   the same,
> A pall-like silence fell upon the patrons of the game.
>
> A straggling few got up to go in deep despair. The rest
> Clung to that hope which springs eternal in the
>   human breast;
> They thought, "If only Case could but get a whack
>   at that—
> We'd put up even money now, with Casey at the bat."

ERNEST LAWRENCE THAYER

Ballads are listed in the Booklist at the end of the chapter.

• • RIDDLE POEMS • •

Students nurtured on poetry have meaningful experiences with complicated poetic forms like ballads, but many prefer simpler riddle poems. J. Patrick Lewis and Elizabeth Spires have contributed excellent material for riddle lovers. In *Riddle-Lightful* (P–I), Lewis says, "The middle of table / The end of a tub /// In front of a battleship / In back of a sub /// A bus to start off with / A cab at the end /// I hope you will be my / B-you-tiful friend." (Answer: the letter *b*.) In *Riddle Road: Puzzles in Poems and Pictures* (P–I), Spires tells us, "I eat words wherever/I find them but am no wiser,/Keep your books under lock and key/or they'll be devoured by me! (Answer: bookworm). Students enjoy creating their own riddles and delight in asking others to guess the answer. Riddle poems are listed in the Booklist at the end of the chapter.

• • NOVELS IN VERSE • •

Several authors have recognized that using line breaks and poetic language helps them write compelling and evocative novels. A novel in verse is a collection of poems that when read sequentially conveys the plot, setting, and characterization of an intricate story. Karen Hesse won the 1998 Newbery Award for *Out of the Dust* (A), a stirring novel in verse about the hardships of life on the Great Plains during the Great Depression. Also written in verse, Hesse's *Witness* (A) describes the racial tensions that existed in New England during the 1920s. Lindsay Lee Johnson's *Soul Moon Soup* (I–A) depicts through poetry the struggles of a contemporary protagonist, as does *Locomotion* (A), by Jacqueline Woodson. *Love That Dog* (I), by Sharon Creech, *Shakespeare Bats Cleanup* (A), by Ron Koertge, and *Bronx Masquerade* (A), by Nikki Grimes, all present young narrators who uncover the power of poetry in their lives. The Booklist at the end of this chapter includes novels in verse you might consider adding to your classroom poetry collection.

Building a Poetry Collection

Teachers need to build their own poetry collection to fit their curriculum and their students. Poetry books come in different formats and sizes. Some poems are published in a single volume with beautiful illustrations; such books provide a good opportunity to explore excellent poetry accompanied by fine artists' work. Teachers need anthologies in order to provide their students with a variety of poems and yet hold their collections to manageable sizes. It is easy to locate a poem in a themed anthology with subject, title, author, and first-line indexes.

Anthologies are particularly useful in the classroom. The specialized anthology, with works by several poets on one subject; the generalized anthology, with works by many poets on many subjects; and the individual anthology, which contains the works of only one poet, all allow young readers to browse through poetry and discover favorites. Teachers find anthologies useful for incorporating poetry across the curriculum.

Specialized anthologies are popular. The plethora of collections of poems and verses about holidays, monsters, dinosaurs, horses, sports, and other special topics bears witness to this. Three excellent anthologists, Lee Bennett Hopkins, Paul Janeczko, and Jane Yolen, add immeasurably to the wealth of resources. Lee Bennett Hopkins has collected more than 100 specialized anthologies from easy-to-read verse to poetry by Carl Sandburg and Langston Hughes. Among his most popular collections are *Good Books, Good Times!* (P–I), *Hand in Hand: An American History through Poetry* (I), *Side by Side: Poems to Read Together* (P–I), and *My America: A Poetry Atlas of the United States* (I–A). Paul Janeczko has collected many specialized anthologies, such as *The Music of What Happens, Poetspeak, The Place My Words Are Looking For, Poetry from A to Z, Brickyard Summer,* and *Wherever Home Begins* (all I–A), as well as *I Feel a Little Jumpy around You* (A), coedited with Naomi Shihab Nye. Janeczko's individual anthologies include *Stardust Otel* (A) and *That Sweet Diamond: Baseball Poems* (I). Jane Yolen gives us a multicultural collection in *Street Rhymes around the World* (P–I). She presents her own poetry along with that of others in *Alphabestiary* (P–I), *Sky Scrape/City Scape* (P–I–A), *Water Music* (I), *Weather Report* (I), *Color Me a Rhyme* (P–I), *Snow, Snow* (I), *Mother Earth Father Sky* (I), and *Once upon Ice and Other Frozen Poems* (I). Jane Yolen has produced numerous individual and collective anthologies that enrich our poetry resources.

Alvin Schwartz uses a different kind of theme to organize his anthology *And the Green Grass Grew All Around* (P–I–A). This collection of more than 250 folk poems contains autograph rhymes, work poems, story poems, nonsense, and much more. The Booklist at the end of the chapter lists specialized anthologies.

A traditional generalized poetry anthology, *The Scott, Foresman Anthology of Children's Literature* (1983), is a comprehensive volume with verse on many subjects. Best-loved poems of childhood include those about people, animals, adventures, games, jokes, magic and make-believe, wind and water, holidays and seasons, and wisdom and beauty. Anthologies help librarians and teachers make poetry central to children's lives. Two books by X. J. Kennedy and Dorothy Kennedy, *Talking Like the Rain* (P–I) and *Knock at a Star: A Child's Introduction to Poetry* (I), contain poems arranged under informative headings. The books are a pleasure to skim, read, or savor. Several general anthologies are listed in the Booklist at the end of the chapter.

David McCord's book *One at a Time* (P–I) is an individual anthology composed solely of his work. An impressive volume, it is a collection of most of his poetry. McCord's wit and thoughtful perception sing in the music of his words. *One at a Time* is a timeless resource to use for cultivating poetic taste and for encouraging children to read poetry for pleasure. See the Booklist at the end of the chapter for general and individual anthologies.

All teachers and groups of students have personal favorite anthologies they like to use. We believe some poets' works are basic to the curriculum. These are listed in the Booklist; the level designations should be considered flexible. Poetry, especially, appeals to a wide age range.

Reading reviews in professional journals and noting the winners of the NCTE poetry award will keep you up-to-date on poetry for children. Being familiar with the body of work of the award-winning poets is a prerequisite for building a sound poetry curriculum in the classroom.

As described earlier, Cullinan conducted a national survey of 3,500 students to find out which poems among the award-winning poets' work they liked best. Children's top five favorites from each poet appear in *A Jar of Tiny Stars: Poems by NCTE Award-Winning Poets* (I–A). Cullinan also conducted a similar survey of Aileen Fisher's poetry. Published in 2001, the book is titled *Sing of the Earth and Sky: Poems about Our Planet and the Wonders Beyond* (P–I).

Using Poetry in the Classroom

• • ENCOURAGE STUDENTS • •
TO EXPLORE POETRY

The first thing you need to do to create student poetry lovers is to love it yourself. Students will like what you like. Students need to feel comfortable using the books you have gathered; talk about the books and display their covers to attract readers. Shelve poetry with other books by the same author or the same subject. Your students need time and space to browse, to pull out several volumes at once, and to compare poems or look for favorites. Having tape recorders close by will stimulate oral interpretation of favorite poems. Give students time to browse through the poetry collection during a free period or to look up a poem for a particular occasion or for independent reading. Allowing and encouraging students to enjoy poetry together, and to talk quietly while doing so, forges strong bonds in a community of readers. It also helps students learn how to read poetry and increases their contact with poetry and poets. Teaching Idea 4.4

Teaching Idea 4-4

Celebrate with Poetry

Whatever the occasion, celebrate with poetry—it captures the right feeling. Celebrate a holiday, the season, the weather, writers, and poets. Poems make celebrations special and memorable.

Celebrate Holidays

Hopkins, Lee Bennett, *Good Morning to You, Valentine* (P)

_____, *My America* (P–I–A)

_____, *Ring Out, Wild Bells: Poems about Holidays and Seasons* (P–I)

Katz, Bobbi, *We the People* (P–I–A)

Livingston, Myra Cohn, *Halloween Poems* (P)

Moore, Clement C., *The Night before Christmas* (P)

Yolen, Jane, *Best Witches: Poems for Halloween* (I)

Celebrate the Seasons

Adoff, Arnold, *In for Winter, Out for Spring* (P–I)

Bruchac, Joseph, *Thirteen Moons on Turtle's Back: A Native American Year of Moons* (I)

Frost, Robert, *Poetry for Young People* (I–A)

Hopkins, Lee Bennett, *Easter Buds Are Springing* (P)

Jacobs, Leland B., *Just around the Corner: Poems about the Seasons* (P–I)

Morrison, Lillian, *Whistling the Morning In* (I)

Singer, Marilyn, *Turtle in July* (P–I)

Thomas, Joyce Carol, *Gingerbread Days* (P)

Turner, Ann, *Moon for Seasons* (P–I)

Updike, John, *A Child's Calendar* (I)

Yolen, Jane, *Weather Report* (I)

Celebrate Families

Adoff, Arnold, *Black Is Brown Is Tan* (P–I)

Hopkins, Lee Bennett, *Been to Yesterdays: Poems of a Life* (P–I–A)

Livingston, Myra Cohn, *Poems for Mothers* (P–I)

Merriam, Eve, *Daddies at Work* (P)

_____, *You Be Good and I'll Be Night* (P)

Smith, William Jay, *Around My Room and Other Poems* (P–I)

Stevenson, James, *Sweet Corn: Poems* (I)

Strickland, Dorothy, and Michael Strickland, *Families: Poems Celebrating the African American Experience* (I–A)

Strickland, Michael, *Haircuts at Sleepy Sam's* (P–I)

---

offers some suggestions for celebrating with poetry in the classroom.

Children learn to love poetry when they are allowed to explore it freely. Unfortunately, some learn to dislike poetry because a teacher insists they search for elusive meanings or rhyme schemes that make no sense to them. Close attention to children's comments can supply a basis for thought-provoking questions that will lead children to discover the substance of poetry for themselves. The object is to develop a child's liking for the music of words; detailed analysis detracts from the splendor of poetry. Explanation that destroys appreciation is no improvement over misconceptions. The magic that words can exercise on the imagination is more valuable than accuracy at the beginning stages. Appropriate discussions of poetry take children back into a poem, not away from it.

A love of poetry is contagious. The way you read and respond to poetry has a tremendous effect on the way students read and respond. If students see you enjoy poetry, they will be more likely to approach poetry with the expectation of joy. If you turn to poetry to illustrate the multicultural nature of our world—reading, for example, Isaac Olaleye's *The Distant Talking Drum* (I)—students will be more likely to do the same. If they see you making connections to real experiences and feelings, they will be more likely to make poetry connections. Perhaps the most important thing that teachers can do with poetry is to make a human connection with a poet's words.

Two books, *Salting the Ocean: 100 Poems by Young Poets* (I–A) and *What Have You Lost?* (A), show the results of Naomi Shihab Nye's work with young people. She exposed students to excellent poetry and helped them release their thoughts and feelings in poetry.

> ONE
>
> *We had a*
> *"Most commonly misspelled word"*
> *Spelling test*
> *Yesterday in English*
> *Fourth Period.*

I commonly misspelled them all.
   Except one.
   Loneliness
Was the only one I got right.

BUTCH MCELROY

Poems for two voices make good material for choral reading. Divide students into groups to read from Paul Fleischman's books *Joyful Noise: Poems for Two Voices, I Am Phoenix,* and *Big Talk: Poems for Four Voices* (all I–A). Also use Georgia Heard's poems for two voices in *Creatures of Earth, Sea, and Sky* (I). Teaching Idea 4.5 offers more ideas for enjoying poetry with students.

Teaching Idea 4-5

Play with Poetry: Act It Out

Students like to perform poetry if we make it fun and nonthreatening. Here are some steps to follow:

* First, perform the poem—model it for students.

* Next, invite students to recite the poem as a group.

* Then invite individuals to say parts of the poem.

* Finally, ask individuals to recite the poems of their own choosing.

At all stages, students should hold a copy of the poem in their hands—to use or not use as they choose. Tell children to relax and let their faces and bodies convey the emotions of a poem. How they feel is how they should look.

Books of Poems to Dramatize

All books and poems are appropriate for primary–intermediate–advanced readers.

Bagert, Brod, *Let Me Be the Boss*

Ciardi, John, *Mummy Slept Late and Daddy Fixed Breakfast*

Esbensen, Barbara, *Words with Wrinkled Knees*

Fleischman, Paul, *I Am Phoenix: Poems for Two Voices*

_____, *Joyful Noise: Poems for Two Voices*

Gunning, Monica, *Not a Copper in Me House*

Olaleye, Isaac, *The Distant Talking Drum*

Spilka, Arnold, *Monkeys Write Terrible Letters*

Springer, Nancy, *Music of Their Hooves*

Thayer, Ernest L., *Casey at the Bat: A Centennial Edition*

Students explore how poetry works by examining what poets do, and they like to experiment with poetry in their own writing. Provide opportunities for students to play with various poetic forms, elements, and devices to help them understand and enjoy a variety of poetry.

Children enjoy collecting their own favorite poetry and copying it onto Post-its, file cards, or notebooks. Primary-grade teachers put favorite poems on charts to be read over and over; teachers of intermediate and advanced grades encourage students to create individual anthologies of favorite poems, adding to them throughout the year. Students illustrate their anthologies, some with their own art, photographs, or pictures cut from magazines. Personal anthologies become part of the classroom library so that peers read and discuss each other's favorites. As anthologies grow, students experiment with classifying the contents.

When poetry is a part of the daily life of the classroom, children spontaneously learn their favorite poems by heart. Do not require them to memorize and recite poems. Instead, casually recite your own favorites and invite your students to do the same. They will soon be eager to share a poem with others. We also discuss using poetry in the classroom in Chapter 14.

• • IMMERSE STUDENTS • • IN POETRY

Immerse, or as poet Ralph Fletcher (2000) says, "marinate" students in poetry. Begin with poems that research shows to be favorites: humorous poems and narrative poems with strong rhyme, rhythm, and sound elements. Gradually expand children's experiences with poetry by exposing them to a broad range of forms. As students hear and read poetry, encourage them to experiment with oral interpretation, such as paired reading, choral reading, choral speaking, and dramatization.

Teachers who want their students to develop an appreciation for poetry immerse them in it. They collect poems that they and their students like; they read them aloud several times a day, put poems on charts for group reading, and sprinkle poetry throughout the curriculum. Teaching Idea 4.6 presents some ideas for integrating science and poetry.

Poetry is best understood when it is read aloud. Children who hear poetry read aloud and read it aloud themselves discover more about poetry. Children need to understand how to read this new style of written language. Work with your students to teach them how to read poetry aloud; it is not the same as reading prose. Illustrate the differences by reading poetry aloud in a number of ways. Read it by pausing at the end of every line regardless of the punctuation. Then read it from a prose format to demonstrate the impact of punctuation.

Remember that we communicate our own expectations through body language, gestures, and how and what we say. If a teacher reads poems in a spirited, enthusiastic manner, children respond positively. If the reader is boring, children are bored. Demonstrate the effect of bad readings: Read poetry in a sing-song fashion. Read it in an icky sweet "poetry voice." Then read it to interpret the meaning. Work with poetry can link the experiences of listening, oral interpretation, silent reading, and writing. Experiences with poetry build on each other. Listening to a poem read aloud well brings

Teaching Idea 4-6

Integrate Science and Poetry

Acquaint students with unrhymed verse by reading several poems from Georgia Heard's *Creatures of Earth, Sea, and Sky* (I) and Pat Moon's *Earth Lines: Poems for the Green Age* (I). Such poems put students in a poetry mood and give them a sense of the poets' concern for the environment. Reread the poems and talk about the poems and the issues they raise.

When students complete informational reports about a science subject, ask them to think about their topic in a poetic way. You can help them do so by doing the following:

✳ Read many examples of science poetry and discuss them.

✳ Ask students to go back to their reports and think as poets about the topic of their report.

✳ Ask them to find five facts about the subject in their report, and write those five facts down.

✳ Explain to students that the five facts are the essence of their subject. That's what poetry is—the essence—the distilled substance of a subject.

✳ Ask students to put the five facts into phrases, and to write them out on the page in different ways, with different line breaks. Ask them to consider how the words look and how they sound.

✳ Then have students share their writing in small groups and revise their work. They can publish their science poems in any manner that makes sense.

Source: The child-written examples came from Marilyn Scala's students. Developed by Marilyn Scala, Munsey Park School, Manhasset, NY.

① Horshoe crabs have been around for 400 millions

② They are called living fossils

③ There reletives are also very old

④ They eat small plants and animals

⑤ They molt

⑥ When babies get to big for there shell they molt

⊗ Horshoe crabs have been around for 400 million years because they haven't been hunted for any part of there body. Also they are called living fossils because they have around since the dinous. Also those reletive the spider crab has been around for so long because they haven't been tampered with either.

The Fossil of the Sea

Horseshoe crabs
have been around
for 400 million years,
because they haven't
been hunted for any part of their body.
They are called

LIVING FOSSILS

because they have been around since the

DINOS!!!

Their relatives, the
spider crabs,
have been around for so long,
because they haven't been
tampered with either.

Pat Turano

insight into how poetry works, what a poem might mean to another reader, techniques for oral interpretation, and strategies for reading that can be employed silently. Before reading a poem aloud to an audience, practice by reading it aloud to yourself several times to get the feel of the words and rhythm, reading in your natural voice. Pay attention to line breaks, but pause when you need to in order to make sense. That is, emphasize the meaning with your voice.

Poetry, perhaps more than any other genre, must be explored through both oral and written language activities. Choral reading can help students discover how important sound is to many poems as they experiment with different approaches and explore how pitch, stress, and rate influence the overall effect of the poem. These experiences can lead naturally to discussions of rhythm and other elements of sound. The rhythm of poetry is a natural springboard into movement. Young children will spontaneously move to the beat of highly metrical poetry, and older children can be encouraged to clap or tap pencils as they hear the beat in the poems they read. These experiences can lead to discussions of variations in rhythm, how rhythm contributes to meaning and overall effect, and word choice in relation to rhythm.

Drawing pictures in response to poems can help children formulate their own meanings. Poems that are rich in figurative language can lead to discussions of metaphor, simile, and imagery. Discussions of "how" a poem means can spring naturally from discussions of "what" a poem means to individual readers, especially when these readers are writers as well.

Writing poetry also helps children appreciate how poetry works and is best accomplished by building on a firm foundation of reading and listening experiences. Poetry writers read poetry with greater understanding. Children who read a lot of poetry will want to try writing it themselves. In the introduction to *Dogs and Dragons, Trees and Dreams* (1), Karla Kuskin says

The poetry reader often becomes a poetry writer. What could be better? No imagination is freer than a child's; no eye is sharper. The conversation of young children is a constant reminder that they are natural poets. But fitting unrestrained thoughts into rigid forms can be discouraging and may cramp the eccentric voice that makes a child's work (any work) unique. Read rhymes to children, but encourage them, as they begin to write, to write without rhyming. To write any way at all. And to read every thing, anything . . . more poetry. (1980, unpaged)

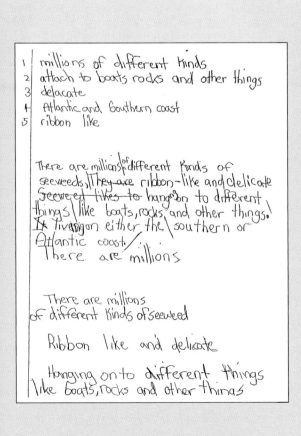

There are Millions

There are millions
Of different kinds of seaweed,

Ribbon-like and delicate,

Hanging on to different things
Like boats, rocks and pinkish shells,

Living on either

The southern or Atlantic coasts.

There are
millions.

Cathy Perifimos

Creative teachers find many ways to immerse children in poetry. One group of primary-grade teachers noticed their students' interest in studying weather and asked, "Why not have a poetic weather report as well as one based on meteorology?" The teachers assigned a poetry reporter to select a poem that best expressed the foggy, sunny, windy, snowy, or rainy day; the poems extended the meaning of the weather symbols attached to the classroom calendar. Talented poet Jane Yolen makes their search easier with *Weather Report* (P–I), a collection of poems about fog, rain, snow, wind, and sun.

Poets themselves have good suggestions for aspiring poets. When Eve Merriam accepted the NCTE poetry award, she encouraged children with these words:

Read a lot. Sit down with anthologies and decide which pleases you. Copy out your favorites in your own handwriting. Buy a notebook and jot down images and descriptions. Be specific; use all the senses. Use your whole body as you write. It might even help sometime to stand up and move with your words. Don't be afraid of copying a form or convention, especially in the beginning. And, to give yourself scope and flexibility, remember: It doesn't always have to rhyme.

You don't need gimmicks, elaborate plans, or detailed instructions. You do need lots of poetry books, time to savor them, and pleasurable poetry experiences. Teaching Idea 4.7 contains suggestions for helping students become poets.

Teaching Idea 4-7

Fifteen Minutes, Fifty Poems!

Teachers who write poetry have students who write poetry. Let them see you write! This teaching idea is perfect for those fifteen-minute intervals between specials or as a warm-up activity before a language arts lesson. Teachers find that it works well with both primary and more advanced students.

Before the Lesson

✳ Be sure each student has a poetry notebook (a blank composition notebook) and a pencil.

✳ Prepare a poetry notebook for yourself as well.

✳ Place an overhead projector in a location where all students will be able to see its projection from their desks.

During the Lesson

✳ Invite students to sit at their desks with their poetry notebooks and pencils.

✳ Dim the lights to create a "writing" mood.

✳ Tell students that you have a poem on your mind; invite them to watch as you try to capture it in words.

✳ Talk out loud as you project your writing on the overhead projector. Scribble out words. Sketch ideas in the margins. Consider line breaks and talk about how you will use them to convey meaning.

✳ Keep writing, even if you are not sure what words will come next. Remember, you are modeling for students what to do if they become "stuck" while writing. Demonstrate how to play with language until your words match your thoughts.

✳ Stop at a point when you are visibly excited about what you will next compose. Tell students that your poem simply cannot wait to emerge on paper and that you must spend the next 10 minutes writing silently in your poetry notebook.

✳ Invite your students to write poems in their poetry notebooks as you write in yours.

✳ Continue writing in your poetry notebook as students work independently. It will be tempting to circulate to observe students at work, but students need to observe *you* writing. When they glance up from their notebooks during moments of frustration, they will need to see that their teacher is a writer—and that writers persevere, even when the words do not come easily. They will also need to see you smile to yourself when you write something "really good"; they will do the same when they write words that please them. Your actions teach your students how to *be* poets—keep your pencil moving!

After the Lesson

✳ When students ask you (and they most likely will) if they can bring their poetry notebooks outside for recess or home for the weekend, say yes! Your 15 minutes of modeling will lead students to create a multitude of poems that they may share with you, with friends, or with the class. The more you model, the more your students will write. The more poems your students write, the more poetic devices and forms they will notice in the poems they read. It is a cycle that sweeps children into exploring and experimenting with language. Teachers have the power to set the cycle in motion.

Resources for Teachers

Graves, Donald, *Explore Poetry: The Reading/Writing Teacher's Companion*

Grossman, Florence, *Listening to the Bells: Learning to Read Poetry by Writing Poetry*

McClure, Amy, with Peggy Harrison and Sheryl Reed, *Sunrises and Songs: Reading and Writing Poetry in an Elementary Classroom*

Poetry is a valuable tool for fully realizing life's many and varied experiences. It allows us to participate in the imaginative experience of others and thereby better understand our own experiences. The more readers participate, the more they create, and the more personal and enjoyable the experience of poetry becomes. The rewards are more than worth the effort.

Summary

Listening to, reading, and writing poetry helps us learn about the world, about ourselves, and about the power and potential of language. Poems make us smile, create memorable images, and express feelings in an understandable way. Poets use devices of sound, rhythm, and meaning to present their own unique visions. Poetry comes in varied forms and is available in many formats. Children are attracted to poetry, and teachers can build on this attraction, providing experiences with poetry that will lead children to enjoy poetry and thus to consider how poetry works. Children who experience a poetry-rich environment will become lifelong readers and writers of poetry.

Read the tribute to David McCord in the November/ December 2001 issue of *The Horn Book Magazine*. Add to your knowledge of McCord and other poets you enjoy by using the reference aids presented in Appendix B and by discovering resources on the World Wide Web.

Watch the video segment in which Lindsay Lee Johnson discusses her verse novel, **Soul Moon Soup**. In this interview Johnson talks about the power of poetic language, and especially narrative poetry, to help young readers connect to books.

Booklist

Poems That Stir Emotions

Selections in this section are appropriate for primary–intermediate readers unless otherwise noted.

LAUGHTER

Bagert, Brod, *Chicken Socks and Other Contagious Poems*
_____, *Elephant Games and Other Playful Poems to Perform*
_____, *Let Me Be the Boss*
Ciardi, John, *Someone Could Win a Polar Bear*
Cole, William, *A Zooful of Animals*
Crews, Nina, *The Neighborhood Mother Goose*
Florian, Douglas, *Beast Feast* (I)
_____, *Bing Bang Boing* (I)
_____, *Laugh-eteria* (I)
_____, *Mammalabilia* (I)
_____, *On the Wing* (I)
Fyleman, Rose, *Mary Middling and Other Silly Folk: Nursery Rhymes and Nonsense Poems*
Giovanni, Nikki, *Shimmy, Shimmy, Shimmy Like My Sister Kate* (A)
Harrison, David, *The Boy Who Counted Stars*
_____, *Somebody Catch My Homework*
_____, *A Thousand Cousins*
Hughes, Shirley, *Rhymes for Annie Rose*
Kennedy, X. J., *Exploding Gravy: Poems to Make You Laugh*
_____, *The Forgetful Wishing Well*
_____, *Fresh Brats*
_____, *Ghastlies, Goops and Pincushions: Nonsense Verse*
_____, *The Kite That Braved Old Orchard Beach*
Kherdian, David, *Beat Voices: An Anthology of Beat Poetry* (A)
Lewis, J. Patrick, *Ridicholas Nicholas: Animal Poems*
McNaughton, Colin, *Who's Been Sleeping in My Porridge? A Book of Wacky Poems and Pictures*
Merriam, Eve, *Poem for a Pickle*
Prelutsky, Jack, *Baby Uggs Are Hatching*
_____, *The Frogs Wore Red Suspenders*
_____, *For Laughing Out Loud*
_____, *The New Kid on the Block*
_____, *A. Nonny Mouse Writes Again!*
_____, *A Pizza the Size of the Sun*
_____, *Scranimals*
Silverstein, Shel, *Falling Up*
_____, *A Light in the Attic*
_____, *Where the Sidewalk Ends*
Smith, William Jay, *Behind the King's Kitchen: A Roster of Rhyming Riddles*
Soto, Gary, *Neighborhood Odes* (A)
Steig, Jeanne, *Consider the Lemming*
Stevenson, James, *Corn Chowder*

SENSORY IMAGES

Adoff, Arnold, *In for Winter, Out for Spring*
Dickinson, Emily, *Poems for Youth* (A)

Esbensen, Barbara Juster, *Dance with Me*

_____, *Who Shrank My Grandmother's House?*

_____, *Words with Wrinkled Knees*

Fisher, Aileen, *Always Wondering*

George, Kristine O'Connell, *Toasting Marshmallows: Camping Poems*

Giovanni, Nikki, *Knoxville, Tennessee*

_____, *Spin a Soft Black Song*

Gordon, Ruth, *Pierced by a Ray of Sun: Poems about the Times We Feel Alone* (A)

Greenfield, Eloise, *Honey, I Love and Other Poems*

_____, *Nathaniel Talking*

Gunning, Monica, *Not a Copper Penny in Me House*

Heard, Georgia, *Creatures of Earth, Sea, and Sky* (I)

Hopkins, Lee Bennett, *Home to Me: Poems across America*

Huck, Charlotte, *Secret Places*

Hughes, Langston, *The Block,* selected by Lowery S. Sims and Daisy Murray Voigt (A)

James, Simon, *Days Like This: A Collection of Small Poems*

Janeczko, Paul, *Stone Bench in an Empty Park* (A)

Levy, Constance, *A Tree Place and Other Poems*

Livingston, Myra Cohn, *Call Down the Moon: Poems of Music* (I–A)

_____, *Sea Songs* (I–A)

Mado, Michio, *The Magic Pocket: Selected Poems*

Merriam, Eve, *Higgle Wiggle: Happy Rhymes*

Morrison, Lillian, *Whistling the Morning In*

Osofsky, Audrey, *Free to Dream: The Making of a Poet: Langston Hughes* (A)

Rosenberg, Liz, *Roots and Flowers: Poets and Poems on Family* (A)

Sidman, Joyce, *The World according to Dog: Poems and Teen Voices* (A)

Smith, William Jay, *Around My Room*

Sneve, Virginia Driving Hawk, *Dancing Tepees*

Stevenson, James, *Candy Corn*

_____, *Cornflakes*

_____, *Popcorn*

_____, *Sweet Corn: Poems*

Worth, Valerie, *All the Small Poems*

_____, *Peacock and Other Poems*

FEELINGS AND EMOTIONS

Adoff, Arnold, *Black Is Brown Is Tan*

Berry, James, *Isn't My Name Magical? Sister and Brother Poems*

Bierhorst, John, *In the Trail of the Wind: American Indian Poems and Ritual Orations* (I–A)

Brooks, Gwendolyn, *Bronzeville Boys and Girls*

de Regniers, Beatrice Schenk, *Way I Feel . . . Sometimes*

Dunning, Stephen, *Reflections on a Gift of Watermelon Pickle and Other Modern Verse* (A)

Fletcher, Ralph, *I Am Wings: Poems about Love* (A)

_____, *Relatively Speaking: Poems about Family*

Gasztold, Carmen Bernos de, *Prayers from the Ark*

George, Kristine O'Connell, *Little Dog Poems*

_____, *Swimming Upstream* (I)

Glaser, Isabel Joshlin, *Dreams of Glory: Poems Starring Girls*

Greenfield, Eloise, *Nathaniel Talking*

_____, *Night on Neighborhood Street*

_____, *Under the Sunday Tree*

Grimes, Nikki, *A Dime a Dozen*

_____, *Hopscotch Love: A Family Treasury of Love Poems*

_____, *Meet Danitra Brown*

_____, *My Man Blue*

_____, *Stepping Out with Grandma Mac*

Hoberman, Mary Ann, *Fathers, Mothers, Sisters, Brothers*

_____, *The Cozy Book*

Hopkins, Lee Bennett, *Been to Yesterdays: Poems of a Life* (A)

_____, *Still as a Star: A Book of Nighttime Poems*

Hughes, Langston, *The Block,* selected by Lowery S. Sims and Daisy Murray Voigt (A)

_____, *The Dream Keeper* (I–A)

Janeczko, Paul, *Wherever Home Begins: 100 Contemporary Poems* (A)

Kurtz, Jane, *River Friendly, River Wild*

Livingston, Myra Cohn, *I Like You, If You Like Me: Poems of Friendship* (I)

_____, *Roll Along: Poems on Wheels*

Margolis, Richard J. *Secrets of a Small Brother*

Medina, Jane, *My Name Is Jorge: On Both Sides of the River*

Newsome, Effie Lee, *Wonders: The Best Children's Poems of Effie Lee Newsome,* compiled by Rudine Sims Bishop

Nye, Naomi Shihab, *The Space between Our Footsteps: Poems and Paintings from the Middle East* (A)

Ormerod, Jan, *Jan Ormerod's To Baby with Love*

Pomerantz, Charlotte, *If I Had a Paka: Poems in Eleven Languages*

_____, *The Tamarindo Puppy and Other Poems*

Prelutsky, Jack, *Nightmares: Poems to Trouble Your Sleep*

Rosenberg, Liz, *Light-Gathering Poems* (A)

Vecchione, Patrice, *Revenge and Forgiveness: An Anthology of Poems* (A)

Wong, Janet, *The Rainbow Hand: Poems about Mothers and Children*

Zolotow, Charlotte, *Snippets: A Gathering of Poems, Pictures, and Possibilities*

Poems That Promote School Learning

Selections in this section are appropriate for primary–intermediate readers unless otherwise noted.

Ackerman, Diane, *Animal Sense*

Berry, James, *A Nest Full of Stars*

Levy, Constance, *Splash! Poems of Our Watery World* (I)

Lewis, J. Patrick, *Scien-Trickery: Riddles in Science* (I)

_____, *A World of Wonders: Geographic Travels in Verse and Rhyme* (I)

Longfellow, Henry Wadsworth, *The Midnight Ride of Paul Revere* (I)

Major, Kevin, *Ann and Seamus* (A)

Myers, Walter Dean, *blues journey* (I–A)

Nelson, Marilyn, *Carver: A Life in Poems* (A)
Olaleye, Isaac, *The Distant Talking Drum* (I)
Scieszka, Jon, *Math Curse,* illustrated by Lane Smith (I)
_____, *Science Verse,* illustrated by Lane Smith (I)
Yolen, Jane, *Fine Feathered Friends*

Language, Sound, and Other Poetic Devices

Selections in this section are appropriate for primary–intermediate readers unless otherwise noted.

Ciardi, John, *You Read to Me, I'll Read to You*
Esbensen, Barbara Juster, *Words with Wrinkled Knees*
Fleischman, Paul, *Joyful Noise: Poems for Two Voices* (I–A)
_____, *Big Talk: Poems for Four Voices* (I–A)
_____, *I Am Phoenix* (I–A)
Florian, Douglas, *Bow Wow, Meow Meow: It's Rhyming Cats and Dogs*
_____, *In the Swim* (I)
Heard, Georgia, *Creatures of Earth, Sea, and Sky*
Hoberman, Mary Ann, *You Read to Me, I'll Read to You: Very Short Stories to Read Together*
Hopkins, Lee Bennett, *Hoofbeats, Claws, and Rippled Fins: Creature Poems*
_____, *Small Talk: A Book of Short Poems*
_____, *A Song in Stone: City Poems*
McCord, David, *One at a Time*
Merriam, Eve, *It Doesn't Always Have to Rhyme*
Moore, Lilian, *I Thought I Heard the City*
_____, *Something New Begins*
Morrison, Lillian, *Whistling the Morning In*
Neil, Philip, *Songs Are Thoughts: Poets of the Inuit*
Nye, Naomi Shihab, *This Same Sky: A Collection of Poems from around the World* (I–A)
Wong, Janet S., *Night Garden: Poems from the World of Dreams*
Worth, Valerie, *All the Small Poems*
Yolen, Jane, *Sky Scrape/City Scape* (P–I–A)

Poetry in Many Forms

Selections in this section are appropriate for primary–intermediate readers unless otherwise noted.

NARRATIVE POETRY

Field, Rachel, *General Store*
Greenfield, Eloise, *Night on Neighborhood Street*
Grimes, Nikki, *Come Sunday*
Johnson, Angela, *The Other Side: Shorter Poems* (I–A)
Kuskin, Karla, *James and the Rain*
Lear, Edward, *The Owl and the Pussycat*
_____, *The Pelican Chorus and Other Nonsense*
Leslie-Spinks, Tim, and Alice Andres, *Treasures of Trinkamalee*
Longfellow, Henry Wadsworth, *Paul Revere's Ride*

Nash, Ogden, *The Adventures of Isabel*
_____, *The Tale of Custard the Dragon*
Poe, Edgar Allan, *Annabel Lee* (A)
Prelutsky, Jack, *The Headless Horseman Rides Tonight*
_____, *The Mean Old Mean Hyena*
Steig, Jeanne, *Tales from Gizzard's Grill* (I–A)
Thomas, Joyce Carol, *Brown Honey in Broomwheat Tea*
_____, *Gingerbread Days*
Whittier, John Greenleaf, *Barbara Frietchie* (I–A)
Williams, Vera B., *Amber Was Brave, Essie Was Smart*

LYRIC POETRY

Bolden, Tonya, *Rock of Ages*
Delacre, Lulu, *Arroro, Mi Niño: Latino Lullabies and Gentle Games*
de la Mare, Walter, *Peacock Pie*
Cunningham, Julia, *The Stable Rat and Other Christmas Poems*
Farjeon, Eleanor, *The Children's Bells*
Frost, Robert, *Stopping by Woods on a Snowy Evening* (I–A)
_____, *Swinger of Birches: Poems of Robert Frost for Young People* (I–A)
_____, *You Come Too: Favorite Poems for Young Readers*
Greenfield, Eloise, *Honey, I Love and Other Love Poems*
Hoberman, Mary Ann, *A House Is a House for Me*
Hollyer, Belinda, *Dreamtime: A Book of Lullabies*
Larrick, Nancy, *I Heard a Scream in the Street*
Myers, Walter Dean, *Here in Harlem* (I–A)
O'Neill, Mary, *Hailstones and Halibut Bones*
Schertle, Alice, and Kathryn Sky-Peck, *Who Has Seen the Wind? An Illustrated Collection of Poetry for Young People*
Thomas, Joyce Carol, *Hush Songs: African American Lullabies*
Wolman, Bernice, *Taking Turns: Poetry to Share*

FREE VERSE

Adoff, Arnold, *Black Is Brown Is Tan*
_____, *Chocolate Dreams* (I–A)
_____, *Eats: Poems* (I–A)
_____, *Hard to Be Six*
_____, *In for Winter, Out for Spring*
_____, *Sports Pages* (I–A)
George, Kristine O'Connell, *Fold Me a Poem*
Hopkins, Lee Bennett, *Been to Yesterdays: Poems of a Life*
Janeczko, Paul, *Pocket Poems* (I–A)
_____, *That Sweet Diamond: Baseball Poems* (I)
Johnson, Angela, *Running Back to Ludie* (A)
Johnson, Linda Lee, *Soul Moon Soup* (I–A)
Soto, Gary, *Canto Familiar* (I–A)
_____, *Fire in My Hands* (A)
_____, *Neighborhood Odes* (A)

HAIKU AND CINQUAIN

Atwood, Ann, *Haiku: The Mood of Earth*
Cassedy, Sylvia, *Red Dragonfly on My Shoulder*

Fukuda, Hanako, *Wind in My Hand: The Story of Issa, Japanese Haiku Poet* (I)

Gollub, Matthew, *Cool Melons—Turn to Frogs! The Life and Poems of Issa* (I)

Grimes, Nikki, *A Pocketful of Poems*

Issa, *Don't Tell the Scarecrow*

Janeczko, Paul, *Stone Bench in an Empty Park* (A)

Lewis, J. Patrick, *Black Swan White Crow: Haiku* (I)

Livingston, Myra Cohn, *Sky Songs* (I)

Prelutsky, Jack, *If Not for the Cat* (I)

Schertle, Alice, *I Am the Cat* (I)

CONCRETE POEMS

Adoff, Arnold, *Street Music: City Poems*

Esbensen, Barbara, *Echoes for the Eye: Poems to Celebrate Patterns in Nature*

Froman, Robert, *Seeing Things: A Book of Poems* (I–A)

Graham, Joan Bransfield, *Flicker Flash*

_____, *Splish Splash*

Janeczko, Paul, *A Poke in the I* (I–A)

Lewis, J. Patrick, *Doodle Dandies: Poems That Take Shape*

Livingston, Myra Cohn, *O Sliver of Liver* (I–A)

Merriam, Eve, *Out Loud*

Morrison, Lillian, *The Sidewalk Racer and Other Poems of Sports and Motion*

Romer, Heidi B., *Come to My Party and Other Shape Poems*

LIMERICKS

Ciardi, John, *The Hopeful Trout and Other Limericks*

Hubbell, Patricia, *Boo! Halloween Poems and Limericks*

Lear, Edward, *Nonsense,* illustrated by Valorie Fisher (I–A)

Lewis, J. Patrick, *A Hippopotamusn't and Other Animal Verses*

Livingston, Myra Cohn, *Lots of Limericks*

Lobel, Arnold, *The Book of Pigericks*

Marshall, James, *Pocketful of Nonsense*

Nims, Bonnie Larkin, *Just beyond Reach and Other Riddle Poems*

BALLADS

Bryan, Ashley, *Sing to the Sun: Poems and Pictures*

Child, Lydia Maria, *Over the River and through the Wood*

dePaola, Tomie, *Tomie dePaola's Book of Christmas Carols*

Fox, Dan, arranger, *We Wish You a Merry Christmas: Songs of the Season for Young People*

Key, Frances Scott, *The Star-Spangled Banner*

Lessie, Pat, *Fablesauce: Aesop Reinterpreted in Rhymed Couplets*

Livingston, Myra Cohn, *Abraham Lincoln: A Man for All the People*

_____, *Keep on Singing: A Ballad of Marion Anderson*

_____, *Let Freedom Ring: A Ballad of Martin Luther King, Jr.*

Philip, Neil, *Singing America: Poems That Define a Nation*

_____, *Songs Are Thoughts: Poems of the Inuit*

Plotz, Helen, *Imagination's Other Place: Poems of Science and Mathematics*

_____, *A Week of Lullabies*

Sandburg, Carl, *The American Songbag* (A)

Thayer, Ernest Lawrence, *Casey at the Bat*

RIDDLE POEMS

Lewis, J. Patrick, *Riddle-Lightful: Oodles of Little Riddle Poems*

Spires, Elizabeth, *Riddle Road: Puzzles in Poems and Pictures*

Smith, William Jay, and Carol Ra, *Behind the King's Kitchen: A Roster of Rhyming Riddles*

Swann, Brian, *The House with No Door: African Riddle Poems*

NOVELS IN VERSE

Creech, Sharon, *Love That Dog* (I)

Grimes, Nikki, *Bronx Masquerade* (A)

Hesse, Karen, *Out of the Dust* (A)

_____, *Witness* (A)

Johnson, Lindsay Lee, *Soul Moon Soup* (I–A)

Koertge, Ron, *Shakespeare Bats Cleanup* (A)

Soto, Gary, *Fearless Fernie: Hanging Out with Fernie and Me* (I–A)

Testa, Maria, *Becoming Joe DiMaggio* (I)

Woodson, Jacqueline, *Locomotion* (A)

Specialized, General, and Individual Anthologies

Selections in this section are appropriate for primary–intermediate–advanced readers unless otherwise noted.

SPECIALIZED ANTHOLOGIES (WORKS BY SEVERAL POETS ON ONE SUBJECT)

Carter, Anne, *Birds, Beasts, and Fishes: A Selection of Animal Poems*

de Regniers, Beatrice Schenk, *So Many Cats!*

Duffy, Carol Ann, *Stopping for Death: Poems of Death and Loss*

Hopkins, Lee Bennett, *Hand in Hand: An American History through Poetry*

_____, *Good Books, Good Times!* (P–I)

_____, *My America: A Poetry Atlas of the United States* (I–A)

_____, *Ragged Shadows: Poems of Halloween Night*

_____, *Side by Side: Poems to Read Together*

Huck, Charlotte S., *Secret Places*

Janeczko, Paul, *Brickyard Summer* (I–A)

_____, *The Music of What Happens: Poems That Tell Stories* (I–A)

_____, *The Place My Words Are Looking For: What Poets Say about and through Their Work* (I–A)

_____, *Poetspeak* (I–A)

_____, *Poetry from A to Z: A Guide for Young Writers* (I–A)

_____, *Very Best (Almost) Friends: Poems of Friendship* (I–A)

_____, *Wherever Home Begins* (I–A)

Janeczko, Paul, and Naomi Shihab Nye, *I Feel a Little Jumpy around You* (A)

Livingston, Myra Cohn, *Dog Poems*

_____, *If You Ever Meet a Whale*

Nye, Naomi Shihab, *Is This Forever, or What? Poems and Paintings from Texas* (A)

_____, *What Have You Lost?* (A)

Rogasky, Barbara, *Winter Poems*

Schwartz, Alvin, *And the Green Grass Grew All Around*

Strickland, Dorothy, and Michael Strickland, *Families: Poems Celebrating the African American Experience*

Vecchione, Patrice, *The Body Eclectic: An Anthology of Poems* (A)

Yolen, Jane, *Alphabestiary* (P–I)

_____, *Color Me a Rhyme* (P–I)

_____, *Mother Earth Father Sky* (I)

_____, *Once upon Ice* (I)

_____, *Sky Scrape/City Scape* (I)

_____, *Snow, Snow* (I)

_____, *Street Rhymes around the World* (P–I)

_____, *Water Music* (I)

_____, *Weather Report* (I)

GENERAL ANTHOLOGIES (WORKS BY MANY POETS ON MANY SUBJECTS)

Selections in this section are appropriate for primary–intermediate readers unless otherwise noted.

Cole, Joanna, *A New Treasury of Children's Poetry: Old Favorites and New Discoveries*

Cullinan, Bernice, *A Jar of Tiny Stars: Poems by NCTE Award-Winning Poets*

Hall, Donald, *The Oxford Book of Children's Verse in America*

Kennedy, X. J., and Dorothy Kennedy, *Knock at a Star: A Child's Introduction to Poetry* (I)

_____, *Talking Like the Rain*

Lalicki, Barbara, *If There Were Dreams to Sell*

MacKay, David, *A Flock of Words: An Anthology of Poetry for Children and Others*

Nye, Naomi Shihab, *This Same Sky: A Collection of Poems from around the World* (I–A)

_____, *Salting the Ocean: 100 Poems by Young Poets* (I–A)

Paladino, Catherine, *Land, Sea, and Sky: Poems to Celebrate the Earth*

Prelutsky, Jack, *The Random House Book of Poetry*

Sutherland, Zena, editor, *The Scott, Foresman Anthology of Children's Literature*

INDIVIDUAL ANTHOLOGIES (THE WORKS OF ONE POET)

Selections in this section are appropriate for primary–intermediate readers unless otherwise noted.

Adoff, Arnold, *Sports Pages* (I–A)

Angelou, Maya, *Soul Looks Back in Wonder* (I–A)

Bodecker, N. M., *Water Pennies and Other Poems*

Cassedy, Sylvia, *Zoomrimes: Poems about Things That Go*

Ciardi, John, *Monster Den: or Look What Happened at My House—and to It*

Dotlich, Rebecca Kai, *Sweet Dreams of the Wild: Poems for Bedtime*

Florian, Douglas, *Summersaults*

George, Kristine O'Connell, *Little Dog and Duncan*

Hillert, Margaret, *The Sky Is Not So Far Away*

Hopkins, Lee Bennett, *Home to Me: Poems across America*

Janeczko, Paul, *Stardust Otel* (A)

_____, *That Sweet Diamond: Baseball Poems* (I)

Katz, Bobbi, *We the People*

Kuskin, Karla, *The Animals and the Ark*

_____, *Soap Soup and Other Verses*

Livingston, Myra Cohn, *Space Songs* (I–A)

McCord, David, *One at a Time*

Prelutsky, Jack, *Beneath a Blue Umbrella*

_____, *Dragons Are Singing Tonight*

Ridlon, Marci, *Sun through the Window*

Rosenthal, Betsy R., *My House Is Singing*

Silverstein, Shel, *Falling Up*

Spinelli, Eileen, *Where Is the Night Train Going? Bedtime Poems*

Willard, Nancy, *A Visit to William Blake's Inn: Poems for Innocent and Experienced Travelers* (I–A)

Wong, Janet, *Behind the Wheel: Poems about Driving*

_____, *Knock on Wood: Poems about Superstitions*

_____, *Night Garden: Poems from the World of Dreams*

Building a Poetry Collection

Berry, James, *When I Dance* (A)

Clinton, Catherine, *I, Too, Sing America: Three Centuries of African American Poetry* (A)

Dunbar, Paul Laurence, *Jump Back, Honey: The Poems of Paul Laurence Dunbar,* selected by Ashley Bryan and Andrea Davis Pinkney (P)

Dyer, Jane, *Animal Crackers* (P)

Elledge, Scott, *Wider Than the Sky: Poems to Grow Up With* (I)

Esbensen, Barbara Juster, *Cold Stars and Fireflies: Poems of the Four Seasons* (I)

Field, Edward, *Magic Words* (P)

Fleischman, Paul, *Big Talk: Poems for Four Voices* (I–A)

Gillooly, Eileen, *Robert Browning: Poetry for Young People* (A)

Gordon, Ruth, *Time Is the Longest Distance* (A)

Hall, Donald, *The Oxford Illustrated Book of American Children's Poems* (P)

_____, *The Oxford Book of Children's Verse in America* (I)

Hoberman, Mary Ann, *A House Is a House for Me* (P–I)

_____, *The Llama Who Had No Pajama: 100 Favorite Poems* (P)

Hopkins, Lee Bennett, *Climb into My Lap: First Poems to Read Together* (P)

_____, *My America: A Poetry Atlas of the United States* (I)

_____, *Side by Side: Poems to Read Together* (P)

_____, *Voyages: Poems by Walt Whitman* (A)

Hughes, Ted, *The Mermaid's Purse* (A)

Janeczko, Paul B., *Looking for Your Name: A Collection of Contemporary Poems* (A)

_____, *The Music of What Happens: Poems That Tell Stories* (A)

_____, *The Place My Words Are Looking For: What Poets Say about and through Their Work* (A)

_____, *Preposterous: Poems of Youth* (A)

_____, *Stardust Otel* (A)

Katz, Bobbi, *We the People: Poems by Bobbi Katz* (I)

Kennedy, X. J., and Dorothy M. Kennedy, *Talking Like the Rain: A First Book of Poems* (I)

_____, *Knock at a Star: A Child's Introduction to Poetry* (I)

Lawrence, Jacob, *Harriet and the Promised Land* (P)

Lear, Edward, *The Complete Nonsense of Edward Lear* (I)

_____, *Nonsense,* illustrated by Valorie Fisher (I–A)

Lewis, J. Patrick, *The Snowflake Sisters,* illustrated by Lisa Desimini (P–I)

Livingston, Myra Cohn, *I Like You, If You Like Me: Poems of Friendship* (I)

Moss, Jeffrey, *Butterfly Jar* (I)

Myers, Walter Dean, *Brown Angels: An Album of Pictures and Verse* (I)

Nikola-Lisa, W., *Bein' with You This Way* (P)

Opie, Iona, *My Very First Mother Goose* (P)

Pomerantz, Charlotte, *Halfway to Your House* (P)

Prelutsky, Jack, *New Kid on the Block* (I)

_____, *Read-Aloud Rhymes for the Very Young* (P)

_____, *Something Big Has Been Here* (I)

_____, *The 20th Century Children's Poetry Treasury* (P)

Rosen, Michael, *Classic Poetry: An Illustrated Collection* (P–I)

Sandburg, Carl, *Poems for Children Nowhere Near Old Enough to Vote* (I)

_____, *Poetry for Young People* (I)

Schertle, Alice, *How Now, Brown Cow?* (P)

Silverstein, Shel, *Falling Up* (I)

_____, *A Light in the Attic* (I)

_____, *Where the Sidewalk Ends* (I)

Stevenson, Robert Louis, *A Child's Garden of Verses* (P)

Wong, Janet S., *Good Luck Gold and Other Poems* (A)

Worth, Valerie, *All the Small Poems and Fourteen More* (P–I)

Resources for the Poetry Teacher

Booth, David, and Bill Moore, *Poems Please! Sharing Poetry with Children*

Brown, Bill, and Malcolm Glass, *Important Words: A Book for Poets and Writers*

Chatton, Barbara, *Using Poetry across the Curriculum*

Cullinan, Bernice, Marilyn Scala, and Virginia Schroder, with Ann Lovett, *Three Voices: An Invitation to Poetry across the Curriculum*

Denman, Gregory A., *When You've Made It Your Own: Teaching Poetry to Young People*

Esbensen, Barbara Juster, *A Celebration of Bees: Endless Opportunities for Inspiring Children to Write Poetry*

Fletcher, Ralph, *Poetry Matters: Writing a Poem from the Inside Out*

Fox, Mem, *Radical Reflections*

Grossman, Florence, *Listening to the Bells: Learning to Read Poetry by Writing Poetry*

Janeczko, Paul, *Seeing the Blue Between: Advice and Inspiration for Young Poets*

Kuskin, Karla, *Dogs and Dragons, Trees and Dreams*

Harrison, David L., and Bernice Cullinan, *Easy Poetry Lessons That Dazzle and Delight*

Harwayne, Shelley, *Lasting Impressions: Weaving Literature into the Writing Workshop*

_____, *Children's Visions of 9/11*

Heard, Georgia, *Awakening the Heart: Exploring Poetry in Elementary and Middle School*

_____, *For the Good of the Earth and Sun: Teaching Poetry*

_____, *Writing toward Home: Tales and Lessons to Find Your Way*

Hewitt, Geof, *Today You Are My Favorite Poet: Writing Poems with Teenagers*

Hopkins, Lee Bennett, *Pass the Poetry, Please*

_____, *Pauses: Autobiographical Reflections of 101 Creators of Children's Books*

Janeczko, Paul, *The Place My Words Are Looking For: What Poets Say about and through Their Work*

Kennedy, X. J., and Dorothy M. Kennedy, *Knock at a Star: A Child's Introduction to Poetry*

Larrick, Nancy, *Let's Do a Poem*

Livingston, Myra Cohn, *Climb into the Bell Tower*

_____, *Poem-Making: Ways to Begin Writing Poetry*

McClure, Amy, with Peggy Harrison and Sheryl Reed, *Sunrises and Songs: Reading and Writing Poetry in an Elementary Classroom*

McVitty, Walter, *Word Magic: Poetry as a Shared Adventure*

Nye, Naomi Shihab, *Salting the Ocean: 100 Poems by Young Poets*

Swartz, Larry, *Classroom Events through Poetry*

Folklore

This chapter was revised and updated by Rebecca Rapport.

Now in this village there lived a poor man who had three daughters. The two older daughters were cruel and hard-hearted, and they made their youngest sister sit by the fire and feed the flames. When the burning branches popped, the sparks fell on her.

—RAFE MARTIN, *The Rough-Face Girl,* unpaged

IN SANDY'S FOURTH-GRADE CLASS, THE STUDENTS BEGIN THEIR UNIT ON Cinderella by brainstorming and discussing the elements of fairy tales. They decide that these stories usually include a prince, giants and other magical creatures, someone who is treated unfairly, a stepfamily, the number three, animals that take on human characteristics, a problem and a resolution, and of course, a happy ending. When they consider Cinderella stories, they decide that they usually center on one main female character, the youngest daughter, who is treated unfairly by members of her stepfamily. Sandy shows them her collection of Cinderella books that come from countries all over the world and tells them that the story of Cinderella is probably at least a thousand years old. The children are amazed at the number and variety of books. Sandy reads aloud Rafe Martin's *The Rough-Face Girl,* an Algonquin Cinderella story that she predicts is probably quite different from the version with which most of her students are familiar. The children are eager to compare this version to the European and movie versions of the Cinderella story they know. After reading many more of the tales in Sandy's collection in small groups and during independent reading times, the students begin considering characteristics that distinguish Cinderella tales, what the stories have in common, and what the students can learn about the cultures represented through the stories.

When Sandy presents the idea of writing their own versions of Cinderella, her students are excited to begin. First, Sandy and the children talk about the best way to plan their own stories. Each child invents a main character who has a problem; he or she crafts a good lead, then decides on a resolution and begins writing details that support the story. The children write complete descriptions of the main character, and they plan the events that will take the main character from the beginning of the story to the end. They learn the art of the writing process by conferring with Sandy and their peers, revising and editing many times. When they are finished, the children type their stories on a computer. Once the stories are printed, they are ready to be illustrated. The children take care to match the illustrations to the printed words. Once the books are complete, each child compiles a cover page, a copyright page, a dedication page, and a page about the author before finally binding his or her book.

Sandy and her students celebrate by having a Cinderella Author's Tea. The children write invitations to their families, and they hold the tea in the gym, where four children are seated at each round table along with their guests. Each child reads his or her story, and when all are finished, the group celebrates with a light breakfast of bagels, fruit, coffee, tea, and juice. It's a fitting ending for a unit on that most appealing form of literature, the fairy tale.

Defining Folklore: A Literary Heritage

All people tell stories, and everyone has his or her own story to tell. Parents and grandparents tell children embellished stories from their childhoods, about how they had to walk miles to and from school—uphill both ways!—in torrential rain and even blizzards. They settle on a child's bed in a darkened room and tell the magical stories they were told when they were children. Families gather around the Thanksgiving table, reminiscing about celebrations long ago. Quilts and other heirlooms and their accompanying stories are passed down from one generation to the next. Even the simple query, "How was your day today?" leads to the sharing of stories. Creating stories is an essential part of being human. Today when we think of stories, we often think of books, of stories that are written down and frozen just as they are for all time. Long ago, long before most people could write, stories were told aloud to captivated listeners. Each time a teller told the tale, it was revised and reborn. Many of these tales have survived over the centuries and have found their way into the books we share with children; some are still shared today through the ancient art of storytelling.

Folklore, or traditional literature, includes those tales, nursery rhymes, myths, epics, legends, jokes and riddles, fables, and songs and ballads that have been passed down by storytellers for hundreds, even thousands, of years to enlighten and entertain many generations of listeners, young and old. No one knows who the first teller of any particular story was, only that with countless tellers, over long periods of time, the stories evolved into the written, literary tales that we know today. Jane Yolen writes that

the oldest stories were transmitted and transmuted, the kaleidoscope patterns of motif changed by time

and by the times, by the tellers and by the listeners, by the country in which they arose and the countries to which they were carried. The old oral tales were changed the way culture itself changes, the way traditions change, by an erosion/eruption as powerful in its way as any geological force. (2000, p. 22)

Stories of the folk of many different world cultures explained why the world is as it is, showed that wishes could come true, gave hope to the young and the powerless, made even the fiercest fiend vulnerable, proved that good could vanquish evil, and taught all who listened how to live and work in harmony. In a speech given for Book Week at the University of Minnesota, folklorist and children's author Lise Lunge-Larsen (2004) affirmed, "Folktales grow out of the shadowy borderland between what is known and what is unknown. Or as ancient maps warned: Beyond here there be dragons."

Storytelling began with the songs and tales early societies composed to describe their daily work. "The first primitive efforts," notes storyteller Ruth Sawyer (1962, pp. 45–46), "consisted of a simple chant set to the rhythm of some daily tribal occupation such as grinding corn, paddling a canoe or kayak, sharpening weapons for hunting or war, or ceremonial dancing." As they speculated about the power of nature, the forces behind it, and human behavior, the people of primitive societies created stories to explain the unexplainable. These were the stories that grew into pourquoi tales, hero legends, and myths. When the ancient Greeks, for instance, were frightened by thunder, they invented a story about an angry god who shook the heavens. When they did not understand how and why the sun moved, they imagined a god who drove a chariot across the sky. Love, hate, heroic acts, values, morality, and other human qualities and concerns play an important part in myths of all cultures. With the passage of time and the growth of tribes, the desire to preserve ancestral stories increased, and the folklore that had been passed from one generation to the next became our cultural heritage.

At one time, common belief held that all folklore emerged from one prehistoric civilization. The Grimm brothers, who collected tales from all over Germany, subscribed to this view, speculating that as people migrated, they took their stories with them. This theory would account for regional differences in folktales, such as the evolution of West Africa's trickster Ananse the spider to Anansi in the Caribbean and Aunt Nancy in the United States. As folklorists studied the tales of many diverse cultures, however, it became apparent that some stories must have originated spontaneously in a number of separate places, which would account for the hundreds of variants of the Cinderella tale told all over the world. Today, cultural anthropologists believe that both theories about the origin of folktales are correct. Distinguished folklore scholars Iona and Peter Opie (1974) note that no one theory "is likely to account satisfactorily for the origin of even a majority of the tales. Their wellsprings are almost certainly numerous, their ages likely to vary considerably, their meanings—if they ever had meanings—to be diverse" (p. 18). What we do know is that people everywhere tell and listen to stories and have done so for a long, long time.

Folklore in Children's Lives

Though very few tales were originally intended for children alone, folklore is a rich source of literature for today's children. In the same way that it explained the world to early people, folklore helps modern children understand their world and all that is good and bad within it. Children struggle with the notion of evil, firmly believing that justice and goodness will prevail. Preschool children often believe that magic accounts for the things they do not understand. They even give inanimate objects human characteristics. F. Andre Favat (1977), who studied the moral development of children, draws a parallel between the perceptions of morality in fairy tales and those held by children. Children under the age of six, he posits, have an "eye for an eye" mentality; because the fairy tale shares that vision, it is particularly suited for children in that developmental stage (pp. 38, 50). Older children are able to explore feelings of anger and joy, despair and elation through these stories of long ago. They are no longer so innocent and already know the world can be a wonderful yet sometimes violent place. They can talk about this knowledge when considering and discussing folklore, stories Jane Yolen deems "the lively fossils" (2000, p. 21). These timeless tales present the world as it was and as it still is.

Psychoanalytic writers and psychologists have explored the meaning of folklore in children's lives. According to Freud, the characters in fairy tales symbolize a child's subconscious urges. Bettelheim, too, argues that fairy tales tap into unconscious desires—the wellspring of repressed emotions. Fairy tales, he says, help children deal with emotional insecurities by supplying images about which they can fantasize. Jung (1976/1916, p. 6) suggests that dreams, fantasy, imagination, and vision stem from the collective unconscious, a part of the mind common to all people. Because of the universal nature of the unconscious, he says, diverse people share common stories. The mythical figures and conflicts are archetypes, or original models, of racial memories.

Although most adults today recognize the importance of sharing folklore with children, some try to censor the tales because they feel they are too sexist or too violent. Historically, though the tales were shared orally by all classes of people for many centuries, by the 1600s, many adults did not approve of them, finding the stories crude, brutal, dishonest, and of questionable moral value—certainly not appropriate for children. Jack Zipes (1979) points out in his discussion of these early complaints about fairy tales that "the tales were often censored and outlawed during the early phase of the rise of the middle classes to power because their fantastic components which encouraged imaginative play and free exploration were contrary to the precepts of capitalist rationalization and the Protestant ethos" (p. 196). In *Written for Children,* John Rowe Townsend (1987) reports that a woman wrote to Mrs. Trimmer's *Guardian of Education:* "Cinderella paints some of the worst passions that can enter into the human breast, and of which little children should if possible be totally ignorant; such as envy, jealousy, a dislike of mothers-in-law and half-sisters, vanity, a love of dress, etc., etc." (p. 32). It wasn't until the end of the 19th century that the tales were no longer generally considered dangerous to young minds and became widely available in print. These are the stories on which so many modern stories are based, the stories of the people, all the people, that continue to play a vital role in the lives of children. Children know what they know about human nature and have a keen sense of what is fair and right. The symbolic violence and absolute justice in these ancient tales where heroes prevail and evil is vanquished suit their sensibilities and assure them that the world is a place where good is rewarded and the seemingly powerless win out in the end, the kind of world where they can feel secure. Further, these stories and rhymes are but one part of children's literary experience. Children can read and hear other stories that reflect modern perceptions of gender equity and nonviolence.

Researcher Arthur Applebee (1979), who has studied the child's concept of story, reasons that children search for structures and patterns that suggest order and consistency in the world around them. They are reassured by the repeated pattern of three characters, three events, and three trials. Traditional stories are one means of transmitting these patterns. Children derive pleasure from mastering the rules, and this concept is a particularly important factor in formula stories such as fairy tales. Going out from home, encountering three trials, and returning home successfully is a satisfying pattern for a child.

Whatever the explanation of the origins or purposes of the tales, it is clear that similar archetypes—images, plot patterns, themes, or character types that recur in the oldest stories—appear in the myths, legends, and folktales of all people across time and place. For example, the normal process of maturing finds its psychological expression in the archetype of the hero's quest—slaying the dragon or winning a princess. Traditional heroes from many cultures share similar traits: they often have unusual births, leave home to go on a quest, have magical help, have to prove themselves through many trials, and are richly rewarded for their heroism. Other familiar character examples that reappear in many tales include the good mother (fairy godmother), the bad mother (wicked stepmother or old witch), and the evil underside of every person (the shadow). The same archetypes of these primal stories appear in realistic and fantasy novels; characters continue to battle the forces of evil to ensure the survival of good.

Motifs, the smallest recurring elements of these archetypal stories, have been used by folklorists such as Stith Thompson (1955–58) to categorize and analyze the tales. Many stories share similar stock characters—the youngest son, the trickster; they also may contain magical objects, such as flying carpets, cooking pots, or boots and other footwear; or they include episodes in which characters sleep for a very long time or make wishes. Beasts and frogs are really princes, and evil creatures and human beings are easily tricked. These are the folklore elements that make these stories so appealing to children from one generation to the next. Margaret Read MacDonald and Brian W. Sturm have created *The Storytellers Sourcebook: A Subject, Title, and Motif Index to Folklore Collections for Children, 1983–1999* (2001), a valuable resource for teachers and librarians who want students to compare folktale variants and their motifs. See Teaching Idea 5.1 for further suggestions on exploring archetypes and motifs in folklore.

Criteria for Evaluating Folklore

When evaluating folklore, look for qualities of authenticity and excellence in language, structure, theme, and illustration, as presented in Figure 5.1. These old tales are at their best when the language reflects their oral origins. Listen for language that sounds natural when read aloud, and text that includes vivid imagery and melodious rhythms and that maintains the cultural integrity of early retellings. Avoid simplified, controlled vocabulary versions that reduce the

Teaching Idea 5-1

An Exploration of Theme in Folklore

Reading a wide range of folklore helps students develop a sense of its basic elements. Gradually they become aware of various archetypes and motifs in the folklore they read and are able to identify images, characters, and patterns that occur frequently. To develop an awareness of the dominant themes in folklore, ask students to identify the important lessons that are conveyed through the tales and to list them along with the titles of the stories. Compare their discoveries with those of other students. Ask students which themes and stories appeal to them most. Why do these big ideas resonate? What do they say about what students value and believe to be true? About who they are? Some books that contain evocative themes include the following:

Hero's Quest

Hodges, Margaret, *St. George and the Dragon: A Golden Legend*

McKinley, Robin, *The Outlaws of Sherwood*

McVitty, Walter, *Ali Baba and the Forty Thieves*

Pyle, Howard, *The Story of King Arthur and His Knights*

Wicked Witch/Wicked Stepmother

Grimm, Jacob, and Wilhelm Grimm, *Hansel and Gretel*

_____, *Snow White and the Seven Dwarfs,* translated by Randall Jarrell

Perrault, Charles, *Cinderella*

San Souci, Robert D., *The Talking Eggs*

Good versus Evil

Galdone, Paul, *The Three Little Pigs*

Steptoe, John, *Mufaro's Beautiful Daughters*

Yolen, Jane, *Tam Lin*

Young, Ed, *Lon Po Po*

Transformations and the Power of Love

Brett, Jan, *Beauty and the Beast*

Cooper, Susan, *The Selkie Girl*

Ormerod, Jan, and David Lloyd, *The Frog Prince*

Steptoe, John, *The Story of Jumping Mouse*

Yagawa, Sumiko, *The Crane Wife,* translated by Katherine Paterson

Figure 5-1

Checklist for Evaluating Folklore

Language

✿ Sounds like spoken language, with rich, natural rhythms

✿ Reflects the cultural integrity of early retellings

Structure

✿ Preserves the simple, straightforward plot structure of oral stories

Theme

✿ Explores significant universal themes

Illustrations

✿ Serve as examples of artistic excellence

✿ Complement and extend the narrative

✿ Reflect the cultural heritage of the tale

stories to trite episodes for the sake of making them easy for beginning readers to read on their own. Fortunately, talented illustrators often choose folklore to showcase their art. Artists present an immense amount of cultural detail in their illustrations—detail that the honed language of folklore may not provide. Further, they have a unique opportunity to create their own visions because the oft-told tales present only general descriptions of setting and character. Look for artistically excellent illustrations that complement and extend the narrative with accuracy and reflect the cultural heritage of the tale.

✳ ✳ ✳

A CLOSE LOOK AT

The Rough-Face Girl

Folklore structured around the basic Cinderella motif is common; approximately 1,500 versions of the tale have been recorded by folklorists. Rafe Martin retells the Algonquin Indian version of Cinderella in **The Rough-Face Girl** (1), illustrated by David Shannon. In this retelling, both the Algonquin culture and the voice of the storyteller are apparent in illustrations and text.

*David Shannon captures the relationship between the human-sized Rough-Face Girl and the overwheming grandeur and beauty of nature in **The Rough-Face Girl**, by Rafe Martin.*

Summary

The story begins "long ago" in a "village by the shores of Lake Ontario." Many women of the village want to marry the remarkable Invisible Being, but first they must be able to see him and answer questions that his sister asks. Two of the village women are cruel and haughty sisters who torment their younger sister, forcing her to keep the fire going, a job that results in scars on her face and hands. After the sisters fail in their attempt to marry the Invisible Being, the younger sister goes to his tent. When questioned by the Invisible Being's sister, the girl answers correctly. She is married to the Invisible Being and "they lived together in great gladness and were never parted."

Structure

The simple structure of an oral tale is preserved in this retelling. The story begins with a simple statement of setting and moves immediately to the problem: Only the woman who can see the Invisible Being can marry him. On the third page we are introduced to the characters: a poor man with three daughters, two cruel and heartless, one sweet and submissive. The story then moves immediately to the action, briefly detailing the unsuccessful attempts of the haughty sisters to convince the Invisible Being's sister that they have seen him, and the subsequent triumph of the Rough-Face Girl. This economy of detail reflects the oral origins of the tale; brief statements of setting and the use of stereotypical characters allow the teller to get right to the exciting part—the action—thus holding the attention of the audience.

Language

The language, too, reflects the oral origins of the tale. The story makes use of dialogue and of prosodic features that indicate tone and volume when the sister of the Invisible Being speaks:

> "All right, then," she said quietly, "if you think you've seen him, then tell me, WHAT'S HIS BOW MADE OF?" And suddenly her voice was swift as lightning and strong as thunder!

Rafe Martin

© 2000 Rafe Martin

*S*ometimes people ask me— *"Why are folktales important? Why should they be shared, retold, recreated, put in books today? Are they just remnants of outdated cultures, quaint and charming stories of little current relevance? Why do you so often write recreations of folktales, anyway?" My answer to that is that folktales, perhaps better called traditional tales, return us, not to the literal world but to the imagined one. They are the doorways into a constant realm of universal dreaming through which archetypes may be embodied, characters and roles and life paths explored. (from "Why Folktales?")*

Rafe Martin believes possibility is born of imagination. Traditional tales, with their deeply rooted human archetypes and patterns, nourish the imagination, thus allowing us to dream beyond our present situations (1999). An award-winning reteller of traditional tales, Martin has been helping children stretch toward possibility for over a decade.

In retelling traditional tales, Martin selects stories from around the world. His culturally diverse collection of work includes folklore from India, such as *The Brave Little Parrot,* illustrated by Susan Gaber, and *Foolish Rabbit's Big Mistake,* illustrated by Ed Young. *Dear as Salt, The Language of Birds, Mysterious Tales of Japan,* and *The Shark God* draw on the oral traditions of Italy, Russia, Japan, and Hawaii. Martin retells a Chinook tale in *The Boy Who Lived with Seals,* and *The Rough-Face Girl* is a Cinderella story in the Algonquin tradition.

"In a Cinderella tale," notes Martin, ". . . we can experience justice—see good rewarded and evil punished. When was the last time reading the newspaper brought that? How could it? Our daily news is built on tales of injustice. That is the world. But not the world we wish for. Traditional tales put us into a real human world; not the literal one, but one we really wish might be. That wish is part of our truth as human beings. If we lose it we lose a deep part of ourselves, the very part, perhaps, that motivates our constant effort to improve society and recreate the world to accord with wish—to bring into being a world of integrity and equality. Traditional tales keep the flame of such possibility alive" (1999). Martin's commitment to capturing these traditional tales in writing helps ensure that children's literature will continue to be a vehicle for keeping hope alive for young readers.

Source: Martin, R. (1999, January). Why folktales? *Storytelling Magazine.* [www.rafemartin.com/articles.htm#folk]. Accessed October 23, 2004.

There is also repetition. The Rough-Face Girl asks her father the same question that her older sisters have already asked, she makes the same journey they did, and she is asked the same questions by the sister. Yet sharp contrasts are also made apparent. Her father has nothing to give her, the villagers laugh at her as she walks by in her odd clothing, and she answers the questions correctly and marries the Invisible Being. By repeating the events and the dialogue, the storyteller heightens the drama of the tale.

Perhaps the most moving passage comes when the Invisible Being enters his wigwam and sees the Rough-Face Girl:

> And when he saw her sitting there he said, "At last we have been found out." Then, smiling kindly, he added, "And oh, my sister, but she is beautiful." And his sister said, "Yes."

Read aloud, these words ring with emotion.

Illustrations

The voice of the storyteller comes through the words, but the culture of the people comes through both the words and the beautiful full-color realistic paintings that illustrate this tale. The first page, on which the setting is introduced in one sentence, exemplifies how text and illustrations work together to form this tale. Above the text is a painting of an Algonquin village. If you look closely you can see men in canoes and men carrying game; women carrying water, tending fires, scraping skins, and cooking; and children playing. Surrounding the village are tall pines and firs, and mist is rising from the lake. Thus, in one line the story is set, and the setting is elaborated in the detailed illustration. In subsequent illustrations we see wigwams and their symbolic decorations, details of clothing, and beautiful natural images that inspired much of Algonquin folklore. These images speak of the people and the culture that first told this haunting tale. We also see the pride and meanness of the two sisters, the humility of the Rough-Face Girl, and the awesome nature of the Invisible Being. The illustrations not only reflect but also elaborate and extend the story, providing readers with details that are not easily incorporated in a brief oral text.

The Rough-Face Girl demonstrates the close relationship that the reteller and artist have with the original tale. The combination of a riveting story, a skillful retelling, and beautiful, detailed illustrations results in a book that children remember and reread numerous times.

*   *   *

Patterns in Folklore

Students who read widely soon recognize recurring patterns in the folklore of many countries. As characters, events, and resolutions recur in their reading, students begin to recognize the conventions, motifs, and themes that form these tales. They then use this literary knowledge in their own writing. Teachers and librarians can help students recognize these patterns if they provide exposure to a wide array of stories that exemplify the characteristic structure.

• • C O N V E N T I O N S • •

Literary devices called *conventions* are the cornerstones of folktales. One of the easiest conventions children recognize and adapt in their own writing is the story frame, such as the one that begins with "Once upon a time" and ends with "They lived happily ever after." Opening variations such as "Long ago and far away," or "Once there was and once there was not," which are used by storytellers in some cultural groups, contribute to children's ability to generalize the patterns; seeing a different frame serve the same purpose helps children appreciate the flexibility of the device. Early in their literary education, children search for formulaic patterns in language, plots, and characters that they can identify.

© 1992 David Shannon

*David Shannon's art quickly establishes the setting of a village by the lake. The time of "long ago" is reflected in the shelter and food preparation scenes in **The Rough-Face Girl,** by Rafe Martin.*

The repeated use of the number three is another familiar convention. In addition to three main characters—three bears, three billy goats, three pigs—there are usually three events. "Goldilocks and the Three Bears" contains three bears, of course, but also three more sets of three: three bowls of porridge, three chairs, and three beds. Goldilocks tries each bowl of porridge and each chair and bed before deciding which is "just right." Many other folktales feature three tasks, three adventures, three magical objects, three trials, or three wishes. The number seven appears frequently, too, as in "Snow White and the Seven Dwarfs," "The Seven Ravens," and "The Seven Swans." Teaching Idea 5.2 offers ideas for exploring numbers in folklore.

Teaching Idea 5-2

Have Fun with Numbers in Folklore

Numbers in folklore are believed to have mystical qualities. Folktales center on numbers from 1 to 12, although there are more stories dealing with numbers 3, 7, and 12 than there are stories about other numbers. With your class, search for and categorize folktales that repeat numbers. Make a comparison chart for folktales and numbers. Can you identify any common themes or trends? Do certain cultures prefer certain numbers? Can you discover why?

Folktales and Folk Songs with Numbers

1 Puss in Boots
2 Jorinda and Joringel
   Perez and Martina
3 Three Wishes
   Three Little Pigs
   Three Billy Goats Gruff
   Goldilocks and the Three Bears
4 Bremen Town Musicians
   Four Gallant Sisters
5 Five Chinese Brothers
6 Six Foolish Fishermen
7 Seven Blind Mice
   Her Seven Brothers
   Seven at One Blow
   Snow White and the Seven Dwarfs
12 Twelve Dancing Princesses
   Twelve Days of Christmas

• • MOTIFS • •

A *motif* is a recurring salient element, the smallest unit used to classify tales: the intentional repetition of a word or phrase, an event or unit of action, characters, objects, or ideas that run through a story. Many stories contain a number of different motifs that students can identify when comparing folktales. Cinderella stories often contain a small shoe, a flight from a ball, a youngest daughter who is ill-treated, a prince, a wicked stepmother, and a fairy godmother. Characters—gods, witches, fairies, tricksters, noodleheads, or stepmothers—behave in stereotypical ways, so readers learn to predict how they will act in certain situations. A representative human (such as a busybody or a country bumpkin) is often used to stand for a trait or character type.

A second kind of motif focuses on magical objects, spells, curses, or wishes as the center of the plot. Beans tossed carelessly out a window lead the way to a magical kingdom in "Jack and the Beanstalk." "The Magic Porridge Pot" and its variants hinge on a secret ritual. Sometimes the magical element is a spell or enchantment. Both Snow White and Sleeping Beauty are victims of a witch's evil curse and are put to sleep until a kiss from a handsome prince awakens them. In some stories, the evil spell causes a transformation; only love and kindness can return the frog, donkey, or beast to its former state. "The Frog Prince," "The Donkey Prince," "The Seven Ravens," "The Six Swans," "Jorinda and Joringel," and "Beauty and the Beast" are all transformation tales.

A third type of motif involves trickery, or outwitting someone else. A spider man is the trickster in African and Caribbean tales, a rabbit in West African tales, and a tortoise in the Brazilian tale *Jabuti the Tortoise* (P–I), by Gerald McDermott. Trickery and cunning also appear in French and Swedish folktales such as "Stone Soup" and "Nail Soup," and in Jon Muth's Far Eastern version, *Stone Soup* (P–I), featuring three Buddhist monks instead of soldiers. The wiliest trickster of all, Brer Rabbit, is always able to outsmart his larger opponents.

• • THEMES • •

Themes in folktales, obvious although not stated explicitly, express the values of the people who created them and reflect their philosophy of life. The theme in a folktale revolves around a topic of universal human concern. Time and time again, the struggle between good and evil is played out: hate, fear, and greed contrast with love, security, and generosity. The themes are usually developed through stereotyped characters who personify one trait. For example, the bad fairy in "Sleeping Beauty," the witch in "Hansel and Gretel," and the stepmother in "Snow White" all represent evil. Each is destroyed, and the virtuous characters triumph.

Such themes are reassuring to young children. In enchantment and transformation tales, the struggle between good and evil materializes as a contrast between surface appearances and deeper qualities of goodness. A beautiful princess sees the goodness of the prince hidden beneath the loathsome or laughable guise of a beast, frog, or donkey. In other stories, such as some versions of "Sleeping Beauty," the entire world lies under an evil spell, veiled and hidden from clear view until goodness triumphs.

Another theme, that of the quest, centers on the hero's search for happiness or lost identity, which he undertakes in order to restore harmony to life. The hero succeeds only after repeated trials, much suffering, and extended separation, and he often exhibits courage, gallantry, and sacrifice.

Types of Folklore

Folklore has many categories. Those most commonly available to children include nursery rhymes; folktales, including fairy tales, tall tales, and animal tales; fables; myths; legends; and folk songs. Beginning in infancy and continuing through the primary grades, children delight in nursery rhymes. As they grow and develop a literary background, they understand and enjoy folktales, tall tales, myths, legends, and the simple stories and morals of fables. Teachers often introduce children to fairy and animal tales in the primary grades and subsequently move to legends and myths in the upper grades. Today's sophisticated retellings and artwork make such age distinctions unnecessary. Primary-grade children enjoy myths presented in an engaging format; when they study myths later, they have a foundation on which to build their understanding. Similarly, students in the intermediate and advanced grades profit from a study of folktales, especially ones with which they are familiar from childhood.

• • MOTHER GOOSE AND • • NURSERY RHYMES

Mother Goose and nursery rhymes form the foundation of a child's literary heritage. Surprising as that may sound, the rhythm and rhyme of the language, its compact structure and engaging characters produce bountiful models for young children learning language. As they chant the phrases, mimic the nonsense words, and endlessly recite the alliterative rhymes and repetitions, children develop phonemic awareness—the ability to segment sounds in spoken words, something that is a prerequisite to phonics instruction and proficient reading. Researchers MacLean, Bryant, and Brad-

ley (1987) show that exposure to nursery rhymes improves children's phonological skills and thereby their later reading ability. More important, children delight in language play. Poet Walter de la Mare (1962) declared that Mother Goose rhymes "free the fancy, charm the tongue and ear, delight the inward eye, and many of them are tiny masterpieces of word craftsmanship. . . . They are not only crammed with vivid little scenes and objects and living creatures, but, however fantastic and nonsensical they may be, they are a direct short cut into poetry itself" (p. 21). Children learn about characters, themes, and structures that become the foundation stones for subsequent literary education.

Origins

As is true of all folklore, we do not have conclusive evidence of the origins of Mother Goose rhymes, nor do we know whether a woman with that name actually existed. According to Iona and Peter Opie (1951), authors of *The Oxford Nursery Rhyme Book* and *The Oxford Dictionary of Nursery Rhymes,* the rhymes have been linked with social and political events, and numerous attempts have been made to identify the nursery characters with real people. "The bulk of these speculations are worthless," they write. "Fortunately the theories are so numerous they tend to cancel each other out" (p. 27). Whatever the rhymes' origins or original intent, children have always enjoyed them because of their interesting people with unusual names—Georgie Porgie and Jack Sprat and Little Miss Muffet—and the fascinating events they portray. Why would someone want to eat 4-and-20 blackbirds baked in a pie? And poor Humpty Dumpty!

Many of the rhymes probably have a simple origin. They may have been written with the aim of teaching children to count, to learn the alphabet or the days of the week, to share important customs and beliefs, or to remind them to say their prayers. Others—riddles, tongue twisters, and nonsense—were probably intended simply for amusement. The literary name "Mother Goose" was probably first associated with Charles Perrault's 1697 publication of *Histoires ou Contes du Temps Passé, avec des Moralités (Stories or Tales of Times Past, with Morals).* The frontispiece shows an old woman spinning and telling stories and is labeled *Contes de ma Mere l'Oye (Tales of My Mother Goose).* Today the name Mother Goose is associated primarily with nursery rhymes and no longer with the folktales first recorded in the late 1600s.

Mother Goose and nursery rhymes know no regional, ethnic, cultural, or language boundaries. People around the world have crooned similar verses to their young children. The magic of Mother Goose is still handed down by word of mouth, though there are many collections available. When selecting books to share with children, it is essential to choose versions that maintain the original, robust language.

Characteristics

The *rhythmic words* of Mother Goose rhymes strengthen a child's sense of language. The rhythm invites a physical response long before a child can attach meaning to the words. The cadence of the language—its beat, stress, sound, and intonation—is reinforced by the bounce of an adult's knee, as literary critic Northrop Frye (1963) points out:

> The infant who gets bounced on somebody's knee to the rhythm of "Ride a Cock Horse" does not need a footnote telling him that Banbury Cross is twenty miles northeast of Oxford. He does not need the information that "cross" and "horse" make (at least in the pronunciation he is most likely to hear) not a rhyme but an assonance. He does not need the value judgment that the repetition of "horse" in the first two lines indicates a rather thick ear on the part of the composer. All he needs is to get bounced. (p. 25)

A second major characteristic of Mother Goose is the *imaginative use of words and ideas*. Nothing is too preposterous! Children delight in the images conjured up by

> Hey diddle, diddle,
> The cat and the fiddle,
> The cow jumped over the moon;
> The little dog laughed
> To see such sport,
> And the dish ran away with the spoon.

Anything can happen in the young child's unfettered world. The verses feed their fancy, spark their creativity, and stretch their imagination: three wise men of Gotham go to sea in a bowl; an old woman is tossed up in a basket, 19 times as high as the moon; another old woman lives in a shoe with her entire brood of children. Anything can happen in nursery rhymes too.

A third characteristic, the *compact structure*, establishes the scene quickly and divulges the plot at once. In four short lines we hear an entire story:

> Jack Sprat could eat no fat,
> His wife could eat no lean,
> And so between them both, you see,
> They licked the platter clean.

As in all folklore, the consolidation of action and the economy of words result from the rhymes' being said aloud for many generations before being set in print. As the verses were passed from one teller to the next, they were honed to their present simplicity.

The *wit and whimsy* of the characters also account for the popularity and longevity of Mother Goose. Children appreciate the obvious nonsense in

> Gregory Griggs, Gregory Griggs,
> Had twenty-seven different wigs.

> He wore them up, he wore them down,
> To please the people of the town;
> He wore them east, he wore them west,
> But he never could tell which he loved best.

The humor appeals both to children and adults. Surprise endings provide clever resolutions, as in

> Peter, Peter, pumpkin eater,
> Had a wife and couldn't keep her;
> He put her in a pumpkin shell,
> And there he kept her very well.

Collections

Such old favorites as Alice and Martin Provensen's *The Mother Goose Book,* Blanche Fisher Wright's *The Real Mother Goose,* Arnold Lobel's *The Random House Book of Mother Goose,* and Iona and Peter Opie's *Tail Feathers from Mother Goose* (all N–P) provide many familiar and some less familiar rhymes to share. More recently, Rosemary Wells and Iona Opie worked together to produce *My Very First Mother Goose* and *Here Comes Mother Goose* (both N–P), and Nina Crews has added a lively urban collection, *The Neighborhood Mother Goose* (P–I). *The Charles Addams Mother Goose* (A), with its darkly droll, comic illustrations, will appeal to older students who will see the familiar rhymes in a totally novel way.

Authors, editors, and publishers, aware of the international makeup of our population and the global-village view of our world, search for new books to reflect that vision. Schools need several Mother Goose and nursery rhyme collections for teachers to read aloud and for children to look at, hold, share, and love. Patricia Polacco includes verses and images from her Russian grandmother in *Babushka's Mother Goose;* Nancy Van Laan depicts a mother and a child from seven different continents in *Sleep, Sleep, Sleep: A Lullaby for Little Ones around the World;* and Jane Yolen selects from an international palette in *Sleep Rhymes around the World* (all N–P). For their collection *Chinese Mother Goose Rhymes* (N–P), illustrator Ed Young and editor Robert Wyndham have chosen rhymes from the Chinese oral tradition that may sometimes seem familiar even to modern American children. *¡Pío Peep! Traditional Spanish Nursery Rhymes* (N), by Alma Flor Ada and F. Isabel Campoy, with English adaptations by poet Alice Schertle, is a bilingual collection of rhymes that may be well known to Hispanic children and will appeal to children from other cultures as well.

Other excellent Mother Goose books in single editions and edited collections are listed in the Booklist at the end of the chapter.

THAILAND

Chao non bai
Yen pra-pai ma ruay-ruay
Mae cha pa pai non duay
Cha klom hai chao non
Mue-sai cha pad wee
Mue-kwa nee pen Chamorn
Sao-noy chao ya on
Chao puan-non kong mue—euy

Take an afternoon nap, my baby.
When the cool, constant breeze caresses you
I'll cuddle you to sleep, very near to me.
I'll lull you to sleep with my songs.
With my left hand as a fan I'll cool you,
With my right hand as a whisk I'll protect you.
Don't cry, my baby,
Dear sleeping friend of mine.

*Sleep rhymes work at bedtime for children everywhere. This illustration is from Jane Yolen's **Sleep Rhymes around the World.***

• • FOLKTALES • • •

Origins

The transition from oral retelling to printed versions of folktales dates back centuries. Some Eastern stories appeared in print as early as the ninth century. In Europe, Straparola (1480–1557), author and duke of Milan, Italy, gathered one of the earliest and most important collections of traditional tales in mid-16th-century Venice in *Piacevoli Notti,* vols. 1 and 2 (published in 1550 and 1553). The work contains 20 folktales, including "Beauty and the Beast" and "Puss in Boots." Straparola's work was followed by Basile's *Pentameron or Entertainment for the Little Ones* in 17th-century Naples. Perrault's French publication of *Histoires ou Contes du Temps Passé* in 1697 helped folk literature flourish in Europe. Perrault included "Sleeping Beauty," "Little Red Riding Hood," "Cinderella," and "Puss in Boots" along with other familiar tales in his collection. During the 18th century, La Fontaine's *Fables,* Countess d'Aulnoy's *Fairy Tales,* and Madame de Beaumont's *Beauty and the Beast* were published. Folktales have deep literary roots.

Toward the end of the 18th century, philologists studied folklore to find out about customs and languages in different societies. The German brothers Jacob and Wilhelm Grimm traveled through the countryside asking people to tell stories they remembered. The Grimms eventually wrote a German dictionary and a book of grammar, but they are best remembered for their retellings of the stories they

heard. The two volumes of the first edition of *Kinder-und Hausmarchen* were published in 1812 and 1815.

German Popular Stories, an English translation of the Grimm's tales illustrated by George Cruikshank, became an instant success when it was published in 1823. It raised the respectability of the old tales among scholars and educators, who had held them to be "an affront to the rational mind" (Opie & Opie, 1974, p. 25). Wanda Gag translated and illustrated the stories in her *Tales from Grimm* (I–A) in 1936 and *More Tales from Grimm* (I–A) in 1947, and in 1973 Maurice Sendak handsomely illustrated Lore Segal's translation *The Juniper Tree and Other Tales from Grimm* (vols. 1 and 2), a collection containing many grim tales most suited for adolescent readers. Many others have retold and illustrated single tales from the Grimm brothers, such as *Snow White and the Seven Dwarfs* (I), translated by Randall Jarrell and illustrated by Nancy Ekholm Burkert. In *The Annotated Brothers Grimm,* Maria Tatar translates 37 of the 210 tales, along with 9 adult tales, from the Grimms' final edition of the stories, giving readers valuable background information for each.

Following the popularity of the Grimm brothers' tales, enthusiasm for collecting folklore spread around the world. Joseph Jacobs and Andrew Lang collected folktales in England; Jacobs's *English Fairy Tales* includes many best-loved stories, and Lang's series, in which the books are identified by color—*The Blue Fairy Book,* for example—continues to serve as a primary source of British tales. During the mid-1800s, Norse scholars Peter Christian Asbjornsen and Jorgen E. Moe collected most of the Scandinavian tales we have today. George Webbe Dasent's translation of *East o' the Sun and West o' the Moon* (I) into English retains the vitality of spoken language. Many of the same tales appear in Ingri and Edgar Parin d'Aulaire's *East of the Sun and West of the Moon* (I), which contains illustrations echoing Norwegian folk art. Nancy Willard converted the tale into a dramatic play (A) of the same name, illustrated by Barry Moser. More recently, Lise Lunge-Larsen has collected Norwegian troll stories in *The Troll with No Heart in His Body* (I), with rough-textured woodcuts by Betsy Bowen that echo the age of the tales. Isaac Bashevis Singer's collections of Yiddish tales, in such books as *Naftali the Storyteller and His Horse, Sus* (P–I), and *When Shlemiel Went to Warsaw* (I), are inspired by old Jewish stories he heard as a boy in Warsaw.

Characteristics

Folktales are narratives in which heroes and heroines triumph over adversity by demonstrating virtues like cleverness or bravery, or loveable vices like supreme silliness. Their themes, obvious though not always stated explicitly, express the values of the people who created them. The stories have an artistic yet simple form that derives from the oral tradition. The *plot structure* is clean and direct. The first paragraph establishes characters and setting, the body develops the problem and moves toward the climax, and the ending quickly resolves the problem without complications. Folktales are, in fact, minidramas. See Teaching Idea 5.3 for ideas for involving students in folklore theatre.

Folktales unfold with little ambiguity: the good characters are supremely good; the evil ones are outrageously evil; and justice prevails without compromise. The conflict is identified early, and only incidents that build on the problem or add complexity to it have survived oral transmission. Problems are resolved decisively, with little denouement, resulting in classic happily-ever-after endings. Margaret Willey's books set in the far north woods, *Clever Beatrice* and *Clever Beatrice and the Best Little Pony* (both P–I), which introduce a spunky and very capable young girl who first outsmarts a giant and then a lutin, a cunning little man, are excellent examples of tales that fit this pattern.

Because folktales are more concerned with situation than personality, characters are delineated economically. Few subtleties interrupt the intentional stereotyping that quickly establishes character traits. These one-dimensional, or "flat," characters crystallize in the form of the foolish, the wise, the wicked, or the virtuous. All perform in predictable ways and rarely change throughout the course of a story. Children tolerate the idea that a different range of possibilities existed in the distant past. In Applebee's study (1978) young children said, "Witches and giants lived a long time ago." They know that giants do not live in today's world, but they readily accept the possibility that they might have lived at one time.

The language—direct, vivid vernacular—is uncluttered by awkward constructions or convolutions. Gail E. Haley's retelling of *Mountain Jack Tales* (I) reflects the Appalachian regional dialect of their origin. Colloquialisms add to the

---

Teaching Idea 5-3

Create a Folklore Performance

Folklore is ideal material for readers' theatre, puppetry, or choral reading. Folktales contain simple plot lines, a limited cast of well-defined characters, and decisive endings, making them ideal for young scriptwriters and dramatists. To create a folklore performance with your students:

1. Ask book groups to choose several folktales to read.
2. Generate criteria for selecting a good story for dramatizing. What elements make stories easier to tell?
3. Have them choose their favorite folktale that fits the selection criteria to share through creative drama.
4. Prepare a script for readers' theatre, a puppet play, or choral reading.
5. Practice and share the performance with others.

Fractured folktales and myths add a note of hilarity to a story. Some versions with dramatic possibilities include the following:

Scieszka, Jon, *The Stinky Cheese Man and Other Fairly Stupid Tales*

_____, *The True Story of the Three Little Pigs*

Wells, Rosemary, *Max and Ruby's First Greek Myth: Pandora's Box*

_____, *Max and Ruby's Midas: Another Greek Myth*

The befuddled giant can't believe that Clever Beatrice has won their first bet.

© 2001 Heather Solomon

Folktale Characteristics

✳ Heroes and heroines employ such traits as cleverness, bravery, or supreme silliness to triumph over adversity.

✳ Plot lines are direct and are uncluttered by side issues.

✳ Stories contain very little ambiguity: good is good; evil is outrageously evil.

✳ Conflict is identified early.

✳ Resolution is decisive.

✳ Characters are delineated economically.

✳ Themes express the values of the people who created them.

✳ Language is direct, vivid vernacular.

✳ Setting is geographically vague; time is vague.

flavor and reflect the heritage of the tale; they are tempered to the tongue, having been honed and polished through centuries.

Although folktales use precise language, the *setting* remains geographically vague, leaving an impression of a world that is complete in itself. The stories take place in unidentified times, in places defined by minimal detail. Young children do not question the truthfulness of story—it is a *story,* and it really happened. Folktales know no geographical or temporal boundaries; they come to life everywhere for each new generation of children. Figure 5.2 summarizes folktale characteristics.

Types of Folktales

CUMULATIVE TALES Each incident in a cumulative tale grows from the preceding one, as in "This Is the House That Jack Built" and "The Old Woman and Her Pig." Jeanette Winter's *The House That Jack Built* (N–P) uses rebus characters in the text so that even younger children can predict what is coming next. These stories are often called "chain tales," because each part of the story is linked to the next. The initial incident reveals both central character and problem; each subsequent scene builds on the previous one, continuing to a climax and then unraveling in reverse order or stopping with an abrupt surprise ending. Cat is so very hungry in Meilo So's Indian folktale, *Gobble, Gobble, Slip, Slop: A Tale of a Very Greedy Cat* (P–I), that he eats every-

thing and everyone he encounters, with ridiculous results. Chain tales often have repetitive phrases like "Run, run as fast as you can. You can't catch me. I'm the Gingerbread man," from "The Gingerbread Boy" and its variants, "Johnny Cake," "The Pancake," and "The Bun." More examples of cumulative tales are listed in the Booklist at the end of the chapter.

TALKING ANIMALS In this type of tale, animals talk with human beings or with each other. Like human characters, the talking animals may be good or evil, wise or silly. Those who are good and wise are rewarded. Young children especially enjoy talking animals. Perennial favorites include "The Three Little Pigs," "The Three Billy Goats Gruff," "Henny Penny," "Brer Rabbit," and the Anansi spider stories. Jessica Souhami retells a traditional tale from India in *No Dinner! The Story of the Old Woman and the Pumpkin* (N–P). With the help of her granddaughter, the old woman outsmarts a bear, wolf, and tiger that want to eat her for dinner.

Children appreciate the humorous situations and rhythmic language of Eric Kimmel's retelling of the West African trickster tale, *Anansi Goes Fishing* (P), an exemplary talking animal tale, as is his tale *Anansi and the Moss-Covered Rock* (P), with Janet Steven's humorous illustrations of the scheming spider and all the animals he tricks and is tricked by. Native American tribal tales also have tricksters, such as coyote and raven. Gerald McDermott's *Coyote* tells the story of a prideful, comic mischief-maker with "a nose for trouble." The rabbit in *Brother Rabbit: A Cambodian Tale* (P–I), by Minfong Ho and Saphan Ros, is clever enough to repeatedly outsmart the hungry crocodile. Animal tricksters such as these are common in stories from many different cultures. Julius Lester (2004) writes that "a prime characteristic of the trickster tale is the absence of morality. Uncle Remus said, 'Creatures don't know nothing about that's good and that's bad. They don't know right from wrong. They see what they want and they get it if they can, by hook or crook'" (p. 114). Perhaps tricksters and their stories are so appealing to children for just that reason: tricksters will do anything to get what they want.

Brer Rabbit trickster stories traveled from Africa and Jamaica to the American rural South, and were originally popularized by storyteller Joel Chandler Harris. Van Dyke Park's outstanding renditions of these traditional tales include *Jump! The Adventures of Brer Rabbit, Jump Again! More Adventures of Brer Rabbit,* and *Jump on Over: The Adventures of Brer Rabbit and His Family* (all P–I), all illustrated by Barry Moser. Julius Lester's retellings, *The Tales of Uncle Remus, More Tales of Uncle Remus,* and *Further Tales of Uncle Remus* (all I–A) are also marked by melodious language that reflects the authentic speech patterns of the culture that gave rise to the stories. *The Butter Tree: Tales of Bruh Rabbit* (I), retold by Mary Lyons and illustrated by

Mireille Vautier, and *Bruh Rabbit and the Tar Baby Girl* (p–i), retold by Virginia Hamilton and illustrated by James Ransome, show that Brer Rabbit is just as sly as ever. Other talking animal stories appear in the Booklist at the end of the chapter.

NOODLEHEAD TALES Humorous noodlehead stories focus on characters who are pure hearted but lacking in good judgment. In *Noodlehead Stories from around the World* (i), M. A. Jagendorf describes a noodlehead as a simple blunderer who does not use good sense or learn from experience. Every cultural group has noodlehead stories that provoke hearty laughter: the wise men of Gotham in England, the fools in the Jewish ghetto of Chelm in Poland, Juan Bobo in Puerto Rico, the Connemara Man in Ireland, and the Montieri in Italy. Other examples of noodlehead stories are listed in the Booklist at the end of the chapter.

FAIRY TALES Fairy tales are magical narratives replete with supernatural beings, such as trolls, ogres, dragons, elves, and sometimes even fairies, as well as humans, such as the youngest son; poor, widowed mothers; and wicked half-sisters. Fairy tales originated long ago from the oral tradition, but today are primarily written and told for the amusement and enlightenment of children. Though fairy tales are structured like other folktales, their deeply magical character sets them apart. Wee people, fairy godmothers, and other magical beings intervene to make things happen. Enchantment aside, these stories paint an ideal vision of life based on the hope that virtue will be recognized and hard work rewarded. Fairy tales show children that courage, honesty, and resourcefulness are valued. Paul Hazard (1967), literary critic and author of *Books, Children, and Men,* said, "Fairy tales are like beautiful mirrors of water, so deep and crystal clear. In their depths we sense the mysterious experience of a thousand years" (p. 157).

Examples of fairy tales include Robert D. San Souci's *The Talking Eggs* (p–i), a Creole variant of Cinderella illustrated by Jerry Pinkney, and *The Turkey Girl* (i), a Zuni version retold by Penny Pollock and illustrated by Ed Young. In *A Handful of Beans* (i–a), Jeanne Steig retells six popular European tales, including "Little Red Riding Hood" and "Rumpelstiltskin," that she makes her own by sprinkling them with witty verse. Lise Lunge-Larsen's collection, *The Hidden Folk: Stories of Fairies, Dwarves, Selkies, and Other Secret Beings* (p–i–a), with lushly patterned, folkloric

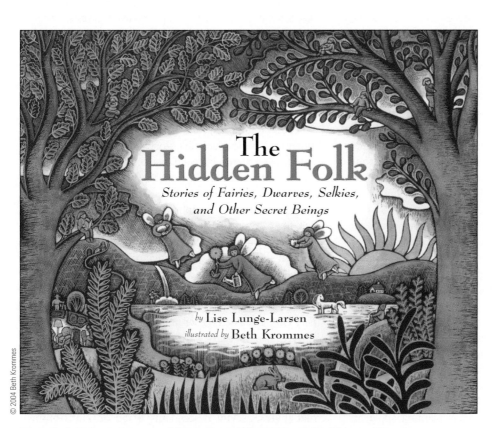

Through the informative text and illustrations of **The Hidden Folk,** *children will become quite familiar with the gnomes, fairies, selkies, and sprites who may be hiding nearby.*

scratchboard illustrations by Beth Krommes, is a comprehensive introduction to the folk characters who populate many European fairy tales. Jane Yolen shares a dozen tales of strong women in *Not One Damsel in Distress: World Folktales for Strong Girls* (I), and Judy Sierra has gathered enchanting tales in *Nursery Tales around the World* (N–P). The editor of Virginia Hamilton's *The People Could Fly: The Picture Book* (P–I) states in an opening note about the story, based on a letter Hamilton wrote in 1984, that it is "one of the mythical old tales of 'things that never were,' as opposed to characters and events that were once actual." Magical stories of slaves flying from their enslavement are still very fitting in a world where slaves still suffer and people long to be free. Other examples of fairy tales and their variants are listed in the Booklist at the end of the chapter.

TALL TALES Tall tales are primarily indigenous to the United States and are a peculiarly American form of folktale. They are a combination of history, myth, and fact. Tall tales gave the early American settlers symbols of strength, and offset with a little humor the harsh realities of an untamed land. The exaggerated strength and blatant lies in tall tales added zest and lightened a life of hard labor. As the settlers built a new country, they created heroes who were the mightiest, strongest, and most daring lumberjacks, railroad men, coal miners, riverboat drivers, and steel workers possible.

Many heroes of tall tales were real people, but their improbable stories have made them larger than life. Davy Crockett, Daniel Boone, and Johnny Appleseed accomplished feats no mortal would dare. John Henry, Pecos Bill, and Mike Fink exemplify the Yankee work ethic, the brawn and muscle required to develop America. Children love the exaggerated humor and lies that mark the tall tales. They laugh when Paul Bunyan's loggers tie bacon to their feet and skate across the huge griddle to grease it. The thought of Slewfoot Sue bouncing skyward every time her bustle hits the ground produces giggles. And when the infant Pecos Bill falls out of the covered wagon, children can picture the abandoned baby scrambling toward the coyote mother, who eventually raises him with the rest of the coyote pack. The heroes in tall tales are all-powerful, so readers know they will overcome any problem. The suspense is in *how* the problem will be solved.

Julius Lester describes the mighty battle between a steam drill and the legendary hero in *John Henry* (P–I), illustrated by Jerry Pinkney. Steven Kellogg's tall tale biography, *Johnny Appleseed* (P–I), and Reeve Lindbergh's poetic version, *Johnny Appleseed: A Poem* (P–I), illustrated by Kathy Jakobsen, both tell the story of John Chapman, who traveled across the Allegheny Mountains planting apple orchards. Alvin Schwartz gathered his entertaining and informative research into the language, superstition, and folk

history of America's legendary past in many books, including *Whoppers: Tall Tales and Other Lies, Witcracks: Jokes and Jests from American Folklore,* and *Flapdoodle: Pure Nonsense from American Folklore* (all I–A). Glen Rounds presented many larger-than-life stories of Paul Bunyan and Babe in his book *Ol' Paul the Mighty Logger* (P–I). Not all the heroes are male: Robert D. San Souci collected 20 tales about strong women in *Cut from the Same Cloth: American Women of Myth, Legend, and Tall Tale* (I). Other tall tales are listed in the Booklist at the end of the chapter.

Variants of Folktales

Although the origins of folktales are clouded in prehistory, variants can be traced to many cultures. Contemporary writers and artists breathe new life into the many versions of ancient folktales. Many stories have hundreds of variants from countries all over the world. Comparing the motifs, characters, and themes of the different versions can be a very illuminating activity for students.

CINDERELLA Folklorist M. R. Cox, a pioneer in folklore research during the 1890s, revealed the Cinderella motif in his book for adults, *Cinderella: Three Hundred and Forty-Five Variants* (1893). In the foreword to the Cox collection, Andrew Lang, a Scottish scholar who lived from 1844 to 1912 and who was noted for his own collections of fairy tales, states, "The marchen [fairy tale] is a kaleidoscope: the incidents are the bits of coloured glass. Shaken, they fall into a variety of attractive forms; some forms are fitter than others, survive more powerfully, and are more widely spread" (p. x).

The romantic rags-to-riches versions of "Cinderella," based on Charles Perrault's story, have been illustrated by noted artists Marcia Brown, Susan Jeffers, and Errol Le Cain, among others. In the German version by the Brothers Grimm, *Cinderella* (I–A), illustrated by Nonny Hogrogian, the story takes on a macabre tone. In order to make their feet fit into the tiny glass slipper, the sisters take drastic measures: One cuts off her toe, and the other cuts off her heel. In the end they are blinded. Other versions include Appalachian, Chinese, Creole, Yiddish, Egyptian, English, Indonesian, Irish, Korean, Persian, Spanish American, and Vietnamese, as well as the Algonquin variant, *The Rough-Face Girl,* discussed earlier in this chapter.

SLEEPING BEAUTY In *Once upon a Time: On the Nature of Fairy Tales,* Max Luthi (1970), a notable folklorist, presents an insightful analysis of the many variants of "Sleeping Beauty." Luthi speaks of fairy tales as remnants of primal myths, playful descendants of an ancient, intuitive vision of life and the world. The story of Sleeping Beauty, who is mysteriously threatened and who suffers a sleep similar to death but is then awakened, parallels the story of death and resurrection. The awakening of the sleeping maiden can also represent the earth's awakening from winter to blossom anew when touched by the warmth of spring. Trina Schart Hyman's *The Sleeping Beauty* (P–I–A) interprets the story through elegant, mysterious art and graceful text. "The Princess grew up so gracious, merry, beautiful, and kind that everyone who knew her could not help but love her. And because she was mischievous and clever as well, she was called Briar Rose."

Luthi describes how "Sleeping Beauty" is more than an imaginatively stylized love story portraying a girl whose love breaks a spell. The princess is an image for the human spirit: The story portrays her natural gifts, talents, and personal strengths; it describes the fall and the redemption not just of one girl but of humankind. Sleeping Beauty's recovery symbolizes that the human soul can be revived, healed, and redeemed despite suffering repeated setbacks. The fairy tale is a miniature universe that reflects the wisdom of the ages in an enchanting tale.

GOOD SISTER–BAD SISTER More than 900 versions of the "kind sister–unkind sister" theme have been recorded. Charlotte Huck's *Toads and Diamonds* (P–I), illustrated by Anita Lobel, shows the younger Rene walking a mile and a half twice a day to carry water for her stepmother and stepsister. Along the path, Rene feeds bread crumbs to a friendly rabbit and to a bird that flies to her shoulder. One day an old peasant woman sits near the spring and asks for a drink. When Rene quenches the old woman's thirst, the woman says, "Because you are as kind as you are beautiful, I have a gift for you. For every word you speak, a flower or jewel will drop from your lips. And this will happen as long as there will be a need for it." The stepmother sends her other daughter to receive the same gift, but her behavior—and the gifts she receives—are dreadfully different. John Steptoe's *Mufaro's Beautiful Daughters* (P–I) and Robert D. San Souci's *The Talking Eggs* are variants on this theme. Teachers at primary, intermediate, and advanced grade levels find that students are fascinated by discovering variants of familiar tales. Students gain an understanding of folklore, culture, literary structures, and genre characteristics through discussion of these discoveries. We discuss working with variants later in this chapter.

RUMPELSTILTSKIN The story of the little man who, for a cruel fee, helps a poor girl spin straw or flax into skeins of gold is another well-loved tale. The best-known version, Grimm's *Rumpelstiltskin* (I), retold and illustrated by Paul Zelinsky, tells the story of a dwarf who demands the queen's firstborn child as payment for his help. Joseph Jacobs's *Tom Tit Tot* (P), retold and illustrated by Evaline Ness, is a version from Suffolk, England, in which an impet (dwarf) spins

© 1987 John Steptoe

Kindly Nyasha, Mufaro's good, beautiful daughter, greets a small green snake, assuring him that he is welcome in her garden.

five skeins of gold from flax. In Devonshire and Cornwall, England, the devil knits stockings, jackets, and other clothing for the Squire, as recounted in *Duffy and the Devil* (P), retold by Harve Zemach. The character that corresponds to Rumpelstiltskin is called Trit-a-Trot in Ireland and Whuppity Stoorie in Scotland. Each version's cultural origins are reflected in the clothing, dialect, and settings. Virginia Hamilton uses a colloquial style to present a West Indian variant in *The Girl Who Spun Gold* (P–I). Leo and Diane Dillon illustrate the book in magnificent paintings made with acrylic paint on acetate overpainted with gold. The embossed paintings appear on pages edged with gold leaf. The gold of the art conveys the importance of gold in the story.

JACK AND THE BEANSTALK "Jack and the Beanstalk" first appeared in Joseph Jacobs's collection of English folktales. It has since been illustrated by many contemporary artists. In Lorinda Bryan Cauley's *Jack and the Beanstalk* (N–P), the beanstalk is a lush green forest peopled with dour folks who sense danger and are heavy with foreboding. In contrast, Paul Galdone's characters in *Jack and the Beanstalk* (N–P) are oafish, laughing bunglers who create a lighthearted story.

© 2000 Leo & Diane Dillon

Leo and Diane Dillon illustrate an elegant edition of an ancient tale in **The Girl Who Spun Gold.**

Many Americanized versions of Old World tales revolve around a boy named Jack and are therefore known as "Jack Tales." One of the most familiar is a variant of "Jack and the Beanstalk" known as "Jack's Bean Tree." It is found in Richard Chase's *Jack Tales* and in *Jack and the Wonder Beans* (both P–I), by James Still. Appalachian dialect permeates these versions of the familiar tale. For example, the giant's refrain in *Jack and the Wonder Beans* is "Fee, fie, chew tobacco, I smell the toes of a tadwhacker." Gail E. Haley's Appalachian retelling, *Jack and the Bean Tree* (P), is set in the context of a storyteller's tale. Family and neighbors gather round Grandmother Poppyseed, who gives a local flavor to her tales: A banty hen lays the golden eggs; the giant chants "Bein' he live or bein' / he dead, / I'll have his bones / To eat with my pones." Haley paints her bold, energetic illustrations on wood, and the brilliant colors reflect the intensities of light and shadow.

Mary Pope Osborne chose a girl to climb the beanstalk in *Kate and the Beanstalk* (P), illustrated by Giselle Potter. Kate outsmarts the giant and makes a fortune for herself and her mother. Raymond Briggs wrote a parody of the Jack Tales in *Jim and the Beanstalk* (P–I). The giant has grown old and has lost his appetite, his teeth, and his eyesight. Jim helps him get false teeth and glasses. Variants of this tale and others appear in the Booklist at the end of the chapter.

• • FABLES • •

A fable is a brief tale that presents a clear and unambiguous moral. Fables make didactic comments on human nature using dramatic action to heighten the effect. They differ from other traditional literature in that the moral of the story is explicitly stated.

Many common sayings come from fables. "Better beans and bacon in peace than cakes and ale in fear" comes from "Town Mouse, Country Mouse," one version of which is illustrated by Jan Brett. "Slow and steady wins the race" is from "The Tortoise and the Hare," one of the tales retold and illustrated by Jerry Pinkney in *Aesop's Fables* (P–I). "Knowing in part may make a fine tale, but wisdom comes from seeing the whole," is illustrated in *Seven Blind Mice* (P–I), by Ed Young. "Do not put off until tomorrow what you should do today" is one of the morals from *Unwitting Wisdom: An Anthology of Aesop's Fables* (P–I), by Helen Ward. Such injunctions, explicitly stated as morals, are taught by allegory, or symbolic narrative. Animals or inanimate objects take on human traits in stories that clearly show the wisdom of the simple lessons. Folklorists therefore relate fables to beast tales—stories in which characters are animals with human traits—which were used for satiric purposes and in some cases taught a moral. In the single-

In her intricately detailed watercolors in **Unwitting Wisdom: An Anthology of Aesop's Fables,** *Helen Ward aptly captures Fox's disappointment.*

incident story typical of the fable, we are told not to be vain, not to be greedy, and not to lie.

Joseph Jacobs (1854–1916), the Australian-born scholar of English folklore, traces the origins of fables to both Greece and India. Reputedly, a Greek slave named Aesop used fables for political purposes, and though some scholars doubt that he ever lived, his name has been associated with fables since ancient times. Jean de La Fontaine, a 17th-century French poet, adapted many of Aesop's fables into verse form. Brian Wildsmith illustrated several of these, including *The Hare and the Tortoise* (P).

The source of early collections from the East is the Indian "Panchatantra" (literally five *tantras,* or books), known to English readers as the "Fables of Bidpai" or "Jataka Tales." The Jatakas are stories of the Buddha's prior lives, in which he took the form of various animals. Each story is intended to illustrate a moral principle. *Foolish Rabbit's Big Mistake* (P–I), by Rafe Martin, is an early version of a "sky is falling" tale, with frenetic action vividly illustrated by Ed Young.

Several collections of fables for younger children are available, but some educators question whether primary-grade children understand the subtle abstractions. Because

fables are short and are told in simple language, some teachers mistakenly give fables to children who are too young to comprehend or fully appreciate them. Researcher Arlene Pillar (1983) found that seven-year-olds often missed the point of widely used fables. Because fables are constructed within the oblique perspective of satire, allegory, and symbolism, their intent may elude young children's literal understanding. Examples of individual and collected fables appear in the Booklist at the end of the chapter.

• • M Y T H O L O G Y • •

The special group of stories we call myths developed as humans sought to interpret both natural phenomena and human behavior. They were used to answer fundamental questions concerning how human beings and their world were created. Myths express the beliefs and religious customs of ancient cultures and portray their visions of destiny. Unlike other stories, myths relate to each other; taken together, they build a complex picture of an imaginative world (Frye, 1970). They are once-sacred stories that feature capricious gods and goddesses who were believed to control people's everyday lives. Many myths are so integral to Western culture that they appear as literary allusions, as discussed in Teaching Idea 5.4.

Penelope Farmer (1979), translator of many myths, describes their purpose this way:

> Myths have seemed to me to point quite distinctly—yet without ever directly expressing it—to some kind of unity behind creation, not a static unity, but a forever shifting breathing one. . . . The acquisition by man of life or food or fire has to be paid for by the acceptance of death—the message is everywhere, quite unmistakable. To live is to die; to die is to live. (p. 4)

The great archetypal theme of life and death appears again and again throughout the stories told by all cultures. Children are familiar with the bare branches and frozen ground of winter giving way to the rebirth of flowers and trees in the spring. Most of them have buried a seed in the ground and watched for it to sprout. In images and symbols, mythic themes reappear under many guises that children can recognize through their study of myth. Literature throughout the ages echoes the themes of the ancient myths. Northrop Frye (1970) traces the origins of all literature back to one central story: how man once lived in a golden age or a garden of Eden or the Hesperides or a happy island kingdom in the Atlantic, how that world was lost, and how we some day may be able to get it back again (pp. 53, 57).

The literary value of myths lies in their exciting plots, well-developed characters, heroic actions, challenging situations, and deep emotions. They are compelling stories of love, carnage, revenge, and mystery. At the same time, they transmit ancient values, symbols, customs, art, law, and language. Isaac Asimov explores the roots of hundreds of mythic images in *Words from the Myths* (I), a handy reference for students interested in etymology. Penelope Proddow compiled *Art Tells a Story: Greek and Roman Myths* (I–A), a collection of myths accompanied by photographs of the artwork they inspired. *Gods, Goddesses and Monsters: A Book of World Mythology* (A), by Sheila Keenan, provides information about mythic characters from countries all around the globe.

In myths, as in all folklore, a great deal depends on the telling. Much also depends on the illustrating, and myths offer artists an excellent opportunity for presenting their own interpretation of some elemental stories. Jeanne Steig's lively, often poetic collection, *A Gift from Zeus: Sixteen Favorite Myths* (A), showcases the witty illustrations of William Steig. Gods, goddesses, humans, and beasts suffer and cavort, lament and sing in the wry watercolors and lush language of this book.

Creation myths are popular and are suitable for students in elementary and middle school. They describe the origin of the earth and the phenomena that affect it. Some books are collections of creation myths from around the world; others focus on myths from one culture. Jacqueline Morley collected 11 creation myths in *Egyptian Myths* (I), illustrated by Giovanni Caselli. Her graceful retellings focus on the struggle between good and evil, the creation of the world, and the relationships between gods and humans. Virginia Hamilton's definitive collection, *In the Beginning: Creation Stories from around the World* (I–A), gives students many different cultures' explanations of how the world began and how people were created.

Teaching Idea 5-4

Search for Mythical Allusions

Students who read widely recognize frequently used *allusions* (references to a literary figure, event, or object) drawn from mythology. Classical allusions—such as Pandora's box, an Achilles' heel, the Midas touch, the Trojan horse, and the face that launched a thousand ships—appear in our language, literature, and culture; they are part of our common vocabulary. A winged horse (Pegasus) appeared on old gas station signs, Mercury delivers flowers, Vulcan repairs tires, and many of us wear our Nike shoes to work or play every day.

The English language reflects origins in Greek, Roman, and Norse myths: *erotic* comes from Eros, *titanic* comes from the Titans, and *cereal* comes from Ceres. The days of the week derive from myths: Sunday = Sun-day; Monday = Moon-day; Tuesday = Tiu's-day; Wednesday = Odin's-day; Thursday = Thor's-day; Friday = Freya's-day; Saturday = Saturn's-day. In *Words from the Myths,* Isaac Asimov presents many words that have their origins in myths. To encourage students to learn more about allusions:

1. Have students notice words, symbols, and allusions to myths as they read newspapers, magazines, and books, and as they watch television and movies.

2. Instruct them to keep a list of words and mythological referents.

3. Have them find out who Odysseus, Medea, Achilles, Antigone, Oedipus, Hector, and other mythical characters are and why their names are important to us today.

4. Have students post the allusions on a bulletin board as they find them. Who can find the most unusual?

© 2001 Jeanne & William Steig

Pandora realizes too late that she has unleashed Carbuncles, Pestilence, Fleas, Flatulence, and other hideous creatures depicted with gruesome wit by William Steig in A Gift from Zeus.

Pourquoi Stories

The simplest myths are *pourquoi* stories, from the French word for "why." They tell how the earth began and why the seasons change, how animals got their colors and why they behave as they do. Pierre Grimal (1965) notes in his comprehensive *Larousse World Mythology* that we humans lose our fear of things we can name and explain:

> Given a universe full of uncertainties and mysteries, the myth intervenes to introduce the human element: clouds in the sky, sunlight, storms at sea, all extra-human factors such as these lose much of their power to terrify as soon as they are given the sensibility, intentions, and motivations that every individual experiences daily. (p. 9)

Why the Sky Is Far Away: A Nigerian Folktale (N–P), by Mary-Joan Gerson, illustrated by Carla Golembe, and *Why Mosquitoes Buzz in People's Ears* (P), by Verna Aardema, illustrated by Leo and Diane Dillon, are two excellent examples of African pourquoi tales. Native Americans also have many stories to explain animals' traits, human conduct, and natural phenomena. Joseph Bruchac's stories, such as *The First Strawberries* or *How Chipmunk Got His Stripes: A Tale of Bragging and Teasing,* or Paul Goble's *The Gift of the Sacred Dog* (I) will give students an idea of the significance

of this type of story to North American tribes. More pourquoi tales are listed in the Booklist at the end of the chapter.

Greek and Roman Mythology

Myths are only tenuously related to historical fact and geographical location. However, they played an important role in the lives of the ancients, especially in the art, music, architecture, and culture of ancient Greece. The Greeks believed that gods and goddesses controlled the universe. Zeus, the most powerful god, controlled the weather—the lightning and thunder—and ruled over all the other gods who lived on Mount Olympus and the mortals who lived around it. Figure 5.3 lists the Greek gods and goddesses, the functions and powers attributed to them, and the names later given to them by the Romans, who adopted the Greek deities as their own.

Greek myths are replete with wondrous monsters. Children are fascinated by these half-human, half-beast creatures that frightened early people and wreaked havoc on their lands. Just as young children delight in tales of witches and giants, older students, too, love to read about Medusa, who grew hissing snakes on her head instead of hair; Cerberus, the huge three-headed dog; and the horrible one-eyed Cyclops.

Stories of individual heroes tell of great adventures, tests, victories, and losses. They feature relationships between gods and mortals and show how life must be lived with morality and conscience. Countless myths focus on the love between a god or goddess and a mortal, like that between Psyche and Cupid. Students familiar with this myth recognize its presence in many modern romances.

In *Dateline: Troy* (I–A), Paul Fleischman shows that the ancient tabloids are as fresh as today's news. Fleischman sets the ancient story of the Trojan War and today's headlines side by side—they are strikingly similar!

> The first book to be printed in English appeared in 1475 and recounted the Trojan War. In 1873 the site of Troy was discovered in western Turkey, facing Greece across the Aegean Sea. The city long thought mythical was real. Listeners and readers had always found real human nature in what had transpired there. Envy-maddened Ajax, love-struck Paris, crafty Odysseus, and all the others have walked the earth in every age and place. They live among us today. Though their tale comes from the distant Bronze Age, it's as current as this morning's headlines. The Trojan War is still being fought. Simply open a newspaper. (pp. 8–9)

Superior retellings of Greek myths include Shirley Climo's *Atalanta's Race: A Greek Myth* (I–A), illustrated by Alexander Koshkin. In *Olympians: Great Gods and Goddesses of Ancient Greece* (I–A), Leonard Everett Fisher presents

Figure 5-3

Greek and Roman Gods

Greek Name	Title	Roman Name
Aphrodite	Goddess of love and beauty	Venus
Apollo	God of sunlight, music, prophecy, and poetry	Apollo
Ares	God of war	Mars
Artemis	Goddess of the hunt	Diana
Athena	Goddess of wisdom	Minerva
Demeter	Goddess of the harvest	Ceres
Dionysus	God of wine	Bacchus
Eos	Goddess of the dawn	Aurora
Eros	God of love	Cupid
Hades	God of the underworld	Pluto
Hecate	Goddess of the dark and magic	Trivia
Hephaestus	God of fire and patron of craftsmen	Vulcan
Hera	Goddess of marriage	Juno
Hermes	Messenger of the gods	Mercury
Hestia	Goddess of hearth and home	Vesta
Kronos	God of time	Saturn
Nike	Goddess of victory	Victory
Persephone	Goddess of spring	Prosperine
Poseidon	Lord of the sea	Neptune
Selene	Goddess of the moon	Luna
Zeus	King of the gods, lord of the sky	Jupiter

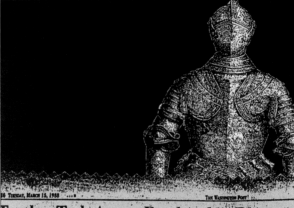

© 1996 Gwen Frankfeldt & Glenn Morrow

In **Dateline: Troy**, *Paul Fleischman shows that universal issues of the ancient past are still alive, appearing in today's newspapers. His strategy makes the connection between the ancient story of Achilles and the armor being developed by the Pentagon.*

handsome portraits and describes the origins and characteristics of the deities. In *King Midas* (I–A), illustrated by Isabelle Brent, Philip Neil brings the king's sorrowful curse to life. Jane Yolen's *Wings* (I–A) tells the story of Daedalus, a mortal who is exiled to the island of Crete.

Most myths are seldom fully appreciated until the later years of elementary school. Even then, they may not be embraced by all students. The stories of King Midas, Pandora's Box, and Jason and the Golden Fleece are, however, basic material for students' literary education.

Norse Mythology

Equally rich stories exist among other cultures, most notably the Vikings. The tales that grew from the cold, rugged climate of northern Europe burn with man's passionate struggle against the cruelty of nature and the powerful gods and monsters that ruled the harsh land.

In *Favorite Norse Myths* (I–A), Mary Pope Osborne explains how the universe began, according to the creation story of Norway. She quotes from the *Poetic Edda,* the oldest written source of Norse mythology. In it, Odin, the Norse war god, trades an eye for all the world's wisdom. Thor, god of thunder, defeats a vicious giant with a hammer, and mischief-maker Loki creates trouble wherever he goes. Padraic Colum, an Irish poet and master storyteller, first published *The Children of Odin: The Book of Northern Myths* (I) in 1920; his classic collection remains available today. Ingri and Edgar Parin d'Aulaire have told these bold stories in *Norse Gods and Giants* (I–A), an entertaining account based on Norse mythology.

Mythology from Other Cultures

Although Greek, Roman, and Norse mythologies have traditionally been the most studied and the most readily available, today we have access to books of mythology from many cultures. Mythology from Africa has taken its place alongside European stories, and hauntingly beautiful versions of Native American and Inuit myths are being published with increasing frequency.

Ngangur Mbitu and Ranchor Prime have collected the myths of Africa in *Essential African Mythology* (I). Isaac Olaleye describes a contest on a rainfield in Africa in *In the Rainfield: Who Is the Greatest?* (P–I), illustrated by Ann Grifalconi. Wind, fire, and rain are portrayed as regal Africans competing to determine who is the greatest. Richard Lewis retells the Aztec myth that explains how music came to earth in *All of You Was Singing* (I–A), a poetic version that is infused with his own imagination. Ed Young's illustrations combine Lewis's images, Aztec cultural motifs, and his own vision. The result is a stunningly beautiful book that echoes the splendor of creation. John Bierhorst has gathered many other Aztec tales in *The Hungry Woman: Myths and Legends of the Aztecs* (A). Myths from many cultures are listed in the Booklist at the end of the chapter.

• • HERO TALES: • • EPICS AND LEGENDS

Epics, also known as hero tales, focus on the courageous deeds of superhuman mortals in their struggles against each other or against gods or monsters. The heroes embody universal human emotions and represent the eternal contest between good and evil. Hero tales contribute to an appreciation of world history and literature, to an understanding of national ideals of behavior, and to our understanding of valor and nobility.

Epics are usually written in verse and consist of a cycle of tales that center on a legendary hero. Some well-known epics include those of Beowulf, King Arthur and Camelot, and Robin Hood, and the account of the Trojan War retold in Homer's *Iliad* and *Odyssey*. Language is often key in setting the drama of the tales, as is evident from the first line of

Robert Sabuda's *Arthur and the Sword* (I): "Long ago in a time of great darkness, a time without a king, there lived a fair boy called Arthur." The elegant language foretells the majesty in the story. *Merlin and the Making of the King* (I–A), retold by Margaret Hodges and illustrated by Trina Schart Hyman, introduces three of the famous Arthurian legends that chronicle Arthur's life from his birth until his death. The dramatic tales are accompanied by equally dramatic illustrations surrounded by tiny flowered borders inspired by illuminated manuscripts. Kevin Crossley-Holland has written an authoritative resource on Camelot, Arthur, his knights, and the history of chivalry in *The World of King Arthur and His Court: People, Places, Legend and Lore* (A), a book that gives historical knowledge of England at the time Arthur may have lived as well as information about the Arthurian ideal created by storytellers through the ages. The illustrations by Peter Malone, inspired by medieval art, clarify the information provided by the text.

The epic of the hero Gilgamesh, who travels the world with his friend Enkidu fighting monsters, is the oldest known recorded story in the world. In the foreword to her retelling, *Gilgamesh the Hero* (I–A), Geraldine McCaughrean relates that the story was carved onto 12 tablets that were smashed into thousands of shards over thousands of years. The story of this ancient Sumerian king of Mesopotamia (now Iraq), which may not be complete, was painstakingly restored by scholars. Gilgamesh, though a powerful hero, suffers terribly: "Gilgamesh knelt on the bank of the pool vomiting his misery in great retching sobs. He beat his torn fists on the ground and howled like a wild animal" (p. 88). Like the theme of so many others to follow, his story ends, "He walked through darkness and so glimpsed light" (p. 95).

Hero tales that are not technically epics are often referred to as *legends*. Legendary heroes may be real or imaginary people. Even if legends have some factual basis, they are often so fanciful that it becomes difficult to tell where fact stops and imagination takes over. Many storytellers elaborated on reports of their hero's exploits until the stories became full-blown legends that interwove fact and fiction yet contained a grain of truth at their core. Davy Crockett, Johnny Appleseed, and Daniel Boone were real people, but their stories have made them larger than life.

In *La Llorona/The Weeping Woman* (I–A), Joe Hayes retells the Hispanic legend of La Llorona (the Weeping Woman), the jilted wife who turned her rage against her beloved children and is still believed to wander the banks of the river where she died of grief after she drowned them. Hayes asserts that no one knows whether or not the story is true, but in notes to the reader at the end of the book he writes, "When children ask me if I believe in La Llorona, I answer as I do whenever I'm asked about a story: I don't think the things I told you really did happen, but if you

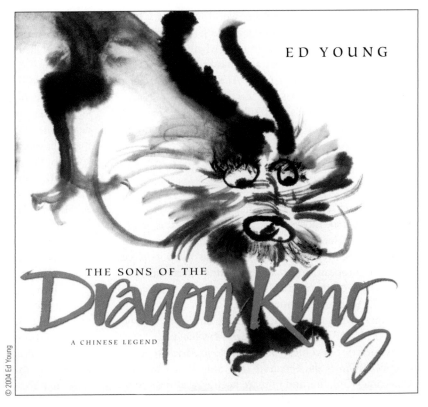

ED YOUNG

THE SONS OF THE
Dragon King
A CHINESE LEGEND

Using the bold, economical brushstrokes of traditional Chinese art, Young brings the wise father to life in the Chinese legend **The Sons of the Dragon King.**

think about the story you can find a lot of truth in it." In Demi's tale **The Hungry Coat** (I), Nasrettin Hoca, a legendary wise Turkish hero, teaches an old friend and his guests, "If you want to look deeply, look at the man and not at his coat. You can change the coat, but you cannot change the man." Students will appreciate the humor in Demi's tale enhanced by her illustrations, inspired by Turkish art.

Legends also grow around places and phenomena. Barbara Juster Esbensen's poem about the aurora borealis, **The Night Rainbow** (P), presents images from many cultures, including white geese, dancers, whales, and battles. Esbensen also provides scientific explanations as well as information about the legends in this celebration of the northern lights. **The Sons of the Dragon King** (I–A), retold and illustrated by Ed Young, shows how the many tribes of China were combined into one by the Dragon King and his nine sons, and thus an entire culture is influenced by an ancient story.

• • F O L K S O N G S • •

Songs serve as powerful vehicles for both shaping and preserving our cultural heritage. Ballads and folk songs inform and unify people. Work songs, often developed as a diversion from boredom, capture the rhythm and spirit of the labor in which their creators were engaged. They sing of the values and lifestyles of the people who laid the railroads, dug the tunnels and canals, sailed the ships, and toted the bales.

Folklorist Benjamin A. Botkin (1944) observed in *A Treasury of American Folklore* that we sing folk songs for self-gratification, power, or freedom (pp. 818–819). We also sing songs to lighten our labor, fill our leisure time, record events, and voice praise or protest. Civil rights marchers led by Martin Luther King Jr. were united by the experience of singing "We Shall Overcome" together.

We use songs to teach young children to count or to say the ABCs and, most often, to soothe them and sing them to sleep. Joyce Carol Thomas collected African American songs for **Hush Songs: African American Lullabies** (N–P–I), illustrated by Brenda Joysmith. These songs have worked their sleepy-time magic for generations. Jane Hart compiled 125 songs in her splendid **Singing Bee! A Collection of Favorite Children's Songs** (N–P–I), which is beautifully illustrated by Anita Lobel. She augments the nursery rhymes, lullabies, finger plays, cumulative, holiday, and activity songs with piano accompaniments and guitar chords. Lobel uses historical settings, 18th-century garb, and stage production scenes to illustrate the traditional songs.

Children celebrate their own culture or learn about others through song; they can even learn a second language through song. The best published versions include guitar or piano scores, historical notes, and appropriate illustrations that coordinate with the text. Lulu Delacre selected and illustrated *Arroz con Leche: Popular Songs and Rhymes from Latin America* (P), with English lyrics by Elena Paz and musical arrangements by Ana-Maria Rosada. Jose-Luis Orozco selected, arranged, and translated Latin American songs for *De Colores and Other Latin American Folk Songs for Children* (P), illustrated by Elisa Kleven. Gary Chalk chose humorous illustrations depicting events of the American Revolution to accompany the original verses of "Yankee Doodle" in *Yankee Doodle* (P). Gerald Milnes shares traditional songs, rhymes, and riddles from the mountains of West Virginia in *Granny Will Your Dog Bite and Other Mountain Rhymes* (I–A). Other collectors of folk songs include Robert Quackenbush, Aliki, Glen Rounds, John Langstaff, and Peter Spier.

Fractured Fairy Tales and Literary Folklore

Many writers, especially those who write fantasies, have been influenced by the structure, motifs, problems, and characters of tales from the oral tradition. Hans Christian Andersen, Rudyard Kipling, Oscar Wilde, and contemporary author Jane Yolen have created their own fairy tales and pourquoi stories, sometimes referred to as fakelore, patterned after those tales they heard when they were young and still took pleasure in as adults. Other writers create parodies and fractured versions of favorite tales. David Wiesner's *The Three Pigs* (P–I) relies on the fact that readers know something about the original tale so that they can fully enjoy the pigs' plight and ingenious means of escape in his story. Jon Scieszka's *The True Story of the Three Little Pigs* (P–I), illustrated by Lane Smith, is told from the point of view of a harmless-looking and misunderstood wolf. Similarly, Robert Munsch's *The Paper Bag Princess* is much funnier because it turns the traditional Cinderella-style ending upside down. Older readers enjoy the twists to Cinderella in *Ella Enchanted* by Gail Carson Levine. Writers also are inspired by mythology. Gerald McDermott's *Creation* (P–I–A) and Phyllis Root's *Big Momma Makes the World* (N–P–I) echo Genesis and other cultures' creation myths while inventing their own joyous celebrations of the beginning of life. In *Wings* (P–I-A), Christopher Myers tells the modern story of Ikarus Jackson, who proudly flies using his powerful wings just as did his namesake in Greek

Christopher Myers creates a modern story with ancient roots in Wings.

mythology. Teaching Idea 5.5 gives suggestions for helping children identify folkloric style in more contemporary stories that are not from the oral tradition. Other narratives based on folklore traditions are considered in Chapter 6.

Using Folklore in the Classroom

Because traditional literature is a foundation for future literary understanding, it is critical that children spend time reading from the vast body of folklore. We shortchange children if we deny them the background information necessary for understanding the countless references to folklore in contemporary books and society. Children who do not comprehend the significance of the wolf in folklore will not understand the meaning of the wolf-shaped bush in Anthony Browne's *Piggybook* (P–I). They will not know why their

Teaching Idea 5-5

Identify Folkloric Style

Contemporary stories are often written in a folkloric style: they contain elements, themes, or recurring patterns found in folklore. Read aloud and discuss fiction containing folklore elements, motifs, or allusions to illustrate the idea. Encourage book discussion groups to continue the search for transformations, magic objects, wishes, trickery, and other folklore conventions. Do the following to help students learn about folkloric style:

✳ Collect stories written in folkloric style.

✳ Discuss folklore elements. What characteristics suggest that a work is folklore?

✳ Have students work in groups to discover folklore elements.

✳ Discuss the devices, allusions, and patterns found. Make a list of commonly used folklore elements.

✳ Encourage students to use the elements in stories they write.

Consult the books listed here to get started.

Arnold, Caroline, *The Terrible Hodag*

Bang, Molly, *Dawn*

_____, *The Paper Crane*

Cowley, Joy, *The Wishing of Biddy Malone*

Della Chiesa, Carol, *Adventures of Pinocchio*

French, Fiona, *Anancy and Mr. Dry-Bone*

Gregory, Valiska, *Through the Mickle Woods*

Isaacs, Anne, *Swamp Angel*

Melmed, Laura Krauss, *Rainbabies*

Nolen, Jerdine, *Big Jabe*

Paterson, Katherine, *The King's Equal*

Wisniewski, David, *The Warrior and the Wise Man*

Yolen, Jane, *The Girl Who Touched the Wind*

---

classmates say "uh-oh" when they discover that the babysitter in Mary Rayner's *Mr. and Mrs. Pig's Evening Out* (P) turns out to be a wolf. And they will not appreciate the humor of folktale parodies, such as Jon Scieszka's *The True Story of the Three Little Pigs.* Children should be aware that common phrases like "sour grapes" and "slow and steady wins the race" come from Aesop's fables and that "Pandora's box" and "the Midas touch" originated in Greek mythology.

Good teachers give children opportunities to *discover* recurring patterns; they do not *tell* them what to recognize. Teachers who facilitate students' discovery of archetypes find that the primal patterns, themes, and characters become the structural framework for viewing all literature as one story. The most effective approach is to immerse students in traditional stories until they begin to recognize similarities, distinguish patterns, and make predictions. Children who have heard many folktales will tell you that they often begin "Once upon a time" and end "They lived happily ever after," that the good people win, and that the youngest son gets the princess. These responses show that children recognize the motifs, themes, and story conventions of folklore.

Folklore provides an opportunity for increasing multicultural understanding; it reflects the values, hopes, fears, and beliefs of many cultures. By recognizing recurring themes in folklore from around the world, we can begin to build a bridge of understanding among all people. Also, the oral origins of folklore make it a wonderful resource for storytelling and language development. Dramatic readings or performances offer one venue for creativity. Teaching Idea 5.6 presents suggestions on how to select stories for telling and become a storyteller. Children who are familiar with folklore also learn to use similar patterns and conventions in their own writing, borrowing and exploring folkloric frameworks and characters for their own personal stories.

Teaching Idea **5-6**

The Ancient Art of Storytelling

Teachers and students can become proficient story-tellers of the tales they enjoy most, the ones that say the most about who they are and what they believe and value. To hear how the best storytellers tell tales that engage their audiences, students can listen to tapes such as those by Robert Munsch, Michael Parent, or the many actors, such as Robin Williams and Denzel Washington, who tell tales for the Rabbit Ears series *We All Have Tales*. Rafe Martin tells the story of *The Rough-Face Girl* on *Rafe Martin Tells His Children's Books* (Yellow Moon Press).

The Student Storyteller

1. With an audience in mind (maybe children in another class below theirs), students can pore over folklore looking for the perfect tale to tell. It may be one that has cultural significance to them or one that is particularly funny or exciting or that mirrors their values.

2. After discovering the ideal tale, students should read it aloud a few times to really hear the language and become familiar with the characters and plot.

They should also recognize the climax and the slower parts of the tale.

3. Students should then memorize any recurring refrains and learn important events to recognize the pattern of the story.

4. After putting the book aside, students can practice telling the story a few times, making the story theirs.

5. They should decide how to introduce the story to the audience to help them get ready to listen.

6. Then students can tell the story often to as many people as they can.

There are also many storytelling resources available, including *The Way of the Storyteller,* by Ruth Sawyer (1962), and *The Story Vine: A Source Book of Unusual and Easy-to-Tell Stories from around the World,* by Anne Pellowski (1984).

• • • Summary • • •

Folklore began as stories and poems told across the generations, as people sought to entertain, to explain the world, and to transmit cultural values and beliefs. Folklore helps us understand not only ourselves but people from other cultures and other times. Tales, myths, legends, and fables add depth to our literary knowledge.

Each type of folklore has its own characteristics. Rhythmic Mother Goose rhymes enchant young children. Folktales—which include fairy tales, talking animal stories, noodlehead tales, cumulative tales, and tall tales—have universal themes and motifs and appear in different guises around the world. Fables incorporate explicit moral statements that are intended to guide behavior. Myths explain the origins of the world, natural phenomena, and human behavior. Hero tales reveal cultural beliefs and values. Folk songs celebrate the values and circumstances of those who first sang them.

Teachers in all grades recognize that folklore, in addition to being a source of pleasure for students of all ages, is a valuable resource for developing language, learning about literature, and learning about other cultures. As it did in the past, folklore today continues to educate and entertain. Every child should share in the same captivating experience that Wanda Gág describes in the introduction to her *Tales from Grimm:*

The magic of Marchen is among my earliest recollections. The dictionary definitions—tale, fable, legend—are all inadequate when I think of my little German Marchenbuch and what it held for me. Often, usually at twilight, some grown-up would say, "Sit down, Wanda-chen, and I'll read you a Marchen."

Then, as I settled down in my rocker, ready to abandon myself with the utmost credulity to whatever I might hear, everything was changed, exalted. A tingling, anything-may-happen feeling flowed over me, and I had the sensation of being about to bite into a big juicy pear. (1947, p. vii)

Above all else, these are stirring stories that have entertained listeners for centuries because they are filled with harrowing adventures and horrific monsters as well as mythic and everyday heroes who triumph in the end. When teachers share these memorable stories with their students, they link them to people in the distant past from all corners of the world.

In the January/February 2002 issue of *The Horn Book Magazine,* Nancy Willard writes about how fairy tales shape our lives in "A Tale out of Time." Read her article and then discuss with a peer the folklore that you remember. Why do you think you remember those particular tales? What shaped your perception of them?

Folklore from the World's Geographical Regions

WORLDWIDE COLLECTIONS

Hamilton, Virginia, *The Dark Way: Stories from the Spirit World* (I–A)

_____, *In the Beginning: Creation Stories from around the World* (I–A)

Keenan, Sheila, *Gods, Goddesses and Monsters: A Book of World Mythology* (A)

Kherdian, David, *Feathers and Tails: Animal Fables from around the World* (P–I)

Norman, Howard, *Between Heaven and Earth: Bird Tales from around the World* (I)

Rosen, Michael, *How the Animals Got Their Colors: Animal Myths from around the World* (P–I)

Shannon, George, *Stories to Solve* (I–A)

_____, *More Stories to Solve* (I–A)

_____, *True Lies: 18 Tales for You to Judge* (I–A)

_____, *More True Lies: 18 Tales for You to Judge* (I–A)

Sierra, Judy, *Nursery Tales around the World* (N–P)

Van Laan, Nancy, *Sleep, Sleep, Sleep: A Lullaby for Little Ones around the World* (N)

Yolen, Jane, *Mightier Than the Sword: World Folktales for Strong Boys* (I)

_____, *Not One Damsel in Distress: World Folktales for Strong Girls* (I)

_____, *Sleep Rhymes around the World* (N–P)

_____, *Street Rhymes around the World* (P–I)

NORTH, SOUTH, AND CENTRAL AMERICA

Aardema, Verna, *Borreguita and the Coyote: A Tale from Ayutla, Mexico* (P–I)

Ada, Alma Flor, *Mediopollito/Half-Chicken* (P–I)

_____, *Three Golden Oranges* (P–I)

Anaya, Rudolfo, *My Land Sings: Stories from the Rio Grande* (I)

Bang, Molly, *Wiley and the Hairy Man* (P–I)

Bierhorst, John, *Is My Friend at Home? Pueblo Fireside Tales* (P–I)

_____, *The Naked Bear: Folktales of the Iroquois* (I)

_____, *The People with Five Fingers: A Native Californian Creation Tale* (P–I)

Bernier-Grand, Carmen T., *Juan Bobo: Four Tales from Puerto Rico* (N–P–I)

Bruchac, Joseph, *Between Earth and Sky: Legends of Native American Sacred Places* (P–I)

_____, *The Boy Who Lived with the Bears and Other Iroquois Stories* (I)

_____, *Gluskabe and the Four Wishes* (P–I)

_____, *The Story of the Milky Way: A Cherokee Tale* (P–I)

Brusca, María Cristina, and Tona Wilson, *When Jaguars Ate the Moon and Other Stories about Animals and Plants of the Americas* (P–I)

Bryan, Ashley, *Turtle Knows Your Name* (P–I)

DeSauza, James, *Brother Anansi and the Cattle Ranch* (P–I)

Gerson, Mary-Joan, *People of Corn: A Mayan Story* (P–I)

Goble, Paul, *Adopted by the Eagles: A Plains Indian Story of Friendship and Treachery* (P–I)

_____, *Crow Chief: A Plains Indian Story* (P–I)

_____, *Iktomi and the Boulder* (I)

Hamilton, Virginia, *Her Stories: African American Folktales, Fairy Tales, and True Tales* (I–A)

_____, *The People Could Fly: American Black Folktales* (I–A)

_____, *The People Could Fly: The Picture Book* (P–I)

_____, *When Birds Could Talk and Bats Could Sing* (I–A)

Hayes, Joe, *La Llorona/The Weeping Woman: An Hispanic Legend Told in Spanish and English* (I–A)

_____, *A Spoon for Every Bite* (P–I)

Hooks, William, *Moss Gown* (P–I)

Hunter, C. W., *The Green Gourd: A North Carolina Folktale* (P)

Jaffe, Nina, *The Golden Flower: A Taino Myth from Puerto Rico* (P)

Joseph, Lynn, *The Mermaid's Twin Sister: More Stories from Trinidad* (I–A)

Kimmel, Eric A., *The Two Mountains: An Aztec Legend* (P–I)

Lester, Julius, *John Henry* (P–I)

Lyons, Mary E., *The Butter Tree: Tales of Bruh Rabbit* (I)

_____, *Raw Head and Bloody Bones: African-American Tales of the Supernatural* (A)

McDermott, Gerald, *Arrow to the Sun* (P–I)

_____, *Raven: A Trickster Tale from the Pacific Northwest* (P–I)

McKissack, Patricia C., *The Dark-Thirty: Southern Tales of the Supernatural* (A)

Milnes, Gerald, *Granny Will Your Dog Bite and Other Mountain Rhymes* (I–A)

Moreles, Yuyi, *Just a Minute: A Trickster Tale and Counting Book* (N–P)

Moses, Will, *Johnny Appleseed: The Story of a Legend* (I)

Philip, Neil, *Horse Hooves and Chicken Feet: Mexican Folktales* (I)

Rockwell, Anne, *The Boy Who Wouldn't Obey: A Mayan Legend* (P–I)

Rodanas, Kristina, *Dance of the Sacred Circle: A Native American Tale* (I)

_____, *Dragonfly's Tale* (P)

Ross, Gayle, *How Turtle's Back Was Cracked: A Traditional Cherokee Tale* (P–I)

San Souci, Robert D., *The Faithful Friend* (P–I)

_____, *Six Foolish Fishermen* (P–I)

_____, *Sukey and the Mermaid* (P–I)

_____, *The Talking Eggs* (P–I)

Schwartz, Alvin, *I Saw You in the Bathtub and Other Folk Rhymes* (P–I)

Sierra, Judy, *Wiley and the Hairy Man* (P–I)

Sloat, Teri, *The Eye of the Needle* (P–I)

Stevens, Jane, *Old Bag of Bones: A Coyote Tale* (P–I)

Van Laan, Nancy, *In a Circle Long Ago: A Treasury of Native Lore from North America* (I–A)

_____, *With a Whoop and a Holler: A Bushel of Lore from Way Down South* (I)

EUROPE, AFRICA, AND THE MIDDLE EAST

Aardema, Verna, *The Lonely Lioness and the Ostrich Chicks* (P)

_____, *Misoso: Once upon a Time: Tales from Africa* (I–A)

_____, *Why Mosquitoes Buzz in People's Ears: A West African Tale* (P)

Bryan, Ashley, *Ashley Bryan's African Tales, Uh-Huh* (I)

_____, *Beat the Story Drum, Pum-Pum* (I)

_____, *Beautiful Blackbird* (P)

_____, *Lion and the Ostrich Chicks* (I)

Cauley, Lorinda Bryan, *The Pancake Boy: An Old Norwegian Folk Tale* (P)

Cooper, Susan, *Tam Lin* (P–I)

Doyle, Malachy, *Tales from Old Ireland* (I–A)

Gerson, Mary-Joan, *Why the Sky Is Far Away: A Nigerian Folktale* (N–P)

Gregor, C. Shana, *Cry of the Benu Bird: An Egyptian Creation Story* (P–I)

Grifalconi, Ann, *The Village of Round and Square Houses* (P)

Haley, Gail E., *A Story, a Story* (P–I)

Huck, Charlotte, *The Black Bull of Norroway: A Scottish Tale* (P–I)

Huth, Holly Young, *The Son of the Sun and the Daughter of the Moon: A Saami Folktale* (P–I)

Hutton, Warwick, *The Trojan Horse* (P–I)

Janisch, Heinz, *The Merry Pranks of Till Eulenspiegel* (P–I)

Kimmel, Eric A., *The Adventures of Hershel of Ostropol* (I)

_____, *Count Silvernose: A Story from Italy* (P–I)

Lupton, Hugh, *Pirican Pic and Pirican Mor* (P)

McDermott, Gerald, *The Magic Tree: A Tale from the Congo* (P)

_____, *Tim O'Toole and the Wee Folk* (P)

McVitty, Walter, *Ali Baba and the Forty Thieves* (I–A)

Mollel, Tololwa M., *The Orphan Boy: A Maasai Story* (P–I)

_____, *Shadow Dance* (P–I)

_____, *Subira Subira* (P–I)

Morley, Jacqueline, *Egyptian Myths* (I–A)

Onyefulu, Obi, *Chinye: A West African Folk Tale* (P–I)

Paye, Won-Ldy, and Margaret Lippert, *Head, Body, Legs: A Tale from Liberia* (P–I)

_____, *Mrs. Chicken and the Hungry Crocodile* (P–I)

Philip, Neil, *Celtic Fairy Tales* (I–A)

Sierra, Judy, *The Beautiful Butterfly: A Folktale from Spain* (P–I)

Singer, Isaac, *When Shlemiel Went to Warsaw and Other Stories* (I)

_____, *Zlateh the Goat and Other Stories* (I)

Souhami, Jessica, *The Leopard's Drum: An Ashanti Tale from West Africa* (P)

Taback, Sims, *Joseph Had a Little Overcoat* (N–P–I)

Tchana, Katrin, *Sense Pass King: A Story from Cameroon* (I)

Washington, Donna, *A Pride of African Lions* (I)

Willard, Nancy, *East of the Sun and West of the Moon* (A)

Wisniewski, David, *Elfwyn's Saga* (I)

_____, *Golem* (I–A)

Yolen, Jane, *Tam Lin* (I)

CENTRAL ASIA

Bider, Djemma, *A Drop of Honey: An Armenian Fable* (I)

Brett, Jan, *The Mitten: A Ukrainian Folktale* (P)

Demi, *Firebird* (P–I)

_____, *The Hungry Coat: A Tale from Turkey* (I)

Hastings, Selina, *The Firebird* (P–I)

Hodges, Margaret, *The Little Humpbacked Horse: A Russian Tale Retold* (P)

Hogrogian, Nonny, *The Contest* (P)

_____, *One Fine Day* (P)

Hort, Lenny, *The Fool and the Fish* (I)

Kismaric, Carole, *The Rumor of Pavel and Paali: A Ukrainian Folktale* (I–A)

Ransome, Arthur, *The Fool of the World and the Flying Ship: A Russian Tale* (P–I)

Shah, Idries, *The Boy without a Name* (P–I)

_____, *The Clever Boy and the Terrible, Dangerous Animal* (P–I)

_____, *Neem the Half-Boy* (P–I)

_____, *The Old Woman and the Eagle* (P–I)

Sherman, Josepha, *Vassilisa the Wise: A Tale of Medieval Russia* (I)

Tresselt, Alvin R., *The Mitten: An Old Ukrainian Folktale* (P)

Winthrop, Elizabeth, *Vasilissa the Beautiful: A Russian Folktale* (P–I)

THE FAR EAST

Demi, *The Empty Pot* (P)

_____, *The Magic Boat* (P–I)

Ginsburg, Mirra, *The Chinese Mirror* (P–I)

Greene, Ellin, *Ling-Li and the Phoenix Fairy: A Chinese Folktale* (P–I)

Heyer, Marilee, *Weaving of a Dream: A Chinese Folktale* (I)

Ho, Minfong, and Saphan Ros, *Brother Rabbit: A Cambodian Tale* (P–I)

_____, *The Two Brothers* (P–I)

Ishii, Momoko, *The Tongue-Cut Sparrow,* translated by Katherine Paterson (I)

Kajikawa, Kimiko, *Yoshi's Feast* (P–I)

Kimmel, Eric, *Three Samurai Cats: A Story from Japan* (P–I)

Mahy, Margaret, *The Seven Chinese Brothers* (P–I)

McDermott, Gerald, *The Stonecutter: A Japanese Folktale* (P)

Muth, Jon, *Stone Soup* (P–I)

Paterson, Katherine, *The Tale of the Mandarin Ducks* (P–I)

Quayle, Eric, *The Shining Princess and Other Japanese Legends* (I)

Souhami, Jessica, *No Dinner! The Story of the Old Woman and the Pumpkin* (N–P)

Xiong, Blia, *Nine-in-One Grr! Grr!* (P–I)

Yacowitz, Caryn, *The Jade Stone: A Chinese Folktale* (I)

Yep, Laurence, *Tongues of Jade* (I–A)

Young, Ed, *The Lost Horse: A Chinese Folktale* (I)

_____, *Seven Blind Mice* (P–I)

_____, *The Sons of the Dragon King: A Chinese Legend* (I–A)

Mother Goose and Nursery Rhymes

Addams, Charles, *The Charles Addams Mother Goose* (A)

Crews, Nina, *The Neighborhood Mother Goose* (P–I)

dePaola, Tomie, *Tomie dePaola's Mother Goose* (N–P)

Downes, Belinda, *A Stitch in Rhyme: A Nursery Rhyme Sampler with Embroidered Illustrations* (N–P)

Galdone, Paul, *Three Little Kittens* (N–P)

Griego, Margot C., Betsy Bucks, Sharon Gilbert, and Laurel Kimball, *Tortillas para Mama and Other Nursery Rhymes: Spanish and English* (P–I)

Larrick, Nancy, *Songs from Mother Goose* (N–P)

Lobel, Arnold, *Random House Book of Mother Goose* (N–P)

Marcus, Leonard, and Amy Schwartz, *Mother Goose's Little Misfortunes* (N–P)

Marshall, James, *James Marshall's Mother Goose* (N–P)

_____, *Old Mother Hubbard and Her Wonderful Dog* (N–P)

Opie, Iona, *Here Comes Mother Goose* (N–P)

_____, *My Very First Mother Goose* (N–P)

_____, *Tail Feathers from Mother Goose: The Opie Rhyme Book* (N–P–I–A)

Opie, Iona, and Peter Opie, *I Saw Esau: The Schoolchild's Pocket Book* (N–P–I)

_____, *The Oxford Dictionary of Nursery Rhymes* (N–P–I–A)

Polacco, Patricia, *Babushka's Mother Goose* (N–P)

Potter, Beatrix, *Beatrix Potter's Nursery Rhyme Book* (N–P)

Rojankovsky, Feodor, *The Tall Book of Mother Goose* (N–P)

Slier, Debby, *The Real Mother Goose: Book of American Rhymes* (N–P)

Spier, Peter, *To Market! To Market!* (N–P)

Sutherland, Zena, *The Orchard Book of Nursery Rhymes* (N–P)

Watson, Wendy, *Father Fox's Pennyrhymes* (N–P)

_____, *Wendy Watson's Mother Goose* (N–P)

Wildsmith, Brian, *Brian Wildsmith's Mother Goose* (N–P)

Wright, Blanche Fisher, *The Real Mother Goose* (N–P)

Wyndham, Robert, editor, *Chinese Mother Goose Rhymes* (N–P)

Yolen, Jane, *Jane Yolen's Mother Goose Songbook* (N–P)

Folktales

CUMULATIVE TALES

Aardema, Verna, *Bringing the Rain to Kapiti Plain: A Nandi Tale* (N–P)

Butler, Stephen, *Henny Penny* (N–P)

Galdone, Paul, *The Gingerbread Boy* (N–P)

Gonzalez, Lucia, *The Bossy Gallito: A Traditional Cuban Folktale* (N–P)

Hogrogian, Nonny, *One Fine Day* (N–P)

So, Meilo, *Gobble, Gobble, Slip, Slop: A Tale of a Very Greedy Cat* (P–I)

Stobbs, William, *The House That Jack Built* (N–P)

Taback, Sims, *This Is the House That Jack Built* (N–P)

Winter, Jeanette, *The House That Jack Built* (N–P)

TALKING ANIMALS

Asbjornsen, Peter C., and Jorgen Moe, *The Three Billy Goats Gruff* (N–P)

Faulkner, William J., *Brer Tiger and the Big Wind* (I–A)

Galdone, Paul, *The Three Little Pigs* (N–P)

Grimm, Jacob, and Wilhelm Grimm, *The Bremen Town Musicians,* retold and illustrated by Ilse Plume (N–P)

Hamilton, Virginia, *Bruh Rabbit and the Tar Baby Girl* (P–I)

Kimmel, Eric, *Anansi and the Moss-Covered Rock* (P–I)

Knutson, Barbara, *Sungura and Leopard: A Swahili Trickster Tale* (P–I)

Lester, Julius, *The Tales of Uncle Remus: The Adventures of Brer Rabbit* (I–A)

_____, *More Tales of Uncle Remus: Further Adventures of Brer Rabbit, His Friends, Enemies, and Others* (I–A)

_____, *Further Tales of Uncle Remus: The Misadventures of Brer Rabbit, Brer Fox, Brer Wolf, the Doodang, and Other Creatures* (I–A)

McDermott, Gerald, *Coyote: A Trickster Tale from the American Southwest* (P–I)

_____, *Zomo the Rabbit: A Trickster Tale from West Africa* (P–I)

McGill, Alice, *Sure as Sunrise: Stories of Bruh Rabbit and His Walkin' Talkin' Friends* (P–I)

Parks, Van Dyke, *Jump Again! More Adventures of Brer Rabbit* (P–I)

_____, *Jump on Over! The Adventures of Brer Rabbit and His Family* (P–I)

Parks, Van Dyke, and Malcolm Jones, *Jump! The Adventures of Brer Rabbit* (P–I)

Perrault, Charles, *Puss in Boots,* illustrated by Marcia Brown (N–P)

Rascol, Sabina, *The Impudent Rooster* (I)

Stevens, Janet, *The Three Billy Goats Gruff* (N–P)

NOODLEHEAD AND SIMPLETON STORIES

Asbjornsen, Peter C., and Jorgen Moe, *The Squire's Bride* (N–P–I)

Cole, Joanna, *It's Too Noisy* (N–P–I)

Hague, Kathleen, and Michael Hague, *The Man Who Kept House* (N–P–I)

Kellogg, Steven, *The Three Sillies* (N–P–I)

Lurie, Alison, *Clever Gretchen and Other Forgotten Folktales* (P–I)

San Souci, Robert D., *Six Foolish Fishermen* (N–P–I)

Shulevitz, Uri, *The Golden Goose* (N–P–I)

Singer, Isaac Bashevis, *Mazel and Shlimazel, or The Milk of a Lioness* (P–I)

_____, *Naftali the Storyteller and His Horse, Sus* (P–I)

FAIRY TALES

Brown, Marcia, *Once a Mouse* (P)

Gàg, Wanda, translator, *More Tales from Grimm* (I–A)

_____, *Tales from Grimm* (I–A)

Grimm, Jacob, and Wilhelm Grimm, *The Annotated Brothers Grimm,* translated and edited by Maria Tatar (A)

_____, *Hansel and Gretel,* translated by Elizabeth Crawford (N–P)

_____, *The Juniper Tree and Other Tales from Grimm,* translated by Lore Segal and Randall Jarrell (A)

_____, *Rapunzel,* adapted by Barbara Rogasky (N–P)

_____, *The Shoemaker and the Elves,* translated by Wayne Andrews (N–P)

_____, *Snow White,* retold by Paul Heins (I)

_____, *Snow White and the Seven Dwarfs,* translated by Randall Jarrell (I)

Jacobs, Joseph, *Tom Tit Tot,* illustrated by Evaline Ness (P)

Lunge-Larsen, Lise, *The Hidden Folk: Stories of Fairies, Dwarves, Selkies, and Other Secret Beings* (P–I–A)

Manna, Anthony, and Christodoula Mitakidou, *Mr. Semolina-Semolinus: A Greek Folktale* (I)

Mayer, Marianna, *The Twelve Dancing Princesses* (I)

Perrault, Charles, *Beauty and the Beast,* adapted by Jan Brett (N–P–I)

_____, *Beauty and the Beast,* adapted by Nancy Willard (N–P–I)

Sierra, Judy, *Nursery Tales around the World* (N–P)

Steig, Jeanne, *A Handful of Beans: Six Fairy Tales* (I–A)

Willey, Margaret, *Clever Beatrice* (P–I)

_____, *Clever Beatrice and the Best Little Pony* (P–I)

TALL TALES

Arnold, Caroline, *The Terrible Hodag* (P–I)

Blair, Walter, *Tall Tale America: A Legendary History of Our Humorous Heroes* (I)

Cohen, Caron Lee, *Sally Ann Thunder Ann Whirlwind Crockett* (P–I)

Jaquith, Priscilla, *Bo Rabbit Smart for True: Tall Tales from the Gullah* (P–I–A)

Johnson, Paul Brett, *Old Dry Frye: A Deliciously Funny Tall Tale* (N–P–I)

Kellogg, Steven, *Paul Bunyan* (P)

_____, *Pecos Bill* (P)

Lester, Julius, *John Henry* (P–I)

Osborne, Mary Pope, *American Tall Tales* (P–I)

San Souci, Robert D., *Cut from the Same Cloth: American Women of Myth, Legend, and Tall Tale* (I)

Schwartz, Alvin, *Kickle Snifters and Other Fearsome Creatures from American Folklore* (I)

_____, *Whoppers: Tall Tales and Other Lies* (I–A)

Stoutenberg, Adrien, *American Tall-Tale Animals* (I)

_____, *American Tall Tales* (I)

Walker, Paul Robert, *Big Men, Big Country: A Collection of American Tall Tales* (A)

Fables

Books in this section are appropriate for primary–intermediate readers unless otherwise noted.

Anno, Mitsumasa, *Anno's Aesop: A Book of Fables by Aesop and Mr. Fox*

Bierhorst, John, *Doctor Coyote: A Native American Aesop's Fables*

Brett, Jan, *Town Mouse, Country Mouse*

Cauley, Lorinda Bryan, *The Town Mouse and the Country Mouse*

Climo, Shirley, *The Little Red Ant and the Great Big Crumb: A Mexican Fable*

Demi, *A Chinese Zoo: Fables and Proverbs*

Galdone, Paul, *The Monkey and the Crocodile*

Heins, Ethel, *The Cat and the Cook and Other Fables of Krylov*

La Fontaine, Jean de, *The Hare and the Tortoise*

_____, *The Lion and the Rat*

MacDonald, Suse, and Bill Oakes, *Once upon Another: The Tortoise and the Hare/The Lion and the Mouse*

Martin, Rafe, *Foolish Rabbit's Big Mistake*

McDermott, Gerald, *The Fox and the Stork*

Pinkney, Jerry, *Aesop's Fables*

Stevens, Janet, *The Tortoise and the Hare: An Aesop Fable*

_____, *The Town Mouse and the Country Mouse: An Aesop Fable*

Storr, Catherine, *Androcles and the Lion*

Wang, M. L., *The Ant and the Dove: An Aesop Tale Retold*

Ward, Helen, *The Hare and the Tortoise: A Fable from Aesop*

_____, *Unwitting Wisdom: An Anthology of Aesop's Fables*

Young, Ed, *Seven Blind Mice*

Myths, Legends, and Pourquoi Tales from Many Cultures

GREEK AND ROMAN

Books in this section are appropriate for intermediate–advanced readers unless otherwise noted.

Barth, Edna, *Cupid and Psyche: A Love Story*

Climo, Shirley, *Atalanta's Race: A Greek Myth*

Colum, Padraic, *Golden Fleece and Heroes Who Lived Before Achilles*

d'Aulaire, Ingri, and Edgar Parin d'Aulaire, *Ingri and Edgar Parin d'Aulaire's Book of Greek Myths*

Evslin, Bernard, *Hercules*

_____, *Jason and the Argonauts*

_____, *Theseus and the Minotaur*

Fisher, Leonard Everett, *Olympians: Great Gods and Goddesses of Ancient Greece*

Fleischman, Paul, *Dateline: Troy*

Gates, Doris, *Lord of the Sky: Zeus*

_____, *Two Queens of Heaven: Aphrodite and Demeter*

Hodges, Margaret, *The Arrow and the Lamp: The Story of Psyche*

Hutton, Warwick, *Odysseus and the Cyclops*

_____, *Persephone*

_____, *Theseus and the Minotaur*

McDermott, Gerald, *Daughter of the Earth: A Roman Myth*

Orgel, Doris, *Ariadne, Awake!*

Philip, Neil, *King Midas*

Steig, Jeanne, *A Gift from Zeus: Sixteen Favorite Myths* (A)

Weil, Lisl, *Pandora's Box*

NORSE

Books in this section are appropriate for intermediate–advanced readers unless otherwise noted.

Barth, Edna, *Balder and the Mistletoe: A Story for the Winter Holidays*

Climo, Shirley, *Stolen Thunder: A Norse Myth*

Colum, Padraic, *The Children of Odin: The Book of Northern Myths*

Crossley-Holland, Kevin, *Norse Myths*

d'Aulaire, Ingri, and Edgar Parin d'Aulaire, *Norse Gods and Giants*

de Gerez, Toni, *Louhi, Witch of North Farm* (P–I)

Mayer, Marianna, *Iduna and the Magic Apples*

Osborne, Mary Pope, *Favorite Norse Myths*

AFRICAN

Books in this section are appropriate for primary–intermediate readers.

Aardema, Verna, *Princess Gorilla and a New Kind of Water*

_____, *Why Mosquitoes Buzz in People's Ears: A West African Tale*

Dayrell, Elphinstone, *Why the Sun and the Moon Live in the Sky: An African Folktale*

Gerson, Mary-Joan, *Why the Sky Is Far Away: A Nigerian Folktale*

Knutson, Barbara, *How the Guinea Fowl Got Her Spots*

_____, *Why the Crab Has No Head*

Lester, Julius, *How Many Spots Does a Leopard Have? And Other Tales*

Troughton, Joanna, *How Stories Came into the World: A Folk Tale from West Africa*

NATIVE AMERICAN

Books in this section are appropriate for primary–intermediate readers.

Connolly, James E., *Why the Possum's Tail Is Bare and Other North American Indian Nature Tales*

dePaola, Tomie, *The Legend of the Bluebonnet: An Old Tale of Texas*

Esbensen, Barbara Juster, *Ladder to the Sky: How the Gift of Healing Came to the Ojibway Nation*

Goble, Paul, *Her Seven Brothers*

_____, *Mystic Horse*

_____, *Star Boy*

Lattimore, Deborah Nourse, *Why There Is No Arguing in Heaven: A Mayan Myth*

Martin, Rafe, *The Boy Who Lived with the Seals*

Oughton, Jerrie, *How the Stars Fell into the Sky: A Navajo Tale*

Troughton, Joanna, *How Rabbit Stole the Fire: A North American Indian Folktale*

_____, *How the Birds Changed Their Feathers: A South American Indian Folktale*

Vogel, Carole Garbuny, *Legends of Landforms: Native American Lore and the Geology of the Land*

Hero Tales and Epics

Books in this section are appropriate for intermediate–advanced readers unless otherwise noted.

Crossley-Holland, Kevin, *Beowulf*

_____, *The World of King Arthur and His Court: People, Places, Legend and Lore* (A)

de Gerez, Toni, *Louhi, Witch of North Farm* (P–I)

Gretchen, Sylvia, *Hero of the Land of Snow*

Hodges, Margaret, *The Kitchen Knight: A Tale of King Arthur*

_____, *Merlin and the Making of the King*

_____, *St. George and the Dragon*

Hodges, Margaret, and Margery Evernden, *Of Swords and Sorcerers: The Adventures of King Arthur and His Knights*

Jaffrey, Madhur, *Seasons of Splendour: Tales, Myths, and Legends of India*

Lunge-Larsen, Lise, *The Race of the Birkebeiners*

Malory, Sir Thomas, *Le Morte d'Arthur*

McCaughrean, Geraldine, *Gilgamesh the Hero* (A)

McKinley, Robin, *The Outlaws of Sherwood*

Perham, Molly, *King Arthur: The Legends of Camelot*

Philip, Neil, *Tale of Sir Gawain*

Pyle, Howard, *Merry Adventures of Robin Hood of Great Renown in Nottinghamshire*

_____, *Story of King Arthur and His Knights*

Running Wolf, Michael B., and Patricia Clark Smith, *On the Trail of Elder Brother: Glous'gap Stories of the Micmac Indians*

Sabuda, Robert, *Arthur and the Sword*

San Souci, Robert D., *Cut from the Same Cloth: American Women of Myth, Legend, and Tall Tale*

_____, *Larger Than Life: The Adventures of American Legendary Heroes*

_____, *Young Guinevere*

Sutcliff, Rosemary, *The Light beyond the Forest: The Quest for the Holy Grail*

_____, *The Road to Camlann*

_____, *The Sword and the Circle: King Arthur and the Knights of the Round Table*

_____, *Tristan and Iseult*

Williams, Marcia, *King Arthur and the Knights of the Round Table*

Yolen, Jane, *Camelot*

Young, Ed, *Monkey King*

Folk Songs

Aliki, *Go Tell Aunt Rhody* (P)

_____, *Hush Little Baby: A Folk Lullaby* (P)

Axelrod, Alan, *Songs of the Wild West* (P–I)

Bryan, Ashley, *All Night, All Day: A Child's First Book of African-American Spirituals* (P–I)

Chalk, Gary, *Mr. Frog Went a-Courting: Discover the Secret Story* (P–I)

Delacre, Lulu, *Arroz con Leche: Popular Songs and Rhymes from Latin America* (P)

Durell, Ann, compiler, *The Diane Goode Book of American Folk Tales and Songs* (P–I)

Glazer, Tom, *Eye Winker, Tom Tinker, Chin Chopper: Fifty Musical Fingerplays* (P)

Hoberman, Mary Ann, *The Eensy-Weensy Spider* (P)

Kellogg, Steven, *Yankee Doodle* (P)

Larrick, Nancy, *The Wheels of the Bus Go Round and Round: School Bus Songs and Chants* (P)

Plotz, Helen, *As I Walked Out One Evening: A Book of Ballads* (I–A)

Watson, Clyde, and Wendy Watson, *Father Fox's Feast of Songs* (P–I)

Yolen, Jane, *The Lullaby Songbook* (N–P)

_____, *Street Rhymes around the World* (N–P)

Zemach, Harve, *Mommy, Buy Me a China Doll* (N–P)

Religious Stories and Songs

Armstrong, Carole, *Lives and Legends of the Saints* (P–I–A)

Bach, Alice, and J. Cheryl Exum, *Miriam's Well: Stories about Women in the Bible* (P–I)

_____, *Moses' Ark: Stories from the Bible* (P–I)

Bierhorst, John, *Spirit Child: A Story of the Nativity* (I–A)

Cohen, Barbara, *The Donkey's Story: A Bible Story* (I–A)

Cole, Joanna, *A Gift from Saint Francis: The First Creche* (I–A)

dePaola, Tomie, *Christopher: The Holy Giant* (I–A)

_____, *Francis: The Poor Man of Assisi* (I–A)

_____, *The Lady of Guadalupe* (P–I)

_____, *The Legend of the Poinsettia* (P–I)

_____, *Mary: The Mother of Jesus* (I–A)

_____, *Tomie dePaola's Book of the Old Testament: New International Version* (I–A)

Fisher, Leonard Everett, *The Seven Days of Creation* (I–A)

Ganeri, Anita, *Out of the Ark: Stories from the World's Religions* (I–A)

Hennessy, B. G., *The First Night* (P–I–A)

Higginsen, Vy, *This Is My Song: A Collection of Gospel Music for the Family* (I–A)

Hodges, Margaret, *Brother Francis and the Friendly Beasts* (I–A)

_____, *St. Jerome and the Lion* (I–A)

Hutton, Warwick, *Adam and Eve: The Bible Story* (I–A)

Johnson, James Weldon, *The Creation* (I–A)

Kimmel, Eric A., *Wonders and Miracles: A Passover Companion* (A)

Laird, Elizabeth, *The Road to Bethlehem: An Ethiopian Nativity* (I–A)

Langstaff, John, *Climbing Jacob's Ladder: Heroes of the Bible in African-American Spirituals* (N–P)

_____, *What a Morning! The Christmas Story in Black Spirituals* (P–I)

Mayer, Marianna, *Young Mary of Nazareth* (I–A)

McDermott, Gerald, *Creation* (P–I–A)

Mohr, Joseph, *Silent Night, Holy Night: A Christmas Carol* (P–I)

Muhlberger, Richard, *The Christmas Story: Told through Paintings* (P–I–A)

Rock, Lois, *Words of Gold: A Treasury of the Bible's Poetry and Wisdom* (I–A)

Sawyer, Ruth, *The Remarkable Christmas of the Cobbler's Sons* (P–I–A)

Schwartz, Howard, and Barbara Rush, *The Sabbath Lion: A Jewish Folktale from Algeria* (I–A)

Segal, Lore, *The Book of Adam to Moses* (I–A)

Vivas, Julie, *The Nativity* (P–I)

Wensel, Ulises, *They Followed a Bright Star* (I–A)

Wildsmith, Brian, *A Christmas Story* (P–I)

Wolkstein, Diane, *Esther's Story* (I–A)

NOAH STORIES

Baynes, Pauline, *Noah and the Ark* (P–I)

Gauch, Patricia Lee, *Noah* (P–I)

Godden, Rumer, *Prayers from the Ark: Selected Poems* (I–A)

Hogrogian, Nonny, *Noah's Ark* (P–I)

Ludwig, Warren, *Old Noah's Elephants: An Israeli Folktale* (P–I)

Olson, Arielle, *Noah's Cats and the Devil's Fire* (P–I–A)

Pinkney, Jerry, *Noah's Ark* (P–I)

Ray, Jane, *Noah's Ark: Words from the Book of Genesis* (I–A)

Reid, Barbara, *Two by Two* (P–I)

Singer, Isaac Bashevis, *Why Noah Chose the Dove* (P–I)

Spier, Peter, *Noah's Ark* (P–I)

Folklore Variants, Parodies, and Fractured Fairy Tales

BABA YAGA

Arnold, Katya, *Baba Yaga: A Russian Folktale* (N–P–I)

Mayer, Marianna, *Baba Yaga and Vasilisa the Brave* (N–P–I)

Polacco, Patricia, *Babushka Baba Yaga* (N–P–I)

Rael, Elsa Okon, *Marushka's Egg* (N–P–I)

CINDERELLA

Climo, Shirley, *The Egyptian Cinderella* (N–P–I)

_____, *The Irish Cinderella* (N–P–I)

_____, *The Korean Cinderella* (N–P–I)

Greaves, Margaret, *Tattercoats* (N–P–I)

Hayes, Joe, *Little Gold Star/Estrellita de Oro: A Cinderella Cuento* (N–P–I)

Hooks, William, *Moss Gown* (N–P–I)

Huck, Charlotte, *Princess Furball* (N–P–I)

Jacobs, Joseph, *Tattercoats* (N–P–I)

Jungman, Ann, *Cinderella and the Hot Air Balloon* (N–P–I)

Louie, Ai-Ling, *Yeh Shen: A Cinderella Story from China* (N–P–I)

Lowell, Susan, *Cindy Ellen: A Wild Western Cinderella* (N–P–I)

Martin, Rafe, *The Rough-Face Girl* (N–P–I)

Perrault, Charles, *Cinderella and Other Tales from Perrault* (N–P–I)

San Jose, Christine, *Cinderella* (N–P–I)

San Souci, Robert D., *Cendrillon: A Caribbean Cinderella* (P–I)

_____, *Cinderella Skeleton* (I–A)

_____, *Sootface: An Ojibwa Cinderella Story* (P–I)

Silverman, Erica, *Raisel's Riddle* (P–I)

FROG PRINCE

Cecil, Laura, *Frog Princess* (N–P–I)

Isadora, Rachel, *The Princess and the Frog* (N–P–I)

Ormerod, Jan, and David Lloyd, *The Frog Prince* (N–P–I)

Scieszka, Jon, *The Frog Prince Continued* (N–P–I)

Tarcov, Edith H., *Frog Prince* (N–P–I)

GOLDILOCKS AND THE THREE BEARS

Aylesworth, Jim, *Goldilocks and the Three Bears* (N–P)

Barton, Byron, *Three Bears* (N–P)

Lowell, Susan, *Dusty Locks* (P–I)

Marshall, James, *Goldilocks and the Three Bears* (N–P)

Muir, Frank, *Frank Muir Retells Goldilocks and the Three Bears* (N–P)

Tolhurst, Marilyn, *Somebody and the Three Blairs* (N–P)

Turkle, Brinton, *Deep in the Forest* (N–P)

JACK TALES

Briggs, Raymond, *Jim and the Beanstalk* (P–I)

Compton, Kenn, and Joanne Compton, *Jack the Giant Chaser: An Appalachian Tale* (P–I)

Fleischman, Sid, *McBroom and the Beanstalk* (P–I)

Haley, Gail E., *Jack and the Fire Dragon* (I)

_____, *Mountain Jack Tales* (P–I)

Howe, John, *Jack and the Beanstalk* (N–P)

Kellogg, Steven, *Jack and the Beanstalk* (N–P)

Osborne, Mary Pope, *Kate and the Beanstalk* (P–I)

Wildsmith, Brian, and Rebecca Wildsmith, *Jack and the Meanstalk* (N–P)

RED RIDING HOOD

Crawford, Elizabeth D., *Little Red Cap* (N–P)

de Regniers, Beatrice Schenk, *Red Riding Hood* (N–P)

Ernst, Lisa Campbell, *Little Red Riding Hood: A Newfangled Prairie Tale* (N–P)

Hyman, Trina Schart, *Little Red Riding Hood* (N–P)

Langley, John, *Little Red Riding Hood* (N–P)

Perrault, Charles, *Little Red Riding Hood* (N–P)

Young, Ed, *Lon Po Po: A Red Riding Hood Story from China* (N–P)

Zeifert, Harriet, *Little Red Riding Hood* (N–P)

RUMPELSTILTSKIN

Stanley, Diane, *Rumpelstiltskin's Daughter* (P–I)

Zelinsky, Paul, reteller, *Rumpelstiltskin* (I)

Zemach, Harve, *Duffy and the Devil: A Cornish Tale* (I)

SLEEPING BEAUTY

Early, Margaret, *Sleeping Beauty* (N–P–I)

Minters, Frances, *Sleepless Beauty* (N–P–I)

Yolen, Jane, *Sleeping Ugly* (N–P–I)

SNOW WHITE AND THE SEVEN DWARFS

Andreason, Dan, *Rose Red and the Bear Prince* (N–P–I)

French, Fiona, *Snow White in New York* (N–P–I)

Grimm, Jacob, and Wilhelm Grimm, *Snow White and the Seven Dwarfs,* translated by Randall Jarrell (I)

Watts, Bernadette, *Snow White and Rose Red* (N–P–I)

THREE LITTLE PIGS

Bucknall, Caroline, *Three Little Pigs* (N–P)

Hooks, William H., *The Three Little Pigs and the Fox* (N–P)

Marshall, James, *The Three Little Pigs* (N–P)

Moser, Barry, *The Three Little Pigs* (P–I)

Scieszka, Jon, *The True Story of the Three Little Pigs* (P–I)

Trivizas, Eugene, *Three Little Wolves and the Big Bad Pig* (N–P)

Wiesner, David, *The Three Pigs* (P–I)

Zemach, Margot, *The Three Little Pigs: An Old Story* (N–P–I)

COLLECTIONS OF VARIANTS AND FRACTURED FAIRY TALES

Anno, Mitsumasa, *Anno's Twice Told Tales: The Fisherman and His Wife and the Four Clever Brothers* (P–I)

Brooks, William, *A Telling of the Tales* (I)

Galloway, Priscilla, *Truly Grim Tales* (I–A)

King-Smith, Dick, *The Topsy Turvy Storybook* (P–I)

Scieszka, Jon, *The Stinky Cheese Man and Other Fairly Stupid Tales* (I)

Chapter

6

Fantasy and Science Fiction

Do you remember when Despereaux was in the dungeon, cupped in Gregory the jailer's hand, whispering a story in the old man's ear?

I would like it very much if you thought of me as a mouse telling you a story, this story, with the whole of my heart, whispering it in your ear in order to save myself from the darkness, and to save you from the darkness, too.

"Stories are light," Gregory the jailer told Despereaux. Reader, I hope you have found some light here.

—KATE DiCAMILLO, *The Tale of Despereaux,* p. 270

*J*ACOB'S FOURTH/FIFTH GRADE CLASS HAS JUST FINISHED LISTENING TO HIM read *The Tale of Despereaux* (P–1), and the final words of the coda still linger in their heads. Not all of the 27 students in the class were excited about reading the book when Jacob began just two weeks ago. Some thought it was too much like a fairy tale, with a princess and a king and a villain, and thus too "babyish" for them. Others were disgruntled because it was fantasy, and they prefer realistic fiction. But as the tale unfolded, all were caught up in the story of this unlikely hero—a small mouse with big ears—and his determination to follow his heart. Since the end of the first reading session they have been listening raptly. Now, the last word has been read.

Jacob asks his class if DiCamillo did what she hoped to do: Had they found some light in the story? The class choruses an enthusiastic yes, and he then tells them to take a minute to think about what kind of light they found, then turn and share their ideas with their neighbor. In just a few minutes the room is buzzing as students exchange ideas. Then Jacob calls the class back together with a request to share some of those ideas with the whole group. Amy begins by saying, "I don't know if this is exactly light, but the story did make me think about things, and it did make me happy, not sad, so I guess that's light." Elijah adds, "Yeah, it was a happy story, and funny, too. And I kind of understood what Gregory meant about stories being light because they kind of make you see things, if they're good."

Jacob is interested in Amy's and Elijah's comments and responds, "Ah, stories make you think about things and see things. That's interesting. Do the rest of you agree with this? What are some of the things you thought about or saw?" The students offer several suggestions. They considered how brave Despereaux was, that he was on a quest and so had to persevere because "you keep doing what you need to do." Lauren makes everyone laugh when she adds, "And soup helps you be brave." They have been talking about soup off and on throughout the reading of the book. There has even been some talk about a "Soup for Bravery" cookbook compilation. The conversation continues as they discuss how Despereaux was different from the other mice, and that it took courage to be different. They then circle back to stories as bringers of light.

Larissa tells the group that she likes to read stories when she's sad or lonely or bored because they "take her away." Marcus adds, "Sometimes to exciting places." Elijah completes the idea with "And you can see yourself there, just like Despereaux saw himself in the empty knight armor."

Jacob ends the discussion by complimenting them for their great ideas and asking them to continue to think about these ideas. "Just look back over the story and jot down things that Despereaux did that make you think he was brave. Then do a journal entry about that, or about a time when you had to be brave."

Although Jacob began by asking his students to talk about stories being light, it was easier for them to talk about courage. They did, eventually, circle back to thinking about the light that stories bring. Over the next few days they continued to work with this idea, finding places in the story in which DiCamillo uses light to tell about characters or as a symbol. And they talked about what light does—illuminate—and what that means. They built on this idea as they went on to other stories, other authors, always asking themselves what a particular story was making them think about. The story of a small mouse with big ears became a touchstone for thinking about how books can open new worlds.

Defining Fantasy and Science Fiction

Fantasy and science fiction are imaginative narratives that explore alternate realities. Science fiction explores scientific possibilities, asking and answering the question, "If this, then what?" Fantasy suspends scientific explanations and natural laws; it contains some element of character, setting, or plot not found in the natural world as it asks age-old questions about life, goodness, and balance. Both fantasy and science fiction are often set in worlds that do not correspond to present realities, but science fiction differs from fantasy in that the future realities it depicts are based on extrapolation from scientific principles. As Robert Heinlein (1953) describes it,

The author takes as his first postulate the real world as we know it, including all established facts and nat-

ural laws. The result can be extremely fantastic in content, but it is not fantasy; it is legitimate—and often very tightly reasoned—speculation about the possibilities of the real world. (p. 1118)

Of course it is sometimes difficult to draw the line between what is scientifically possible and what is not, and some critics talk about "science fantasy" books in which the line between the fantastic and a scientific possibility is a fine one. Madeleine L'Engle's *A Wrinkle in Time, A Wind in the Door,* and *A Swiftly Tilting Planet* (all A) all involve travel through time and space. Is this fantasy? Or, because this travel is theoretically possible, is it science fiction? What is truly important is that L'Engle's powerful novels, however one chooses to classify them, offer readers opportunities to think about the power of love in a deeper, more profound way than our daily lives permit.

Fantasy and science fiction are rooted in folklore but differ in that they are written by an individual author, rather than handed down by word of mouth. These genres build on and derive their strength from traditions established in ancient myths and legends. Just as our ancestors created a myth to explain the sun's apparent movement—describing how Apollo drove a chariot of fire across the sky—so modern writers spin imaginative tales to explain things we do not fully understand and to probe the dimensions of areas we do not fully know. As Jane Yolen (1999, p. 15) puts it, "stories lean on stories."

Just as the heroes of ancient legend confront great danger and rise to impossible challenges, modern heroes take on a larger-than-life nature as they are depicted in fantasy and science fiction. For example, in Philip Pullman's magnificent trilogy *The Golden Compass, The Subtle Knife,* and *The Amber Spyglass* (all A), Lyra and Will, the youthful heroes, battle powerful forces as they seek to fulfill their own destinies. These stories and many others also rely on structural patterns found in the oral tradition. The characters go on a quest that turns out differently from what they expected, they rise to the occasion, and they return home transformed in some way. In the Pullman trilogy, Lyra and Will travel to several worlds, including the world of the dead, and they end up discovering the magnificence of love.

There is a significant difference, however, between stories that came to us through oral tradition and ones we call fantasy or science fiction. Ancient tales were shaped and honed through cultural belief and the voice of the storyteller. Modern tales are shaped through the author's artistic vision and stylistic choices. Egoff (1981) calls this the difference between a public dream (folklore) and a private, metaphorical vision (modern fantasy and science fiction). For example, the appearance of the Holy Grail in Thomas Malory's *Le Morte d'Arthur* was not taken as fantasy in the 15th century; it was a public dream, meant to be believed. Weaving this and other legends from Arthurian days into the fabric of modern life, Susan Cooper creates fantasies that dramatize the risks of failing to stand up for what is right and just. Cooper bases her stories on English and Celtic myth, beginning with *Over Sea, Under Stone* and continuing with *The Dark Is Rising, Greenwitch, Silver on the Tree,* and *The Grey King* (all A).

The Role of Fantasy and Science Fiction in Children's Lives

Fantasy and science fiction open doors to worlds of imagination. They enrich and illuminate children's lives because the stories deal with the great complexities of existence: the relativity of size, time, and space; the interdependence of all things in the universe; good versus evil; the strength and courage of the individual; and integrity. Fantasy and science fiction writers often treat problems of the universe with a high seriousness. They can also deal lightheartedly with capricious supernatural events—adventures in space, as in Jane Yolen's *Commander Toad in Space* (P); stuffed animals that talk, as in Margery Williams's *The Velveteen Rabbit* (P–I); or miniature lives, as in John Peterson's *The Littles* (I).

For many children, fantasy is the first literature they love. Children in preschool and primary grades love books with animal characters who act like human beings. William Steig's *Sylvester and the Magic Pebble* (P), Russell Hoban's *Bread and Jam for Frances* (P), Rosemary Wells's *Max's First Word* (N), and many other beloved books for young children are fantasies—in this case books about talking animals, characters that could not really exist. Children have

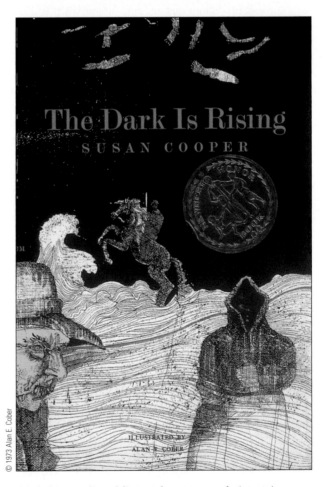

© 1973 Alan E. Cober

Susan Cooper spins a delicate web to create an elusive tension between physical reality and an imaginative world where good struggles against evil. Cooper's skill at manipulating myth and reality is unparalleled.

no trouble understanding what the stories are about and what questions they raise about real life.

As they mature, children experience many kinds of literature. Sometime during the elementary school years, some children become enraptured with realistic fiction, giving themselves completely over to this genre. Others become avid consumers of nonfiction and biography. Some continue to enjoy fantasy, moving from picture books to more fully developed narratives. As children mature they either move toward science fiction and fantasy or learn to avoid them entirely in their personal selection of books (Galda, 1990; Sebesta & Monson, 2003). Those who like these genres love them passionately, and those who do not are just as passionate. For some children, these genre preferences may last the rest of their lives; others will become more eclectic with development and will once again enjoy fantasy. The record-breaking popularity of J. K. Rowling's **Harry Potter** (I–A) series has enticed many readers to fantasy and perhaps converted some of them into avid readers of fantasy. It has certainly spawned increased interest in writing and publishing fantasy, and there is an abundance of outstanding books from which to choose.

Why do some readers prefer this unrealistic and sometimes disturbing literature over other genres? Susan Cooper, noted fantasy writer, speaks of fantasy as "the metaphor through which we discover ourselves" (1981, p. 16). She argues that rather than helping us escape out of our selves and into a fantasy world, fantasy draws readers into themselves, pushing them to consider who they are and what the world is. Serious fantasy "is probably the most complex form of fiction [readers] will ever find" (p. 16) and demands a great deal from its readers. Fantasy, she contends, satisfies our hunger for myth (1996).

Children don't expect fantasy to help them solve their daily social problems; rather, they read and enjoy fantasy because it reaches for their souls (May, 1984). Lloyd Alexander, himself a much honored writer of fantasy, feels that fantasy even has the power to encourage social change (1970). Because fantasy can explore the big issues of our world, it can be a vital force for moral and spiritual growth.

The imaginative speculation that marks science fiction stretches the minds of readers as they consider ethical dilemmas that might result from physical and technological advances. Stories set in worlds never before known deal with problems that children may someday face—the rights of extraterrestrials whose planets are colonized, the consequences of diminishing resources in a world of rapidly growing populations, the social and moral effects of medical advances—and thus prompt readers to rethink choices and directions of our society. Science fiction, a literature about change and the attendant moral issues that change brings, is important for the children of a rapidly changing world.

Criteria for Evaluating Fantasy and Science Fiction

As with all quality narrative literature, good fantasy and science fiction tell an interesting story, have well-developed characters, an engaging plot, and an identifiable theme, all presented through a well-crafted style. Authors manipulate these elements to create a fantasy world. If the writer is successful, readers willingly suspend disbelief. We judge the quality of a writer's private vision by how thoroughly it convinces us of its reality, by how long it haunts our memory, and by how deeply it moves us to new insights. Figure 6.1 presents characteristics of excellent imaginative fiction.

• • **SETTING** • •

No matter how fantastic they are, settings are believable when an author provides rich details that enable a reader to envision them. Some authors provide detailed maps of fantasy lands, complete with place names that are consistent with the fantasy. Others gradually lead readers from the real world into the fantasy world through some device, such as a magic door, a magic object, or the belief of realistic characters in the fantasy setting. In science fiction the setting is some time in the future, and that future has been shaped by a present-day scientific possibility that has been realized.

Figure 6-1

Checklist for Evaluating Fantasy and Science Fiction

✿ The story meets the criteria for excellence in narrative fiction.

✿ The fantasy world is detailed and believable within the context of the story.

✿ The story events are imaginative, yet logically consistent within the story world.

✿ The characters are multidimensional, with consistent and logical behavior.

✿ There are vivid images and solid, understandable structures.

✿ The themes are meaningful, causing readers to think about life.

It may be a world that has become overcrowded due to medical advances, or in which genetic engineering has run amuck, or that has been devastated by global warming. Effective settings are detailed and believable within the context of the story. Teaching Idea 6.1 suggests ideas for examining some believable settings with your students.

• • PLOT • •

Even though events might not be realistic, what happens in a story must be logically consistent within the story world. If characters move through time, they do so for a reason; they may walk through a door, press a magic button, or visit a particular place. If the fantastic operates in the real world, then there must be consistency in how real people are affected by the fantastic events. In science fiction, the plot is usually driven by the problems that scientific advances have created for the characters in the story world.

• • CHARACTERS • •

Excellent fantasy and science fiction stories contain characters, human and nonhuman, who are recognizable beings with strong emotions. These main characters are multidimensional personalities who behave consistently, respond to events in a believable fashion, and grow and change across the course of the story. Who they are both influences and is influenced by the plot. If a character that lives in a realistic story world enters a fantasy situation, the character does not magically change, but remains consistent across both worlds. Characters in science fiction struggle with scientific advances as they try to live in a future world. Even if characters are superheroes within a story, they are so carefully delineated that readers accept their otherworldly powers. Memorable characters are well developed, with behavior that is consistent and logical within the story world.

• • STYLE • •

How a writer chooses to tell a story—through structure, syntax, and word choice—makes the difference between a mediocre book and an excellent one. Some of the best writing in children's books appears in fantasy and science fiction. Style works to establish the setting; rich images and vivid figurative language help readers envision the created world. Style makes the characters and the plot believable; authentic dialogue and clear structure help readers build characterizations and follow the action. Well-written stories have clear structures supported by vivid, interesting images and rich language.

Teaching Idea **6-1**

Teaching Genre: Setting in Fantasy and Science Fiction

Good fantasy writers establish believable settings by carefully presenting them in intricate detail. Because the reader must envision the fantasy world, a writer's words ought to stimulate pictures in the mind's eye. Some writers add a map or make a scale drawing of an area; some paint scenes that are so vivid you can smell them.

Read outstanding fantasies to savor the descriptive language used to establish setting. If you work with young students, read aloud scenes and ask them to create dioramas, paintings, or three-dimensional scenes of the ones described. Ask students to describe in writing the scene they envision. Discuss these and other examples of vivid writing in a writing workshop to show effective techniques and then ask young writers to create their own vivid settings.

Suggested books and pages where you will read vivid scenes:

Farmer, Nancy, *The House of the Scorpion.* See p. 324, chap. 33, "The Boneyard."

Grahame, Kenneth, *Wind in the Willows.* See p. 9, the passage that begins, *The Mole had been working. . . .*

Jacques, Brian, *Redwall.* See the frontispiece: *Redwall stood foursquare along the marches of the old south border, flanked on two sides by Mossflower Wood's shaded depths. . . .*

Jansson, Tove, *Tales from Moominvalley.* See p. 11: *The brook was a good one. . . .*

White, E. B., *Charlotte's Web.* See p. 13: *The barn was very large. It was very old. It smelled of hay and it smelled of manure. It smelled of the perspiration of tired horses and the wonderful sweet breath of patient cows.*

• • THEME • •

Although some fantasy and science fiction is lighthearted, many other books have serious themes of great import. The monumental struggle between good and evil, what it means to be human, and the consequences of pride are all examples of recurring fantasy themes. The themes in science fiction make us consider the emotional, psychological, and mental effects of scientific advances; they help us keep an open mind so that we can consider the unlimited possibilities science offers us. In both cases, these themes are woven throughout the story, logically radiating from character and plot. At their best, these stories ask questions that arise naturally from the unity of character and action and are meaningful for readers, causing them to ask questions about life.

✳ ✳ ✳

A CLOSE LOOK AT

The Tale of Despereaux

Kate DiCamillo's *The Tale of Despereaux: Being the Story of a Mouse, a Princess, Some Soup, and a Spool of Thread* (P–I), winner of the 2004 Newbery Medal, is an engaging, multilayered story that asks fundamental questions about life. On the surface this is a story about a very small mouse with very large ears, his love for a princess, his quest through the dungeon to rescue her, and a mostly happily-ever-after

Kate DiCamillo's story of an unlikely hero with big ears not only pleased the young boy who asked her to write it but also went on to please many others and win the 2004 Newbery Medal.

ending. Beneath the surface tale, important questions about love, honor, perfidy, self-worth, and determination combine to elevate the story to one that explores the human heart with great seriousness.

Synopsis

The story begins with the birth of a small mouse with large ears and wide-open eyes—our hero, Despereaux. It is soon apparent that he is not like the other mice, preferring to read instead of eat the pages of books in the castle library, becoming enchanted by the music that he hears, and eventually breaking all mouse codes by revealing himself to humans—the king and Princess Pea—and even talking with them. For this he is banished to the rat-infested dungeon by the other mice, denounced by his own father, and led to his doom by his brother. The story then pauses and goes backwards, introducing the rat Chiaroscuro, who is fascinated by light, which is not a ratlike thing, and who has inadvertently caused the demise of the queen by falling from a chandelier into her soup, scaring her to death. DiCamillo then pauses and goes backwards again, telling the story of Miggory Sow, a slow and unbeautiful girl who has been sold as a servant by her father and ends up working in the castle. Miggory, however, has a heart's desire—to be a princess—and the rat Chiaroscuro uses this desire to gain revenge on the humans who have banished him to the dungeon. Together they kidnap the princess and hide her in the dungeon. Despereaux rescues her at great peril, Chiaroscuro is repentant, Miggory Sow is reunited with her father, and all is well, if not perfect.

Setting

In this fantasy, the setting is in many ways a generic castle, but the imagery is so evocative that the reader feels the darkness and smells the stench of the dungeon, while also hearing the music and seeing the light of the castle. The kitchen, where two important scenes take place, is easy to visualize, as are the dark, dark stairs leading to the dungeon. Through DiCamillo's description of Despereaux's descent, we feel his despair when he arrives at the bottom of the steps:

> He got to his feet and became aware of a terrible, foul, extremely insulting smell. The dungeon, reader, stank. It stank of despair and suffering and hopelessness. Which is to say that the dungeon smelled of rats. And it was so dark. Despereaux had never before encountered darkness so awful, so all-encompassing. (p. 73)

Characterization

DiCamillo clearly cares about her characters, and this empathy helps charm the reader. Despereaux is the hero on a quest, and, as in all good quests, his mettle is tested, allowing him to grow and develop from a small mouse who faints into a brave hero. The sweetness of Despereaux's love for the princess, his pleasure in music and books, and his wavering but ultimately resolute determination to rescue the princess raise the mouse above a stock hero and elevate his quest beyond the confines of a fairy tale. When he re-

turns to the dungeon to save the princess, he gathers his courage by telling himself a story:

"I will tell myself a story," said Despereaux. "I will make some light. Let's see. It will begin this way: Once upon a time. Yes. Once upon a time, there was a mouse who was very, very small. Exceptionally

Courtesy Candlewick Press, Cambridge, MA

Kate DiCamillo

*K*ate DiCamillo's writing career began with a childhood lie. Not exactly a lie, *she was quick to explain in a speech she delivered at the University of Minnesota. A misunderstanding, really. Having found a story in a children's magazine that she particularly liked, a young Kate transcribed the words in her own notebook. When her family found the notebook, they were impressed with the story. They asked if she had written it. Her answer, of course, was yes. She had written that story— in the literal sense of the word. That was her handwriting! News circulated quickly: Kate was talented. Caught in a snowball of assumptions, Kate knew the only way to keep from disappointing her family, friends, and teachers was to actually begin writing. Her own stories.*

"When I write," explained DiCamillo in *Something about the Author,* "I sometimes stop and cup my hands, as if I am drinking water. I try, I want desperately to capture

the world, to hold it for a moment in my hands." According to DiCamillo, *looking* at the world is an essential step in capturing the stories surrounding all of us:

In "Birches," Robert Frost says, "Earth is the right place for love, I don't know where it's likely to go better." Earth is also the right place for story ideas. All you have to do is look around you.

Years ago, when I was living in Florida, I was driving home late one night, so late that it was really early morning. There was fog everywhere. . . .

I was sitting at a stoplight and I looked over at the car idling next to me. It was a huge, old Chevrolet Impala. Green. And in the front seat, there was a boy with hair so blond it was almost white. While I was looking, the boy slid close to the man and bent his head and looked up at the man, and the man, after a small minute, reached out and put a hand on the boy's head. That was it. That's all that happened. Nothing more. The light changed. The Impala and the boy floated away into the fog. The man's hand was still on the boy's head.

I kept that image with me for years, until finally it turned itself into my second novel, **The Tiger Rising.** *And all I had to do to get the characters, the idea, was to move my head to the left early one morning and look out my car window at the fog and the car next to me and wonder about the people in it. (from "Look, Listen, Lie," p. 4)*

DiCamillo's ability to read the world and to translate its details

into stories has been widely appreciated by audiences. Her first novel, *Because of Winn-Dixie* (1), was a Newbery Honor book. *The Tiger Rising* (1) was a 2001 National Book Award finalist. She won the 2004 Newbery Medal for her fantasy, *The Tale of Despereaux.*

It was while drafting the manuscript for *The Tale of Despereaux* that DiCamillo happened to be traveling by airplane. On board the airplane, she sat next to a passenger who asked her what she did for a living. She dreaded this question. At a time when the world seemed filled with tumult and despair, writing a fantasy novel felt inconsequential, silly even. She explained she was writing a story. The passenger pressed her to explain what the story was about. A mouse. A story about a mouse. Later, the passenger found DiCamillo in the terminal and encouraged her to keep writing her story, that a story might offer just what the world needed: a ray of hope. DiCamillo agreed that stories could help people survive in the world. "The world is dark, and light is precious," begins *The Tale of Despereaux.* "Come closer, dear reader. You must trust me. I am telling you a story."

Sources:

DiCamillo, K. (2002). Look, listen, lie. *A View from the Loft, 25*(8), 4–5.

Peacock, S. (Ed.). (2001). Kate DiCamillo. *Something about the Author: Facts and Pictures about Authors and Illustrators of Books for Young People, 121,* 74–75. New York: Gale Research.

Profile

small. And there was a beautiful human princess whose name was Pea. And it so happened that this mouse was the one who was selected by fate to serve the princess, to honor her, and to save her from the darkness of a terrible dungeon." This story cheered up Despereaux considerably. (p. 237)

Chiaroscuro, the rat, is a villain, but a villain with weaknesses, and it is difficult not to sympathize with him, at least a little. Miggory Sow is selfish, not too bright, and clumsy, but she has had a hard life and thus evokes some sympathy as well. The others are stock characters, but each has a bit of personality. The king loves music, his daughter, and his late wife, but he is obstinate and rather silly. The princess is sweet and charming, but she is also demanding and imperious; her heart harbors unsavory emotions. The cook is wonderful—inciting mouse murder in one scene, feeding Despereaux her special soup in another. Though clearly not real, these characters each reflect the combination of darkness and light that rests in the human heart.

Plot

The plot structure in *Despereaux* is unusual in that it is not linear. The story is divided into four "books," with the first being a linear recounting of Despereaux's life from birth through his descent into the dungeon. "Book the second" begins several years before the birth of Despereaux, with the birth of Chiaroscuro, and chronicles his fascination with light and the eventual death of the queen. "Book the third" goes back in time yet again, beginning with the death of Miggory's mother and recounting her squalid life with her father and subsequently as a servant. This book ends in the present, with Chiaroscuro and Miggory planning the abduction of the princess, while Despereaux listens in. Book the fourth, "Recalled to the Light," takes the action forward from there, culminating in the happy ending. By using such markers of time as "Again, reader, we must go backward before we can go forward," DiCamillo helps her readers follow the sequence of events. The intricacy of the plot, with the strands of three lives interweaving to propel the plot to the climax, is carefully, perfectly, and satisfyingly realized.

Style

The book is distinguished in many ways, one of which is the use of the narrator's personal asides to bring readers into the story, even as they are sent off to the dictionary to enlarge their vocabulary:

> Reader, you may ask this question; in fact, you must ask this question: Is it ridiculous for a very small, sickly, big-eared mouse to fall in love with a beautiful human princess named Pea? (p. 32)

The narrator's voice is funny, imperious, and often sarcastic, yet serves to remind readers that this fantasy may seem to be about a mouse and a princess, but relates directly to our lives. DiCamillo's use of imagery and symbol, such as in the constant interplay between dark and light, heightens the impact of her tale. She names the rat "Chiaroscuro" as a way to highlight the idea that he was, in fact, not all bad, but rather a combination of good and evil, light and darkness:

> Reader, do you know the definition of the word "chiaroscuro"? If you look in your dictionary, you will find that it means the arrangement of light and dark, darkness and light together. (p. 85)

Not only does the name serve as a symbol, it is integral to the action of the story, as the rat's obsession with light precipitates the queen's death as well as his own eventual redemption. Other images of light and dark appear throughout the story, echoing the epic struggle between good and evil that fills stories of high fantasy.

Theme

Important questions about love, honor, perfidy, self-knowledge, and determination permeate the story. How powerful is love? How does honor spur action? How does one forgive someone for doing one a great harm? How does one stand up for what one believes in, despite the approbation of others? Where does one find the strength to begin a quest despite overwhelming fear? These and other questions are asked and answered, and linger long in readers' thoughts.

The book is also carefully designed. Timothy Basil Ering's beautiful pencil illustrations decorate the text and remind us that our hero is, after all, only a small mouse with big ears. The book's old-fashioned cover and deckle-edged pages complement the classic feel of the tale.

✳ ✳ ✳

A CLOSE LOOK AT

The House of the Scorpion

Nancy Farmer's *The House of the Scorpion* (A), a Newbery Honor book for 2003, is science fiction at its best. Building on the scientific possibility of cloning to prolong life and on the social possibility of drug cartels' making political deals in order to create their own laws and countries, Farmer creates a future in which wealthy, powerful drug lords "farm" their own clones for future organ harvesting.

Synopsis

Matteo Alacrán is the clone of El Patrón, drug lord of the state of Opium and ruler of the Alacrán empire. Farmer's novel chronicles Matteo's maturation from a six-year-old who doesn't understand why he can't leave his house, to his eventual discovery of his origins and status, his mistreatment at the hands of the ruling family and their friends, his dramatic escape, and his final return.

Setting

Farmer carefully details her setting, the mountains and desert along the sliver of the Colorado River that separates the southwestern tip of Arizona from Mexico. The mountains and sky, the endless fields of poppies that produce the opium that supports the Alacráns, the heat and sun and dust of the southwestern desert are all described so vividly that one sees, feels, and tastes what Matt does. El Patrón's estate and the oasis to which Tam Lin takes Matt are also vividly depicted, a virtual map drawn in the head of the reader. This vivid setting allows readers both to visualize the story world and to realize that this world looks quite like our world today; in fact, it is identical except for the poppy fields.

Characterization

Matt, the protagonist, is a complex and dynamic character who grows and changes across the course of the story. He is in charge of his own destiny even at six, when he breaks a

Nancy Farmer

© Harold Farmer

According to the Shona, the Africans among whom we lived, I had been visited by a shave (pronounced "shah-vay") or wandering spirit. Shaves come from people who haven't received proper burial rites. They drift around until they find a likely host, possess whoever it is, and teach him or her a skill. In my case I got a traditional storyteller. Now I am a full-time professional storyteller myself. (from Something about the Author)

Nancy Farmer was 40 years old when she first began writing. "I had been reading a novel by Margaret Forster," Farmer told *Something about the Author,* "and thought: *I could do that.* Three hours later I emerged with a complete story. The experience was so surprising and pleasant I did it again the next day." In an online biography, Farmer said she knew her first story "wasn't good, but it was fun." Although her first stories were not award-winning pieces, they did spark in Farmer a passion that would lead her to write acclaimed novels. "Since that time [in my forties], I have been absolutely possessed with the desire to write. I can't explain it," Farmer commented in her online biography, "only that everything up to then was a preparation for my real vocation."

Farmer's preparation was rich. She spent her childhood living and working in the hotel her family owned in Arizona. "I remember cages of lions and wolves in the parking lot. Once, when I was nine, the circus vet invited me to attend an elephant autopsy and he discovered that the animal had two hearts. Life there was a wonderful preparation for writing" (www.barnesandnoble.com/writers).

As an adult, Farmer served for two years as a Peace Corps volunteer in India. She also spent many years working as a scientist in Africa. "The character, viewpoint and zany sense of humor of the people I met there have had a major effect on my writing," she said (Peacock, 2000, p. 57).

Farmer won a Newbery Honor for *The Ear, the Eye, and the Arm,* a science fiction novel set in Zimbabwe. Audiences also applauded her science fiction novel, *The House of the Scorpion,* which was a Newbery Honor book, a National Book Award winner, and a Printz Honor book. "One of my main themes," Farmer told *Locus* magazine, "is self-reliance, the ability to compete against odds and to beat them. A lot of kids' books have somebody who learns to come to terms with some dreadful situation, and it's all about them continuing to suffer at the end of the book. I don't want to write 'victim' books. I want a triumph, a hero or heroine, and that's what I write about."

Farmer's other works for children and young adults include *Do You Know Me? The Warm Place, Runnery Granary, A Girl Named Disaster, Casey Jones's Fireman,* and *Sea of Trolls.*

Sources:

Locus Online. (2004, January). [Excerpts from an interview with Nancy Farmer]. [www.locusmag.com/2004/Issues/01Farmer.html]. Accessed July 21, 2004.

Nancy Farmer. (n.d.). *Meet the Writers.* [www.barnesandnoble.com/writers]. Accessed July 21, 2004.

Reid, A. H. (n.d.). Nancy Farmer. *Meet the Writers.* [www.barnesandnoble.com/writers]. Accessed July 21, 2004.

Peacock, S. (Ed.). (2000). Nancy Farmer. *Something about the Author: Facts and Pictures about Authors and Illustrators of Books for Young People,* 117, 56–59. New York: Gale Research.

window with a cooking pot in order to talk and play with the children who discover him locked in his house in the middle of the fields. This "birth" into the real world triggers his dawning understanding of what he is and his gradual realization of what that means. He comes to understand that most people around him consider him a beast, with "Property of the Alacrán Estate" tattooed on his foot, and treat him as such. He discovers that he was born from a cow. And finally he realizes the extent of the evil of El Patrón and understands that he himself will be killed in order for El Patrón to continue to live. Confronted with these horrifying facts, he responds as any child would, with anger, denial, and bewilderment. Finally, however, Matt acts with resolve to resist the fate planned for him.

He is the epitome of a resilient child. When he is imprisoned in a room full of chicken litter, he creates games, makes friends with roaches, and keeps his spirit alive despite his despair. Surrounded by people with twisted morals, he sometimes stumbles into anger and revenge, but he carefully creates a soul for himself, building on the love of Celia, who took care of him as a baby; the example of Tam Lin, the bodyguard who cares for Matt; and his love for Maria, daughter of one of El Patrón's supporters. By the time he escapes it is not surprising that he has the resources to confront new dangers and challenges, or that he is determined, once he returns to Opium, to change it for the better.

Plot

This novel is not only science fiction but also adventure story and quest. The bulk of it occurs on the Alacrán estate, where the action centers around Matt coming to realize the situation he is in as he grows from boy to young man. As the central conflict is revealed, smaller conflicts that heighten the tension occur. Matt is abused by one of the servants and taunted by others, especially Tom, who vies against him for the heart of Maria. These subplots increase the distance between Matt, the beast, and others who are fully human. When Matt escapes from Opium he finds himself in dangerous circumstances, yet these dangers allow him to prove his courage and resolve. This ending section of the book reflects the age-old quest story: Matt leaves home, albeit a home that wasn't very welcoming, and goes out into the world, only to return a changed and better person.

Style

The world that Farmer creates is a brutal one, full of ugliness, horrifying to contemplate. Contrasted with that world is the friendship between Matt and Tam Lin, and Matt's love for Maria. Matt himself also stands in contrast, as his soul seems indomitable; it enables him to survive the brutality of body and spirit that he endures. These carefully crafted contrasts throw light on the questions that Farmer explores. Her careful use of language, including Spanish words and

phrases appropriate to the region, and vivid descriptions of characters, places, and events, add to the power of her story.

Theme

What does it mean to be human? Who is more fully human, the clone or the drug lord and his compatriots? Is humanity an accident of birth or the result of one's conduct in the world? What does it mean to know oneself and chart one's own course in spite of great odds? The beast is, ironically, the most human of them all. All these questions, and more, add dimension and texture to Farmer's deft characterization and complex plot. The age-old struggles between good and evil, powerful and powerless are depicted here in terms of the future, a future that comes closer every day (Galda, 2002).

Both *The Tale of Despereaux* and *The House of the Scorpion* offer many opportunities to explore powerful questions about life. One of the themes that students who have read these books often discuss is self-knowledge. This is not

*Nancy Farmer creates an all too believable futuristic setting and forces readers to consider some complex questions in **The House of the Scorpion**.*

Teaching Idea 6-2

Thematic Exploration: Self-Knowledge

In *The Tale of Despereaux,* Despereaux finds himself at odds with his community. Rather than hide from humans, he visits with them; rather than eat books, he reads them; and he can hear music. In *The House of the Scorpion,* Matteo soon discovers that, unlike the other Alacrán family and friends, he has been cloned and born from a cow. His differences are all too apparent. Both of these heroes realize their differences and discover their strengths. Despereaux is brave and has great perseverance. Matteo has a brave and loving heart. As you read, discuss passages from either book in which the heroes discover something about themselves and act on it. Ask students to write or talk about the following general questions:

✳ What did (the protagonist) discover about himself in this passage?

✳ How did (the protagonist's) actions reflect his increasing self-knowledge?

✳ What are some of the special things that define you as a person?

✳ Have you ever felt as different from others as (the protagonist) felt?

at all surprising, as this audience is frequently concerned with discovering who they are, who they want to be, and who they might become. Teaching Idea 6.2 offers some suggestions for writing prompts or discussion questions that can lead to a consideration of how Despereaux and Matteo discovered who they were, decided what they wanted to be, and acted on this self-knowledge.

The World of Fantasy

As we have seen, fantasy can be deeply serious. This type of fantasy is sometimes called "high" fantasy. High fantasy lies closely beside ancient folklore and contains archetypal themes. It explores the struggle between good and evil or follows a quest for personal identity. More lighthearted fantasy uses a veil of unreality to disguise the real world in some way. The fantastic element may be as simple as animals that act like humans or as complex as fully developed miniature worlds that reflect real life with a small twist.

Fantasy writers use such devices as time slips and magic, fully developed fantasy settings, or supernatural characters to create the fantasy. By creating a fantasy, writers are able to freely explore issues that might be too disturbing when considered in realistic settings. The metaphorical nature of fantasy allows children to consider prejudice, death, war, the consequences of beauty, and other serious issues in a manageable way. It is the seriousness of the questions that a story raises that determines whether a fantasy is "light" or "high." In either case, authors may create their fantasy using a variety of literary devices.

✳ ✳ ANIMAL FANTASY ✳ ✳

Animal fantasy attributes human thought, feeling, and language to animals. Children like to see animals dressed like people and believe in them readily. Actually, young children are often willing to invest any kind of creature or object with human characteristics. Because books that extend and enrich this normal developmental tendency strike a responsive chord in children, animal fantasy is a well-loved form. Like the folktale, it becomes part of children's literary experiences before they make clear distinctions between fact and fancy. This early pleasure in animal fantasy often continues as children mature into readers who devour fantasy novels.

Some of the most memorable characters from children's literature populate animal fantasy. Naive Wilbur, incorrigible Toad of Toad Hall, mischievous Peter Rabbit, Babar, and Winnie-the-Pooh call to mind many modern classics of this genre. Animal fantasies for older readers create an allegorical world in which the human scene is replayed to amuse and, often, to instruct. Such books as *Charlotte's Web* (I), by E. B. White, *Wind in the Willows* (I), by Kenneth Grahame, *The Mob: Feather and Bone Chronicles* (A), by Clem Martini, and *Watership Down* (A), by Richard Adams, use animal fantasy to comment on human frailties and foibles. In *Charlotte's Web,* for example, we find not only a delightful picture of the power of friendship and love but also a reminder that in the midst of life there is also death. In *Watership Down* we confront, among other issues, the consequences of war. And in *The Mob* we explore how social organizations must examine traditional rules in the light of new challenges.

Jill Barklem's **Brambly Hedge** (P) series presents realistic, everyday events, as experienced by a community of mice. The detailed, beautiful illustrations create a setting that heightens the pleasure. In books for slightly older readers, Dick King-Smith examines issues of individual difference in *Babe, the Gallant Pig* (I) and tolerance in *Martin's Mice* (I). Avi's **Tales from Dimwood Forest** series, which includes *Poppy, Poppy and Rye, Ragweed,* and *Ereth's Birthday* (all I), follows the adventures of one special mouse, Poppy, and her friends. As they seek to make a safe home in Dimwood Forest, they encounter many dangers from humans and other predators. The combination of humorous dialogue, notable characters, and a vividly detailed setting makes these books perfect for readers who enjoy animal fantasy and are ready for short novels. Once they have read this series, many will want to go on to Brian Jacques's **Redwall** (I–A) books, a multivolume series that provides high adventure, memorable characters, and intriguing descriptions of battles and weapons, all within an animal fantasy. Two new additions to the series are *Loamhedge* (I–A) and *Triss* (I–A). These books are devoured by boys from fourth through seventh grade who enjoy animal fantasy. Because this series is so extensive, many children never run out of good books to read!

In contrast to the epic battles in the **Redwall** books, *The Improbable Cat* (I), a small but rather dark animal fantasy by Allan Ahlberg, tells the tale of a family that is quite taken with a sweet gray kitten who appears one day. As the cat rapidly grows to an enormous size, it soon takes over the lives of everyone except David and his infant brother. They are the only ones who have not stroked the cat, and because of this they can resist it. Upper elementary grade readers enjoy talking about just what the cat symbolizes. The Booklist at the end of this chapter contains a number of memorable animal fantasies.

• • MINIATURE WORLDS • •

Every cultural group has its folkloric sprites, elves, trolls, brownies, or leprechauns, which go unseen about houses and villages. Tales about these small beings charm audiences, young and old alike. Just as older readers continue to enjoy novel-length animal fantasy, they also continue to respond to the call of miniature worlds. There is something compelling about smallness that pulls readers into a story world. What and how do small people eat, dress, move about? How does smallness transform daily life as we know it? What extra challenges does it pose? Miniature worlds, like animal fantasy, fascinate readers interested in details. Stories set in miniature worlds might take a lighthearted look at what life in miniature would be like or seriously explore human needs and desires. Fantasies about toys or miniature beings highlight human emotions by displaying them in action on a miniscule scale. From Arrietty in *The Borrowers* (I), by Mary Norton, to the Minnipins in *The Gammage Cup* and *The Whisper of Glocken* (both I), by Carol Kendall, the best and worst in human nature are magnified by the small size of the characters.

Carnegie Medalist Terry Pratchett has added to his popular **Discworld Series** with *The Wee Free Men* (A). Pratchett is a master at combining suspense and humor, and this story does not disappoint. In Fairyland, the six-inch-high Wee Free Men battle the forces of evil alongside Tiffany, a young human girl who, in her world, is a witch in training,

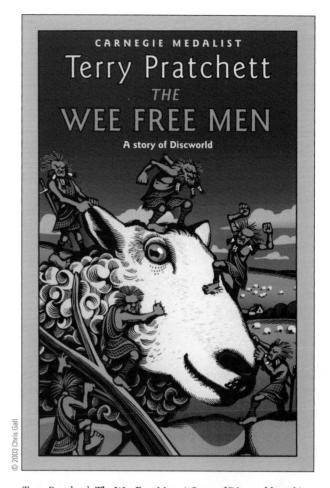

Terry Pratchett's **The Wee Free Men: A Story of Discworld** *combines humor and suspense in a story that is completely engaging.*

in spite of which she confronts contemporary issues such as sexist assumptions about courage.

• • TIME SLIPS AND MAGIC • •

Many fantasy writers use the device of time slips, or characters traveling through time, to create and sustain the fantasy in their stories. Still others use magic of some kind to propel the action. These devices help create a fantasy world and can be found in all types of fantasy, including animal fantasy, stories of miniature worlds, and epic quest tales and literary lore.

In some stories, time is the element that is carried beyond the realm of everyday experience, as characters move between their current reality and other times and places. For many writers, the past and future are part of the present; by challenging our understanding of time as sequential, these authors are making a statement about the meaning of time itself. One such writer, Eleanor Cameron (1969), describes a globe of time in which the past, present, and future are perceived as a whole.

Authors of fantasy invent a dazzling variety of devices to permit their characters to move in and out of conventional time. The children in C. S. Lewis's *The Lion, the Witch, and the Wardrobe* (I) enter the land of Narnia through a wardrobe; while they are in Narnia, time does not pass in their real world. Jon Scieszka plays with time in his **Time Warp Trio** series (I), in which Joe, Fred, and Sam, ordinary boys all, manage to travel through time to a series of unlikely places. The eight books in this series, including *It's All Greek to Me,* are lighthearted fun.

Several time-slip fantasies focus on a central character going through a difficult adjustment period; loneliness, alienation, and extraordinary sensitivity seem to be associated with time travel. In Philip Pullman's trilogy, *The Golden Compass, The Subtle Knife,* and *The Amber Spyglass,* Lyra and Will travel between worlds as well as through time as they engage in their epic quest.

Magic is also a basic ingredient in fantasy. Often the magic is mixed with humor, and readers respond avidly to both. Children recognize the possibilities that magic entails; they willingly enter a world that does not operate by natural law. Bruce Coville's **Magic Shop** series (I) uses the device of a shop that caters to would-be magicians to allow realistic characters to enter fantasy worlds. Dragons figure prominently in *Jeremy Thatcher, Dragon Hatcher* (I), and talking toads are featured in *Jennifer Murdley's Toad* (I).

Natalie Babbitt's classic fantasy, *Tuck Everlasting* (I), postulates a magic spring that, like the water so long sought by explorer Ponce de León, bestows eternal life. The magical water has given eternal life to the Tuck family, and young Winnie Foster discovers their secret. What she learns about the impact of eternal life on the Tucks influences the deci-

© 1975 Natalie Babbitt

This beautifully written novel raises powerful questions about the cycle of life . . . and death.

sion she makes—not to drink from the spring. The magic in this tale allows Babbitt to explore some important life questions. Young readers discuss this story with great seriousness, pondering such questions as those listed in Teaching Idea 6.3.

Teaching Idea 6-3

Everlasting Questions

Powerful discussions arise from reading *Tuck Everlasting,* by Natalie Babbitt. Here are some suggested book discussion group topics:

✳ Would you want to live forever? What age would you choose to be?

✳ If someone promised you everlasting life, would you do what was required to obtain it? What would you do with your life?

✳ Why does Winnie Foster confide in the toad?

✳ How does the toad help Winnie make up her mind about drinking the spring water, which promises eternal life?

✳ What does the man in the yellow suit represent?

✳ How does the Tuck family feel about Winnie Foster?

✳ Do you think Winnie made the right choice?

✳ What would you say to Winnie if you could meet her?

✳ Is killing someone ever justified?

There are an increasing number of books that make use of magical realism, blurring the line between contemporary realistic fiction and fantasy, just as years ago Jane Yolen blurred the line between historical fiction and fantasy through the use of a time slip in her Holocaust novel, *The Devil's Arithmetic* (A). The magical realism of David Almond's *Skellig* (A), a beautifully haunting, moving tale, involves a being that seems to be an angel, at least to the two young protagonists who see and talk with him. How you categorize this book depends on your perception of who Skellig was and where you place magical realism. For some, this is a fantasy novel; for others, it is grippingly realistic.

J. K. Rowling's *Harry Potter and the Sorcerer's Stone* (I), *Harry Potter and the Chamber of Secrets* (I), *Harry Potter and the Prisoner of Azkaban* (I–A), *Harry Potter and the Goblet of Fire* (A), and *Harry Potter and the Order of the Phoenix* (A) contain a vast array of magical devices, such as Harry's famous Quidditch broom, owls that deliver mail, invisibility cloaks, and a map that shows people and their locations. The books are also firmly anchored in the well-developed fantasy world of Hogwarts School of Witchcraft and Wizardry, which is peopled by teachers and students who practice an assortment of bizarre and intriguing magic. All of this magic is carefully placed, and the actions within the fantasy world are ultimately logical. Rowling never violates the rules she creates, and readers devour these books with a passion rarely seen.

Three recent books create their fantasy worlds around the magic of books. Cornelia Funke's *Inkheart* (A) and Roderick Townley's *The Great Good Thing* (I) and *Into the Labyrinth* (I) play with the idea that not only can readers enter a story world, but the characters in a book can enter the real world as well. In these books the story characters come alive, and journey between the story world and the real world, affecting both. These writers extend our conception of how stories and the imagination can influence life. These and other fantasies that use devices such as time slips and magic to create the fantasy world are included in the Booklist at the end of the chapter.

• • **L I T E R A R Y   L O R E** • •

The literary tale, a story crafted by a writer who intentionally imitates the traditional qualities of ancient folklore, has become increasingly popular over the past several years. Teaching Idea 6.4 offers suggestions for exploring these tales with students. As discussed in Chapter 5, these stories appeared initially as "fractured fairy tales," stories that were not cultural variants of well-known folktales but rather the deliberate construction of a writer intending to imitate, embellish, or alter traditional folktales. Today there are many full-length novels with characters and action based on traditional lore, elaborated to create a wholly original version of a traditional tale.

It takes a reader to make a book come alive, but what happens when a book character goes to live in a reader's dreams?

Jon Scieszka's *The True Story of the Three Little Pigs* and *The Stinky Cheese Man* (both I) are well-loved examples of this type of story for younger readers. Increasingly, writers for middle school and young adult readers have created stories that weave around traditional tales. Robin McKinley's *Beauty* (A), an early example of this phenomenon, has been followed by *Rose Daughter* and *Spindle's End* (both A). Older readers can appreciate Donna Jo Napoli's mastery of style in such books as *Crazy Jack, Beast, Spinners, Zel,* and *The Magic Circle* (all A). Gail Carson Levine's *Ella Enchanted* (I), a delightful twist of the Cinderella tale, won a Newbery Honor.

Jane Yolen is one of the masters of literary lore. Her novels in **The Young Merlin Trilogy** recreate the legend of King Arthur with her own deft touches. In *Sword of the Rightful King: A Novel of King Arthur* (I), she recreates the story of Excalibur with a new twist, creating ultimately human characters out of the stuff of legend. Kevin Crossley-Holland's new trilogy, *The Seeing Stone, At the Crossing Places,* and *King of the Middle March* (all I–A), moves between the often uncomfortable, filthy reality of the Middle Ages and the magical world described in the legend of King Arthur. These novels are a unique blend of historical fiction and fantasy.

Teaching Idea 6-4

Literary Tales and Folkloric Themes

It is easy to confuse literary tales with folklore because the two genres are quite similar. Modern writers intentionally use folkloric elements in their stories, and sometimes they do this so well that their work is often mistaken for folktales. For example, Hans Christian Andersen captures the essence of folktales so artfully that it's hard to distinguish his work from the massive body of anonymous traditional literature. Other authors, such as Donna Jo Napoli, Jane Yolen, and Kevin Crossley-Holland, build on essential elements of well-known folklore, and craft novel-length stories around their central core. As you read literary tales with your students, build on their knowledge of folklore elements and discuss those that they notice in the literary tales they are reading. After you have read several literary tales with your students, ask them to consider the following questions:

✳ What folklore elements do the tales contain?

✳ How subtly does the author weave in the folklore elements? Give an example.

✳ Compare a literary tale to the original piece of folklore on which it was modeled.

✳ Discuss the differences between the original and the elaborated tale.

Another gifted writer who retells ancient tales, Gerald Morris brings to life both the Middle Ages and the famous story of the doomed love of Tristram and Iseult in *The Ballad of Sir Dinadan* (A). He has recently added to his Arthurian series with *The Princess, the Crone, and the Dung-Cart Knight* (I–A), a magical, sometimes funny, bittersweet tale.

Even more ancient legends are at the core of other examples of literary lore. Mary Pope Osborne's **Tales from the Odyssey** series retells and embellishes well-known stories from Homer's epic poem. *The One-Eyed Giant, The Land of the Dead, Sirens and Sea Monsters, The Gray-Eyed Goddess,* and *Return to Ithaca* (all I) are written with verve and style in a manner that appeals to middle-grade readers. Adele Geras's *Troy* (A) casts the story of the siege of Troy from the perspective of two young handmaidens living through it, complete with humorous comments from the

gods and goddesses who are manipulating people and events. Michael Cadnum brings classic legends from Ovid to life in *Starfall: Phaeton and the Chariot of the Sun* (A); Jean Thesman bases her novel *Singer* (A) on an ancient Gaelic tale. These writers echo the sounds from storytellers' tongues of ages past.

• • QUEST TALES • •

Many stories that we call literary lore are also quest tales. T. A. Barron's **The Last Years of Merlin** five-book epic (all A) is a magnificent quest based on legend. His new book, *The Great Tree of Avalon: Child of the Dark Prophecy* (A), the first of a planned series, is set in a wholly imagined world that was created when Merlin planted a seed and the tree of Avalon sprang into being.

Franny Billingsley, winner of the Boston Globe–Horn Book Award, builds on ancient Selkie (seal maiden) tales in *The Folk Keeper* (A), a hauntingly beautiful story of a young girl who disguises herself as a boy in order to keep herself safe as a folk keeper, a person who controls the damage that the folk can create when they are hungry and unhappy. When she moves to a wild island to control the folk there, she discovers her own heritage and her true powers, even as she is forced to acknowledge her femininity as she matures and falls in love. This quest tale epitomizes the depth of emotion and complexity of ideas that mark high fantasy.

Archetypal quest themes from folklore become vividly evident in high fantasy. Here again is the misty outline of a story in which we search for the golden age, or we have lost—and seek to regain—our identity. Victory in the battle between good and evil depends on finding the missing heir, recognizing a prince or princess in disguise, or achieving utopia under the rule of a king whose coming has been foretold. Quest stories that are most memorable describe characters' outer and inner struggles and may involve Herculean journeys during which they overcome obstacles and vanquish enemies. Quests often become a search for an inner, rather than an outer, enemy. Inner strength is required as characters are put to a variety of challenges that often seem endless and unbeatable. It is the indomitable goodness of character that prevails. Books such as *The Book of Three* from Lloyd Alexander's beloved series, **The Prydain Chronicles** (I), which has been reissued in beautiful matched editions, continue to enchant young readers eager to test their metaphorical mettle against all odds. Monica Furlong's classic quest tales, *Juniper, Wise Child,* and *Colman* (all A), have been recently published in hardcover U.S. editions.

Some of the most remarkable books of this type published in the recent past are Philip Pullman's **His Dark Materials** trilogy (all A). Readers are introduced to Lyra, the young and engaging protagonist, in *The Golden Compass.*

Lyra is an interesting blend: she is both a street urchin and the highly intelligent daughter of eminent and powerful people. She thinks herself an orphan but soon discovers to her horror who her mother and father really are. Lyra sets out on her quest to save herself and the children who are being kidnapped and sent north to be the victims of a horrible experiment. By the end of the story she has come to realize that her quest is bigger than this, and she unhesitatingly steps into a new world, determined to carry on. Continue she does, in *The Subtle Knife,* where she meets her partner, Will, a hero not unlike herself but from a different world. They pursue their quest, moving between worlds, aided by witches and angels, running from the evildoers of the Church, until the triumphant ending of *The Amber Spyglass.* This series has it all: child heroes, alternate worlds, time slips, magic objects, fantastic creatures, imagination at its height. It is all anchored within an overarching theme of the struggle between good and evil, mirrored in the poet John Milton's story *Paradise Lost,* and the overwhelming power of love. These and other quest tales appear in the Booklist at the end of this chapter. Teaching Idea 6.5 offers a way to help children link their own lives and concerns with the heroes of some of these quest tales by exploring the power of naming.

Themes in Science Fiction

As with fantasy, some science fiction is light; it relies on technological advances, such as space travel, to create the story. Many children are introduced to science fiction through some of these lighter stories. Science fantasy, that blend of fantasy and science fiction that is often set in other worlds but is uncomplicated by elaborate scientific theories, provides a good entree for beginning science fiction readers. As they read and enjoy these stories they will become interested in moving on to more complex stories that explore significant issues. Young readers enjoy Jane Yolen's **Commander Toad** (P) series, as well as such books as Betsy Duffey's *Alien for Rent* (P–I) or Louis Sachar's *Marvin Redpost: A Flying Birthday Cake?* (I), all humorous science fantasy. Other science fiction for younger readers is more serious, while still not overly complex. In *The Green Book* (I), a beautifully written story by Jill Paton Walsh, young Pattie takes her green-covered blank book with her when she and her family escape from the dying planet Earth. When they arrive at their new settlement, Pattie and her friends explore their new world, Shine. Their courage and perseverance

Teaching Idea 6-5

The Power of Naming

According to traditional lore, there is power in knowing someone's true name; to know a true name is to hold that person's life in your hands. *Rumpelstiltskin* (Grimm) and *Duffy and the Devil* (Zemach) illustrate the folkloric power of naming. In high fantasy, the secrecy of a name and the true identity of a hero are heavily guarded. Only trusted friends know the hero's true name. Locate books in which naming is integral to the plot. Start with these:

Alexander, Lloyd, *The Black Cauldron*

_____, *The Book of Three*

_____, *The Castle of Llyr*

_____, *The High King*

_____, *Taran Wanderer*

Le Guin, Ursula, *The Farthest Shore*

_____, *Tombs of Atuan*

_____, *Wizard of Earthsea*

L'Engle, Madeleine, *Wind in the Door*

Sutcliff, Rosemary, *The Road to Camlann*

Questions for book discussion:

✳ If people who knew your name held power over you, who would you allow to know your name?

✳ What kind of people would you trust to know your true name?

✳ From what kind of people would you keep your name secret?

You can encourage your students to notice the importance of names in the literature of many cultures. For example, Native peoples often kept their true names secret from all but those closest to them. Others from the Far East have two names—one that is their true name and one for the outside world to use. Many immigrants to this country use nicknames to help them fit into American culture more readily. The power of naming can be seen everywhere.

lead the community to find a way to exist, and Pattie's book becomes the place where the community can write the story of their survival. The occasional soft illustrations by Lloyd Bloom help describe what life is like in Shine.

Science fiction for older readers offers the same kind of deep questioning that fantasy offers, although in this case, the questions asked relate to scientific possibilities. In Andrew Clements's *Things Not Seen* (A), the 15-year-old protagonist is used to being "invisible." His parents are busy, the popular kids at school look right through him, and he doesn't think much of himself, either. When he wakes up one morning to find himself invisible, due, we eventually discover, to a flaw in the current in his electric blanket, he and his parents are shaken. Although the book is filled with very humorous episodes, it also considers serious questions about society. His growing relationship with a blind girl and his experience being truly invisible push him and the reader to consider what it means to see and to have others truly see you.

Most category systems, including ones for dividing science fiction into types, are arbitrary; many novels fit into more than one classification. There are, however, three major themes treated in science fiction—mind control, life in the future, and survival—one of which often dominates a particular book even when all are present.

✳ ✳ MIND CONTROL ✳ ✳

Several science fiction writers deal with themes of mind control, telepathy, ESP, and other forms of communication across time and space. As computers, television, and other forms of communication reach more and more people across the globe, and advances in medicine make possible genetic and nervous system alterations, the potential increases for mind control on a grand scale.

One early example is John Christopher's **White Mountain** trilogy. This series about extraterrestrial invaders of Earth appeals to today's readers in the upper elementary grades. *The White Mountains, The City of Gold and Lead,* and *The Pool of Fire* (all I–A), are set in the 21st century in a world ruled by the Tripods, dreaded robots. When humans are 14, the Tripods implant steel caps in their skulls that keep them submissive, docile, and helpless. Christopher's narrative impels readers to ponder the values of life and science.

Lois Lowry's *Messenger* (A) continues her exploration of the possibilities of controlled communities that began in *The Giver* and continued in *Gathering Blue* (both A). In this final book in the trilogy, Lowry brings together characters from the first two books and creates a new hero, a young boy named Matty, who is on the brink of discovering his true power. Lowry's dystopian novels probe issues of mind

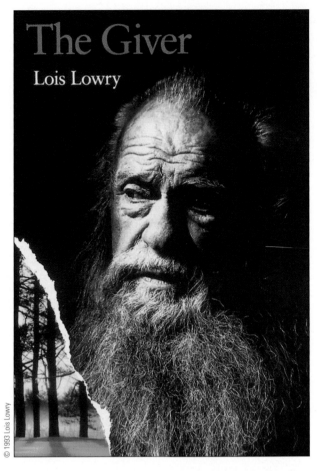

© 1993 Lois Lowry

The Giver, the receiver of memories in a planned community, tries to hand down those memories to his successor and thereby changes the community forever.

control, individuality, honor, and courage in a future world, the seeds of which are visible today.

The futuristic dystopia in M. T. Anderson's *Feed* (A) may not be as futuristic as we might hope. In this story world, consumer profiling has run amuck, and over half the American population has a transmitter implanted in the brain to feed information to corporations eager to sell what people, especially teenagers, want, and what they want is controlled by the feed that they get. This unusual examination of the consequences of mind control offers young readers the opportunity to think about what they really need and want.

✳ ✳ LIFE IN THE FUTURE ✳ ✳

Some science fiction examines anthropological and sociological aspects of life in the future and considers questions of individual commitment and ethical behavior. The results of aggression and competition as opposed to peace and co-operation, a consideration of what it means to be human, the quality of life in an increasingly crowded world, comparisons among cultures at different levels of development, and finding one's purpose in life are all ideas that science fiction writers explore.

Margaret Peterson Haddix explores sociological themes—in this case population control—in her **Shadow Children** series, *Among the Hidden, Among the Betrayed, Among the Imposters,* and *Among the Barons* (all I–A). The future world that she creates is crowded, so crowded that the government has mandated that only two children can be born to any one family. The mandate is not always followed, however, and third, or shadow, children live their lives in hiding, never knowing who or what might betray them. These stories are filled with engaging young characters who have many of the same hopes and dreams as contemporary readers.

The Sterkarm Handshake (A), by Susan Price, winner of the 1999 *Guardian* Fiction Prize, blends the future and the past. The Elves, time travelers from the 21st century, return to the 16th century to plunder the rich natural resources of the border country between England and Scotland. When Andrea, a 21st-century anthropologist, takes Per, her 16th-century lover, through time in order to save his life, she creates an unmanageable situation. Cultures clash, both societies and individuals, and there are no easy answers. The sequel, *A Sterkarm Kiss* (A), continues the adventure.

Teaching Idea 6.6 describes a way to get students to think about the effects of scientific advances in their own lives, and how these advances might influence their own futures.

• • SURVIVAL • •

Both gloomy and hopeful views of the future are apparent in the literature of survival. Although most nuclear scenarios are extremely depressing, an entire body of books exists that shows children surviving a nuclear war. Postnuclear holocaust books such as Louise Lawrence's *Children of the Dust* (A) offer young readers the opportunity to consider deep, abiding questions.

Stories about survival are not limited to the horrors of life after a nuclear war. The problems of life as it is today—the overcrowding, the pollution, the extinction of animal and plant species, and the question of an adequate food supply—provide science fiction writers with unlimited opportunities to project how humans will survive on earth. Some propose that the new frontier lies in outer space. Others propose that if we remain here on earth, the new frontier might be what we could do to make earth more livable.

The Ear, the Eye, and the Arm (A), by Nancy Farmer, deals with life in the year 2194 when people live in armed fortresses and in tunnels under toxic waste dumps. Thirteen-year-old Tendai and his younger sister and brother are kidnapped and forced to work in miserable surroundings. Their parents engage the Ear, Eye, and Arm detective agency to find them, but the detectives get near to the children only moments after they have moved on. The mystery and close calls keep readers turning the pages to find out what happens.

A future in which the sea is reclaiming the land, genetic engineering has erased most individual differences, and the intellectual pursuit of the science of archaeology is close to illegal is the setting for Jan Mark's *Useful Idiots* (A). There are many levels of struggle for survival. One is the physical one, in which human beings confront the awesome power of nature's storms and seas, trying to keep nature at bay. Another is the struggle for the survival of science, in this case the science of history and archaeology. Like the Lowry trilogy, Mark's novel presents a future in which the government tries to control what people know about the past. Survival of cultures is yet another layer, as the Aboriginal, or "Inglish," people who inhabit the sea's edge in what used to be England struggle to maintain both their history and their independence. Finally, the physical and emotional survival

Teaching Idea 6-6

Science Changes the World

Many people believe that each small change in our world results in a chain reaction of changes. We cannot foresee subsequent changes, nor can we control them. Some may bring good results; others, undesirable ones. Science fiction writers take the possibility of change to its ultimate extreme.

After reading several science fiction novels that use new scientific and technological advances as the premise for their futuristic depictions, discuss how these writers extrapolate from a possibility to a fully realized depiction of what might happen. Such books as *Feed, The House of the Scorpion, The Giver, The Exchange Student, Dancing with an Alien,* and *Singularity* (all A) will promote interesting discussions. Then ask students to consider both the pros and cons of the new technology they use and to describe application of that technology in a possible future world. How might such technology affect life?

This can become an interesting writing exercise if you ask students to select one piece of technology, imagine the furthest limits of its application, and create a future scenario that describes what might happen.

of the protagonist is also at stake in this fast-paced mystery set in a future world that no one wants to see. This and other engaging science fiction stories are listed in the Booklist at the end of this chapter.

Fantasy and Science Fiction in the Classroom

Once children have enjoyed and made their own the many picture books that are also fantasy, it is an easy step into longer, more complex stories. Many children will find these stories on their own, moving naturally from books like Mem Fox's *Possum Magic* (N–P) to such books as E. B. White's *Charlotte's Web* (I), Natalie Babbitt's *Tuck Everlasting* (I), or Kate DiCamillo's *The Tale of Despereaux* (P–I). As children develop as readers and thinkers, they discover the intellectual enchantment of Ursula Le Guin's **Earthsea** novels, ponder the questions of Nancy Farmer's *The House of the Scorpion* (A), or relive ancient stories with such books as Adele Geras's *Troy* (A). They are intrigued by the powerful questions that fantasy and science fiction writers ask and answer.

Some children, however, will leave fantasy behind as they grow older and will never discover the joys of science fiction unless they are helped into these genres by knowledgeable teachers. In many cases reading aloud is the very best way to encourage readers to expand their interests. The newfound interest in fantasy engendered by the **Harry Potter** series can be built on by teachers who know and enjoy fantasy and science fiction and who plan read-aloud programs that offer children the opportunity to experience books that move beyond magic into thoughtful considerations of some of life's most important questions. Intermediate-grade teachers might want to read some of the lighter fantasy and science fiction books, and upper-grade teachers might want to select science fiction short stories to read aloud. The books that we discuss and list in this chapter are both well written and thought-provoking, and thus are excellent choices to read aloud, both to pique and to fuel developing interest in these genres.

Fantasy and science fiction books can also be read and discussed by literature groups, an idea that is discussed in Chapter 12. These books fit well into genre studies as well as within many thematic units. The kinds of questions about values, selfhood, good and evil, and courage that fantasy and science fiction writers consider are also themes in contemporary realism and historical fiction, as our series of thematically related Teaching Ideas demonstrates. Looking at books from various genres that contain similar themes can be a powerful reading experience.

Benefits of fantasy and science fiction include the flexibility and expansion of the imagination that they encourage and the important questions that they push readers to consider. As children read stories about people and events that are real and familiar to them, they also need to read stories that make them wonder, that cause them to reassess values and ideals, and that stretch their souls. Fantasy and science fiction can do just that.

• • • Summary • • •

Fantasy is concerned with people, places, or events that could not occur in the real world. Science fiction is concerned with the impact of present-day scientific possibilities on the world of the future. In both genres we find many excellent stories that are well written, that present multi-dimensional characters engaging in exciting plots, and that contain profound themes. Although some children move naturally from their favorite picture-book fantasies into more complex fantasies and science fiction, some need to be helped into the more complex books by their teachers. In either case the rewards are well worth the effort.

Locate Kate DiCamillo's Newbery Medal acceptance speech in the July/August 2003 issue of *The Horn Book Magazine*. After you have read her speech, in which she discusses how children need to think about both the light and the dark side of their human nature, and the biographical sketch of DiCamillo in the same volume, think back to your experience with *Despereaux*. In a small group, discuss the idea of children considering the dark side of human nature in light of her story and other fantasy you may have read. Look at Susan Cooper's "There and Back Again: Tolkien Reconsidered" (*The Horn Book Magazine,* March/April 2002) and John Rowe Townsend's examination of Pullman's **His Dark Materials** trilogy in "Paradise Reshaped" (*The Horn Book Magazine,* July/August 2002) for information about the history and scope of modern fantasy.

In our interview with Kate DiCamillo, she speaks about how young readers can, and need to, think about powerful ideas when reading fantasy, and realistic fiction for that matter, and how fantasy can provide these readers with the opportunity to do so. Listen to what Kate has to say and bring that into your discussion of the power of fantasy to shape our ideas.

Animal Fantasy

Adams, Richard, *Watership Down* (A)

Ahlberg, Allan, *The Improbable Cat* (I)

Avi, *The End of the Beginning: Being the Adventures of a Small Snail (and an Even Smaller Ant)* (P–I)

_____, *Ereth's Birthday* (I)

_____, *Perloo the Bold* (I)

_____, *Poppy* (I)

_____, *Poppy and Rye* (I)

_____, *Ragweed* (I)

Barklem, Jill, *Brambly Hedge* (P)

Bell, Clare, *Ratha's Creature* (A)

DiCamillo, Kate, *The Tale of Despereaux* (P–I)

Grahame, Kenneth, *Wind in the Willows* (I)

Hearne, Betsy, *Wishes, Kisses, and Pigs* (I)

Howe, James, *Bunnicula* (I)

Jacques, Brian, *Lord Brocktree* (A)

_____, *Marlfox* (A)

_____, *Redwall* (A)

Jarrell, Randall, *Animal Family* (I)

King-Smith, Dick, *Babe, the Gallant Pig* (I)

_____, *Martin's Mice* (I)

Lawson, Robert, *Rabbit Hill* (A)

Lisle, Janet Taylor, *Forest* (A)

Lofting, Hugh, *The Story of Doctor Doolittle* (P–I)

Milne, A. A., *Winnie-the-Pooh* (I)

Oppel, Kenneth, *Firewing* (I)

_____, *Silverwing* (I)

_____, *Sunwing* (I)

Pearce, Philippa, *The Little Gentleman* (I)

Potter, Beatrix, *The Tale of Peter Rabbit* (P)

Said, S. F. *Varjak Paw* (I)

Selden, George, *Cricket in Times Square* (I)

_____, *Old Meadow* (I)

_____, *Tucker's Countryside* (I)

White, E. B., *Charlotte's Web* (I)

Miniature Worlds, Time Slips, Unreal Worlds, and Magic

Almond, David, *Heaven Eyes* (I)

_____, *Kit's Wilderness* (A)

_____, *Skellig* (A)

Babbitt, Natalie, *Search for Delicious* (I)

_____, *Tuck Everlasting* (I)

Bell, Hilari, *The Goblin Wood* (I)

Bosse, Malcolm, *Cave beyond Time* (A)

Boston, Lucy M., *Children of Green Knowe* (I)

Brittain, Bill, *Wizards and the Monster* (I)

Bruchac, Joseph, *The Dark Pond* (I)

Cassedy, Sylvia, *Behind the Attic Wall* (A)

_____, *Lucie Babbidge's House* (A)

Conrad, Pam, *The Tub People* (P)

_____, *Zoe Rising* (I)

Coville, Bruce, *Jennifer Murdley's Toad* (I)

_____, *Jeremy Thatcher, Dragon Hatcher* (I)

Cross, Gillian, *The Dark Ground: Book One* (I)

Curry, Jane Louise, *Dark Shade* (A)

Dahl, Roald, *Charlie and the Chocolate Factory* (I)

_____, *James and the Giant Peach* (I)

_____, *Matilda* (I)

Dexter, Catherine, *Mazemaker* (A)

Downer, Ann, *Hatching Magic* (I)

Dunlop, Eileen, *Webster's Leap* (A)

Ferris, Jean, *Once upon a Marigold* (A)

Fleischman, Paul, *Time Train* (P)

_____, *Westlandia* (P)

French, Jackie, *Somewhere around the Corner* (A)

Funke, Cornelia, *Inkheart* (A)

Hamilton, Virginia, *The Magical Adventures of Pretty Pearl* (A)

Herman, John, *Labyrinth* (I)

Ibbotson, Eva, *The Haunting of Granite Falls* (I)

James, Mary, *Shoebag* (I)

Jansson, Tove, *Finn Family Moomintroll* (I)

Jones, Diana Wynne, *The Merlin Conspiracy* (A)

Joyce, William, *George Shrinks* (P)

Juster, Norton, *The Phantom Tollbooth* (I)

Kendall, Carol, *The Gammage Cup* (I)

_____, *The Whisper of Glocken* (I)

Kindl, Patrice, *Goose Chase* (I)

King-Smith, Dick, *The Water Horse* (I)

Lewis, C. S., *The Lion, the Witch, and the Wardrobe* (I)

Lindbergh, Anne, *The Hunky Dory Dairy* (I)

_____, *Three Lives to Live* (A)

_____, *Travel Far, Pay No Fare* (I)

Lisle, Janet Taylor, *Afternoon of the Elves* (A)

_____, *Lampfish of Twill* (A)

Mahy, Margaret, *Alchemy* (A)

Nesbit, E., *Enchanted Castle* (I)

Norton, Mary, *The Borrowers* (I)

Oppel, Kenneth, *Airborn* (A)

Pearce, Philippa, *Tom's Midnight Garden* (I)

Pierce, Meredith Ann, *Treasure at the Heart of Tanglewood* (I)

Pierce, Tamora. *Shatterglass* (I)

_____, *Street Magic* (I)

Peterson, John, *The Littles* (I)

Pratchett, Terry, *A Hat Full of Sky* (I–A)

_____, *The Wee Free Men* (I)

Prue, Sally, *Cold Tom* (I)

_____, *The Devil's Toenail* (I)

Rowling, J. K., *Harry Potter and the Chamber of Secrets* (I)

_____, *Harry Potter and the Goblet of Fire* (A)

_____, *Harry Potter and the Order of the Phoenix* (A)

_____, *Harry Potter and the Prisoner of Azkaban* (I–A)

_____, *Harry Potter and the Sorcerer's Stone* (I)

Rubenstein, Gillian, *Under the Cat's Eye: A Tale of Morph and Mystery* (A)

Scieszka, Jon, *It's All Greek to Me* (I)

Shusterman, Neal, *Full Tilt* (A)

Slade, Arthur, *Dust* (I)

Steig, William, *Sylvester and the Magic Pebble* (P)

Townley, Roderick, *The Great Good Thing* (I)

_____, *Into the Labyrinth* (I)

Van Allsburg, Chris, *The Garden of Abdul Gasazi* (I)

_____, *Jumanji* (I)

_____, *The Wreck of the Zephyr* (I)

Walsh, Jill Paton, *Chance Child* (A)

Waugh, Sylvia, *The Mennyms* (I)

Wiesner, David, *Sector 7* (P–I)

_____, *Tuesday* (P–I)

Winthrop, Elizabeth, *Battle for the Castle* (I)

_____, *Castle in the Attic* (I)

Wooding, Chris, *The Haunting of Alaizabel Cray* (A)

Wrede, Patricia, *Dealing with Dragons* (A)

Wrightson, Patricia, *The Nargun and the Stars* (A)

Yorinks, Arthur, *Hey, Al* (P)

Literary Lore

Aidenoff, Elsie, *The Garden* (A)

Cadnum, Michael, *Starfall: Phaeton and the Chariot of the Sun* (A)

Crossley-Holland, Kevin, *At the Crossing Places* (I)

_____, *King of the Middle March* (I–A)

_____, *The Seeing Stone* (I)

Hodges, Margaret, *The Kitchen Knight: A Tale of King Arthur* (P–I)

_____, *Merlin and the Making of a King* (P–I)

Levine, Gail Carson, *Ella Enchanted* (I)

McKinley, Robin, *Beauty* (A)

_____, *Rose Daughter* (A)

_____, *Spindle's End* (A)

Morris, Gerald, *The Ballad of Sir Dinadan* (A)

_____, *Parsifal's Page* (I)

_____, *The Princess, the Crone, and the Dung-Cart Knight* (I–A)

_____, *The Savage Damsel and the Dwarf* (A)

_____, *The Squire, His Knight, and His Lady* (A)

_____, *The Squire's Tale* (A)

Napoli, Donna Jo, *Beast* (A)

_____, *Breath* (A)

_____, *Crazy Jack* (A)

_____, *The Magic Circle* (A)

_____, *The Prince of the Pond* (I)

_____, *Spinners* (A)

_____, *Zel* (A)

Osborne, Mary Pope, *The Gray-Eyed Goddess* (I)

_____, *The Land of the Dead* (I)

_____, *The One-Eyed Giant* (I)

_____, *Return to Ithaca* (I)

_____, *Sirens and Sea Monsters* (I)

Pullman, Philip, *I Was a Rat* (I)

Scieszka, Jon, *The Stinky Cheese Man and Other Fairly Stupid Tales* (I)

_____, *The True Story of the Three Little Pigs* (I)

Spinner, Stephanie, *Quiver* (A)

Springer, Nancy, *I Am Mordred: A Tale from Camelot* (A)

_____, *I Am Morgan LeFay: A Tale from Camelot* (A)

_____, *Rowan Hood: Outlaw Girl of Sherwood Forest* (I)

Swope, Sam, *Jack and the Seven Deadly Giants* (I)

Thesman, Jean, *Singer* (A)

Yolen, Jane, *Hobby* (I)

_____, *Merlin* (I)

_____, *Passager* (I)

_____, *Sword of the Rightful King* (I)

Quest Stories

Alexander, Lloyd, *The Black Cauldron* (I)

_____, *Book of Three* (I)

_____, *The Castle of Llyr* (I)

_____, *Foundling and Other Tales of Prydain* (I)

_____, *The High King* (I)

_____, *The Rope Trick* (I)

_____, *Taran Wanderer* (I)

Barron, Thomas, *The Ancient One* (A)

_____, *Heartlight* (A)

_____, *The Great Tree of Avalon: Child of the Dark Prophecy* (A)

_____, *The Merlin Effect* (A)

Bass, L. G. *Sign of the Qin: Outlaws of the Moonshadow Marsh, Book One* (I–A)

Billingsley, Franny, *The Folk Keeper* (A)

Cooper, Susan, *The Dark Is Rising* (A)

_____, *Greenwitch* (A)

_____, *The Grey King* (A)

_____, *Over Sea, Under Stone* (A)

_____, *Silver on the Tree* (A)

Divakaruns, Chitra Banerjee, *The Conch Bearer* (I)

Farmer, Nancy, *The Sea of Trolls* (A)

Fisher, Catherine, *The Oracle Betrayed* (A)

_____, *Snow-Walker* (A)

Funke, Cornelia, *Dragon Rider* (A)
Furlong, Monica, *Colman* (A)
_____, *Juniper* (A)
_____, *Wise Child* (A)
Hoffman, Alice, *Green Angel* (I)
Jones, Diana Wynne, *Cart and Cwidder* (A)
_____, *The Crown of Dalemark* (A)
_____, *Dark Lord of Dorkhdim* (A)
_____, *Drowned Ammet* (A)
_____, *The Spellcoats* (A)
Kaaberbol, Lene, *The Shamer's Daughter* (A)
Le Guin, Ursula, *The Farthest Shore* (A)
_____, *Gifts* (A)
_____, *Tehanu: The Last Book of Earthsea* (A)
_____, *The Tombs of Atuan* (A)
_____, *Wizard of Earthsea* (A)
Levine, Gail Carson, *The Two Princesses of Bamarre* (I)
Lewis, C. S., *The Horse and His Boy* (I)
_____, *The Last Battle* (I)
_____, *The Lion, the Witch and the Wardrobe* (I)
_____, *The Magician's Nephew* (I)
_____, *Prince Caspian* (I)
_____, *The Silver Chair* (I)
_____, *The Voyage of the Dawn Treader* (I)
Lisle, Janet Taylor, *The Lost Flower Children* (I)
McKinley, Robin, *The Blue Sword* (A)
_____, *The Hero and the Crown* (A)
Pierce, Meredith, *Darkangel* (A)
_____, *A Gathering of Gargoyles* (A)
Pierce, Tamora, *Alanna, the First Adventure* (A)
_____, *The Emperor Mage* (A)
_____, *In the Hand of the Goddess* (A)
_____, *Lioness Rampant* (A)
_____, *Magic Steps* (A)
_____, *Squire* (A)
_____, *Trickster's Choice* (A)
_____, *Wild Magic* (A)
_____, *Wolf Speaker* (A)
_____, *The Woman Who Rides Like a Man* (A)
Pullman, Philip, *The Amber Spyglass* (A)
_____, *The Golden Compass* (A)
_____, *The Subtle Knife* (A)
Rodda, Emily, *Rowan of Rin* (I)
Taylor, G. P., *Shadowmancer* (A)
Tolkien, J.R.R., *The Hobbit* (A)
_____, *The Lord of the Rings* (A)
Yolen, Jane, *The Dragon's Boy* (I)

Science Fantasy and Short Stories

Asimov, Isaac, *Norby the Mixed-Up Robot* (I)
Asimov, Isaac, Martin Harry Greenberg, and Charles Waugh, editors, *Time Warp* (A)
Atwater, Richard, *Mr. Popper's Penguins* (I)

Duffey, Betsy, *Alien for Rent* (I)
Fox, Helen, *Eager* (I)
Griffin, Peni, *The Ghost Sitter* (I)
Jones, Diana Wynne, *Mixed Magics: Four Tales of Chrestomanci* (I)
November, Sharyn, *Firebirds: An Anthology of Original Fantasy and Science Fiction* (I–A)
Pearce, Philippa, *Who's Afraid? And Other Strange Stories* (I)
Rubenstein, Gillian, *Space Demons* (A)
Service, Pamela F., *Stinker from Space* (I)
_____, *Weirdos of the Universe, Unite!* (A)
Sleator, William, *Marco's Millions* (I)
Slote, Alfred, *My Trip to Alpha One* (I)
_____, *Omega Station* (I)
Wynne-Jones, Tim, *Some of the Kinder Planets* (A)
Yolen, Jane, *Commander Toad in Space* (P)
Yolen, Jane, editor, *Things That Go Bump in the Night: A Collection of Original Stories* (A)

Science Fiction

Anderson, M. T., *Feed* (A)
Asimov, Isaac, *Fantastic Voyage: A Novel* (I)
Brooks, Bruce, *No Kidding* (I)
Christopher, John, *City of Gold and Lead* (A)
_____, *The Pool of Fire* (A)
_____, *When the Tripods Came* (A)
_____, *The White Mountains* (A)
Clements, Andrew, *Things Not Seen* (A)
Cross, Gillian, *New World* (A)
Dickinson, Peter, *Eva* (A)
DuPrau, Jean, *The City of Ember* (I–A)
_____, *The People of Sparks* (I–A)
Engdahl, Sylvia, *Enchantress from the Stars* (A)
_____, *The Far Side of Evil* (A)
Farmer, Nancy, *The Ear, the Eye, and the Arm* (A)
_____, *The House of the Scorpion* (A)
Gilmore, Kate, *The Exchange Student* (A)
Grunwell, Jeanne Marie, *Mind Games* (I)
Haddix, Margaret Peterson, *Among the Barons* (I–A)
_____, *Among the Betrayed* (I–A)
_____, *Among the Hidden* (I–A)
_____, *Among the Imposters* (I–A)
Hautman, Pete, *Hole in the Sky* (A)
Heinlein, Robert A., *Citizen of the Galaxy* (A)
_____, *Door into Summer* (A)
_____, *Tunnel in the Sky* (A)
Hoover, H. M., *The Shepherd Moon* (A)
_____, *Winds of Mars* (A)
Hughes, Monica, *The Golden Aquarians* (I)
_____, *Invitation to the Game* (A)
_____, *Keeper of the Isis Light* (A)
Lawrence, Louise, *Children of the Dust* (A)

L'Engle, Madeleine, *Swiftly Tilting Planet* (A)
_____, *Wind in the Door* (A)
_____, *Wrinkle in Time* (A)
Logue, Mary, *Dancing with an Alien* (A)
Lowry, Lois, *Gathering Blue* (A)
_____, *The Giver* (A)
_____, *Messenger* (A)
Mark, Jan, *Useful Idiots* (A)
McCaffrey, Anne, *Dragondrums* (A)
_____, *Dragonsinger* (A)
_____, *Dragonsong* (A)
Nix, Garth, *Abhorsen* (A)
_____, *Lirael* (A)
_____, *Sabriel* (A)
O'Brien, Robert C., *Mrs. Frisby and the Rats of NIMH* (I)
_____, *Z for Zachariah* (A)
Paton Walsh, Jill, *The Green Book* (I)

Price, Susan, *The Sterkarm Handshake* (A)
_____, *A Sterkarm Kiss* (A)
Reeve, Philip, *Mortal Engines* (A)
_____, *Predator's Gold* (A)
Rubenstein, Gillian, *Galax-Arena: A Novel* (I)
Sedgwick, Marcus, *Floodland* (I)
Seuss, Dr., *The Lorax* (P)
Sleator, William, *Singularity* (A)
Waugh, Sylvia, *Who Goes Home?* (I–A)

Fantasy Classics

Barrie, James M., *Peter Pan* (P–A)
Baum, L. Frank, *The Wizard of Oz* (P–A)
Carroll, Lewis, *The Adventures of Alice in Wonderland* (P–A)
Dickens, Charles, *A Christmas Carol* (P–A)
Lofting, Hugh, *The Story of Doctor Doolittle* (P–I)

Chapter

7

Contemporary Realistic Fiction

"I want to show you something," I told Steven. I reached into my pocket for the crumpled-up W picture I had taken out of my backpack before I'd left. "I've had it since I was six."

We sat on a ledge, our feet dangling, and he smoothed the picture on his knee, stared at it, then looked over at me.

"We had to find pictures with W words," I said.

"It's a wishing picture," he said slowly, "for a family."

I could feel my lips trembling. Oh, Mrs. Evans, I thought, why didn't you see that?

"It's too bad you didn't come when you were six." He smiled. "I knew you had to stay with us when you let me win that checkers game."

His hair was falling over his forehead and his glasses were crooked, almost hiding his eyes. I thought of the X-picture day and walking out of school. I thought of sitting in the park on a swing, my foot digging into the dirt underneath.

"I run away sometimes," I said. "I don't go to school."

He kicked his foot gently against the ledge, his socks down over his sneakers.

"Someone called me incorrigible."

Now that I'd begun, I didn't know how to stop. "Kids never wanted to play with me. I was mean. . . ."

Steven pulled his glasses off and set them down on the ledge next to him. He rubbed the deep red mark in the bridge of his nose.

I stopped, looking out as far as I could, miles of looking out. For a moment I was sorry I'd told him. But he turned and I could see his eyes clearly, and I wondered if he might *be blinking back tears. I wasn't sure, though. He reached out and took my hand. "You ran in the right direction this time, didn't you?"*

And that was it. He knew all about me, and he didn't mind.

—Patricia Reilly Giff, *Pictures of Hollis Woods*, pp. 123–125

Sarah had to stop a few times to wipe the tears from her eyes as she read this climactic scene aloud to her fourth-grade class. Several students wipe away tears too, but they don't seem at all ashamed. The moving story of the foster child, Hollis, and her missed opportunity to be part of a loving family has captured them all. They have been talking about family, and loving relationships, and what it is like for Hollis never to have experienced them. They have been talking about how Josie, an elderly artist with whom Hollis eventually goes to live, helps her understand that she is a good person with a special talent. And now they are about to discover why Hollis ran away from her one chance at being part of a family, fled the love and understanding that were offered to her.

When they hear the end of the scene, in which Steven and Hollis are about to have an accident, they erupt with comments and questions: "Oh, no! Steven is going to die!" "Giff's been hinting at this all along, this about the truck." "It's not Hollis's fault! It's not!" "How can this happen to her?" Ms. Hansen lets the comments flow freely for a minute, then brings the class back together. She begins, "I can tell that you were all engrossed in the scene as I was reading. I was even crying, wasn't I? I heard someone say that Giff has been hinting at this event. Was that you, Joelle? You're right; she has been hinting at this. This kind of hinting is called foreshadowing. How did she foreshadow this accident with the pickup?" Various students tell her about parts of the story in which either Steven or his father talks about his lack of skill as a driver and the danger of the road up the mountain. Ms. Hansen then changes the focus a bit, commenting, "I also heard someone say, 'How could this happen to her?' and I felt that way, too. What had just happened to Hollis before they got into the truck?" The class continues to talk, noting how Hollis had finally realized that Steven cared for her even though she wasn't perfect, and how that seemed like a big breakthrough for her. They have been discussing how little she liked or valued herself, and this scene seemed to resolve some of that. And then the accident occurs. "We could say that this is ironic," comments Ms. Hansen, "that just when Hollis realizes that the Regan family really does like her for who she is, she and Steven crash in the truck. What do you think will happen next? Remember, we already know that she runs away from them. Take a few minutes to write in your response log and speculate on what happens. There are only 41 pages left before we see how Giff ends it herself."

Characterization is the soul of great literature. When readers connect with the emotions of the characters in a book, they experience the events of the story as though they were happening to them. Thus, through the magic of fiction, children accumulate the experience of many lives and grow wise beyond their years. These fourth graders empathized with the loneliness and despair of Hollis as the story unfolded, and at this point they are so involved that this climactic event evoked their cries of protest. Fortunately for them, a happy ending is only pages away.

Defining Realistic Fiction

Realistic fiction has a strong sense of actuality. Its plausible stories are about people and events that could actually happen. Good contemporary realistic fiction illuminates life, presenting social and personal concerns in a fully human context.

Realistic fiction portrays the real world in all its dimensions; it shows the humorous, the sensitive, the thoughtful, the joyful, and the painful sides of life. By its very nature, it deals with the vast range of sensitive topics prevalent in today's world. Lloyd Alexander (1981) reminds us that stories explore polarities, such as love and hate, birth and death, joy and sorrow, loss and recovery. Life's raw materials, questions, and polarities appear most starkly in realistic fiction. Consequently, controversy often surrounds realistic fiction for children and adolescents.

Good stories do not resolve complex problems with easy answers; they consider these problems with the seriousness they require. Because literature reflects the society that creates it, children's contemporary realistic fiction reflects many of the problems that our society is concerned with today. It also reflects the things that we value in our lives: love, personal integrity, family, and friends. Thus, although many realistic novels are problem laden, many are also stories of courage in which people grapple with their problems and transform their lives into something worthwhile by drawing on their inner strength. And many are accounts of ordinary people living ordinary lives; their stories are illuminated through the careful consideration of a talented author.

No definition of realism is simple, and to say that realism is fiction that could happen in the real world—as opposed to fantasy, which could not—is simplistic. Every work of fiction, like the stories we tell ourselves, is part fanciful and part realistic. We selectively remember and reshape events of our past and present; the same thing happens in books. A realistic story is an author's vision of what might really happen (the plot) in a particular time and place (the setting) to particular people (the characters).

Realistic Fiction in Children's Lives

For many young readers, the sense of actuality in realistic fiction makes it easy to live the story as it is being read, to experience the story in a virtual manner. Realistic fiction presents stories that can act as windows through which we see the world, and as mirrors in which we see ourselves. Readers who engage with these stories often report seeing themselves in a realistic fiction story: "The whole time I was reading I was thinking, 'Yes, that's right. That's exactly how I feel.'" This intense connection with a book causes many young readers, especially those in the intermediate grades, to prefer realistic fiction above other genres (Sebesta & Monson, 2003).

Children unabashedly ask for books "about a person just like me" who is confronting familiar issues. The connection between book and reader, however, hinges not on age, time, or place but on the validity of the emotions presented. Feelings must ring true in the reader's mind; they are more important than surface actuality. Children and adolescents who read widely, testing and tasting various circumstances and life experiences, have many opportunities to try out roles vicariously through realistic books. When they read books that show others searching for self, young readers find they are not alone. They learn that life will be what they make of it. They search for an identity and look for a yardstick against which to measure themselves, and they turn to realistic fiction to help them define the person they want to become.

Realistic stories can help us reflect on life. While reading, we unconsciously participate in a story, drawing analogies between what we are reading and our own lives. These comparisons help us understand our lives and prepare us for the future by creating expectations and models. The expectations influence our reactions to real events as we rehearse experiences we might live someday. A fifth grader talked about this when she said, "When I wasn't reading, I was thinking what it would be like if that really happened, because it's such a big thing that happened, . . . like if it happened to me or something. Like if I had a sister, or if my mother died or something, how that would affect me." Younger readers also make connections between realistic fiction and life, asking questions or making statements that let you know they, too, are thinking about "what it would be like *if*." As one young reader expressed after hearing Lucille Clifton's *My Friend Jacob* (P), "Mommy, if I had a friend who needed extra special help, I'd be very nice to him."

Realistic stories can illuminate lifestyles that are different from our own. We can try them on for size through the

Teaching Idea 7-1

Keep a Writer's Notebook

Authors of realistic fiction develop plot lines in which they portray real people with real feelings. To do this, they observe themselves and others living their lives and record their observations in journals—not only when they are working on a story, but every day.

Ask your students to collect material for future stories by recording their observations in small notebooks that they can carry around with them. Follow this procedure:

1. Have students start notebooks of their own by recording events that happen to them. Have them describe events they observe, as well as their feelings about what they see happening.

2. After they have kept the notebook for a period of time, have them go back through their notes and highlight

items that might lead to a story. At the same time, read what established authors have to say about where they get their ideas for writing. The July/August issue of *The Horn Book Magazine* always contains the acceptance speech of that year's Newbery winner; in these speeches, authors frequently talk about why they wrote their books.

3. Have students discuss in groups what ideas might lead to interesting stories. Then they can proceed to write.

4. Find resources that will help you and your students develop their writer's notebook. Ralph Fletcher's *Writer's Notebook* is an excellent place to begin, as is Janet Wong's book for younger readers, *You Have to Write*.

---

books we read. We can discover that others living in different environments have done, thought, and felt the same things that we ourselves have done, thought, and felt. Realistic fiction helps us experience things we would never experience in real life, allowing us many experiences in the safe harbor of our role as reader: We can escape a war-torn country without fear of death or fall in love without heartbreak, while still probing the emotions of the moment. Realistic stories can put us in touch with our lives. Teaching Idea 7.1 shows how students can use a writer's notebook to keep track of their own observations of life as they live it, compiling ideas that they might one day turn into a realistic story.

Criteria for Selecting Realistic Fiction

Realistic fiction, like many other genres, needs to be evaluated in terms of the setting, characters, plot, theme, style, and point of view. If the book is illustrated, the quality of the art is important as well. Specific considerations for realistic fiction include the plausibility of characters, plot, and setting. It is this quality of plausibility that also necessitates a consideration of community standards when selecting these stories.

• • SENSITIVITY TO • • COMMUNITY STANDARDS

In realistic fiction for children from nursery school through high school, we can find explicit language, earthy dialogue, unseemly behavior, and sensitive issues. The issues that appear in literature for children reflect the concerns of the culture: abandoned children, drugs, alcoholism, divorce, abortion, death, homelessness, teenage sexuality, child abuse, and violence all appear in realistic stories for children and adolescents. Some adults prefer to shield children from subjects like these. Others believe that children can benefit from reading and having a safe experience that is removed from reality. Both positions have merit. It is important to consider books in light of what they *say* about the subjects they explore. For example, if a story is about adolescents who take drugs, as in Walter Dean Myers's ***The Beast*** (A), what happens to them? Are drugs seen as good or bad? Is the book expressing the general idea that children shouldn't take drugs because they're dangerous? Adults who complain about a book that examines a controversial subject often haven't looked to see what the author says about that topic. In many cases the "message" that a controversial realistic book contains is actually one that the community would approve.

Individual parents and communities will set the standards for what they believe to be suitable for their own children. We, as teachers and librarians, need to be sensitive to the standards of our community while at the same time protecting children's right to read books that stimulate, inform, and delight. This is an important and difficult task, and we discuss ways to respond sensitively to censorship in Chapter 1 because it is an issue that confronts teachers and librarians of all grades and that concerns all genres.

When selecting realistic fiction, look for books that contain developmentally appropriate topics, and language, events, and themes that are in keeping with the community's standards. Think as well about how you are planning to use the books. Some are good candidates for a read-aloud experience; others might be more suitable as individual, independent reading, and some might work in a small-group setting. But first, always consider the literary quality of such books and evaluate the setting, characters, plot, theme, and style.

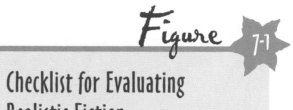

• • SETTING • •

Authors of realistic stories choose a time and place that actually does or could possibly exist as a setting. The setting may be general or specific, depending on the needs of the story. When evaluating setting in realistic fiction, look for a vivid, realistic setting that supports the events of the story.

• • CHARACTER • •

Characters in realistic fiction reflect human beings we know; they are circumscribed by the natural powers and failings of a real person in a real world. When evaluating characterization in realistic fiction, look for main characters that are credible, authentic, and not stereotypical, are fully developed as multidimensional human beings, and show change or development during the course of the story. Who the characters are and what they do is influenced by the events of the plot.

• • PLOT • •

The central conflict in a realistic fiction story is one that is probable in today's world and that matters to today's children. When selecting realistic fiction, look for plot structures that can be understood by the target audience, and events that are probable given the setting and characters of the story. How the plot evolves is influenced by who the characters are and the actions they take.

• • THEME • •

Realistic fiction is often categorized by theme, which is how we discuss it later in this chapter. Themes in realistic fiction reflect important issues of contemporary society. When selecting realistic fiction, look for books with themes that

Figure 7-1

Checklist for Evaluating Realistic Fiction

✿ The story meets the criteria for excellence in narrative fiction.

✿ There is a vivid, realistic setting that supports the events of the story.

✿ The characters are credible and nonstereotypical.

✿ The main characters are multidimensional. They change and develop over time.

✿ The problems are believable and are solved in realistic, culturally grounded ways.

✿ The intended age group can understand the plot structure.

✿ There is a theme that is applicable to children's lives, and it is intrinsic to the story.

✿ The dialogue and thoughts of the characters sound natural, with dialect and diction that do not overwhelm the reader.

are intrinsic to the story situation and that matter to young readers' lives.

• • STYLE • •

The dialogue of the characters in realistic fiction should reflect today's language forms, including current slang and appropriate dialect variations. Yet strict adherence to current slang or faithful reproduction of dialect eventually can date a good story or make it inaccessible to many readers. Look for books with a language style that engages the reader and an oral quality that is appropriate to the characters and their cultural milieu.

Figure 7.1 summarizes the criteria for evaluating a work of contemporary realistic fiction.

✳   ✳   ✳

A CLOSE LOOK AT
Pictures of Hollis Woods

Patricia Reilly Giff's *Pictures of Hollis Woods* (I–A) is an outstanding example of contemporary realistic fiction. Winner of a 2003 Newbery Honor, this book meets and exceeds the criteria for excellence in realistic fiction. It engages young readers in a search for love and acceptance that is sure to change the way they regard their own family lives.

Synopsis

Hollis Woods, named for the place where she was abandoned as an infant, has shuffled through too many foster homes. Almost 12 years old, this "mountain of trouble" just can't seem to find a family, until she spends a summer with the Regans: Izzy, the mom; "the Old Man"; and Steven, whom she comes to love as her just-barely-older brother. Over the course of the summer, Izzy and the Old Man make it clear that they have come to love Hollis, as does Steven, and she allows herself to feel that she has at last found the family she has longed for, the one she imagined when she was six years old and her teacher asked her to make a "W" picture out of cut-up magazine images. Hollis's picture was of a family, and her W was for "wish."

Yet Hollis runs from the Regans and the love they offer because she feels responsible for events that seem to disrupt the family, one of which also almost kills Steven. Though they try to persuade her to return, she is obstinate in her resolve and is sent by a social worker to stay with Josie, a beautiful, eccentric elderly artist. Hollis is drawn to Josie and is content to stay with her, while also longing for the Regans as she explores the memories triggered by a series of pictures she drew when she was with them.

Josie's eccentricities become more pronounced, and she is increasingly forgetful. The social worker decides that Hollis must move. Unwilling to leave Josie, who can't fend for herself, Hollis runs away with her to the one place where Hollis has felt wholly happy—the Regans' summer house on the Delaware River (Galda, 2003).

Setting

The story is set in two different places: the primary setting is the Regans' house in upstate New York, by the East Fork of the Delaware River; Josie's house is the secondary setting. Both are described vividly, with a great deal of visual imagery that makes both come alive for the reader. Josie's house is full of color and odd bits and pieces of her long life. The Delaware house is old, somewhat decrepit, and full of warmth and color. The river and the mountain that the house rests beside are also clearly depicted, and much of the action takes place there.

Plot

The story is told as a series of flashbacks that are interspersed with Hollis's ongoing life with Josie, until the final climax. These are not ordinary flashbacks, however, but are triggered by Hollis's looking at the pictures that she drew during her summer with the Regans. As she looks and remembers, we learn of her past life, how she came to spend

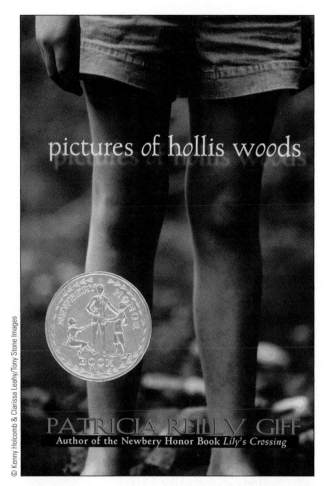

Patricia Reilly Giff creates a heartbreakingly real story in **Pictures of Hollis Woods.**

the summer with the Regans, how she gradually became a part of their family, and why she left them. This is juxtaposed with her growing love of Josie, and her decision to stay with her. Tragically, Josie's deteriorating mental health precipitates yet another move for Hollis, and she flees with Josie to the only other place she has ever felt loved—the Delaware River house. It is there, in the middle of winter, the day after Christmas, that the two parts of her life come together and the conflict is resolved.

The conflict in the story is primarily an internal one, as Hollis struggles with herself, caught between her intense longing for family and the fear of the potential for pain that loving others opens us up to. Minor conflicts between Hollis and her former foster mothers as well as her case workers help set up her character as a difficult child, but her internal dialogue allows us to understand that her actions spring from this desire to be loved. Finally, the climax of her story with the Regans, when she and Steven crash trying to drive down the mountain, pits the two children against this formidable force of nature, a conflict that has been foreshadowed throughout her time with them.

Characterization

Because we are experiencing the story through Hollis's point of view, and in part through her direct memories, we feel immediate sympathy for her. From the outset, we see her as a loving child in untenable circumstances. Like the heroes in the ancient Greek dramas, she carries within herself the seeds of her own downfall. Her habit of running away from unhappy foster homes is repeated with the Regans when Hollis feels responsible for the crash and again when she flees with Josie from a new placement. Her lifelong intense desire for a family has led her to idealize family life, and that idealization causes her to feel guilty about her role in the arguments that Steven and his father have, even though they have nothing to do with Hollis. The seeds of her redemption are also within her. Hollis is an artist, and it is through her drawings that she comes to understand her life. Her own vision, realized in her art, allows her to see those whom she loves with a clarity that is not typical of a 12-year-

© Tim Keating

Patricia Reilly Giff

I want to write books that children will laugh over even if their own lives are not happy, books that say ordinary people are special. (from Viking Penguin Children's Books, n.d.)

Patricia Reilly Giff believes ordinary children have exceptional stories to share, and she uses her writing as a vehicle to express this conviction (Bantam Doubleday Dell, n.d.; Olendorf & Telgen, 1993). Her characters, full of authentic spunk, adroitly demonstrate how ordinary people are special in everyday ways.

The genuineness of Giff's characters reflects her tendency to build books around the people in her life (Bantam Doubleday Dell). A pamphlet for Viking Children's Picture Books describes how Giff met the protagonist of her **Ronald Morgan** books in a school cafeteria:

It was my turn for cafeteria duty . . . that half-hour in the lunchroom with its overpowering smell of tomato soup and peanut butter sandwiches. It was raining, of course. It always seemed to rain when I had duty. I struggled with the window pole as the room filled with children carrying trays or lunch bags.

"I can close that for you, teacher," a voice said behind me. I looked down at the second-grader pulling at my arm. His yellow slicker hung from his shoulders like a cape, as he balanced his tray with one hand.

"It's an indoor day," I said. "Why didn't you leave your raincoat in the classroom?"

"It's new." He raised one shoulder in the air. "I'm the window pole monitor," he said, reaching out for the pole. The soup sloshed over the side of the cup onto the tray.

"Watch out," I said.

"Oops." He pushed his tray onto the table. "Let me do it. I know how."

I stood next to him, guiding his hands as he leaned against the pole, intent on fitting the hook into the round hole in the window.

Victorious finally, we rammed the window shut.

I watched him wolf down his sandwich and gulp his soup, talking first to someone on one side and then to someone on the other. Once in a while, he'd look up at me and grin.

What a kid, I thought. A good kid, a kid who tried hard. I watched him. Tomato soup ringed his mouth and cracker crumbs dotted his T-shirt. A kid who'd drive his teacher crazy.

He was the first one finished. He went to the front and slid his tray onto the counter.

"I have to tell you something," he said as he passed me.

I smiled down at him.

"I'm not really the window pole monitor. I do the wastepaper basket."

"Wait," I called after him as he raced out the door. "What's your name?"

"Ronald," he called back, "R-O-N-A-L-D," and disappeared out the door.

A kid to write a book about.

Giff hopes her books inspire young readers to write the stories of their own lives: "I want [children] to make the connection that books are people's stories, that writing is talking on paper, and I want them to write their own stories. I'd like my books to provide that connection for them" (Bantam Doubleday Dell, n.d.).

Giff has written prolifically since 1979, producing over 60 books for children. Her popular series include *Kids of the Polk Street School, New Kids at the Polk Street School,* and *Polka Dot, Private Eyes.* She has won Newbery Honor awards for *Lily's Crossing* and for *Pictures of Hollis Woods.*

Sources:

Bantam Doubleday Dell. (n.d.). Patricia Reilly Giff [Promotional brochure]. New York: Author.

Olendorf, D., & Telgen, D. (Eds.). (1993). Patricia Reilly Giff. *Something about the Author, 70,* 71–72. New York: Gale Research.

Viking Penguin Children's Books. (n.d.). Patricia Reilly Giff [Promotional brochure]. New York: Author.

Profile

old. These tight causal connections between character and plot create a unity of character and action that helps make this a very compelling novel.

The character of Hollis is primary, but Giff also pays close attention to Josie, Izzy, the Old Man, and Steven as well, creating characters that we recognize as human beings, complete with foibles as well as strengths, characters that we would like to know. Just as Hollis does, we come to love these people in her life.

Style

Giff's lyrical, intensely visual style is filled with imagery so strong that colors and shapes are almost palpable. Hollis sees the world in precise colors: French blue, iridescent silver, the yellow kitchen, the mix of greens and grays and blues of the river and the mountain. This imagery allows Giff to develop the character of Hollis, the unity of character and action that is evident in the novel, and the themes that permeate the novel. The sustaining metaphor of art as a clearer vision of life becomes the vehicle through which Hollis grows and changes.

At one point in the story, Beatrice, Josie's cousin and best friend, remarks to Hollis that "drawing is what you see of the world, truly see. . . . And sometimes what you see is so deep in your head you're not even sure of what you're seeing. But when it's down there on paper, and you look at it, really look, you'll see the way things are" (p. 45). When Hollis remarks that a friend (the Old Man) once said, "Look at a picture one way and you'll see one thing. Look again and you might see something else," Beatrice adds, "And something else. You, the artist, can't hide from the world, because you're putting yourself down there too" (p. 45). As Hollis looks at the pictures she has created, she also looks at herself and discovers that, through her art, she has captured things she didn't know she was seeing, important things that she realized with her heart and her eyes, if not with her conscious mind (Galda, 2003).

Theme

Art as a means for seeing life truly is certainly one of the central themes in this powerful story. Through this sustaining metaphor, Giff also explores what it means to be a family; the importance of loving and being loved and how to love oneself; belonging; how actions lead to consequences; and how the misinterpretations of actions and events can lead to destruction rather than redemption. This ultimately triumphant story of the power of art and love to transform life stays in the hearts of readers long after they read the final words, as they look with Hollis at the last picture, the one that doesn't exactly match that W picture she's been holding on to for so long:

> But the picture, and why it doesn't match the first one, the W picture: It's because I'm holding my sister,

Christina, six weeks old, in my arms. . . . So there are five of us now: a mother, a father, a brother, and two sisters. A family. (p. 166)

✳   ✳   ✳

Types of Contemporary Realistic Fiction

Like other genres, realistic fiction includes a variety of literature. A realistic story also could be labeled an adventure story, mystery, animal story, sports story, humorous story, or romance because of its content. Contemporary realistic fiction varies in format as well, and can be found in picture books, series books, novels in verse, and short stories, as well as in prose novels. Of course, many books fall into more than one category, such as a mystery that is embedded in an adventure story. Because children often ask for books by saying that they want "an adventure story," or "a real story about animals," we discuss contemporary realistic fiction in this manner. We begin, however, with a discussion of three formats that are available in contemporary realistic fiction: picture books; series books, many of which are transitional chapter books; and novels in verse. No matter what type, good books measure up to the criteria discussed here. Some of the best are listed in the Booklist at the end of this chapter.

• • PICTURE BOOKS • •

Picture storybooks can also be excellent realistic fiction, and Jane Yolen's *Owl Moon* (P–I) is a perfect example of a realistic story rendered outstanding by carefully selected words and evocative illustrations. Yolen tells the story of a father and his young child going out late one night to see owls. They walk together quietly into the woods, the father imitates the call of a great horned owl, and they see the owl. Afterward, they walk back home.

The story is deceptively simple, for poetic prose evokes powerful images of the cold, dark winter night; the silence; the beauty of the woods white with snow; and the adventure that child and father undertake. John Schoenherr's Caldecott Medal–winning illustrations take these images and transform them into an intensely beautiful visual experience. His pictures correspond to what the text is saying, but they also transcend it. His use of light and white space is extraordinary, making the dark spruce woods and winter night seem lit from within. In most of the pictures the father and child are small, insignificant intruders in the forest of towering trees and pristine snow. In contrast, the mysterious

© 1988 John Schoenherr

*John Schoenherr's strikingly dramatic watercolors capture the wonder when father and child go in search of owls on a cold, silent night in Jane Yolen's **Owl Moon**.*

For one minute,
three minutes,
maybe even a hundred minutes,
we stared at one another.

majesty of the owl fills three-quarters of a double-page spread. The owl is shown poised for flight, intensely staring as it allows itself to be glimpsed by the father and child and also by the reader.

The final picture shows the father carrying the child, whose arms are twined around his father's neck as they return to their farmhouse. The text is framed by two bare saplings that reach to the top of the white page like supplicating arms around the words. Text and pictures work together to create an unforgettable experience that many children might otherwise never have—unless they read this book.

Many other picture books contain wonderful realistic stories. Some are listed along with books for intermediate- and advanced-grade readers in the Booklist at the end of this chapter; others are listed in Chapters 2 and 3.

• • BOOKS IN SERIES • •

Books that contain the same characters in varying situations across many different books are called *series books.* Obviously, series books may comprise animal, sports, humorous,

adventure, mystery, romance, and other kinds of stories as well, but their distinguishing feature is that their main characters appear in several books rather than in just one. The best of these books contain memorable, vivid characters that readers remember from book to book. Many have school settings and explore peer relationships, and many series books for younger readers are also transitional chapter books that support these readers as they venture into longer texts.

Many children like to read series books; their familiarity makes readers comfortable. Feitelsen, Kita, and Goldstein (1986) studied the effects of reading series books on first-grade readers. They found that series books facilitate reading comprehension because the reader knows the character and setting, the framework, and the background of the story. Knowing the characters and what to expect from them makes reading easier; it's like meeting a good friend again. Series books also motivate reluctant readers. Knowing that there are other books in the series increases the anticipation; if the first book was good, then the new one is sure to be.

Although a number of series books are formula fiction, several high-quality series are available, such as Cynthia

Rylant's **Henry and Mudge** and **Mr. Potter and Tabby** books (P), Johanna Hurwitz's **Aldo** books (P–I), Paula Danziger's **Amber Brown** books (P), and Patricia Reilly Giff's **Polk Street School** series (P). These are very popular with young readers. Intermediate-grade readers also enjoy the comfort of familiarity, and devour books such as Betsy Byars's **Blossom Family** and **Bingo Brown** (I) series, Jamie Gilson's **Hobie Hanson** books (I), and Jack Gantos's **Jack** books (I).

Michele Edwards's **Jackson Friends** (P–I) series is narrated by a young African American girl who attends a contemporary American magnet school, and young readers relate to the multicultural school environment that Edwards creates. Lois Lowry's **Anastasia** (I) books are so popular that she has also written several books about Anastasia's little brother, Sam, such as *Zooman Sam* (P–I). Phyllis Reynolds Naylor's **Alice** books, like Lowry's, follow a young girl as she grows up. The books at the beginning of this series appeal to intermediate-grade readers; those at the end are more appropriate for advanced readers.

• • NOVELS IN VERSE • •

As we discuss in Chapter 1, the past several years have seen a surge in the number of novels that are written in verse. Are these novels poetry? Yes, many are narrative poetry, but they can also be considered contemporary realistic fiction. Sharon Creech's *Love That Dog* (I) is a beautifully told story of a young boy who at first resists his teacher's attempts to get him to write poetry. As the year progresses, he learns to express himself through poetry, and we watch as he comes to terms with the loss of a beloved companion. Lindsay Lee Johnson uses poetry to tell the story of Phoebe, abandoned by both mother and father, in *Soul Moon Soup* (I–A). This hauntingly beautiful novel follows Phoebe as she discovers her inner resources and the healing power of art and nature.

In *Locomotion* (I–A), Jacqueline Woodson tells the story of 11-year-old Lonnie Collins Motion, who lost both of his parents in a deadly fire. He lost his little sister, too, even though she survived the fire, because they were placed in different foster homes. His pervasive grief and loneliness begin to lift when his teacher gives him a great gift—she asks him to "write it down before it leaves your brain," and Lonnie begins to write his life in free verse. This exquisite award-winning book reminds us of the power of words to shape our lives. Teaching Idea 7.2 offers suggestions for using contemporary realistic fiction to help students consider what they can learn about themselves.

Picture books, series books, and novels in verse are three formats for presenting the realistic fiction story. Contemporary realistic fiction also contains many different types of stories in these formats, ranging from animal stories to sports stories, adventure stories to romance.

Teaching Idea 7-2

Thematic Connections: Discovering the Self

In *Pictures of Hollis Woods,* Hollis is engaged in a journey of self-discovery. Ask your students to list the things that Hollis discovers about herself and how she did so. Then ask them to compare their own journeys of self-discovery with Hollis's. Is their own easier? More difficult? Have they completed it? Do they think they will? Other books that lend themselves to this same question are *Soul Moon Soup, Shakespeare Bats Cleanup, Heartbeat,* and *Locomotion.* Compare the way that art helps the protagonists of *Soul Moon Soup, Heartbeat,* and *Pictures of Hollis Woods* heal themselves, and the way that writing helps the protagonists of *Shakespeare Bats Cleanup* and *Locomotion.* Ask students to think about what they can do to help them come to know themselves and to heal their own emotional wounds.

• • ADVENTURE • • AND SURVIVAL STORIES

Marked by especially exciting, fast-paced plots, adventure and survival stories captivate readers, who can't wait to discover what happens. Often the central problem is a conflict between person and nature. The best adventure stories also contain multidimensional characters who control much of the action and who change as a result of the action. Many young readers who enjoy a compelling plot prefer adventure stories.

Gary Paulsen's *Hatchet* (I–A) is still one of the most popular adventure stories today. Engaged readers also enjoy *Brian's Winter* and *Brian's Return* (both I–A), in which Paulsen explores possible endings to this exciting adventure story set in the woods of northeastern Canada. These novels focus on Brian's conflict with nature, but also include some internal conflict as Brian struggles with himself in an attempt to cope with his parents' divorce. In Tor Seidler's *Brothers below Zero* (I), sibling rivalry results in two brothers struggling to stay alive in a terrible snowstorm, with the interpersonal conflict leading to the conflict with nature.

Sharon Creech's novel *The Wanderer* (I–A), a Newbery Honor book, revolves around several conflicts: internal struggles with the self, struggles between individuals, and a struggle with nature—in this case the sea. Sophie, 13, is sailing across the ocean with her uncles and two 13-year-old cousins, Cody and Brian, when a tremendous storm threatens their lives and calls forth courage that they did not know they possessed. Told in a series of journal entries from Sophie and Cody, this is a complex, beautifully crafted story.

In *Red Midnight* (I), Ben Mikaelsen's young protagonist, 12-year-old Santiago, and his younger sister demonstrate great courage and resourcefulness as they flee Guatemala after guerrilla soldiers attack their village. The overland adventure soon gives way to their struggle with the ocean as they try to reach the United States by sea kayak. Michael Morpurgo's *Kensuke's Kingdom* (I–A) is an exciting survival story with a twist. When Michael and his dog are washed up on an island in the Pacific, they soon discover that there is another castaway sharing the island—Kensuke, who has lived there since Nagasaki was bombed. How these two learn to understand one another is as compelling as how they manage to survive.

• • MYSTERIES • •

A *mystery* is marked by suspense: Will the mystery be solved? The focus in a mystery story is a question—Who did it? Where is it? What happened?—and the action centers on finding the answer to that question. The best mysteries revolve around an intriguing problem and contain well-developed characters who work to solve the problem. They feature fast-paced action and a logical solution that is foreshadowed through the careful presentation of clues. Many children go through a phase in which mysteries are all they want to read. Fortunately, there are some excellent mysteries for children of all ages.

Young readers who love mysteries are happy to find that mysteries are often also series books. Elizabeth Levy, Donald Sobol, Seymour Simon, and Marjorie Sharmat are some of the writers who have provided younger readers with brief, exciting mysteries that satisfy their desire to figure things out. As these young readers mature, they continue to enjoy series, such as the very popular **Sammy Keyes** (I) books, by Wendelin Van Draanen. In *Sammy Keyes and the Psycho Kitty Queen,* Sammy finds a dead cat on her 13th birthday and gets involved in solving yet another mystery. She is a super sleuth with a great sense of humor who navigates with verve the life of a young adolescent.

Blue Balliett's first novel, *Chasing Vermeer* (I), is a puzzle, an adventure, and a mystery that needs solving. From the beginning of this intriguing novel, Balliett invites readers to participate in helping the young protagonists solve the mystery of the missing Vermeer, and they are more than willing to give it a try. These and other books, such as James Howe's popular **Sebastian Barth** (I–A) series and Betsy

Byars's **Herculeah Jones** (I), keep intermediate-grade children reading and guessing, and provide alternatives to augment the many formula mystery series, such as the time-tested **Nancy Drew** and **Hardy Boys** books.

Joan Lowry Nixon's psychic mysteries, Lois Duncan's eerie novels, and books by Eve Bunting satisfy older readers. E. L. Konigsburg's *Silent to the Bone* (A), Carol Plum-Ucci's *The Body of Christopher Creed* (A), and Tim Bowler's *Storm Catchers* (A) provide adolescent mystery fans with intriguing books to read and think about. Robert Cormier's chilling *The Rag and Bone Shop* (A) is both a mystery and a gripping exploration of the human psyche. Told from two alternating points of view, this novel probes the nature of guilt and innocence.

• • ANIMAL STORIES • •

Animal stories are about realistic relationships between human beings and animals, most commonly horses or dogs, or about realistic animal adventures. When they focus on an animal-human relationship, this relationship is usually a vehicle for maturation by the central human character. Good animal stories have engaging characters that grow and change as a result of their experience with an animal. Many of these books are very moving, often provoking a strong emotional response.

The protagonist of Kate DiCamillo's *Because of Winn-Dixie* (I), 10-year-old India Opal Buloni, loves her new dog from the first moment she sees him in the Winn-Dixie grocery store. His canine companionship eases her longing for her mother, helps her develop friendships in her new town, and opens up communication with her taciturn father.

Phyllis Reynolds Naylor's *Shiloh* (I–A) is an outstanding example of a realistic animal story. Winner of the 1992 Newbery Medal, *Shiloh* presents a profound ethical dilemma as experienced by 11-year-old Marty Preston, who rescues and then falls in love with a stray dog that has been abused. His family and community expect him to return the dog to his rightful owner, even though Judd has mistreated Shiloh. Marty, however, feels that a higher principle supports his keeping the dog. Intermediate-grade readers, in the midst of developing their own moral code as they begin to encounter ideas and experiences that cause them to think about values, can do so in the safety of the story world of *Shiloh.*

Mary Casanova tells animal stories of a different kind in *Moose Tracks* and *Wolf Shadows* (both I), in which she explores poaching, the ethics of hunting, and the protection of wild animals. These two novels are unique in that they look at hunting from a balanced perspective, something that most other books for young readers do not do. These and other fine animal stories are in the Booklist at the end of this chapter.

*Marty struggles with the conflicting demands of his conscience and his heart in Phyllis Reynolds Naylor's **Shiloh.***

© 1991 Lynne Dennis

• • SPORTS STORIES • •

In sports stories, the action revolves around a sport and the thrills and tensions that accompany that particular sport. Like mysteries, many sports stories are series books as well. Also like mysteries, many of the available sports stories are not particularly well written, but they are devoured by young enthusiasts nonetheless. A small but increasing number of sports books with girls as central characters have broadened the scope of the genre, and some recent sports stories examine social issues like sexism. The best of these books, such as Walter Dean Myers's *Slam!* (A), balance the descriptions of the sport with the development of the story, in which the central character grows in some way as a result of the challenges he or she faces because of participation in the sport.

Rich Wallace writes sports stories that especially appeal to adolescent males. His *Wrestling Sturbridge* (A) explores life in a small Pennsylvania town, the trials of adolescence, and the anxiety and exhilaration of being a member of a top-notch wrestling team in a sports-crazy town. That same small town is also the setting for *Shots on Goal,* about an

underdog high-school soccer team; *Playing without the Ball;* and his short stories cum novel, *Losing Is Not an Option* (all A). Wallace's riveting descriptions of the sports and his outstanding character development make his books excellent examples of this genre. Chris Crutcher is another master of the sports story genre. In *Whale Talk* (A) Crutcher deftly combines a story about swimming with an exploration of male friendships and high school social stratification, in a gripping coming-of-age story.

Rather than describing how sports shape a child's life, Ron Koertge explores how being unable to continue a beloved sport shapes a young boy's life in *Shakespeare Bats Cleanup* (I–A). Combining poetry and sports in a moving contemporary story, Koertge presents a young man driven to writing by boredom. He is home with mononucleosis, unable to play baseball, and he begins to read and write poetry, trying out different poetic forms. Like Lonnie in *Locomotion,* he uses his writing to come to terms with the recent death of his mother and with his changing role among his peers when his illness leaves him too weak to resume his role as baseball star. These and other sports stories are listed in the Booklist at the end of this chapter.

• • HUMOROUS STORIES • •

The real world has both laughter and tears, happiness and sadness, and children's books reflect this wide range of emotional experience. A world made up of all problems and no joy is just as unrealistic as the vision of the happily-ever-after world we gave children a generation ago, when so many books exhibited the happy-ending-no-matter-what syndrome. Children need and want humorous books. When you ask primary- and intermediate-grade children, "What kinds of stories do you like to read?" many will answer, "*Funny* stories!" Many teachers choose a humorous story to read aloud to remind children of the pure pleasure of enjoying a good book. In the annual Children's Choices sponsored by the International Reading Association and the Children's Book Council, humorous books repeatedly top the list.

Some of the best-known humorous stories for the elementary grades are Beverly Cleary's **Ramona** (P–I) series and Judy Blume's **Fudge** (P–I) series. Recently, other gifted authors have created characters who appear in a series of books that look with humor at some of the problems associated with growing up. Louis Sachar's **Marvin Redpost** (P) and **Wayside School** (P–I) books, Johanna Hurwitz's popular **Ozzie** books (I), and Stephanie Greene's **Owen Foote** (P–I) series offer children who are ready for simple chapter books the opportunity to read—and laugh—about someone they could easily know. Other transitional chapter books, such as Bonnie Graves's *Taking Care of Trouble* (P), tickle the funny bone of many newly independent readers.

Louis Sachar's humor extends beyond his series books. He has written several very funny yet poignant novels for intermediate-grade readers, such as *There's a Boy in the Girls' Bathroom* (I) and his Newbery Medal winner, *Holes* (I). This book breaks many of the rules—it is both contemporary and historical; the characters are ludicrous; the circumstances are implausible; there are too many coincidences; and it's not really realistic—which serves only to heighten the humor. By the end of the story, readers are cheering for Stanley Yelnats and laughing as they do.

Since the success of *Holes,* a number of humorous books for intermediate readers have appeared. Polly Horvath, author of *The Trolls, The Canning Season,* and *The Pepins and Their Problems* (all I), makes readers laugh by exaggerating the wackiness of her characters and their situations. Esme Raji Codell's *Sahara Special* and *Sing a Song of Tuna Fish* (both I) are wonderfully funny school stories. All these stories make use of humor to explore real and important human issues. Carl Hiassen combines mystery, environmental protection, and knee-slapping humor in *Hoot* (I), a 2003 Newbery Honor book. That same year Stephanie Tolan's *Surviving the Applewhites* (I–A) also won a Newbery Honor. Tolan tells the story of the redemption of a difficult boy when his grandfather forces him to be homeschooled by the very odd Applewhite family, which results in some extremely hilarious consequences.

There are also a number of humorous books that appeal to older readers. Hilary McKay's books about the Conroy sisters, *The Exiles, The Exiles at Home,* and *Exiles in Love* (I–A), tell engaging family stories laced with gentle humor. In *True Confessions of a Heartless Girl* (A), Martha Brooks uses humor to lighten the mood and illuminate a cast of characters in the small town of Pembina Lake, Manitoba, in this affecting story about love and forgiveness. These and other humorous books can be found in the Booklist at the end of this chapter.

• • ROMANCE STORIES • •

The action in romance stories centers on falling in love. Often an element of self-discovery is also involved, as when an intense relationship with another person helps the central character come to know himself or herself better. Adolescent readers, especially girls, often prefer romance stories, and there are a myriad of formula romance series, such as **Sweet Valley High,** for them to read. There are also some superbly crafted stories that appeal to girls and boys alike, such as Marcus Zusak's *Getting the Girl* (A), in which the younger brother of an accomplished young man is quite smitten with his older brother's girlfriend.

In the best of these books, the romance is interwoven with themes of growing up and family, and the characters are strongly drawn and multidimensional. Sharon Flake manages to do this through the medium of the short story in *Who Am I without Him? Short Stories about Girls and the Boys in Their Lives* (A). This is a hard-hitting look at the dynamics of love relationships for black adolescents. In the 10 first-person narratives that make up this collection, we see girls both weak and strong as they are engaged in figuring out how romantic relationships can work in today's world.

Romance isn't always wonderful, and two novels for adolescents explore the difficulties inherent in falling in love while you are still discovering who you are. Liz Rosenberg's *17* (A) is a compelling portrait of a young woman with many issues to work out before she can be comfortable with herself and thus able to love someone else. Told in a series of prose poems, the novel is a collection of beautifully written pieces that stand alone, but together create a cohesive story. Sarah Dessen's protagonist in *The Truth about Forever* (A) is coping with the death of her father and with her mother's obsessive desire to control life; she's also on her own, as her boyfriend is gone for the summer. Her mother's immersion in work during this unwelcome separation from her boyfriend gives the young woman the time to discover what it means to love without fear.

Themes in Contemporary Realistic Fiction

The themes in contemporary realistic fiction are as many and varied as life itself. In fact, events in authors' own lives may influence what they write, as pointed out in Teaching Idea 7.3. Most books explore more than one theme. How would you classify *Pictures of Hollis Woods*? Is it a story about family, coming-of-age, friendship, or self-discovery? It is all of these and more, depending on the story an individual reader creates during reading. Despite this sort of difficulty, it is helpful to group books loosely by themes, as children often want to read several books that relate to a single theme; many teachers, too, enjoy constructing thematic units (discussed in Chapters 13 and 14) with their students. The thematic Teaching Ideas, such as Teaching Idea 7.3, are examples of how these connections can be made. Some common themes in realistic fiction for children center on issues embedded in growing up, peer relations, and family relations. As society changes, themes in contemporary realistic fiction change. Recently, a number of realistic novels have explored the experiences of young people caught up in wars and forced to flee everything familiar to reconstruct their lives in a new place.

Teaching Idea 7-3

Study an Author's Work and Life

Choose an author who writes realistic fiction, both novels and picture storybooks, and has also written an autobiography. With your students, read the autobiography and some of the realistic fiction books and discuss how events in the author's life influenced his or her books. For example, there is a clear link between Cynthia Rylant's early years and some of her early picture books and novels, and the same is true of Patricia Polacco. In her autobiography, Lois Lowry makes clear connections between her life and her writing, as do Chris Crutcher, Jack Gantos, and Walter Dean Myers.

The following are some questions you might want to pursue:

✳ What were the major influences in the author's life?

✳ How did events from the author's life influence her or his writing?

✳ What parallels can you find between her stories and her life?

✳ What does the author say about the relation between his life and his art?

* * COMING-OF-AGE * *

Not surprisingly, some of the most popular books for children and adolescents are about growing up. Because our society has few formalized rites of passage, the way to adulthood is less clear for our children; they must mark their own paths. Books that portray a character struggling toward adulthood allow readers to see themselves reflected, and provide a rehearsal for real life. There are numerous picture storybooks for primary-grade readers that depict realistic characters trying to cope with growing up. Many of these books deal with children's increasing independence from adults, and with the fear and delight that accompany that independence. We discuss these in Chapter 3.

Older readers continue to struggle for independence, often confronting conflicting feelings, difficult moral choices, and personal challenges along the way. Young people are engaged in a process of trying to find out who they are, what they like and do not like, and what they will and will not do. They are passionately preoccupied with themselves and may look to literature for solutions to or escape from their preoccupations. They enter into books in ways they cannot with television; reading is a far more personal and creative experience. When students want to understand themselves, they can use story to help them do so, experiencing lives vicariously and thinking about how they might act.

In *Granny Torrelli Makes Soup* (I), Sharon Creech juxtaposes the stories that Granny Torrelli tells about her own adolescence and the conflicted feelings that 12-year-old Rosie has about her best friend, Bailey, a boy she has known all her life. As Rosie struggles with feeling competitive, angry, and jealous, Granny cooks soup and dispenses wisdom through her stories. Martha, the protagonist in Kevin Henkes's *Olive's Ocean* (I), a 2004 Newbery Honor winner, is also 12; she is about to spend the summer at her grandmother's house in Cape Cod when she is given a diary entry written by Olive, a recently deceased classmate, in which Olive had written that she had hoped to become Martha's friend. This precipitates Martha's thoughts about herself, life, her peers, and the world. As she wonders about what might have been, she is also thrust into what will be, as she awakens to her first crush and to the truth that her beloved

Kevin Henkes won a Newbery Honor for his portrayal of a young girl on the brink of adolescence in **Olive's Ocean***.*

grandmother is getting old. Martha's realization that she is not the center of the universe is compellingly perceptive.

Coming-of-age always involves change, and change is what has the protagonist of *Ida B . . . and Her Plans to Maximize Fun, Avoid Disaster, and (Possibly) Save the World* (I) so upset. Katherine Hannigan paints a picture of an almost perfect life—home schooling, freedom to roam the family's land, loving parents—disrupted by her mother's cancer diagnosis and treatment. Ida B has to go to school in town, and her father is forced to sell some of their land, land that contained some of the many trees that she has named and talked with. This plunges her into the depths of despair and anger, and her slow realization that life will go on and she can be happy is a mesmerizing read.

A different kind of coming-of-age is portrayed in Angela Johnson's *The First Part Last* (A), in which 16-year-old Bobby becomes a father and realizes what that means. Told from Bobby's first-person point of view, this complex novel speaks to the rarely considered bond between a teenage father and his child. These and other coming-of-age stories appear in the Booklist at the end of the chapter.

• • PEER RELATIONSHIPS • •

Part of growing up involves learning to interact with ever-widening worlds and with a wide variety of people. Books that explore peer relationships mirror many of the concerns that young readers have about their own lives. Today's books explore a wide range of relationships among peers; some characters are noble, some are loyal, but most are simply ordinary beings. Because young people value acceptance by their friends, they are highly susceptible to peer pressure. The literature reflects their vulnerability and their strengths. Understandably, a number of realistic books dealing with peer relationships are set in school or revolve around a school-related problem. Many picture storybooks involve peer relationships; making new friends, going to school, and learning to share are some of the things that children learn to do as they widen their circle of friends. These books are discussed in Chapter 3.

Many books about peer relationships for intermediate-grade students are easy to read and offer humor and satisfaction as well as reassurance that boys and girls are not alone in their feelings. These "school stories," many of them also series books, form a solid foundation for the more complex stories and relationships that students will encounter as they mature. In Kathleen O'Dell's *Ophie out of Oz* (I), fourth-grader Ophie is confident that she will become one of the popular kids in her new school. She has just moved from California to Oregon, she's friendly, and she has a natural talent for the theater. The popular girls do not welcome her, however, and she is forced to make do with two other outsiders. When she is finally invited to become one of the popular crowd she jumps at the chance, only to reconsider and do the right thing. Kathe Koja's *Buddha Boy* (A) explores the same issue—popularity—through the unexpected friendship between Justin, a popular boy, and Jinsen, considered a freak by the boys who control the social scene at school. As Justin discovers Jinsen's wonderful artistic talent and learns more about his beliefs, he realizes that Buddha Boy is someone whom he admires. When Justin stands up for Jinsen, his shame at his own complicity in and anger at the meanness of others is wholly believable.

As children mature, their relationships become more complex. Often the unevenness of the onset of adolescence creates gulfs between good friends: One is interested in the opposite sex, one isn't; one is physically mature, one isn't. Adolescence also brings with it increasing pressures to experiment with the dangerous side of life—drugs and alcohol, sex, brushes with the law—and books for advanced readers often contain characters who struggle with a per-

© 2003 Rick Lieder

Kathe Koja

Kathe Koja's use of first-person narration in **Buddha Boy** *creates a compelling sense of immediacy.*

sonal crisis as they seek to stand up for what they value and at the same time maintain their friendships. Sharon Draper explores popularity, peer pressure, and hazing in *The Battle of Jericho* (A). Jericho is thrilled to be asked to become a member of the most prestigious club in school. When the initiation becomes frightening and dangerous, he begins to question what he is doing, but it's too late.

• • FAMILY RELATIONSHIPS • •

Family relationships are also important to children and adolescents, and contemporary books present a varied picture of family life and probe new dimensions of realism. These books portray not only two-parent families but also communal, one-parent, and extended families, families headed by divorced or separated parents, families headed by homosexual parents, and children living alone without adults. Although there have always been books in which each family member stays in formerly culturally assigned roles, as these roles have evolved and changed, so too have books for young readers. Modern readers find both mirrors and windows in the wealth of family stories available today.

Family stories have changed in other ways as well. Fathers receive increasing attention in books for children and adolescents. Where they had once been ignored, they are now recognized as viable literary characters. Fictional mothers now run the full range of likeable to despicable characters, just as they do in real life. Stories about siblings have also changed with the times. Children growing up in the same home must learn to share possessions, space, and parents or guardians. Stories of the idyllic relationships portrayed in books like *Little Women* (A) are seldom found in today's books. More often, contemporary novels treat such subjects as sibling rivalry or learning to accept stepsisters or stepbrothers. In addition to happy, well-adjusted children from safe, loving homes, there are children who are victims of child abuse, abandonment, alcoholism, neglect, and a whole range of society's ills. These characters are often cynical, bitter, disillusioned, and despondent, but sometimes courageous and strong.

Frances, the protagonist in Julie Schumacher's *Grass Angel* (I), had a perfect summer planned, until her mother changed everything with her decision to spend some time at a spiritual retreat center. When Frances's mother and younger brother drive off without her, Frances goes to live with her odd Aunt Blue and begins to worry that her mother and brother are happier without her. The perfect summer is, of course, not perfect at all, but Frances learns a lot about love, family, and herself. In Colby Rodowsky's *Not Quite a Stranger* (A), Tottie is quite happy with her life until she answers the door one Saturday afternoon to find Zach, a teenage boy who looks very much like a younger version of her father. Told in alternating chapters by Zach and Tottie, this novel explores what it means to be a family.

Sharon Creech's novel in verse, *Heartbeat* (I–A), describes a transitional year in the life of 12-year-old Annie. Her grandfather is declining, her mother is awaiting the birth of Annie's first sibling, and her peers are changing, especially her friend Max. Annie is an artist, and it is through following her assignment to draw an apple 100 times over 100 days that she begins to understand that life will change, and so will she, but that it will be all right.

In Kimberly Willis Holt's *Keeper of the Night* (A), Isabel's family is shattered when her mother commits suicide. As Isabel tries to cope with her own grief, she also tries to help her father, brother, and younger sister regain their lives. The setting is Guam, where the author lived for two years as a child, and the meticulous descriptions of place through the eyes of Isabel enhance the reality of this story of a family trying to stay together despite tragedy. These books offer students the opportunity to think about their relationships with their own parents, as we consider in Teaching Idea 7.4.

Teaching Idea 7-4

Considering Parents in Realistic Novels

Parents are portrayed in both positive and negative ways in realistic novels, just as parents in real life are both good and bad. Students are either close to or distanced from their parents, admire them or are embarrassed by them. Parents are an interesting topic of conversation, especially when it begins with the parents in a book. It's easy to make personal connections. Ask your students to consider the following questions:

* How do the girls get along with their fathers? their mothers?

* How do the boys get along with their fathers? their mothers?

* What descriptions or actions from the books best demonstrate what the parents are like? Why?

* How are the parents perceived by the main character(s)?

* Do you think the main character is seeing his or her parents clearly?

* How do the parents in the book compare to your family?

These and many other books that explore family life appear in the Booklist at the end of this chapter.

• • CURRENT THEMES • •

As we have said, as the world changes, themes in literature change with it. Today, drug use is an ever-increasing concern. Melvin Burgess explores this in his novel *Smack* (A), and Walter Dean Myers does the same in *The Beast* (A). Spoon lives in Harlem, and he loves it, but he accepts the opportunity to go to a prep school in Connecticut. He has always known that drugs were pretty much everywhere, but now he sees it clearly, and when his first love, Gabi, succumbs to heroin, he battles to save her from the Beast. The first-person narration makes this an especially powerful look at what heroin can do to people's lives.

Yet another contemporary issue is violence, in and out of school, and Jamie Adoff's *Names Will Never Hurt Me* (A) is unsparing in its depiction of the daily humiliations and power plays that seem to trigger some of that violence. The four teenage voices that tell this story are all too real. Walter Dean Myers explores the same idea in *Shooter* (A), as he presents readers with a school board's "Threat Analysis" report, consisting of newspaper articles, interviews with students, the shooter's journal, and police and medical examiner's reports. This multilayered look at violence in high schools, like Adoff's book, provokes important conversations.

War and the consequences of war have sparked several novels for middle and high school readers. As in John Marsden's *Tomorrow, When the War Began* (A), an unnamed enemy invades a country in Meg Rosoff's *How I Live Now* (A), winner of the 2005 Printz Award. Life as she knows it changes dramatically for 15-year-old Daisy, an American girl sent to England to live with four cousins on their farm, as the children are evacuated. The war serves as a crucible for Daisy, and she grows from being self-absorbed to generous, from child to young adult. The recent past in Afghanistan is the backdrop for Deborah Ellis's *The Breadwinner* and *Parvanna's Journey* (both I), highlighting both the horrible circumstances of that country and the courageous resilience of children. Arthur Dorros's *Under the Sun* (A) follows one boy's struggle to survive in war-torn Bosnia. ·

Many of today's children straddle two cultures—the one they were born into and the one they are living in—and this is the theme of several novels for young readers. The issue of cultural dislocation and biculturalism is not a simple one, and there are no simple answers given in Andrea Cheng's *Honeysuckle House* (I), the story of two young Chinese American girls and their families. When fourth grader Sarah is assigned the role of special friend to Tina, a newly arrived immigrant from China, Sarah resents her. She is justly upset at her teacher's assumption that a shared first-culture heritage will make the girls friends. As Sarah and Tina get to know one another, they do become friends, but not because they are both of Chinese origin. This story explores growing up and the immigrant experience, complete with incidents of subtle racism and the trauma of adjusting to new family circumstances.

Uma Krishnaswami looks at biculturalism from a different perspective in *Naming Maya* (I–A). In this story, a young Indian American girl travels from New Jersey to Chennai, in southern India, when her mother must return to sell her father's house. Not only does Maya have to contend with leaving her home and reconnecting with her friends in Chennai, she is traveling with her mother, and they haven't really spoken much since her parents' bitter divorce. Once in India, Maya discovers a lot about herself and her family, and also learns that she can be herself in two very different parts of the world. A different look at this same issue, Jane Kurtz's *Jakarta Missing* (I–A) explores the realities of adjusting to life in the United States after living in Africa, and how this adjustment varies tremendously. Not everyone, it seems, can be happy in one place.

Two picture books, Aliki's *Marianthe's Story: Painted Words/Spoken Memories* (P) and Helen Recorvitz's *My Name is Yoon* (P), consider how young children adjust to life in an American school when they move with their families from another country. Although these books are suitable for primary-grade children, they can certainly be the beginning of a conversation about the topic with older children as well. Jackie Brown's *Little Cricket* (I) recounts the story of a 12-year-old Hmong girl who flees her home in Laos for a refugee camp in Thailand and three years later immigrates to St. Paul, Minnesota, with her older brother and grandfather. Their adjustment to life in America is not easy. The protagonist of Kashmira Sheth's *Blue Jasmine* (I) is also 12, and misses her home in India terribly when she and her family relocate to Iowa City, Iowa. Both of these books offer realistic yet hopeful depictions of the challenges that learning to live in a new culture can create.

An Na's Printz Award–winning *A Step from Heaven* (A) tells the story of Young Ju's wrenching departure from Korea and her beloved grandmother, her childhood and adolescence in the United States, and her eventual triumph over her abusive father and the grinding poverty that has plagued her family. Told in a series of short, present-tense, first-person narratives, this story has an immediacy that almost compels readers to feel the emotions with which Young Ju wrestles.

Contemporary realistic fiction reflects the contemporary world, with its joys, triumphs, and dangers. For many readers, contemporary realistic fiction is a passport to experiences in all parts of the world.

Contemporary Realistic Fiction in the Classroom

Children enjoy contemporary realistic fiction, and this genre is often a way to entice reluctant readers to taste the joys of a good book. The books are often passed around from reader to reader as children discover themselves in these books. Such books can also open windows on other people and other worlds, offering children the opportunity to "try on" other lives for the space of time it takes them to read a book and to ponder it later.

Reading and discussing contemporary realistic fiction provides an opportunity to connect children's lives with the classroom, as children use their own experiences to help them understand the books they read. Many teachers find that discussing contemporary realistic fiction opens new paths of communication among students and between students and teachers.

Contemporary realistic fiction can also acquaint children with other cultures and communities. Reading contemporary realistic fiction stories that are set in different parts of the country or the world, contain characters that are culturally diverse, and explore the lives of a variety of people helps children learn about others. Knowing people from diverse cultures through books is a first step toward building understanding and tolerance. It is also a first step toward recognizing our common humanity—the wishes, fears, and needs we all share, regardless of culture. Culturally diverse titles are discussed in this chapter, and many more are presented in Chapter 11.

Any well-stocked classroom library contains many contemporary realistic fiction titles. These books should represent a wide range of reading levels, a diversity of authors, and a range of types and themes. Comparing books of similar types or themes can help students learn about literature and writing, as they closely examine how different authors approach comparable tasks. Reading a wide range of books can also help students develop knowledge of their own preferences. Having many titles on hand means that teachers can readily incorporate realistic fiction in thematic units, building on students' interests or curricular demands by making available numerous appropriate and timely books.

Fine contemporary realistic fiction rings with truth. It offers readers multiple lenses through which to view the world and themselves, allowing them to become finer people—more compassionate, more knowledgeable, more heroic than they are in real life. Britton (1970) argues that the virtual experience possible through reading fiction is an important vehicle for constructing personal values. Freed from the necessity of action that real life demands, readers engaged with stories can contemplate feelings, consider actions, and make value judgments. Realistic fiction can be the mirror and the window in which we readers see our better selves.

• • • Summary • • •

Books of contemporary realistic fiction are plausible stories set in today's world. The characters often seem like people we know, and the plots consist of events and actions that can and do occur in everyday life. Realistic fiction includes adventure stories, mysteries, animal stories, sports stories, humorous stories, and romances. Several series are extremely popular with young readers, each with a memorable character who ties the books together. Contemporary realism explores a number of themes, including growing up, peer and family relationships, and other contemporary, sometimes sensitive issues. Children enjoy realistic fiction, and teachers find these books an essential part of a classroom library.

In the September/October 2002 issue of *The Horn Book Magazine,* Lauren Adams explores some of the innovative narrative structures employed by writers for adolescents. Read her essay, "Disorderly Fiction," and then discuss or write about the Western notion of narrative. From early childhood we learn that stories have a beginning, a middle, and an end (usually happy); a problem and a solution; and a temporal sequence. How do the innovative structures Adams discusses challenge this concept of narrative? Find and read some of these innovative books, and be sure to look for picture books too.

Bonnie Graves, author of several transitional chapter books for young readers, talks about how she develops and maintains a young voice in her books *Taking Care of Trouble* and *No Copycats Allowed.* Before you watch the video, take the time to read one of these books to hear the voice and humor in her work.

Adventure and Survival Stories

Creech, Sharon, *The Wanderer* (I–A)

Crews, Donald, *Shortcut* (P)

Fox, Paula, *Monkey Island* (I–A)

George, Jean Craighead, *Julie of the Wolves* (A)

_____, *My Side of the Mountain* (A)

Hobbs, Will, *The Maze* (A)

Holman, Felice, *Slake's Limbo* (I–A)

Lester, Alison, *The Quicksand Pony* (I)

Marsden, John, *Tomorrow, When the War Began* (A)

Mickelson, Ben, *Red Midnight* (I)

Morpurgo, Michael, *Kensuke's Kingdom* (I–A)

Paulsen, Gary, *Brian's Return* (I–A)

_____, *Brian's Winter* (I–A)

_____, *Dog Song* (I–A)

_____, *Hatchet* (I–A)

Philbrick, Rodman, *The Young Man and the Sea* (I–A)

Salisbury, Graham, *Lord of the Deep* (I–A)

Seidler, Tor, *Brothers below Zero* (I)

Mystery Stories

Balliett, Blue, *Chasing Vermeer* (I)

Bauer, Marion Dane, *Ghost Eye* (A)

Bloor, Thomas, *The Memory Prisoner* (A)

Bowler, Tim, *Storm Catchers* (A)

Byars, Betsy, *The Dark Stairs: A Herculeah Jones Mystery* (I)

Cormier, Robert, *The Rag and Bone Shop* (A)

Duncan, Lois, *Stranger with My Face* (A)

Griffith, Helen, *Cougar* (I)

Howe, James, *What Eric Knew* (I–A)

Joose, Barbara, *Ghost Trap: A Wild Willie Mystery* (P)

Konigsburg, E. L., *From the Mixed-Up Files of Mrs. Basil E. Frankweiler* (I)

_____, *Silent to the Bone* (A)

L'Engle, Madeleine, *The Arm of the Starfish* (A)

_____, *Troubling a Star* (A)

Lester, Julius, *When Dad Killed Mom* (A)

Naylor, Phyllis Reynolds, *Ice* (A)

Nixon, Joan Lowry, *The Haunting* (A)

_____, *Spirit Seeker* (A)

Plum-Ucci, Carol, *The Body of Christopher Creed* (A)

Raskin, Ellen, *The Westing Game* (I)

Roberts, Willo Davis, *The View from the Cherry Tree* (I)

_____, *What Could Go Wrong?* (I–A)

Sharmat, Marjorie, *Nate the Great* (P)

Sobol, Donald, *Encyclopedia Brown Takes the Cake* (I)

Stevenson, James, *The Bones in the Cliff* (I)

Van Draanen, Wendelin, *Sammy Keyes and the Hollywood Mummy* (I)

_____, *Sammy Keyes and the Psycho Kitty Queen* (I)

_____, *Sammy Keyes and the Skeleton Man* (I)

Wells, Rosemary, *When No One Was Looking* (A)

Werlin, Nancy, *Double Helix* (A)

_____, *The Killer's Cousin* (A)

Wright, Betty Ren, *The Ghost Comes Calling* (I)

_____, *A Ghost in the Family* (I)

Wynne-Jones, Tim, *Stephen Fair* (A)

Animal Stories

Blades, Ann, *Mary of Mile 18* (P)

Burnford, Sheila, *The Incredible Journey* (A)

Casanova, Mary, *Moose Tracks* (I)

_____, *Wolf Shadows* (I)

Corcoran, Barbara, *Wolf at the Door* (I)

DiCamillo, Kate, *Because of Winn-Dixie* (I)

Farley, Walter, *The Black Stallion* (I–A)

George, Jean Craighead, *The Cry of the Crow* (I)

Godwin, Laura, *Forest* (P–I)

Haas, Jessie, *Beware the Mare* (I)

_____, *Beware and Stogie* (I)

_____, *Runaway Radish* (I)

Hall, Lynn, *The Soul of the Silver Dog* (I)

Hearne, Betsy, *The Canine Connection: Stories about Dogs and People* (A)

_____, *Eliza's Dog* (I)

Henry, Marguerite, *Misty of Chincoteague* (I)

Hesse, Karen, *Sable* (P)

Hurwitz, Johanna, *One Small Dog* (I)

Levin, Betty, *Look Back, Moss* (I)

Naylor, Phyllis Reynolds, *Shiloh* (I–A)

Rodowsky, Colby, *Not My Dog* (P–I)

Sports Stories

Avi, *S.O.R. Losers* (I)

Brooks, Bruce, *The Moves Make the Man* (A)

Crutcher, Chris, *Ironman* (A)

_____, *Running Loose* (A)

_____, *Whale Talk* (A)

Deuker, Carl, *Heart of a Champion* (A)

_____, *Night Hoops* (A)

Duder, Tessa, *In Lane Three, Alex Archer* (A)

Koertge, Ron, *Shakespeare Bats Cleanup* (I–A)
Lipsyte, Robert, *The Brave* (A)
_____, *The Contender* (A)
Lynch, Chris, *Ice Man* (A)
_____, *Shadow Boxer* (A)
Myers, Walter Dean, *Slam!* (A)
Powell, Randy, *Run If You Dare* (A)
_____, *Three Clams and an Oyster* (A)
Russo, Marisabina, *House of Sports* (I)
Wallace, Rich, *Losing Is Not an Option* (A)
_____, *Playing without the Ball* (A)
_____, *Shots on Goal* (A)
_____, *Wrestling Sturbridge* (A)
Zusak, Marcus, *Fighting Ruben Wolfe* (A)

Humorous Stories

Blume, Judy, *Superfudge* (I)
_____, *Tales of a Fourth-Grade Nothing* (I)
Brooks, Martha, *True Confessions of a Heartless Girl* (A)
Byars, Betsy, *The Not-Just-Anybody Family* (I)
_____, *The SOS File* (I)
Codell, Esme Raji, *Sahara Special* (I)
_____, *Sing a Song of Popcorn* (I)
Duffey, Betsy, *Cody Unplugged* (P–I)
Ferris, Jean, *Love among the Walnuts* (A)
Gauthier, Gail, *Saving the Planet and Stuff* (A)
Gilson, Jamie, *Hobie Hanson, You're Weird* (I)
Graves, Bonnie, *Taking Care of Trouble* (P)
Greene, Stephanie, *Owen Foote: Frontiersman* (P–I)
Haddix, Margaret Peterson, *Say What?* (P–I)
Hiassen, Carl, *Hoot* (I)
Horvath, Polly, *The Canning Season* (I)
_____, *Everything on a Waffle* (I)
_____, *The Pepins and Their Problems* (I)
_____, *The Trolls* (I)
Hurwitz, Johanna, *Adventures of Ali Baba Bernstein* (I)
_____, *Aldo Applesauce* (I)
Korman, Gordon, *No More Dead Dogs* (I)
_____, *Son of the Mob* (I)
Kurzweil, Allen, *Leonard and the Spitting Image* (I)
Manes, Stephen, *Be a Perfect Person in Just Three Days!* (I)
McKay, Hilary, *The Exiles* (I–A)
_____, *The Exiles at Home* (I–A)
_____, *The Exiles in Love* (I–A)
Nelson, Theresa, *Ruby Electric* (I–A)
Rennison, Louise, *Angus, Thongs and Full-Frontal Snogging: Confessions of Georgia Nicolson* (A)
Sachar, Louis, *Holes* (I)
_____, *Marvin Redpost #7: Super Fast, out of Control!* (P)
_____, *There's a Boy in the Girls' Bathroom* (I)
Tolan, Stephanie, *Surviving the Applewhites* (I–A)
Yee, Lisa, *Millicent Min, Girl Genius* (I)

Romance Stories

Corbet, Robert, *Fifteen Love* (A)
Dessen, Sarah, *The Truth about Forever* (A)
Flake, Sharon, *Who Am I without Him? Short Stories about Girls and the Boys in Their Lives* (A)
Koertge, Ron, *Margaux with an X* (A)
_____, *Stoner and Spaz* (A)
Koja, Kathe, *The Blue Mirror* (A)
Nilsson, Per, *Heart's Delight* (A)
Oneal, Zibby, *In Summer Light* (A)
Plummer, Louise, *The Unlikely Romance of Kate Bjorkman* (A)
Rosenberg, Liz, *17* (A)
Spinelli, Jerry, *Star Girl* (A)
Williams-Garcia, Rita, *Every Time a Rainbow Dies* (A)
Zusak, Marcus, *Getting the Girl* (A)

Stories about Coming-of-Age

Atkins, Catherine, *Alt Ed* (A)
Bauer, Cat, *Harley, Like a Person* (A)
Bauer, Joan, *Hope Was Here* (A)
_____, *Rules of the Road* (A)
_____, *Stand Tall* (A)
Bauer, Marion Dane, *On My Honor* (A)
Blume, Judy, *Are You There God? It's Me, Margaret* (I)
_____, *Then Again, Maybe I Won't* (I)
_____, *Tiger Eyes* (A)
Bond, Nancy, *Truth to Tell* (A)
Brooks, Bruce, *All That Remains* (A)
_____, *What Hearts* (I–A)
Brooks, Martha, *Traveling on into the Light and Other Stories* (A)
Clements, Andrew, *Frindle* (I)
_____, *The Janitor's Boy* (I)
_____, *The Landry News* (I)
Creech, Sharon, *Chasing Redbird* (A)
_____, *Granny Torrelli Makes Soup* (I)
_____, *Love That Dog* (I)
_____, *Walk Two Moons* (I–A)
Cummings, Priscilla, *The Red Kayak* (I–A)
Duffey, Betsy, *Coaster* (I)
Earls, Nick, *48 Shades of Brown* (A)
Fleischman, Paul, *Whirligig* (A)
Fox, Paula, *The One-Eyed Cat* (I)
Frank, E. R., *Life Is Funny* (A)
Frank, Lucy, *I Am an Artichoke* (A)
Gantos, Jack, *Jack on the Tracks: Four Seasons of Fifth Grade* (I)
Hamilton, Virginia, *Plain City* (A)
Hannigan, Katherine, *Ida B* (I)
Hartinger, Brent, *Geography Club* (A)
Henkes, Kevin, *Olive's Ocean* (I)

Horniman, Joanne, *Mahalia* (A)

Johnson, Angela, *The First Part Last* (A)

_____, *Gone from Home: Short Takes* (A)

Konigsburg, E. L., *The Outcasts of 19 Schuyler Place* (A)

Lowry, Lois, *Rabble Starkey* (A)

_____, *A Summer to Die* (A)

MacLachlan, Patricia, *The Facts and Fictions of Minna Pratt* (A)

Mass, Wendy, *Leap Day* (I–A)

Mead, Alice, *Junebug* (I)

Moore, Martha, *Under the Mermaid Angel* (A)

Myers, Walter Dean, *145th Street Stories* (A)

_____, *Monster* (A)

Naylor, Phyllis Reynolds, *Achingly Alice* (A)

_____, *Alice the Brave* (A)

_____, *Lovingly Alice* (I)

Rosenberry, Vera, *Vera Rides a Bike* (P)

Singer, Marilyn, *Stay True: Short Stories for Strong Girls* (A)

Tashjian, Janet, *Multiple Choice* (A)

Thesman, Jean, *The Rain Catchers* (A)

Weeks, Sarah, *Guy Time* (I)

Wolff, Virginia Euwer, *True Believer* (A)

Zeises, Lara, *Contents under Pressure* (I–A)

Zephaniah, Benjamin, *Gangsta Rap* (I–A)

Koja, Kathe, *Buddha Boy* (A)

Koss, Amy Goldman, *The Girls* (I–A)

Lewis, Maggie, *Morgy Makes His Move* (I)

Marchetta, Melina, *Looking for Alibrandi* (A)

McGhee, Alison, *Snap* (I)

McKay, Hilary, *Indigo's Star* (A)

Moriarty, Jaclyn, *The Year of Secret Assignments* (A)

Naylor, Phyllis Reynolds, *Alice Alone* (I)

_____, *Alice on the Outside* (A)

_____, *The Grooming of Alice* (A)

Nelson, Teresa, *The Empress of Elsewhere* (I)

O'Connor, Barbara, *Fame and Glory in Freedom, Georgia* (I)

O'Dell, Kathleen, *Ophie out of Oz* (I)

Paterson, Katherine, *Bridge to Terabithia* (I)

_____, *Flip-Flop Girl* (I)

Perkins, Lynn Ray, *All Alone in the Universe* (I–A)

Spinelli, Jerry, *Crash* (I)

Voigt, Cynthia, *Bad Girls* (A)

Walter, Mildred Pitts, *Suitcase* (I)

Williams, Dar, *Amalee* (I)

Wittlinger, Ellen, *Heart on My Sleeve* (A)

Woodson, Jacqueline, *I Hadn't Meant to Tell You This* (A)

_____, *Last Summer with Maizon* (A)

Yumoto, Kazumi, *The Friends* (A)

Stories about Peer Relationships

Anderson, Laurie Halse, *Speak* (A)

Anderson, M. T., *Burger Wuss* (A)

Bauer, Marion Dane, *The Double-Digit Club* (I)

Bloor, Edward, *Crusader* (A)

_____, *Tangerine* (A)

Bradby, Marie, *Some Friend* (I)

Brashares, Ann, *The Second Summer of the Sisterhood* (A)

_____, *The Sisterhood of the Traveling Pants* (A)

Cole, Brock, *The Goats* (A)

Coleman, Michael, *Weirdo's War* (I)

Crutcher, Chris, *Staying Fat for Sarah Byrnes* (A)

Dessen, Sarah, *Someone Like You* (A)

Dowell, Frances O'Roark, *The Secret Language of Girls* (I)

Draper, Sharon, *The Battle of Jericho* (A)

Fletcher, Ralph, *Flying Solo* (I)

Going, K. L., *Fat Kid Rules the World* (A)

Gorman, Carol, *Dork in Disguise* (I)

Greenfield, Eloise, *Koya Delaney and the Good Girl Blues* (I)

Hamilton, Virginia, *Bluish* (I)

Hautman, Pete, *Stone Cold* (A)

Hurwitz, Johanna, *Roz and Ozzie* (I)

Kantor, Melissa, *Confessions of a Not It Girl* (A)

Kerr, M. E., *What Became of Her* (A)

Kimmell, Elizabeth Cody, *Visiting Miss Caples* (I–A)

Stories about Family Relationships

Avi, and Rachel Vail, *Never Mind! A Twin Novel* (I)

Brooks, Bruce, *Everywhere* (I)

_____, *Vanishing* (I)

Brooks, Martha, *Being with Henry* (A)

Cart, Michael, *Necessary Noise: Stories about Our Families as They Really Are* (A)

Cheng, Andrea, *The Key Collection* (P–I)

Clements, Andrew, *The School Story* (I)

Coloumbis, Audrey, *Getting Near to Baby* (I)

Conly, Jane Leslie, *Trout Summer* (I)

_____, *While No One Was Watching* (I–A)

Creech, Sharon, *Heartbeat* (I–A)

_____, *Ruby Holler* (I)

Dessen, Sarah, *Dreamland* (A)

Fine, Anne, *Flour Babies* (A)

_____, *The Jamie and Angus Stories* (P)

Fleischman, Paul, *Seek* (A)

Fletcher, Ralph, *Uncle Daddy* (I)

Flinn, Alex, *Nothing to Lose* (A)

Giff, Patricia Reilly, *Pictures of Hollis Woods* (I–A)

Hamilton, Virginia, *Second Cousins* (I)

Henkes, Kevin, *The Birthday Room* (I)

_____, *Protecting Marie* (A)

Hermes, Patricia, *Cheat the Moon: A Novel* (I–A)

Holt, Kimberly Willis, *Keeper of the Night* (A)

Johnson, Angela, *Songs of Faith* (I)

Johnson, Lindsay Lee, *Soul Moon Soup* (I–A)

Koss, Amy Goldman, *Stranger in Dadland* (I)

Kurtz, Jane, *Jakarta Missing* (I–A)

Lisle, Janet Taylor, *How I Became a Writer and Oggie Learned to Drive* (I)

MacLachlan, Patricia, *Baby* (I–A)

_____, *Journey* (I–A)

McKay, Hilary, *Saffy's Angel* (A)

Namioka, Lensey, *Yang the Third and Her Impossible Family* (I–A)

Nelson, Vaunda Micheaux, *Possibles* (A)

Paterson, Katherine, *The Great Gilly Hopkins* (I–A)

_____, *Jacob Have I Loved* (A)

_____, *The Same Stuff as Stars* (I)

Paulsen, Gary, *The Winter Room* (A)

Peck, Richard, *Bro* (I–A)

_____, *Strays Like Us* (I–A)

Pennebaker, Ruth, *Both Sides Now* (A)

Plummer, Louise, *A Dance for Three* (A)

Powell, Randy, *Tribute to Another Dead Rock Star* (A)

Rodowsky, Colby, *Hannah in Between* (A)

_____, *Sydney, Invincible* (A)

Ryan, Pam Muñoz, *Becoming Naomi Leon* (I)

Rylant, Cynthia, *Missing May* (I–A)

Shumacher, Julie, *Grass Angel* (I)

Sones, Sonya, *One of Those Hideous Books Where the Mother Dies* (I–A)

_____, *What My Mother Doesn't Know* (A)

Thesman, Jean, *Calling the Swan* (A)

Woodson, Jacqueline, *Miracle's Boys* (A)

Current Themes

DRUGS

Burgess, Melvin, *Smack* (A)

Myers, Walter Dean, *The Beast* (A)

VIOLENCE

Adoff, Jamie, *Names Will Never Hurt Me* (A)

Myers, Walter Dean, *Shooter* (A)

Woods, Brenda, *Emako Blue* (I–A)

WAR AND THE CONSEQUENCES OF WAR

Dorros, Arthur, *Under the Sun* (A)

Ellis, Deborah, *The Breadwinner* (I)

_____, *Parvanna's Journey* (I)

Marsden, John, *Tomorrow, When the War Began* (A)

Rosoff, Meg, *How I Live Now* (A)

SPANNING TWO CULTURES

Aliki, *Marianthe's Story: Painted Words/Spoken Memories* (P)

Brown, Jackie, *Little Cricket* (I)

Cheng, Andrea, *Honeysuckle House* (I)

Krishnaswami, Uma, *Naming Maya* (I–A)

Kurtz, Jane, *Jakarta Missing* (I–A)

Na, An, *A Step from Heaven* (A)

Perkins, Mitale, *Monsoon Summer* (I–A)

Recorvitz, Helen, *My Name Is Yoon* (P)

Sheth, Kashmera, *Blue Jasmine* (I)

Historical Fiction

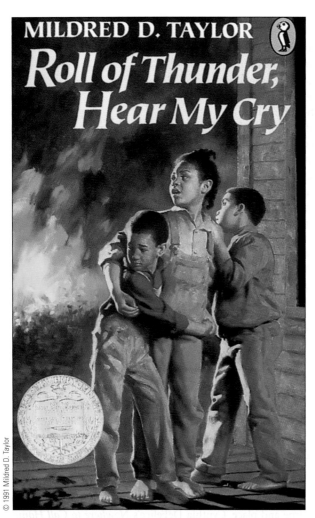

Cassie Logan tries to shelter her brothers from the racism and hatred that enflame her 1930s rural neighborhood in Mildred Taylor's Roll of Thunder, Hear My Cry.

for *A Single Shard* (A), a novel about a medieval Korean boy who becomes a master potter. Although her ancestors were Korean, she still had to do a great deal of research to be able to capture the place and time accurately. Family experience may have triggered these stories, but it took a great deal of research to turn those memories into good historical fiction.

Historical fiction sometimes surprises readers because it can also take the form of an adventure story, as in Kate McMullan's *My Travels with Capts. Lewis and Clark by George Shannon* (I–A) or Michael Cadnum's *Blood Gold* (I–A); a mystery, as in Jen Bryant's *The Trial* (I–A); or a romance, as in Dianne Gray's *Together Apart* (A). Historical fiction may be an animal story, as in Rosemary Wells's adaptation, *Lassie Come-Home* (I); it may be written in poetic form, as in Karen Hesse's *Out of the Dust* (A); or it may contain fantasy elements like time travel, as in Jane Yolen's *The Devil's Arithmetic* (A). What makes these books historical

is their historical setting and the importance of that setting to the story.

Several series, such as the Scholastic **Royal Diaries** (I) and **Dear America** (I) books, or the Morrow **American Adventures** (I) series, have been developed and marketed to attract growing numbers of young readers to historical fiction. These books have created an interesting debate among children's literature scholars. Some of these books, such as Siobhan Parkinson's *Kathleen: The Celtic Knot* and Jane Kurtz's *Saba: Under the Hyena's Foot* (both I) are very well done, written by outstanding authors and filled with a masterful blend of historical fact and period detail within an engaging fictional story. Kathryn Lasky's *Elizabeth I: Red Rose of the House of Tudor* (I), which presents Elizabeth's life in the years immediately preceding the death of her father, Henry VIII, is another series book that stands on its own merits as an excellent piece of historical fiction. Some other series books are less well documented and may present misinformation to young readers. Native American scholars and children's book critics have faulted Ann Rinaldi's *My Heart Is on the Ground: The Diary of Nannie Little Rose, a Sioux Girl, Carlisle Indian School, PA 1880* (I) for glossing over the horrors of the Indian schools in 19th-century America. Others point out that Rinaldi has told one girl's story and does not presume to speak for all the children at the Carlisle School. Still other critics decry the fact that the diaries are presented as real diaries, with some even containing a ribbon for marking the day's entry! On balance, however, these series, with their brief entries and engaging format, offer young readers an important introduction to reading historical fiction. The best of them also offer readers a glimpse of life as it was lived by a historical, albeit fictional, child, someone whose voice is rarely heard in other histories.

In 1982 Scott O'Dell, a noted writer of award-winning historical fiction, established the Scott O'Dell Award for Historical Fiction, to be given to a writer from the United States for a meritorious book published the preceding year. O'Dell hoped that this award would interest new writers in working within the historical fiction genre and thus provide young readers more books that would help them understand the historical background that has helped shape their world. It seems that his desire has been realized, for historical fiction seems to be enjoying renewed popularity; many new novels set in the past are published for young readers each year.

No matter what form it takes, outstanding historical fiction shows that history is created by people, that people experience historical events in individual ways, that people living now are tied to those who lived in the past through a common humanity, and that human conditions of the past shape our lives today. Historical fiction offers readers the opportunity to travel across time and place and thus to find themselves.

Historical Fiction in Children's Lives

History is made by people—people with strengths and weaknesses who experience victories and defeats. It reflects what they do, what they say, and what they are. Authors of books set in the past want children to know historical figures as human beings—real people like themselves who have shortcomings as well as strengths. Historical events sometimes affected the common people even more than they did kings and military leaders; the way the common folk responded to history's traumas shows adaptability and gives modern children a sense of reality concerning times past.

Today's children don't know a world without computers, video technology, rapid transportation, and modern communication. When they read good historical fiction, however, children can imagine themselves living in another time and place. They can speculate about how they would have reacted and how they would have felt. They can read about ordinary people acting heroically. By doing so, they begin to understand the impact one person can have on history.

There are strong links between children's family histories and the historical fiction that they read. Children are interested in finding out about what life was like in the "olden" days, and reading historical fiction is like listening to a grandmother's stories. Knowing stories of a grandmother's childhood, of a great-great-grandfather's escape from slavery through the Underground Railroad, or of a great-aunt's journey across the ocean to America is knowing history. Just as family stories help children discover their own place in the history of their family, historical fiction can help children discover their own place in the history of their world; it can give them a sense of the historical importance of their own lives. Well-written historical fiction can make the past alive, real, and meaningful to children who are living today and who will shape the world of tomorrow.

Historical fiction relates to children's lives both in and out of school. Stories of life in the past that are set in the place where they live help children see their home with new eyes. Knowing the details of daily life in the past enables children to understand and appreciate the magnitude of the industrial, technological, and medical advances that shape their lives. So much good historical fiction is available that the study of virtually any time in history can be enriched. Historical fiction can relate to children's lives through the themes that it explores. Many thematic connections can be made between historical fiction and contemporary realistic fiction, just as thematic connections can be made between children's lives and what they read. For example, big ideas such as freedom, prejudice, self-knowledge, interdependence, or social justice appear in many works of historical fiction and in many works of contemporary realism, and are certainly important in the lives of today's students. Historical fiction can help those students understand that our contemporary desires and concerns have come to us through our history.

By relating trade books to topics in social studies and other curriculum areas, we strengthen children's understanding with a wealth of material that far exceeds the limited view of any single text. We can do the same in other curricular areas by reading stories, for example, that are set in times during which important scientific breakthroughs occurred. Poetry, biography, and nonfiction (discussed in Chapters 4, 9, and 10) can also support historical fiction and extend children's understanding of our past. Nonfiction books about important events in the history of science, mathematics, art, language, medicine, and many other fields provide factual information to add to the emotional information that historical fiction conveys. Historical fiction provides insights into the panoply of history; it is a lively and fascinating way to transmit the story of the past to the guardians of the future.

Criteria for Evaluating Historical Fiction

The best historical stories come from good storytellers who are well acquainted with the facts; good historical fiction is grounded in facts but not restricted by them. An author may use historical records to document events, but the facts merely serve as a framework for the story. Many books that present historical facts do not qualify as historical fiction. To do so, a text must meet the criteria for *all* good narratives: It must have well-developed characters and integral themes; it must tell an engaging story with well-crafted language; and, in the case of picture books, it must contain beautiful and accurate art. Beyond this, it must meet criteria that are particular to the genre. Figure 8.1 is a checklist for evaluating historical fiction.

• • HISTORICAL ACCURACY • •

Historical fiction should be consistent with historical evidence. The story, though imaginative, must remain within the limits of the chosen historical background, avoiding distortion and anachronism. Historical accuracy, however, presents an interesting dilemma, one we discuss again in Chapter 9. Although we can know so-called facts about our past, we know these facts only in light of the present. Every

Checklist for Evaluating Historical Fiction

General

❧ The work meets the criteria for all good narratives.

Historical Accuracy

❧ Events and attitudes are consistent with historical evidence and appropriate to the time period.

❧ Social issues are portrayed honestly, without condoning racism and sexism.

Setting

❧ The setting is integral to the story.

❧ The story evokes a vivid historical setting consistent with historical and geographical evidence.

Language

❧ The language patterns are historically authentic and in keeping with the mood and characterization, yet are still understandable to young readers.

Characterization

❧ Characters are well developed, with feelings, values, and behavior that reflect the period.

Plot and Theme

❧ The plot is based on authentic facts that are subordinate to the story itself.

❧ The theme echoes larger historical concerns.

Illustrations

❧ The illustrations enhance an understanding of plot, setting, and characterization through the use of realistic details.

---

generation of historians, to some degree, reinterprets the past by using the concerns of the present as a lens. For example, a book like Esther Forbes's classic Revolutionary War story, *Johnny Tremain* (A), written during a time of great patriotic fervor (1946), is not at all critical of war. James Lincoln Collier and Christopher Collier's *My Brother Sam Is Dead* (A), written during the Vietnam conflict (1974), presents a very different picture of the same war (Taxel, 1984). Both stories deal with the same set of "facts," but their implications are radically different because they are written from different perspectives. Any presentation of history is an interpretation, but good historical fiction creates as true a picture of the past as an author can craft. The interpretive nature of historical fiction is even more complicated when issues of "authority" are considered in terms of cultural group membership, which we discuss further in Chapter 11. Historical "accuracy," then, is always influenced by who the author is and when the author is writing, by how the author understands the historical experience within his or her own life.

Historical accuracy can create problems with racism and sexism. When writing about periods of time in which racism and sexism abounded, authors must take care to portray these social issues honestly while at the same time not condoning them. In Ann Turner's *Nettie's Trip South* (I–A), the issue of slavery is foregrounded; it is slavery that marked the South before the Civil War, and it is slavery that sickens

young Nettie. In *Walks Alone* (I), Brian Burks describes the often vicious approach to the Apache taken by the U.S. Army. Jerry Spinelli's *Milkweed* (A) and Gary Schmidt's *Mara's Stories: Glimmers in the Darkness* (I–A) depict the racism and violence of Nazi-occupied Europe but do so in a way that helps readers understand how horrible it was as well as appreciate the personal courage of those caught up in the Holocaust. Historical fiction may have to portray racism and sexism for historical accuracy, but the stories themselves should not be racist or sexist.

Noteworthy historical novels do not overgeneralize; they do not lead the reader to believe, for example, that all Native Americans are like those portrayed in any one story. Each character is unique, just as each of us is, and although the novelist focuses on one person in a group, it should be clear that the character is only a person, not a stereotype.

When evaluating historical fiction, look for events and attitudes that are appropriate to the time period and for stories that portray social issues honestly, without condoning racism and sexism.

• • SETTING • •

Setting is a crucial element in evaluating historical fiction, because it is setting that distinguishes this form most

Teaching Idea 8-1

Writing Connection: Descriptive Techniques

Select several historical fiction books to compare literary descriptions of historical settings. Then

* Read aloud several books that describe the same region or historical period.

* Ask students to compare selections and illustrations.

* Discuss with students which descriptions are more evocative, which use the most sensory details.

* Ask students to decide which books help them understand the place and time best.

* Have students use the techniques they have discussed to create original descriptions of a real place that they know.

Any number of books with vivid settings, grouped by period or place, are appropriate. Often the historical fiction that you select can be complemented by nonfiction and other genres. For example, Cynthia Rylant's *Appalachia: Voices of Sleeping Birds* (I) is nonfiction and describes both place and people. So do many of her picture storybooks, such as *When I Was Young in the Mountains* (P–I), and novels, such as *Missing May* (I–A). Ruth White's books, such as *Buttermilk Hill* (I), are set in the same location, as is Phyllis Reynolds Naylor's *Shiloh* (I–A).

dramatically from other literary forms. Details of setting must be spelled out so clearly that readers can create mental images of the time and place in which the events occur. These elements are integral to the plot of historical fiction; they determine characters' beliefs and actions. The setting must also be authentic and consistent with historical and geographical evidence. In evaluating historical books, look for settings that are integral to the story and authentic in historical and geographical detail. Teaching Idea 8.1 describes a way to explore settings and help students learn about descriptive writing.

• • LANGUAGE • •

Language should be in keeping with the period and the place, particularly in dialogue. However, today's readers have difficulty understanding archaic language. Accom-

plished authors synthesize language that has the right tone or sound for a period but is understandable to contemporary readers. Rosemary Sutcliff explains how she works appropriate language into her writing:

I try to catch the rhythm of a tongue, the tune that it plays on the ear, Welsh or Gaelic as opposed to Anglo-Saxon, the sensible workmanlike language which one feels the Latin of the ordinary Roman citizen would have translated into. It is extraordinary what can be done by the changing or transposing of a single word, or by using a perfectly usual one in a slightly unusual way: "I beg your pardon" changed into "I ask your pardon." . . . This is not done by any set rule of thumb; I simply play it by ear as I go along. (1973, pp. 307–308)

The character's thoughts should also reflect the time and place. Any metaphors, similes, or images that describe what a character is thinking or feeling must be appropriate to the setting. In Michael Dorris's *Morning Girl* (I), set in 1492 on a Bahamian island that will soon be visited by Christopher Columbus, Morning Girl, a young Taino, thinks about her brother:

The world fits together so tightly, the pieces like pebbles and shells sunk into the sand after the tide has gone out, before anyone has walked on the beach and left footprints.

In our house, though, my brother was the footprints. (p. 14)

Morning Girl's world is bounded by the sand and the sea; it is fitting that she think of life in those terms.

When evaluating language in historical fiction, look for language patterns and word choices that are authentic and in keeping with the mood and characterization.

• • CHARACTERIZATION • •

Characters in historical fiction should believe and behave in a manner that is in keeping with the times in which they live. Authors who attribute contemporary values to historical figures run the risk of creating an *anachronism,* mistakenly placing something in the wrong historical period. Sometimes this is difficult to determine. When Karen Cushman's *Catherine, Called Birdy* (A) was published, several critics took Cushman to task for creating a character who was a literate female living in the Middle Ages. Women, they said, weren't literate and, what's more, didn't act independently. In fact, most women weren't literate and were completely under the control of men. However, some noted historical figures were different, and it was these whom Catherine most resembles. She is not meant to represent "all" medieval women, but rather to stand as one specific, fictional woman. In historical fiction, the characters' feelings, behavior, values, and language should reflect the period, but also the individuality of the character.

• • PLOT AND THEME • •

History is filled with a tremendous amount of raw material for exciting plots and themes. Yet an abundance of historical facts may overburden a story. The trick is to make the facts such a part of the background—in the setting, the events, the characterizations, the language, and the ideas—that readers may not consciously notice most of them, yet they are fundamental in shaping the story. Although the facts must be accurate, they should not bog down the plot. Instead, they should help propel the narrative line. The themes that are developed through facts and narrative often reflect both a macrocosm of the era (for example, a war for independence) and the microcosm of the story (for example, a struggle for personal independence). In the best historical fiction, the theme is evident in both the individual story and the larger historical context as it is presented.

In evaluating historical fiction, look for books that interweave factual background information to support the story and that contain a theme that echoes larger historical concerns.

• • ILLUSTRATIONS • •

In recent years, a number of excellent historical fiction picture storybooks have been published. These books contain not only well-written, riveting stories but also beautiful illustrations that support and enhance the story. Illustrations in picture storybooks of historical fiction must meet the criteria for quality of illustration in any picture book. In addition, they must be historically accurate, providing realistic details of life in the historical period as well as reflecting and interpreting character and action. Look for illustrations that enhance the story and that use realistic details to reflect an understanding of the setting, plot, and characterization.

✳ ✳ ✳

A CLOSE LOOK AT

Crispin: The Cross of Lead

Avi's 50th book and winner of the 2003 Newbery Medal, *Crispin: The Cross of Lead* (I–A), is an outstanding example of historical fiction. Set in medieval England, this is a riveting adventure, an intriguing mystery, and a moving coming-of-age story.

Historical Accuracy

A great deal of research underlies the story of *Crispin,* research so meticulous and precise that both small details and the larger historical context are accurate. Avi reveals what people of the time wore, how and what they ate, how they spoke, how they thought, and how the feudal system operated, among other things. All of this information is woven seamlessly into the story so that it is unobtrusive. To prepare to write this book, Avi listened to lectures, read countless works on the Middle Ages, visited England, and read and listened to literature from the period. His familiarity with the time and place is evident in the setting, plot, character development, and themes that permeate this novel.

Setting

The setting is integral to the story; without it the events could not have occurred. The character of Crispin is forged by when and where he lived. Avi provides many details of time and place. The book begins with the date—England, A.D. 1377—and the sentence, "The day after my mother died, the priest and I wrapped her body in a gray shroud and carried her to the village church." Within the first four pages the scene is set: a dismal, dreary, wet, muddy village where people worked in the fields and were cruel to Crispin. We discover that the village is part of a manor owned by a lord and managed by an evil steward, John Aycliffe. We learn that punishment is swift and severe, that when someone died a death tax was owed the lord, that God and the church were a central part of life, and that Crispin wore a gray wool tunic and leather shoes. We learn that Crispin believes that God directs every action, even that of tripping and falling onto a stone. And a careful reader will realize that Crispin has no name other than "Asta's son."

As the story develops and Crispin leaves his village, the sights, sounds, tastes, and smells of medieval England come vividly to life as readers travel along the road with Crispin and his companion, Bear. As Crispin sees new sights, and wonders about what he sees, Bear offers explanations. Through Crispin's comments and questions, and Bear's answers, the setting is elaborated in a natural manner.

Language

One of the most difficult stylistic aspects of historical fiction is the language the characters speak. It is difficult to strike a balance between authentic and understandable, especially when the language a character would actually speak is as different from modern English as the Middle English of the medieval period. Avi manages to capture a cadence of speech that marks the language as different from modern English without making it difficult to understand. He also

Profile

© Avi

Avi

Writing is hard. And writing very well is very hard. Never believe any writer who suggests otherwise. Scratch the surface of any successful author. Just below—in fetal position, sucking a thumb—is an insecure writer. For all of us writing well is always a struggle. (from Avi's Newbery Medal acceptance speech, Toronto, June 22, 2003)

Avi knows what it means to write well. Since 1975 he has engaged in the struggle to create award-winning literature for children. His 50th book, *Crispin: The Cross of Lead,* won the 2003 Newbery Medal. In his acceptance speech, Avi suggested that a successful story is one that the writer begins and the reader completes. He explained what it means for writers to be in partnership with readers by sharing a metaphor developed by the author Donald Hall:

The writer in his writing, tries to create the letter O. But he does so by writing the letter C. Which is to say there is a gap. Where there is nothing. Dark matter perhaps. The writer's words on the page create structure,

character, and voice—but there are the gaps, the dark matter, the unknown, and the not written. It is the reader who fills this gap.

If the gap's too large, the reader cannot fill it. If the gap is too small, the reader need not fill it. But if the gap is just right, the reader fills it with—self. And the circle is complete. Thus—writer and reader have joined together to make the writing whole.

For Avi, the best literature contains gaps that challenge readers to consider, for the first time, aspects of themselves or their surroundings that are familiar but unexamined. "Great writing," he said, "reveals what we know—but never noticed before. Great writing identifies that most elusive of all things—that which we have seen but had not noticed, that which did not seem to exist until it was named."

Over the past 50 years, Avi has invited readers to complete gaps in more than 13 historical fiction pieces. Some of his popular titles include ***Don't You Know There's a War On? Emily Upham's Revenge, Night Journeys,*** and ***The True Confessions of Charlotte Doyle,*** which won a Newbery Honor in 2000. In an interview for Hyperion, Avi discussed the challenge of writing historical fiction. "We don't know fully what life was like," he says, and you have to build a whole style and language to convey something. In other words, the whole thing is a stylistic construction, and you almost invent the language." In writing *Crispin,* Avi first composed his text "in verse." "[B]ut it would have been six hundred pages," Avi laughed. "So I took the linguistic structure and recast it back into a traditional narrative."

In an interview, Avi also discussed the challenge of writing *Crispin* in a way that would enable readers to complete the gaps in a story that takes place in the late 1300s. "I think the problem of writing historical fiction for young people in particular is how to convey the strictures of that earlier society," he said. "The rules of life in the fourteenth century are so radically different from today that you have to create a context that is understandable." Avi found that music was one way for 20th-century readers to see themselves in Crispin. "Music," says Avi, "is something kids do relate to, and figuring out that there was music at that time is a way for them to connect."

Avi works hard to help kids connect with books. "I've published at least one book a year," he said in his Newbery acceptance speech. "Since *Crispin* I've written and published more. But though I may tire at the end of the day, I never tire of this great enterprise." His infatuation with stories motivates him to keep writing: "I have a passion for books, the smell of ink, the turn of the page—with words, and beyond all else, stories. I love the whole process, from sitting down and writing the first sentence, to seeing kids absorbed in my books, my story—not me." By creating texts in which readers help complete his stories, Avi has contributed books that strengthen readers' aesthetic experiences of literature.

Source: *Crispin: The cross of lead. Teacher's guide.* (2003). Hyperion Books for Children Lesson Plan Series. New York: Hyperion.

uses words appropriate to the period—steward, reeve, pestilence—that are easily understood within the context of the story. Finally, there are Bear's songs, songs that reflect the language of the time and enrich the setting.

Characterization

As the protagonist, Crispin is a fully developed, dynamic character. We understand his feelings, values, and attitudes, and they reflect the milieu in which he lives. His growth across the story is tremendous: from an ignorant, fearful, unnamed slave who knew nothing of his heritage to a courageous, curious, free man who is sure that his name is Crispin and who knows who he is. When Crispin flees the village he is running out of fear, trying to get to a city and obtain his freedom, but he has little idea of how to get there or what freedom really means. When he stumbles upon Bear, a huge, red-bearded juggler, his life begins to improve. As he travels with him, Crispin begins to realize that Bear juggles ideas as well as balls, and for the first time in his life, Crispin begins to question, to think for himself. As Bear explains the political realities of the day, Crispin begins to sense possibilities

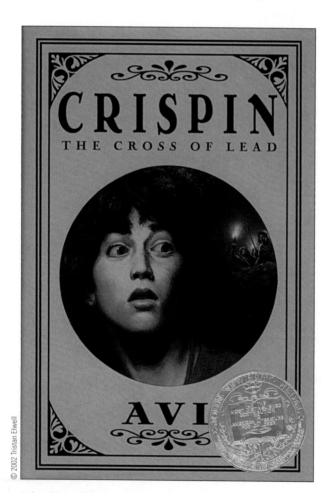

When his mother dies, Crispin embarks on a journey of self-discovery.

© 2002 Tristan Elwell

he has never considered and to question things he has taken for granted—such as the right of one human being to own another. Bear challenges Crispin to think for himself, and the boy begins to rely more on his own judgment than on the rules of others or their assumptions about what God wants done. Crispin's quest for freedom—of both mind and body—is thoroughly shaped by his historical context.

The story is told from Crispin's point of view. This enables Avi to apprise the reader of what Crispin is thinking. Thus, when Crispin is frightened and confused, the reader is also confused and aware of danger. When Crispin slowly begins to figure out why Aycliffe is chasing him, when his new experiences cause him to question old ideas, the reader is privy to those thoughts and realizations. This allows us to know Crispin well and to believe in his transformation.

Plot

The story opens with a series of major events: the death of Crispin's mother, his realization that Aycliffe wants him killed, learning that he has a name and that his mother could read and write, and his subsequent discovery of the body of the village priest. These events both create an immediate interest in what might happen and propel Crispin out of his village and into the wider world. His journey from village to city is exciting not only because he is seeing and learning new things but because he is being pursued by Aycliffe for some unknown reason. The combination of adventure and mystery serves to heighten the tension and propel the plot toward its rousing conclusion.

Although Crispin knows that Aycliffe has declared him a "wolf's head," which means that anyone can kill him and claim a reward, he does not know why. In fact, there is a large price on his head, though Crispin can't imagine why he is worth anything. As Crispin begins to realize that Aycliffe's pursuit has something to do with who Crispin really is, he also begins to see that his own actions have consequences. As the plot and the mystery unfold, Crispin learns from his experiences and grows accordingly. This unity of character and action works to make the plot believable and the character of Crispin fully human.

Theme

Crispin's quest for freedom is shaped by his historical context, but it echoes across the ages. This quest is one that all humans pursue. We might call it growing up or becoming free from the constraints of childhood and the control of adults. It is often a larger freedom that we struggle for, such as the freedom of independent thought, the freedom of equality, or perhaps the freedom to live in peace and to develop and grow as a human being. Crispin is seeking all these freedoms, in spite of terrible odds, and his attainment of freedom is a triumph. His journey to self-discovery is literal as well as figurative, and one that young readers rec-

Teaching Idea 8-2

Thematic Exploration: Self-Knowledge

One of the themes that is woven through the story of Crispin is his discovery of who he is. He discovers this literally as he learns his name and the truth about his mother and his heritage. This is one kind of self-knowledge that he acquires during the course of the story. He also discovers his own interests, desires, abilities, and strengths, coming to know his emotional self. Ask students to consider the knowledge of themselves that they have. They might want to create a coat of arms for Crispin or for their own family with emblems that signify important aspects of their lives; Crispin might include, for example, a cross on his coat of arms. They might want to write a list poem or an acrostic, or name poem, for Crispin or for themselves, in which they list character traits. Crispin's name poem might begin "Courageous / Ready to learn / Inquisitive." Or they might simply write a journal entry discussing what Crispin discovered about himself or what they have discovered about themselves. This activity can also be linked to books in other genres that explore this same theme.

ognize and share. Teaching Idea 8.2 offers ways to help students explore the theme of self-knowledge.

The seamless interweaving of setting, plot, and character as they center around a universal theme of the search for freedom and self-awareness is supported by impeccable writing that offers just enough flavor of the times.

* * *

History through Historical Fiction

Much historical fiction is set in one particular historical period, but a few excellent books are intergenerational sagas. Walter Dean Myers's *The Glory Field* (A) begins in 1753 with the harrowing story of a young man traveling from West Africa on a slave ship, and ends at a family reunion in 1994. Each story he tells is rich with historical details reflecting the various times in the lives of the Lewis family, and each involves a turning point in an adolescent family member's life. Themes of family unity, pride, and freedom connect the stories into a coherent whole.

Holding Up the Earth (A), by Dianne Gray, also spans a considerable amount of time, but the story is anchored in one place: the Nebraska farm that five generations of young women have loved. Janet Hickman's *Jericho* (A) is yet another emotionally satisfying intergenerational story; it explores the lives of three generations of women—grandmother, mother, and daughter.

Historical fiction can be studied in many ways: as a genre, by theme, by chronological period, or according to the topics in a social studies curriculum. In any case, well-written stories will "establish human and social circumstances in which the interaction of historical forces may be known, felt, and observed" (Blos, 1992). We present historical fiction chronologically and then consider how to explore particular historical settings as well as important themes across history.

• • PREHISTORIC AND • • ANCIENT TIMES

Prehistoric times, the ancient period before written records were kept, are wrapped in the shrouds of antiquity. Scientists theorize about the daily life and culture of ancient peoples by observing fragments of life and making inferences from shards of pottery, weapons, or bits of bone. Authors draw from the findings of archaeologists, anthropologists, and paleontologists to create vivid tales of life as it might have been.

Many novels of prehistoric times are set in distant lands around the Mediterranean Sea or in ancient Britain. The best fiction about prehistoric people does more than re-create possible settings and events of the past. It engages itself with themes basic to all persons everywhere: the will to survive, the need for courage and honor, the growth of understanding, the development of compassion. Peter Dickinson's series **The Kin**, which includes *Suth's Story, Noli's Story, Po's Story,* and *Mana's Story* (all I–A), takes readers back 200,000 years but grapples with issues important today. War and peace, the power of language and the thought it enables, loving relationships, and community are some of the themes that connect these stories with our own times. These and other stories of prehistoric times are listed in the Booklist at the end of this chapter.

Stories of ancient times often focus on life in the Mediterranean civilizations. Julius Lester's *Pharaoh's Daughter: A Novel of Ancient Egypt* (A) is a fictional account of the biblical story of Moses that contains well-developed characters and complex themes. Susan Fletcher writes imaginatively of life in a Persian harem during the time of Sheherazade in *Shadow Spinner* (A), a suspenseful story with a resourceful female protagonist and intriguing details of time and place.

Some stories of ancient civilizations merge with mythology (see chapters 5 and 6), such as Adele Geras's narrative *Troy* (A). Other authors attempt to retain a more factual base for their work. Rosemary Sutcliff's novels of ancient Britain, such as *The Eagle of the Ninth, The Shining Company,* and *The Lantern Bearers* (all A), are masterful evocations of their time; they also provide sensitive insights into the human spirit. Each story reverberates with an eternal truth and lasting theme. Sutcliff's heroes live and die for values and principles that we embrace today. Much like high fantasy, a very different genre, her stories reveal the eternal struggle between goodness—that which we value—and evil—the forces that work to destroy it. Sutcliff's books, and other fine stories of ancient times, are listed in the Booklist at the end of this chapter.

• • THE MIDDLE AGES • •

The dissolution of the Roman Empire signaled the beginning of that part of the medieval period sometimes referred to as the Middle Ages, spanning roughly from 500 to the early 1500s A.D. There is some recorded history of these times, and writers breathe life into the shadowy figures of the history of this period to construct novels that blend fact and legend with an artistic touch, as in Michael Morpurgo's retelling of *Sir Gawain and the Green Knight* (I–A). In the past 10 years there have been a number of outstanding narratives set in the Middle Ages, both fantasy or literary lore, as discussed in Chapter 6, and more realistic fictional narratives.

Elizabeth Wein links ancient Britain and ancient Africa in her acclaimed Arthurian/Aksumite cycle. The first three books, *The Winter Prince, A Coalition of Lions,* and *The Sunbird* (all A) move from sixth-century Britain to sixth-century Africa as Goewin, princess of Britain, travels to African Aksum (Eritrea and Ethiopia) and helps forge an alliance between ancient Britain and the African kingdom. With the third book the plague has come to Britain, and Aksum is under threat from many sides. Steeped in Arthurian legend but based on facts about the history of Britain and Ethiopia, these riveting narratives postulate a believable connection between the two ancient kingdoms, forged by unforgettable characters.

Many historical fiction narratives are set in the Western world, especially Great Britain. Karen Cushman's *The Midwife's Apprentice* (I–A), winner of the 1996 Newbery Medal, weaves an array of details about daily life into a compelling narrative. The mundane, often distasteful details of the lives of the common folk in the Middle Ages form the rich background against which a young girl discovers her worth. Cushman's other two books set in the Middle Ages, *Matilda Bone* and *Catherine, Called Birdy* (both A), are also filled

with details that sweep readers into the midst of life in England at that time. Readers who have enjoyed these books and Avi's *Crispin* (I–A) might want to go on to read Odo Hirsch's *Yoss* (A), a novel of the Middle Ages for slightly older readers that explores many of the themes that appear in *Crispin.*

Mollie Hunter's *The King's Swift Rider* (A) grapples with the conflicts that arise from having personal commitments to both nonviolence and a free Scotland. Jane Yolen and Robert Harris present the same general time and place in *Girl in a Cage* (I–A), a gripping story in which Robert the Bruce and his followers match wits and strength with Edward I of England. Narrated by 11-year-old Marjorie Bruce, a princess now imprisoned in a cage, this novel makes history real and vivid.

Other fine stories explore the medieval period in other parts of the world. Frances Temple's *The Beduin's Gazelle* (A) is set in the midst of a war between Beduin tribes in 1302. Jill Paton Walsh tells the story of the fall of Constantinople in 1453 in *The Emperor's Winding Sheet* (I–A). Tracy Barrett's

© 2002 Trina Schart Hyman

One aspect of the Scots' struggle for freedom is seen through the eyes of a young girl in **Girl in a Cage.**

Anna of Byzantium (A) is a graphic novel of the life of a brilliant woman in the 11th-century Byzantine Empire, a difficult time in history for strong women. Janet Rupert's *The African Mask* (A) is set in 11th-century Nigeria. Linda Sue Park's *A Single Shard* (A), set in medieval Korea, won a Newbery Medal for her exquisite description of time and place and development of a protagonist whom readers come to care about. Mette Newth's *The Transformation* (A), set in Greenland in the mid-1400s, explores the impact of Christian Europeans on the beliefs and culture—indeed on the well-being—of the Inuit. This is a novel that presents a place and time that is unfamiliar to most readers, considers profound questions of theology and culture, and is also a riveting adventure and a tender love story. These and other stories are included in the Booklist at the end of this chapter.

• • THE RENAISSANCE AND • • THE AGE OF EXPLORATION

Whether in real life or in books, mysterious or dangerous explorations of the unknown mesmerize us all. Accounts of navigation of the earlier world intrigue today's children as much as travels to the moon or Mars do. Explorers of the past and present need the same kind of courage and willingness to face the unknown. Stories of explorations range from tales of the early Vikings to those set in the age of European exploration—Columbus and after.

In 1992, the 500th anniversary of Columbus's famous 1492 voyage brought forth many books to mark the anniversary. These books also reflected a growing trend in children's literature: Some told the "other side" of the story, presenting Columbus from the point of view of the Native Americans who were present when he landed, or of Europeans who were skeptical of his motives. Books like Jane Yolen's *Encounter* (I–A) and Pam Conrad's *Pedro's Journal* (I) help present a more balanced picture of the impact of the age of exploration. The powerful writing and clever structure of Michael Dorris's *Morning Girl* (I) allows young readers to experience "firsthand" the shock of Columbus's invasion of the Taino Indian islands.

Michael Cadnum's *Ship of Fire* (I–A) is based on actual events during Sir Francis Drake's raid on the Spanish port of Cadiz in 1587. The protagonist, a young doctor, not only finds adventure and acts courageously but also is forced to question the English hero, Drake. Is he truly a hero or simply a pirate, stealing for Queen Elizabeth? These questions elevate this exciting novel beyond just an adventure story.

The Renaissance is a fascinating time in history, but few books for children explore this era in Europe, and even fewer are set in other parts of the world. Pilar Molina Llorente's *The Apprentice* (I) is set in Renaissance Florence and depicts the lives of middle-class merchants and famous artists

alike. Linda Sue Park sets *The Kite Fighters* (I) in Seoul, Korea. These and other stories are included in the Booklist at the end of this chapter.

• • COLONIAL THROUGH • • POST-REVOLUTIONARY WAR TIMES

Immigrants began sailing to America in the late 16th century, some seeking adventure and financial gain, some escaping religious persecution, some traveling as missionaries, and some seeking political freedom. Economic and social conditions made the New World attractive to people who were willing to sacrifice the known for the possibilities of a promising unknown. The settlements by the English at Roanoke, Jamestown, Plymouth, and Boston are vivid settings for stories based on early colonial life.

By the end of the 17th century, the early settlers were well established in their new communities and were stern guardians of their religious views, pious behavior, and moral standards. The hysteria that gripped the people of Salem, Massachusetts, in the days of the witch hunts grew out of the political, economic, and social forces of the community. Kathryn Lasky's *Beyond the Burning Time* (A) explores some of the hidden passions that might have stoked the fires of Salem, and brings to life the way people lived, believed, and sometimes died in that place and time. In her classic *The Witch of Blackbird Pond* (I–A), winner of the 1959 Newbery Medal, Elizabeth George Speare reveals how guilt by association occurs in Old Salem when a young girl and the old woman she has befriended are accused of witchcraft. Both books artfully blend fact and fiction to create a vivid picture of people and their lives during colonial times.

The history of America is incomplete without stories of Native Americans. In the past their story was told, if at all, by European Americans who often characterized them in stereotyped ways. A growing number of writers now give more accurate portrayals of Native American cultures and a more objective picture of the 500-year clash between the European and Native American cultures. Stories for younger children may present a simple view of the interaction between Europeans and Native Americans, but this view should not rely on stereotypes. Stories for older readers often consider the complexities inherent in the clash between two cultures, such as Elizabeth George Speare's compelling novel about the faltering friendship of a white boy and an Indian boy in the 1700s, *The Sign of the Beaver* (I–A). Although some people criticize Speare for her non-Native point of view, others find the book to be a rewarding catalyst for discussion about the clash of cultures.

Stories that reflect a Native American point of view concerning these times are still scarce, however, as are those that depict the lives and struggles of the many Africans brought as slaves before the turn of the century. Notable exceptions include Michael Dorris's *Guests* and *Sees Behind Trees* (both I), as well as Joseph Bruchac's *The Arrow over the Door* (I). In Joyce Rockwood's *To Spoil the Sun* (A), recently reissued, the story of the devastation of smallpox is vivid and moving. Rain Dove, a young Cherokee girl, finds her life destroyed when the disease arrives along with the white man.

The 18th century was an interesting and tumultuous time, with disease wreaking havoc in Europe and ships carrying people around the globe with greater and greater frequency. L. A. Meyer captures the dangers and excitement of mid-18th-century life in *Bloody Jack: Being an Account of the Curious Adventures of Mary "Jacky" Faber, Ship's Boy* and its sequel, *Curse of the Blue Tattoo: Being an Account of the Misadventures of Jacky Faber, Midshipman and Fine Lady* (both I–A). These tales of high adventure on the seas differ from most others in one remarkable way—the protagonist is female.

There was also great upheaval in many countries around the world during this time, including Great Britain. Jane Yolen and Robert Harris again combine their talents in *Prince across the Water* (I–A), set during the Scottish rebellion to replace King George with Bonnie Prince Charlie. The age-old desire of young men to go to war to prove their mettle plays itself out against a meticulously detailed setting and a thorough understanding of the role of clan and honor in the Highlander culture of the day. Another collaboration between Yolen and Harris, *The Queen's Own Fool: A Novel of Mary Queen of Scots* (I–A), brings another exciting piece of Scottish history to young readers.

Wars wrapped the globe in this period, and the American Revolutionary War was one of the most significant. Stories of this war were once quite one sided; the Tories, or loyalists, were bad, the patriots good. A more balanced picture began to appear in the 1970s with *My Brother Sam Is Dead* (A), and this trend has continued. Since then, the divided loyalties in colonial families or communities and the true horror of war have usually been foregrounded in fiction about this era. Janet Lunn, one of Canada's best-known writers for children, explores just these topics in *The Hollow Tree* (A), a gripping account of a young girl's harrowing journey north from New Hampshire to Canada to join other loyalist families even though her own family is divided in its allegiance.

Writers of historical fiction sometimes choose to tell more localized stories. *Fever 1793* (I–A), by Laurie Halse Anderson, graphically depicts the terrors of the yellow fever epidemic that killed nearly 5,000 people in Philadelphia. Anderson's heroine, a spunky and engaging 16-year-old, draws readers into her story; the informational notes at the end of the book offer the facts to interested readers. These and other stories that illuminate life in North America at this time are listed in the Booklist at the end of this chapter.

• • WESTWARD EXPANSION • • AND THE CIVIL WAR

The 19th century saw North America experiencing severe growing pains as the country expanded westward. National identity was seriously challenged; the question of slavery became a national debate; and immigrants from Europe, Africa, and Asia (both voluntary and involuntary) brought their despair and sometimes their hopes and dreams to a new land. It was an interesting century, filled with amazing contradictions. As the United States grew, the native peoples' lands shrank, and their cultures were almost obliterated. As the nation expanded, indentured Chinese, lured to America by the promise of work, were exploited as they built the transcontinental railroad. As the new nation prospered, Africans and others were ripped from their homelands, forcibly transported, and doomed to endure a life of slavery. As the nation became industrialized, the quality of life improved for some and grew worse for many. Children's books explore these contradictions from many viewpoints, telling the story of the growth of a nation and the consequences of that growth.

The Westward Migration

Americans were on the move from the beginning. Those moving called it expansion; those who were displaced saw it as invasion. In either case, life required great physical strength and, often, the ability to endure loneliness. Pioneer families worked hard by necessity, providing their own food, clothing, shelter, and entertainment. Themes of loneliness, hardship, and acceptance of what life brings are threaded through many excellent novels about the pioneers and their struggle to tame a wild land.

These themes are evident in Joyce Carol Thomas's descriptions of the courage and dignity of a young black woman determined to own her own land. *I Have Heard of a Land* (P–I) presents the inspiring story of one woman who symbolizes all who homesteaded the American West, braving isolation, the wilderness, and nature's vagaries to forge a home for themselves. Loretta Ellsworth's *The Shrouding Woman* (I), set on the prairie, presents a quiet story of grief and recovery along with a description of a job that is all but extinct today—the shrouding of the dead by women trained to do so. In *Prairie Whispers* (I), Frances Arrington uses the setting to create a mood of foreboding and isolation. Young Colleen's baby sister dies soon after birth, and when Colleen is begged by a dying woman to take her baby girl, she takes the baby home and gives it to her unconscious mother. When the baby's father arrives looking for the money that his wife fled with, Colleen confronts a series of ethical choices as she tries to keep him from also taking the baby. *Nothing Here But Stones* (I–A), by Nancy Oswald, tells the fictional story of a real group of Russian Jews who struggled to create a new home in the Colorado mountains.

Going west was an adventure story to many, and Will Hobbs's *Jason's Gold* (A) is a spine-tingling account of a young boy's adventures in the Klondike during the Alaskan gold rush. Michael Cadnum explores a similar story in the California gold fields in *Blood Gold* (I–A). This gripping adventure story takes readers from Panama to San Francisco by ship and then on to the gold fields, as the young narrator pursues an acquaintance who left his pregnant girlfriend in Philadelphia. The suspense is high, the plot twists and turns, and the settings are vivid.

During these times, the clash of cultural values between European settlers and Native Americans resulted in numerous conflicts, from grisly battles in which hundreds were killed, to more personal conflicts in which individuals who had come to know each other as friends had to choose between friendship and loyalty to their own people.

The famous 1804–1805 voyage of Meriwether Lewis and William Clark is emblematic of the interest the U.S. government had in expanding westward. Until recently, stories of their expedition were told from the viewpoint of the two leaders or the soldiers who accompanied them. However, with the minting of the Sacajawea "gold" dollar came not one but several stories about this brave Native American woman who helped lead Lewis and Clark through a large part of the upstream Missouri River and into the Rocky Mountains. Joseph Bruchac's *Sacajawea* (I–A) is a brilliant, thoughtful recounting of the voyage told in alternating points of view—Sacajawea's and William Clark's. Clark's chapters begin with excerpts from the diaries he kept on the journey; Sacajawea's begin with stories that her people told. Each brings a unique perspective to the grand adventure, and their mutual respect and growing friendship are evident.

The 200th anniversary of this epic journey occurred in 2004–2005, accompanied by the appearance of more books. Kate McMullan tells the story of the journey from the point of view of the youngest member of the group in *My Travels with Capts. Lewis and Clark by George Shannon* (I–A). McMullan used not only public records but also family documents—she is a direct descendant of George Shannon—to create a first-rate adventure story. The story is, however, also filled with great detail about people and places and is a chronicle of the growth of a boy, called Pup because he was so young, into a man. Stephen Ambrose also creates a fictional diary of George Shannon in *This Vast Land* (A). Allan Wolf tells the same story from the perspective of 13 participants in the journey, one of which is the dog, Seaman, in *New Found Land: Lewis and Clark's Voyage of Discovery* (A).

Fortunately, some stories about the westward expansion reflect the views of someone other than the white settlers. Laurence Yep writes of the life of the Chinese laborers in *The Traitor: 1885* (I–A), part of his **Gold Mountain Chroni-** cles series. Cornelia Cornelissen tells of the forcible removal of the Cherokee to Oklahoma in *Soft Rain: A Story of the Cherokee Trail of Tears* (I), and Louise Erdrich tells of the effects of smallpox, brought by the white man to the Native Americans, in *The Birchbark House* and *The Game of Silence* (both I). Teaching Idea 8.3 offers a way to help students notice how varying perceptions of events influence the way we think of those events. These and other stories that reflect the negative aspects of the westward expansion, as well as those that depict the vigorous growth of a new nation, are listed in the Booklist at the end of this chapter.

Slavery, the Civil War, and Its Aftermath

Slavery was a part of American life from early colonial days until long after the Emancipation Proclamation. Many chapters of American history are grim, but those involving slavery and the Civil War are among the worst; the war was a long, savage contest that tore the country apart and caused many deaths. Historical fiction of this period describes antebellum life as well as the turmoil and tragedy of the bloody war years and the reverberations that are still felt today. The years immediately preceding the Civil War were a bleak period in American history, although individual acts of compassion and heroism did occur. A notable children's book that has captured the antebellum period is Ann Turner's picture book *Nettie's Trip South* (I–A), which depicts the horror of slavery as seen through the eyes of a white girl from the North who is on a train trip to the South.

Teaching Idea 8-3

Discussion: Compare Perceptions of an Historical Event

Collect several books, both historical fiction and nonfiction, that describe an historical event such as the first Thanksgiving, the westward expansion on the Great Plains, or the Civil War. Read these with your students. Compare them, considering such questions as the following:

* Who is telling the story?
* What is the narrator's perception of the events?
* What factors influence that perception?
* How do perceptions differ across books?

An effective follow-up activity is to ask students to role-play from different perspectives.

Although *The River Between Us* (A) begins and ends in 1916, Richard Peck recreates life during the Civil War in a small Illinois town on the Mississippi River. When 15-year-old Howard, his father, and his two younger brothers arrive in Grand Tower, Illinois, to visit his grandparents and Great Aunt Delphine and Grand Uncle Noah, he and the reader are immediately swept up in Grandma Tilly's stories and transported into the world of the Civil War. Border states, such as Illinois, especially the southern regions of those states, reflected the larger division in the country. Further, the Mississippi was the main thoroughfare for the center of the country, and North and South mingled, even after the beginnings of the war, through the trade between New Orleans and the North. This setting is integral to the story that Grandma Tilly unfolds of the mysterious Calinda and the beautiful Delphine who came north from New Orleans on one of the last riverboats. With this story, Peck raises questions about how the United States considers race and what it meant to be a free person of color in that time and place.

The story of *Pink and Say* (I–A) is one that has been passed down over the generations in Patricia Polacco's own family. Her great-great-grandfather, Sheldon Russell Curtis,

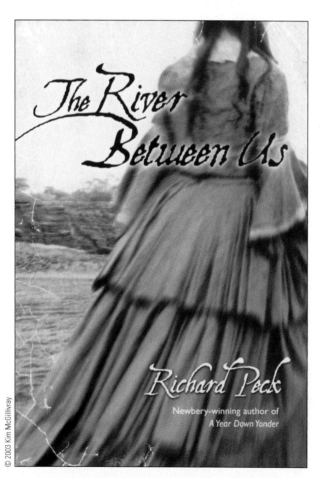

Richard Peck examines issues of race in the United States in **The River Between Us,** *a gripping novel of the Civil War.*

called Say, had been left for dead on a Civil War battlefield in Georgia when he was rescued by an African American Union soldier, Pinkus Aylee. Pink took Say to his home, where his mother, Moe Moe Bay, a slave, nursed Say back to health. The three became close. Say confided in Moe Moe that he was a deserter, and Pink told Say that he knew how to read. Say told Pink and his mother the story of how he shook the hand of Lincoln. Shortly after Moe Moe was killed by marauders, Pink and Say were captured and transported to Andersonville, where Pink was hanged.

Polacco's illustrations focus on the emotional highs and lows of the characters and provide enough details to visually anchor the story in the period. The story is told in Say's country dialect, and the dialogue reflects the times without being overwhelming to the reader. The final few pages are an afterword, when we learn what happened to Pink and Say and are asked to remember Pink.

Mildred Taylor has reached back in time in her ongoing chronicle of the Logan family in *The Land* (A), the story of Paul-Edward, Cassie Logan's grandfather. The son of a white man and his former slave, Paul-Edward is privileged and educated, but also a young black man in the post–Civil War South. Blacks distrust his whiteness, whites discriminate against him because of his blackness, and he needs to find in himself the strength to craft the life that he wants, for society is determined to thwart him. Taylor, arguably one of our most important contemporary authors, is unflinching in her examination of what life was like for African Americans in the postwar era (Galda, 2001).

• • THE TURN OF THE • • CENTURY: IMMIGRATION AND THE INDUSTRIAL REVOLUTION

Continuing the Logan family saga, Mildred Taylor's *The Well: David's Story* (A) is set in the rural South in the early 20th century and tells the story of David, the son of Paul-Edward. Focused on discrimination and injustice, Taylor's story is emotionally draining and raises important issues for older readers to think about and discuss. As in *The Land,* the social, political, and physical setting is richly detailed.

With the aftereffects of the Civil War at work in the South and the continued westward expansion, the East was changing as well. Millions of immigrants came from distant lands, dreaming of freedom and hoping to create a better life. Their stories are our stories, repeated over and over at family gatherings where young children cluster around their elders. Historical fiction contains a wealth of immigrant stories for all ages. Many books describe the conditions that led families to leave their country and migrate to America; others focus on the difficulties and hardships endured during immigration.

Patricia Reilly Giff sets *Nory Ryan's Song* (I–A) in 1845 in Ireland, just at the beginning of the potato famine. Although Nory is only 12, her strength of character and gritty determination help her save her family and friends from starvation before she begins her own journey to America. That journey and its happy ending are described in the sequel, *Maggie's Door* (I–A). In *A House of Tailors* (I–A), Giff relates the story of 13-year-old Dina, who flees Germany after being accused of spying against the Germans during the Franco-Prussian War. Dina hopes to leave her work as a seamstress, but when she arrives in Brooklyn in 1870, she finds that her uncle's house is as full of sewing as her father's was. As Dina adjusts to life in America, she also comes to value her talent as a seamstress and to realize that although she may love her American life, she will always long to return to Germany. This duality in the immigrant experience is beautifully captured by Allen Say in his Caldecott Medal–winning picture book, *Grandfather's Journey* (P–I–A), set in the early part of the 20th century.

While the West was being settled and immigrants were pouring into the thriving cities of the East, rural and small-town America seemed quiet and peaceful. Several stories set at the turn of the century give a glimpse of life as it was lived in small towns in the East, away from the high drama of life on the frontier or in bustling urban centers. One of these is Jennifer Donnelly's *A Northern Light* (A). This novel is at once a coming-of-age story, an evocation of the world of the summer hotels of upstate New York in 1906, and a murder mystery, the same murder that inspired Theodore Dreiser to write *An American Tragedy*.

Gary Schmidt bases the Newbery Honor book *Lizzie Bright and the Buckminster Boy* (I–A) on a true story as well. In 1911, Maine officials forced African American, Native American, and foreign-born residents to leave Malaga Island because they wanted to use the island as a tourist attraction. Schmidt takes this incident and weaves the story of Turner Buckminster III, son of the new Congregational preacher, and Lizzie Bright Griffin, granddaughter of Malaga's African American preacher. The gripping drama contains multiple conflicts—not the least between Turner and his father—that reveal both the worst and the best sides of humanity, as townspeople engage in a struggle for human dignity that is sparked by the desire for money and power.

In *The Silent Boy* (I–A), Lois Lowry's evocation of time and place in a small town outside Philadelphia between 1908 and 1911 is masterful. Told by the narrator as an old woman in a series of brief stories that span the years, this novel seems slow and quiet, as quiet as the brain-damaged boy who does not speak and who so fascinates young Katy. In the brief glimpses of her young life, we see Katy coming of age in a time and place that were changed forever by the impending entry of America into World War I. These and other books of this era appear in the Booklist at the end of the chapter.

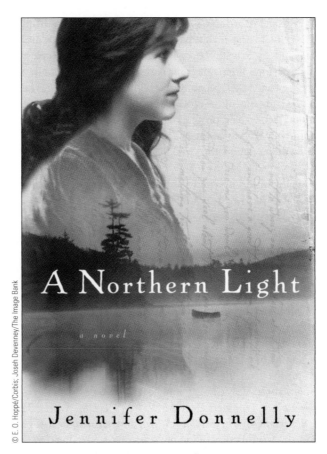

© E. O. Hoppé/Corbis; Joseh Devenney/The Image Bank

*Readers not yet ready for Dreiser's **An American Tragedy** will be intrigued by the mystery in **A Northern Light**.*

• • WORLD WAR I • • AND ITS AFTERMATH

There are not many books set during World War I, in either picture book or novel form, but the books that do exist are outstanding. Recently, there have been several new books that examine both the events and the nature of this war from the perspective of those left behind as well as those on the front lines. In Iain Lawrence's *Lord of the Nutcracker Men* (I–A), young Johnny's world has been profoundly affected. With his father in France and his mother working in a distant munitions plant, Johnny must leave London for the safety of his aunt's countryside home. He takes with him the nutcracker men and toy soldiers that his father made for him before leaving, and his army grows with each soldier that his father carves and sends him from the front. As the war continues, both the soldiers and the letters from his father get more and more frightening, while Johnny learns to take responsibility for himself. Although Johnny's anguish is foregrounded, his father's letters also reveal the true horrors of the front.

Michael Morpurgo's *Private Peaceful* (A) moves from the front to the idyllic past of turn-of-the-century rural England as Private Thomas Peaceful spends a sleepless night trying to remember his past. His memories, told in a series of vignettes, recount his childhood and adolescence in the company of his older brother, Charlie, and their best friend, Molly. The brothers are so close that even though Tommo loves Molly, Charlie's marriage to her does not destroy their relationship. When Charlie goes to war, Tommo lies about his age to follow him. Morpurgo explores the brutality of not only the war but the people who engage in it. The ending is a profound condemnation of the killing of others, for any reason.

✷ ✷ THE GREAT DEPRESSION ✷ ✷

Stories of the Depression years portray America in times of trouble. The beginning of the period is generally considered to be the stock market crash of 1929. Then, stories of ruined businessmen jumping from skyscrapers filled the headlines of daily newspapers. Now, stories for children describe the grim effects of living in poverty. Mildred Taylor's books about Cassie Logan and her family, *Song of the Trees* (I), *Roll of Thunder, Hear My Cry* (A), *Let the Circle Be Unbroken* (A), *The Friendship* (A), and *Mississippi Bridge* (A), show rural poverty and prevailing racism. Young Cassie and her extended family, including Paul-Edward's widow, who is Cassie's grandmother, and David Logan, who is her father, live on their own farm. Owning their own land was unusual for African Americans in Mississippi at that time, and it is a source of pride for Cassie. However, she doesn't really understand why her father has to leave the family to find work to pay the taxes. Nor does she understand the prevalent racism that surrounds her, for she has been protected by her loving family. In Newbery Medal–winning *Roll of Thunder,* Taylor vividly portrays the physical, social, and political setting through Cassie's eyes as Cassie begins to discover the truth about where she lives and the compelling reasons for holding on to their land. The Logan saga is the most complete chronicle of the Jim Crow era that is available for young readers. As such, it illuminates key threads of our history and identity as a nation.

Jen Bryant builds on a specific incident—the kidnapping and subsequent death of the Lindbergh baby in 1932—in *The Trial* (I–A). This novel in poems introduces us to 12-year-old Katie and the world of small-town New Jersey during the Depression as seen through Katie's eyes. Katie finds herself inside the courtroom at the Hauptmann trial, helping her Uncle Jeff, a reporter who needs help taking notes because he has broken his arm. Because Katie, in all her innocence, is there, we can see the trial through fresh eyes, eyes that wonder about guilt and innocence.

Karen Hesse's Newbery Medal–winning *Out of the Dust* (A), one of the earliest novels in verse for young readers, is unrelenting in its depiction of life in the Oklahoma dust bowl; the story is softened only by the sensitivity of its heroine and its own poetic form. Told through the poems of young Billie Jo, the novel captures the combination of hope and despair that reflects both the time and place and the pain of adolescence at any time, in any place.

Other stories set during this time are less grim. In Gennifer Choldenko's *Al Capone Does My Shirts* (I–A), Moose worries about his father losing his job and their home, but he also copes with his sister's autism and their mother's emotional trauma; the daily life of his family, living on Alcatraz; and his increasing maturity. Although Christopher Paul Curtis's Newbery Medal–winning *Bud, Not Buddy* (I) does involve death, homelessness, and racism, its overall tone is one of hope mixed with poignant humor. Richard Peck's Newbery Medal–winning *A Year down Yonder* and Newbery Honor–winning *A Long Way from Chicago: A Novel in Stories* (both I–A) are set in the Depression-era small-town Midwest. In both books, the characterization and humor, as well as the sense of place and time, are outstanding. Fifteen-year-old Mary Alice spends the year 1937 with her grandmother, the indomitable Grandma Dowdel, while her older brother, Joey, is working for the Conservation Corps. *A Long Way from Chicago,* a series of stories spanning the years 1929 to 1942, ends poignantly with Joey's journey by train to fight in World War II. In many stories set during the Depression, homelessness is one of the central themes. Teaching Idea 8.4 offers suggestions for exploring that theme across different genres.

✷ ✷ WORLD WAR II ✷ ✷
AND ITS AFTERMATH

The years 1933 to 1946 encompassed Adolph Hitler's rise and fall in Germany and Japanese military activity in the Pacific. World War II brought into vivid awareness humanity's potential inhumanity, particularly toward our fellow human beings. The horrors of the period were so unthinkable that it was several decades before the story was told in books for young people. The children who read these books today are reading about the world of their grandparents and great-grandparents; these stories connect with their family histories.

Stories Set in Europe and Asia

The familiar adage that those who do not know the past are condemned to repeat it is adequate cause for attending to the tragedy of the Holocaust. The books describing Hitler's reign of terror, with its effects ultimately on all people, are a

Teaching Idea 8-4

Genre Study: Compare Treatment of a Theme across Genres

Select a theme that crosses the boundaries of time, such as the effects of homelessness on people's lives. Gather primary sources, such as current or historical newspapers and magazines and contemporary and historical fiction and nonfiction. Ask students to read and respond to their reading, then to compare these experiences to their reading of a textbook or encyclopedia on the same topic. Discuss the different ways of knowing—cognitive and emotional—that these readings generate.

The following are titles that deal with homelessness during the Great Depression and today:

Contemporary Fiction

Bunting, Eve, *Fly Away Home* (I)

Fox, Paula, *Monkey Island* (A)

Johnson, Lindsay Lee, *Soul Moon Soup* (I–A)

Tolan, Stephanie, *Sophie and the Sidewalk Man* (I)

Historical Fiction

Bartoletti, Susan Campbell, *Christmas Promise* (P)

Choldenko, Gennifer, *Al Capone Does My Shirts* (I–A)

Curtis, Christopher Paul, *Bud, Not Buddy* (I)

DeFelice, Cynthia, *Nowhere to Call Home* (I–A)

Peterson, Jeanne Whitehouse, *Don't Forget Winona* (I)

Nonfiction

Coombs, Karen Mueller, *Children of the Dust Days* (I)

Wroble, Lisa, *Kids during the Great Depression* (I)

---

good place to begin. Many emphasize—some in small ways, others in larger—that in the midst of inhumanity there can be small acts of human kindness.

Despite their grimness, some books are affirmative: Young people work in underground movements, strive against terrible odds, plan escapes, and struggle for survival. Some books show heroic resistance, in which characters fight back or live with dignity and hope in the face of a monstrous future. Some teachers will agonize over the place of literature in teaching about the Holocaust. The following are valid questions for them to consider: Is mass murder a suitable subject for a children's or adolescent novel? What is the proper place for it in the school curriculum? What are the possible consequences of not informing young people about one of history's most bitter lessons?

Jane Yolen's *The Devil's Arithmetic* (A) is a graphic, moving account of being a Jew in Poland during the Nazi persecution. Using the fantasy device of a time slip, Yolen plunges her young protagonist into the life that her aunt and her aunt's best friend endured at the hands of the Nazis. A less graphic book appropriate for upper elementary school readers is Lois Lowry's Newbery Medal–winning *Number the Stars* (I). Lowry tells the story of how one Danish family saves the lives of their friends the Rosens. The young daughters of each family are best friends, and they are initially unaware of the danger in which they are living. The contrast between the implications of Nazi rule for the Jewish Ellen and the Danish Annemarie is striking.

Karen Hesse, intrigued by an article she read, began to research the Warsaw Ghetto and Jewish resistance in Poland and wrote *The Cats in Krasinski Square* (I), a picture book with a spare, poetic text and muted, lovely illustrations. The illustrations fill in details of time and place, and Hesse's words convey fear, determination, and the small joys of life in this small story of resistance.

Stories about life in Europe after the war explore how people began to mend their shattered lives. Mirjam Pressler's *Halinka* (A) explores the emotional damage of war through the eyes of a young girl sent to a home for troubled girls in Germany in the postwar years. This story, translated from the German, is truly a universal tribute to the power of love.

Despite the fact that American armed forces fought for four years in the Pacific, few children's and adolescent novels are set in this locale. Two especially outstanding novels, Yoko Kawashima Watkins's *So Far from the Bamboo Grove* and *My Brother, My Sister, and I* (both A), are set in North Korea and postwar Japan. The horror and hardships that Watkins and her family faced underscore the horror of war for those on both sides of the battle lines but also serve to illustrate the strength of love in adversity.

Another novel set in Korea under the control of the Japanese, Linda Sue Park's *When My Name Was Keoko* (A), chronicles the life of the children of a Korean scholar, revealing the small, quiet triumphs and the abiding fear of an oppressed people. Set within the larger historical context of the war, the struggles of Sun-hee, forced to take the Japanese

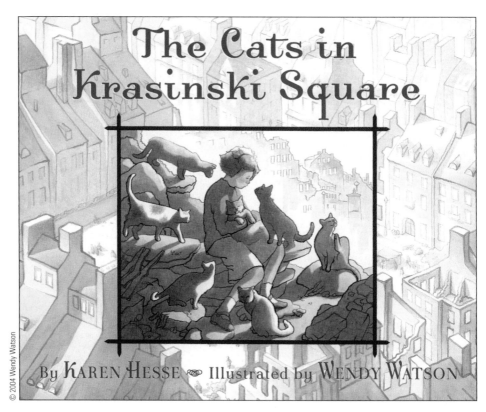

Karen Hesse's story of Jewish resistance in the Warsaw Ghetto is beautifully illustrated by Wendy Watson.

name of Keoko, and her brother Tae-yul, renamed Nobuo, are revealed in alternating first-person points of view. What is happening in Korea is mirrored in the family's life, and the hope at the end of the novel is only slightly dimmed by the communist threat in the north.

Stories Set in North America

Some stories that take place during World War II are set in North America. Many of these are about children who were evacuated from Europe. Others chronicle the shameful internment of Japanese Americans, and still others explore the lives of children whose fathers, uncles, and big brothers were fighting in the war abroad. Kit Pearson's *The Sky Is Falling* (I–A) tells the story of a brother and sister who are evacuated from England to Canada. They miss their family, and their adjustment is slow, but eventually they learn to live with their hearts in two worlds.

Some stories explore the ugly side of life in the United States during the war. Ken Mochizuki's *Baseball Saved Us* (I) describes how one Japanese American family was uprooted and transported to an internment camp in the middle of the desert. Even when the war was over, ugly feelings against Japanese Americans ran high, especially on the West Coast. Virginia Euwer Wolff's *Bat 6* (I–A), set in 1949 in a small Oregon town, explores how the wounds that were

opened by the war continued to fester long after the war's end, culminating in a terrible incident during a girls' community baseball game. There were strong feelings on the East Coast as well, with German Americans as the target. Janet Taylor Lisle's *The Art of Keeping Cool* (A), which takes place in a community located on the heavily fortified Rhode Island coast, explores the hatred in the community through the character of Abel Hoffman, a refugee artist. The story also depicts the havoc that hatred has wreaked in the life of one family.

• • THE 1950S THROUGH THE 1980S: POLITICAL AND SOCIAL TURMOIL

The end of World War II brought with it change in the social organization of the world and the lifestyles of many people. Peace was not long lasting; soon the world was disturbed by the Cold War and the Korean, Vietnam, and Cambodian conflicts, as well as by other, less publicized wars. In the United States, the civil rights movement forever altered the status quo, and the role of women in society also changed dramatically. Books set amid the issues and events of these decades are becoming more plentiful. David

Almond's *The Fire-Eaters* (I–A) captures the tension of the Cold War at a specific time—when Kennedy and Kruschev were arguing over Cuba and it seemed that nuclear war was inevitable. Set in rural England, this spellbinding novel brings this historical time to young readers who live with their own set of global tensions.

Ann Martin's *Here Today* (I–A) is set in the same time—the early 1960s—but in the United States. Ellie is struggling with adolescence; she is being bullied at school, her mother wants a more glamorous life than her family can provide, and then John Kennedy is assassinated. Ellie, desperate for things to settle down and be "normal," tries to keep her family together. Her slow realization that she won't be able to do so, but that nevertheless she will be fine, is very moving.

People like Mildred Taylor's Cassie Logan and her brothers were at the front of the line during the civil rights movement, and many authors now tell their stories. Christopher Paul Curtis's *The Watsons Go to Birmingham—1963* (I–A), a Newbery Honor book, explores the experiences and feelings of 10-year-old Kenny and his family as they drive from Flint, Michigan, to Birmingham, Alabama, to visit Grandma. Alternately funny and deadly serious, the novel captures the tenor and the tragedy of the times.

There are a number of novels that evoke the everyday life in small-town America in the middle of the 20th century. Bonnie Geisert's novel, *Prairie Summer* (I), illustrated by her husband, Arthur Geisert, depicts Rachel's summer between fourth and fifth grade on the family farm and her complex relationship with her father. Along the way, details of life on the farm and in their small town in South Dakota create a vivid setting.

Cynthia Kadohata's *Kira-Kira* (I–A) is set in the early 1960s and follows Katie and her family as they move from a Japanese community in Iowa to the Deep South of Georgia, where they encounter racism and unabashed curiosity. When Katie's beloved older sister, Lynn, dies, Katie helps her family realize that there is, indeed, hope in the future. As Lynn has taught her, the world is kira-kira, shining. Kadohata won a Newbery Medal for this moving depiction of one family's experience.

Kimberly Willis Holt's *When Zachary Beaver Came to Town* (A), winner of the National Book Award, is set in a sleepy Texas town during the Vietnam conflict. The historical details are rich, and the characters' lives reflect the times in which they live even as the novel focuses on life issues rather than historical ones. Ruth White does the same for life in rural North Carolina in the early 1970s in her novel *Buttermilk Hill* (I).

Historical fiction set during the conflict in Vietnam and the aftermath in Cambodia is becoming more plentiful. Like those about World War II, some of these books are set in the midst of the conflict and consider the lives of children in the war zones. Others are set in North America, Australia, or other countries and deal with such issues as children flee-

© 2004 Julia Kuskin

Katie Takeshima helps her family remember that there is always a shining hope in the world in **Kira-Kira.**

ing the war to find a new life; the experiences of children whose grandfathers, uncles, and fathers went to war; the impact of returning veterans on family life; and the deep divisions in America during the Vietnam conflict. Such books as Eve Bunting's *The Wall* (I) and Minfong Ho's *Rice without Rain, The Clay Marble,* and *Gathering the Dew* (all A) remind us of a war that divided America and shattered lives across the Far East. Walter Dean Myers explores issues of race as well as issues surrounding the Vietnam conflict in his powerful *Fallen Angels* (A). In *Letters from Wolfie* (A), Patti Sherlock effectively portrays the deep divisions in the United States during the Vietnam conflict. When Mark's older brother leaves for Vietnam, Mark becomes convinced that he should send his beloved dog, Wolfie, to the army to be used as a scout dog. Mark's reasons for doing so are as jumbled as his feelings in this emotionally wrenching story.

There is no time period that young readers cannot explore through historical fiction. These stories offer us a wonderful resource for helping children, and ourselves, discover our own connections with humanity throughout history, to makes sense of our present through our past, and to think about our future in new ways.

Historical Fiction in the Classroom

Reading historical fiction can help children realize that they are players on the historical stage and that their lives, too, will one day become part of history. As they read historical fiction, they come to realize the human drama inherent in history as well as the common themes that reach across time and cultures. Historical fiction offers students opportunities that history textbooks do not. Students who read trade books in addition to textbooks learn more than students who do not.

There are several ways to incorporate historical fiction into the curriculum. Middle school teachers can coordinate English language arts and social studies classes, assigning historical fiction that corresponds to the times and places focused on in the social studies curriculum. Elementary school teachers who have self-contained classes can easily link their students' reading material with the social studies topics they explore. Groups of children can read and discuss books set in a particular period of history, individual children can read independently from a collection of historical fiction, and the teacher can read aloud from a book that explores the time and place that the class is studying. In Chapter 14, we describe Book Club, an effective method for integrating the language arts and social studies curricula.

• • PRESENTING • • HISTORICAL ERAS THROUGH MULTIPLE GENRES

Historical fiction can also be linked to other genres: poetry, folklore, fantasy, realistic fiction, biography, and nonfiction can be combined with historical fiction in the study of a particular time and place. For example, teachers who want their students to come to know about life in medieval England might want to combine folklore, such as the legends that surround King Arthur, with fantasy, such as the novels of Jane Yolen and Kevin Crossley-Holland discussed in Chapter 6, and with historical fiction, such as *Crispin, Yoss, Catherine Called Birdy,* and *The Midwife's Apprentice.* Together, these books provide a series of reading experiences that leave young readers so steeped in the time and place that they understand how people lived and thought, and how that influenced subsequent generations.

The first time one fifth-grade teacher tried using historical fiction, poetry, biography, and nonfiction instead of the social studies text for the study of the American Revolution, she was unsure of the possible outcomes. She asked students to read one novel, some poetry, one biography, and one informational book on that historical period. In addition, they read an encyclopedia account of one of the events described in the novel. The students then critically examined the presentations in the various sources. The teacher modeled the process, and they worked in collaborative learning groups to discuss their findings. The class concluded that no single book could have given them the basis for understanding that they gained from their wide reading. Even more exciting, the children begged their teacher to use the same approach for the next social studies unit.

Another teacher worked with her third-grade children to develop a study plan for a unit on early settlers in America. She filled the room with many sources of information, including books, records, poetry, films, and pictures. The students spent several days exploring the material and making suggestions about topics that interested them. Their list included the Pilgrims, Plymouth Rock, the *Mayflower,* and the first Thanksgiving. The group organized the ideas into reasonably logical categories, and students chose topics they wanted to pursue, identified sources of information, and began the research for the study. Examining the past in this way helped students begin to understand human behavior, the ways that people and societies interact, the concept of humans as social beings, and the values that make people human.

When studying the same period of time with his eighth-grade students, another teacher successfully combined historical fiction set in colonial times with some of the excellent nonfiction available about those times, specifically the work of Marc Aronson, discussed in Chapter 10. This allowed his students to understand how the political systems and religious thought in England influenced the structures and thought of colonial America.

• • EXPLORING THEMES • • WITH HISTORICAL FICTION AND OTHER GENRES

Thematically organized instruction is yet another way to explore historical fiction. History is always repeating itself, and many stories set in the past explore issues that are important to people today. Understanding human nature and social patterns can result from thinking about themes found in historical fiction and linking them to books in other genres and to our own lives. People have common needs that must be met; these universal needs can be identified as themes that permeate social interactions. For example, the quest for freedom and respect, the struggle between good and evil or between love and hate, and the determination to seek a better life are themes that are as old as time and as current as today. Historical fiction contains the stories of many people caught up in such struggles. Reading a number of books that explore the same theme across different periods of history allows students to understand the similarities of human needs across time; looking at books that explore the same theme in different cultures allows students to understand the similarities of human needs across peoples.

Prejudice, for example, is an issue that permeates many of the books discussed in this chapter, many of the books of contemporary realism discussed in Chapter 7, and even some of the fantasy and science fiction novels discussed in Chapter 6. You will find issues of prejudice in the biographies of people who faced racism and sexism and in the nonfiction accounts of segregation, women in the workforce, and life for immigrants, to name but a few subjects. The cultural dislocation experienced by immigrants is both a timeless and a contemporary issue. The contemporary fiction presented in Chapter 7 can be combined with historical fiction about the immigrant experience to explore this theme. Teaching Idea 8.5 offers ideas for thematic study.

The possibilities for thematic combinations across genres as well as within the historical fiction genre are many, as are the times and places that young readers can explore. There are resources available to help teachers identify books to use. An annotated bibliography published yearly by the Children's Book Council and the National Council of the Social Studies, *Notable Children's Trade Books in the Field of Social Studies,* is one such resource. This is available from either organization and is also published in the April/May issue of the journal *Social Education.* Other resources, such as the National Council of Teachers of English publication *Adventuring with Books,* present books by theme. These and other resources mentioned in Chapter 1 and Appendix B will help you construct powerful reading experiences for your students.

Teaching Idea 8-5

Explore Themes in Historical Fiction

Grouping historical fiction by theme allows students to see how people from diverse times and places grapple with common issues. You can also work with contemporary fiction and fantasy that consider the same themes. Here we present titles that explore aspects of prejudice, but historical fiction can be organized around many themes and also linked with other genres.

Bunting, Eve, *Spying on Miss Muller* (A)

Byars, Betsy, *Keeper of the Doves* (I)

Curtis, Christopher Paul, *The Watsons Go to Birmingham—1963* (I–A)

Franklin, Kristine, *The Grape Thief* (A)

Hesse, Karen, *Witness* (A)

Mochizuki, Ken, *Heroes* (I)

Taylor, Mildred, *The Friendship* (A)

_____, *Mississippi Bridge* (A)

_____, *Roll of Thunder, Hear My Cry* (A)

Wolff, Virginia Euwer, *Bat 6* (I–A)

• • • Summary • • •

When teachers put wonderful stories set in the past into the hands of children, the past comes alive for their students. By reading historical fiction, students see that history was lived by people who, despite their different dress, customs, and habits, were a lot like we are. Whether they are confronting the plague in Europe during the Middle Ages, fleeing from soldiers in the American West, or watching a young father go to war, readers of today can vicariously experience the events of the past. When children are immersed in a compelling story, history comes to life. It is only then that it becomes real and important, that it becomes meaningful for young readers.

Read Avi's Newbery Medal acceptance speech in the July/August 2003 issue of *The Horn Book Magazine.* At the end of his speech he suggests that what he and other writers do is "create stories that will enable our young readers to find the stirrings of their souls." Do you think *Crispin* does this? Discuss *Crispin* and other books you have read that have made you think about yourself.

In our interview with Avi, we talk about the research he did to enable him to capture the world of medieval England. Listen to how Avi worked to re-create language patterns as well as details of time and place without having them intrude on his well-told story.

Prehistoric Times

Crowley, Marjorie, *Dar and the Spear Thrower* (I)
Dickinson, Peter, *Mana's Story* (I–A)
_____, *Noli's Story* (I–A)
_____, *Po's Story* (I–A)
_____, *Suth's Story* (I–A)
Steele, William, *The Magic Amulet* (I–A)
Sutcliff, Rosemary, *Warrior Scarlet* (A)

Ancient Times

Barrett, Tracy, *Anna of Byzantium* (A)
Behn, Harry, *The Far Distant Lurs* (I–A)
Carter, Dorothy, *His Majesty, Queen Hatshepsut* (I)
Fletcher, Susan, *Shadow Spinner* (A)
Haugaard, Erik Christian, *The Samurai's Tale* (A)
Lester, Julius, *Pharaoh's Daughter* (A)
Speare, Elizabeth George, *The Bronze Bow* (A)
Sutcliff, Rosemary, *The Eagle of the Ninth* (A)
_____, *The Lantern Bearers* (A)
_____, *The Shining Company* (A)

The Middle Ages

Avi, *Crispin: The Cross of Lead* (I–A)
Burkert, Nancy Ekholm, *Valentine and Orson* (A)
Cadnum, Michael, *The Book of the Lion* (A)
Cushman, Karen, *Catherine, Called Birdy* (A)
_____, *Matilda Bone* (A)
_____, *The Midwife's Apprentice* (I–A)
De Angeli, Marguerite, *The Door in the Wall* (I)
Gray, Elizabeth Vining, *Adam of the Road* (A)
Hirsch, Odo, *Yoss* (A)
Hoobler, Dorothy, and Thomas Hoobler, *The Demon in the Teahouse* (I)
Hunter, Mollie, *The King's Swift Rider* (A)
Jenks, Catherine, *Pagan in Exile* (A)
Kelly, Eric, *The Trumpeter of Krakow* (A)
McCaffrey, Anne, *Black Horses for the King* (A)
McCaughrean, Geraldine, *The Kite Rider* (A)
Morpurgo, Michael, *Sir Gawain and the Green Knight* (I–A)
Newth, Mette, *The Dark Light* (A)
_____, *The Transformation* (A)
Park, Linda Sue, *A Single Shard* (A)
Sauerwein, Leigh, *Song for Eloise* (A)
Springer, Nancy, *I Am Mordred* (A)
Temple, Frances, *The Beduin's Gazelle* (A)

_____, *The Ramsay Scallop* (A)
Walsh, Jill Paton, *The Emperor's Winding Sheet* (I–A)
Wein, Elizabeth, *A Coalition of Lions* (A)
_____, *The Sunbird* (A)
_____, *The Winter Prince* (A)
Yolen, Jane, and Robert Harris, *Girl in a Cage* (I–A)

The Renaissance and the Age of Exploration

Blackwood, Gary, *The Shakespeare Stealer* (I)
Cadnum, Michael, *Ship of Fire* (I–A)
Chibbaro, Julie, *Redemption* (A)
Conrad, Pam, *Pedro's Journal* (I)
Cooper, Susan, *King of Shadows* (I)
Dorris, Michael, *Morning Girl* (I)
Garden, Nancy, *Dove and Sword: A Novel of Joan of Arc* (I–A)
Konigsburg, E. L., *A Proud Taste for Scarlet and Miniver* (A)
Park, Linda Sue, *The Kite Fighters* (I)
Yolen, Jane, *Encounter* (I–A)
Yolen, Jane, and Robert Harris, *The Queen's Own Fool* (A)

Colonial through Post–Revolutionary War Times

Anderson, Laurie Halse, *Fever 1793* (I–A)
Avi, *Encounter at Easton* (I)
_____, *The Fighting Ground* (I)
_____, *Night Journeys* (I)
Bowen, Gary, *Stranded at Plimoth Plantation 1626* (I)
Bruchac, Joseph, *The Arrow over the Door* (I)
Carbone, Elisa, *Storm Warriors* (I)
Clifton, Lucille, *The Times They Used to Be* (I–A)
Collier, James Lincoln, and Christopher Collier, *My Brother Sam Is Dead* (A)
_____, *War Comes to Willie Freeman* (I)
Dorris, Michael, *Guests* (I)
_____, *Sees Behind Trees* (I)
Fleischman, Paul, *Saturnalia* (A)
Forbes, Esther, *Johnny Tremain* (A)
Fritz, Jean, *Early Thunder* (A)
Jacques, Brian, *The Angel's Command* (I)
Krensky, Stephen, *The Printer's Apprentice* (I)
Lasky, Kathryn, *Beyond the Burning Time* (A)
Levitin, Sonia, *Roanoke: A Novel of the Lost Colony* (I–A)
Lunn, Janet, *The Hollow Tree* (A)
Martin, Jacqueline Briggs, *Grandmother Bryant's Pocket* (P)
Meyer, L. A., *Bloody Jack* (I–A)
_____, *Curse of the Blue Tattoo* (I–A)
Monjo, F. N., *The House on Stink Alley* (I)

Petry, Ann, *Tituba of Salem Village* (I)

Rinaldi, Ann, *A Break with Charity: A Story about the Salem Witch Trials* (A)

Rockwood, Joyce, *To Spoil the Sun* (I–A)

Speare, Elizabeth George, *The Sign of the Beaver* (I–A)

_____, *The Witch of Blackbird Pond* (I–A)

Updale, Eleanor, *Montmorency: Thief, Liar, Gentleman?* (I–A)

Yolen, Jane, and Robert Harris, *Prince across the Water* (I–A)

Slavery, the Civil War, and Its Aftermath

Alcott, Louisa May, *Little Women* (A)

Armstrong, Jennifer, *The Dreams of Mairhe Mehan* (I–A)

_____, *Mairhe Mehan, Awake* (I–A)

_____, *Steal Away* (A)

Beatty, Patricia, *Charlie Skedaddle* (A)

_____, *Jayhawker* (A)

_____, *Turn Homeward, Hannalee* (A)

_____, *Who Comes with Cannons?* (A)

Blos, Joan, *A Gathering of Days: A New England Girl's Journal, 1830–32* (A)

Climo, Shirley, *A Month of Seven Days* (A)

Collier, James Lincoln, and Christopher Collier, *With Every Drop of Blood* (A)

Cox, Clinton, *Undying Glory* (I–A)

Elliott, L. M., *Annie between the States* (I–A)

Fleischman, Paul, *Bull Run* (I–A)

Fox, Paula, *The Slave Dancer* (A)

Fritz, Jean, *Brady* (I–A)

Gaeddert, Louann, *Breaking Free* (I–A)

Gauch, Patricia Lee, *Thunder at Gettysburg* (I)

Hahn, Mary Downing, *Hear the Wind Blow: A Novel of the Civil War* (A)

Hansen, Joyce, *The Heart Calls Home* (A)

_____, *Out from this Place* (A)

_____, *Which Way Freedom?* (A)

Hesse, Karen, *A Light in the Storm: The Civil War Diary of Amelia Martin* (I)

Hopkinson, Deborah, *Sweet Clara and the Freedom Quilt* (P)

Houston, Gloria, *Bright Freedom's Song* (I–A)

Hunt, Irene, *Across Five Aprils* (A)

Hurmence, Belinda, *Tancy* (I–A)

Johnson, Dolores, *Now Let Me Fly: The Story of a Slave Family* (I)

Johnston, Tony, *The Wagon* (I)

Keith, Harold, *Rifles for Watie* (A)

Lester, Julius, *Day of Tears* (I–A)

_____, *Long Journey Home* (A)

Lyons, Mary E., *Letters from a Slave Girl: The Story of Harriet Jacobs* (A)

Monjo, F. N., *The Drinking Gourd* (P–I)

Paulsen, Gary, *Soldier's Heart* (A)

Peck, Richard, *The River between Us* (A)

Polacco, Patricia, *Pink and Say* (I–A)

Reeder, Carolyn, *Shades of Gray* (A)

Ruby, Lois, *Soon to Be Free*

_____, *Steal Away Home* (A)

Siegelson, Kim, *Trembling Earth* (I–A)

Taylor, Mildred, *The Land* (A)

Turner, Ann, *Nettie's Trip South* (I–A)

Winter, Jeanette, *Follow the Drinking Gourd* (P–I)

Westward Migration

Ambrose, Stephen, *This Vast Land* (A)

Armstrong, Jennifer, *Black-Eyed Susan* (I)

Arrington, Francis, *Bluestem* (I)

_____, *Prairie Whispers* (I)

Avi, *The Barn* (I–A)

Beatty, Patricia, *Wait for Me, Watch for Me, Eula Bea* (A)

Brink, Carol Ryrie, *Caddie Woodlawn* (I–A)

Burks, Brian, *Runs with Horses* (A)

Cadnum, Michael, *Blood Gold* (I–A)

Coerr, Eleanor, *Buffalo Bill and the Pony Express* (P)

_____, *The Josephina Story Quilt* (P)

Conrad, Pam, *Prairie Songs* (A)

Cushman, Karen, *The Ballad of Lucy Whipple* (A)

_____, *Rodzina* (I)

Ellsworth, Loretta, *The Shrouding Woman* (I)

Erdrich, Louise, *The Birchbark House* (I)

_____, *The Game of Silence* (I)

Figley, Marty Rhodes, *The Schoolchildren's Blizzard* (P)

Fritz, Jean, *The Cabin Faced West* (I)

Goble, Paul, *Death of the Iron Horse* (I)

Gray, Dianne, *Holding Up the Earth* (A)

_____, *Together Apart* (A)

Harvey, Brett, *Cassie's Journey: Going West in the 1860s* (P–I)

_____, *My Prairie Christmas* (P–I)

_____, *My Prairie Year: Based on the Diary of Elenore Plaisted* (P–I)

Howard, Ellen, *The Chickenhouse House* (P–I)

_____, *Edith Herself* (P–I)

_____, *Sister* (P–I)

Irwin, Hadley, *Jim-Dandy* (I–A)

Johnston, Tony, *The Quilt Story* (P)

LaFaye, Alexandra, *Worth* (I–A)

MacLachlan, Patricia, *Caleb's Story* (P–I)

_____, *More Perfect Than the Moon* (P–I)

_____, *Sarah, Plain and Tall* (P–I)

_____, *Skylark* (P–I)

_____, *Three Names* (P)

McCaughrean, Geraldine, *Stop the Train!* (I)

McMullan, Kate, *My Travels with Capts. Lewis and Clark by George Shannon* (I–A)

Meyer, Carolyn, *Where the Broken Heart Still Beats* (A)

Myers, Walter Dean, *The Righteous Revenge of Artemis Bonner* (I–A)

O'Dell, Scott, *Sing Down the Moon* (A)

_____, *Thunder Rolling in the Mountains* (A)

Oswald, Nancy, *Nothing Here But Stones* (I)
Paulsen, Gary, *Call Me Francis Tucket* (I)
Turner, Ann, *Dakota Dugout* (P–I)
_____, *Grasshopper Summer* (I–A)
Van Leeuwen, Jean, *Bound for Oregon* (I–A)
_____, *Going West* (P)
Warner, Sally, *Finding Hattie* (I)
Whelan, Gloria, *Next Spring an Oriole* (I)
_____, *Night of the Full Moon* (I)
Wilder, Laura Ingalls, **Little House** series (I)
Wolf, Allan, *New Found Land: Lewis and Clark's Voyage
    of Discovery* (A)
Yep, Laurence, *The Traitor: 1885* (I–A)

The New Century

Blos, Joan, *Brooklyn Doesn't Rhyme* (I)
Boling, Katharine, *January 1905* (I–A)
Byars, Betsy, *Keeper of the Doves* (I)
Cameron, Eleanor, *Julia and the Hand of God* (I)
_____, *Julia's Magic* (I)
_____, *The Private Worlds of Julia Redfern* (I)
_____, *A Room Made of Windows* (I)
_____, *That Julia Redfern* (I)
Crew, Linda, *Brides of Eden: A True Story Imagined* (A)
DeFelice, Cynthia, *Lostman's River* (A)
Donnelly, Jennifer, *A Northern Light* (A)
Fleischman, Paul, *The Borning Room* (A)
Giff, Patricia Reilly, *A House of Tailors* (I–A)
_____, *Maggie's Door* (I–A)
_____, *Nory Ryan's Song* (I–A)
Hahn, Mary Downing, *Anna on the Farm* (I)
Hall, Donald, *Lucy's Christmas* (P)
_____, *Lucy's Summer* (P)
Howard, Elizabeth Fitzgerald, *Aunt Flossie's Hats
    (and Crab Cakes Later)* (P)
_____, *Chita's Christmas* (P)
_____, *Papa Tells Chita a Story* (P)
Ibbotson, Eva, *The Star of Kazan* (I)
Jocelyn, Marthe, *Mable Riley: A Reliable Record
    of Humdrum, Peril, and Romance* (I)
Levinson, Riki, *I Go with My Family to Grandma's* (P)
_____, *Watch the Stars Come Out* (P)
Levitin, Sonia, *Journey to America* (I)
_____, *Silver Days* (I)
Lovelace, Maud Hart, *Betsy-Tacy* (I)
_____, *Betsy-Tacy and Tib* (I)
Lowry, Lois, *The Silent Boy* (I–A)
Martin, Jacqueline Briggs, *The Camp, the Ice, and the Boat
    Called Fish* (I)
_____, *On Sand Island* (P)
Mayerson, Evelyn, *The Cat Who Escaped from Steerage* (I)
McDonald, Megan, *The Potato Man* (P–I)

McKissack, Patricia, *Mirandy and Brother Wind* (P)
Moeri, Louise, *The Devil in Ol' Rosie* (I)
Nagell, Judy, *One Way to Ansonia* (A)
Oneal, Zibby, *A Long Way to Go* (A)
Paterson, Katherine, *Lyddie* (A)
Peck, Richard, *The Teacher's Funeral: A Comedy
    in Three Parts* (I–A)
Sandin, Joan, *The Long Way to a New Land* (P)
_____, *The Long Way Westward* (P)
Schmidt, Gary, *Lizzie Bright and the Buckminster Boy* (I–A)
Skurzynski, Gloria, *The Tempering* (A)
Taylor, Mildred, *The Well: David's Story* (A)

World War I and Its Aftermath

Doyle, Brian, *Mary Ann Alice* (I–A)
Franklin, Kristine, *The Grape Thief* (A)
Harlow, Joan Hiatt, *Thunder from the Sea* (I)
Houston, Gloria, *The Year of the Perfect Christmas
    Tree* (P–I)
Kinsey-Warnock, Natalie, *The Night the Bells Rang* (I)
Lawrence, Iain, *Lord of the Nutcracker Men* (I–A)
Morpurgo, Michael, *Private Peaceful* (A)
Rostkowski, Margaret, *After the Dancing Days* (A)
Smith, Barry, *Minnie and Ginger* (P)
Whelan, Gloria, *The Impossible Journey* (I)
Wulffson, Don, *Soldier X* (A)

The Great Depression

Avi, *Smugglers' Island* (I)
Bryant, Jen, *The Trial* (I)
Disher, Garry, *The Bamboo Flute* (I–A)
Durbin, William, *The Darkest Evening* (A)
French, Jackie, *Somewhere around the Corner* (A)
Griffin, Adele, *Hannah, Divided* (I)
Hale, Marian, *The Truth about Sparrows* (I–A)
Hesse, Karen, *Out of the Dust* (A)
Houston, Gloria, *Littlejim* (I–A)
Levinson, Riki, *Boys Here—Girls There* (I)
Mitchell, Margaree King, *Uncle Jed's Barbershop* (P–I)
Parkinson, Siobhan, *Kathleen: The Celtic Knot* (I)
Peterson, Jeanne Whitehouse, *Don't Forget Winona* (I)
Reeder, Carolyn, *Grandpa's Mountain* (I–A)
_____, *Moonshiner's Son* (A)
Taylor, Mildred, *Let the Circle Be Unbroken* (A)
_____, *Mississippi Bridge* (A)
_____, *The Road to Memphis* (A)
_____, *Roll of Thunder, Hear My Cry* (A)
_____, *Song of the Trees* (I)
Turner, Ann, *Dust for Dinner* (P)
Wells, Rosemary, *Wingwalker* (I)

World War II and Its Aftermath

Ackerman, Karen, *When Mama Retires* (P)

Avi, *Who Was That Masked Man, Anyway?* (A)

Bunting, Eve, *Spying on Miss Muller* (A)

Chotjewitz, David, *Daniel Half Human and the Good Nazi* (A)

Cormier, Robert, *Other Bells for Us to Ring* (I–A)

Degens, T., *On the Third Ward* (A)

_____, *Transport 451-R* (A)

Doyle, Brian, *Boy O'Boy* (I–A)

Gallico, Paul, *The Snow Goose* (A)

Hautzig, Esther, *The Endless Steppe* (A)

Holt, Kimberly Willis, *My Louisiana Ski* (I)

Houston, Gloria, *But No Candy* (P)

Innocenti, Robert, *Rose Blanche* (I–A)

Janeczko, Paul, *Worlds Afire* (A)

Johnston, Julie, *Hero of Lesser Causes* (I–A)

Kerr, Judith, *When Hitler Stole Pink Rabbit* (I–A)

Kositsky, Lynne, *The Thought of High Windows* (I–A)

Laird, Christa, *But Can the Phoenix Sing?* (A)

_____, *Shadow of the Wall* (A)

Lawrence, Iain, *B for Buster* (A)

Levitin, Sonia, *Room in the Heart* (A)

Lingard, Joan, *Between Two Worlds* (A)

_____, *Tug of War* (A)

Lowry, Lois, *Number the Stars* (I)

Magorian, Michelle, *Back Home* (A)

_____, *Good Night, Mr. Tom* (A)

Matas, Carol, *After the War* (A)

_____, *Daniel's Story* (A)

Mazer, Harry, *A Boy at War: A Novel of Pearl Harbor* (A)

Mochizuki, Ken, *Baseball Saved Us* (I)

Morpurgo, Michael, *Waiting for Anya* (A)

Mosher, Richard, *Zazoo* (A)

Oppenheim, Sulamith Levey, *The Lily Cupboard* (P)

Orlev, Uri, *The Island on Bird Street* (A)

_____, *The Lady with the Hat* (A)

_____, *Lydia, Queen of Palestine* (A)

_____, *The Man from the Other Side* (A)

Park, Linda Sue, *When My Name Was Keoko* (A)

Pearson, Kit, *The Lights Go On Again* (I–A)

_____, *Looking at the Moon* (I–A)

_____, *The Sky Is Falling* (I–A)

Pressler, Mirjam, *Halinka* (A)

_____, *Malka* (A)

Recorvitz, Helen, *Where Heroes Hide* (I)

Reiss, Johanna, *The Upstairs Room* (A)

Rylant, Cynthia, *I Had Seen Castles* (A)

Schmidt, Gary, *Mara's Stories: Glimmers in the Darkness* (I–A)

Spinelli, Jerry, *Milkweed* (A)

Stevenson, James, *Don't You Know There's a War On?* (P)

Thesman, Jean, *Molly Donnelly* (A)

Uchida, Yoshiko, *The Invisible Thread* (A)

_____, *Journey Home* (A)

_____, *Journey to Topaz* (A)

Vos, Ida, *Anna Is Still Here* (I–A)

_____, *Dancing on the Bridge of Avignon* (A)

_____, *Hide and Seek* (I–A)

Watkins, Yoko Kawashima, *My Brother, My Sister, and I* (A)

_____, *So Far from the Bamboo Grove* (A)

Westall, Robert, *The Kingdom by the Sea* (A)

Yolen, Jane, *All Those Secrets of the World* (P–I)

_____, *The Devil's Arithmetic* (A)

The 1950s through the 1980s: Political and Social Turmoil

Almond, David, *The Fire-Eaters* (A)

Baille, Allan, *Little Brother* (A)

Bunting, Eve, *The Wall* (I)

Crowe, Chris, *Mississippi Trial, 1955* (A)

Curtis, Christopher Paul, *The Watsons Go to Birmingham— 1963* (I–A)

Dahlberg, Maurine, *Escape to West Berlin* (I–A)

Geisert, Bonnie, *Prairie Summer* (I)

Harrington, Janice, *Going North* (I)

Ho, Minfong, *The Clay Marble* (A)

_____, *Gathering the Dew* (A)

_____, *Rice without Rain* (A)

Lyon, George Ella, *Sonny's House of Spies* (I)

Martin, Ann, *A Corner of the Universe* (I)

_____, *Here Today* (I)

McCord, Patricia, *Pictures in the Dark* (I–A)

McKissack, Patricia, *Tippy Lemming* (P)

Mochizuki, Ken, *Baseball Saved Us* (I)

_____, *Heroes* (I)

Myers, Walter Dean, *Fallen Angels* (A)

Nelson, Theresa, *And One for All* (A)

Nelson, Vaunda Micheaux, *Mayfield Crossing* (A)

Oughton, Jerrie, *Music from a Place Called Half Moon* (I–A)

Paek, Min, *Aekyung's Dream* (P)

Paterson, Katherine, *Park's Quest* (A)

Paulsen, Gary, *Harris and Me* (A)

Rostkowski, Margaret, *The Best of Friends* (A)

Sherlock, Patti, *Letters from Wolfie* (A)

Smothers, Ethel Footman, *Moriah's Pond* (I–A)

Thesman, Jean, *Rachel Chance* (A)

White, Ruth, *Buttermilk Hill* (I)

_____, *Tadpole* (I)

Wiles, Deborah, *Freedom Summer* (I)

Biography

But even if drastic social conditions produced a new leader like Hitler, there's no reason the world should extend the same leeway to him that it did toward his predecessor. With the hindsight of history, it's clear that the Führer's rise to power could have been stopped, or at least braked, at many places along the way. If the moderate political parties in Germany had put aside their differences and joined forces against him, he might have been defeated at the polls in the crucial elections of the early 1930s. Later, if France and Britain had taken a strong stand, he might not have dared to reoccupy the Rhineland, or invade Austria and Czechoslovakia, or launch a Blitzkreig attack on Poland.

Above all, if more of Germany's Jews—not to mention the religious and political leaders of other countries—had taken seriously what Hitler wrote in Mein Kampf when it first appeared, the worst effects of the Holocaust might have been lessened if not averted entirely. So many ifs. The trick will be to apply them before rather than after the fact, should another Hitler come to power in a time of crisis.

At the end of the political testament he dictated in the last days of his life, Adolf Hitler refused to accept the reality of Germany's defeat. Instead, he said the six-year war the country had waged would one day be recognized as "the most glorious and valiant manifestation of a nation's will to existence." Going further, he predicted that National Socialism would rise again, and that the sacrifices he and his

> *soldiers had made in the struggle against "international Jewry" would be vindicated at last.*
>
> *The challenge to the world's peoples couldn't be clearer. Now and in the future, every possible step must be taken to ensure that the Führer's final predictions never come true.*
>
> —JAMES CROSS GIBLIN, *The Life and Death of Adolf Hitler*, pp. 222–223

WHEN SUSAN DECIDED TO READ GIBLIN'S SIEBERT AWARD–WINNING biography of Hitler with her eighth-grade class, she sent a letter home to the parents of her students, explaining why they would be spending time learning and talking about the life of a man whom most people consider evil. In that letter she talked about how a study of Hitler's life related to the history that students were learning in social studies, and also about how she had developed a thematic organization for the semester that centered around tolerance. She didn't know a more powerful example of what happens when people act on their prejudice than the Holocaust, she told them, and she wanted to read this biography to spark conversations about the consequences of acts of bigotry against others. She wanted her students to link what happened in Germany to the experiences of Native Americans and African Americans, almost all immigrant groups that came to the United States, and to religious, racial, and social intolerance today. Her letter was so persuasive that all parents gave permission, and her students embarked on a study of power gone terribly wrong.

As they discussed the information that Giblin presents, the students came to realize that Hitler was not born a monster, but that his attitudes and experiences, as well as the times in which he lived, made him into one. Perhaps more than anything else, this shook their confidence as they realized that human beings are capable of evil on both a small and a grand scale.

Defining Biography

Biography, autobiography, and memoir all tell the story of the life or a portion of the life of a real person. Biographies and autobiographies can be either mostly fictional or authentic—they straddle the boundary between fiction and nonfiction. Memoirs are based on events in the life of the author, but are interpretive accounts in which events are selected, arranged, and constructed in order to bring out a particular theme or personality trait. Biographies may be episodic; that is, the author highlights a particular part of a life to illustrate the subject's character or an important event in the life of the subject. In episodic biographies, writers can present a number of details within a manageable length, providing young readers the details they relish without sacrificing authenticity. Robert Burleigh's *Langston's Train Ride* (1) is an excellent example of this type of biography. It focuses on one event in the life of Langston Hughes, the train trip when he wrote his poem "The Negro Speaks of Rivers" and realized that he was a poet. Through the device of Langston's reflection about his life as he traveled, Burleigh is able to present other facts about him as well.

Other biographies are complete, spanning the entire life of a subject. Some, for primary- and intermediate-grade readers, are simplified, presenting what is in effect an outline of the subject's life. David Adler's many biographies for primary-grade readers, such as *A Picture Book of Benjamin Franklin* (P), are examples of simplified biography; they contain few details and are most useful as an introduction to important people in history, although some argue that their very simplification amounts to distortion. On the other hand, Jeanette Winter's small biography *Beatrix: Various Episodes from the Life of Beatrix Potter* (P) is simple, yet full of details of the life and thoughts of this special writer. Winter uses Potter's own words in her letters and journals to portray her subject. Even simplified biographies can rely on fact and present original source material.

Today, most biographies for young readers are authentic biographies, well-documented stories about individuals in which even the dialogue is based on some record of what was actually said or written by particular people at particular times. Russell Freedman is an accomplished biographer, and his work, such as Newbery Medal–winning *Lincoln: A Photobiography* and Siebert Award–winning *The Voice That Challenged a Nation: Marian Anderson and the Struggle for Equal Rights* (both I–A), is filled with archival photographs, documented through multiple sources, and written with passion and verve.

Some very engaging biographies are biographical fiction, consisting almost entirely of imagined conversations and reconstructed events in the life of an individual. Francesco D'Adamo's *Iqbal* (I–A) is a fictionalized account of the life of an actual person, 13-year-old Iqbal, who worked to change the conditions of the child laborers who create Pakistani rugs. Joseph Bruchac's *Pocahontas* (I–A), told in alternating chapters by Pocahontas and John Smith, is another intriguing work of biographical fiction. Both books are classified as fiction, but they are based in part on factual evidence about a real person's life.

Memoirs are an increasingly popular form of writing in which an individual explores his or her own life; they are truthful, without necessarily being completely true. Francisco Jiménez's memoirs, *The Circuit* and *Breaking Through* (I–A), are stories about his life as a migrant child. They are classified as fiction. In contrast, Chris Crutcher's *King of the Mild Frontier: An Ill-Advised Autobiography* (A) is classified as nonfiction, yet both are stories about their lives as recalled by the authors. The line is a fine one, and is made even more complicated by such books as Milton Meltzer's *Lincoln: In His Own Words* and *Frederick Douglass: In His Own Words* (A), in which the author uses selections from the speeches and writings of his subjects, connected by his own commentary, to create a form very much like a memoir.

Biographies also vary according to presentation. Some biographies focus on a single individual, whereas others are collective biographies, or biographies about several individuals. These usually focus around a theme or other unifying principle. Catherine Thimmesh has gathered brief biographical sketches of women in politics in *Madam President: The Extraordinary, True (and Evolving) Story of Women in Politics* (I) and arranged them so that young readers can learn about some important women and their accomplishments while also understanding the realities and possibilities of today. Joyce Hansen creates a rich portrait of 13 strong African American women who might inspire others to follow their visions in *Women of Hope: African Americans Who Made a Difference* (I–A). Sometimes the titles clearly indicate the purpose of a collective biography, as in Phillip Hoose's *It's Our World, Too! Young People Who Are Making a Difference (How They Do It—How You Can, Too!)* (I–A).

We find all kinds of biographies—authentic, fictionalized, or memoir; individual or collective; episodic, simplified, or complete—in picture books as well. Picture-book biographies present a subject through both text and art. Malcah Zeldis's folk art paintings brilliantly depict the important moments of King's life in Rosemary Bray's *Martin Luther King* (P–I) and evoke the spirit of the times and of the man himself.

Any good biography illuminates the interaction between an individual and historical events, demonstrating how a person's time and culture influence his or her life even as that person influences his or her time and culture. Vivid

© 2003 Jeanette Winter

Jeanette Winter's small biography of this beloved writer presents Potter's life through her own words.

and accurate portrayals of the *people* of history make history come alive for young readers.

Biography in Children's Lives

Biography was once regarded as an opportunity for young people to read about people they might emulate. For example, they might strive to be as honest as Abraham Lincoln or as brave as Lewis and Clark. Biographers in the 19th and early 20th centuries wrote only about the good qualities of their subjects. During this period of intense nationalism, these writers deified America's heroes in a self-conscious effort to provide children with a set of role models. Fortunately, contemporary biographers are more likely to consider their subjects in a less adulatory and more realistic manner. We now view biography not as an opportunity for moral enlightenment but as a chance for children to learn about themselves as they learn about the lives and times of people who made or are making a significant impact on the world (Herman, 1978). With this altered view of the role of biography have come books that focus on people who are not heroes. Today there are biographies of contemporary people living out their lives, such as Trish Marx's *One Boy from Kosovo* (I), in which she details pivotal events in the life of a refugee. There are also biographies of villains, such as James Cross Giblin's *The Life and Death of Adolf Hitler* (A). Biographies of all kinds of people allow young readers to understand both history and the contemporary world.

Biography can help children develop their concepts of historical time; they can discover ideas and empathize with historical characters. Children who read biographies learn that all people have the same basic needs and desires. They begin to see their lives in relation to those of the past, learn a vast amount of social detail about the past, and consider the human problems and relationships of the present in the light of those in the past.

Milton Meltzer hopes that reading well-written biographies will help children learn that they, like the subjects of the biographies, can make a difference in their own lives and in the lives of others:

> I want to give young readers vision, hope, energy. I try to do it honestly, without concealing the weaknesses, the false starts, the wrong turns of my heroes and heroines. Even those who try their best not to engage in selfish attempts to outsmart their fellows can make tragic mistakes. Still, I write about them because they share a deep respect for the rights, the dignity, the value of every human being. (1989, p. 157)

Good biographies can enrich young readers' understanding of their history and potential.

Criteria for Evaluating Biographies

Biographies are stories of people's lives and, like all narratives, are evaluated in terms of the characterization, the presentation of plot and setting, the style of the writing, the unifying theme, and, in the case of picture books or illustrated books, the quality and contribution of the illustrations. As biographies, they are also subject to special considerations. Biographies need to be portraits of real people, complete with both strengths and weaknesses. They must present accurate depictions of the time and place in which the subject lived. Even biographical fiction should be grounded in source material and should present authentic information about a person's life and times in an engaging style. Figure 9.1 presents a brief list of criteria for evaluating biographies.

Figure 9-1

Checklist for Evaluating Biography

Accuracy and Social Details
- The story is grounded in source material, or there is enough truthful information to make it worth reading.
- The facts and story line are integrated.
- The social details are vivid, accurate, and linked to the individual's accomplishments.

Portrayal of the Subject
- The subject's character is well developed and multidimensional.
- The author avoids stereotypes.

Style
- The writing style is comprehensible and engaging.
- Complex topics are explained adequately.

Theme
- There is a unifying theme.
- The theme highlights the special qualities of the subject.

Illustrations
- The illustrations help the reader visualize the time and place.
- The illustrations illuminate the character of the subject.

• • ACCURACY • •

Although not all biographers for children rely solely on primary sources, good biographies are always grounded in fact. Biographies need to present both a vivid and an accurate picture of the life and the times of the subject. As is true of historical fiction, accuracy is a complex criterion. Careful biographers do not go beyond the facts as we know them today, but they do interpret these facts through the eyes of the present. Consider, for example, the d'Aulaires' biography *Columbus* (P–I), written in 1955, which refers to Native Americans as savages; the biographers seemingly saw no need to consider the humanity of the native people when assessing Columbus's life. Likewise, early biographies of Rosa Parks present her as a woman who sat down in the front of the bus because she was tired. Later biographies, such as *Rosa Parks: My Story* (I), were influenced by society's acknowledgment of the careful organization of the civil rights movement, and present her action as the planned, deliberate attempt to confront unjust practices and laws that it was.

Authentic biographies are anchored by primary sources: letters, diaries, collected papers, and photographs. They usually contain lists of sources the author consulted and address the author's process. Biographical fiction goes well beyond what is known about a subject; it would be a mistake to think of it as a factual resource. Memoirs, too, are not meant to be a source of facts, but rather an evocation of a subject's life, in the subject's own words. Both biographical fiction and memoir, however, should be truthful.

Russell Freedman's *Lincoln: A Photobiography* (I–A) exemplifies what an authentic biography should be. Freedman is always careful to distinguish fact from opinion and truth from legend. He presents a significant amount of interesting historical detail. His text includes many direct quotations from Lincoln, all set off with quotation marks. These quotations, the historical facts, and social details are all taken from sources listed at the end of the book. Freedman follows the text with a sampling of Lincoln's famous quotations, with sources indicated, along with the sources for the quotations that begin each chapter. After these are a list and description of historic sites having to do with Lincoln's life, a description of source books about Lincoln, acknowledgments, and a useful five-page index. This end material and the photographs of historical documents that appear throughout the text all attest to the integrity and thoroughness of this biography.

In an interesting departure from the norm, Candace Fleming uses archival material not only to support but actually to format her book *Ben Franklin's Almanac: Being a True Account of the Good Gentleman's Life* (I–A). Fleming patterns her book on Franklin's own *Poor Richard's Almanack,* organizing her information around the major interests in Franklin's life—science, public service, family, time in France—and including reproductions of etchings, paintings, and cartoons of the time along with Franklin's own words. The originality in the design of the book is matched by the authenticity of its content.

Judging the accuracy of a biographer's presentation is not easy unless one happens to be an expert on the subject. When evaluating a biography, ask these questions: What sources did the author use? Are these sources documented? Does the account of the subject's life seem truthful according to what you already know? Are unnecessary generalizations about the people of the time or stereotypes of gender, ethnic, or racial groups evident?

• • SOCIAL DETAILS: • •
SETTING AND PLOT

A subject's personality and accomplishments are more understandable when they are presented against a rich and vivid depiction of the social details of life. Children often read for these social details, relishing the minutiae of another person's life. Careful biographers find a balance between telling everything and telling just enough to portray a person's life accurately. Many subjects of biographies for children had lives that were touched with pain, suffering, and great hardship; many great achievements were won at great cost. These issues must be carefully presented in biographies for children. For example, the times that shaped Dr. Martin Luther King were not happy times; he grew up in a country deeply divided by racism. In any biography of King written for young readers, the social climate needs to be honestly portrayed in a way that is understandable to children without being overwhelming. Balancing the needs of the audience and the accuracy of the story is especially difficult when writing for primary-grade readers. Rosemary Bray's *Martin Luther King* is an outstanding example of the achievement of this balance, in part because of the strength of the illustrations. So too are Doreen Rappaport's *Martin's Big Words: The Life of Dr. Martin Luther King* (P), with illustrations by Bryan Collier, and *My Brother Martin* (P–I), written by King's sister Christine King Farris.

Look for settings that are clearly and accurately depicted, full of interesting social details, and linked to the development of the subject's character and accomplishments.

The particular events that shape a subject's life form the basis of a biographical plot. Some biographies are chronological and present the subject's entire lifetime, but having to plod through tedious detail about everything that hap-

By selecting key events in a subject's life and presenting them vividly, biographers illuminate their subject and keep a reader's interest. Look for plots that blend factual background with a good story.

*Malcah Zeldis's folk art paintings vibrantly depict the important moments of King's life in Rosemary Bray's **Martin Luther King.***

• • P O R T R A Y A L   O F • •
T H E   S U B J E C T

Biographers must consider their subjects as individuals rather than as paragons, and individuals are multidimensional. The strengths *and* weaknesses of individuals are presented in excellent biographies, such as ***This Land Was Made for You and Me: The Life and Songs of Woody Guthrie*** (A), by Elizabeth Partridge. Guthrie's failings as well as his strengths and the harsh times in which he created his songs are vividly portrayed. Good biographies also avoid implying that the greatness of the subject was implicit from birth. They avoid weaving background knowledge or prescient knowledge of latent talents into unlikely conversations (Herman, 1978). Exaggerating the good qualities of a subject results in *hagiography*—the telling of the life of a saint—or the creation of a legend. Biographies are about real people, not legendary figures.

The biographer's point of view and interest in the subject should be apparent, as should the biographer's purpose. The same subject may be treated differently by different biographers. Teaching Idea 9.1 explores this idea. When selecting biographies, look for subjects that are well developed and multidimensional, brought to life through the presentation of vivid details.

• • S T Y L E • •

Authors make choices about what they say and how they say it. Even when a story is well grounded in verifiable fact, as in authentic biography, it still represents an author's choice of facts and can still be told in an engaging fashion. Good biographies incorporate the language and customs of the times. The dialogue should reflect how the subject is likely to have talked, with enough authenticity that readers get a true picture but are not overwhelmed by archaic or idiosyncratic speech patterns. For example, Joseph Bruchac's biography of Sitting Bull, *A Boy Called Slow: The True Story of Sitting Bull* (I), is told in the cadence of the storyteller and includes some Lakota words. Robert Burleigh captures Langston Hughes's voice by quoting from his poetry in *Langston's Train Ride* (I), and Deborah Kogan Ray uses William Bartram's journals in *The Flower Hunter* (P–I). Look for language that rings true to the characters but is not overwhelmingly archaic or full of dialect.

pened in a subject's life makes a book unwieldy. At the same time, however, oversimplification often results in an incomplete picture of both the individual and the times (Saul, 1986). Biographers have an array of facts available to them; how they select from those facts and craft an engaging story is up to them. Certainly whatever events are presented as facts should be accurate. Good authors document their facts and also differentiate between fact and opinion, or fact and legend. Diane Stanley and Peter Vennema do an excellent job of this in their biography *Bard of Avon: The Story of William Shakespeare* (I). In a foreword, they alert their readers to the problems of fact they encountered; not much is known about the details of Shakespeare's early life. In their text, they make careful use of qualifying words and phrases, such as *if so* and *perhaps,* to alert readers to theory, opinion, and educated guesses.

In *The Flower Hunter: William Bartram, America's First Naturalist* (P–I), Deborah Kogan Ray highlights the expeditions that William so enjoyed, first with his father and later as an adult. It was on these expeditions that he made his botanical discoveries; thus, selecting these key events helped Ray portray her subject in some detail in only 32 pages.

Teaching Idea 9-1

Compare Biographies about One Person

Ask your students to compare and evaluate different biographies about the same person by doing the following:

1. Choose two biographies about the same person and read them.

2. Decide which biography gives the best idea of what the person was really like. How does it accomplish this?

3. Decide which tells the most about the person's accomplishments.

4. Decide which is more informative and which is more interesting.

Students can also compare biographies written from different perspectives:

1. Compare a biography written before 1970 with one written within the past five years.

2. Describe the differences in the way the subject is viewed or the way similar events are reported.

3. Decide which is more informative and which is more interesting.

Many biographies have been written about historical figures, such as George Washington, Abraham Lincoln, and Martin Luther King. Select those best suited to your students and have them form small groups to compare what they find.

• • THEME • •

The theme of a biography is the unifying element behind the story. Facts are merely facts until they are subordinated to a theme and a structure that allows them to make a statement with universal application and appeal. Fighting against injustice, struggling for independence, or working for human rights happens around the world and in many different ways. Each individual story builds its own theme; combined, the stories highlight the resilience and courage of human beings. Look for books that contain a theme with universal application and appeal.

• • ILLUSTRATIONS • •

If the biography is a picture book, the illustrations must present the setting and the subject in an accurate manner.

Illustrations often provide the interesting details that the brief text of a picture-book biography lacks. For example, in *Woody Guthrie: Poet of the People* (P–I), Bonnie Christensen captures the mood of the time and presents many small details in her powerful illustrations.

Biographers also make use of archival photographs, when they are available, to highlight their subject's personalities and lives. Orbis Pictus Award–winning *Through My Eyes* (I–A), by Ruby Bridges, contains reproductions of photographs taken during the tense times when schools in the South were forcibly integrated. They allow readers to compare the innocence and courage of a young girl with the hatred and ugliness of the adults who opposed integration. Look for illustrations that include interesting details and illuminate the character of the subject.

* * *

A CLOSE LOOK AT

The Life and Death of Adolf Hitler

In 2003, the American Library Association bestowed the Siebert Award for nonfiction on James Cross Giblin's stunning biography of one of history's greatest villains. The award committee recognized both Giblin's accuracy and his artistry.

Setting and Plot

Giblin chose to tell the story of Hitler's entire life, from birth to death, but he carefully selected facts that would build on each other to present an accurate and vivid picture. Giblin frames Hitler's life in the present, thereby increasing a reader's perception of the relevance of this biography. He begins with a discussion of why we don't know where Hitler's remains are, the evolution of the idea of dictatorship, and the questions that frame the book: "What sort of man could plan and carry out such horrendous schemes? How was he able to win support for his deadly ventures? And why did no one try to stop him until it was almost too late?" (pp. 2–3). In like manner, he ends the book with a discussion of the neo-Nazi movement of today and the hope that the world will never see another Hitler. The framing of the story of Hitler's life by chapters that are contemporary supports one of Giblin's primary themes—that this could happen again.

As the successive chapters unfold, Giblin not only recounts Hitler's life but sets it within the context of European history of the time. Because one of his theses is that Hitler was shaped by the time and place in which he lived, Giblin takes great pains to explain the attitudes, opportunities, and beliefs that surrounded Hitler as a boy and a young man. He describes life in Vienna, where Hitler had hoped to become an artist, and the excitement of Munich just before World War I, through the rise of Hitler and the Nazi party and the

Courtesy Clarion Books/Houghton Mifflin Co.

James Cross Giblin

Although James Cross Giblin has authored a retelling of the King Arthur legend, as well as dramatic pieces and short stories, he is best known for his nonfiction writing. Among his long list of nonfiction titles are award-winning biographies, including *Charles A. Lindbergh: A Human Hero* and *The Amazing Life of Benjamin Franklin.* Both books received ALA notable citations and were named National Council of Teachers of English Orbis Pictus Honor books. In 2003, Giblin won the Robert F. Sibert Award for *The Life and Death of Adolf Hitler.*

"Nonfiction books for children aged eight through twelve," Giblin told *Something about the Author,* "[give] me the opportunity to pursue my research interests, meet interesting and stimulating experts in various fields, and share my enthusiasms with a young audience. I try to write books that I would have enjoyed reading when I was the age of my readers" (Peacock, 2001, p. 89). As a child coming of age in the 1940s, Giblin was fascinated by World War II: "My favorite [movies] weren't films made for children but spy movies set in Germany and Nazi-occupied areas such as Casablanca. I also liked melodramas starring emotional actresses like Bette Davis and Greer Garson, especially if they took place in exotic settings . . . or had to do with World War II" (p. 92).

When asked in a *Publishers Weekly* interview (Frederick, 2002) why he chose to write about Adolf Hitler, Giblin referred to his childhood experiences. "I was six," said Giblin, "when Hitler invaded Poland. At 12, I remember our teacher bringing a radio into the classroom so we could hear Germany surrender in May of 1945. My childhood was shaped by the war, and Hitler was a big part of that. In going back to write about him, it was almost like reliving an important chunk of my past."

Giblin feels that an author's fascination with his or her subjects leads to good nonfiction books for children. "In writing nonfiction, as with other types of books," noted Giblin, "I believe it's absolutely essential for the author to be enthusiastic about his or her topic. Only then can one hope to generate enthusiasm in readers" (Crowell Junior Books, n.d.).

Throughout his writing career, Giblin has felt passionate about a number of figures in American history. His earlier biographies include *Edith Wilson: The Woman Who Ran the United States, George Washington: A Picture Book Biography,* and *Thomas Jefferson: A Picture Book Biography.*

Nearly two decades ago, Giblin expressed the joy he experienced while researching nonfiction texts (Crowell Junior Books, n.d.). "I only hope my pleasure communicates itself to young readers," he said, "and makes them want to read more books. If it does, I'll be repaying the debt I owe all the fine writers who nurtured my love of reading when I was a child." With his contribution of over 20 exemplary informational books for children, James Cross Giblin is fulfilling his debt while expanding the literary lives of young readers.

Sources:

Crowell Junior Books. (n.d.). James Cross Giblin [Promotional brochure]. New York: Author.

Frederick, H. V. (2002, April 1). PW talks with James Cross Giblin. *Publishers Weekly.* [http://static.highbeam.com/p/publishersweekly/april012002]. Accessed July 16, 2004.

Ohio Reading Road Trip. (n.d.). James Cross Giblin. [www.ohioreadingroadtrip.org/giblin/index.html]. Accessed March 7, 2005.

Peacock, S. (Ed.). (2001). James Cross Giblin. *Something about the Author: Facts and Pictures about Authors and Illustrators of Books for Young People, 122,* 89–93. New York: Gale Research.

World War II years. As he paints a broad picture of the setting and the historical events, Giblin also includes small details that bring the bigger picture into manageable focus. We learn of Hitler's infatuation with his niece and then with Eva Braun; we are privy to the scene in which he became a vegetarian. These small details serve to heighten the tension between Adolf the human being and Hitler the monster.

Portrayal of the Subject

There is no danger of hagiography in this portrayal of subject; it is clear from the outset that Giblin considers Hitler to be a very evil man, but a man nonetheless. As he presents Hitler's life, he highlights events that might be considered influential or perhaps even causal in the development of this dictator. We discover that Hitler's father beat him; that he was extraordinarily close to his mother, who died when he was a young man; that he experienced debilitating failure early in life; and that he was attracted to beautiful young women but had difficulty developing relationships. Hitler's eccentricities hinted at an emotionally disturbed young man; his magnetism and oratorical skills propelled him to the forefront of the Nazi party in the chaos of postwar Germany. Thus Giblin's portrayal of Hitler emphasizes the

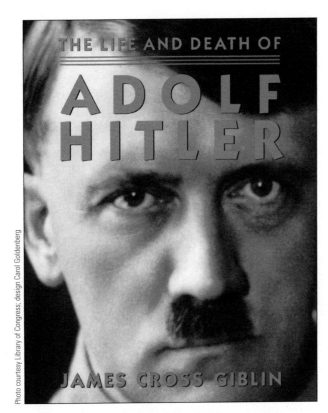

Photo courtesy Library of Congress; design Carol Goldenberg

THE LIFE AND DEATH OF
ADOLF HITLER
JAMES CROSS GIBLIN

Giblin's chilling and remorseless account of the making of a monstrous dictator ends with the hope that the world never sees another Hitler.

transformation from child to dictator and the interaction of personality and social milieu.

Accuracy and Style

Giblin is careful to distinguish between fact and supposition. For example, he states, "It's not clear what role, if any, Adolf Hitler played in the Munich revolution and its suppression." Giblin also presents speculations as to why, other than because of the prevailing attitude of the times, Hitler might have developed such hatred for the Jewish people. For example, he mentions that some suggest that it was because the doctor who treated his mother during her final illness was Jewish; Giblin also notes, however, that Hitler had "nothing but praise" for the doctor.

Giblin faces the particular difficulty of reporting the thoughts of a man whose ideas are repugnant. At times he reminds the reader that what Hitler thought was not true, or even close to accurate, as in the scene in which Hitler wonders what had happened to the patriotic spirit of Munich by the third year of the war:

> He soon decided he'd found the answer: the Jews. "The offices were filled with Jews," he wrote in *Mein Kampf.* "Nearly every clerk was a Jew, and nearly every Jew was a clerk. I was amazed at this plethora

of warriors of the chosen people and could not help but compare them with their rare representatives at the front." (Which was not an accurate observation: Many Jews served with distinction in the German army in the First World War.)

Each chapter in the text is filled with quotes from various sources, and the end material contains source notes for each chapter, both supporting Giblin's scholarship and extending to readers the possibility of exploring the source material themselves. The chapters are also filled with archival photographs that support the text and add visual interest.

The liberal use of photographs, generous trim size, and 12-point font make this a physically attractive book. The cover, in which Hitler's eyes stare directly at the reader in an eerie and unsettling manner, presages the disturbing nature of the story that Giblin tells. And he tells it well, with chapters that spill naturally from one to the other, each chapter ending with a thought or question that the subsequent chapter takes up. Scholarship, artistry, and passion are evident throughout the book, and it comes as no surprise to read in the introduction to the source notes and bibliography that Giblin had a lifelong fascination with Hitler.

Theme

One of the themes that permeate this biography is that Hitler was not always Hitler. He began life, as we all did, as a baby. The first line of Chapter 2 makes this theme explicit: "It's hard to find hints in the young Adolf Hitler of the cruel dictator he was to become" (p. 4). Giblin's portrait of this deeply disturbed man who was also a charismatic leader serves to remind us that this could happen again, and that it's crucial not to forget the lesson this dictator's life has taught us.

* * *

Exploring Biography

Looking at biography in terms of historical period is perhaps the most common way of using biography in the classroom. Like historical fiction, biography can help students envision what life was like in the past. We recognize this use of biography in the organization of the Booklist; many titles are presented by historical period. Here, however, we explore biography according to the people that biographies portray. Because the subject is the reason for biography, we look to the subject as a way to classify biographical narratives.

Doing so also makes it easier to talk about biography in terms of broad human themes. Political and military lead-

Teaching Idea 9-2

Thematic Connection: Self-Knowledge

There are many biographies in which one of the pivotal events is the subject's recognition of his or her own talent or strength. This is evident in Francisco Jiménez's *Breaking Through* (I–A), Robert Burleigh's *Langston's Train Ride* (I), and William Miller's *Zora Hurston and the Chinaberry Tree* (P–I). As you read books such as these with your students, ask them to consider how the subject's realization altered his or her life. Then ask them to think about themselves. Do they have a dream? A special talent? A special strength?

ers seek either to control or to lead their people toward specific goals; issues of power, vision, and honor permeate biographies of these leaders. Philosophers and religious leaders seek to articulate principles on which we might live; their lives are spent considering the role of human beings and higher beings. Many of these leaders exemplify or demonstrate their principles simply by living a holy life, however that might be defined, thus convincing others of the truth of their ideas. Artists of all kinds—musicians, dancers, writers, painters, craftsmen, filmmakers—all try to present their inner visions to the world; they often struggle to realize their talent and to find acceptance for their innovations. Scientists and inventors, too, seek to discover, understand, and create new ideas and opportunities for their fellow human beings; they often face a long struggle for recognition during which they must persevere to reach their goals. Adventurers and explorers, propelled by their innate curiosity, spend their lives exploring new places and new challenges. Sports heroes work hard to attain a level of excellence that allows them to succeed. And the extraordinary ordinary people who live lives with dignity and strength change the world, one person at a time. An exploration of all these types of biographical subjects can inspire readers to think about their place in the world today.

• • POLITICAL AND MILITARY LEADERS

For good or for ill, political and military leaders help shape the course of history. One such leader is the subject of Diane Stanley's *Saladin: Noble Prince of Islam* (I). Her por-

trayal of this courageous yet merciful man brings to life a person and a time in history that is not well known to most of the Western world. Stanley carefully describes major events in the history of the Middle East through to the time of the Second Crusade, the world into which Saladin was born. Through charisma and courage, Saladin succeeded in uniting the Arab world to fight against the barbarians of the West and regain Jerusalem. As he did so, he distinguished himself by his generous and merciful treatment of those he fought. Throughout the text, Stanley reminds readers that three faiths—Jewish, Muslim, and Christian—share the same regard for the Holy Land, then and now.

A political leader who never held office, Frederick Douglass inspired a movement toward abolition and became one of the greatest, if not the greatest, African Americans of the 19th century. Peter Burchard's *Frederick Douglass: For the Great Family of Man* (A) chronicles the life of this American hero, from his childhood as a slave, to his rise to prominence as counselor to presidents, to his death. Although Burchard portrays Douglass's great strengths and influence, he also depicts his personal struggles. Douglass was, in many ways, an icon of the century that moved from slavery to a taste of freedom in the post-Reconstruction South. He died knowing that the promise of emancipation had not truly been fulfilled.

Biographies of these and other important political and military figures appear in the Booklist at the end of the chapter.

• • PHILOSOPHERS AND RELIGIOUS LEADERS

Many great philosophers and religious leaders have left their mark on the world. Born 2,555 years ago, Confucius was one of them. Russell Freedman celebrates his influence in *Confucius: The Golden Rule* (I). Although Confucius was born poor and had a homely appearance, his charm and intelligence helped him become a revered teacher and philosopher. His progressive ideals, such as equality and treating others as oneself, have been studied and argued for more than 25 centuries. Freedman teaches us not only who Confucius was but how he thought and how his precepts have echoed across time, as, for example, Jesuit missionaries read his teachings during the 16th century and realized the similarities between Confucius's thinking and their own Christian precepts. The liberal use of quotations from the *Analects* of Confucius helps present the man while also stimulating the minds of readers: "Do you want to know what knowledge is? When you know something, recognize that you know it, and when you don't know something, recognize that you don't know it. That's knowledge."

As we live in an increasingly interconnected world, it is increasingly important to understand the thought and beliefs of other people. Books such as this help introduce young readers to timeless ideas and new ones.

• • SCIENTISTS • • AND INVENTORS

Just as philosophers seek to articulate their particular beliefs and share them with the world, scientists and inventors seek to discover, understand, and create new knowledge and possibilities. Often their search begins with careful observation of the world around them. Galileo observed the heavens and came to the conclusion that the earth was not the center of the universe. Peter Sis uses his considerable talents as an artist to present the genius of Galileo in *Starry Messenger: Galileo Galilei* (I). The story can be read in several ways. Sis's spare text reveals the basic details of Galileo's life, his illustrations present the main ideas of the text, and Galileo's own words present his experiences and ideas. All together, this is a remarkable introduction to the man who, in spite of punishment by the Pope, puzzled out the workings of the solar system by observing the stars, and changed the way we see the world.

John Harrison defied tradition and prevailing scientific opinion to understand how to measure longitude, one's east-west position on the globe. In 1714 Britain offered the Longitude Prize, a sizeable fortune, to the person who could discover the secret and make it safer for the ships that sailed the globe. In *The Man Who Made Time Travel* (I), Kathryn Lasky tells the story of Harrison, an uneducated clockmaker who had a wonderful idea and the perseverance to continue to perfect his chronometer. Kevin Hawkes's beautiful paintings provide a visual record of Harrison's persistence. Older readers interested in this topic enjoy Joan Dash's *The Longitude Prize* (A).

• • ADVENTURERS • • AND EXPLORERS

Those who leave home to confront physical challenges or explore unknown places often become heroes. Grand exploits, such as climbing Mt. Everest or crossing the South Pole by dogsled, capture the imagination of the world. Sometimes, however, the adventure lies closer to home. Mordicai Gerstein's Caldecott Medal–winning *The Man Who Walked between the Towers* (P–I) presents the extraordinary feat of Philippe Petit's walk on a wire strung between the almost completed towers of the World Trade Center in August 1974. Defying the rules, as well as gravity, Petit did something extraordinary, something that captured the imagination of the world. This and other books that recount the exploits of adventurers and explorers are listed in the Booklist at the end of the chapter.

• • PRACTITIONERS • • OF THE ARTS

There are many wonderful biographies of painters, sculptors, musicians, filmmakers, dancers, artisans, and writers who have successfully presented their visions to the world. The success is often hard won, however, and stories about these individuals often portray their struggles as thoroughly as they celebrate their successes.

Increasingly, those who write for children and young adults are creating autobiographies and memoirs that allow young readers to see the struggles of authors they admire. Jack Gantos is brutally honest about his life, which includes a time in prison, in *Hole in My Life* (A), a riveting story of a young man who makes a series of bad decisions that land him in prison, only to be saved by his need to write. Chris Crutcher's life was less dramatic, but the trials and tribulations of growing up as a dweeb are poignantly funny in *King of the Mild Frontier: An Ill-Advised Autobiography* (A). Rather than telling his life story in a chronology, Crutcher organizes his memories thematically, exploring how experiences he had as a child were complemented by those he had as an adolescent and often appear in his writing as an adult. Crutcher's signature sense of humor and keen eye for the ridiculous and pathetic make this an occasionally sidesplitting read. Biographies about writers are important resources for exploring what it means to be a writer and for extending children's knowledge of the authors whose works they enjoy reading.

Sometimes those who have great artistic talent use their talent to do more than delight or entertain. Marian Anderson was one such artist, and two recent biographies present her life and times and celebrate the profound impact she had on the struggle for civil rights over the course of her long life (1897–1993). Pam Muñoz Ryan's picture-book biography *When Marian Sang: The True Recital of Marian Anderson, the Voice of a Century* (I) presents Marian's early life with simplicity and honesty, depicting a young African American girl with great talent being denied access to the training she needed because of the racist attitudes prevalent in the United States at that time. These trials and tribulations make all the more satisfying her brilliant performance on the steps of the Lincoln Memorial in Washington, D.C. Brian Selznick's brilliant illustrations frame the story as a play—the curtain closed at the beginning, yet remaining open in the final, triumphant scene of Marian's debut with the Metropolitan Opera.

In a more detailed biography for older readers, Russell Freedman's perspective on Anderson's life is clear from the very beginning, as the title sums it up: *The Voice That Challenged a Nation: Marian Anderson and the Struggle for Equal Rights* (I–A). Freedman begins with the concert at the Lincoln Memorial in 1939: 75,000 people standing in front of the memorial on a cool Easter Sunday, an ovation,

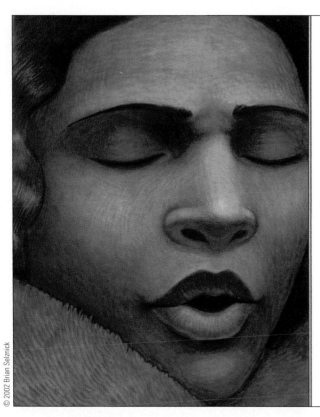

Marian looked out on a river of 75,000 people. Her heart beat wildly. Would she be able to utter one note?

She took a deep breath and felt the power of her audience's goodwill surge toward her. Marian's sisters were there, and Mother too. Marian stood straight and tall. Then she closed her eyes and sang,

"My country 'tis of thee
Sweet land of liberty . . .
Let freedom ring!"

A roaring cheer followed every song. At the end of the program, the people pleaded for more.

When she began her thought-provoking encore,

"Oh, nobody knows the trouble I see
Nobody knows my sorrow...."

. . . silence settled on the multitudes.

Brian Selznick's brilliant illustrations capture the power of Marian Anderson's voice in **When Marian Sang,** *by Pam Muñoz Ryan.*

a moment of silence, and then Marian singing. This dramatic introduction is followed by an effectively brisk recounting of her childhood and young adulthood, focusing on her dedication to her talent and on the obstacles she had to overcome. The emphasis, however, is on Marian as a singer; Freedman does not presume to cast her as an active player in the civil rights movement that was just beginning to develop, but rather portrays her as an artist whose great talent put her in a position to make a powerful statement simply by using that talent, as she did.

These and other outstanding biographies of those who practice the arts appear in the Booklist at the end of the chapter.

• • SPORTS HEROES • •

Sports heroes, like famous artists, often have the opportunity to work for a better world because of the esteem in which others hold them. Jackie Robinson epitomizes both the talent that it takes to be a heroic sports figure and the dedication that is necessary to use that position to benefit others. Sharon Robinson's moving tribute to her father, *Promises to Keep: How Jackie Robinson Changed Amer-*

ica (I–A), combines narrative reconstruction of the major events in his life with family photographs and letters. She presents the life of the man who broke the color barrier in major league baseball and who then went on to become an activist in politics and the struggle for civil rights. Although not all sports heroes have the opportunity to affect the world in the manner Jackie Robinson did, good sports biographies are more than just sources of information about heroic exploits in the sports arena.

• • EXTRAORDINARY • • ORDINARY PEOPLE

Recently, several books that celebrate the lives of ordinary people who live their lives with a particular dignity and grace have become available for young readers. Memoirs such as Alan Grovenar's *Osceola: Memories of a Sharecropper's Daughter* (I), authentic biographies like Alison Leslie Gold's *A Special Fate: Chiune Sugihara: Hero of the Holocaust* (A), and biographical fiction such as Joseph Bruchac's *Sacajawea* (I–A) depict the acts of ordinary people. The heroes of these stories are not sports or movie stars, politicians or generals, artists or philosophers, but persons whose

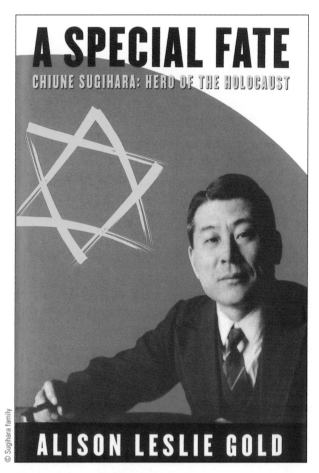

© Sugihara family

Chiune Sugihara quietly defied his own government and the other Axis powers when he issued 6,000 transit visas to Jews caught in the madness of Nazi Europe.

strength of character makes them extraordinary in some way. Sacajawea's knowledge, bravery, and intelligence made her an integral part of Lewis and Clark's expedition instead of just the wife of one of their interpreters. Osceola Mays's courage and strength allowed her to triumph over poverty and a cruelly racist society. Chiune Sugihara's sense of decency and personal courage led him to defy his government and save thousands of Jews of Eastern Europe during World War II.

Sometimes it surprises us that people who are now considered famous or heroic, such as Ruby Bridges, Rosa Parks, or Malcolm X, were in fact people with no particular reputation, talent, or position that would indicate eventual fame. Others whose lives are worth reading and thinking about still aren't famous—but they are exemplary. Quietly told stories of people who did not create headlines can also have a strong and lasting impact on young readers. The memoir *Leon's Story* (I–A), written by Leon Walter Tillage and illustrated with collage art by Susan L. Roth, won a Boston Globe–Horn Book Award for nonfiction. In this small book, Tillage tells the story of his life as the son of an African

American sharecropper, growing up in North Carolina during the 1940s. As a young boy he learns to endure the racism and bigotry of his surroundings while keeping intact his own dignity and sense of worth. His experiences lead him directly to being involved in the civil rights movement.

These and other biographies about ordinary people leading extraordinary lives, including contemporary children struggling with repression or working to change the world, appear in the Booklist at the end of this chapter. Teaching Idea 9.3 presents suggestions for helping students create a memoir of their own.

Biography in the Classroom

Biography can enliven a social studies curriculum; in conjunction with historical fiction and nonfiction, it can illuminate a time and place by telling the story of an individual. It can also support studies in music and art; many fine biog-

Teaching Idea **9-4**

Who Becomes a Biographical Subject?

Ask your students to consider what types of people are most likely to become the subjects of biographies. What people are most likely to have several biographies written about them? Ask students to consider whether the subjects of biography have changed in the past 30 years. Have them follow this procedure:

1. Go to the library or on the Internet to find out how many biographies have been written about a particular individual. List authors, titles, and dates of publication.

2. Check the school library holdings to ascertain what kinds of people are subjects of biographies written within the past 30 years. List subjects, authors, titles, and dates of publication.

3. Summarize the data from items 1 and 2 and make generalizations based on the data.

4. Discuss the findings, considering these questions: Who is in favor? Who is not? What kinds of people are the subjects of biography or memoir in any given year? Are there any observable trends?

---

raphies of artists and musicians explore both their lives and their creative endeavors. An exploration of themes is enriched by including biographies.

Memoirs can serve as models for children as they develop their own or those of an older friend or family member. Other biographies serve as excellent examples of how to use source material to craft an engaging and accurate story. Some provide access to primary source material for students to use in their own research. A biography collection is an important part of any classroom or school library.

• • BUILDING A • • BIOGRAPHY COLLECTION

Individual biographies are judged according to the criteria explained at the beginning of this chapter. A collection of biographies needs to be assessed in terms of its scope and representation of diverse people. As you gather biographies, be sure to evaluate the breadth of your selection in terms of gender and cultural representation as well as representation of different types of people. Biography for children was once dominated by the stories of American white men. This has changed significantly in the past few decades, and there are now good biographies available of women and people of color as well as biographies that bring the entire world to the classroom. Balancing your collection across gender and race is important, as we discuss in Chapter 11. If there are biographies of women and people of color that speak to your subject, be sure to include them in your collection. If there are not, you may want to consider with your students why there are no biographies of, for example, ancient female explorers, and why biographies of modern female explorers are now available. Taking into account the biog-

raphies and memoirs of ordinary people that are available today, consider with your students why someone might become the subject of a biography, an idea that is explored in Teaching Idea 9.4. Using this approach, children can begin to see how the world has changed and how historical and current social conditions influence individuals' potential.

• • USING BIOGRAPHY • • WITH OTHER GENRES TO STUDY AN ERA

As we have discussed in other chapters, it is often quite effective to read across genres. When you do this, students not only learn about the focus of study but also further develop their understanding of genre constraints and possibilities. If, for example, you link literature with social studies, you can combine historical fiction, biography, and nonfiction to study a particular time or place. Experiences in each genre offer readers different opportunities that, taken together, can help them learn not only the "facts" about particular people and particular places but also the human story that has become history.

If, for example, you want students to really understand the reasons for and the impact of the civil rights movement, you might want to read biographies of Gandhi, Martin Luther King, and Malcolm X. Trace the development of Gandhi's ideas in the work of King, and compare King with Malcolm X. Then bring in the stories of such people as Rosa Parks, Leon Tillage, and Ruby Bridges, some poetry from Langston Hughes (and his biographies), and historical fiction such as *Roll of Thunder, Hear My Cry* (A) or *The Watsons Go to Birmingham, 1963* (I–A). Nonfiction, such as Chris Crowe's *Getting Away with Murder: The True Story of the Emmett Till Case* (A) and other books discussed in Chapter 10, supplements biography to provide added facts, while the stories told in biographies enhance the fiction.

• • ORGANIZING • • BIOGRAPHY BY THEME

Biography, like fiction, includes stories of people who explore their world, fight for freedom, revolt against oppression, immigrate, establish new nations, and struggle for survival and human rights. Biographies can complement historical and realistic fiction that studies similar themes, or themes can be explored primarily through biographies. There are several biographical series—for example, the **Extraordinary People** series, published by Children's Book Press; the **Black Americans of Achievement** series, published by Chelsea; and Enslow's **African-American Biography, Hispanic Biography, World Writers,** and **Historical Americans** series—that present biographies about various people engaged in similar struggles. There are also collective biographies, mentioned earlier in this chapter, which present brief biographies of a number of people who are linked in some way. Nathan Aaseng's collective biography *Black Inventors* (A) and Patricia Calvert's *Great Lives: The American Frontier* (A) offer readers a glimpse of the lives of people who share attributes, desires, and achievements. These and other series and collective biographies are listed in the Booklist at the end of this chapter.

You can also collect books that illustrate a particular theme, such as the struggle for human rights. By studying the lives of diverse people from around the world and across history, students can come to understand the universal struggles of humankind. Why do people around the world struggle for human rights? How are these struggles similar across nations and time? How do they vary according to age and culture? Exploring these kinds of questions can lead to a better understanding of humanity and one's place in it.

For example, you might want to consider the human desire to explore new places. Many biographies focus on explorers, both ancient and modern. Sir Walter Raleigh explored the New World; Sally Ride explored space. The theme of exploration can be widened to include those who explore the boundaries of science. Those people who have made scientific and technological breakthroughs are curious, dedicated individuals, just as many geographic explorers are. Biographies of famous scientists and inventors can enrich students' concepts of what it means to be an explorer. Artists and musicians who break new ground can also be considered explorers. Thus a general theme like exploration or human rights can be woven from many varying biographies and even complemented by fiction and nonfiction.

Biographies of artists and musicians also can support the study of art and music. They can be compared in terms of the driving force that shaped the lives of their subjects: What caused them to pursue their talents with such passion and success? Biographies of female artists and musicians can be explored as examples of triumph over discrimination and then related to the general theme of human rights.

A great number of writers and illustrators of books for children have written biographies and memoirs, including a series of autobiographies for primary-grade readers published by Richard Owens. These biographies can be read for any number of purposes—to discover information about the writers, to learn about the effect of the time and place in which the writer lived on the writer's work, to develop an understanding of what it means to be a writer, and to extend knowledge of the authors whose works children enjoy reading.

Biography has become one of the most diverse, interesting, and popular genres in literature for young readers. Wise adults build on children's fascination with real stories and the details about the lives of others by using biography to explore both contemporary and historical people, events, and ideas.

• • • Summary • • •

Biographies tell the stories of the people who shaped and are shaping our history. Reading fine biographies helps children understand that people make history and that these people have strengths and weaknesses, as we all do. Understanding the humanity behind the greatness allows children to dream of their own accomplishments and to know they are possible.

Russell Freedman and Jonda C. McNair had an interesting exchange regarding how biographers and historians select the information they present and what the effects of that selection are. Read "An Interview with Russell Freedman" in the November/December 2002 issue of *The Horn Book Magazine,* then follow with the letters to the editor in the March/April 2003 issue and "Will the Real Abe Lincoln Please Stand Up?" in the May/June 2003 issue. Discuss the issues raised in this exchange, considering the influence of contemporary culture on how we think about historical figures and whether widely held opinions about these figures can color our understanding of our own history.

Biographies Arranged by Historical Period

THE COLONIAL PERIOD AND THE AMERICAN REVOLUTION

Adler, David, *A Picture Book of Benjamin Franklin* (P)

_____, *A Picture Book of Thomas Jefferson* (P)

Bober, Natalie, *Abigail Adams: Witness to a Revolution* (A)

Fritz, Jean, *And Then What Happened, Paul Revere?* (I)

_____, *Can't You Make Them Behave, King George?* (I)

_____, *The Great Little Madison* (A)

_____, *Traitor: The Case of Benedict Arnold* (A)

_____, *What's the Big Idea, Ben Franklin?* (I)

_____, *Why Don't You Get a Horse, Sam Adams?* (I)

_____, *Will You Sign Here, John Hancock?* (I)

Giblin, James Cross, *The Amazing Life of Benjamin Franklin* (I)

_____, *George Washington: A Picture Book Biography* (P–I)

_____, *Thomas Jefferson: A Picture Book Biography* (P–I)

Jacobs, William Jay, *Washington* (I–A)

Lawson, Robert, *Ben and Me* (I)

McGill, Alice, *Molly Bannacky* (I)

Meltzer, Milton, *The American Revolutionaries: A History in Their Own Words* (A)

_____, *George Washington and the Birth of Our Nation* (A)

_____, *Thomas Jefferson: The Revolutionary Aristocrat* (A)

Monjo, F. N., *Poor Richard in France* (I)

Osborne, Mary Pope, *The Many Lives of Benjamin Franklin* (A)

Pinkney, Andrea Davis, *Dear Benjamin Banneker* (I)

Wallner, Alexandra, *Betsy Ross* (P)

THE CIVIL WAR

Archer, Jules, *A House Divided: The Lives of Ulysses S. Grant and Robert E. Lee* (I–A)

Burchard, Peter, *Charlotte Forten: A Black Teacher in the Civil War* (I–A)

_____, *Lincoln and Slavery* (A)

Chang, Ina, *A Separate Battle: Women and the Civil War* (A)

Everett, Gwen, *John Brown: One Man against Slavery* (I)

Freedman, Russell, *Lincoln: A Photobiography* (I–A)

Fritz, Jean, *Harriet Beecher Stowe and the Beecher Preachers* (I)

_____, *Stonewall* (A)

Hamilton, Virginia, *Anthony Burns: The Defeat and Triumph of a Fugitive Slave* (A)

_____, *Many Thousand Gone: African Americans from Slavery to Freedom* (I–A)

Lawrence, Jacob, *Harriet and the Promised Land* (P–I)

Lester, Julius, *Long Journey Home* (I–A)

_____, *To Be a Slave* (I–A)

Marrin, Albert, *Unconditional Surrender: U. S. Grant and the Civil War* (A)

_____, *Virginia's General: Robert E. Lee and the Civil War* (A)

McCurdy, Michael, *Escape from Slavery: The Boyhood of Frederick Douglass in His Own Words* (I)

McKissack, Patricia, and Fredrick McKissack, *Sojourner Truth: Ain't I a Woman?* (I–A)

Meltzer, Milton, *Abraham Lincoln* (A)

_____, *Frederick Douglass: In His Own Words* (A)

Miller, William, *Frederick Douglass: The Last Day of Slavery* (P–I)

Reit, Seymour, *Behind Rebel Lines: The Incredible Story of Emma Edmonds* (I–A)

Rockwell, Anne, *Only Passing Through: The Story of Sojourner Truth* (P–I)

Schroeder, Alan, *Minty: A Story of Young Harriet Tubman* (P–I)

WESTWARD EXPANSION

Bruchac, Joseph, *A Boy Called Slow: The True Story of Sitting Bull* (P–I)

_____, *Crazy Horse's Vision* (P)

Conrad, Pam, *Prairie Visions: The Life and Times of Solomon Butcher* (I–A)

Freedman, Russell, *Indian Chiefs* (I–A)

_____, *The Life and Death of Crazy Horse* (I–A)

Fritz, Jean, *Bully for You, Teddy Roosevelt* (I–A)

_____, *Make Way for Sam Houston* (I)

Harvey, Brett, *My Prairie Year: Based on the Diary of Elenore Plaisted* (P–I)

Jakes, John, *Susanna of the Alamo: A True Story* (P–I)

Katz, William Loren, *Black Women of the Old West* (I)

Klausner, Janet, *Sequoyah's Gift: A Portrait of the Cherokee Leader* (I–A)

Marrin, Albert, *Sitting Bull and His World* (A)

Monceaux, Morgan, and Ruth Katcher, *My Heroes, My People: African Americans and Native Americans in the West* (I)

Pelz, Ruth, *Black Heroes of the Wild West* (I)

San Souci, Robert D., *Kate Shelley: Bound for Legend* (P)

Schlissel, Lillian, *Black Frontiers: A History of African American Heroes in the Old West* (I)

Yates, Diana, *Chief Joseph: Thunder Rolling down from the Mountains* (I)

IMMIGRATION, WORLD WAR I, AND THE GREAT DEPRESSION

Burleigh, Robert, *Flight: The Journey of Charles Lindbergh* (P–I)

Fradin, Dennis Brindell, and Judith Bloom Fradin, *Ida B. Wells: Mother of the Civil Rights Movement* (I–A)

Freedman, Russell, *The Wright Brothers: How They Invented the Airplane* (I–A)

Fritz, Jean, *You Want Women to Vote, Lizzie Stanton?* (I)

Govenar, Alan, *Osceola: Memories of a Sharecropper's Daughter* (I)

Greenfield, Eloise, *Mary McLeod Bethune* (I)

Kraft, Betsy Harvey, *Mother Jones: One Woman's Fight for Labor* (I–A)

McKissack, Patricia, *Mary McLeod Bethune* (I)

WORLD WAR II

Adler, David, *A Picture Book of Eleanor Roosevelt* (P)

Besson, Jean-Louis, *October 45: Childhood Memories of the War* (I)

Cooney, Barbara, *Eleanor* (P)

Faber, Doris, *Eleanor Roosevelt: First Lady of the World* (I–A)

Freedman, Russell, *Eleanor Roosevelt: A Life of Discovery* (A)

_____, *Franklin Delano Roosevelt* (A)

Giblin, James Cross, *The Life and Death of Adolf Hitler* (A)

Gold, Alison Leslie, *A Special Fate: Chiune Sugihara: Hero of the Holocaust* (A)

Greenfeld, Howard, *The Hidden Children* (I–A)

Lobel, Anita, *No Pretty Pictures* (A)

Marrin, Albert, *Hitler* (A)

Pressler, Mirjam, *Anne Frank: A Hidden Life* (A)

Reiss, Johanna, *The Journey Back* (I–A)

_____, *The Upstairs Room* (I–A)

Rosenberg, Maxine, *Hiding to Survive: Fourteen Jewish Children and the Gentiles Who Rescued Them from the Holocaust* (I–A)

Uchida, Yoshiko, *The Invisible Thread* (A)

Van der Rol, Ruud, and Rian Verhoeven, *Anne Frank: Beyond the Diary* (I)

THE 1950S TO THE PRESENT

Bray, Rosemary, *Martin Luther King* (I)

Demi, *The Dalai Lama: A Biography of the Tibetan Spiritual and Political Leader* (P)

Harrison, Barbara, and Daniel Terris, *A Twilight Struggle: The Life of John Fitzgerald Kennedy* (A)

Haskins, James, *Thurgood Marshall: A Life for Justice* (I–A)

McKissack, Patricia, *Jesse Jackson: A Biography* (I)

Medearis, Angela Shelf, *Dare to Dream: Coretta Scott King and the Civil Rights Movement* (I)

Meltzer, Milton, *Winnie Mandela: The Soul of South Africa* (A)

Mills, Judie, *Robert Kennedy* (A)

Myers, Walter Dean, *Malcolm X: By Any Means Necessary* (I–A)

_____, *Malcolm X: A Fire Burning Brightly* (I–A)

Ringgold, Faith, *My Dream of Martin Luther King* (P–I)

Winner, David, *Desmond Tutu* (A)

Collective and Series Biographies

Aaseng, Nathan, *Black Inventors* (A)

Archer, Jules, *Breaking Barriers: The Feminist Revolution from Susan B. Anthony to Margaret Sanger to Betty Friedan* (A)

Bland, Celia, *Peter MacDonald: Former Chairman of the Navajo Nation,* from the **North American Indians of Achievement** series (I)

Bryant, Jennifer Fisher, *Louis Braille: Inventor,* from the **Great Achievers: Lives of the Physically Challenged** series (I)

Calvert, Patricia, *Great Lives: The American Frontier* (A)

Caras, Roger, *A World Full of Animals: The Roger Caras Story,* from the **Great Naturalists** series (I)

Cedeno, Maria, *Cesar Chavez: Labor Leader,* from the **Hispanic Heritage** series (I)

Elish, Dan, *James Meredith and School Desegregation,* from the **Gateway Civil Rights** series (I)

Gulotta, Charles, *Extraordinary Women in Politics,* from the **Extraordinary People** series (I)

Hoose, Phillip, *It's Our World, Too! Young People Who Are Making a Difference (How They Do It—How You Can, Too!)* (I–A)

Krull, Katherine, *Lives of Extraordinary Women: Rulers, Rebels (and What the Neighbors Thought)*

_____, *Lives of the Presidents: Fame, Shame (and What the Neighbors Thought)* (I)

_____, *They Saw the Future: Oracles, Psychics, Scientists, Great Thinkers, and Pretty Good Guessers* (I)

Lazo, Caroline, *Elie Wiesel,* from the **Peacemakers** series (I)

Lyons, Mary E., *Starting Home: The Story of Horace Pippin, Painter,* from the **African-American Artists and Artisans** series (I)

McKissack, Patricia, and Fredrick McKissack, *African-American Scientists,* from the **Proud Heritage** series (I)

Meltzer, Milton, *Ain't Gonna Study War No More: The Story of America's Peace Seekers* (A)

Pinkney, Andrea Davis, *Let It Shine: Stories of Black Women Freedom Fighters* (I–A)

Thimmesh, Catherine, *Madame President: The Extraordinary, True (and Evolving) Story of Women in Politics* (I)

Turner, Robyn Montana, *Georgia O'Keeffe,* from the **Portraits of Women Artists for Children** series (P–I)

Whitelaw, Nancy, *Mr. Civil Rights: The Story of Thurgood Marshall* (**Notable Americans** series) (I)

Yolen, Jane, *Letter from Phoenix Farm* (**Meet the Author** series) (P)

Biographies Arranged by Type of Subject

POLITICAL AND MILITARY LEADERS

Andronik, Catherine, *Hatshepsut, His Majesty, Herself* (I)

Burchard, Peter, *Frederick Douglass: For the Great Family of Man* (A)

Cooper, Ilene, *Jack: The Early Years of John F. Kennedy* (I–A)

Demi, *Chingas Khan* (I)

Donnelly, Matt, *Theodore Roosevelt: Larger Than Life* (A)

Fleming, Candace, *Ben Franklin's Almanac: Being a True Account of the Good Gentleman's Life* (I–A)

King Farris, Christine, *My Brother Martin: A Sister Remembers Growing Up with the Rev. Dr. Martin Luther King Jr.* (P–I)

Kraft, Betsy Harvey, *Theodore Roosevelt: Champion of the American Spirit* (A)

Krull, Kathleen, *Harvesting Hope: The Story of Cesar Chavez* (P–I)

Marrin, Albert, *Old Hickory: Andrew Jackson and the American People* (A)

McCurdy, Michael, *Escape from Slavery: The Boyhood of Frederick Douglass in His Own Words* (I)

Rumford, James, *Sequoyah: The Cherokee Man Who Gave His People Writing* (I)

Stanley, Diane, *Saladin: Noble Prince of Islam* (I)

Stanley, Diane, and Peter Vennema, *Good Queen Bess: The Story of Elizabeth I of England* (I)

_____, *Shaka, King of the Zulus* (I)

St. George, Judith, *You're on Your Way, Teddy Roosevelt* (P–I)

Thomas, Jane Resh, *Behind the Mask: The Life of Queen Elizabeth* (A)

PHILOSOPHERS AND RELIGIOUS LEADERS

Demi, *Buddha* (I)

_____, *The Dalai Lama: A Biography of the Tibetan Spiritual and Political Leader* (I)

_____, *Gandhi* (I)

_____, *Muhammad* (I)

Freedman, Russell, *Confucius: The Golden Rule* (I)

SCIENTISTS AND INVENTORS

Armstrong, Jennifer, *Audubon: Painter of Birds in the Wild Frontier* (P–I)

Brown, Don, *Odd Boy Out: Young Albert Einstein* (P)

Collins, Mary, *Airborne: A Photobiography of Wilbur and Orville Wright* (I)

Davies, Jacqueline, *The Boy Who Drew Birds: A Story of John James Audubon* (P–I)

Fisher, Leonard Everett, *Alexander Graham Bell* (I)

_____, *Galileo* (I)

_____, *Gutenberg* (I)

_____, *Marie Curie* (I)

Fleischman, Paul, *Townsend's Warbler* (I–A)

Freedman, Russell, *The Wright Brothers: How They Invented the Airplane* (I–A)

Gerstein, Mordicai, *Sparrow Jack* (I)

Lasky, Katherine, *The Man Who Made Time Travel* (I)

Lucas, Eileen, *Jane Goodall: Friend of the Chimps* (I)

Matthews, Tom, *Always Inventing: A Photobiography of Alexander Graham Bell* (I)

Old, Wendie, *To Fly: The Story of the Wright Brothers* (I–A)

Ray, Deborah Kogan, *The Flower Hunter: William Bartram, America's First Naturalist* (P–I)

Reef, Catherine, *Sigmund Freud: Pioneer of the Mind* (A)

Severance, John, *Einstein: Visionary Scientist* (I)

Sis, Peter, *Starry Messenger: Galileo Galilei* (I)

_____, *The Tree of Life: A Book Depicting the Life of Charles Darwin: Naturalist, Geologist and Thinker* (I–A)

Stanley, Diane, and Peter Vennema, *Leonardo da Vinci* (I)

St. George, Judith, *Dear Dr. Bell . . . Your Friend, Helen Keller* (A)

Towle, Wendy, *The Real McCoy: The Life of an African-American Inventor* (P–I)

Ventura, Piero, *Darwin: Nature Reinterpreted* (I–A)

Wadsworth, Ginger, *Rachel Carson: Voice for the Earth* (I)

ADVENTURERS AND EXPLORERS

Aronson, Marc, *Sir Walter Raleigh and the Quest for El Dorado* (A)

Blumberg, Rhoda, *The Remarkable Voyages of Captain Cook* (I)

_____, *York's Adventures with Lewis and Clark: An African-American's Part in the Great Expedition* (I)

Ceserani, Gian Paolo, *Marco Polo* (I)

Grimes, Nikki, *Talkin' about Bessie: The Story of Aviator Elizabeth Coleman* (I)

Marrin, Albert, *The Sea King: Sir Francis Drake and His Times* (A)

Roth, Susan, *Marco Polo: His Notebook* (I)

Sis, Peter, *Follow the Dream: The Story of Christopher Columbus* (P–I)

Zaunders, Bo, *Feathers, Flaps, and Flops: Fabulous Early Fliers* (I)

ARTISTS, ARTISANS, AND FILMMAKERS

Bonafoux, Pascal, *A Weekend with Rembrandt* (I)

Brown, Don, *Mack Made Movies* (P–I)

Cech, John, *Jacques-Henri Lartigue: Boy with a Camera* (P–I)

Cummings, Pat, *Talking with Artists* (Vols. 1 and 2) (I)

Debon, Nicolas, *Four Pictures by Emily Carr* (I–A)

Everett, Gwen, *Li'l Sis and Uncle Willie: A Story Based on the Life and Paintings of William H. Johnson* (P)

Greenberg, Jan, *Romare Bearden: Collage of Memories* (P–I)

Greenberg, Jan, and Sandra Jordan, *Action Jackson* (P–I)

_____, *The American Eye: Eleven Artists of the Twentieth Century* (I–A)

_____, *Andy Warhol: Prince of Pop* (A)

Greenfeld, Howard, *Paul Gauguin* (A)

Krull, Kathleen, *Lives of the Artists: Masterpieces, Messes (and What the Neighbors Thought)* (I)

Le Tord, Bijou, *A Blue Butterfly: A Story about Claude Monet* (P)

Lyons, Mary E., *Master of Mahogany: Tom Day, Free Black Cabinetmaker* (I)

_____, *Stitching Stars: The Story Quilts of Harriet Powers* (I)

Oneal, Zibby, *Grandma Moses: Painter of Rural America* (I–A)

Raboff, Ernest, *Albrecht Dürer* (I–A)

_____, *Michelangelo* (I–A)

Rodari, Florian, *A Weekend with Picasso* (I)

Ross, Michael Elsohn, *Salvador Dali and the Surrealists: Their Lives and Ideas* (A)

Sills, Leslie, *Visions: Stories about Women Artists* (P)

Skira-Venturi, Rosabianca, *A Weekend with van Gogh* (I)

Slaymaker, Melissa Eskridge, *Bottle Houses: The Creative World of Grandma Prisbrey* (P)

Stanley, Diane, *Michelangelo* (I)

Turner, Robyn, *Mary Cassatt* (P–I)

Walker, Lou Ann, *Roy Lichtenstein: The Artist at Work* (I)

Wallner, Alexandra, *Grandma Moses* (P)

Warhola, James, *Uncle Andy's: A Fabulous Visit with Andy Warhol* (P)

Winter, Jeanette, *Diego* (P)

MUSICIANS AND DANCERS

Anderson, M. T., *Strange Mr. Satie* (P)

Christensen, Bonnie, *Woody Guthrie: Poet of the People* (P–I)

Ferris, Jeri, *What I Had Was Singing: The Story of Marian Anderson* (I)

Freedman, Russell, *Martha Graham: A Dancer's Life* (A)

_____, *The Voice That Challenged a Nation: Marian Anderson and the Struggle for Equal Rights* (I–A)

Gerstein, Mordicai, *What Charlie Heard* (P–I)

Jones, Hettie, *Big Star Fallin' Mama: Five Women in Black Music* (A)

Kamen, Gloria, *Hidden Music: The Life of Fanny Mendelssohn* (I)

Krull, Kathleen, *Lives of the Musicians: Good Times, Bad Times (and What the Neighbors Thought)* (I)

McKissack, Patricia, *Marian Anderson: A Great Singer* (P–I)

Medearis, Angela Shelf, *Little Louis and the Jazz Band: The Story of Louis "Satchmo" Armstrong* (I)

Nichol, Barbara, *Beethoven Lives Upstairs* (P)

Partridge, Elizabeth, *This Land Was Made for You and Me: The Life and Songs of Woody Guthrie* (A)

Pinkney, Andrea Davis, *Alvin Ailey* (I)

_____, *Duke Ellington* (I)

_____, *Ella Fitzgerald: The Tale of a Vocal Virtuosa* (P–I)

Rappaport, Doreen, *John's Secret Dreams: The Life of John Lennon* (P–I)

Reich, Susanna, *Clara Schumann: Piano Virtuoso* (I)

Ryan, Pam Muñoz, *When Marian Sang* (P–I)

Schroeder, Alan, *Satchmo's Blues* (P–I)

Tallchief, Maria, *Tallchief: America's Prima Ballerina* (I)

Winter, Jeanette, *Sebastian: A Book about Bach* (P)

WRITERS

Burleigh, Robert, *Langston's Train Ride* (I)

Cooper, Floyd, *Coming Home: From the Life of Langston Hughes* (I)

Crutcher, Chris, *King of the Mild Frontier: An Ill-Advised Autobiography* (A)

Gantos, Jack, *Hole in My Life* (A)

Herrera, Juan Felipe, *The Upside Down Boy/El Niño de Cabeza* (P)

Kerley, Barbara, *Walt Whitman: Words for America* (I)

Krull, Kathleen, *The Boy on Fairfield Street: How Ted Geisel Grew Up to Become Dr. Seuss* (P–I)

_____, *Lives of the Writers: Comedies, Tragedies (and What the Neighbors Thought)* (I)

Lasky, Kathryn, *A Brilliant Streak: The Making of Mark Twain* (I)

Lowry, Lois, *Looking Back: A Book of Memories* (I)

Lyons, Mary E., *Keeping Secrets: The Girlhood Diaries of Seven Women Writers* (A)

_____, *Sorrow's Kitchen: The Life and Folklore of Zora Neale Hurston* (I–A)

Meltzer, Milton, *Langston Hughes: An Illustrated Edition* (A)

Miller, William, *Zora Hurston and the Chinaberry Tree* (P)

Murphy, Jim, *Into the Deep Forest with Henry David Thoreau* (I)

_____, *Pick and Shovel Poet: The Journeys of Pascal D'Angelo* (I–A)

Myers, Walter Dean, *Bad Boy* (A)

Paulsen, Gary, *Guts: The True Stories behind Hatchet and the Brian Books* (I–A)

Reef, Catherine, *Walt Whitman* (I–A)

Rylant, Cynthia, *But I'll Be Back Again* (I)

Shapiro, Miles, *Maya Angelou* (I)

Spinelli, Jerry, *Knots in My Yo-Yo String: The Autobiography of a Kid* (I)

Stanley, Diane, and Peter Vennema, *Bard of Avon: The Story of William Shakespeare* (I)

_____, *Charles Dickens: The Man Who Had Great Expectations* (I)

Walker, Alice, *Langston Hughes, American Poet* (A)

Wallner, Alexandra, *Laura Ingalls Wilder* (P)

Winter, Jeanette, *Beatrix: Various Episodes from the Life of Beatrix Potter* (P)

Younger, Barbara, *Purple Mountain Majesties: The Story of Katharine Lee Bates and "America the Beautiful"* (P)

SPORTS HEROES

Adler, David, *Jackie Robinson: He Was the First* (P)

_____, *A Picture Book of Jesse Owens* (P)

Bolden, Tonya, *The Champ* (I)

Bruchac, Joseph, *Jim Thorpe's Bright Path* (I)

Cooper, Floyd, *Jump! From the Life of Michael Jordan* (P–I)

Goedicke, Christopher, *The Wind Warrior: The Training of a Karate Champion* (I)

Golenbock, Peter, *Teammates* (P–I)

Greenberg, Keith Elliot, *Magic Johnson: Champion with a Cause* (I)

Hopkinson, Deborah, *Girl Wonder: A Baseball Story in Nine Innings* (P)

Krull, Kathleen, *Wilma Unlimited: How Wilma Rudolph Became the World's Fastest Woman* (P–I)

Lipsyte, Robert, *Joe Louis: A Champ for All America* (A)

_____, *Michael Jordan* (I–A)

Littlefield, Bill, *Champions: Stories of Ten Remarkable Athletes* (I–A)

Macht, Norman, *Christy Mathewson* (I)

Myers, Walter Dean, *The Greatest: Muhammad Ali* (A)

Robinson, Sharon, *Promises to Keep: How Jackie Robinson Changed America* (I–A)

Walker, Paul Robert, *Pride of Puerto Rico: The Life of Roberto Clemente* (I)

Weissberg, Ted, *Arthur Ashe* (A)

EXTRAORDINARY ORDINARY PEOPLE

al-Windawi, Thura, *Thura's Diary: My Life in Wartime Iraq* (I–A)

Bang, Molly, *Nobody Particular: One Woman's Fight to Save the Bays* (I–A)

Bridges, Ruby, *Through My Eyes* (I–A)

Brown, Don, *Kid Blink Beats the World* (P–I)

Bruchac, Joseph, *Pocahontas* (I–A)

_____, *Sacajawea* (I–A)

Coleman, Evelyn, *The Riches of Osceola McCarty* (I)

Coles, Robert, *The Story of Ruby Bridges* (I)

D'Adamo, Francesco, *Iqbal* (I–A)

Dash, Joan, *The World at Her Fingertips: The Story of Helen Keller* (A)

Erdich, Lise, *Sacagawea* (P–I)

Filipovic, Zlata, *Zlata's Diary: A Child's Life in Sarajevo* (A)

Fradin, Dennis Brindell, and Judith Bloom Fradin, *Fight On! Mary Church Terrell's Battle for Integration* (I)

Greenfield, Eloise, *How They Got Over: African Americans and the Call of the Sea* (P)

Greenfield, Eloise, and Lessie Jones Little, *Childtimes: A Three-Generation Memoir* (I)

Hoose, Phillip, *It's Our World, Too! Young People Who Are Making a Difference (How They Do It—How You Can, Too!)* (I–A)

Hoyt-Goldsmith, Diane, *Hoang Anh: A Vietnamese-American Boy* (I)

Hurst, Carol Otis, *Rocks in His Head* (P–I)

Jiménez, Francisco, *Breaking Through* (I–A)

_____, *The Circuit* (I–A)

Marx, Trish, *One Boy from Kosovo* (I)

McMahon, Patricia, *Chi-Hoon: A Korean Girl*

Say, Allen, *Music for Alice* (P–I)

Steig, William, *When Everybody Wore a Hat* (P)

Tillage, Leon Walter, *Leon's Story* (I–A)

Warren, Andrea, *Escape from Saigon: How a Vietnam War Orphan Became an American Boy* (I–A)

Wolf, Bernard, *Coming to America: A Muslim Family's Story* (P)

Chapter

10

Nonfiction

We began as tiny round cells,
and we've changed a lot since then.
But we carry with us reminders
of each step of our past.

That's how it is with families.
And ours goes back a long, long way.

—LISA WESTBERG PETERS, *Our Family Tree:*
An Evolution Story, unpaged

WHEN JOHANNA DECIDED TO USE READING ALOUD TO HER SECOND-GRADE class as a way to explore the questions they often asked, she began to look for books that might help her youngsters consider some of the mysteries that seemed to so fascinate them. Why is the sky blue? What makes it snow? Where did I come from? It was this last question that took her to *Our Family Tree.* Johanna knew that "Where did I come from?" could mean many things: birth, adoption, even evolution. So she gathered a number of books that she could read and discuss with her students, among them Laurence Pringle's *Everybody Has a Belly-button* (N–P), an excellent explanation of gestation and birth for young readers; and Ann Turner's *Through Moon and Stars and Night Skies* and Rose Lewis's *I Love You like Crazy Cakes* (both N–P), two wonderful books about international adoption. When she found *Our Family Tree,* she knew she had the perfect book for introducing the concept of evolution to her students. Parents were invited to read and discuss the book as well, and many decided to buy their own copies to share with their other children. The book was a wonderful introduction to the concept, and interested readers could follow up with Joanna Cole's *Evolution* (P) and Peter Sis's *The Tree of Life* (I). In Johanna's class, the question "Where did I come from?" sparked both interesting discussions and a lot of reading.

Defining Nonfiction

Children have a desire to *know,* and when they discover that books are a place to find answers, they embark on a journey of lifelong learning. They turn to nonfiction literature to feed their hunger for facts, ideas, and concepts. The term *nonfiction* describes books of information and fact. Nonfiction, or informational, books are distinguished from fiction by their emphasis. Both may tell a story, and both may include fact. In nonfiction, the facts and concepts are uppermost, with storytelling perhaps used as an expressive technique; in fiction, the story is uppermost, with facts sometimes used to support it.

The nonfiction now being published has great appeal to young readers. Writers select topics that interest children, and many of the topics they select fit nicely into an existing curriculum. Nonfiction today includes books with spacious, well-designed pages and intriguing illustrations that enhance and extend the reader's understanding of the topic. The texts present writing at its best: interesting language used in varied ways. Metaphor and descriptive language allow readers to link what they are reading about with what they already know.

The structure of nonfiction varies widely. Some books, such as Joanna Cole's popular **Magic School Bus** series (I), use fantasy devices and parallel texts to interest young readers. Others, such as Laurence Pringle's *An Extraordinary Life: The Story of a Monarch Butterfly* (I), winner of the 1998 Orbis Pictus Award, use a narrative frame to impart information. Lisa Westberg Peters's *The Sun, the Wind and the Rain* (P) explores geology with young readers and includes a parallel narrative thread in which a young girl builds a sand castle on the beach. In *Dear Rebecca, Winter Is Here* (P), Jean Craighead George presents her information about the changing seasons in a letter from a grandmother to her granddaughter.

Because of these variations, nonfiction is sometimes difficult to distinguish from fiction. Indeed, children often wonder how books with talking dinosaurs or magic school buses can be called nonfiction. The key lies in the emphasis of the writer, which in nonfiction should be on the facts and concepts being presented. It is these that must be truthful, verifiable, and understandable.

Nonfiction available today is appealing, attractive, and abundant. Most collections in elementary school libraries and in the children's sections of public libraries are 60 to 70 percent nonfiction—a surprise to most people. Even so, nonfiction writers complain, justifiably, that their work receives less attention than fiction. The Orbis Pictus Award, presented annually since 1990 by the National Council of Teachers of English to the most outstanding work of nonfiction published in the preceding year; the Boston Globe–Horn Book Award for nonfiction; and the Sibert Award, presented by the American Library Association for the first time in 2001, are awards that call attention to the many wonderful nonfiction titles that are published each year.

Nonfiction in Children's Lives

Adults selecting books for children often give short shrift to nonfiction, assuming that stories and poetry are more appealing or are in some way superior to nonfiction. They aren't. Many children prefer nonfiction to fiction; their insatiable curiosity about the world is fueled by nonfiction books. As they mature, many young readers continue to prefer nonfiction, wanting to read to learn. When nonfiction books are well written, children learn not only about the topic being considered but also about good expository writing. And when the topics in nonfiction match children's interests, reading nonfiction is fun, just as reading stories is fun.

You probably remember only isolated fragments of information from your elementary school textbooks. You probably remember more from projects you associated with a special interest or had to research and develop for a presentation, science fair, or demonstration. We learn best when our emotions are involved and when we are actively engaged, and we learn more readily when we pursue our own—rather than someone else's—interests. We remember facts better when they are integrated into our conception of reality, and we often learn and retain them longer when they are part of a meaningful experience. Teaching Idea 10.1

Teaching Idea 10-1

Thematic Connection: Learning about Family History

Students are always interested in finding out about themselves and their families and friends. Ask students to interview their older family members about family history. Then, after students have described that history—either orally or in writing—have them use their research skills, with the help of the school librarian, to find nonfiction books that offer information about some aspect of that history. For example, if a student's great-grandparents immigrated from eastern Europe at the turn of the century, look for books that present that history. If a student's uncle fought in the Vietnam conflict, look for books about that war. Students' family histories can then be put in the context of what the students discovered through their research. For upper elementary and middle school students, this can take the form of a paper, but one that is grounded in personal history.

suggests one way to help students connect their lives to research and report writing through nonfiction.

We learn best by fitting new information into a coherent frame or schema. Nonfiction makes information available to children in ways that facilitate the creation of meaningful category systems. The especially fine nonfiction books published today illuminate children's paths. When children seek out information for themselves, identify what is relevant, and use it for meaningful goals, they become more efficient at storing and retrieving facts. Furthermore, trade books are readily available on virtually any topic and for almost any level of understanding. This rich and vast array of materials generates an interest and excitement that encourages children to find out about their world.

Criteria for Evaluating Nonfiction

Each year, committees of subject area specialists and children's literature specialists select the outstanding examples of books in their respective disciplines. The work, coordinated by the Children's Book Council, involves the National Science Teachers Association, the National Council of Social Studies, the International Reading Association, and the National Council of Teachers of English. Lists of outstanding books that can enhance teaching and learning in each discipline are published in the professional journals of each organization. These lists help teachers select quality trade books for their curriculum.

The science committee, for example, evaluates books using three criteria: (1) the book must be accurate and readable; (2) its format and illustrations must be pleasing; and (3) information must be consistent with current scientific knowledge. In areas of controversy, a book should present different points of view, and information should not be distorted by personal biases or values. Facts must be clearly distinguished from theories, generalizations must be supported by facts, and significant facts must not be omitted. If experiments are a feature of a book, the science committee considers whether they lead to an understanding of basic principles. Moreover, experiments discussed in the book must be appropriate for the reader's age group and must be both feasible and safe. The committee eschews anthropomorphized animals and plants. It also rejects books that are racist or sexist or that extol violence.

The Orbis Pictus Award for Outstanding Nonfiction for Children is an award for nonfiction of all types, and thus the criteria are broad enough to be applicable to books from varied disciplines. The award committee considers four criteria: accuracy, organization, design, and style. The following discussion expands on those criteria. Figure 10.1 contains a checklist of general criteria for evaluating all types of nonfiction.

Figure 10-1

Checklist for Evaluating Nonfiction

Accuracy
✿ Facts are current and complete, with a balance of fact and theory. When appropriate, differing viewpoints are represented.
✿ The scope is appropriate to the audience and the subject.
✿ The author's qualifications and resources are apparent.

Organization
✿ Ideas are logically developed and are presented in a clear sequence and in an understandable and appropriate fashion.
✿ The author indicates interrelationships between facts and between facts and theories.

Design
✿ The format of the book is attractive and reader-friendly, with appropriate illustrations that are strategically placed.
✿ Illustrations illuminate the facts and concepts.

Style
✿ The writing is interesting, revealing the author's enthusiasm about the subject.
✿ The terminology is appropriate. The writer uses rich language that stimulates a reader's curiosity.

• • ACCURACY • •

The criterion of accuracy comprises several facets. First, the facts presented must be current and complete, with a balance between fact and theory, and authenticity of detail. If applicable, varying points of view should be presented. Second, stereotypes should be avoided. Third, the scope of the book should be appropriate to the target audience and to the topic being presented. Fourth, the author's qualifications should be adequate and should be stated in reference lists, acknowledgments, and notes describing the research process.

In excellent nonfiction, facts and theories are clearly distinguished. Highly qualified writers state clearly and succinctly what is known and what is conjectured; they do not mislead by stating as fact what is still a theory or hypothesis. Careful writers use qualifying phrases when they are tentative about the information. For example, some will use such phrases as "many scientists [or historians] believe," "probably could not," "we think that," and "the evidence to date suggests" to indicate that experts in the field are not certain about all things. Good writers also describe the changing status of information about a topic.

In *Wolves* (P), Seymour Simon lets his readers know what is fact and what is supposition: "Wolves make all kinds of sounds besides howling; they bark, growl, whine, and squeak. Barking seems to be a warning when a wolf is surprised at its den. Growling is common among pups when they play." A careful reader realizes that scientists *suppose* that barking serves as a warning, but *know* that pups growl when they play.

Nonfiction writers with integrity acknowledge other opinions of value; they present different views about their topic, discussing their strengths and weaknesses, if this type of discussion is appropriate for the intended audience. For example, many books about dinosaurs for older readers present differing ideas about the extinction of the dinosaurs; those for younger readers simply use verbs such as "think" or "suppose" to indicate that they are presenting theory rather than fact.

Russell Freedman, in *In Defense of Liberty: The Story of America's Bill of Rights* (I–A), explores the freedoms that Americans are entitled to under the Bill of Rights and the many challenges and controversies that have surrounded them. As he discusses these freedoms, he raises issues about them: free speech means that people who say things we don't agree with must be granted the freedom to say them; the right to privacy might mean that people who are concealing a crime can't be searched. This is a book that pushes

Beautiful photography illustrates the way wolves live in the wild in Seymour Simon's **Wolves.**

young readers to consider multiple facets of ideas—one that asks them to be critical thinkers.

The appropriateness of the scope of a book is related to its target audience. What might be said about a topic for very young children is quite different from what might be said about the same topic for older children. For example, in Laurence Pringle's *Everybody Has a Bellybutton* (N–P), the topic of human reproduction is explored in a manner that is appropriate for young children. The information presented is accurate, but the level of detail is minimal in both text and illustration. Seymour Simon's *Gorillas* (P) conveys information about these creatures in ways that young children can understand. He combines stunning photographs with a text that uses comparisons with humans that make sense to children.

In *Shutting Out the Sky: Life in the Tenements of New York, 1880–1924* (I–A), Deborah Hopkinson tells the story of the vast wave of immigrants that came to this country at the turn of the century. Her book is crammed with facts, and she makes them meaningful to and understandable by young readers through her vivid writing, her recreation of the voices of young people who lived through this era, and liberal use of period photographs. In her afterword, she speaks directly to her readers, telling them why she wrote the book and inviting them to find and tell their own family stories. The further reading and bibliography that she provides helps them understand both this particular era and Hopkinson's process.

When evaluating accuracy in nonfiction, consider the author's expertise, the sources the author used, the presentation of fact and theory, and the acknowledgment of alternative viewpoints, as appropriate to the scope of the book.

• • ORGANIZATION • •

The organization of a book refers to the logical development of the content. Ideas should be presented according to a clear sequence and pattern that informs the structure of the text. Interrelationships among facts or events should be clearly indicated.

How content is organized and presented affects the overall value of a piece of nonfiction. Good informational books are clearly organized. A brief look through a piece of nonfiction reveals how the content of a book is arranged. Does it illuminate concepts and build understanding? Does it have a table of contents to show readers what it contains? Some books have additional features, such as a glossary, a subject index (and perhaps an author index as well), a bibliography for further reading, and appendixes with further information. Readers are able to retrieve information or build on the information presented in the book by going to other sources.

The unity of a book results from the relationships among the ideas in the text. The degree of unity hinges on how the author has organized ideas to convey information. Careful, logical development of concepts is essential. Ideas should follow a logical pattern, moving, for example, from simple to complex or general to specific. Well-organized texts also make use of helpful transitions that guide the reader from one idea to the next. And all elements should tie to a central theme.

In Phillip Hoose's *The Race to Save the Lord God Bird* (I–A), the bulk of the chapters are arranged chronologically, a logical organization in a recounting of the extinction of a species over time. Before the chronology begins, however, we read an introduction, "A Bird of the Sixth Wave," that briefly describes the first five waves of extinction and foregrounds how the current, sixth wave is different. Hoose then presents the prologue, a vivid recounting of a naturalist's discovery of several ivory-billed woodpeckers in 1809, all of which he kills, one especially tragically. In Chapter 1, the story jumps ahead almost 100 years to discuss ivory-billed woodpecker specimens that had been collected in 1899; Hoose writes of his discovery of these specimens and of the questions this encounter raised about the fate of these magnificent birds. With this extended introduction setting the predominant theme—extinction and what it means for all of us—the chronology begins. This is more than just the story of the futile attempt to save the ivory-billed woodpecker, more than the stories of the biologists and ornithologists who tried to track, understand, and save the bird, but a story of the impact of extinction on our world. Written with passion, beautifully organized, and bolstered by reproductions of period photographs and art, *The Race to Save the Lord God Bird* is an outstanding work of nonfiction. The end material includes a timeline, glossary, source notes, and index.

A book's organization, of course, should be related to its intended audience. Responsible writers respect their readers and know that children, no matter what their age, can understand important ideas and concepts if they are presented clearly, in an organized fashion. Look for books that have a logical development, with a clear sequence of ideas organized in an identifiable pattern.

© Barbara Grzeslo

Chock-full of information about the ivory-billed woodpecker as well as the work of biologists and conservationists, Phillip Hoose's The Race to Save the Lord God Bird *also contains a powerful message about extinction.*

• • DESIGN • •

The design of an excellent nonfiction book is attractive, with illustrations that complement the text. These illustrations are of an appropriate medium and format to support and extend the ideas and concepts developed in the text. Further, this illustrative material is appropriately placed.

Nonfiction books should be as appealing in layout and design as fiction books. Verbal information can be elaborated by photographs, diagrams, maps, sketches, graphs, or other visual support. The illustrations help readers visualize the information contained in the text. Effective layout means that illustrations appear in close proximity to the text they illuminate, headings and subheadings are clearly presented, and the amount of text and illustration on a page does not make the page appear crowded or overwhelming. Russell Freedman's *Give Me Liberty! The Story of the Declaration of Independence* (A) is beautifully designed, with a lucid text complemented by carefully selected period art.

Many design variations are available today. In the **Eyewitness** series and the **Visual Timeline** series, each double-page spread has clear color photographs, small explanatory notes for each photograph, a brief introduction, and drawings. David Macaulay's *Mosque* (I–A), like his earlier architectural books, is a combination of lucid text and meticulous drawings to pore over. Ranging from drawings of details to colored double-page spreads, the illustrations present not only the architectural structure but also the people who built it, as the text presents both the physical and human aspects of building such a huge edifice.

Look for books in which the design enhances the presentation of information and is visually appealing. Teaching Idea 10.2 suggests an easy way for teachers to help students notice the beauty in many works of nonfiction.

• • STYLE • •

A work of nonfiction is also judged by style, or how the information is presented. The writing should be interesting and stimulating, and should reveal the author's enthusiasm for the subject. Appropriate terminology and rich language should generate curiosity and wonder in young readers.

Even when a book deals with hard facts, graceful language and a fresh vision are important components of excellent literature. Descriptive words used in interesting yet precise ways are a mark of good nonfiction. The tone of the book reveals the thrust and significance of an author's work as well as the author's relationship to the subject. Milton Meltzer (1976), an outstanding biographer and historian, puts it this way:

> What literary distinction, if any, does the book have? And here I do not mean the striking choice of word or image but the personal style revealed. I ask whether the writer's personal voice is heard in the book. In the writer who cares, there is a pressure of feeling which emerges in the rhythm of the sentences, in the choice of details, in the color of the language. Style in this sense is not a trick of rhetoric or a decorative daub; it is a quality of vision. (pp. 21–22)

The literary value of a nonfiction book depends in large part on how much passion an author brings to the work. Laurence Pringle (1986) acknowledges that his passions enter his work:

> When I'm writing, I write about my values and feelings. Many people ask what nonfiction has to do with feelings. If you want feelings, they would say, turn to fiction. But I don't think that has to be true. (p. 26)

Teaching Idea 10-2

Genre Study: Noting the Aesthetic in Nonfiction

So much nonfiction today is beautiful as well as educational. As you work with students who are reading nonfiction, help them get into the habit of noticing how their books are designed. The best way to do this is for *you* to notice and comment on books. Point out an especially beautiful photograph or illustration, commenting not only on its informational value but also on its aesthetic quality. Note the way archival material is placed in a text, even as you comment on what you learn from it. In the case of nonfiction picture books, look at the illustrations as "pictures on a wall" as well as funds of information.

You and your students can talk about the art in nonfiction in terms of line, shape, texture, color, and design, just as you would a picture storybook.

You can do the same with the writing in nonfiction. Note the metaphors that an author uses, commenting on their beauty along with their explanatory power. Discuss how an author "hooks" you, just as you would discuss the "hook" at the beginning of a story. If you note the artistry in the nonfiction that you and your students read, they will, too.

Both of Sophie Webb's books, *My Season with Penguins: An Antarctic Journal* (P–I) and *Looking for Seabirds: Journal from an Alaskan Voyage* (I), convey Webb's delight in her world through lively text and appealing watercolor illustrations. They also present a model of a field-based research journal, complete with Webb's humorous commentary on life in the field. Another strength of these books is Webb's dual perspective as both artist and scientist, with each complementing the other.

Nonfiction writers often use a narrative structure to tell the story of a person, event, or series of events. Jim Murphy uses this technique brilliantly in his many outstanding works of nonfiction, including *An American Plague: The True and Terrifying Story of the Yellow Fever Epidemic of 1793* (I–A), which won a Newbery Honor, an award rarely bestowed on a work of nonfiction. Jennifer Armstrong's riveting *Shipwreck at the Bottom of the World: The Extraordinary True Story of Shackleton and the* Endurance (I) is another outstanding work of nonfiction that employs a narrative frame.

Many nonfiction writers directly address their audience, using the pronoun *you* to draw readers into the book. Joanne Ryder asks readers to become a snail in *The Snail's Spell* (P). Other authors offer readers ideas for doing their own experiments or research, or challenge them to evaluate ideas and arguments based on the facts presented. This technique creates active readers. Look for books that contain language which both conveys and generates excitement about the subject.

JENNIFER ARMSTRONG

SHIPWRECK AT THE BOTTOM OF THE WORLD
THE EXTRAORDINARY TRUE STORY OF SHACKLETON AND THE ENDURANCE

© 1998 Jennifer M. Armstrong

Intriguing details, factual accuracy, interesting characters, and a monumental conflict with nature make this story of the Shackleton expedition to Antarctica one that most book lovers read without stopping.

✴ ✴ ✴

A CLOSE LOOK AT

Our Family Tree: An Evolution Story

Our Family Tree (P) begins at the beginning of life on earth and presents a basic outline of the complicated theory of evolution in a manner that young children can understand.

Accuracy

Although the text is minimal and the description of evolution is not detailed, Lisa Westberg Peters presents accurate facts. The end of the book contains a double-page spread with scientific explanations of nine of the major ideas in the book, another double-page spread that presents a timeline of evolution from single cells to modern humans, and a final page in which both Peters and illustrator Lauren Stringer talk about where they got their information and who reviewed the manuscript. Just as Peters meticulously researched before writing, so too did Stringer in preparation for creating her illustrations. Both text and illustrations were checked and rechecked for accuracy. The central concepts that underlie evolutionary theory—change, adaptation, chance, and interdependence—are also clearly and accurately presented.

Organization

The text is organized chronologically, the only logical way to present a theory of evolution. The minimal space of a picture-book format prohibits a full explanation, so Peters very carefully chose what information to present. Keeping the intended audience in mind, Peters compresses vast amounts of time, saying, for example, "As the seas rose and fell, our family changed again." The timeline at the end of the book indicates the number of years that this took, but within the text, that detail is not crucial, only the fact that it happened. Because Peters wanted to make evolution understandable by young children, she chose to introduce it by connecting the idea of evolution to the image of a human family tree. Stringer begins her illustrations on the title page with an image of a mother and two children—a family—on the beach, where one of them picks up a piece of driftwood and begins to draw their family tree. The text and illustrations end with the same image and the same immediacy.

© Lisa Westberg Peters

Lisa Westberg Peters

I wanted to write about evolution. I knew that this subject pulled on my emotions and made me wonder what it means to be human. Whatever I wrote, I wanted to make room for that emotion and that sense of wonder. ("The Evolution of Our Family Tree," p. 10)

The Saint Croix River flowed through Lisa Westberg Peters's childhood. She spent her summer months by its banks, discovering the nooks and crannies of the Wisconsin outdoors. "All those days of endless swimming, camping on the beach, making forts in the trees, and exploring by canoe," explains Peters in her website biography, "left a deep impression on me. Some of those experiences have found their way into my books."

Many of Peters's books for children reflect her passion for researching and writing about the natural world. The National Science Teachers Association named both *The Sun, the Wind and the Rain* and *This Way Home* Outstanding Science Trade Books. *Water's Way* was a Children's Choice Book. *Our Family Tree: An Evolution Story* won the 16th annual Minnesota Book Award, and the *Riverbank Review* recognized this piece of nonfiction as a 2004 Children's Book of Distinction.

Our Family Tree developed over the course of 13 years, during which

Peters studied geology and garnered information about evolution through reading, lectures, and field trips. "The subjects of evolution and earth and life history were all so new to me," comments Peters (2004). "Everything was startlingly fresh. I'm a curious person, so whenever I learn something new, it always leads me to ask more questions. Many writers are natural researchers and it's a trip to a candy store to sit in a library poring over the books."

Peters (2004) feels that "curiosity fuels the nonfiction writer, more so than the fiction writer." Teachers, she thinks, can help young writers explore nonfiction by modeling for them how to wonder and ask questions about the world:

Say for example, that a student wants to write about his favorite basketball player. A teacher might worry that this student is interested in basketball, only basketball, and that's not enough. But here's what might happen, given the right encouragement and a sense of curiosity:

If he reads enough about the player, he finds out plenty of interesting things. Maybe the player has injured a particular muscle or joint. What are some of the other injuries common to basketball players? Or maybe the player and several others came from a particular neighborhood or region of the country. What is it about that area that spawns basketball players? Without too big a leap, the young writer is now exploring sports medicine or social issues.

To create an outstanding picture book about evolution, Peters had to combine curiosity with creativity. "The hardest part of this process," says Peters (2004), "was finding a way to translate what I was learning into a text that might be accessible and appealing to even the youngest readers. This was the part that took the longest time—more than a dozen years." In her article for *Riverbank Review*, Peters writes that "[the] family album approach provided the frame of reference I was looking

for, since children often see family albums at home or make family trees at school." She goes on to explain that "despite having found a familiar frame of reference, I knew I would be entering territory foreign to most children. I wanted to engage readers by writing a clear, simple story, not a list of facts. As a picture-book writer, I also needed to write a story that offered plenty of visual opportunities and inspiration to an artist, because images would play a critical role in introducing this subject to children" (2003, pp. 11–12).

Although the illustrator, Lauren Stringer, and Peters did not directly collaborate to make decisions about the book's appearance, they did communicate about the text in a way that helped *Our Family Tree* develop into a uniquely unified piece of nonfiction. "The text was finished before Lauren knew about the project," explains Peters (2004). "Once she accepted the project, she needed time and distance from me to learn about the subject and to make the book her own. However, we communicated regularly. I often sent her relevant clippings with images that might be helpful to her. We both sent each other letters and postcards. From the time I first met her and talked about the book," notes Peters, "I felt she had the right soul to illustrate *Our Family Tree*."

With Stringer's meticulously researched illustrations, Peters's depiction of humanity's long ancestry is both aesthetically engaging and scientifically accurate. The book's artistic value and the questions it asks about the world combine to make *Our Family Tree* an exemplary piece of nonfiction for children.

Sources:

Peters, L. W. (n.d.). Biography. [www.lisawestbergpeters.com/bio.html]. Accessed March 2, 2005.

Peters, L. W. (2003). The evolution of *Our Family Tree. Riverbank Review*, 6(1), 10–12.

Peters, L. W. (2004, August 22). E-mail correspondence.

© Matthew Smith

Lauren Stringer

When I finally began painting the original paintings for [Our Family Tree] I had memorized my research enough that it came from inside me. I felt as if I had taken walks through the Devonian swamps and across the arid landscape of Pangaea. When I painted the dancing volcanoes, I knew I would be able to blend my personal vision with the scientific facts and still be accurate. I knew I had done my research well when I felt a deep connection to each of our ancestors and could picture in my mind where they lived, how they moved about, and what they ate. The day I painted the Permian Extinction I found myself in tears thinking about such an enormous loss of life on this earth. (2004)

Lauren Stringer was a painter and sculptor for many years before becoming a children's book illustrator. "As an artist," she told *Something about the Author* (Peacock, 2002, p. 187), "I have always tried to make my paintings and sculptures a kind of visual poetry that can add to or alter the way we perceive the world around us."

Stringer's first book for children, *Mud*, written by Mary Lyn Ray, won the Minnesota Book Award for illustration in 1996. Her other works include illustrations for the fifth

and sixth editions of Galda and Cullinan's *Literature and the Child;* Cynthia Rylant's *Scarecrow;* Mary Lynn Ray's *Red Rubber Boot Day;* Linda Ashman's *Castles, Caves and Honeycombs;* and Lisa Westberg Peters's *Our Family Tree.*

"Upon first reading *Our Family Tree,*" notes Stringer (2004), "I loved it and was terrified by it at the same time. I knew I would need to do a tremendous amount of research before I could even begin to paint this book in my own way. I am not a science illustrator, nor do I have a science/biology background, so I knew I would have to start with the 'ABC's' of evolution." Researching the illustrations for Peters's non-fiction book about evolution was a monumental task, leading Stringer on a journey from the children's science sections of libraries to the academic offices of anthropologists and geologists.

The journals and studio wall space Stringer usually uses to collect and organize artifacts and sketches for new books proved too small a space to contain the four-and-a-half billion years' worth of information she needed in order to illustrate *Our Family Tree.* Her research began to sprawl:

It became very clear early on that there was not enough room to sort and organize all my research and images on one wall. Just outside my studio on the second floor of our old Victorian house is a long wall that goes down the hall and turns to continue down the stairs. I hung sheets of paper on this wall to create a timeline that was 4 feet high by 20 feet long, placing Lisa's text at intervals that coincided with geological eras. I then began to collage images found from books on evolution, art history books, biology books, present day ancestors who still resemble ancient ancestors (e.g., the salamander for the amphibian stage that evolved lungs for us to breathe with). With this timeline I could make

note of when the landscape was frozen and arid because of glaciers or when it was more tropical and hot. I could see when the first deciduous trees and the first flowers evolved. These details were extremely important because often, when I'm working on a book, I will decide to add a flower or a tree for color or texture—but what if they didn't exist yet?! (2004)

Finding the right format for the picture book and trying to make the scientific aspects of evolution "artful" overwhelmed Stringer. She explains that it was only after taking the advice of her editor to shift her focus from illustrating "the entire world" to a more intimate portrayal of a mother and children learning about their larger family tree that she found the mood and outline to match Peters's text. "The day after [my editor] left," says Stringer (2004), "... I found a postcard of a drawing in the sand which the author Debra Frasier had sent to me. A light went on in my head as I remembered how much I used to love drawing in the sand by the seashore, and since all of life comes from the ocean and the metaphor of 'the sands of time, shifting and changing' seemed appropriate to the story of evolution, the idea of drawing our family tree in the sand became the key to the inside/outside patterns of the story."

Stringer's artistic impression of her scientific findings makes even our most distant ancestors seem familiar. Her ability to synthesize research with artistic vision culminates in a nonfiction text for children that is both accurate and aesthetically engaging.

Sources:

Peacock, S. (Ed.). (2002). Lauren Stringer. *Something about the author: Facts and pictures about authors and illustrators of books for young people, 129,* 186–188. New York: Gale Research.

Stringer, L. (2004, September 8). E-mail correspondence.

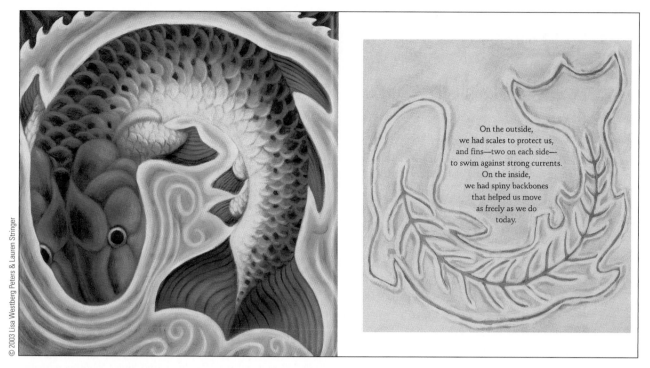

On the outside,
we had scales to protect us,
and fins—two on each side—
to swim against strong currents.
On the inside,
we had spiny backbones
that helped us move
as freely as we do
today.

Full-color paintings accompanied by paintings of sand drawings allowed Lauren Stringer to combine scientific fact and beauty in her illustrations for **Our Family Tree: An Evolution Story,** *by Lisa Westberg Peters.*

This organizational frame allows young readers to understand the larger idea of "family" that evolutionary theory suggests.

Design

The book is beautifully illustrated and designed. Stringer pays close attention to details. For example, the first four images of the family on the beach are enclosed in circles that mirror the shape of our beginnings as single-celled creatures. As the text progresses, Stringer juxtaposes sand sketches of the scientific details that the text is presenting. The genetic code is sketched in the sand, as are the backbone of the fish, the lungs of the amphibian, and the rest of the major points in our evolution that are described in the text. Through the sand sketches, Stringer portrays details without making them too graphic; the accompanying full-color paintings reflect the more general information presented in the text. The sand drawings reappear just before the end of the book in a double-page spread that recapitulates the major stages of evolution.

Style

Although many nonfiction books directly address the reader with the pronoun *you,* Peters uses the first-person pronouns, *we, our,* and *us,* to reinforce the idea of the family of man. The title is **Our** *Family Tree* rather than **The** *Family Tree.* The book begins, "All of us are part of an old, old fam-ily," and as Peters tells the story of evolution, it is happening to us. "We" were tiny round cells. "We" eventually developed big brains. This technique serves to heighten the sense of connectedness, illuminate a central concept of evolution, and keep the reader engaged. Finally, choosing to use a narrative frame to present the idea of evolution—"an evolution story"—creates a familiar structure in which to embed new ideas. Stringer's illustrations build on the story frame by depicting the progression of the day and the elaboration of the drawings that the family makes on the beach, ending with sunset as they walk away together, the sun behind them, their shadows ahead.

Nonfiction across the Curriculum

So many wonderful books are available today that children can use nonfiction trade books to explore almost any topic that interests them. Here we discuss nonfiction (excluding biography, which is covered in Chapter 9) that presents information about a multitude of topics in science, social studies, mathematics, language study, and the fine arts. Teaching Idea 10.3 applies to any topic found in the nonfiction that is available for young readers.

Teaching Idea 10-3

Make an Alphabet Book or Glossary

Every discipline, topic, or subject area has a vocabulary of its own. In order to read and comprehend text, students exploring a new area need to become familiar with its vocabulary. One way to develop vocabulary related to a particular topic is to create an ABC book or a glossary, depending on the topic. This can be done as an individual or group project, and it is a good alternative to the standard "report" by which students demonstrate their expertise.

1. Have students explore a new area of study by having them read widely in nonfiction trade books.

2. Have students select an area within the broader topic in which they would like to specialize.

3. Ask students to list all the new or important words related to the topic under study.

4. Then have them create a book that has a letter on each page, listing topical vocabulary that begins with that letter.

5. Students can draw pictures, list synonyms (if appropriate), and write definitions for each word. Use each word in a sentence that explains something about the topic.

6. Students can read the book to peers or younger students and display the handmade books in the classroom.

• • SCIENCE • •

Science, like any other discipline, evolves over time, and books for children reflect the changes in the discipline. For example, books about the environment began to increase in number about 15 years ago, as environmental issues garnered increasing attention. As politicians and the public began to take more notice of environmental issues, the numbers of books about these issues decreased. Now, with fewer restrictions regarding pollution and the recognition of the threat of global warming, the number of books about the environment, such as *The Race to Save the Lord God Bird,* may begin to increase again.

Advances in science and technology also affect children's books. Seymour Simon's wonderful series about the solar system, which includes *Mercury* and *Venus* (both i), is illustrated by stunning photographs taken during the many explorations of space that have occurred in the past several years. Sally Ride and Tam O'Shaughnessy present some of the interesting information that has been gathered during recent space explorations in *Exploring Our Solar System* (i–a). Some books about timely topics such as space exploration have to be revised in light of new information. Seymour Simon's *Destination: Mars* (i), an updated version of the original published almost 20 years ago, became necessary because of recent exploration of and thinking about the red planet. Reissues of *Earth: Our Planet in Space* and *The Moon* (both i) include new photographs obtained since their original publication 20 years ago. Other books introduce entirely new topics. Recently, there have been several interesting books about medical challenges, such as Jim Murphy's *An American Plague,* discussed earlier, and Albert Marrin's *Dr. Jenner and the Speckled Monster: The Search for the Smallpox Vaccine* (i–a).

The scientific method itself is presented in several books for young readers, including Sophie Webb's books, discussed earlier, and Stephen Swinburne's *The Woods Scientist* (i), part of the **Scientists in the Field** series. Many of Jim Arnosky's books, such as *Field Trips: Bug Hunting, Animal Tracking, Bird-Watching, and Shore Walking with Jim Arnosky* (i), are intended to help young readers learn to be keen observers. Sy Montgomery focuses on how scientists study particular species in *The Snake Scientist* and *The Tarantula Scientist* (both i).

Such topics as plants, animals and their habitats, and dinosaurs have remained popular over the years. As what we know changes, so too change the books to incorporate new information, yet the topics seem timeless. For example, a number of books about dinosaurs have been popular for years. Yet new dinosaur books continue to be written, such as Douglas Henderson's *Asteroid Impact* (i), Sandra Markle's *Outside and inside Dinosaurs* (p), Vivian French's *T. Rex* (p), and Nic Bishop's *Digging for Bird Dinosaurs: An Expedition to Madagascar* (i). It seems that some topics will never go out of favor.

Science books are so popular that HarperCollins has published for many years the **Let's Read and Find Out** series of science books for primary-grade readers. Two new offerings in this series are Wendy Pfeffer's *Dolphin Talk: Whistles, Clicks, and Clapping Jaws* and *Wiggling Worms at Work* (both p).

A list of outstanding science trade books can be obtained from the Children's Book Council and is also published every March in *Science and Children,* a journal of the National Science Teachers Association for elementary and middle school teachers. Other journals, such as *The Reading Teacher, Language Arts,* and *The Horn Book Magazine,* regularly review books that treat science topics. The Booklist at the end of this chapter includes some titles of interesting books appropriate for a science curriculum. There are many more available.

• • SOCIAL STUDIES • •

Just as in science, the content of social studies evolves as changes in the world result in new configurations of countries and people. New communications technology makes the world seem much smaller than it used to be and increases our interest in other people and places. Children have more books than ever to select from as they pursue their interests in the past and present.

In addition to the many fine biographies and works of historical fiction available, many nonfiction books cover such topics as geography and maps, life in the past, and the social structures and customs of various cultures. Children are quite naturally interested in who they are and where they come from; this natural curiosity and openness to people makes them receptive to books that explore the global community, past and present.

American history is presented from fresh perspectives in such books as Tom Feelings's *Middle Passage: White Ships/Black Cargo* (A) and Patricia McKissack and Fredrick McKissack's *Christmas in the Big House, Christmas in the Quarters* (I). Marc Aronson explores the connections between the social and political thought of England and that of colonial America in *Sir Walter Raleigh and the Quest for El Dorado* (A), winner of the first Siebert Award for nonfiction, and in the subsequent *John Winthrop, Oliver Cromwell, and the Land of Promise* (A), the second in a planned trilogy. Although the history isn't new, Aronson's treatment

of it is. New facts are presented in Chris Crowe's *Getting Away with Murder: The True Story of the Emmett Till Case* (A) in which the 1955 murder of a young black boy and the speedy acquittal of his white murderers are portrayed. Crowe also discusses how this incident galvanized people across the nation and helped provoke the civil rights movement of the 1960s.

Seemingly mundane topics are given depth and breadth in good nonfiction. Sylvia Johnson's *Mapping the World* (I) takes a historical and cultural perspective on maps and mapping. Rather than looking at maps as tools for getting from one place to another, Johnson sees them as artifacts that tell about the cultures that produced them. By taking an historical perspective, Johnson allows readers to understand how maps reflect advances in scientific knowledge and the evolution of knowledge about the world that occur over time. By ending with a discussion of geography information systems (a computer mapping system), Johnson invites her readers to join with Ptolemy and Mercator as cartographers of the world as they know it.

Current issues find their way into children's books, as Judith St. George's *So You Want to Be President?* (I–A) aptly demonstrates. David Small's funny cartoon-style illustrations perfectly match the witty text in which St. George imparts information about the office, offers humorous tidbits, and makes some forthright political statements. In the Booklist at the end of this chapter, we include some books that indicate the breadth of choice that exists for the social

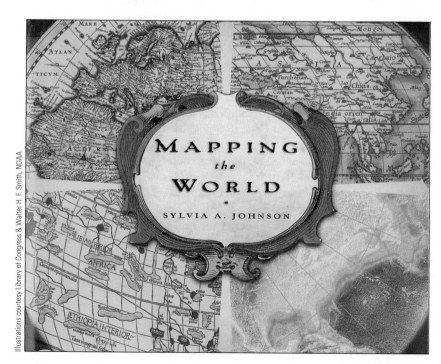

Illustrations courtesy Library of Congress & Walter H. F. Smith, NOAA

Reproductions of maps from across the ages create the visual appeal of this intriguing book.

studies teacher today. Other books that focus on various cultures are discussed in Chapter 11, and biographies are presented in Chapter 9. Further, the Children's Book Council's "Notable Trade Books in Social Studies" list is available from the council and published in the April/May issue of the journal *Social Education*.

• • MATHEMATICS • •

Fewer nonfiction books support a study of mathematics than support either science or social studies, although growing numbers are published each year. Mathematics programs today reflect a philosophy in which fiction and nonfiction literature fit naturally. Earlier mathematics instruction involved practicing isolated skills endlessly, calculating answers, memorizing combinations of numerals, and watching for a place to apply memorized routines. Today, we also present mathematical problems in context, draw on children's background knowledge to solve them, and model strategies for alternate ways to solve problems.

Many mathematics lessons begin with a story—a story with a problem that can be solved through a mathematical process. Teachers invite children to propose as many different strategies as possible to try to solve the problem. Together, they apply each strategy and evaluate its accuracy and efficiency. They learn that there are alternative ways to come up with the right answer. Stories that are structured around numbers and counting, such as Pat Hutchins's *The Doorbell Rang* (P), are especially useful for primary teachers who want to link mathematics and reading.

There are also many beautiful counting books and books that allow children to practice numeral recognition, such as Stephen Johnson's *City by Numbers* (P). These books encourage children to develop their visual skills as they look for numerals or count items on the artistically beautiful pages.

Other books explain mathematical concepts, such as Bruce McMillan's *Eating Fractions* (P–I). McMillan illustrates fractions with mouth-watering photographs of children sharing—and eating—food. The concept of one-fourth is understandable when it means the difference between a whole pizza and only part of one!

Measurement and size are explored in David Schwartz's *Millions to Measure* (P) and Steve Jenkins's *Actual Size* (P–I). Jenkins's amazing cut-paper collages appear again in this oversize book containing life-size illustrations of 18 creatures, or parts thereof. The white backdrop emphasizes the relative sizes of the creatures in the book as compared to each other, and invites young readers to compare themselves to the creatures depicted. Just how big is a gorilla's hand, anyway?

Jon Scieszka's *Math Curse* (I), illustrated by Lane Smith, is a wonderfully funny book that underscores how we use mathematics in our daily lives and presents interesting mathematical puzzles for children to figure out. The outrageous humor in the book is so infectious that children enthusiastically engage in the mental arithmetic the book calls for.

The journal *Teaching Children Mathematics* reviews books that can be linked to mathematics instruction. The Booklist at the end of this chapter includes the titles of books for mathematics learning.

• • LANGUAGE STUDY • •

Children's books that explore language are wonderful resources for an integrated language arts curriculum. Alphabet books, books about traditional parts of speech, histories of language, and books about writing are becoming more plentiful. Even punctuation takes on a new dimension in Robin Pulver's *Punctuation Takes a Vacation* (P), a primary-grades version of the popular adult book *Eats, Shoots and Leaves*. Books such as these support the study of language and, most important, support children's explorations of language as they engage in reading and writing.

Books like Brian Cleary's *Hairy, Scary, Ordinary: What Is an Adjective?* (P) help young readers understand the parts of speech. Ruth Heller is known for her brightly illustrated, eye-catching books about the parts of speech, such as *Mine, All Mine: A Book about Pronouns* (P–I). The rhyming text is surrounded by double-page illustrations visually depicting the pronouns. Heller's books give concrete and intriguing examples of what many students feel is boringly remote.

A series of books by Marvin Terban explores wordplay, such as *Guppies in Tuxedos: Funny Eponyms* (I). Jon Agee's books, such as *Elvis Lives! and Other Anagrams* (I), are also interesting to students exploring what we can do with the English language. Loreen Leedy and Pat Street present interesting sayings in *There's a Frog in My Throat! 440 Animal Sayings a Little Bird Told Me* (P) with illustrations to increase the fun.

Studies of books and authors often accompany composition instruction. These studies work best if they transcend the usual biographical information to get at the essence of what writers do—write. Leonard Marcus does just that in a series of interviews with contemporary authors contained in *Author Talk: Conversations with Judy Blume, Bruce Brooks, Karen Cushman, Russell Freedman, Lee Bennett Hopkins, James Howe, Johanna Hurwitz, E. L. Konigsburg, Lois Lowry, Ann M. Martin, Nicholasa Mohr, Gary Paulsen, Jon Scieszka, Seymour Simon, and Laurence Yep* (I–A). Reading about childhood aspirations as well as details of these writers' contemporary lives helps make clear the human struggle inherent in writing. Marcus explores how authors and illustrators work together to create picture books in *Side by Side: Five Favorite Picture-Book Teams Go to Work* (P–I–A).

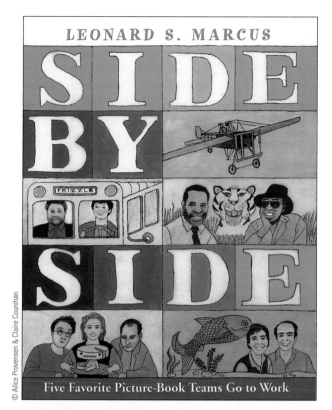

LEONARD S. MARCUS

SIDE BY SIDE

FRIZZLE

Five Favorite Picture-Book Teams Go to Work

© Alice Provensen & Claire Counihan

Leonard Marcus takes readers behind the scenes to discover how five picture-book teams work together.

These books help students not only understand the complexities of the writing process but also recognize the artistry of the books they read and enjoy.

In Chapters 13 and 14, we demonstrate how literature—both fiction and nonfiction—is a crucial component of a language arts program. In the Booklist at the end of this chapter, we include a variety of books about language that indicates the breadth of materials available. Other books on this topic can be found by consulting any reference source organized by subject.

• • **THE ARTS** • •

In addition to the many fine biographies of musicians and artists listed in Chapter 9, a variety of nonfiction books explore aspects of music and art. Just as science, social studies, mathematics, and language study are enhanced when well-written and beautifully designed books become a part of the curriculum, the study of art and music is made more vivid when accompanied by beautiful books. Several series books that explore elements of art, including Philip Yenawine's *Lines* (P–I), and books that help readers learn to look at paintings, such as Gladys Blizzard's *Come Look with Me: Animals in Art* (I), are excellent resources for those inter-

ested in learning more about fine art. Jean Tucker introduces children to photography in *Come Look with Me: Discovering Photographs with Children* (I), another book in the **Come Look with Me** series.

The **Looking at Paintings** series, by Peggy Roalf, is organized around what a viewer sees in a painting. Two books in this series are *Children* and *Flowers* (both I). Each volume contains 19 full-color reproductions of paintings accompanied by a text that presents a history of the artist and information about technique and style.

The Painter's Eye: Learning to Look at Contemporary American Art (A) is a fascinating book that explains complicated concepts in an understandable fashion. Jan Greenberg and Sandra Jordan define and give examples of the elements of art and principles of design that artists use to create paintings. They also present the postwar American artists themselves through conversations, photographs, and brief anecdotes about their childhood and their work. The text begins with a useful table of contents and includes brief biographies of the artists, a list and description of the paintings discussed, a glossary, a bibliography, an index, and suggestions for further reading. Greenberg and Jordan's *The Sculptor's Eye: Looking at Contemporary American Art* (A) is an excellent introduction to the concepts of contemporary sculpture.

A number of books explain different artistic processes and the creation of different products, inviting children to create collages, make paper, or design structures. Others explore bridges, buildings, and other objects as architectural art. David Carter and James Diaz's *The Elements of Pop-Up* (I) is much more than just a how-to manual on pop-ups. It combines clever paper engineering with lucid explanations to create a book that inspires mechanically minded readers to create their own pop-ups.

By using nonfiction books about art in conjunction with picture books that contain fine art, teachers can help children become visually literate. The Booklist at the end of this chapter includes some books about art that will open children's eyes.

Books about music also are becoming increasingly available. Many of these books look at instruments, their development, and how they work; others explore musical groups, such as the band or the symphony. Aliki's *Ah, Music* (I) is a wonderful book to share with primary-grade children. Neil Ardley's **Eyewitness** book *Music* (I–A) contains a wealth of information about how music is made. Topics range from "seeing sound" to detailed presentations of how specific instruments—from early instruments to today's electronic synthesizers—make music. The photographs and sketches that illustrate the various instruments help clarify some of the complex information. Other books about music are included in the Booklist at the end of this chapter.

In *Dance* (P), Bill T. Jones and Susan Kuklin add few words to visually stunning photographs of Jones dancing.

Aliki's *William Shakespeare and the Globe* (I) brings alive Shakespeare's life, times, and theater as she tells the story of how Sam Wanamaker's desire to build an accurate replica of the Globe Theatre results in our being able to imagine theater as it was in Elizabethan England.

Whether the subject is science, social studies, language, or the arts, many beautiful nonfiction children's books present more depth of information than can be contained within the pages of a textbook. The well-written texts of these books don't just inform; they provide models of good expository prose. The illustrations illuminate concepts and present information visually, bringing life and vitality to the topic under scrutiny. Children learn about the world from the many fine nonfiction books that are available, including how to be critical consumers of information.

Nonfiction in the Classroom

Children learn best to think, read, write, speak, and listen when instruction in all curriculum areas is integrated—when, for example, a teacher exploring plant life in a science lesson grasps the opportunity to relate the term *phototropism* to other words with the prefix *photo*. This kind of integration in instruction parallels the way children actually learn—not by seeing facts in isolation, but rather by seeing them as parts of a meaningful whole.

Teachers fashion learning activities that cut across the curriculum and that draw on books of fiction, nonfiction, and poetry in ways that encourage children in an active search for meaning. We discuss integrated instruction in Chapters 13 and 14.

Reading for information is related to other language uses; it is part of the scheme of the total language system. Children do read to learn in assigned textbooks, but they read to learn with enthusiasm and excitement in specialized trade books of quality. Compared to a textbook, a trade book can reveal the point of view of the author more directly, focus on an individual or a topic with a sharper light, and present specialized information that often gives readers a fuller understanding. Trade books provide reading and learning opportunities for readers of all ages and skill levels. Textbooks, written with a generic grade-level student in mind, cannot. Trade books also provide the opportunity for greater depth of study, as they offer more information about individual topics than any one textbook could hold. Excellent nonfiction provides many rich opportunities for learning. Rosemary Bamford and Janice Kristo's *Making Facts Come Alive: Choosing Quality Nonfiction Literature K–8* presents some of these opportunities. Betty Carter's *From Delight to Wisdom: Nonfiction for Young Adults* offers others.

Learning is more than the laying on of discrete areas of information; it requires an active response from students, an interpretation or reconstruction of new information in relation to what they already know. Rather than simply teaching a body of facts for students to memorize, effective teachers help students learn to think critically. Teaching Idea 10.4 offers some suggestions for helping students recognize what they are learning from nonfiction texts, put it in their own words, and determine what they still need to know as they become an expert about a particular topic in preparation for writing about it.

Critical reading and thinking are basic to a lifetime of learning. The schemata we develop as we learn to read and

---

Teaching Idea   10-4

Read First, Write Later

Teachers often discover that students' science and social studies reports sound all too much like the entries in their encyclopedias. The ideas offered here will help students learn to write in their own voice, use a variety of resources, and synthesize information instead of copying it from an encyclopedia.

Collect many resources on science and social studies topics for the classroom library. Keep in mind the following suggestions for enriching students' learning experience:

✳ Have your students keep journals as they read, in which they write down what they are learning *and* what they think about what they are learning. They can do this by using the left-hand side of each double-page spread for notes and the right-hand side for comments.

✳ At regular intervals, have students answer these questions in writing: "What do I know already?" "What do I want to learn?"

✳ Have students explain to a classmate what they have learned and what they are still trying to find out.

✳ Be sure that students use a variety of books to search for answers to their questions. As they read for this purpose, have them take notes about their discoveries.

✳ When they have read widely, talked about their discoveries, and written about what they are learning and how they feel about it, then it is time for them to draft a report. Talk with them about the importance of writing it in their own voice. Give them guidelines for what you want them to produce.

read to learn influence all subsequent knowledge. Thinking readers, called critical readers, evaluate new information in light of what they already know, compare many sources instead of accepting only one point of view, and make judgments about what they read. They can discriminate fact from opinion. If one goal of education is to develop informed, thinking, participating citizens, then helping children learn to read critically is essential.

The skill of reading critically is invaluable. The child who believes that anything found in print is the truth—the whole truth—is at a disadvantage relative to one who has learned to check sources, compare reports, and evaluate. Children do not question what they read when they are given one textbook that is held up as embodying the final and complete truth on its subject. They do learn to question and evaluate as they read if we encourage them to make comparisons among different sources, including nonfiction trade books.

We can engender unquestioning respect for the authority of the textbook by the way we respond to students' questions. When heard over and over again, replies such as "Look it up in the book" or "What does the book say?" may inadvertently teach students to pay abject homage to textbooks in general, at the expense of their own thinking power. Rather, we can encourage critical thinking by asking students to see what different books have to say about the same topic, or to use their own knowledge and experiences to judge the quality of an idea or piece of information.

Developmental differences in children's ability to think critically are not so much a matter of kind as of degree. Long before they turn to information found in books, very young children can make comparisons. They can consider such ideas as who is taller, which coat is warmer, which cookie is bigger. Listening to stories or looking at books, all readers can attend to details, make comparisons, and draw inferences with the help of their teacher and peers. Children of all ages can and do think critically, especially when encouraged.

Children of all ages can verify information found in books by checking it against observations made in real life. They can also assess an author's qualifications, look at the documentation provided, and critically evaluate the books they read, much as we suggest in Figure 10.1, the evaluation checklist at the beginning of this chapter. Many of the nonfiction books we've discussed here encourage readers to adopt a critical stance based on observing, collecting, and analyzing data, drawing conclusions, making inferences, and testing hypotheses. Books that draw the reader into observation and hypothesis testing help children develop an observant critical stance that spills over from books into daily life.

Children can also compare one book with others and decide which they prefer—and why. Although students in advanced grades make more complex comparisons than do younger students, the spontaneous remarks of young children show how natural it is for them to compare books. Several Teaching Ideas in earlier chapters suggest ways to compare nonfiction texts with other genres.

• • • Summary • • •

When children are given excellent nonfiction books to explore topics of interest, they learn a great deal about those topics. They learn more than they would from textbooks or encyclopedias alone because the intriguing formats of nonfiction books make them intrinsically more interesting to read and because trade books contain more detailed information. When reading nonfiction, children also have the opportunity to experience well-written, organized expository prose that can then serve as a model for their own informational writing. Further, reading several nonfiction books provides a perfect opportunity to think critically—evaluating and verifying information by making comparisons with experience and with other books. Children who learn to check multiple sources for the information they need are less likely to believe everything they see in print. Instead, they develop a healthy attitude of critical judgment.

In the May/June 2004 issue of *The Horn Book Magazine,* Betty Carter's article, "Grownup Reading," explores the recent phenomenon of nonfiction books for young readers that are based on nonfiction books for adults. Read her article and then consider her argument. Do you think that these books present an avenue for adolescent readers to join the grownups?

In the May/June 2002 issue of *The Horn Book Magazine,* Danielle Ford, in "More than the Facts: Reviewing Science Books," brings up a number of interesting points about evaluating nonfiction science books. Read this essay and think about the science nonfiction you have read. Would Ms. Ford think your selections were good ones?

Lisa Westberg Peters talks about how the idea for *Our Family Tree* percolated for quite a long time and then came together in a very short amount of time. She also discusses her research process. Lauren Stringer does the same, discussing her struggle to paint something beautiful as well as accurate. After you watch Lisa's and Lauren's interviews, go back to the book and read it again. What do you notice now that you understand the care with which the book was created?

Books for a Science Curriculum

PLANTS AND ANIMALS

Aliki, *My Visit to the Zoo* (P)

Arnold, Caroline, *Camel* (I)

_____, *Elephant* (I)

Arnosky, Jim, *All about Owls* (P)

_____, *Field Trips* (I)

_____, *I See Animals Hiding* (P)

_____, *Watching Water Birds* (P)

Bash, Barbara, *Shadows of Night: The Hidden World of the Little Brown Bat* (P)

Bernhard, Emery, *Eagles: Lions of the Sky* (P)

_____, *Prairie Dogs* (P)

Bowen, Betsy, *Tracks in the Wild* (P)

Brandenburg, Jim, *To the Top of the World: Adventures with Arctic Wolves* (I)

Brenner, Barbara, and May Garelick, *The Tremendous Tree Book* (P)

Budiansky, Stephen, *The World According to Horses: How They Run, See, and Think* (I)

Cerullo, Mary, *Lobsters: Gangsters of the Sea* (I)

Chrustkowski, Rick, *Hop Frog* (N–P)

Cole, Joanna, *My New Kitten* (P)

Cowcher, Helen, *La Tigresa* (P)

Cowley, Joy, *Red-Eyed Tree Frog* (P)

Davies, Nicola, *Surprising Sharks* (P)

Dewey, Jennifer Owings, *Poison Dart Frogs* (I)

Dowden, Anne Ophelia, *The Blossom on the Bough: A Book of Trees* (I)

Dowson, Nick, *Tigress* (P)

Ehlert, Lois, *Waiting for Wings* (P)

Esbensen, Barbara Juster, *Playful Slider: The North American River Otter* (P)

Facklam, Margery, *Creepy, Crawly Caterpillars* (P)

_____, *Spiders and Their Web Sites* (P)

French, Vivian, *Caterpillar, Caterpillar* (P)

_____, *Growing Frogs* (P)

George, Lindsay Barrett, *Around the World: Who's Been Here?* (P)

Gibbons, Gail, *Bats* (P)

Hodgkins, Fran, *Animals among Us: Living with Suburban Wildlife* (I)

Jenkins, Steve, *Biggest, Strongest, Fastest* (P)

_____, *Life on Earth: The Story of Evolution* (P–I)

Jessel, Camilla, *The Kitten Book* (P)

Johnson, Sylvia, *A Beekeeper's Year* (I)

_____, *Raptor Rescue! An Eagle Flies Free* (P)

Jolivet, Joelle, *Zoo-ology* (P)

King, Elizabeth, *Backyard Sunflower* (I)

Lasky, Kathryn, *Interrupted Journey: Saving Endangered Sea Turtles* (P–I)

_____, *Monarchs* (I)

Lauber, Patricia, *Who Eats What? Food Chains and Food Webs* (P)

Lavies, Bianca, *The Atlantic Salmon* (I)

Lerner, Carol, *Backyard Birds of Summer* (I)

_____, *Backyard Birds of Winter* (I)

Lewin, Ted, *Tooth and Claw: Animal Adventures in the Wild* (I)

Lewin, Ted, and Betsy Lewin, *Elephant Quest* (P)

_____, *Gorilla Walk* (I)

Ling, Mary, *Butterfly* (P)

_____, *Foal* (P)

Machotka, Hana, *Breathtaking Noses* (N–P)

_____, *Terrific Tails* (N–P)

Mallory, Kenneth, *Swimming with Hammerhead Sharks* (I)

Markle, Sandra, *Growing Up Wild: Wolves* (P)

_____, *Outside and inside Bats* (P–I)

Matthews, Downs, *Arctic Foxes* (P)

McMillan, Bruce, *The Baby Zoo* (I)

_____, *My Horse of the North* (P)

McNulty, Faith, *How Whales Walked into the Sea* (P)

_____, *When I Lived with Bats* (P)

Micucci, Charles, *The Life and Times of the Ant* (P)

Montgomery, Sy, *The Man-Eating Tigers of Sundarbans* (I)

_____, *The Snake Scientist* (I)

_____, *The Tarantula Scientist* (I)

Patent, Dorothy Hinshaw, *The American Alligator* (I)

_____, *The Bald Eagle Returns* (I)

Peters, Lisa Westberg, *Our Family Tree: An Evolution Story* (P)

Pfeffer, Wendy, *Dolphin Talk: Whistles, Clicks, and Clapping Jaws* (P)

_____, *Wiggling Worms at Work* (P)

Pringle, Laurence, *A Dragon in the Sky: The Story of a Green Darner Dragonfly* (I)

Rauzon, Mark, *Horns, Antlers, Fangs, and Tusks* (P)

Ryden, Hope, *Wildflowers around the Year* (I)

Ryder, Joanne, *Little Panda: The World Welcomes Hua Mei at the San Diego Zoo* (P)

Sattler, Helen Roney, *The Book of North American Owls* (I)

Sayre, April Pulley, *Dig, Wait, Listen: A Desert Toad's Tale* (P)

Simon, Seymour, *Gorillas* (P)

_____, *Wolves* (P)

Sinclair, Sandra, *Extraordinary Eyes: How Animals See the World* (I)

Tresselt, Alvin, *The Gift of the Tree* (P)

Wexler, Jerome, *Jack-in-the Pulpit* (I)

_____, *Wonderful Pussy Willows* (P)

ECOLOGY AND HABITATS

Ashabranner, Brent, *Morning Star, Black Sun: The Northern Cheyenne Indians and America's Energy Crisis* (I–A)

Bang, Molly, *Common Ground: The Water, Earth, and Air We Share* (P)

Brandenburg, Jim, *An American Safari: Adventures on the North American Prairie* (I)

Dewey, Jennifer Owings, *Antarctic Journal: Four Months at the Bottom of the World* (I)

_____, *Mud Matters: Stories from a Mud Lover* (I)

Gibbons, Gail, *Exploring the Deep, Dark Sea* (P)

Guiberson, Brenda, *Rain, Rain, Rain Forest* (P)

Hoose, Phillip, *The Race to Save the Lord God Bird* (I–A)

Montgomery, Sy, *Search for Golden Moon Bear* (I)

Pringle, Laurence, *Living Treasure: Saving Earth's Threatened Biodiversity* (I–A)

Quinlan, Susan, *The Case of the Monkeys That Fell from the Trees and Other Mysteries in Tropical Nature* (I–A)

Simon, Seymour, *Oceans* (P–I)

Swinburne, Stephen, *Once a Wolf: How Wildlife Biologists Fought to Bring Back the Grey Wolf* (I–A)

_____, *The Woods Scientist,* from the **Scientists in the Field** series (I)

Webb, Sophie, *Looking for Seabirds: Journal from an Alaskan Voyage* (I)

_____, *My Season with Penguins: An Antarctic Journal* (P–I)

SPACE, TECHNOLOGY,
AND MEDICAL ADVANCES

Borden, Louise, *Sea Clocks: The Story of Longitude* (I)

Branley, Franklin, *The International Space Station* (P)

Cole, Joanna, *The Magic School Bus and the Electric Field Trip* (P)

Dash, Joan, *The Longitude Prize* (A)

Fleischman, John, *Phineas Gage: A Gruesome but True Story about Brain Science* (I–A)

Gallant, Roy, *The Day the Sky Split Apart: Investigating a Cosmic Mystery* (A)

Jenkins, Alvin, *Next Stop, Neptune: Experiencing the Solar System* (I)

Lauber, Patricia, *You're aboard Spaceship Earth* (P)

Macaulay, David, *The New Way Things Work* (I)

Marrin, Albert, *Dr. Jenner and the Speckled Monster: The Search for the Smallpox Vaccine* (I–A)

Ride, Sally, and Tam O'Shaughnessy, *Exploring Our Solar System* (I–A)

_____, *The Mystery of Mars* (I)

_____, *The Third Planet: Exploring the Earth from Space* (I)

Scott, Elaine, *Close Encounters: Exploring the Universe with the Hubble Space Telescope* (I)

Simon, Seymour, *Comets, Meteors, and Asteroids* (I)

_____, *Destination: Jupiter* (I)

_____, *Destination: Mars* (I)

_____, *Mercury* (I)

_____, *Neptune* (I)

_____, *Our Solar System* (I)

_____, *Uranus* (I)

_____, *Venus* (I)

Skurzynski, Gloria, *Zero Gravity* (I)

OTHER SCIENCE TOPICS

Arnold, Caroline, *Dinosaurs All Around: An Artist's View of the Prehistoric World* (I)

Bang, Molly, *My Light* (P)

Berger, Melvin, *Germs Make Me Sick!* (P)

Bishop, Nic, *Digging for Bird Dinosaurs: An Expedition to Madagascar* (I)

Blackstone, Margaret, and Elissa Haden Guest, *Girl Stuff: A Survival Guide to Growing Up* (I–A)

Cobb, Vicki, *I Face the Wind* (N–P)

Cole, Joanna, *How You Were Born* (P)

_____, *The Magic School Bus Explores the Senses* (P)

Farrell, Jeanette, *Invisible Enemies: Stories of Infectious Disease* (I–A)

Floca, Brian, *Dinosaurs at the Ends of the Earth: The Story of the Central Asiatic Expeditions* (P)

Frasier, Debra, *The Incredible Water Show* (P)

French, Vivian, *T. Rex* (P)

Harris, Robie, *It's Perfectly Normal: A Book about Changing Bodies, Growing Up, Sex, and Sexual Health* (I)

_____, *It's So Amazing! A Book about Eggs, Sperm, Birth, Babies, and Families* (I)

Jackson, Donna, *The Bone Detectives: How Forensic Anthropologists Solve Crimes and Uncover Mysteries of the Dead* (I)

_____, *In Your Face: The Facts about Your Features* (I)

Jukes, Mavis, *It's a Girl Thing: How to Stay Healthy, Safe, and in Charge* (I)

Kerley, Barbara, *A Cool Drink of Water* (P–I)

Lavies, Bianca, *Compost Critters* (I)

Miller, Margaret, *My Five Senses* (N–P)

Mullins, Patricia, *Dinosaur Encore* (P)

Robbins, Ken, *Air,* from **The Elements** series (I)

_____, *Water,* from **The Elements** series (I)

Sattler, Helen Roney, *Stegosaurs: The Solar-Powered Dinosaurs* (I)

Selsam, Millicent, *How to Be a Nature Detective* (P)

Simon, Seymour, *The Brain: Our Nervous System* (I)

_____, *Muscles: Our Muscle System* (I)

Weninger, Brigitte, *Precious Water: A Book of Thanks* (P)

Wexler, Jerome, *Everyday Mysteries* (P)

Zoehfeld, Kathleen Weidner, *Dinosaur Parents, Dinosaur Young: Uncovering the Mystery of Dinosaur Families* (I)

Books for a Social Studies Curriculum

HISTORICAL EVENTS AND ERAS

Armstrong, Jennifer, *Shipwreck at the Bottom of the World: The Extraordinary True Story of Shackleton and the Endurance* (I)

Aronson, Marc, *John Winthrop, Oliver Cromwell, and the Land of Promise* (A)

_____, *Sir Walter Raleigh and the Quest for El Dorado* (A)

_____, *Witch-Hunt: Mysteries of the Salem Witch Trials* (A)

Ashabranner, Brent, *A Strange and Distant Shore: Indians of the Great Plains in Exile* (I–A)

Barboza, Steven, *Door of No Return: The Legend of Goree Island* (I)

Bartoletti, Susan Campbell, *Kids on Strike!* (I)

Bial, Raymond, *Ghost Towns of the American West* (I)

_____, *The Underground Railroad* (I)

Blumberg, Rhoda, *Bloomers!* (P)

_____, *What's the Deal? Jefferson, Napoleon, and the Louisiana Purchase* (I)

Bober, Natalie, *Countdown to Independence: A Revolution of Ideas in England and Her American Colonies: 1760–1776* (A)

Brimmer, L., and Neil Waldman, *Subway: A Brief History of Underground Mass Transit* (P–I)

Burr, Claudia, Krystyna Libura, and Maria Christina Urritia, *Broken Shields* (I)

Capuzzo, Michael, *Close to Shore: The Terrifying Shark Attacks of 1916* (A)

Cooper, Michael, *Fighting for Honor: Japanese Americans and World War II* (I)

_____, *Indian School: Teaching the White Man's Ways* (I)

Denenberg, Barry, *Voices from Vietnam* (A)

Feelings, Tom, *Middle Passage: White Ships/Black Cargo* (A)

Fisher, Leonard Everett, *The Oregon Trail* (I–A)

_____, *Tracks across America: The Story of the American Railroad, 1825–1900* (I)

Fleischman, Paul, *Dateline: Troy* (I–A)

Frank, John, *The Tomb of the Boy King* (I)

Freedman, Russell, *Give Me Liberty! The Story of the Declaration of Independence* (A)

_____, *An Indian Winter* (I)

_____, *Kids at Work: Lewis Hine and the Crusade against Child Labor* (I)

Giblin, James Cross, *The Century That Was: Reflections on the Last One Hundred Years* (A)

Greenfeld, Howard, *The Hidden Children* (I)

Greenwood, Barbara, *A Pioneer Sampler: The Daily Life of a Pioneer Family in 1840* (I)

Hamanaka, Sheila, *The Journey: Japanese Americans, Racism, and Renewal* (I–A)

Hampton, Wilborn, *Meltdown: A Race against Nuclear Disaster at Three Mile Island* (A)

_____, *September 11, 2001: Attack on New York City* (A)

Hansen, Joyce, and Gary McGowan, *Freedom Roads: Searching for the Underground Railroad* (I)

Jacobs, Francine, *The Tainos: The People Who Welcomed Columbus* (I)

Kalman, Maira, *Fireboat: The Heroic Adventures of the* John J. Harvey (P)

Katz, William Loren, *Black Pioneers: An Untold Story* (I–A)

Kimmel, Elizabeth Cody, *Ice Story: Shackleton's Lost Expedition* (I)

Lalicki, Tom, *Grierson's Raid: A Daring Strike through the Heart of the Confederacy* (I)

Landau, Elaine, *The New Nuclear Reality* (A)

Lanier, Shannon, and Jane Feldman, *Jefferson's Children: The Story of One American Family* (I)

Lauber, Patricia, *Who Came First? New Clues to Prehistoric Americans* (I)

Lavender, David, *Snowbound: The Tragic Story of the Donner Party* (I)

Levine, Ellen, *Darkness over Denmark* (A)

_____, *A Fence away from Freedom: Japanese Americans and World War II* (A)

Maestro, Betsy, and Giulio Maestro, *More Perfect Union: The Story of Our Constitution* (P–I)

Marrin, Albert, *America and Vietnam: The Elephant and the Tiger* (A)

McKissack, Patricia, and Fredrick McKissack, *Black Hands, White Sails: The Story of African American Whalers* (I–A)

_____, *Christmas in the Big House, Christmas in the Quarters* (I)

_____, *Red-Tail Angels: The Story of the Tuskegee Airmen of World War II* (I)

McWhorter, Diane, *A Dream of Freedom: The Civil Rights Movement from 1954 to 1968* (I–A)

Meltzer, Milton, *The Amazing Potato: A Story in Which the Incas, Conquistadors, Marie Antoinette, Thomas Jefferson, Wars, Famines, Immigrants, and French Fries All Play a Part* (I)

_____, *Cheap Raw Material* (A)

_____, *Hear That Train Whistle Blow! How the Railroad Changed the World* (A)

_____, *Witches and Witch Hunts: A History of Persecution* (A)

Morrison, Toni, *Remember: The Journey to School Integration* (I)

Murphy, Jim, *Across America on an Emigrant Train* (I)

_____, *An American Plague: The True and Terrifying Story of the Yellow Fever Epidemic of 1793* (I–A)

_____, *Blizzard: The Storm That Changed America* (A)

_____, *The Boys' War: Confederate and Union Soldiers Talk about the Civil War* (I–A)

Myers, Walter Dean, *USS Constellation: Pride of the American Navy* (I)

Rappaport, Doreen, *Free at Last! Stories and Songs of Emancipation* (I)

Ray, Delia, *A Nation Torn: The Story of How the Civil War Began* (A)

Ritter, Lawrence, *Leagues Apart: The Men and Times of the Negro Baseball Leagues* (I)

Schlissel, Lillian, *Black Frontiers: A History of African-American Heroes in the Old West* (I)

Sewall, Marcia, *People of the Breaking Day* (I)

_____, *The Pilgrims of Plimoth* (I)

_____, *Thunder from the Clear Sky* (I)

Stanley, Jerry, *Children of the Dust Bowl: The True Story of the School at Weedpatch Camp* (I)

_____, *I Am an American: A True Story of Japanese Internment* (I)

St. George, Judith, *Mason and Dixon's Line of Fire* (I–A)

Viola, Herman, *It Is a Good Day to Die: Indian Eyewitnesses Tell the Story of the Battle of the Little Bighorn* (I–A)

Winter, Jeanette, *September Roses* (I)

PEOPLE, PLACES, AND HISTORICAL DOCUMENTS

Aaseng, Nathan, *The Impeachment of Bill Clinton,* from the **Famous Trials** series (A)

Arnold, Caroline, *City of the Gods: Mexico's Ancient City of Teotihuacan* (I)

_____, *Uluru: Australia's Aboriginal Heart* (I)

Ashabranner, Brent, *A Date with Destiny: The Women in Military Service for America Memorial* (A)

Budhos, Marina, *Remix: Conversations with Immigrant Teenagers* (A)

Burleigh, Robert, *Black Whiteness: Admiral Byrd Alone in the Antarctic* (I–A)

Chandra, Deborah, and Madeline Comora, *George Washington's Teeth* (P)

Colman, Penny, *Girls: A History of Growing Up Female in America* (I–A)

Crowe, Chris, *Getting Away with Murder: The True Story of the Emmett Till Case* (A)

Curlee, Lynn, *Brooklyn Bridge* (I)

Fisher, Leonard Everett, *The Architects,* from the **Colonial Craftsmen** series (I)

_____, *The Blacksmiths,* from the **Colonial Craftsmen** series (I)

Ford, Michael Thomas, *Outspoken: Role Models from the Lesbian and Gay Community* (A)

Freedman, Russell, *Give Me Liberty! The Story of the Declaration of Independence* (I–A)

_____, *In Defense of Liberty: The Story of America's Bill of Rights* (I–A)

Fritz, Jean, *The Lost Colony of Roanoke* (I)

Geisert, Bonnie, and Arthur Geisert, *Desert Town* (P)

_____, *Prairie Town* (P)

Giblin, James Cross, *Secrets of the Sphinx* (I)

Hansen, Joyce, and Gary McGowen, *Breaking Ground, Breaking Silence: The Story of New York's African Burial Ground* (A)

Hopkinson, Deborah, *Shutting Out the Sky: Life in the Tenements of New York, 1880–1924* (I–A)

Jenkins, Steve, *The Top of the World: Climbing Mt. Everest* (P)

Karas, Brian, *Atlantic* (N–P)

Leacock, Elspeth, and Susan Buckley, *Journeys in Time: A New Atlas of American History* (I)

_____, *Places in Time: A New Atlas of American History* (I)

Lewin, Ted, *Lost City: The Discovery of Machu Picchu* (P)

Macaulay, David, *Mosque* (I–A)

Marrin, Albert, *George Washington and the Founding of a Nation* (A)

Mochizuki, Ken, *Passage to Freedom: The Sugihara Story* (P)

Munro, Roxie, *The Inside-Outside Book of New York City* (P–I)

_____ *The Inside-Outside Book of Washington, D.C.* (P–I)

Murphy, Jim, *Gone a-Whaling: The Lure of the Sea and the Hunt for the Great Whale* (I–A)

_____, *Inside the Alamo* (I)

Nash, Gary, *Forbidden Love: The Secret History of Mixed-Race America* (A)

O'Connor, Jane, *The Emperor's Silent Army: Terracotta Warriors of Ancient China* (I–A)

Patent, Dorothy Hinshaw, *The Lewis and Clark Trail Then and Now* (I)

Philbrick, Nathaniel, *Revenge of the Whale: The True Story of the Whaleship* Essex (A)

Preston, Diana, *Remember the* Lusitania (I)

Seawell, Marcia, *James Towne: Struggle for Survival* (I)

Severance, John, *Skyscrapers: How America Grew Up* (I)

Siebert, Diane, *Rhyolite: The True Story of a Ghost Town* (P)

Smith, David, *If the World Were a Village: A Book about the World's People* (I–A)

Sneve, Virginia Driving Hawk, *The Seminoles* (I)

Stewart, Gail, *Teen Addicts,* from the **Other America** series (A)

Sullivan, George, *Picturing Lincoln: Famous Photographs That Popularized the President* (I)

Waldman, Neil, *Wounded Knee* (I–A)

Williams, Stanley, *Life in Prison* (I–A)

Wolf, Bernard, *Homeless* (P–I)

Yue, Charlotte, and David Yue, *The Wigwam and the Longhouse* (I)

OTHER HISTORICAL TOPICS

Giblin, James Cross, *Be Seated: A Book about Chairs* (I)

Hamanaka, Sheila, *On the Wings of Peace* (I)

Johnson, Sylvia, *Mapping the World* (I)

Lauber, Patricia, *What You Never Knew about Tubs, Toilets, and Showers* (P–I)

Wolf, Bernard, *Homeless* (P–I)

Books for a Mathematics Curriculum

COUNTING

Anno, Mitsumasa, *Anno's Counting Book* (P)

Bang, Molly, *Ten, Nine, Eight* (N–P)

Ehlert, Lois, *Fish Eyes: A Book You Can Count On* (N–P)

Feelings, Muriel, *Moja Means One: A Swahili Counting Book* (N–P)

Fleming, Denise, *Count!* (N–P)

Geisert, Arthur, *Roman Numerals I to MM* (I)

Giganti, Paul, Jr., *How Many Snails?* (P)

Hoban, Tana, *Count and See* (P)

Hutchins, Pat, *1 Hunter* (P)

Morozumi, Atsuko, *One Gorilla* (N–P)

Tafuri, Nancy, *Who's Counting?* (P)

ADDITION AND SUBTRACTION

Aruego, Jose, and Ariane Dewey, *Five Little Ducks* (P)

Burningham, John, *The Shopping Basket* (P)

Chorao, Kay, *Number One Number Fun* (P)

Christelow, Eileen, *Five Little Monkeys Jumping on the Bed* (N–P)

Peek, Merle, *Roll Over!* (P)

Pinczes, Elinor, *A Remainder of One* (P)

MULTIPLICATION AND DIVISION

Aker, Suzanne, *What Comes in 2's, 3's, and 4's?* (I)

Hulme, Joy, *Sea Squares* (I)

Hutchins, Pat, *The Doorbell Rang* (P)

Leedy, Loreen, *2 3 2 5 Boo! A Set of Spooky Multiplication Stories* (I)

FRACTIONS

Leedy, Loreen, *Fraction Action* (I)

McMillan, Bruce, *Eating Fractions* (P–I)

MONEY AND TIME

Anno, Mitsumasa, *All in a Day* (P–I)

Hoban, Tana, *Twenty-Six Letters and Ninety-Nine Cents* (N–P)

Hutchins, Pat, *Clocks and More Clocks* (P)

Schwartz, David, *How Much Is a Million?* (P–I)

_____, *If You Made a Million* (P–I)

MEASUREMENT AND SIZE

Hoban, Tana, *Is It Larger? Is It Smaller?* (N–P)

Jenkins, Steve, *Actual Size* (P–I)

Markle, Sandra, *Measuring Up! Experiments, Puzzles, and Games Exploring Measurement* (I)

Schwartz, David, *Millions to Measure* (P)

PROBLEM SOLVING

Anno, Masaichiro, and Mitsumasa Anno, *Anno's Mysterious Multiplying Jar* (I–A)

Scieszka, Jon, *Math Curse* (I)

Books about Language

Heller, Ruth, *A Cache of Jewels and Other Collective Nouns* (I)

_____, *Many Luscious Lollipops: A Book about Adjectives* (I)

Leedy, Loreen, and Pat Street, *There's a Frog in My Throat! 440 Animal Sayings a Little Bird Told Me* (P)

Marcus, Leonard, *Author Talk: Conversations with Judy Blume, Bruce Brooks, Karen Cushman, Russell Freedman, Lee Bennett Hopkins, James Howe, Johanna Hurwitz, E. L. Konigsburg, Lois Lowry, Ann M. Martin, Nicholasa Mohr, Gary Paulsen, Jon Scieszka, Seymour Simon, and Laurence Yep* (I–A)

_____, *Side by Side: Five Favorite Picture-Book Teams Go to Work* (P–I–A)

Pulver, Robin, *Punctuation Takes a Vacation* (P)

Terban, Marvin, *The Dove Dove* (I)

_____, *Guppies in Tuxedos: Funny Eponyms* (I)

_____, *Hey, Hay! A Wagonful of Funny Homonym Riddles* (I)

_____, *In a Pickle and Other Funny Idioms* (I)

_____, *I Think, I Thought: And Other Tricky Verbs* (I)

_____, *Mad as a Wet Hen! And Other Funny Idioms* (I)

_____, *Punching the Clock: Funny Action Idioms* (I)

_____, *Time to Rhyme: A Rhyming Dictionary* (I)

_____, *Your Foot's on My Feet! And Other Tricky Nouns* (I)

Books about the Arts

Aliki, *Ah, Music* (I)

_____, *William Shakespeare and the Globe* (I)

Ancona, George, *Cutters, Carvers, and the Cathedral* (I)

Bang, Molly, *Picture This: How Pictures Work* (P–I–A)

Berger, Melvin, *The Science of Music* (A)

_____, *The Story of Folk Music* (A)

Blizzard, Gladys, *Come Look with Me: Animals in Art* (P–I)

_____, *Come Look with Me: Exploring Landscape Art with Children* (P–I)

Carter, David, and James Diaz, *The Elements of Pop-Up* (I)

Christelow, Eileen, *What Do Illustrators Do?* (P)

Cummings, Pat, *Talking with Artists* (Vol. 3) (I)

Florian, Douglas, *A Carpenter* (N–P)

_____, *A Potter* (N–P)

Greenberg, Jan, and Sandra Jordan, *The Painter's Eye: Learning to Look at Contemporary American Art* (A)

_____, *The Sculptor's Eye: Looking at Contemporary American Art* (A)

Guthrie, Woody, *This Land Is Your Land* (P)

Hayes, Ann, *Meet the Orchestra* (P–I)

Isaacson, Philip, *A Short Walk around the Pyramids and through the World of Art* (I)

Jones, Bill T., and Susan Kuklin, *Dance* (P)

Krementz, Jill, *A Very Young Dancer* (I)

_____, *A Very Young Musician* (I)

LeTord, Bijou, *A Bird or Two: A Story about Henri Matisse* (P)

Marcus, Leonard, *A Caldecott Celebration: Six Artists and Their Paths to the Caldecott Medal* (I)

Micklethwait, Lucy, *I Spy a Lion: Animals in Art* (P)

_____, *I Spy Two Eyes: Numbers in Art* (P)

Raboff, Ernest, *Albrecht Dürer* (I–A)

_____, *Leonardo da Vinci* (I–A)

_____, *Pablo Picasso* (I–A)

Raschka, Chris, *Mysterious Thelonious* (I)

Roalf, Peggy, *Children,* from the **Looking at Paintings** series (I)

_____, *Flowers,* from the **Looking at Paintings** series (I)

Tucker, Jean, *Come Look with Me: Discovering Photographs with Children* (I)

Venezia, M., *Francisco Goya* (I–A)

_____, *Picasso* (I–A)

Ventura, Piero, *Great Composers* (I)

Woolf, F., *Picture This: A First Introduction to Paintings* (I)

Yenawine, Philip, *People* (P)

_____, *Places* (P)

Zaunders, Bo, *Gargoyles, Girders, and Glass Houses: Magnificent Master Builders* (I)

..Part 2.........

Children and Books

Chapter

11

Building a Culturally Diverse Literature Collection

"We're not going to give up hope. Those rogues and thieves in our country won't be there forever. One day we shall go home!" He spoke in that steady voice that Sade had always found so comforting. She nestled back close to Papa and Femi. Home. She still found it so difficult to say the word herself. She would have to learn. Now that Papa was with them, England might become their new "home" for a while, if they were allowed to stay. If Papa was to lecture in America, they might make a new "home" there. If they went to South Africa . . . If, if . . . Wherever they went, they would have to become like tortoises who carry their homes on their backs. She thought of Papa's brave tortoise and hoped that at least they would not have to meet any more leopards.

—BEVERLY NAIDOO, *The Other Side of Truth,* p. 245

FRANK'S SIXTH-GRADE CLASS HAS BEEN READING BOOKS THAT TELL THE stories of children who are refugees, forced to flee their homeland because of famine, war, or oppression. They have read historical novels, such as Jane Kurtz's *The Storyteller's Beads* and Patricia Reilly Giff's *Nory Ryan's Song* (both I–A), as well as more contemporary books, such as Minfong Ho's *Gathering the Dew,* Peggy Dietz Shea's *Tangled Threads,* Edwidge Danticat's *Behind the Mountains,* and Ben Mikaelsen's *Red Midnight,* as well as *The Other Side of Truth* (all I–A). Frank has a list of other books for students interested in further reading.

Frank's theme for the year has centered on "home." At a time when they are moving away from their home life and more deeply into their social lives, these students have enjoyed thinking and talking about what makes a home and a family. For them, the plight of Sade and her brother, Femi, who must flee Nigeria when their mother is assassinated by those trying to silence their father's outspoken journalism, resonates with what is happening in their own lives, even though they are not fleeing repression. Frank's students have seen in the two characters echoes of the same feelings that they themselves are experiencing as they venture out on their own into the world. These stories of the loss and rebuilding of a "home" have been oddly comforting to these middle-class American kids.

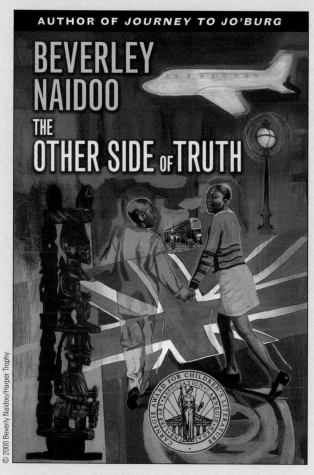

Beverly Naidoo's spellbinding story of two children who flee from Nigeria to London won the Carnegie Award for Children's Literature.

Frank's choice of books is wise; these are exciting stories that captivate readers from the very first page. The characters are engaging, and they are real; young readers recognize their humanity. This is the first year that Frank has used books about political refugees, and he likes the dimension they add to his thematic focus on home. Teaching Idea 11.1 offers some ideas for comparing books about the refugee experience and for linking these books to students' lives, just as Frank has done. As his students are exploring this theme, they are also learning about their world and the stories of others, while linking the experiences and feelings of characters from around the world to their own experiences and feelings. This is possible because Frank selected literature that reflects the diversity of our world.

Culturally Diverse Literature

How lucky we are to be able to explore the diversity and richness that mark children's literature today. As we discussed in Chapter 1, the field of children's books changed considerably during the last half of the 20th century as it

Teaching Idea 11-1

Making Connections with Stories of Refugee Children

Gather a number of books that tell the stories of children who are forced to flee from their homes, and decide how you want to share these books with your students. You might want to read one or two of them aloud to the whole class, or read one aloud and have small groups read different books at the same time. Then pose questions for your students to answer either orally or in writing. Some might be answered with a Venn diagram or a chart highlighting similarities and differences.

✳ What traits do you notice in the main character? Are these traits similar to or different from your own?

✳ What kinds of problems, large and small, does the main character encounter? Have you ever encountered similar problems?

✳ Imagine that you are in the main character's position. What would you do in these circumstances? Would your actions differ from the main character's? Why or why not?

✳ If the main character fled to your state, city, and neighborhood and was going to school with you, do you think he or she would be happy? Why or why not?

If you have read several books, ask students to review their answers to these questions, discuss the books, and see if they can make generalizations that might be universal to all people. For example, they might decide that "Every person needs a home where he or she can feel safe" is a generalization applicable to everyone.

The following is a sampling of books to select from, all appropriate for grades six and up.

Alvarez, Julia, *Before We Were Free*

Armstrong, Jennifer, *Shattered*

Baille, Alan, *Little Brother*

Brown, Jackie, *Little Cricket*

Carlsson, Janne, *Camel Bells*

Danticat, Edwidge, *Behind the Mountains*

Dorros, Arthur, *Under the Sun*

Ellis, Deborah, *Parvana's Journey*

Giff, Patricia Reilly, *House of the Tailors*

_____, *Nory Ryan's Song*

Hesse, Karen, *Aleutian Sparrow*

Hiçyilmaz, Gaye, *Smiling for Strangers*

Ho, Minfong, *The Clay Marble*

_____, *Gathering the Dew*

Kherdian, David, *The Road from Home*

Kurtz, Jane, *The Storyteller's Beads*

Michaelson, Ben, *Red Midnight*

Naidoo, Beverly, *The Other Side of Truth*

Placide, Jaïra, *Fresh Girl*

Pressler, Mirjam, *Malka*

Shea, Peggy Dietz, *Tangled Threads*

Veciana-Suarez, Ana, *Flight to Freedom*

---

began to reflect the diversity that marks North America and to include literature from around the world. Building a culturally diverse collection of books means that we seek out books from many cultures to fill our shelves and to enrich the minds and hearts of our students.

There are many ways to think about diversity. Too often those in the mainstream make the mistake of thinking that cultural diversity refers only to people who are different from them, but it does not! Everyone belongs to a culture, even several cultural communities. Our cultures are woven from many diverse strands; we all live in families and communities that draw on a wealth of knowledge and skills to help them function (Moll, 1994). Culture is much more than race, ethnicity, gender, sexual preference, or exceptionalities, as it also involves values, attitudes, customs, beliefs, and ethics.

From this perspective, all children's books could be considered culturally diverse in relation to each other. The important task is to create a collection that is balanced in terms of diversity, that explores more than just the culture of mainstream, middle-class European Americans, which has for so long dominated children's books. A balanced collection includes books that reflect the rich cultures of Native Americans, African Americans, Asian Americans, Latinos, and others who contribute to the patchwork quilt of North American culture. It includes books that reflect a wide configuration of family structures, explore diverse sexual orientations, make readers think about issues of class and gender, and contain characters with exceptionalities that shape their worlds. A culturally diverse collection also contains international books that reflect the many peoples and places in our world.

Children's and adolescent literature in North America is still largely a literature of the mainstream—middle-class, heterosexual Caucasians living "normal" lives. Although since the mid-20th century we have benefited from an increasing number of books that embrace diversity, the percentage of these books in relation to the entire corpus of books published each year remains woefully low, despite the increasing diversity of our population.

In terms of racial and ethnic diversity, a study of children's books that present pluralistic, balanced racial and ethnic images of children shows that U.S. book publication figures seldom parallel census figures (Bishop, 1994). Although the number of U.S. residents from parallel cultures has increased dramatically, few books representing those groups were published between the 1960s and 1980s. In 1994, Bishop found that only 3 to 4 percent of the children's books published in 1990, 1991, and 1992 related to people of color. Since 1999, less than 3 percent of books published each year were by or about people of color (Hansen-Krening, Aoki, & Mizokawa, 2003). Considering that more than 5,000 books for children and early adolescents are published in the United States alone each year, there are not enough books that reflect diversity published in any given year. Further, many new immigrant groups are severely underrepresented.

The situation is similar in terms of international literature. Although books published in English-speaking countries are often available internationally, less than 1 percent of books published in the United States are books that have been translated (Tomlinson, 2002; see also Stan, 2002, and Tomlinson, 1998). Books that contain characters who are gay, lesbian, bisexual, or transgendered are also few and far between, as are books that contain characters with exceptionalities. Clearly, we have a long way to go.

In spite of the paltry number of books that embrace diversity, we have made some progress. Whereas it was difficult in the 1960s and 1970s to find books that presented girls and women in what at the time were "nontraditional" roles, that is not the case today. Female characters in contemporary realistic fiction reflect a profound change in society's perceptions of roles for women and girls. Social class as presented in contemporary fiction also seems to have been slightly transformed. There are now a greater number of books in which the characters are poor or working class, but again, the numbers do not reflect census figures. Some books, such as Katherine Paterson's *Flip-Flop Girl* (I) or Virginia Ewer Wolff's *Bat 6* (I–A), explicitly grapple with how issues of class affect people's lives.

Although literature by and about people of color, what Virginia Hamilton (1993) calls "parallel cultures," remains a small percentage of all publications, publishing houses devoted to publishing these books are increasing in number. Lee & Low Books recently celebrated their success with *A Tenth Anniversary Celebration of Multicultural Publishing* (2003). Publishing houses that focus on culturally diverse

literature—such as Children's Book Press, Lee & Low Books, Piñata Books, and Arte Público—promise a continued increase in the number of books by and about people of color. Publishers such as North-South Books and Kane/Miller are in the forefront of the effort to bring translated books to an American audience, with sometimes spectacular success. Chih-Yuan Chen's *Guji Guji* (P), first published in Taiwan, where it won the Hsin Yi Picture Book Award, was a *New York Times* bestseller when it became popular in North America. The addresses of these specialized publishers appear in Appendix C. Special recognition of authors and illustrators of particular parallel cultures, such as the Coretta Scott King Awards and the Pura Belpré Award, also help support the production of culturally diverse literature. The Mildred L. Batchelder Award honors the best translated book of any given year. Winners of these awards are listed in Appendix A. Stunning talent, market recognition, stalwart publishers, and the cultural and social changes in the last few decades of the 20th century have come together to create a demand for quality books from parallel cultures that will continue into the future (Bader, 2003b). In a three-part series of articles in *The Horn Book Magazine,* Barbara Bader (2002, 2003a, 2003b) describes the gradual growth of literature from parallel cultures.

In another promising development, teachers, critics, authors, and publishers are becoming increasingly aware of the diversity within diversity, understanding that defining people as belonging to a particular racial group belies the fact that every group contains a wide variety of people, histories, customs, beliefs, and characteristics. It is, however, a convenience to broadly categorize books as "African American" or as about "people with exceptionalities." Within each broad category, however, are wide variations in the ideas and experiences presented. After all, books, especially fictional narratives, are not about groups but about individuals within those groups. As works of culturally diverse literature increase in number and quality, these variations become clearer.

Culturally Diverse Literature in Children's Lives

Readers shape their view of the world and of themselves partly through the books they read. If children never see themselves in books, they receive the subtle message that they are not important enough to appear in books, that books are not for them. Conversely, if children see only themselves in the books they read, the message is that those who are different from them are not worthy of appearing in books. Stereotyped images of an ethnic group, gender, nationality, region, religion, or other subculture also are harmful not only to the children of that group but also to others who then get a distorted view. Culturally diverse literature informs us about ourselves and helps us know each other.

As we discuss in other chapters, literature can act as both mirror and window for its readers (Cullinan, 1982; Galda, 1980). Recently, Bishop (1997) has applied this metaphor to culturally diverse literature. Although it is true that literature allows readers to understand both themselves and those different from themselves, perhaps the best books offer an experience that is more like looking through a window as the light slowly darkens. At first one sees clearly through the window into another's world—but gradually, as the light fades, one's own image becomes reflected too (Galda, 1998). Children's books at their best highlight the unique characteristics of the cultures represented by their characters but also speak to universal experiences. With them we can celebrate differences, call attention to commonly held values and experiences, and promote empathy and a sense of common humanity. The goal of creating a more equitable society requires that people from many cultures learn to live together peaceably. If we understand people of other cultures and other nations, it is difficult to view them as being "on the other side" in times of conflict. Teaching Idea 11.2 offers some suggestions for helping students make links between the books they are reading and their own lives.

Teaching Idea 11-2

Making Thematic Connections: Learning about Yourself

Begin the year by asking students to write down several characteristics that describe themselves, as well as several likes and dislikes. If you plan ahead, you can ask questions that will enable them to think about certain aspects of their lives before they read the books you have selected. As you read books set in different countries depicting various cultures, explicitly talk about the similarities between the experiences, emotions, attitudes, relationships, and personalities that students find in the books and those they find in their lives. Periodically ask students to write about what they have learned about various characters and cultures and what they have learned about themselves. For example, it might surprise some students to realize how terrible it would be not to be able to go to school, or to be separated from a sibling. As a culminating activity, ask students to revisit and revise their original descriptions of themselves.

Children can begin to know people of other cultures through literature. They can recognize similarities between themselves and others; they can understand universal qualities of humankind. Although we do not want literature to explicitly teach lessons of tolerance, thinking about, talking about, and developing an understanding of others are natural outgrowths of reading diverse literature. Further, children who do not have the opportunity to read books from and about different cultures miss a lot of wonderful writing by extraordinary authors.

Criteria for Evaluating Culturally Diverse Literature

Today all genres contain books from different cultural perspectives, which means that it is now possible to make diversity a central tenet of the literature collection in your classroom and in your school library. Books representing many cultures should be a part of children's daily life at school, just as they are an integral part of children's and adolescent literature. Because of this, we discuss those books within the genre chapters in the first section of this book. Here we focus the discussion on how to find and evaluate books that represent diverse cultures so that you can build a rich, useful collection. We explore how to use these books in a classroom setting in Chapters 13 and 14.

There are many aspects to consider when selecting books to build a culturally diverse collection. For example, consider the role of culture in a book. Some books have characters that are from a variety of ethnicities or cultures, and often indicate diversity through visual information, such as color, eye shape, hair color and style, or the presence of a wheelchair, but present no cultural content. You might think of books of this type as "painted faces" books. If the inclusion of culturally diverse characters is gratuitous or stereotyped, the book should be avoided. Sometimes, however, the diversity subtly reinforces the idea that we live in a culturally diverse world, one populated by people of different colors, people in wheelchairs, people who live in a variety of situations. One such book, Rebecca C. Jones's *Matthew and Tilly* (P), illustrated by Beth Peck, is a picture storybook about friends fighting and then resolving their differences. It happens that Matthew is a white male, Tilly a black female; this information comes to us through the illustrations. Culture, as such, is not an important aspect of this book, but the theme of friendship is broadened by the diversity depicted.

Other books are about "culture as a concept"; their theme or unifying idea is that culture is important, that people are different yet the same, that differences need to be bridged. Many of these books explicitly state this idea, such as Mem Fox's *Whoever You Are* (P), Aliki's *Marianthe's Story: Painted Words/Spoken Memories* (P), or Jacqueline Woodson's *The Other Side* (P–I).

Other books are "culturally rich," depicting experiences that are explicitly embedded in a particular culture, with setting, plot, and characters inextricably tied to culture (Bishop, 1997), such as Francisco Jiménez's *La Mariposa* (P–I) or Walter Dean Myers' *blues journey* (I–A), illustrated by Christopher Myers. Ellen Wittlinger's *What's in a Name?* (A) explores class, race, and sexual identity by presenting the perspectives of 10 different adolescents as they react to the same crisis. This novel presents adolescent readers with the opportunity to explore the way life experiences shape the multiple perspectives that are the heart of the book. Culturally rich books allow readers to look through the window at characters just like or different from themselves, to recognize their own culture or learn about another. These are the books that offer the opportunity for a more than superficial experience with diverse characters or concepts, and these are the books that we focus on in this chapter.

Regardless of the role culture plays in a book, the depiction of culture should be accurate, authentic, and free from stereotypes. Culturally diverse literature portrays what is unique to an individual culture and universal to all cultures. It accurately portrays the nuances and variety of day-to-day living in the culture depicted. It does not distort or misrepresent the culture it reflects (Bishop, 1992).

Determining authenticity, accuracy, and the absence of stereotypes can be difficult if you are not of the culture depicted. Fortunately, there are a number of resources that can help you make good decisions about which books to include in your collection. The Multicultural Booklist Committee of the National Council of Teachers of English (NCTE) periodically prepares *Kaleidoscope,* an annotated bibliography of multicultural books (defined as books about people of color residing in the United States, Africa, Asia, South and Central America, the Caribbean, Mexico, Canada, and England) as well as books that focus on intercultural or interracial issues. As they read and evaluate books, the committee eliminates those that demonstrate stereotyped images in text or illustration, demeaning or inaccurate use of language, and inaccuracies in text or illustration. The committee does not consider books multicultural when culture is mere tokenism or when it is reflected through the gratuitous inclusion of a sprinkling of words from another language or an occasional character of color in the illustrations (Bishop, 1994).

Problems with perspective are another concern of the committee and also a source of debate among the children's literature community. Some argue that no one outside a particular cultural group can hope to write with the understanding and knowledge of an insider and therefore should not try. Some grant that being an outsider makes it more difficult, but that good writers such as Paul Goble transcend their outsider status. A good book will "contribute in a positive way to an understanding of the people and cultures portrayed" (Bishop, 1994, p. xx), whether its author is an insider or an outsider to the culture. However, it is important to note the perspective of the author when deciding on the quality of any book. In *Stories Matter: The Complexity of Cultural Authenticity in Children's Literature,* editors Dana Fox and Kathy Short (2003) have collected a number of previously published articles that explore this issue.

Books representing culturally diverse groups must represent them accurately and with depth. Look for books that avoid stereotypes, portray the values and the cultural group in an authentic way, use language that reflects cultural group usage, and validate readers' experiences while also broadening vision and inviting reflection. As you begin to evaluate books for their cultural authenticity, use a checklist such as that in Figure 11.1. You can also consult some of the many sources listed in Figure 11.2 and cited in the next sections of this chapter.

In Chapters 2 through 10, we discuss the criteria for quality literature in each genre and give examples of books that are among the best of the genre. Here we evaluate books not on genre criteria but on criteria that speak to the quality of the cultural content. If you think of the genre criteria as one lens through which to view children's books critically, think of cultural content as a second lens, one that is additional to rather than a replacement for the genre criteria. Each informs the other, and any book can and should be evaluated in terms of both its quality as an example of its genre and its cultural authenticity.

Figure 11-1

Checklist for Evaluating Culturally Diverse Literature

✿ The book is an excellent piece of literature.

✿ The book depicts diversity as an important but not gratuitous backdrop in a nonstereotyped manner, or

✿ The book explores cultural differences and similarities in an accurate and sensitive manner, or

✿ The book explores a particular culture accurately, demonstrating diversity within as well as across cultures if appropriate, and avoiding stereotypes.

✿ The book is a positive contribution to an understanding of the culture portrayed.

Resources for Finding Culturally Diverse Books

The following is a selection of the many books that you might want to consult when selecting culturally diverse literature.

Fox, Dana, and Kathy Short, *Stories Matter: The Complexity of Cultural Authenticity in Children's Literature*

Harris, Violet, *Teaching Multicultural Literature in Grades K–8*

_____, *Teaching with Multiethnic Literature, K–8*

Helbig, Althea, and A. R. Perkins, *Many Peoples, One Land: A Guide to New Multicultural Literature for Children and Young Adults*

Horning, Kathleen, Ginny Moose Kruse, and Megan Schliesman, *Multicultural Literature for Children and Young Adults*

Kaleidoscope (available through the National Council of Teachers of English and now in its fourth edition)

Miller-Lachmann, Lynn, *Our Family, Our Friends, Our World*

Pratt, Linda, and Janice Beaty, *Transcultural Children's Literature*

Quintero, Elizabeth, and Mary Kay Rummel, *American Voices: Webs of Diversity*

Smith, Henrietta, *The Coretta Scott King Awards: 1970–2004*

Stan, Susan, editor, *The World through Children's Books*

Tomlinson, Carl, editor, *Children's Books from Other Countries*

A committee of the International Reading Association also generates a list, "Notable Books for a Global Society," published annually in the February issue of *The Reading Teacher*. See also www.usbby.org/biblioctte.html for a listing of excellent new international titles.

Further, a collection of books—whether in a classroom, a school library, or a public library—can be assessed in terms of both the depth and breadth of the diversity that it represents. It is up to you to select individual books that are of the highest merit, both in literary and in cultural terms. It is also up to you to make sure that the accumulation of these books—your collection—is culturally diverse, no matter who your students are. All students need a collection of outstanding books that are also richly diverse.

Literature from Parallel Cultures

Of the many parallel cultures in North America, African Americans are presented in literature for children and adolescents more frequently and with more variety and fewer stereotypes than other cultural groups. Many recent books with African American characters reflect middle-class American life. There are few strong images of Asian characters of cultures other than Chinese and Japanese, although a handful of books that feature Hmong and Indian characters are recently available. A recent, small increase in the number of books with Latino characters, an increasing number of bilingual English-Spanish books, new Latino writers, and an increase in Latino poetry are welcome indications that this literature will grow. Literature in the Native American tradition continues to be primarily folklore, although there are a few notable new works of contemporary fiction as well.

Folktales still account for about 20 percent of the total number of titles about persons of color. The largest number of books about Asian Americans, Native Americans, and Latinos are folklore. Although these folktales do reflect the values of the people who created them, they say little about the lives of contemporary members of these cultures (Bishop, 1994). Folktales appear in the Booklist at the end of this chapter, but are not discussed here. They are discussed in Chapter 5.

• • AFRICAN AMERICAN • • LITERATURE

Books about African Americans reflect the wide range of African American culture, including the experience and consequences of slavery; the civil rights movement; and life in the 20th century, ranging from inner-city poverty to middle-class African American experiences. There are also several books set in the Caribbean, the West Indies, England, and South Africa, as well as North America. Established authors continue to write, and new voices are being heard. Christopher Paul Curtis won a Newbery Honor for his first novel, *The Watsons Go to Birmingham—1963,* and the Newbery Medal for his second, *Bud, Not Buddy* (both I). His third book, *Bucking the Sarge* (A), is a satirical, humorous story set in contemporary Flint, Michigan, where Curtis used to live. Established African American writers have received high honors: Virginia Hamilton was the first writer for children and adolescents to receive a prestigious MacArthur "genius" grant; Angela Johnson, another prolific

African American author, was recently honored with the same grant.

African American literature spans the genres. Many African American authors and illustrators are noted for their work in a particular genre, whereas others write across genres. Some outstanding African American authors and illustrators and their work are discussed briefly here. Others are included in the Booklist at the end of this chapter; a discussion of many of their books also can be found in Chapters 2 through 10.

Writing in many genres, the late Virginia Hamilton is still one of the most distinguished and influential African American authors today. A noted folklorist, her outstanding collections, such as *The People Could Fly* and *In the Beginning* (both I–A), are an integral part of American folklore. Her posthumously published *Bruh Rabbit and the Tar Baby Girl* (P–I), illustrated by James Ransome and featured in Chapter 2, is a brilliant retelling of a favorite familiar story. She was the first African American to win the Newbery Medal and the world-renowned Hans Christian Andersen Award, an international award given for the body of her work. Her numerous honors include the National Book Award, the Coretta Scott King Award, the Boston Globe–Horn Book Award, and the International Board on Books for Young People (IBBY) Honor List. Her novels include fantasy, mystery, realistic fiction, historical fiction, and biographical works as well as folklore.

Historical fiction at its best is one way to describe Mildred Taylor's books. With the stories of her childhood and her family as her guides, she continues to write books that are powerfully moving. Her Newbery Medal–winning *Roll of Thunder, Hear My Cry* (A) is part of an outstanding series of books about the Logan family. Recently, *The Land* (A) completed the Logan family saga, which spans the period between the Civil War and World War II.

Young readers have devoured books by Walter Dean Myers since the 1970s. He writes across many genres for an upper elementary through adolescent audience. His poetry, short stories, historical and contemporary novels, carefully researched biographies, picture books, and autobiography all attest to his skill and versatility. His powerful book *Monster* (A) was the first recipient of the Printz Award for books for adolescents. His work presents many facets of African American life across the generations, in many different settings.

Several African American authors write in many genres. Folklore, biography, and historical nonfiction are genres in which Patricia McKissack has excelled, often with the co-authorship of her husband, Fredrick McKissack. Her biography and nonfiction reflect careful scholarship, attention to detail, and a storyteller's voice. Her folklore picture books are wonderful retellings of stories she was told when she was a girl. Julius Lester is another outstanding African American author who writes in many genres. His fresh retellings of the Uncle Remus stories, a powerful version of the tall tale of John Henry, and historical and contemporary novels for adolescents are important contributions to the corpus of literature.

Jacqueline Woodson's novels for older readers are quickly becoming classics in the field. She tackles tough subjects—growing up and becoming independent from family, interracial relationships, death, lesbian relationships, class differences—with a grace and style that make her books a joy to read. She won the Coretta Scott King Award for *Miracle's Boys* (A), and her novel in verse, *Locomotion* (I–A), received a Boston Globe–Horn Book honor. Most of her books are contemporary realistic fiction for adolescent readers, but she also has picture books to her credit, such as the thought-provoking *The Other Side* and *Coming On Home Soon* (both P–I), both illustrated by E. B. Lewis. Woodson has also edited a powerful collection of short writings, *A Way Out of No Way: Writings about Growing Up Black in America* (A).

Angela Johnson is another outstanding author of contemporary realistic fiction for adolescents as well as picture books for younger readers, such as *Do Like Kyla* and *When I Am Old with You* (both P). She has received many honors for her books. Her novel *The First Part Last* (A), discussed in Chapter 7, won both the Coretta Scott King Award and the Printz Award for 2004.

Major African American and Caribbean poets include Ashley Bryan, Gwendolyn Brooks, Lucille Clifton, Maya Angelou, Eloise Greenfield, Nikki Grimes, and Nikki Giovanni. Many of these poets write in other genres as well. There are also many authors who explore both contemporary and historical African American experience and folklore in picture storybooks, transitional chapter books, and novels. Books by Jeanette Caines, Sandra Belton, Sharon Draper, Angela Shelf Medearis, Mildred Pitts Walter, Eleanora Tate, and others provide wonderful reading experiences for elementary and middle school children.

Tonya Bolden is the author of several works that present an historical perspective on African American life. Her *Tell All the Children Our Story: Memories and Mementos of Being Young and Black in America* (I–A) is a powerful testimony to both struggle and achievement. Such works as *The Book of African American Women: 150 Crusaders, Creators, and Uplifters* and *Wake Up Our Souls: A Celebration of Black American Artists* (both I–A) offer information and insight into some of the notable achievements of African Americans. Wade Hudson's *Powerful Words: More Than 200 Years of Extraordinary Writing by African Americans* (A) is a rich collection of writing spanning colonial days to contemporary times.

Andrea Davis Pinkney, an editor who began a special imprint, Jump at the Sun, to promote African American literature, is the author of several outstanding biographies for young readers, such as *Alvin Ailey* (I), illustrated by her

© 2000 James Ransome

Quinnie exemplifies a common childhood desire as she seeks to understand the life of the grandmother she was named for.

husband, Brian Pinkney, an award-winning illustrator. Brian is the son of illustrator Jerry Pinkney, one of the best-known African American illustrators. Jerry Pinkney illustrated Julius Lester's **Uncle Remus** tales, including *Uncle Remus: The Complete Tales* (I–A), Patricia McKissack's *Mirandy and Brother Wind* (P), Robert D. San Souci's *The Talking Eggs* (P–I), and Lester's *John Henry* (P–I), as well as many others. He has won numerous other awards, including the Coretta Scott King Award and Caldecott Honors. Some of his picture books were written by his wife, Gloria Jean Pinkney, a talented teller of stories from her own childhood.

James Ransome has graced many books with his powerful oil paintings, including Dinah Johnson's *Quinnie Blue* (P) and Lesa Cline-Ransome's *Satchel Paige* (I). He won the Coretta Scott King Award for illustration with his brilliant visual interpretation of James Weldon Johnson's poem in *The Creation* (P–I–A). His paintings for Hamilton's *Bruh Rabbit and the Tar Baby Girl* (P–I) are vibrant, exploding with the energy of the tale.

Some other outstanding African American illustrators are Ashley Bryan, Bryan Collier, Floyd Cooper, Donald Crews, Leo Dillon, Tom Feelings, E. B. Lewis, Synthia Saint James, and Christopher Myers.

The rich and varied heritage of the African American experience is indeed reflected in its literature for children and adolescents. These and other talented African American writers and illustrators give all readers the gift of wonderful books. The Booklist at the end of this chapter contains titles that represent some of their best efforts.

ASIAN AMERICAN LITERATURE

Although still disproportionately small, the number of high-quality books featuring Asian Americans is increasing. Most of the existing books focus on Asian Americans with Chinese or Japanese heritage, but some other Asian countries, such as Korea, Vietnam, Thailand, and the Pacific Islands, appear with increasing frequency in books for children and adolescents. There is a significant amount of folklore from Asian countries available, and contemporary fiction dealing with Asian American experiences is beginning to appear more frequently. There is some excellent historical fiction, much of which focuses on the Japanese American internment during World War II, and several nonfiction books explore the lives of recent Asian immigrants to North America. *American Eyes: New Asian-American Short Stories for Young Adults* (A), edited by Lori Carlson, contains 10 stories that explore coming-of-age against the clash of cultures. Not only are these stories well written; they also reflect the wide variation in Asian American heritage, with characters who are Korean, Taiwanese, Chinese, Filipino, Japanese, Vietnamese, and Hawaiian.

© 1994 Royce M. Becker

*The stories in Lori Carlson's **American Eyes** remind us that the Asian American experience is not a monocultural one.*

Laurence Yep has been telling the stories of Asian Americans for over 20 years. His historical novels *The Star Fisher* and *Dream Soul* (both I–A), which are based on his Chinese mother's experiences growing up in West Virginia in 1927, chronicle some of the problems that beset Asian American immigrant families. In *Dragon's Gate* (I–A), he goes further back in time to tell the story of a young boy's experiences leaving China for North America and the building of the transcontinental railroad. The rich cultural and social details in these novels add depth to the moving stories. Yep writes across genres, producing folktales, contemporary fiction, fantasy, and mysteries in addition to historical fiction. In many of his contemporary fiction novels, such as *The Cook's Family* and *Thief of Hearts* (both A), Yep explores problems of belonging and alienation in the lives of Asian American and multiracial adolescents. His San Francisco Chinatown mystery series, beginning with *The Case of the Lion Dance* (I–A), is full of rich cultural details. He is also noted for including fantasy elements based on Chinese lore in many of his novels.

Lisa Yee's *Millicent Min, Girl Genius* (I) takes on the "brainy Asian" stereotype with humor and insight as Millicent tries to hide the fact that she is extremely bright so that she can fit in and make friends with another girl. Lensey Namioka also writes about relationships in a contemporary Chinese American family in *Yang the Youngest and His Terrible Ear, Yang the Second and Her Secret Admirers,* and *Yang the Third and Her Impossible Family* (all I), while exploring issues of adjusting to the new customs and experiences that accompany immigration. In a novel for older readers, *April and the Dragon Lady* (A), Namioka explores intergenerational and intergender conflict in a Chinese American family. Marie Lee's novels of contemporary Korean American family life, such as *Necessary Roughness* (A), also explore both cultural and intergenerational conflicts.

An Na won the Printz Award for *A Step from Heaven* (A), a powerful novel that explores the experience of one Korean child who emigrates with her parents to the United States only to find that the streets are not paved with gold for them. Na tackles such issues as cultural dislocation, poverty, gender stereotyping, and abuse as experienced by the protagonist, who grows from childhood to young adulthood in this novel that is nonetheless brimming with hope.

There are several other stories about young people immigrating to North America from various Asian countries, some of which are in turmoil. Peggy Dietz Shea's *Tangled Threads* and Jackie Brown's *Little Cricket* (both I–A) describe the cultural dislocation of two young Hmong girls and how they work to maintain the richness of their original culture while adapting to life in the United States. Minfong Ho's *Gathering the Dew* (I–A), part of a new series, **First Person Fiction,** that focuses on stories of refugees from around the world, begins with life in Phnom Penh, Cambodia, before the Khmer Rouge. Ho tells the story of her young protagonist as she lives through the horrors of war, the challenge of the refugee camp, and the new life that begins when she arrives in America.

Two pieces of contemporary fiction, Sheth Kashmira's *Blue Jasmine* (I) and Uma Krishnaswami's *Naming Maya* (I–A), explore the differences in culture between North America and India. In *Blue Jasmine,* the young protagonist has difficulty adjusting to life in America and then in India when she returns for a visit, whereas in *Naming Maya,* the protagonist is quite content in America. Her difficulty is with her parents' divorce and her mother's insistence that she return to India for a visit.

Yoshiko Uchida, a first-generation Japanese American living in California at the outbreak of World War II, tells the story of her childhood in *Journey to Topaz* and *Journey Home* (both A). These novels provide a vivid and compelling record of the experience of internment. They are complemented by Ken Mochizuki's *Baseball Saved Us* (I).

Janet Wong is a contemporary poet who writes of her experiences growing up as a multiracial young woman in

Good Luck Gold: And Other Poems and *A Suitcase of Seaweed: And Other Poems* (both ɪ). Allen Say also explores being bicultural and biracial in many of his picture books. His several beautiful books about Japanese and Japanese American experiences include *Grandfather's Journey* (ᴘ–ɪ), winner of the Caldecott Medal for its evocative illustrations of a man torn between two beautiful countries—North America and Japan. The text and illustrations portray love and longing in a way that transcends political boundaries. Some of Say's other works, such as *Tree of Cranes* and *Tea with Milk* (both ᴘ–ɪ), explore the blending of cultures.

Several Asian American artists illustrate folklore from Asian countries. Ed Young is a prolific illustrator who won the Caldecott Medal for *Lon Po Po: A Red Riding Hood Story from China* (ɴ–ᴘ–ɪ). His illustrations for Ai-Ling Louie's *Yeh-Shen: A Cinderella Story from China* (ᴘ–ɪ) are richly evocative of the tale's origins.

Although few in number, fiction, nonfiction, and poetry books explore the values and lives of Asian Americans. Some of the best of these books are included in the Booklist at the end of this chapter.

• • LATINO LITERATURE • •

The number of books for children portraying Latino characters stands in stark contrast to the number of Latinos in the population. Only a tiny minority of all children's books published represent a Latino culture (Nieto, 2002). Compared to the number of Latino children who need to see themselves represented in books, and to the number of other children who need to understand something of Latino cultures, there is a dearth of books available. Happily, the situation is changing, however slowly; there are many gifted writers producing high-quality work, such as Victor Martinez, whose novel *Parrot in the Oven: Mi Vida* (ᴀ) won the 1996 National Book Award. Francisco Jiménez's *The Circuit* (ᴀ), a collection of stories based on the author's own experiences as a child in a migrant farmworker family, won the 1998 Boston Globe–Horn Book Award for fiction. Contemporary fiction and poetry are expanding, and the number of Latino writers is increasing. With the increase in the number of Spanish-speaking children in school, there also has been an increase in the number of Spanish-language children's books. However, it is important to remember that many of these books, welcome as they are, are not books that reflect any Latino culture, but rather mainstream children's books translated from English into Spanish.

Latino literature began to become increasingly popular with the paperback publication of *The House on Mango Street* (ᴀ), by Sandra Cisneros, in 1991. This was followed by Judith Ortiz Cofer's *An Island Like You* (ᴀ). Both of these books were originally published by Arte Público, the same house that has recently reissued Nicholasa Mohr's early

books about life in the New York barrio, *Nilda* and *In Nueva York* (both ᴀ), both originally published in the 1970s (Bader, 2003b). Arte Público's juvenile imprint, Piñata Books, publishes bilingual picture books as well as paperback adolescent novels.

Like the literature of other cultures, Latino literature spans folklore, poetry, and all types of fiction and nonfiction, and represents a rich array of subcultures. Gary Soto is one of the primary Latino voices in children's literature today. His work ranges from short stories to novels to poetry. *Baseball in April and Other Stories* and *Local News* (both ᴀ) are collections of short stories that explore growing up as Soto did, poor and Mexican American in central California. *Buried Onions* and its companion novel, *The Afterlife* (both ᴀ), and many other novels explore life for preadolescent and adolescent Latino boys. Soto is also a gifted poet. The poems in *Neighborhood Odes* (ᴀ) center on his early life. Those in *Canto Familiar* (ᴀ) speak of childhood experiences that transcend cultural differences. He has also written several picture storybooks, including the fantasy *Chato's Kitchen* (ɴ–ᴘ), playfully illustrated by Susan Guevara.

Nicholasa Mohr is a Puerto Rican author who explores contemporary issues in the lives of Puerto Rican youth growing up in North America. Her short stories and novels, such as *Going Home* and *Felita* (both ᴀ) and *The Magic Shell* (ɪ), are beautifully written and powerful. Her fantasy

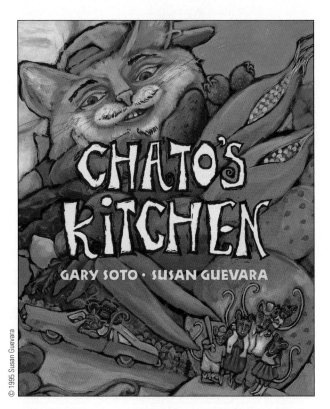

Artist Susan Guevara captures the playful mood of Gary Soto's text in the engaging story **Chato's Kitchen.**

picture book, *Old Letivia and the Mountain of Sorrows* (P), is set in Puerto Rico and based on classic folktale patterns.

Ana Veciana-Suarez's *Flight to Freedom* (A), part of the **First Person Fiction** series, is the moving story of a young girl's experiences as her family is exiled from Cuba and tries to make a new life in North America. Nancy Osa's protagonist in *Cuba 15* (I), Violet Paz, is half Cuban and half Polish, but her Cuban grandmother insists that she must have the traditional quinceanero for her 15th birthday. This event causes Violet to learn about a country she has never lived in and to raise questions that are still being argued today.

In Judith Ortiz Cofer's *Call Me Maria* (I–A), a novel in letters, poems, and prose, Maria, unlike Violet, is caught between two worlds: her mother's beloved Puerto Rico and the New York barrio that has become home to her father.

Alma Flor Ada, Lulu Delacre, and Pat Mora write engaging stories for younger children, and David Diaz, Joe Cepeda, Susan Guevara, and Raul Colón are sought-after Latino illustrators. Pat Mora, a Mexican American author, writes books that appeal to primary-grade children, such as *A Birthday Basket for Tía* (P), as well as some lovely poetry, such as *The Desert Is My Mother* (P) and *Confetti: Poems for Children* (N–P–I). Her Piñata Books publications are bilingual. Alma Flor Ada recounts stories of her Cuban family in *Where the Flame Trees Bloom* (I) and *Under the Royal Palms: A Childhood in Cuba* (P–I). She has retold several notable folktales as well. These and other books offer young readers a more diverse picture of Latino life and culture than was ever before available. They are still not enough. Other Latino authors and illustrators are included in the Booklist at the end of this chapter.

• • NATIVE AMERICAN • • LITERATURE

Native American experiences have been interpreted in literature for children by members of various tribal groups, anthropologists, folklorists, and others who have lived among Native Americans. Unfortunately, until the late 1970s much of the literature that portrayed Native Americans did so with erroneous or stereotyped information and images. Literature by and about Native Americans began to increase in the 1970s as Native American voices, so long suppressed, began to be heard, and mainstream culture developed a new consciousness about Native Americans. Children can now learn about several of the more than 500 different Native American groups.

Children's literature now includes Native American poetry, folklore, historical fiction, and biography, as well as historical nonfiction from a Native American perspective. There are an increasing number of books about contemporary Native American experiences, although not nearly enough. An important resource regarding Native American literature, Beverly Slapin and Doris Seale's *Through Indian Eyes: The Native Experience in Books for Children* (1998), offers essays, poems, and book reviews. Oyate (www.oyate .org), a Native organization, is another source for book reviews. Those at Oyate can help you judge authenticity in Native literature.

Some of the earliest pieces of fiction that truly expressed Native American values, Craig Kee Strete's *When Grandfather Journeys into Winter* and *The Bleeding Man and Other Science Fiction Stories* (both A), offer readers the opportunity to explore issues from a Native American perspective. A later novel by Strete, *Big Thunder Magic* (A), is a contemporary allegory set in city and pueblo. His *The World in Grandfather's Hands* (A), set in the Southwest, is a more recent contemporary novel of family life among urban Native Americans.

Folklore and poetry from Native American cultures are available in anthology and picture-book form. Among the contemporary anthologies available are collections by Richard Erdoes and John Bierhorst. Although an outsider, Paul Goble is one of the most prolific authors and illustrators of Native American folklore. His knowledge of and friendship with the Lakota Sioux Nation enables him to portray their stories and culture accurately.

Hettie Jones's *The Trees Stand Shining: Poetry of the North American Indians* (P–I) is a classic collection that has been reissued. Shonto Begay, a Navajo artist and storyteller, displays his considerable talents in *Ma'ii and Cousin Horned Toad* (P–I), a trickster tale. His beautiful *Navajo: Visions and Voices across the Mesa* (I–A) is a collection of chants, stories, and paintings that express the beliefs and traditions of the Navajo from ancient to contemporary times.

Joseph Bruchac's Abenaki heritage is reflected in his collection *Thirteen Moons on Turtle's Back: A Native American Year of Moons* (I), written in collaboration with Jonathan London. He also tells stories from other Native American groups in such books as *Between Earth and Sky: Legends of Native American Sacred Places* and *Four Ancestors: Stories, Songs, and Poems from Native North America* (both I–A). Bruchac also writes both contemporary and historical stories about Native American people. His contemporary fiction, such as *Eagle Song, The Heart of a Chief, The Dark Pond,* and *Hidden Roots* (all I–A), is a welcome addition to a genre almost devoid of Native American literature. *The Arrow over the Door, The Winter People,* and *Sacajawea* (all I–A) are outstanding pieces of historical fiction. His autobiography, *Bowman's Store* (A), is also excellent.

Other important historical fiction from a Native viewpoint includes Michael Dorris's *Guests, Sees Behind Trees,* and *Morning Girl* (all I); Dorris has also written a contemporary fiction novel, *The Window* (A). *The Birchbark House* (I), by Louise Erdrich, was nominated for the National Book Award for Young People's Literature. Erdrich drew on her Ojibwa heritage and family stories for this book, the first in a series that has been described as a Native version of the **Little House** books, set in northern Wisconsin. The sequel, *The Game of Silence* (I), continues the story of young Omakayas and her family.

Virginia Driving Hawk Sneve's *High Elk's Treasure* (I–A), one of her early works, helped bring books by and about Native Americans to the attention of a larger public. Her *Dancing Teepees: Poems of American Indian Youth* (I–A) is an excellent collection of traditional and modern Native American poetry. She is also a talented writer of nonfiction, and her **First Americans** series, including *The Seminoles* (P–I), provides excellent information sources about many different Native American groups.

Cynthia Leitich Smith is a new author who explores contemporary Native life. Her picture book *Jingle Dancer* (P–I) is enjoyed by young readers of all ethnicities. Her novel for adolescents *Rain Is Not My Indian Name* (I–A) considers issues of growing up and fitting in that are part of almost every adolescent's life. *Indian Shoes* (I), made up of stories about a Cherokee boy and his grandfather in Chicago, explores identity issues in a contemporary setting.

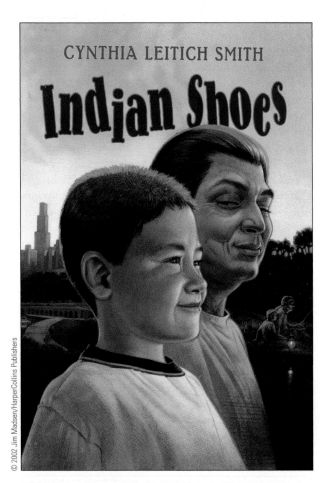

This funny and endearing collection of interlocking stories is a window into what it is like to grow up with both hightops and moccasins.

Teaching Idea 11-3

Study a Regional Culture

Every region of the United States has its natural beauty, cultural traditions, folklore, dialect, traditional foods, and unique manners or mannerisms. Your students will enjoy studying their region's characteristics through literature.

For example, the culture of the southeastern Appalachian region of the United States is one that has been recreated in children's books across many genres. The folklore collections of Richard Chase; new retellings of old tales by such authors as William Hooks; poetry, picture books, and novels by such authors as Cynthia Rylant, Gloria Houston, and Phyllis Reynolds Naylor—all evoke the unique culture of the region, both past and present.

Spend some time finding books that present the flavor of the region in which you teach, and share these books with your students. You can simply enjoy books set in your part of the world or use them as the springboard to a culture study in which you and your students look for aspects of setting, characterization, and values that are common to the books.

Although the number of books by and about people from parallel cultures in America is increasing, we must make special efforts to seek these books out, to include them in our classroom and school libraries and in our curriculum. When we do this, we help children see themselves as members of a larger community. Teaching Idea 11.3 is but one way of helping children explore culture through literature.

International Literature

When Neil Armstrong was hurtling around the world in a capsule in outer space, he said that looking back at Earth was like looking at a big blue marble. His comment made us aware that our "marble" is not a very big one and that what happens in one part of it affects every other part. Viewing our world as a global village makes it clear that literature for children and adolescents should reflect the interdependence of nations and people everywhere.

Books from around the world can give young readers the opportunity to travel to other lands and vicariously experience lives different from their own. Today a wide range of poetry, folklore, fiction, and nonfiction from around the world is available in North America. Although not yet extensive, the exchange of books among nations is becoming more widespread due to the ease of international travel and modern technology, and the efforts of groups such as the IBBY. Publishers from all over the world meet at book fairs in Israel, Italy, Germany, Spain, Mexico, Argentina, Brazil, Colombia, and elsewhere to buy manuscripts and arrange for the copublication of the same book in several languages. Thus children in many countries may read the very same book written in their own native language. Children's literature has become truly international.

This exchange of books and the movement of people from country to country make many wonderful experiences available to North American children. For example, Ifeoma Onyefulu, a Nigerian, brings Nigeria to North America in *Here Comes Our Bride! An African Wedding* (P) and *Saying Good-Bye: A Special Farewell to Mama Nkwelle* (P–I), with lucid writing and clear, full-color photographs. Kyoki Mori's novels *One Bird* and *Shizuko's Daughter* (both A) explore the opportunities and restrictions for women in contemporary Japan. Gaye Hiçyilmaz's contemporary novel set during the war in Yugoslavia, *Smiling for Strangers* (A), follows 14-year-old Nina Topič as she escapes to England. *Thura's Diary: My Life in Wartime Iraq* (I–A), by Thura al-Windawi, brings to a North American audience a picture of life in Baghdad just before and after the American invasion. Adeline Yen Mah tells of her own childhood in *Falling Leaves: The True Story of an Unwanted Chinese Daughter* (A). Christina Bjork takes young readers to Venice in *Vendela in Venice* (I), with help from illustrator Inga-Karin Eriksson. And Mette Newth's *The Transformation* (A) recreates ancient Iceland and the clash between Native and Christian beliefs as well as between humans and nature.

People from the international community discuss books for children and adolescents through their work in professional organizations—namely the IBBY, the United States Board on Books for Young People, the American Library Association, the American Booksellers Association, the Modern Language Association, and the International Reading Association, among others. In Europe, the International Youth Library—located at Blutenburg Castle on the outskirts of Munich, Germany—is devoted to the collection, study, and propagation of international children's literature.

The prestigious Hans Christian Andersen Awards, presented by the IBBY, are given for the entire body of an author's and an illustrator's work. Nominees from all over the world are eligible. Winners are listed in Appendix A. The IBBY magazine, *Bookbird*, provides current information about children's literature from around the world. The Batchelder Award is given in the United States annually to the publisher of the most outstanding book of the year, first published in another country and published in translation in the United States. Batchelder Award winners are found in Appendix A.

Offering young readers literature that originates in other countries gives them an important opportunity to look through that window and see both others and themselves. For example, readers of Mirjam Pressler's *Halinka* (A), translated from the German by Elizabeth D. Crawford, can't help but recognize themselves in this lonely and emotionally fragile young girl living in an orphanage in postwar Germany. Pressler's *Malka* (A), translated by Brian Murdoch, is a frightening and compelling story of sacrifice and survival during World War II, written from a European point of view.

Not all literature from other countries has to be translated, of course, as there are many imports from other English-speaking nations. Books from Canada, the United States, Great Britain, New Zealand, Australia, and other countries are available across the globe. Martha Brooks brings the Canadian prairie to all readers in *True Confessions of a Heartless Girl* (A). Life in Australia for a young adolescent girl is portrayed in Martine Murray's *The Slightly True Story of Cedar B. Hartley (Who Planned to Live an Unusual Life)* (I–A). Decades of apartheid in South Africa are presented in powerful short stories in Beverly Naidoo's *Out of Bounds: Seven Stories of Conflict and Hope* (A). Australian Simon French's *Where in the World* (A), a compelling novel about talent and about finding a home, follows a young musician from his beloved boyhood home in Germany to Australia, where his mother hopes to make a new life for the two of them.

North American writers also set their books in other countries. In *Zazoo* (A), Richard Mosher recreates the idyllic French countryside with its undertones of anger and jealousy left over from World War II. Gloria Whelan's *Homeless Bird* (A), winner of the National Book Award, explores one young girl's coming-of-age in contemporary India. Jane Kurtz combines both North American and African points of view in *Memories of Sun: Stories of Africa and America* (I–A), a collection of stories and poems.

Poet Naomi Shihab Nye brings young readers poems from many places in *This Same Sky: A Collection of Poems from around the World* (I–A). Her *19 Varieties of Gazelle* (I–A), written after the September 11, 2001, tragedy, springs from her Palestinian roots. This is a haunting and wonderful collection of poems that, taken together, illuminate life in another place.

When books present authentic images from another country, children learn an important lesson. They recognize that although all cultures are distinct and different, all people share universal needs for love, belonging, and acceptance. They learn that all people share the need for family, friends, and neighbors and for food, clothing, and shelter. They learn to see themselves as citizens of the world. These and other books that can help young readers do this are included in the Booklist at the end of the chapter.

Literature Exploring Sexual Orientation

Just as issues of sexual identity have become part of the dialogue in the United States, they have also become part of literature for young readers. Although there are a few picture books for younger readers that attempt to help children develop tolerance for different lifestyles, none are without flaws. There are, however, a number of excellent contemporary realistic novels for adolescent readers that explore issues of sexuality.

Sexuality, both straight and gay, is an issue in the lives of many of the several adolescent narrators of Ellen Wittlinger's *What's in a Name?* (A), a powerful collection of interlocking stories; it is also a recurring theme in E. R. Frank's *Life Is Funny* (A), another collection of interlocking stories that spans seven years in the lives of diverse adolescents.

In *Luna* (A), Julie Anne Peters explores the difficulties faced by those who are transgendered. Regan, it seems, is the only one who sees that her older brother Liam is a girl in a boy's body. Their father is constantly disappointed in Liam because he is not athletic; their mother deliberately denies that which she doesn't care to know. As Liam turns into Luna and Regan learns more about transgender issues, readers both learn along with them and come to understand how to love and support someone who, like Liam, is embarking on a transformation.

Jacqueline Woodson's *From the Notebooks of Melanin Sun* and *The House You Pass on the Way* (both A) grapple with the issues that surround homosexuality and race in contemporary culture. Four new novels take a look at gay high school life. Brent Hartinger's *Geography Club* (A) is a bitingly funny and perceptive account of how a diverse group of GLBT students find each other and figure out how to get together without arousing suspicion—by forming the most boring school club they could imagine. David Levithan, in *Boy Meets Boy* (A), creates a setting in which homosexuality is no big deal, a setting in which he can then explore typical high school love relationship issues, only with gay characters. *Rainbow Boys* and *Rainbow High* (both A), by Alex Sanchez, are set in a more realistic high school world. Told in chapters that alternate among the three protagonists, these books offer no simple solutions.

Literature Exploring Exceptionalities

A small but growing number of books for children demonstrate society's increasing awareness of the emotional and physical demands and accomplishments of those with exceptionalities. The trend in the field has shifted from nearly absolute neglect, to the appearance of occasional secondary characters, to the occasional book in which the main character has special needs. In today's literature, people's attitudes toward individuals with special needs are not always positive and do not always improve. At the same time, however, we also find many books in which characters with, for example, mental disabilities are loved and cherished by their families. Betsy Byars's *Summer of the Swans,* Katherine Paterson's *Preacher's Boy,* Lois Lowry's *The Silent Boy,* and Marlene Fanta Shyer's *Welcome Home, Jellybean* (all I–A) all subtly underscore the humanity of those whom many people treat as different. See "The Portrayal of Mental Disability in Children's Literature: An Ethical Appraisal" (Mills, 2002) for a lucid discussion of both the history of literature portraying exceptionalities and a discussion of how we should assess that literature.

Contemporary realistic fiction portrays many kinds of exceptionalities: physical, mental, and emotional. In the Printz Honor book *Stuck in Neutral* (A), an unusual and disturbing novel, Terry Trueman takes readers inside the mind of Shawn, a very bright boy with very bad cerebral palsy—he cannot control his muscles, which means he cannot speak. Those around him think that he is profoundly developmentally disabled, but instead he has the gift of almost total recall of everything he hears. He's afraid that his father is planning to kill him, and he's telling us his story. Trueman informs readers in an afterword that he has a son who is very much like the protagonist in this novel. In a companion novel, *Cruise Control* (A), Trueman tells the other story, the story of the healthy and talented brother and his conflicted feelings about living with a brother like Shawn. A third novel, *Inside Out* (A), is a disturbing portrait of a young man with adolescent-onset schizophrenia.

The 13-year-old protagonist of Ruth White's *Memories of Summer* (A) watches her older sister descend into schizophrenia. This novel, set in 1955, presents the bleak and hopeless outlook for those with mental disorders at that time. Ann Martin explores similar historical attitudes toward mental disabilities in her Newbery Honor–winning *A Corner of the Universe* (I–A), a beautifully written story of the friendship between 12-year-old Hattie and her uncle Adam. Adam returns to the family at age 21, when the school that he has been attending closes. His very existence is a surprise to Hattie, and she quickly learns to love him for his quirkiness; he may be 21, but his mental capability is that of a child. This powerful novel explores the attitudes that kept people with exceptionalities hidden from the rest of society, and the many faces of love. In *So B. It* (I–A), Sarah Weeks presents a loving relationship between Heidi, a "normal" child, and her severely mentally disabled mother. As Heidi searches for the truth of her origins, she encounters a variety of attitudes toward mental disability, not all of them positive.

Mark Haddon won the 2003 Whitbread Book of the Year Award for his portrayal of a young man with Asperger's

A companion book to **Stuck in Neutral,** *Cruise Control explores the feelings of a young man on the brink of adulthood who is learning to recognize just how much he loves his severely disabled brother.*

syndrome, a form of autism, in *The Curious Incident of the Dog in the Night-Time* (A). Haddon wisely decided to tell Christopher's story through Christopher's own eyes, and readers are privy to both the obsession and the brilliance of his mind. As he pursues the solution to the mystery behind the killing of his neighbor's dog, he discovers things about his parents that destroy the world as he has always known it. At the same time, he discovers his own strength. Interestingly, this book is marketed for both adult and adolescent audiences.

Some books explore specific learning disabilities. Jack Gantos writes from the point of view of a young boy with attention deficit hyperactivity disorder in the popular **Joey Pigza** books (all I). Gantos's breathless run-on sentences leave readers almost as frantic as Joey. The first-person point of view allows peers and adults to glimpse what life might be like for children with this disorder. *Joey Pigza Loses Control* is a 2001 Newbery Honor book.

It is important to all of us that these books are available. It is crucial that teachers and other adults put them into the hands of all children. Knowing, through books, the possibilities of life for those with exceptionalities can only increase

our understanding of one another. These and other books are included in the Booklist at the end of this chapter.

• • • Summary • • •

Books for children and adolescents are beginning to reflect the diversity that characterizes North America and the world. As North Americans become more inclusive in attitude toward all peoples, rather than just the mainstream Caucasian middle class, children's literature grows to include wonderful books by and about people of parallel cultures, from other countries, of diverse sexual orientations, and with exceptionalities. Although we do not yet have a body of literature that is as diverse as our population, we do have a good beginning. All classrooms and all libraries can contain collections that reflect this diversity, ones that enable teachers to emphasize diversity through their careful selection of children's literature. After all, good books and good teaching can help change the world.

Read Barbara Bader's history of multicultural literature in *The Horn Book Magazine:* "How the Little House Gave Ground: The Beginnings of Multiculturalism in a New, Black Children's Literature" (November/December 2002), "Multiculturalism Takes Root" (March/April 2003), and "Multiculturalism in the Mainstream" (May/June 2003). Discuss with peers how these changes in children's literature are linked to changes in the greater society, and what that change might mean for literature about sexual orientation and exceptionalities in the future.

Other articles of interest include Cynthia Leitich Smith's "A Different Drum: Native American Writing," in the July/August 2002 issue; Elsa Marston's "A Window in the Wall: Palestinians in Children's Literature," in the November/December 2004 issue; Claudia Mills's "The Portrayal of Mental Disability in Children's Literature: An Ethical Appraisal," in the September/October 2002 issue; and Margaret Chang's "We Like Our Version Better," in the November/December 2002 issue, all in *The Horn Book Magazine.*

Jane Kurtz has written many books that are set in Ethiopia, where she spent her childhood. In our interview with her, Jane talks about how after returning to America and beginning her family and career, she put Ethiopia behind her, only to return to it again through her writing. As you listen to her, think about the concept of culture. How would you describe Jane's culture? She is American, but she didn't grow up here. She's not Ethiopian, but she did spend her childhood there. What implications does this have for the idea of cultural authenticity?

African American Children's Books

FOLKLORE (SEE ALSO CHAPTER 5)

Hamilton, Virginia, *Bruh Rabbit and the Tar Baby Girl,* illustrated by James Ransome (P–I)

_____, *Her Stories: African American Folktales, Fairy Tales, and True Tales,* illustrated by Leo and Diane Dillon (I)

_____, *In the Beginning* (I–A)

_____, *The People Could Fly: American Black Folktales,* illustrated by Leo and Diane Dillon (I–A)

_____, *The People Could Fly: The Picture Book,* illustrated by Leo and Diane Dillon (P–I)

Haskins, James, *The Headless Haunt and Other African-American Ghost Stories,* illustrated by Ben Otero (I)

Hudson, Wade, and Cheryl Hudson, *How Sweet the Sound: African-American Songs for Children,* illustrated by Floyd Cooper (N–P)

Lester, Julius, *Further Tales of Uncle Remus: The Misadventures of Brer Rabbit, Brer Fox, Brer Wolf, the Doodang, and Other Creatures,* illustrated by Jerry Pinkney (I–A)

_____, *John Henry,* illustrated by Jerry Pinkney (I)

_____, *The Last Tales of Uncle Remus,* illustrated by Jerry Pinkney (I–A)

_____, *The Tales of Uncle Remus: The Adventures of Brer Rabbit,* illustrated by Jerry Pinkney (I–A)

McKissack, Patricia, *Flossie and the Fox* (P)

_____, *Mirandy and Brother Wind* (P)

Medearis, Angela Shelf, *The Freedom Riddle,* illustrated by John Ward (P–I)

_____, *Tailypo: A Newfangled Tall Tale,* illustrated by Sterling Brown (P–I)

San Souci, Robert D., *Sukey and the Mermaid,* illustrated by Brian Pinkney (P–I)

_____, *The Talking Eggs,* illustrated by Jerry Pinkney (P–I)

Wahl, Jan, *Little Eight John,* illustrated by Wil Clay (P–I)

_____, *Tailypo!* illustrated by Wil Clay (P)

POETRY AND SONG (SEE ALSO CHAPTER 4)

Adedjouma, Davida, *The Palm of My Heart: Poetry by African American Children,* illustrated by Gregory Christie (P–I–A)

Adoff, Arnold, *The Basket Counts,* illustrated by Michael Weaver (I)

_____, *In for Winter, Out for Spring,* illustrated by Jerry Pinkney (P)

Barnwell, Ysaye, *No Mirrors in My Nana's House,* illustrated by Synthia Saint James (P)

Bishop, Rudine Sims, *Wonders: The Best Poems of Effie Lee Newsome* (P–I)

Boyd, Candy Dawson, *Daddy, Daddy, Be There,* illustrated by Floyd Cooper (N–P–I)

Brooks, Gwendolyn, *Bronzeville Boys and Girls* (P–I)

Bryan, Ashley, *All Night, All Day: A Child's First Book of African-American Spirituals* (P–I–A)

_____, *Ashley Bryan's ABC of African American Poetry* (N–P–I–A)

_____, *Carol of the Brown King: Nativity Poems by Langston Hughes* (N–P–I–A)

_____, *Sing to the Sun* (P)

Clinton, Catherine, *I, Too, Sing America: Three Centuries of African American Poetry,* illustrated by Stephen Alcorn (P–I–A)

Feelings, Tom, *Soul Looks Back in Wonder* (I–A)

Giovanni, Nikki, *Knoxville, Tennessee,* illustrated by Larry Johnson (P)

_____, *The Selected Poems of Nikki Giovanni* (A)

_____, *Shimmy Shimmy Shimmy Like My Sister Kate* (A)

_____, *Spin a Soft Black Song* (P–I)

Greenfield, Eloise, *Angels,* illustrated by Jan Spivey Gilchrist (N–P)

_____, *For the Love of the Game: Michael Jordan and Me,* illustrated by Jan Spivey Gilchrist (N–P–I)

_____, *Honey, I Love and Other Love Poems* (P–I)

_____, *Night on Neighborhood Street,* illustrated by Jan Spivey Gilchrist (P)

Grimes, Nikki, *A Dime a Dozen,* illustrated by Angelo (I–A)

_____, *It's Raining Laughter,* illustrated by Miles Pinkney (N–P)

_____, *Meet Danitra Brown,* illustrated by Floyd Cooper (N–P)

Hudson, Cheryl Willis, *Hold Christmas in Your Heart: African-American Songs, Poems, and Stories for the Holidays,* illustrated by Anna Rich, Cal Massey, Eric Battle, James Ransome, Ron Garnett, Sylvia Walker, and Higgins Bond (N–P)

Hughes, Langston, *The Dream Keeper and Other Poems,* illustrated by Brian Pinkney (I)

Johnson, Angela, *The Other Side: Shorter Poems* (A)

Johnson, James Weldon, *The Creation,* illustrated by James Ransome (P–I–A)

_____, *Lift Ev'ry Voice and Sing,* illustrated by Jan Spivey Gilchrist (N–P–I–A)

Mathis, Sharon Bell, *Red Dog, Blue Fly: Football Poems,* illustrated by Jan Spivey Gilchrist (P–I)

Medearis, Angela Shelf, *Rum-a-Tum-Tum,* illustrated by James Ransome (N–P–I)

_____, *Skin Deep and Other Teenage Reflections,* illustrated by Michael Bryant (A)

Myers, Walter Dean, *Angel to Angel: A Mother's Gift of Love* (N–P–I–A)

_____, *blues journey,* illustrated by Christopher Myers (I–A)

_____, *Brown Angels: An Album of Pictures and Verse* (P–I)

_____, *Harlem,* illustrated by Christopher Myers (P–I–A)

Okutoro, Lydia Omolola, *Quiet Storm: Voices of Young Black Poets* (A)

Strickland, Dorothy, and Michael Strickland, *Families: Poems Celebrating the African American Experience,* illustrated by John Ward (P–I)

Thomas, Joyce Carol, *Brown Honey in Broomwheat Tea,* illustrated by Floyd Cooper (P–I)

_____, *Gingerbread Days,* illustrated by Floyd Cooper (P–I)

PICTURE BOOKS (SEE ALSO CHAPTERS 2 AND 3)

Adoff, Arnold, *Hard to Be Six,* illustrated by Cheryl Hanna (P)

Barber, Barbara, *Allie's Basketball Dream,* illustrated by Darryl Ligasan (P)

_____, *Saturday at the New You,* illustrated by Anna Rich (P)

Barnwell, Ysaye, *No Mirrors in My Nana's House,* illustrated by Synthia Saint James (P)

Battle-Lavert, Gwendolyn, *The Shaking Bag,* illustrated by Aminah Brenda Lynn Robinson (P)

Belton, Sandra, *From Miss Ida's Porch,* illustrated by Floyd Cooper (I)

_____, *May'naise Sandwiches and Sunshine Tea,* illustrated by Gail Gordon Carter (P)

_____, *Pictures for Miss Josie,* illustrated by Benny Andrews (P)

Clifton, Lucille, *Everett Anderson's Christmas Coming,* illustrated by Jan Spivey Gilchrist (P)

_____, *Three Wishes,* illustrated by Michael Hays (P)

Coleman, Evelyn, *White Socks Only,* illustrated by Tyrone Geter (I)

Crews, Donald, *Bigmama's* (P)

_____, *Shortcut* (P)

Cummings, Pat, *Carousel* (P)

_____, *Clean Your Room, Harvey Moon* (P)

Flournoy, Vanessa, and Valerie Flournoy, *Celie and the Harvest Fiddler,* illustrated by James Ransome (P–I)

Greenfield, Eloise, *Easter Parade* (P)

_____, *First Pink Light,* illustrated by Jan Spivey Gilchrist (P)

_____, *Grandpa's Face,* illustrated by Floyd Cooper (P)

_____, *William and the Good Old Days,* illustrated by Jan Spivey Gilchrist (P)

Havill, Juanita, *Jamaica's Blue Marker,* illustrated by Anne Sibley O'Brien (P)

Herron, Carolivia, *Nappy Hair,* illustrated by Joe Cepeda (P)

Hort, Lenny, *How Many Stars in the Sky?* illustrated by James Ransome (P)

Howard, Elizabeth Fitzgerald, *Mac and Marie and the Train Toss Surprise,* illustrated by Gail Gordon Carter (P)

_____, *Papa Tells Chita a Story,* illustrated by Floyd Cooper (P)

Hudson, Wade, *Jamal's Busy Day,* illustrated by George Ford (P)

Johnson, Angela, *Do Like Kyla* (P)

_____, *Just Like Josh Gibson* (P–I)

_____, *The Leaving Morning,* illustrated by David Soman (P)

_____, *One of Three,* illustrated by David Soman (P)

_____, *When I Am Old with You,* illustrated by David Soman (P)

Johnson, Dinah, *Quinnie Blue,* illustrated by James Ransome (P)

_____, *Sunday Week,* illustrated by Tyrone Geter (P)

Johnson, Dolores, *The Best Bug to Be* (P)

_____, *Papa's Stories* (P)

Mathis, Sharon Bell, *The Hundred Penny Box,* illustrated by Leo and Diane Dillon (P–I)

McKissack, Patricia, *Ma Dear's Aprons,* illustrated by Floyd Cooper (P)

_____, *A Million Fish . . . More or Less,* illustrated by Dena Schutzer (P–I)

Medearis, Angela Shelf, *The Adventures of Sugar and Junior* (P)

_____, *Dancing with the Indians,* illustrated by Samuel Byrd (P–I)

_____, *Haunts: Five Hair-Raising Tales,* illustrated by Trina Schart Hyman (I)

_____, *Our People,* illustrated by Michael Bryant (P)

_____, *Poppa's New Pants,* illustrated by John Ward (P)

Mitchell, Margaree King, *Granddaddy's Gift,* illustrated by Larry Johnson (P–I)

Myers, Walter Dean, *Patrol* (I–A)

Pinkney, Brian, *The Adventures of Sparrowboy* (P)

_____, *JoJo's Flying Side Kick* (P)

_____, *Paperboy* (P)

Pinkney, Brian, and Andrea Davis Pinkney, *I Smell Honey* (N)

Pinkney, Gloria Jean, *Back Home,* illustrated by Jerry Pinkney (P–I)

_____, *The Sunday Outing,* illustrated by Jerry Pinkney (P–I)

Ringgold, Faith, *Tar Beach* (I)

Smalls, Irene, *Dawn and the Round To-It,* illustrated by Tyrone Geter (P)

Smalls-Hector, Irene, *Ebony Sea,* illustrated by Jon Onye Lockard (I)

Steptoe, John, *Stevie* (P)

Stroud, Bettye, *Down Home at Miss Dessa's,* illustrated by Felicia Marshall (P)

Tate, Eleanora, *Front Porch Stories at the One-Room School,* illustrated by Eric Velasquez (I)

Thomas, Joyce Carol, *I Have Heard of a Land,* illustrated by Floyd Cooper (P–I)

Walter, Mildred Pitts, *Two and Too Much,* illustrated by Pat Cummings (P)

Williams, Sherley Anne, *Girls Together,* illustrated by Synthia Saint James (P)

_____, *Working Cotton,* illustrated by Carole Byard (P–I)

Woodson, Jacqueline, *The Other Side* (P–I)

_____, *We Had a Picnic This Sunday Past* (P)

NOVELS (SEE ALSO CHAPTERS 6, 7, AND 8)

Boyd, Candy Dawson, *Chevrolet Saturdays* (I)

Curtis, Christopher Paul, *Bucking the Sarge* (A)

_____, *Bud, Not Buddy* (I)

_____, *The Watsons Go to Birmingham—1963* (I–A)

Draper, Sharon, *Forged by Fire* (A)

_____, *Tears of a Tiger* (A)

Fenner, Carol, *Yolanda's Genius* (I–A)

Greenfield, Eloise, *Koya DeLaney and the Good Girl Blues* (I)

Grimes, Nikki, *Jazmin's Notebook* (A)

Hamilton, Virginia, *Bluish* (I–A)

_____, *Cousins* (I–A)

_____, *M. C. Higgins, the Great* (I–A)

_____, *Plain City* (A)

_____, *Planet of Junior Brown* (I–A)

_____, *Second Cousins* (I–A)

_____, *Zeely* (I)

Hansen, Joyce, *The Captive* (I–A)

_____, *I Thought My Soul Would Rise and Fly* (I–A)

Johnson, Angela, *Bird* (A)

_____, *The First Part Last* (A)

_____, *Gone from Home* (A)

_____, *Heaven* (A)

_____, *Humming Whispers* (A)

_____, *Songs of Faith* (A)

_____, *Toning the Sweep* (A)

Lester, Julius, *Pharaoh's Daughter* (A)

_____, *When Dad Killed Mom* (A)

McKissack, Patricia, *Run Away Home* (I–A)

Myers, Walter Dean, *The Beast* (A)

_____, *Fallen Angels* (A)

_____, *Fast Sam, Cool Clyde, and Stuff* (I–A)

_____, *The Glory Field* (A)

_____, *Monster* (A)

_____, *145th Street Stories* (A)

_____, *Slam!* (A)

_____, *Somewhere in the Darkness* (A)

_____, *The Young Landlords* (A)

Pinkney, Andrea Davis, *Hold Fast to Dreams* (I–A)

_____, *Raven in a Dove House* (A)

_____, *Silent Thunder: A Civil War Story* (I–A)

_____, *Solo Girl*, illustrated by Nneka Bennett (P–I)

Robinet, Harriette Gillem, *Forty Acres and Maybe a Mule* (I–A)

_____, *If You Please, President Lincoln* (I–A)

_____, *Mississippi Chariot* (I–A)

Smothers, Ethel Footman, *Moriah's Pond* (I)

Tate, Eleanora, *A Blessing in Disguise* (I–A)

_____, *The Secret of Gumbo Grove* (I)

Taylor, Mildred, *The Friendship* (A)

_____, *The Land* (A)

_____, *Let the Circle Be Unbroken* (A)

_____, *Mississippi Bridge* (A)

_____, *Roll of Thunder, Hear My Cry* (A)

_____, *Song of the Trees* (I)

_____, *The Well: David's Story* (A)

Walter, Mildred Pitts, *Second Daughter: The Story of a Slave Girl* (A)

Wilkinson, Brenda, *Definitely Cool* (I)

_____, *Ludell* (A)

Williams-Garcia, Rita, *Every Time a Rainbow Dies* (A)

_____, *Like Sisters on the Homefront* (A)

Woodson, Jacqueline, *The Dear One* (A)

_____, *From the Notebooks of Melanin Sun* (A)

_____, *I Hadn't Meant to Tell You This* (A)

_____, *Last Summer with Maizon* (A)

_____, *Locomotion* (I–A)

_____, *Maizon at Blue Hill* (A)

_____, *Miracle's Boys* (A)

_____, *A Way Out of No Way: Writings about Growing Up Black in America* (A)

NONFICTION (SEE ALSO CHAPTERS 9 AND 10)

Bolden, Tonya, *The Book of African American Women: 150 Crusaders, Creators, and Uplifters* (I–A)

_____, *Tell All the Children Our Story: Memories and Mementos of Being Young and Black in America* (I–A)

_____, *Wake Up Our Souls: A Celebration of Black American Artists* (I–A)

Cline-Ransome, Lesa, *Satchel Paige*, illustrated by James Ransome (I)

Cox, Clinton, *Undying Glory: The Story of the Massachusetts 54th Regiment* (I)

Golenbock, Peter, *Teammates*, illustrated by Paul Bacon (I)

Greenfield, Eloise, *How They Got Over: African Americans and the Call of the Sea*, illustrated by Jan Spivey Gilchrist (P)

Haskins, Jim, *Black Dance in America: A History through Its People* (A)

_____, *Black Eagles: African Americans in Aviation* (I)

_____, *The Day Martin Luther King, Jr., Was Shot: A Photo History of the Civil Rights Movement* (I–A)

_____, *One More River to Cross: The Stories of Twelve Black Americans* (A)

McKissack, Fredrick, *Black Hoops: The History of African Americans in Basketball* (I)

McKissack, Patricia, and Fredrick McKissack, *Black Diamond: The Story of the Negro Baseball Leagues* (A)

_____, *Christmas in the Big House, Christmas in the Quarters* (I–A)

Miller, William, *Zora Hurston and the Chinaberry Tree*, illustrated by Cornelius Van Wright and Ying-Hwa Hu (P–I)

Monceaux, Morgan, *Jazz: My Music, My People* (I–A)

Myers, Walter Dean, *Bad Boy: A Memoir* (A)

_____, *Malcolm X: By Any Means Necessary* (A)

_____, *Now Is Your Time! The African-American Struggle for Freedom* (I–A)

Parks, Rosa, with Jim Haskins, *Rosa Parks: My Story* (I)

Pinkney, Andrea Davis, *Alvin Ailey*, illustrated by Brian Pinkney (I)

_____, *Bill Pickett: Rodeo-Ridin' Cowboy*, illustrated by Brian Pinkney (P–I)

_____, *Dear Benjamin Banneker*, illustrated by Brian Pinkney (P–I)

_____, *Duke Ellington*, illustrated by Brian Pinkney (P–I)

Rappaport, Doreen, *Escape from Slavery: Five Journeys to Freedom* (I–A)

_____, *Martin's Big Words*, illustrated by Bryan Collier (P)

Walter, Mildred Pitts, *Kwanzaa: A Family Affair* (I)

_____, *Mississippi Challenge* (A)

Asian American Children's Books

FOLKLORE (SEE ALSO CHAPTER 5)

Chang, Margaret, and Raymond Chang, *The Beggar's Magic: A Chinese Tale*, illustrated by David Johnson (N–P)

Demi, *The Dragon's Tale and Other Animal Fables of the Chinese Zodiac* (N–P)

_____, *The Stonecutter* (N–P)

Fang, Linda, *The Ch'I-Lin Purse: A Collection of Ancient Chinese Stories*, illustrated by Jeanne Lee (P–I–A)

Han, Oki, and Stephanie Haboush Plunkett, *Kongi and Potgi: A Cinderella Story from Korea* (N–P)

Ho, Minfong, and Saphan Ros, *Brother Rabbit: A Cambodian Tale,* illustrated by Jennifer Hewitson

_____, *The Two Brothers,* illustrated by Jean Tseng and Mou-Sian Tseng (P–I)

Louie, Ai-Ling, *Yeh-Shen: A Cinderella Story from China,* illustrated by Ed Young (I)

Namioka, Lensey, *The Loyal Cat,* illustrated by Aki Sogabe (P–I)

Uchida, Yoshiko, *The Wise Old Woman,* illustrated by Martin Springett (P–I)

Wang, Rosalind, *The Treasure Chest: A Chinese Tale* (P–I)

Yee, Paul, *Tales from Gold Mountain: Stories of the Chinese in the New World* (I–A)

Yep, Laurence, *The Dragon Prince: A Chinese Beauty and the Beast Tale,* illustrated by Kam Mak (N–P–I)

_____, *The Khan's Daughter: A Mongolian Folktale,* illustrated by Jean Tseng and Mou-sien Tseng (N–P)

_____, *The Rainbow People* (A)

_____, *Tiger Woman,* illustrated by Robert Roth (N–P)

_____, *Tongues of Jade* (A)

Young, Ed, *Cat and Rat: The Legend of the Chinese Zodiac* (N–P)

_____, *Little Plum* (N–P)

_____, *Lon Po Po: A Red Riding Hood Story from China* (N–P–I)

_____, *The Lost Horse: A Chinese Folktale* (N–P)

Zhang, Song Nan, *Five Heavenly Emperors: Chinese Myths of Creation* (N–P–I)

POETRY AND SONG (SEE ALSO CHAPTER 4)

Ho, Minfong, *Maples in the Mist,* illustrated by Jean Tseng and Mou-sien Tseng (P–I–A)

Wong, Janet, *Good Luck Gold: And Other Poems* (I–A)

_____, *The Rainbow Hand: Poems about Mothers and Children* (I)

_____, *A Suitcase of Seaweed: And Other Poems* (I)

PICTURE BOOKS (SEE ALSO CHAPTERS 2 AND 3)

Chinn, Karen, *Sam and the Lucky Money,* illustrated by Cornelius Van Wright and Ying-Hwa Hu (P–I)

Choi, Sook Nyul, *The Best Older Sister,* illustrated by Cornelius Van Wright and Ying-Hwa Hu (N–P)

_____, *Halmoni and the Picnic,* illustrated by Karen Dugan (P)

Hamanaka, Sheila, *Bebop-A-Do-Walk!* (N–P)

Heo, Yumi, *One Afternoon* (N–P)

Mochizuki, Ken, *Baseball Saved Us,* illustrated by Dom Lee (I)

_____, *Heroes,* illustrated by Dom Lee (P–I)

Narahashi, Keiko, *I Have a Friend* (N–P)

_____, *Is That Josie?* (N–P)

Nunes, Susan Miho, *The Last Dragon,* illustrated by Chris Soentpiet (P)

Recorvitz, Helen, *My Name Is Yoon,* illustrated by Gabi Swiatkowska (P)

Rumford, James, *Dog-of-the-Sea-Waves* (P)

_____, *The-Island-Below-the-Star* (P)

Sakai, Kimiko, *Sachiko Means Happiness,* illustrated by Tomie Arai (I)

Say, Allen, *El Chino* (I)

_____, *Grandfather's Journey* (P–I)

_____, *Tea with Milk* (P–I)

_____, *Tree of Cranes* (P–I)

Tan, Amy, *The Moon Lady,* illustrated by Gretchen Schields (I–A)

Wong, Janet, *Buzz,* illustrated by Margaret Chodos-Irvine (N–P)

Yee, Paul, *Roses Sing on New Snow: A Delicious Tale,* illustrated by Harvey Chan (I)

_____, *A Song for Ba,* illustrated by Jan Peng Wang (P–I)

NOVELS (SEE ALSO CHAPTERS 6, 7, AND 8)

Brown, Jackie, *Little Cricket* (I–A)

Carlson, Lori, editor, *American Eyes: New Asian-American Short Stories for Young Adults* (A)

Choi, Sook Nyul, *Gathering of Pearls* (A)

Ho, Minfong, *Gathering the Dew* (I–A)

Kadohata, Cynthia, *Kira-Kira* (I–A)

Kashmira, Sheth, *Blue Jasmine* (I)

Krishnaswami, Uma, *Naming Maya* (I)

Lee, Marie, *Finding My Voice* (A)

_____, *If It Hadn't Been for Yoon Jun* (A)

_____, *Necessary Roughness* (A)

_____, *Night of the Chupacabras* (I–A)

_____, *Saying Goodbye* (A)

Lord, Bette Bao, *In the Year of the Boar and Jackie Robinson* (I)

Na, An, *A Step from Heaven* (A)

Namioka, Lensey, *April and the Dragon Lady* (A)

_____, *Yang the Second and Her Secret Admirers* (I)

_____, *Yang the Third and Her Impossible Family* (I)

_____, *Yang the Youngest and His Terrible Ear* (I)

Okimoto, Jean Davies, *Molly by Any Other Name* (A)

_____, *Talent Night* (A)

Shea, Peggy Dietz, *Tangled Threads* (I–A)

Uchida, Yoshiko, *Journey Home* (I–A)

_____, *Journey to Topaz* (I–A)

Yee, Lisa, *Millicent Min, Girl Genius* (I)

Yep, Laurence, *American Dragons: Twenty-Five Asian American Voices* (A)

_____, *The Case of the Lion Dance* (I–A)

_____, *Child of the Owl* (A)

_____, *The Cook's Family* (A)

_____, *Dragon's Gate* (I–A)

_____, *Dragonwings* (A)

_____, *Dream Soul* (I–A)

_____, *The Ghost Fox* (I–A)

_____, *Hiroshima* (A)

_____, *Mountain Light* (A)

_____, *Sea Glass* (I–A)

_____, *The Serpent's Children* (I–A)

_____, *The Star Fisher* (I–A)

_____, *Thief of Hearts* (A)

NONFICTION (SEE ALSO CHAPTERS 9 AND 10)

Brown, Tricia, *Konnichiwa! I Am a Japanese-American Girl,* illustrated by Kazuyoshi Arai (P)

_____, *Lee Ann: The Story of a Vietnamese-American Girl,* illustrated by Ted Thai (I)

Cha, Dia, *Dia's Story Cloth: The Hmong People's Journey of Freedom,* illustrated by Chue Cha and Nhia Thao Cha (I)

Hamanaka, Sheila, *The Journey: Japanese Americans, Racism, and Renewal* (A)

Hoyt-Goldsmith, Diane, *Hoang Anh: A Vietnamese-American Boy,* illustrated by Lawrence Migdale (P)

Uchida, Yoshiko, *The Invisible Thread* (A)

Yep, Laurence, *The Lost Garden* (I–A)

Latino Children's Books

FOLKLORE (SEE ALSO CHAPTER 5)

Ada, Alma Flor, *The Gold Coin,* illustrated by Neil Waldman (P)

Belpré, Pura, *Perez and Martina/Perez y Martina: A Puerto Rican Folktale,* illustrated by Carlos Sanchez (P)

Bernier-Grand, Carmen, *Juan Bobo: Four Folktales from Puerto Rico,* illustrated by Ernesto Ramos Nieves (N–P)

Gonzalez, Lucia, *The Bossy Gallito/El Gallo de Bodas: A Traditional Cuban Folktale,* illustrated by Lulu Delacre (N–P)

_____, *Señor Cat's Romance and Other Favorite Stories from Latin America,* illustrated by Lulu Delacre (N–P)

Mohr, Nicholasa, *The Song of el Coqui and Other Tales of Puerto Rico,* illustrated by Antonio Martorell (P–I)

Mora, Pat, *The Race of Toad and Deer,* illustrated by Maya Itzna Brooks (N–P)

Orozco, Jose-Luis, *De Colores and Other Latin-American Folk Songs for Children,* illustrated by Elisa Kleven (N–P)

Pitre, Felix, *Paco and the Witch,* illustrated by Christy Hale (N–P)

Schon, Isabel, *Dona Blanca and Other Hispanic Nursery Rhymes and Games* (P)

POETRY AND SONG (SEE ALSO CHAPTER 4)

Alarcón, Francisco X., *From the Bellybutton of the Moon and Other Summer Poems/Del Ombligo de la Luna y Otros Poemas de Verano,* illustrated by Maya Christina Gonzalez (N–P)

_____, *Laughing Tomatoes and Other Spring Poems/Jitomates Risuenos y Otros Poemas de Primavera,* illustrated by Maya Christina Gonzalez (N–P)

Carlson, Lori, *Cool Salsa: Bilingual Poems on Growing Up Latino in the United States* (A)

Cumpian, Carlos, *Latino Rainbow: Poems about Latino Americans,* illustrated by Richard Leonard (P–I)

Gonzalez, Ray, *Touching the Fire: Fifteen Poets of Today's Latino Renaissance* (A)

Mora, Pat, *Confetti: Poems for Children,* illustrated by Enrique O. Sanchez (N–P–I)

_____, *The Desert Is My Mother/El Desierto Es Mi Madre,* illustrated by Daniel Lechón (P)

_____, *Listen to the Desert/Oye al Desierto,* illustrated by Francisco X. Mora (P)

_____, *This Big Sky,* illustrated by Steve Jenkins (P)

_____, *Uno, Dos, Tres: One, Two, Three,* illustrated by Barbara Lavallee (N–P)

Ortiz Cofer, Judith, *Reaching for the Mainland and Selected New Poems* (A)

Soto, Gary, *Canto Familiar* (I–A)

_____, *Fire in My Hands: A Book of Poems* (A)

_____, *Neighborhood Odes,* illustrated by David Diaz (A)

PICTURE BOOKS (SEE ALSO CHAPTERS 2 AND 3)

Ada, Alma Flor, *Gathering the Sun: An Alphabet in Spanish and English,* illustrated by Simon Silva (N–P)

Anaya, Rudolfo, *The Farolitos of Christmas,* illustrated by Edward Gonzales (P–I)

Anzaldua, Gloria, *Prietita and the Ghost Woman/Prietita y la Llorona,* illustrated by Christina Gonzalez (P)

Cisneros, Sandra, *Hairs/Pelitos,* illustrated by Terry Ybanez (P)

Cordova, Amy, *Abuelita's Heart* (N–P–I)

Cruz, Martel, *Yagua Days* (P)

Delacre, Lulu, *Vejigante Masquerader* (P–I)

Delgado, Maria Isabel, *Chave's Memories: Los Recuerdos de Chave,* illustrated by Yvonne Symank (N–P)

Dorros, Arthur, *Abuela,* illustrated by Elisa Kleven (P)

_____, *Radio Man/Don Radio* (P)

Garza, Carmen Lomas, *My Family* (P)

Herrera, Juan Felipe, *Calling the Doves/El Canto de las Palomas,* illustrated by Elly Simmons (N–P–I–A)

Jiménez, Francisco, *La Mariposa,* illustrated by Simon Silva (P–I)

Lachtman, Ofelia Dumas, *Pepita Talks Twice/Pepita Habla Dos Veces,* illustrated by Alex Pardo (N–P)

Mohr, Nicholasa, *Old Letivia and the Mountain of Sorrows,* illustrated by Rudy Gutierrez (P)

Mora, Pat, *A Birthday Basket for Tía,* illustrated by Cecily Lang (P)

_____, *Pablo's Tree,* illustrated by Cecily Lang (P)

_____, *Tomás and the Library Lady,* illustrated by Raul Colón (N–P)

Nodar, Carmen Santiago, *Abuelita's Paradise/El Paraiso de Abuelita,* illustrated by Diane Paterson (P)

Reiser, Lynn, *Tortillas and Lullabies/Tortillas y Cancioncitas,* illustrated by "Corazones Valientes" (N–P)

Roe, Eileen, *Con Mi Hermano/With My Brother,* illustrated by Robert Casilla (P)

Soto, Gary, *Big Bushy Mustache,* illustrated by Joe Cepeda (N–P)

_____, *Chato's Kitchen,* illustrated by Susan Guevara (N–P)

_____, *The Old Man and His Door,* illustrated by Joe Cepeda (N–P)

_____, *Snapshots from the Wedding,* illustrated by Stephanie Garcia (P–I)

NOVELS (SEE ALSO CHAPTERS 6, 7, AND 8)

Ada, Alma Flor, *My Name Is Maria Isabel* (P–I)

_____, *Under the Royal Palms* (P–I)

_____, *Where the Flame Trees Bloom,* illustrated by Antonio Martorell (I)

Belpré, Pura, *Firefly Summer* (A)

Bernardo, Anilu, *Fitting In* (I–A)

_____, *Jumping Off to Freedom* (A)

Bertrand, Diane Gonzales, *Alicia's Treasure* (A)

_____, *Sweet Fifteen* (A)

Cisneros, Sandra, *The House on Mango Street* (A)

Garcia, Lionel, *To a Widow with Children* (A)

Garcia, Pelayo Pete, *From Amigos to Friends* (A)

Hernandez, Irene Beltran, *The Secret of Two Brothers* (A)

Jiménez, Francisco, *Breaking Through* (A)

_____, *The Circuit* (A)

Lachtman, Ofelia Dumas, *The Girl from Playa Blanca* (A)

_____, *Leticia's Secret,* illustrated by Roberta C. Morales (I–A)

Martinez, Floyd, *Spirits of the High Mesa* (I–A)

Martinez, Victor, *Parrot in the Oven: Mi Vida* (A)

Mohr, Nicholasa, *Felita* (A)

_____, *Going Home* (A)

_____, *In Nueva York* (A)

_____, *Nilda* (A)

Ortiz Cofer, Judith, *Call Me Maria* (I–A)

_____, *An Island Like You: Stories of the Barrio* (A)

_____, *The Year of Our Revolution: New and Selected Stories and Poems* (A)

Osa, Nancy, *Cuba 15* (I)

Soto, Gary, *The Afterlife* (A)

_____, *Baseball in April and Other Stories* (A)

_____, *Boys at Work* (I)

_____, *Buried Onions* (A)

_____, *Crazy Weekend* (A)

_____, *Jesse* (A)

_____, *Living Up the Street* (A)

_____, *Local News* (I–A)

_____, *Off and Running* (I–A)

_____, *Pacific Crossing* (A)

_____, *Petty Crimes* (A)

_____, *Pool Party* (I)

_____, *Summer on Wheels* (A)

_____, *Taking Sides* (A)

Tashlick, Phyllis, *Hispanic, Female and Young: An Anthology* (A)

Thomas, Piri, *Stories from el Barrio* (A)

Veciana-Suarez, Ana, *Flight to Freedom* (A)

Velasquez, Gloria, *Juanita Fights the School Board* (A)

_____, *Maya's Divided World* (A)

_____, *Tommy Stands Alone* (A)

NONFICTION (SEE ALSO CHAPTERS 9 AND 10)

Anastos, Phillip, and Chris French, *Illegal: Seeking the American Dream* (A)

Brimner, Larry Dane, *A Migrant Family* (I–A)

Hewett, Joan, *Hector Lives in the United States Now,* illustrated by Richard Hewett (P–I)

Lomas Garza, Carmen, as told to Harriet Rohmer, *Family Pictures/Cuadros de Familia* (P–I)

Native American Children's Books

FOLKLORE (SEE ALSO CHAPTER 5)

Begay, Shonto, *Ma'ii and Cousin Horned Toad: A Traditional Navajo Story* (P–I)

Bierhorst, John, *The Deetkatoo: Native American Stories about Little People* (I–A)

_____, *Lightning inside You: And Other Native American Riddles* (I)

_____, *Naked Bear: Folktales of the Iroquois* (I)

_____, *On the Road of Stars: Native American Night Poems and Sleep Charms,* illustrated by Judy Pedersen (N–P–I)

_____, *The People with Five Fingers: A Native Californian Creation Tale,* illustrated by Robert Andrew Parker (P)

_____, *The Sacred Path: Spells, Prayers and Power Songs of the American Indians* (I)

_____, *The White Deer: And Other Stories Told by the Lenape* (A)

Bruchac, Joseph, *Between Earth and Sky: Legends of Native American Sacred Places,* illustrated by Thomas Locker (I–A)

_____, *The Boy Who Lived with the Bears: And Other Iroquois Stories* (I)

_____, *Flying with the Eagle, Racing the Great Bear: Stories from Native America* (I–A)

_____, *Four Ancestors: Stories, Songs, and Poems from Native North America,* illustrated by S. S. Burrus, Murv Jacob, Jeffrey Chapman, and Duke Sine (P–I)

_____, *Gluskabe and the Four Wishes,* illustrated by Christine Nyburg Shrader (P)

Bruchac, Joseph, and Gayle Ross, *The Girl Who Married the Moon* (I–A)

_____, *The Story of the Milky Way: A Cherokee Tale,* illustrated by Virginia A. Stroud (P)

Caduto, Michael, and Joseph Bruchac, *Keepers of the Earth* (I)

Erdoes, Richard, *The Sound of Flutes and Other Indian Legends* (I–A)

Goble, Paul, *Adopted by the Eagles: A Plains Indian Story of Friendship and Treachery* (I)

_____, *Buffalo Woman* (I)

_____, *Crow Chief: A Plains Indian Story* (I)

_____, *Dream Wolf* (I)

_____, *The Girl Who Loved Wild Horses* (I)

_____, *Iktomi and the Buzzard: A Plains Indian Story* (P–I)

_____, *The Legend of the White Buffalo Woman* (P–I)

_____, *Love Flute* (P–I)

_____, *Star Boy* (I)

Lacapa, Michael, *The Flute Player: An Apache Folktale* (I)

Manitonquat (Medicine Story), *The Children of the Morning Light: Wampanoag Tales,* illustrated by Mary F. Arquette (I)

Rodnas, Kristina, *Dance of the Sacred Circle: A Native American Tale* (I–A)

_____, *Dragonfly's Tale* (P)

_____, *The Eagle's Song: A Tale from the Pacific Northwest* (N–P)

_____, *Follow the Stars: A Native American Woodlands Tale* (N–P)

Ross, Gayle, *How Rabbit Tricked Otter and Other Cherokee Trickster Stories,* illustrated by Murv Jacob (I)

_____, *How Turtle's Back Was Cracked: A Traditional Cherokee Tale,* illustrated by Murv Jacob (N–P–I)

_____, *The Legend of the Windigo: A Tale from Native North America,* illustrated by Murv Jacob (N–P–I)

Smith, Patricia Clark, *On the Trail of Elder Brother: Glous'gap Stories of the Micmac Indians,* illustrated by Michael B. Runningwolf (A)

Ude, Wayne, *Maybe I Will Do Something: Seven Coyote Tales,* illustrated by Abigail Rorer (I)

Yellow Robe, Rosebud, *Tonweya and the Eagles and Other Lakota Indian Tales* (I)

POETRY AND SONG (SEE ALSO CHAPTER 4)

Begay, Shonto, *Navajo: Visions and Voices across the Mesa* (I–A)

Bruchac, Joseph, *The Earth under Sky Bear's Feet: Native American Poems of the Land,* illustrated by Thomas Locker (I–A)

Bruchac, Joseph, and Jonathan London, *Thirteen Moons on Turtle's Back,* illustrated by Thomas Locker (I–A)

Harjo, Joy, *The Woman Who Fell from the Sky: Poems* (A)

Hirschfelder, Arlene, and Beverly Singer, *Rising Voices: Writings of Young Native Americans* (A)

Jones, Hettie, *The Trees Stand Shining: Poetry of the North American Indians,* illustrated by Robert Andrew Parker (P–I–A)

Sneve, Virginia Driving Hawk, *Dancing Teepees: Poems of American Indian Youth,* illustrated by Stephen Gammell (I–A)

Swamp, Chief Jake, *Giving Thanks: A Native American Good Morning Message,* illustrated by Erwin Printup Jr. (P)

Tapahonso, Luci, *Blue Horses Rush In: Poems and Stories* (A)

PICTURE BOOKS (SEE ALSO CHAPTERS 2 AND 3)

Erdrich, Louise, *Grandmother's Pigeon,* illustrated by Jim LaMarche (N–P–I)

Smith, Cynthia Leitich, *Jingle Dancer* (P–I)

Strete, Craig Kee, *Little Coyote Runs Away,* illustrated by Harvey Stevenson (N–P)

Strete, Craig Kee, and Michelle Netten Chacon, *How the Indians Bought the Farm,* illustrated by Francisco X. Mora (N–P)

Stroud, Virginia, *Doesn't Fall Off His Horse* (P–I)

_____, *The Path of Quiet Elk: A Native American Alphabet Book* (N–P)

NOVELS (SEE ALSO CHAPTERS 6, 7, AND 8)

Bruchac, Joseph, *The Arrow over the Door* (I–A)

_____, *Children of the Longhouse* (I–A)

_____, *The Dark Pond* (I–A)

_____, *Dog People: Native American Dog Stories* (I)

_____, *Eagle Song* (I–A)

_____, *The Heart of a Chief* (I–A)

_____, *Hidden Roots* (I–A)

_____, *Sacajawea* (I–A)

_____, *The Waters Between: A Novel of the Dawn Land* (A)

Dorris, Michael, *Guests* (I)

_____, *Morning Girl* (I)

_____, *Sees Behind Trees* (I)

_____, *The Window* (A)

Erdrich, Louise, *The Birchbark House* (I)

_____, *The Game of Silence* (I)

Smith, Cynthia Leitich, *Indian Shoes* (I)

_____, *Rain Is Not My Indian Name* (I–A)

Sneve, Virginia Driving Hawk, *High Elk's Treasure,* illustrated by Oren Lyons (I)

_____, *The Trickster and the Troll* (P–I)

Spinka, Penina Keen, *Mother's Blessing* (A)

Strete, Craig Kee, *Big Thunder Magic* (A)

_____, *The Bleeding Man and Other Science Fiction Stories* (A)

_____, *When Grandfather Journeys into Winter* (I–A)

_____, *The World in Grandfather's Hands* (A)

NONFICTION (SEE ALSO CHAPTERS 9 AND 10)

Ancona, George, *Earth Daughter: Alicia of Acoma Pueblo* (I)

_____, *Powwow* (I)

Broker, Ignatia, *Night Flying Woman: An Ojibway Narrative* (A)

Bruchac, Joseph, *Bowman's Store* (A)

Ekoomiak, Normee, *Arctic Memories* (I–A)

Erdoes, Richard, *Rain Dance People: The Pueblo Indians, Their Past and Present* (A)

Freedman, Russell, *Indian Chiefs* (I–A)

_____, *An Indian Winter,* illustrated by Karl Bodmer (I–A)

Hoyt-Goldsmith, Diane, *Arctic Hunter,* illustrated by Lawrence Migdale (I)

_____, *Cherokee Summer* (I)

_____, *Pueblo Storyteller,* illustrated by Lawrence Migdale (I)

_____, *Totem Pole,* illustrated by Lawrence Migdale (I)

Jacobs, Francine, *The Tainos: The People Who Welcomed Columbus,* illustrated by Patrick Collins (I–A)

Keegan, Marcia, *Pueblo Boy: Growing Up in Two Worlds* (I)

Kendall, Russ, *Eskimo Boy: Life in an Inupiaq Eskimo Village* (P–I)

King, Sandra, *Shannon: An Ojibway Dancer,* from the **We Are Still Here** series (I)

Lazar, Jerry, *Red Cloud: Sioux War Chief,* from the **North American Indians of Achievement** series (I)

Left Hand Bull, Jacqueline, and Suzanne Haldane, *Lakota Hoop Dancer,* illustrated by Suzanne Haldane (P–I)

Littlechild, George, *This Land Is My Land* (P)

Roessel, Monty, *Kinaalda: A Navajo Girl Grows Up,* from the **We Are Still Here** series (I)

Sneve, Virginia Driving Hawk, *The Cherokees,* illustrated by Ronald Himler, from the **First Americans** series (P–I)

_____, *The Seminoles,* illustrated by Ronald Himler, from the **First Americans** series (P–I)

Tapahonso, Luci, and Eleanor Schick, *Navajo ABC* (P)

International Books

POETRY AND SONG (SEE ALSO CHAPTER 4)

Berry, James, *Around the World in Eighty Poems,* illustrated by Katherine Lucas (P–I–A)

_____, *When I Dance,* illustrated by Karen Barbour (A), Caribbean/Britain

Delacre, Lulu, *Las Navidades: Popular Christmas Songs from Latin America* (P–I–A), Latin America

Nye, Naomi Shihab, *19 Varieties of Gazelle* (I–A), Palestine

_____, *This Same Sky: A Collection of Poems from around the World* (I–A)

Tagore, Rabindranath, *Paper Boats,* illustrated by Grayce Bochak (I), India

PICTURE BOOKS (SEE ALSO CHAPTERS 2 AND 3)

Baille, Allan, *Rebel,* illustrated by Di Wu (P–I), Burma

Bjork, Christina, *Vendela in Venice* (I), Italy

Bontemps, Arna, and Langston Hughes, *Popo and Fifina,* illustrated by E. Simms Campbell (I–A), Haiti

Castañeda, Omar, *Abuela's Weave,* illustrated by Enrique O. Sanchez (P–I), Guatemala

Chen, Chih-Yuan, *Guji Guji* (P), Taiwan

_____, *On My Way to Buy Eggs* (P), Taiwan

Daly, Niki, *Not So Fast, Songololo* (P), South Africa

Dematons, Charlotte, *The Yellow Balloon* (P–I)

Eriksson, Eva, *Molly Goes Shopping* (P), Scandinavia

Fox, Mem, *Possum Magic,* illustrated by Julie Vivas (P), Australia

Harel, Nira, *The Key to My Heart,* illustrated by Yossi Abulafia (N–P), Israel

Isadora, Rachel, *At the Crossroads* (P), South Africa

_____, *Over the Green Hills* (P), South Africa

Khan, Rukhsana, *Ruler of the Courtyard,* illustrated by R. Gregory Christie (P), Pakistan

Kurtz, Jane, *Faraway Home,* illustrated by E. B. Lewis (P), Ethiopia

_____, *Fire on the Mountain,* illustrated by E. B. Lewis (P), Ethiopia

Kurtz, Jane, and Christopher Kurtz, *Only a Pigeon,* illustrated by E. B. Lewis (P), Ethiopia

Lee, Jeanne, *Silent Lotus* (I), Cambodia

Merrill, Jean, *The Girl Who Loved Caterpillars: A Twelfth-Century Tale from Japan,* illustrated by Floyd Cooper (P), Japan

Mollel, Tololwa, *Big Boy,* illustrated by E. B. Lewis (P), Tanzania/Masai

_____, *Subira Subira,* illustrated by Linda Saport (P), Tanzania

Onyefulu, Ifeoma, *A Is for Africa* (P), Nigeria

_____, *Chidi Only Likes Blue: An African Book of Colors* (P), Nigeria

_____, *Emeka's Gift* (P), Nigeria

_____, *Here Comes Our Bride! An African Wedding* (P), Nigeria

_____, *Ogbo: Sharing Life in an African Village* (P), Nigeria

_____, *Saying Good-Bye: A Special Farewell to Mama Nkwelle* (P–I), Nigeria

Palacios, Argentina, *A Christmas Surprise for Chabelita,* illustrated by Lori Lohstoeter (P), Panama

Potter, Giselle, *Chloe's Birthday . . . and Me* (P), France

Rumford, James, *Nine Animals and the Well* (P), India

Tomioka, Chiyoko, *Rise and Shine, Mariko-Chan,* illustrated by Yoshiharu Tsuchida (P), Japan

Topooco, Eusebio, *Waira's First Journey* (P–I), Bolivia

Williams, Karen Lynn, *Galimoto,* illustrated by Catherine Stock (P), South Africa/Malawi

Winter, Jeanette, *Elsina's Clouds* (P), South Africa/Basotho

NOVELS (SEE ALSO CHAPTERS 6, 7, AND 8)

Almond, David, *The Fire-Eaters* (I–A), England

al-Windawi, Thura, *Thura's Diary* (I–A), Iraq

Baille, Alan, *Little Brother* (A), Cambodia

Bawden, Nina, *Humbug* (A), England

Berry, James, *Ajeemah and His Son* (A), Jamaica

_____, *The Future-Telling Lady* (A), Jamaica

_____, *A Thief in the Village* (A), Jamaica

Bolden, Tonya, editor, *Rites of Passage: Stories about Growing Up by Black Writers from around the World* (A)

Bredsdorff, Bodil, *The Crow-Girl: The Children of Crow Cove* (I), Denmark

Brooks, Martha, *True Confessions of a Heartless Girl* (A), Canada

Brugman, Alyssa, *Walking Naked* (A), Australia

Cameron, Ann, *The Most Beautiful Place in the World,* illustrated by Thomas Allen (P–I), Guatemala

Castañeda, Omar, *Among the Volcanoes* (I), Guatemala/Mayan

Choi, Sook Nyul, *Year of Impossible Goodbyes* (A), North Korea

Crew, Gary, *Angel's Gate* (A), Australia

_____, *Strange Objects* (A), Australia

Dalokay, Vedat, *Sister Shako and Kolo the Goat* (I), Turkey

de Jenkins, Lyll Becerra, *The Honorable Prison* (A), Colombia

Disher, Garry, *The Bamboo Flute* (A), Australia

Doherty, Berlie, *Granny Was a Buffer Girl* (A), England

Gee, Maurice, *The Fat Man* (A), New Zealand

_____, *The Fire-Raiser* (A), New Zealand

Haugen, Tormod, *Keeping Secrets,* translated by David Jacobs (A), Norway

Hautzig, Esther, *The Endless Steppe* (A), Poland/Russia

Hiçyilmaz, Gaye, *Against the Storm* (I–A), Turkey

_____, *The Frozen Waterfall* (A), Turkey/Switzerland

_____, *Smiling for Strangers* (A), Yugoslavia/England

Hill, Anthony, *The Burnt Stick,* illustrated by Mark Sofilas (I), Australia/Aboriginal

Ho, Minfong, *The Clay Marble* (A), Thailand/Cambodia

_____, *Rice without Rain* (A), Thailand

Holm, Anne, *I Am David* (formerly *North to Freedom*) (I–A), Eastern Europe/Denmark

Huynh, Quang Nhuong, *The Land I Lost: Adventures of a Boy in Vietnam* (I–A), Vietnam

_____, *Water Buffalo Days: Growing Up in Vietnam* (I), Vietnam

Jang, Ji-li, *Red Scarf Girl: A Memoir of the Cultural Revolution* (I–A), China

Jiménez, Juan Ramón, *Platero y Yo/Platero and I,* translated by Myra Cohn Livingston, illustrated by Antonia Frasconi (A), Spain

Kherdian, David, *The Road from Home: The Story of an Armenian Girl* (A), Turkey

Kurtz, Jane, *Memories of Sun: Stories of Africa and America* (I–A), Africa

_____, *The Storyteller's Beads* (A), Ethiopia

Laird, Elizabeth, *Kiss the Dust* (A), Iraq/Kurd

Lawrence, Iain, *B Is for Buster* (A), Canada and England

_____, *The Lightkeeper's Daughter* (A), Canada

Maartens, Maretha, *Paper Bird* (A), South Africa

Mahy, Margaret, *24 Hours* (A), New Zealand

_____, *Underrunners* (A), New Zealand

Marsden, John, *Letters from the Inside* (A), Australia

McKay, Hilary, *Indigo's Star* (A), England

Moeri, Louise, *The Forty-Third War* (A), Central America

Morgenstern, Susie, *A Book of Coupons* (I), France

Mori, Kyoko, *One Bird* (A), Japan

_____, *Shizuko's Daughter* (A), Japan

Mosher, Richard, *Zazoo* (A), France

Naidoo, Beverly, *Chain of Fire* (A), South Africa

_____, *Journey to Jo'burg* (A), South Africa

_____, *The Other Side of Truth* (A), Nigeria and England

_____, *Out of Bounds: Seven Stories of Conflict and Hope* (A), South Africa

Neville, Emily Cheney, *The China Year* (A), China

Newth, Mette, *The Transformation* (A), Greenland

Orlev, Uri, *The Island on Bird Street* (A), Poland

_____, *The Man from the Other Side* (A), Poland

Oz, Amos, *Soumchi,* translated by Amos Oz and Penelope Farmer (A), Israel

Pausewang, Gudrun, *Fall-Out* (A), Germany

Place, François, *The Old Man Mad about Drawing: A Tale of Hokusai,* translated by William Rodarmor (I), Japan

Pressler, Mirjam, *Halinka* (A), Germany

_____, *Malka* (A), Germany

Rana, Indi, *The Roller Birds of Rampur* (A), India

Russell, Ching Yeung, *First Apple* (A), China

_____, *Water Ghost* (A), China

Semel, Nava, *Flying Lessons,* translated by Hillel Halkin (A), Israel

Siegal, Aranka, *Upon the Head of the Goat* (A), Hungary

Staples, Suzanne Fisher, *Haveli* (A), Pakistan

_____, *Shabanu: Daughter of the Wind* (A), Pakistan

Temple, Frances, *Grab Hands and Run* (A), El Salvador

_____, *Taste of Salt* (A), Haiti

_____, *Tonight, by Sea* (A), Haiti

Watkins, Yoko Kawashima, *My Brother, My Sister, and I* (A), Japan

_____, *So Far from the Bamboo Grove* (A), Korea/Japan

Whelan, Gloria, *Good-Bye Vietnam* (A), Vietnam

_____, *Homeless Bird* (A), India

Wrightson, Patricia, *A Little Fear* (A), Australia

Yen Mah, Adeline, *Falling Leaves: The True Story of an Unwanted Chinese Daughter* (A), China

Yumoto, Kazumi, *The Friends* (A), Japan

_____, *The Letters* (A), Japan

_____, *The Spring Tone* (A), Japan

NONFICTION (SEE ALSO CHAPTERS 9 AND 10)

Lekuton, Joseph Lemasolai, with Herman Viola, *Facing the Lion: Growing Up Maasai on the African Savanna* (I), Kenya

Smith, David, *If the World Were a Village: A Book about the World's People* (I–A)

Books Exploring Sexual Orientation

Selections in this section are appropriate for advanced readers.

Bauer, Marion Dane, *Am I Blue? Coming Out from the Silence*

Block, Francesca Lia, *Baby Be-Bop*

Boock, Paula, *Dare, Truth, or Promise*

Frank, E. R., *Life Is Funny*

Garden, Nancy, *Annie on My Mind*

_____, *Holly's Secret*

Hartinger, Brent, *Geography Club*

Kerr, M. E., *Deliver Us from Evie*

Levithan, David, *Boy Meets Boy*

Nelson, Theresa, *Earthshine*

Peters, Julie Ann, *Luna*

Porte, Barbara Ann, *Something Terrible Happened*

Sanchez, Alex, *Rainbow Boys*

_____, *Rainbow High*

Taylor, *The Blue Lawn*

Walker, Kate, *Peter*

Wittlinger, Ellen, *Hard Love*

_____, *What's in a Name?*

Woodson, Jacqueline, *From the Notebooks of Melanin Sun*

_____, *The House You Pass on the Way*

Yamanaka, Lois-Ann, *Name Me Nobody*

Books Exploring Exceptionalities

Anderson, Rachel, *The Bus People* (A)

Banks, Jacqueline Turner, *Egg Drop Blues* (I)

Betancourt, Jeanne, *My Name Is ~~Brain~~ Brian* (I–A)

Birdseye, Tom, *Just Call Me Stupid* (I)

Byars, Betsy, *Summer of the Swans* (I–A)

Caseley, Judith, *Harry and Willy and Carrothead* (P)

Clifton, Lucille, *My Friend Jacob* (P)

Conly, Jane Leslie, *Crazy Lady!* (A)

Covington, Dennis, *Lizard* (I)

Gantos, Jack, *Joey Pigza Loses Control* (I)

_____, *Joey Pigza Swallowed the Key* (I)

Gleitzman, Morris, *Blabber Mouth* (I)

Haddon, Mark, *The Curious Incident of the Dog in the Night-Time* (A)

Johnson, Angela, *Humming Whispers* (A)

Little, Jean, *Mine for Keeps* (I)

Lowry, Lois, *The Silent Boy* (I)

Martin, Ann, *A Corner of the Universe* (I–A)

Mass, Wendy, *A Mango-Shaped Space* (I)

Mazer, Harry, *The Wild Kid* (A)

Metzger, Lois, *Barry's Sister* (A)

_____, *Ellen's Case* (A)

Paterson, Katherine, *Preacher's Boy* (I–A)

Philbrick, Rodman, *Freak the Mighty* (A)

Sachs, Marilyn, *The Bear's House* (I)

_____, *Fran Ellen's House* (I)

Shreve, Susan, *The Flunking of Joshua T. Bates* (I)

_____, *Joshua T. Bates Takes Charge* (I)

Shyer, Marlene Fanta, *Welcome Home, Jellybean* (I–A)

Trueman, Terry, *Cruise Control* (A)

_____, *Inside Out* (A)

_____, *Stuck in Neutral* (A)

Voigt, Cynthia, *Izzy Willy-Nilly* (A)

Weeks, Sarah, *So B. It* (I–A)

White, Ruth, *Belle Prater's Boy* (I–A)

_____, *Memories of Summer* (A)

Chapter 12

Developing Responsive Readers

But the dam still stood, its great bulk defying the puny efforts of the Minnipins.

Glocken could not believe his eyes. His hand went out to the Whisper, and he struck it again, this time from the other side. And then again. And again. And again. And still the dam stood.

Until suddenly—it simply disappeared.

One moment it was there defying them. And the next moment it had gone into a thousand cracks. And the earth, the stone, the washed-limestone simply went to powder and slid away. With a roar, the released river shot out from under them, roaring down the valley, roaring across the waste, roaring to freedom!

In his excitement Glocken struck the Whisper one last time. There was a sudden fearful crack! over their heads.

Then the whole mountain fell down on top of them.

—CAROL KENDALL, **The Whisper of Glocken,** p. 218

ANNA, HER HEAD BENT FORWARD SO THAT HER DARK HAIR MAKES A TENT around her face and the book she is reading, is totally engrossed in the world of *The Whisper of Glocken.* When she gets to the part where Silky finds a little gray creature and calls him Wafer, she looks up, sighs, and says, "Mom, Wafer is a perfect name for a gray kitten." She then goes back to her reading, once more lost to the world. Later, when she is finished with the book, she talks about it, wondering aloud how the Minnipins had the courage to leave their valley and venture out into the bigger world, questioning whether she would be that brave. From one book she's found the perfect name for her new gray kitten, has experienced a dangerous journey into an unknown land, and has thought about her personal courage, all without leaving her own living room.

She's been doing this forever. She careened down a hill in a buggy with Max, Rosemary Wells's captivating rabbit, even as she chewed the corners of the sturdy board book. She went with another Max in his private boat to the land of the wild things, played in the rain with Peter Spier's children, and learned to understand the natural world through Joanne Ryder's imaginative nonfiction. She's laughed, cried, absorbed information, experienced danger, engaged in adventures, solved mysteries, and learned a great deal about the world and about herself as she's read book after book. Anna's a lucky child. She's been engaged with wonderful children's books all her life.

Memories of special books and of those who read them to us stay with us all our lives. The experiences we have during our lives shape and are shaped by the books that are important to us. Like Anna, many children who love to read get so engrossed in their books that the real world disappears. Parents laugh about calling and calling their children to no avail and then discovering them curled up somewhere reading, oblivious to what is going on around them. Teachers recognize that good books excite children about reading, and encourage them to read widely. Librarians are aware that exciting read-alouds lure children into the library to check out books on their own. Teachers appreciate that a child's imagination is fostered by a story's invitation to pretend. But nonnarrative books also play an important role in children's lives. Teachers see how children seek out and devour nonfiction texts and how these books enliven any area of study. Britton (1970) talks of how the language models of well-written books—narrative, poetic, and nonfiction

Anna is totally absorbed in the book she is reading. A frequent traveler in the world of books, she knows the pathway well.

© Lee Galda

texts—help form the language that children use in their own speaking and writing.

As children grow, they learn to understand their world, using language and reasoning to make sense of their experiences, including their experiences with books. Children also develop socially as they come to understand their world, respond to people and books, and adopt feelings and beliefs about themselves. We search for an understanding of ourselves when we read. Literature fosters this development.

The culture in which children live also shapes both cognitive and social development as it influences how they perceive experience as well as what they experience. Culture shapes children's attitudes and understanding about books and the ways that books function in their lives. It also shapes the way the books themselves are written.

Yes, the books children read are formative influences in their lives; it is our responsibility to know their books. It is also our responsibility to know the children, their experiences, how they develop and learn, and how they read and respond to what they read. Useful criteria for choosing literature for children are based on knowledge of children's books and an understanding of children's development and experiences. In this chapter we explore children as readers, and we discuss practices that promote responsive reading. Further discussion of effective classroom practices appears in Chapters 13 and 14.

A critical reason for selecting appropriate books is to foster children's connections with the books they read. When we share excellent literature with children, we must be sure to consider the age of the child. No matter how wonderful the book, children don't want to be seen reading what they consider to be "baby books." If we miss the golden years of two to four when Margaret Wise Brown's *Goodnight Moon* (N) strikes a responsive chord, children may never see the charm of it later. If we lose the chance to share Maurice Sendak's *Where the Wild Things Are* (P) when children are

© 1963 Maurice Sendak

*Five- to seven-year-old children appreciate Max's fun during a wild rumpus in **Where the Wild Things Are.** Sendak says his relatives used to come toward him and say "I'm going to eat you up." He used them as his models. Notice they are all smiling.*

five to seven, they may never appreciate its magic. Fifth-grade students will not be caught reading Arnold Lobel's ***Frog and Toad Are Friends*** (P), nor will older students be seen reading Natalie Babbitt's ***Tuck Everlasting*** (I), but what a shame if students miss them. There are more than 75,000 children's books in print. Children could read omnivorously and still never read an outstanding book. Most importantly, unless children read some of the really good books, they will probably not get hooked as lifelong readers.

We as teachers can observe children's responses to literature and other media, and thus become aware of the broad patterns of intellectual organization that structure their thinking. When we come to know the children in our classrooms, we also can learn to make judgments about the appropriateness of specific books for specific children. Further, when we begin to understand the cultural forces that shape our students' lives, we can begin to enlarge our perceptions of what is "appropriate" so as to include culturally diverse expressions of literacy. Figure 12.1 lists some guidelines for book selection that can help you make initial judgments about appropriate books. No guidelines, however, can substitute for knowing your students well.

A Transactional View of Reading

It is important to know your students well because who they are determines how they read. Readers construct meaning as they read (Goodman, 1985). Instead of absorbing "one right meaning" from a text (an elusive concept at best),

readers rely on their own background knowledge and create unique meanings (Rosenblatt, 1938/1976, 1978). Meaning does not reside in the text alone, waiting for a reader to unearth it; meaning is created in the transaction that occurs between a text and a reader. As a reader reads, personal experiences, feelings, preferences, and reasons for reading guide the selection and construction of meaning. At the same time, the text itself—the words on the page—guide and constrain the meaning that a reader builds. Engaged readers build meaning that is shaped by the text, no matter what kind of book they are reading.

Langer (1990) and others argue that reading is temporal in nature, that the meaning that readers construct is fluid and changes during the act of reading. Readers begin by "being out and stepping into" their "envisionment" of the text. They then move through this envisionment, often stepping back and rethinking their previous understandings. Finally they step out of the envisionment and react to the reading experience (Langer, 1995). This process occurs with all types of text. However, the emphasis and reasoning processes that readers use to construct their envisionments vary, depending on whether the text is informative or narrative (Lander, 1995).

● ● EFFERENT AND ● ● AESTHETIC READING

Efferent and aesthetic reading lie at either end of a continuum that describes how and why people read. When people want to find information about something, they usually look for a nonfiction text. A person might read a recipe to

Figure **12-1**

Guide to Book Selection

Characteristics of Children	Features of Books	Favorite Titles
INFANTS AND TODDLERS (BIRTH TO 2 YEARS)		
Explore world with eyes, ears, hands, feet, and mouth	Invite participation	*Pat the Bunny* (Kunhardt)
Enjoy bouncing rhymes, rhythm, music, and singing	Have brief, rhythmic text	*Mother Goose Songbook* (Yolen)
"Read" pictures as adult reads words; ask "What's that?"	Are colorful and sturdy	*Max's First Word* (Wells)
NURSERY—EARLY CHILDHOOD (2 TO 4 YEARS)		
Understand simple concepts, counting, and ABCs	Have clear, eye-catching pictures and simple concepts	ABC books; counting books
Want to "do it myself"	Present simple plots, songs, and verse	*Goodnight Moon* (Brown)
Hold book and "read" familiar story to self	Have melodic, lilting language	*Have You Seen My Duckling?* (Tafuri)
		Rosie's Walk (Hutchins)
PRIMARY (5 TO 8 YEARS)		
Become independent readers	Have artistically excellent illustrations	*Where the Wild Things Are* (Sendak)
Have vivid imaginations	Have supportive structure in books to read alone	*The Talking Eggs* (San Souci)
Demand strict moral judgments	Have rich language in books to read aloud	*Chrysanthemum* (Henkes)
		Frog and Toad Are Friends (Lobel)
INTERMEDIATE (9 TO 12 YEARS)		
Like mystery, intrigue, and humor	Present realistic view of the world	*Bridge to Terabithia* (Paterson)
Develop strength in independent reading	Develop strong characters, memorable plots	*Tuck Everlasting* (Babbitt)
Form strong friendships outside the family	Stress growing-up and friendship themes	*Hush* (Woodson)
Are concrete thinkers		
ADVANCED (12 YEARS AND UP)		
Accept responsibility for self and action	Deal with social and personal problems	*Dicey's Song* (Voight)
Seek role models and heroes	Show the underside of people and society	*A Wizard of Earthsea* (Le Guin)
Are self-conscious; "everybody's looking at me"	Develop complex plots and strong characterization	*A Wrinkle in Time* (L'Engle)
Are beginning to think abstractly	Vary stylistically	*Monster* (Myers)

discover how to prepare a new dish, a manual to learn how to assemble a bicycle, a factual text about dogs to discover how to care for a new puppy. Rosenblatt (1978) calls this *efferent* reading, reading that is done for the practical purpose of gaining knowledge from the text, much like your reading of this textbook. Just because this kind of reading has a practical purpose, however, does not mean that it isn't pleasurable. Many readers of all ages enjoy reading nonfiction text in an efferent manner.

Stories and poems are also read for pleasure, but with a different purpose and in a different fashion. Rosenblatt calls

this kind of reading *aesthetic*. Reading aesthetically involves being aware of the sound and feeling of a text, as well as identifying with characters and participating in the story world—virtually experiencing the story. Reading aesthetically gives readers the emotional space in which to evaluate the feelings, actions, and decisions of the story world, and thus to construct their own values (Britton, 1970). Reading aesthetically allows readers to make sense of their lives through books.

Efferent and aesthetic reading are not opposites, but lie at either end of a continuum, with most reading comprising a mixture of the two. Whereas efferent reading relates mainly to public, cognitive aspects of meaning, aesthetic reading relates mainly to private, affective aspects of meaning, to the lived-through experience (Rosenblatt, 1991). Different genres signal a predominant stance to a reader, but it is a reader's individual purpose for reading that decides the stance. For example, a cookbook signals an efferent stance—information about how to cook is inside the covers. However, a reader might pick up an especially enticing cookbook and read it for pure pleasure, imagining how good the various dishes might taste and what dishes might go well together; another reader might enjoy the beautiful photographs of food or the accompanying humorous asides. It is a reader's purpose that determines the stance he or she takes. Rosenblatt argues that although both efferent and aesthetic experiences can be present in any reading, it is important that we as teachers are clear about the primary stance appropriate for different purposes for reading. Stories and poems, for example, are meant to be read aesthetically. If a book is meant to be "'literature' for . . . students, it must be experienced" first (Rosenblatt, 1991, p. 447). Think, for example, about reading historical fiction. Certainly we learn facts about a historical period as we read, but the purpose for reading is not to learn the facts but to virtually experience life in a particular time and place. The facts are secondary (Galda & Liang, 2003).

Readers connect with narratives, whether realistic or fantasy, by becoming involved with and caring about the characters, by being engrossed in the events of the story, by experiencing the story they are reading—by feeling as though they are there, in the story world. One young reader described being "inhaled by books," a metaphor that perfectly sums up the single-minded absorption that connecting with a book can provide (Galda, 1982). But just what happens when readers read aesthetically and respond to literature?

• • RESPONSE TO • • LITERATURE

Reading and responding to stories and poems is a complex process that involves readers, texts, and the contexts in which reading occurs. Who is reading, what is being read, the purposes for reading, and the social and cultural factors surrounding reading all influence what a particular reader creates while reading a particular text. Responses are influenced by many factors and come in many forms (Galda, 1988; Galda & Beach, 2004). A text that makes one reader cry might bore another; a book read as a 10-year-old brings a different kind of pleasure when read again as a 13-year-old; and the cultural values that permeate a text will trigger varying responses in culturally diverse readers.

Responses are often hard to preserve; they are present in the moment of reading and are only imperfectly captured later through writing, discussion, art, or dramatic activities. Young children in classrooms sometimes show their responses on their faces, in their bodies, in their laughter; older children often shield themselves by not expressing their responses unless encouraged to do so by a supportive classroom context.

Creating meaning with a literary text involves connecting life and text. And the act of creating meaning while reading a story or poem is at once highly individual and intensely social. This creation, however, always begins with a reader.

The Reader

Who readers are and what they have experienced influence their responses to the books they read. The places they have been, the people they know, the attitudes they hold, who they are, and the way they present themselves to the world all influence how readers read and respond. Research has shown that individuals seem to have "response styles," or characteristic ways of responding. For example, three fifth-grade girls with similar backgrounds and schooling were quite different in their approaches to books, but each was individually consistent (Galda, 1982). Four first- and second-grade students showed remarkably different response styles; for example, one reader exhibited sensitivity toward the feelings of the story characters, and another used the story as a springboard for oral performance (Sipe, 1998).

Past experience with books, both inside and outside the classroom, also influences how children read and respond. For example, years of reading stories in a classroom in which the teacher asks questions that prompt recall of specific information from stories and poems will force young readers away from their naturally aesthetic responses into an inappropriate information-seeking stance. One parent, for instance, talking about how her son learned to hate reading in school, described how he first reads the questions that he has to answer at the end of each reading selection and then scans the story or poem to find the answers to those questions. Reading for information means he misses the story; never connecting with the story means he misses the pleasure that a story can bring. Missing that pleasure, he has not learned to like reading. Another middle school boy, an avid reader of long, complex animal fantasies at home, felt that he had become a "poor" reader because of his performance on the tests in a popular computer-based reading program. He had learned to read for the virtual experience, the pleasure; the tests asked for very specific and often unimportant details. Consequently, he chose less complex novels to read for his school reading.

In contrast, children who have had an array of pleasurable experiences with books will spontaneously compare stories, knowledgeably discuss authors, and bring their ideas about literature to their reading. Many researchers and teachers, such as McGinley and Kamberelis (1996), Sipe (1999), Many and Wiseman (1992), Short and Pierce (1990), and Galda, Rayburn, and Stanzi (2000), have documented the richness of children's responses when children are in an environment that encourages exploration and consideration of books.

Readers' preferences and reading ability also influence the act of reading. Children who like science fiction approach a science fiction text with the expectation of pleasure (and with a storehouse of experience reading science fiction), whereas children who have not read and enjoyed science fiction approach the same text rather doubtfully. Children who read fluently read with an ease that enables them to concentrate fully on the story world they are creating; children who struggle with words often miss the meaning. A group of fourth-grade readers was discussing Madeleine L'Engle's *A Wind in the Door* (I–A), a complex science fantasy that contains some difficult proper nouns, when one reader remarked, "I was doing okay; then I tried to figure out the names and got all mixed up." Another reader responded by describing how he had "replaced" the hard names with familiar ones because, as he put it, "it didn't make any difference to the story" (Galda, 1990, 1992, 1993).

Differences in concepts of story certainly influence response. What readers know about literature—its creations, its forms, its purposes, and its effects—influences the meaning that they create (Galda, 1982). Applebee (1978) describes how children's concepts of story grow in complexity as they mature. As they learn more about literature, children grow in their ability to appreciate different books for different reasons, to step back from their personal preferences and view books in the larger literary context. A third-grade reader who didn't especially enjoy *Charlotte's Web* (I) may learn later to appreciate the style and humor of E. B. White, even if animal fantasies are not a preferred genre.

CHILDREN'S COGNITIVE DEVELOPMENT Cognitive development and learning influence responses to literature. As children grow and learn, they change as people, and certainly as readers. Piaget's theories of intellectual development offer a useful framework for analyzing changes underlying thought processes. He views the acquisition of knowledge as a gradual developmental process in which children actively experience and organize concepts about their environment. Therefore the child is seen as an active, dynamic being who interacts with the environment to create knowledge. Vygotsky (1962, 1978) reminds us that this interaction with the environment is social. Learning happens in the company of others, as children learn from and with knowledgeable peers and adults.

Young children learn through their senses and motor movements; they feel, grasp, taste, touch, smell, see, and hear people and objects in their environment. Books that young children can hold (and chew) and that are congruent with

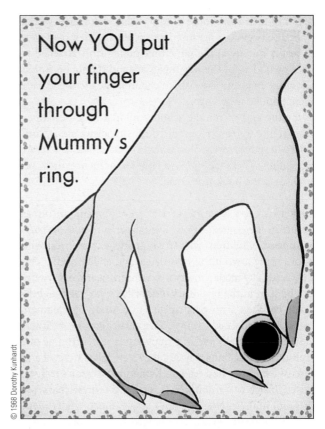

© 1968 Dorothy Kunhardt

Young children won't sit still for long unless they can join in the action. Pat the Bunny *invites them to put a finger through Mummy's ring.*

real-life experiences make sense to them. Board books containing simple stories or pictures of familiar objects, and participation books, such as Dorothy Kunhardt's *Pat the Bunny* (N), incorporate experiences appropriate for children up to five years old. Children are also learning language rapidly when they are very young; this language is learned in real-life contexts, because it serves real needs. Children learn language to tell people what they want, to relate to others, to find out about their world, and to play "let's pretend." Books provide infinite opportunities to engage children in talk about meaningful things.

During preschool and the primary grades, children rapidly develop language, thought, and symbolic representation. Books provide children with rich and varied opportunities for exploring language in many ways, finding out about their worlds, and enjoying the many virtual experiences that stories can impart. At this age, children see stories as true, as presenting the world as it is—not as it might be. Generally, they believe in magic and do not question contradictions. Simple animal fantasies and folklore are often popular with children at this age.

In elementary school, children quickly distinguish between reality and fantasy in literature. They frequently classify literature and can be quite systematic in the way they organize their storehouse of knowledge about their world. They also begin to tolerate contradictions in their own view of reality but are at the same time quite firmly attached to their own ideas of the way things are and should be. Books about the here and now, about children like themselves, are often popular at this age.

By the end of middle school, children have developed their ability to reason logically, deal with abstractions, consider alternative ways of viewing a situation, and tolerate ambiguity. These developing abilities influence their responses to the books they read.

THE ROLE OF EXPERIENCE Development, of course, occurs in the context of our lives; *experience influences development.* Children who have many experiences with books bring a wealth of knowledge and ability to the texts they read. The intertwining of development and experience can be seen in the responses of fourth-, sixth-, and eighth-grade children who participated in a study by Cullinan, Harwood, and Galda (1983). The participants were interviewed individually and in groups of three after reading one realistic and one fantasy novel; they were asked to retell and discuss what they had read. In Katherine Paterson's realistic novel *Bridge to Terabithia* (I), Leslie, a central character, dies, but in their retellings, not a single fourth grader mentioned the death. When encouraged to tell more by nondirective probes, such as, "Anything else?" children added other details from the story but studiously avoided any mention of Leslie's death. When a child in the group questioned "whether she really died," others insisted she had "come back to life" and was right there with Jess at the end of the story. Their strong preference for a happy ending allowed them to create a happy ending even though one was not present in the text.

The sixth-grade boys were disdainful of the emotional intensity of the novel: they saw Jess as an emotional sissy and Leslie as a daredevil show-off. Some said the book sounded "like a Hollywood romance or a soap opera."

The eighth-grade girls read the novel as a romance and hoped that they might someday be the kind of friend to some boy, often a particular boy, that Leslie was to Jess. The eighth-grade boys reacted very differently in the individual interview and the group discussion. Individually, they characterized the relationship between the boy and girl as idyllic, but when in the group, they demeaned both characters as "countrified" and immature. Their concern for their image affected their responses in front of their peers.

These comments demonstrate how children's development, their background of reading and life experiences, and their social milieu all are influential factors in their responses to literature, at least in those they are willing to express in public.

The context in which children read and respond makes a difference in the way they respond; supportive contexts allow children to stretch their ideas. Lehr (1991), for example, found that young children who are in literature-rich classrooms and have many experiences reading and discussing literature over time in a supportive context can, and do, discuss themes and character motivation and make generalizations about stories—behaviors usually associated with older children. Galda, Rayburn, and Stanzi (2000) demonstrated the depth of understanding evident in the discussions of second-grade readers in a safe, supportive literature-based classroom. Although there are certainly differences between child and adolescent cognition, these may be differences in degree rather than in kind. That is, young children may analyze and generalize, but not in an adult way and usually not without support from an adult or more competent peer.

What we have described here are general patterns of response. It is not the case that 8-year-old readers have no understanding of how texts work or that 12-year-old girls read every book as a romance. In literature-rich kindergartens you will hear children earnestly discussing why Maurice Sendak didn't put any words on the wild rumpus pages in *Where the Wild Things Are* (P). Third-grade children who read with a writer's eyes compare different authors' treatments of the same topic. And many seventh-grade girls read and enjoy difficult fantasy novels rather than popular teenage romances. Generic descriptions of how children of varying ages make sense of a story need to be considered in light of the texts the children read and the contexts in which they read and respond; these will always vary from child to child.

CHILDREN'S LANGUAGE DEVELOPMENT Descriptions of children's understandings about literature are based on what children tell us. For example, we make inferences about children's comprehension based on what they say about what they read. These inferences may be good—when what children say closely matches their understanding—or poor—when children understand but cannot express adequately their understandings through language. For example, young children may think about themes or spontaneously compare texts to each other, but unless they know how to talk about these things, they may never be able to express their understandings.

Studies of children's language development provide a broad base for inferences about appropriate literary experiences (Britton, 1970). Three principles guide the way we view language and literature. First, children develop language naturally as they interact with language users—when they are immersed in language and expected to respond to it. Vygotsky's exploration of language and thought (1962, 1978) clearly demonstrates how human beings who are firmly embedded in a social world use language for social purposes and learn language in that social world. Children learn the use, function, and power of words because language users talk to them. Children learn about books by being read to (often when they are being held on a parent's lap) and by talking about what they are doing; they learn about books by seeing what others do with them. Stories told or read to children give them opportunities to hear words in use and, in the process, to support, expand, and stimulate their own experiments with language. As children listen to language, they gradually understand meanings and eventually express meanings through their own sounds. Language development is a process of generalizing and discriminating finer meanings and sounds. As children learn, books can help fulfill their need to make sense of language and the world.

Second, we know that in language development, comprehension generally exceeds production. Though they may not yet be using sentences in their talk, children understand sentences and draw meaning from the contexts in which they are heard. For example, when asked, "Where's your teddy bear?" a child can pick up the toy or point to it long before she can say the words. Similarly, the six-year-old who responds to a question with "I know it in my head, but I can't say it" understands more than he can communicate. Through experience, children assimilate meaning and expand the storehouse of words they use to express meaning. Books, which provide experience beyond the immediate environment, contribute to the meaning base of language. Through books we learn to comprehend more than we actually express in speaking or in writing. Books expand language by providing new words, experiences, and ideas in a context that helps children understand them. Books also provide language models in a variety of well-crafted styles.

Parents and other caregivers who read to children provide a model of the pleasure of reading, what reading is, how language works, and new vocabulary.

Third, language learning never ends. As students mature, their language skills increase and awareness grows in direct proportion to their experiences. Students come to recognize that written material and society affect each other and that language is used in a variety of ways for a variety of purposes. Although they have been using language in any number of ways since their early years, students gradually come to understand and to be able to talk about the persuasive uses of language, the figurative uses of language, the existence of different points of view, and the influence of literature. From wide exposure to books and many other language experiences, students extend their ability to comprehend and appreciate the subtleties and ambiguities of language.

One way to see clearly how experience with books affects language development is to watch young children who learn to read without formal instruction. Children who are read to understand at an early age that books carry meaning and provide fun. Even very young children demonstrate this when they pick up their favorite nursery rhyme book and "read" it aloud to their stuffed animals or the family dog, relying on their memory of the words and the cues in the illustrations to tell them which rhyme belongs on which page. They also come to understand that the words, those black squiggles on the page, carry much of the meaning. They begin to ask such questions as "What's that white space for?" and they note punctuation marks and follow along with their eyes as an adult reads aloud. As they listen to books, they take in the lilt and cadence of book language, develop a sense of structure and form, and begin to recognize words. For many children who have extensive experience with books, it is easy to move into independent reading. We discuss learning to read with literature in Chapter 13.

DEVELOPING A SENSE OF STORY Books also help children extend their understandings about story. Extensive experience with books gives children more resources to draw from as they build a concept of story. Children who hear many stories develop expectations about them; this is called *developing a sense of story*.

For example, research into the stories children tell shows that their ability to tell connected stories develops over time. Applebee (1978) found that children's stories change from disconnected strings to sequential orderings and eventually to focused, sequential stories containing distinct story markers. One such marker is evident when young children signal that they are telling a story by giving a title. Another appears when they begin their stories with a formal opening, such as "Once upon a time," and end with a closing such as "They lived happily ever after." Most children use recognizable opening and closing story frames by the time they are five years old. Many children at this age also use the past tense when they narrate action, and some alter their speaking tone into a dramatic "story voice," using the present tense when they are in a character role. That these story markers appear regularly in children's oral language indicates the extent to which they have assimilated literature, and dramatically illustrates the potential power of literature to affect language as well as cognitive and affective development.

You can see how children's sense of story works if you read Pat Hutchins's *What Game Shall We Play?* (P), a tightly structured story with a repetitive phrase, to a group of five-year-olds. By the time you meet the third character, the children will be "reading" it with you. Hearing only the first few pages, children can recognize the story structure and predict what is coming next. They do this with any highly patterned, repetitive text they hear. They are not memorizing the text, as so many very young children who "read and reread" their favorite story are doing (even when it is held upside down); rather, they know how the story works because of their prior experiences with stories.

In addition to developing an understanding of the sequential structure of stories, children learn to use the content of stories to organize what they encounter in the world. One well-read five-year-old, living in a strange city for a brief period, thought she had figured out just where she was when she saw an old, vine-covered building: "Mommy, are we in Paris?" She, of course, had been reading Ludwig Bemelman's *Madeline* (P).

Duck and Frog went out to play.
"What game shall we play?" asked Duck.
"I don't know," said Frog.
"Let's go and ask Fox."

© 1990 Pat Hutchins

Pat Hutchins invites children to join in saying the familiar phrase that is repeated in each episode of **What Game Shall We Play?**

Our vision of reality is shaped by the stories we tell ourselves. Telling ourselves stories is a primary human activity, one that adults as well as children engage in (Bruner, 1987; Hardy, 1978). Each of us selectively perceives the world from a unique vantage point, and we tell ourselves stories about what we perceive. Children who are sent to bed in a dark room may fear the monsters that lie hidden there, and no amount of logical reassurance convinces them that the stories they have told themselves about the presence of monsters are unfounded. Philosophical treatises debate what "reality" actually is, but there is a consensus that one's own reality is what one perceives it to be; it is largely shaped by what we choose to believe and by the stories we tell ourselves.

As children mature and their experience with literature increases, their understanding about the relations between literature and life is affected. Galda (1990, 1993) found that one dimension that distinguished older readers (grades 8–9) from younger readers (grades 4–5) was that most of the older children consistently discussed the texts as works of art separate from life. The majority of the younger readers compared the characters in Betsy Byars's *The Summer of the Swans* (I) to their own lives. They complained of the lack of exact fit with their own worlds: The characters were "kind of like us," but "they don't act like we act at my house," and "they don't fight like real brothers and sisters." The older readers were more objective when they criticized the book; they understood how literature works. When one girl commented that Charlie's retardation "wasn't necessary" to the story, another countered with "Well, the story did need it because it sort of changed the relationship between Sara and Charlie." The eighth-grade readers in the Cullinan, Harwood, and Galda (1983) study had the same sort of discussion about Katherine Paterson's *Bridge to Terabithia* (I). One said, "She shouldn't have died," and another replied, "But it wouldn't have been the story it was if she hadn't." Rather than dismissing those parts of the stories that they found extraneous, many of these older readers could go beyond their personal reactions to see how parts functioned in the story as a whole. In general, older readers had a more developed understanding of the interrelatedness of literary elements than did the younger readers. Along with this was a diminishing tendency to judge a book according to its fit with one's personal perception of reality. Thus even fantasy came to be understood as being about recognizable people with familiar problems, as being *true* even if not *actual*.

The Text

We have discussed how different kinds of texts signal different kinds of reading, with some texts written for a predominantly efferent stance and others a predominantly aesthetic stance. Reader preferences also influence the way readers approach a book. We have already discussed how children change as readers over time, and certainly their appreciation for different kinds of books changes as well.

We can make some generalizations about children's interests and preferences, about what they *might like* to read or what they *actually select* to read, but within each generalization lies a lot of individual variation. Many children, regardless of age, enjoy humor. Primary-grade children often enjoy stories with animal characters and are usually fond of folklore. There is a period of time during the elementary years when many readers are engrossed in mysteries and will read any book, by any author, as long as it's a mystery. As children enter the intermediate grades and begin to form important friendships outside their immediate families, they often like to read realistic stories about children "just like" themselves, especially stories that are exciting and full of action. Many children and adolescents are likely to choose books with characters a bit older than they are, using their reading to think about what life holds for them.

When Lehman (1989) compared books that were given the Children's Choice Award with those that were honored by adults but not by children, she found that children preferred optimistic texts that were action-oriented and well paced and that offered clear resolutions of conflict. A book, no matter how high its literary quality, must also be engaging to children.

As children mature, boys and girls often show differences in reading interests. Many advanced-grade girls prefer romance and contemporary realistic novels to all other types of books; bright advanced-grade boys are often immersed in the world of science fiction and fantasy, whereas others enjoy biography. These generalizations, however, are just that—generalizations. There are children who never truly like animal stories, children who do not get bitten by the mystery bug, and girls who disdain romance novels. As each individual reader matures and reads an increasing number of books with an increasing degree of understanding, the preferences of that individual will change along lines that reflect the individual's interests, development, and experiences (Galda, Ash, & Cullinan, 2000; Sebesta & Monson, 2003).

As readers' preferences change, so too do their overall responses to literature. When children read widely, they seem to develop an appreciation for a broad range of characters, styles, and genres, regardless of their own specific preferences. Experienced readers often look for interesting characters, and this focus seems to be linked to their developing ability to be "inhaled by books," regardless of character age or sex, and in spite of genre differences.

It is clear that successful guesses about what readers will enjoy reading are only possible if they are based on a clear understanding of individual children and a knowledge of a wide range of books. Even then, we as teachers and librarians can only encourage children to read books; it is entirely up to them to make books their own. In the Booklist at the end of this chapter, we present selected books from the Children's and Young Adult Choices list. These are books that children across America have enjoyed.

The Context

It is vital to understand at least three things about the social nature of reading and responding to literature. First, learning occurs in a social context that depends on interaction; literature plays an important role in that context. Second, children grow in their ability to understand literature as they gain experience with life and literature; this experience often occurs in the company of others. Third, a teacher's influence is a powerful determinant of children's response to literature. How readers read and how they respond to the books they read are influenced by the contexts in which they are reading. Hearing a bedtime story is different from hearing a story at the library's two o'clock story hour; reading on a rainy Saturday afternoon in the most comfortable chair in the house is different from reading from eight-thirty to nine every morning at a school desk. Reading in a classroom that has plenty of books, that provides time to read them, and that includes other readers who support developing ideas is much different from reading for homework, punishment, or contests.

Children will become engaged readers when we surround them with opportunities to read and respond to a variety of genres, styles, and authors; when we appreciate individual differences and offer opportunities to explore and share diverse responses; and when we provide time and encouragement for responding in a variety of ways, such as spontaneous sharing, small- and large-group discussion, writing, art, drama, and movement.

Although response is highly individualistic, it is also intensely social. Reading books is often a solitary activity, but the way we use and talk about books is a natural social response, one that we as readers all share. When we finish reading a good book, it's quite natural to talk about it, and we usually learn from that talk. Talking about books encourages readers to articulate their own responses to books and to find out how other readers responded. In many cases, talking about books adds new dimensions to individual responses, as the ideas of others provide new perspectives. As one young reader remarked, "I never thought about it that way, but now it makes a lot of sense"—a sentiment that anyone who has discussed books with friends can understand.

Children develop feelings and beliefs about themselves and their world through interactions with those around them; this includes their interactions around books. They find out who they are and what role they are to play by interpreting the verbal and nonverbal messages that significant others give them. Children develop a positive self-concept if people around them show them they are loved

Profile

Courtesy of Louise Rosenblatt

Louise Rosenblatt

Louise Rosenblatt was a remarkable woman with exceptional talent. Her work, which presents theories about the nature of reading and the literary experience, substantially shaped the teaching of English in schools and colleges.

Rosenblatt brought a scholarly approach to literary criticism, combined with an active concern for the teaching of English. At a time when it was assumed that the reader's role was to passively receive a "ready-made" meaning from a text, she stressed the idea of the reader actively making meaning by engaging in a transaction with the text. This new vantage point helps us understand that the reader's background and interests play an important part in the development of the ability to read. She also emphasized the difference between reading a poem or story with attention focused on what is being lived through (an aesthetic experience),

and reading material with attention focused on what is to be carried away (an efferent experience), such as information or directions.

Rosenblatt graduated with honors from Barnard College, Columbia University. After several years of graduate work in France (at the University of Grenoble and the Sorbonne, University of Paris), she received her doctorate in comparative literature from the Sorbonne. Her doctoral dissertation on the 19th-century aesthetic movement in England and France led her to see the necessity for a literate reading public. Postdoctoral work in anthropology with Franz Boas and Ruth Benedict at Columbia University inspired her feeling for the contributions of diverse cultures that encourage the creation of a democratic American society.

Rosenblatt's primary professorship was at New York University, where she directed the doctoral program in English education. She also taught at Barnard College, Columbia University, Brooklyn College of the City University of New York, Northwestern University (summer sessions), and Rutgers University.

Rosenblatt received the John Simon Guggenheim Fellowship (1943), the Great Teacher Award from New York University (1972), the Distinguished Service Award from the National Council of Teachers of English (1973), and the National Conference on Research in English Lifetime Award (1990). She was inducted into the Reading Hall of Fame by the International

Reading Association in 1992. On the 50th anniversary of the publication of *Literature as Exploration,* the National Council of Teachers of English honored her with a full day of programs to celebrate her distinguished work. In another major text, *The Reader, the Text, the Poem,* she expanded her theories and implications for practice.

In a letter dated February 7, 1993, Rosenblatt stated:

I believe that if in the early years youngsters get the feel of the aesthetic and efferent ways of reading, if the classroom atmosphere and teacher's interventions permit students to automatically adopt the appropriate stance, then all the other (efferent) things we do with literature— analyze, categorize, criticize, evaluate—will have real literary experiences as their subject or base. So many of the bright students who came into my freshman and sophomore classes at the university level had learned that one reads literature in school in order to do these efferent things (I have nothing against them in their proper place), and they had lost, if they ever had, the delight of aesthetic or literary experience. It's the cumulative effect over the years of the way literature is approached that I am concerned about.

Rosenblatt was married to Sidney Ratner, scholar in philosophy and history, for more than 60 years. They have a grown son and a granddaughter. Rosenblatt died in 2005 at 100 years of age.

and valued. In a similar way, they develop a positive attitude toward books if books are treated as a source of pleasure and knowledge. When children share books with a loving caregiver from early on, they develop positive feelings about books and the joy that can come from them. When children share books with peers and teachers in collaborative, supportive contexts, they develop positive feelings about books and about themselves as readers. The social and cultural context in which children grow and learn shapes their view of the world and the role of literature in it.

Children do not all experience the same social and cultural contexts. Heath (1982, 1983) documents how three very different home cultures—in the same city in North America—influence children's experiences with books and concepts about them and, in turn, their experiences in school. She argues that children learn at home how to define and enact book reading. In many cases, this does not resemble how teachers expect children to read and respond in school. Sensitive teachers recognize individual differences and build on the oral and literate traditions that children bring to school from home, emphasizing a multifaceted conception of literacy. They also clearly explain the additional strategies that they expect children to use in school—demonstrating, for example, how they make connections between their lives and the books they read, or among various books. These teachers view reading as being shaped by one's individual experiences. They recognize that people have varied concepts regarding the functions of literature, the purposes for literature, and the appropriate stance to take toward literature.

As mentioned at the beginning of this chapter, just as literature is *shaped* by readers' views of the world, so too can literature help *shape* readers' views of the world. Frye (1970) underscores the role of literature in "educating" the imagination and shows the necessity of imagination in creating a social vision. He believes that the fundamental job of the imagination in ordinary life is to produce, out of the society we *have* to live in, a vision of the society we *want* to live in. In this sense, we live in two worlds: our ordinary world and our ideal world. One world is around us; the other is a vision inside our minds, born and fostered by the imagination, yet real enough for us to try to make the world we see conform to its shape. Teachers can foster transforming experiences with literature through their own actions and through what they ask of their students.

Helping Children Grow as Responsive Readers

Activities described throughout this text are chosen to help readers develop a deeper understanding of and a greater appreciation for books. Because children's literature is so rich and varied, it can be used to enhance every area of the curriculum. The best kind of activity is one that is intended to bring readers back to books they've read and guide them to others. Rosen and Rosen (1973) state the case well:

> It is as though there is a deep lack of confidence in the power of literature to do its work and a profound conviction that unless literature can be converted into the hard currency of familiar school learning it has not earned its keep. What will take children more deeply into the experience of the book? This is the question we should be asking rather than by what means can I use this book as a launching-pad into any one of a dozen endeavors which leave the book further and further behind, at best a distant sound, at worst forgotten entirely. (p. 195)

This is as true today as it was over thirty years ago.

Linguist M.A.K. Halliday (1982) says that people *learn* language, *learn about* language, and *learn through* language. His model can be applied to literature as well. When we read literature we learn language—the language of story, poem, and well-crafted nonfiction. As readers we also learn *about* language—how language is crafted to suit different purposes, how varied genres are structured, and how particular stylistic choices have different power and effect. And of course readers learn *through* literature; they read about other places, people, and ideas to broaden their knowledge and understanding. Beyond this, readers who are engaged with books learn about themselves and others; they consider the virtual experiences they have through story, and construct their own value systems.

Children will, of course, learn many other things through literature. They can learn how to read, learn about innumerable topics, and learn to be better writers, among other things. They can learn all this, and more, in an atmosphere that does not lose sight of the fact that good books are important in and of themselves and don't always need to "teach" something. The challenge for educators is to teach with literature in a manner that preserves its integrity as well as the integrity of children's responses to it. It is not easy to keep the focus on children and their responses to the books they read. Indeed, children and books can easily get lost in a maze of goals, activities, and assessments if a literature-based curriculum is implemented without careful planning.

Natalie Babbitt (1990) speaks eloquently about some real dangers inherent in a poorly planned literature-based curriculum. One danger she sees is what Rosenblatt (1991) calls *basalizing literature*. Babbitt writes,

> I know that there is a movement underway to stop using texts for the teaching of reading and to start using works of fiction. In the beginning that seemed to me to be a good idea. But now I'm not so sure. The texts had related workbooks with sentences to complete, quizzes, questions to think about, and all kinds of suggested projects. The feeling has been, as I understand it, that these texts and workbooks were making a dry and tedious thing out of learning to read at the very time when concern about literacy levels was growing more and more serious. So it seemed sensible to try using real stories in the classroom—stories that could grab the children's fancies and show them what the joy of reading is all about. But what I see happening now is that these real stories are being used in the same way that the old texts were used. Every once in a while someone sends me something meant to accompany a classroom reading of my story, *Tuck Everlasting,* and here's what I find: a related workbook with sentences to complete, quizzes, questions to think about, and all kinds of suggested projects. I worry that this will make a dry and tedious thing out of fiction. (pp. 696–697)

If teachers use trade books in the curriculum to interest children and to help them become literate in the fullest sense of the word, then it is crucial that we allow the books to be as interesting as they can be, that we not ruin the power of trade books by turning them into material for exercises.

Another concern centers on the individuality of emotional response. Stories and poems are about feelings, about meanings and significances, about questions rather than answers. Most authors write stories to raise questions rather than teach lessons. Certainly, stories deal with values, with morality, but teaching object lessons is not what they are about. Babbitt voices this concern in response to a discussion of the moral lessons in *Tuck Everlasting* when she says,

> I don't think any [young readers of *Tuck*] are coming away with a heightened sense of social responsibility. They could be made to, of course. You can come away from any book with that, if it's thrust upon you. But how sad for the book!
>
> ... What children take away with them when they've finished a book will depend on each child's personal needs and personal quirks. (1990, p. 701)

Katherine Paterson, Marion Dane Bauer, and many other authors say the same thing: Their books are not meant to teach children morals, but are meant, rather, to engage readers, to allow children to discover, explore, and build their own values. The assumption that we can use books to inculcate morals in children, and the tendency to look at books in terms of what moral lessons they might "teach" lead only to practices that ruin the power of a good book.

The primary goal of a response-centered curriculum is to engage readers in the act of reading responsively. The focus is not on the works of literature, nor on the topics or skills, but on "the mind of the reader as it meets the book—the response" (Purves, Rogers, & Soter, 1990). A response-centered curriculum recognizes and encourages diversity among readers, recognizes and encourages connections among readers, and "recognizes that response is joyous" (Purves et al., 1990, p. 56). In this curriculum, the teacher provides a variety of books, time to read and explore them, time to talk and write about them, and time to draw and dramatize from them. In addition, teachers provide opportunities for students to enjoy the collaborative company of peers with whom to explore similarities and differences in responses. The teacher also helps students find the language with which to articulate their responses, and challenges them to understand why they respond as they do (Purves et al., 1990, p. 56). Figure 12.2 states some goals for a response-centered curriculum and some ways to achieve them.

A second goal is to build on the engagement that a response-centered curriculum fosters in order to develop

Figure 12-2

Goals of a Response-Centered Curriculum

A Response-Centered Curriculum Helps Students

* Develop a lasting love of reading
* Establish the lifelong reading habit
* Feel secure in their responses to literature
* Make connections between literature and life
* See connections among texts (intertextuality)
* Recognize commonalities among responses
* See variations of meaning in stories and poems
* Recognize different purposes for reading
* Engage in aesthetic reading (reading to savor experience)
* Engage in efferent reading (reading to do something)
* Recognize different types of reading material—descriptive, expository, narrative, poetic, and so on
* Learn about language and how it is used
* Understand how words work
* Appreciate the beauty of things well said
* Grasp subtleties of language

Ways to Achieve Goals Are

* Encourage students to interact with books
* Provide time to read and explore
* Give time to talk, write, draw, and dramatize
* Provide time to collaborate with peers
* Plan time to explore similarities and differences in responses
* Accept and encourage diversity among readers
* Give students a choice of material to read
* Let them choose from ways to respond (talk, write, draw, dramatize, and so on)
* Provide ways to respond joyously
* Provide a variety of books
* Stimulate motivation to read
* Give book talks to generate enthusiasm
* Integrate reading with other areas
* Create a rich literacy environment
* Help students find language to express responses
* Give students opportunities to learn language
* Help students realize their potential as learners, as language users, and as readers
* Give students the opportunity to learn about themselves and their world

children's awareness of the world of literature and of how words work (Benton, 1984) in literature. This goal is focused on helping children learn language and learn about it and its use in literature through reading.

A third goal is to give children the opportunity to learn about themselves and their world through books, to learn *through* language. The virtual experiences possible through story, the emotional expansion that is possible with poetry, and the exposure to information about the world that comes from nonfiction all increase children's knowledge of themselves and their worlds. And this increased knowledge widens children's horizons and makes even more learning possible.

We advocate a response-centered literature curriculum because it is through such a curriculum that we as teachers can best help our students realize their potential as learners, as language users, and as readers. In an integrated, response-centered literature curriculum, books and readers are at the center of many types of learning. In Chapter 13 we detail specific ideas about a literature-based curriculum in the primary grades. In Chapter 14 we present ways of integrating literature study, reading, writing, oral language development, and other areas of the curriculum into the upper elementary and middle school grades. As a basis for the practices we detail in those chapters, here we broadly describe a response-based curriculum and three of its essential ingredients: time and choice, reading aloud, and activities that support children's developing understanding of literature. Students need time to read, choices about how they read and respond, many experiences hearing you read aloud, and your help as they grow in their understandings of how literature works.

• • TIME AND CHOICE • •

Children need both time to read and choices about what to read, how to read, and whom to read with.

> Allowing children time to be with books in the classroom, rather than assigning them to a certain number of books to be read on their own time, teaches them to value books. When time is set aside for reading and responding to literature, students know that this is viewed as important by their teacher. So, too, does reading to and with a class help to convince students of the value and the pleasures of reading. (Galda, 1988, p. 100)

In many classrooms Sustained Silent Reading (SSR) is one way that teachers build time for individual reading into their busy schedules. SSR is a plan wherein 20 to 30 minutes are set aside each day when everybody in the school reads—the principal, the custodian, the teachers, and all the students. There are many variations of the program: DEAR (Drop Everything and Read), USSR (Uninterrupted Sustained Silent Reading), and READ (Read Everything and Dream). Sometimes SSR operates within an individual classroom rather than throughout the entire school. These programs have consistently produced better readers. Even when students are not fluent independent readers, they need time to explore books independently.

We know that reading independently improves reading fluency, but research suggests that students do not have enough time to read in school. Many students spend up to 70 percent of the time allocated for reading instruction doing seatwork—workbooks and skill sheets, many of which are unrelated to reading and are actually detrimental to children's attitudes toward reading (Anderson, Hiebert, Scott, & Wilkinson, 1985).

A mother described her daughter storming in the door from school, complaining, "Mom, I *hate* reading!" Her mother countered, "But you love reading your Little House and Beverly Cleary books here at home." "Yes, I know that, but I *hate* reading!" What she hated was the class at school called Reading, which would have been more appropriately named Worksheets and which obviously had nothing to do with really reading books. Classroom research shows that the amount of time devoted to worksheets does *nothing* to improve reading proficiency. The amount of *independent* silent reading children do in school, however, is significantly related to gains in reading achievement. Researchers estimate that the typical primary school child reads silently only 7 or 8 minutes per day. By the middle grades, silent reading time still averages only 15 minutes per school day. No one can become skilled at anything practiced only 7 to 15 minutes a day (Taylor, Frye, & Maruyama, 1990; West, Stanovich, & Mitchell, 1993).

We might think that we can solve the problem of tight schedules and too little time for reading in the classroom by assigning reading as homework. Research shows that children who averaged even 10 minutes per day of reading outside the classroom had significantly higher reading achievement scores than those who did not (Fielding, Wilson, & Anderson, 1986). However, few children read even 10 minutes per day. Of the fifth-grade students studied, 50 percent read from books only 4 minutes a day or less, 30 percent 2 minutes a day or less, 10 percent not at all. Students were more likely to read outside of school if the teacher read aloud in school and if they had SSR during school. If we want students to read, we must tempt them with good stories, poems, and nonfiction, and show them that we value reading by devoting a significant amount of time to it in the classroom. Assign reading as homework, but make it classwork, too.

It is vitally important not only that students have a significant amount of regularly scheduled time to read independently and with peers, and to respond to what they have read, but also that they are given time to listen to you read aloud. There are as many ways to schedule reading time as there are classrooms. Reading time, spent on either independent or teacher's oral reading, is often scheduled first thing in the morning, right after recess, or right after lunch as a way of calming and pulling a class together. Some teachers make use of lunchtime by encouraging students to take books with them and read while they eat. This also gives them something positive to do while they're waiting for lunch to end. Other teachers like to end the day by reading aloud to the whole class; ending on a cliff-hanger certainly encourages children to return tomorrow!

Students need opportunities to make choices. As we discussed earlier, responses and preferences are highly individualistic. Although you as a teacher need to be able to help students select books they will like—and certainly you can make suggestions and assign books and response activities—children also need to be able to make their own choices about the books they read. They sometimes should be able to make choices about what they want to do when they are finished with a book. Some children might like to paint, others to talk, and others to sit quietly and think.

Teachers help students become knowledgeable about themselves as readers by providing both guidance and the freedom to choose books. Teachers of young children might present many books to the class during read-aloud time; many of these books might be highly patterned stories or stories that are familiar to the children. Students can then read these stories independently during SSR time, approximating the teacher's reading and gradually developing their ability to read the text independently.

Older readers, too, benefit from hearing stories that the teacher and others enjoy. Reading aloud and creating space and structures that allow children to read and talk with each other about books help promote reading while giving children ideas about books to read. Some teachers allow children a full range of choice; they can choose any book they would like to read. Others provide revolving classroom collections that support curricular study (discussed in Chapters 13 and 14) and ask children to choose from those books. Others carefully gather books that reflect the reading levels in the classroom. Whatever the approach, the idea that they can choose what they want to read has changed the way many children feel about reading.

As children become confident readers, they learn to recognize what books they can read and what books they might like to read. They begin to know which authors and illustrators they like. And they learn where to go for recommendations about books—to the teacher, the librarian, family and friends, other students in their class. Good readers know how to find books for themselves.

The value we place on books is also reflected in the physical environment of the classroom. The books that you have in your classroom should be easily accessible to students and attractively displayed, with many covers facing out-

ward. Children can help devise a simple scheme to organize the books. Comfortable places to sit and relax with a book and attractive displays such as posters and book jackets also make reading inviting.

You as a teacher can show that you value literature by being a reader yourself: by reading along with the children during SSR, talking about books you like, reading bits of your own stories aloud to them, and, of course, reading aloud with pleasure and skill.

• • READING ALOUD • •

One primary way that teachers help children grow as engaged, responsive readers is to read aloud. Reading aloud is one of the most common and easiest means of sharing books and poetry. It is a pleasurable experience for all when done well, and it has a positive impact on students' reading development (Clark, 1976; Durkin, 1966; Wells, 1986). Reading aloud not only helps young children become readers, but also helps older children become better readers. Reading aloud extends students' horizons, introduces them to literature they might not read on their own, offers alternate worlds and lifestyles, increases their experiential base from which to view the world, and models good reading (Galda & Cullinan, 2003). Reading aloud to young children

Children can understand books they cannot read on their own. Read books aloud that are slightly above their reading level to expand their literary experiences. Story time quickly becomes the favorite part of the school day.

also demonstrates print- and book-handling concepts such as left-to-right and top-to-bottom directionality, page turning, and the role of print and pictures in telling a story or presenting a concept. The wealth of available evidence caused the Commission on Reading to conclude that "the single most important activity for building the knowledge required for eventual success in reading is reading aloud to children" (Anderson et al., 1985, p. 23). The many reasons for reading aloud are summarized here:

Reading Aloud . . .

Introduces new words (vocabulary)

Displays interesting sentence patterns

Presents a variety of forms of language

Shows various styles of written language

Develops a sense of story

Motivates children to read more

Provides ideas for students' writing

Enriches students' general knowledge

Models the sound of good reading for students

Adds pleasure to the day

There are some important guidelines to consider when selecting books to read aloud, the most important of which is to select books that are well written. Books of quality abound, and it is a waste of precious time to read second-rate materials. Good books pique children's interest and invite them to read them—or others like them—independently. Sometimes teachers will read an inferior book "because the children love it," but students will love good books even more. Select books that will influence and expand children's literary tastes.

Find out which books are already familiar by asking children to list their favorites and then build from there, selecting books that children will probably not discover on their own. Save read-aloud time for the special books that you want your students to know. Introduce children to all of an author's books by reading aloud from one of them and telling them where to find the rest.

Reading from outstanding examples of all types of literature—realistic fiction, historical fiction, fantasy, science fiction, folklore, poetry, biography, nonfiction—can help expand children's literary tastes. Reading some books slightly above students' reading abilities extends their language; they usually comprehend more than they can read. A good book can be spoiled for children by reading it to them before they can understand its subtleties. Most books can be understood on several levels, but do consider the students' emotional maturity as you choose. Select books that you want to make part of the whole-class experience, books that you want to become part of the shared knowledge in your classroom.

When reading aloud to children, know your material before you begin. Practice reading is important, especially when reading poetry, where the phrasing and cadence carry so much of the meaning. Listen to recordings of poets reading their own work; they know how it should sound. Practice reading also helps you decide on the mood and tone that you want to set and allows you to learn special names or refrains so that you won't stumble over them and thus spoil the story.

It is important to be thoroughly familiar with the content of the material you read aloud. Some books contain words and incidents that might be offensive in some communities or that are best kept as a private interchange between author and individual reader. You can avoid embarrassment by being alert to sensitive issues. Not all books or all scenes from books are for oral group sharing.

When reading, use a natural voice, with inflections and modulations befitting the book. Avoid greatly exaggerated voice changes and overly dramatic gestures. Read slowly, enunciate clearly, project your voice directly, and maintain eye contact with your listeners as much as possible. Teachers who read aloud with their noses in the book soon lose their audience. Some brief guidelines for reading aloud are presented here.

Tips for Reading Aloud

1. Read the book ahead of time; be familiar with it.
2. Give a brief description of the book or character to establish a context for the listeners.
3. Begin reading aloud slowly; quicken the pace as listeners are drawn into the book.
4. Look up from the book frequently to maintain eye contact.
5. Interpret dialogue meaningfully.
6. Read entire books, if possible, or read a chapter or more per day to sustain meaning.

When it comes to reading picture books aloud to children, educators have different points of view. Some teachers believe that because the illustrations are integral to the text, children need to see them while hearing the words. Others read the text aloud and then explore the pictures with children later. Your decision will rest on the qualities of the particular book you choose. If you feel that the illustrations are needed to make sense of the story, hold the book open and to one side as you read. And there is nothing wrong with rereading a favorite book, either immediately or at another time; in fact, it is highly recommended.

Teachers who permit students to draw, read their own books, or do quiet seatwork during read-aloud time diminish the importance of reading aloud by implying that it does not deserve students' full attention. Instead, make read-aloud time a highlight of the day—something special you share. Your enthusiasm and extra preparations for the occasion set the tone; once you have begun, the magic of the book takes over.

Courtesy of Harcourt Brace and Company

The kind of material to be read changes, but the practice of reading aloud to students continues throughout junior high school.

Reading aloud is central to every school day and should continue at least through middle school. Nursery and primary school teachers read aloud many times a day. Intermediate and advanced-grade teachers usually read aloud at one particular time. In one school during noon recess, different teachers read aloud from a novel, biography, or nonfiction book, and students choose the group they want to attend.

· · SUPPORTING · ·
CHILDREN'S
GROWING LITERARY
UNDERSTANDING

Sensitive teachers help children make connections between their own lives and the books they read. Cochran-Smith (1984) documented how one preschool teacher did this with her class as she demonstrated how to make connections between text and life and between life and text. Wolf and Heath (1992) describe the way two children incorporate the literature that is read to them into their own lives. Many

teachers across the grades see this as one of the most important things they do. Asking questions and making such statements as "This story reminds me of the story that you told us about your cousin, Miguel" or "Has anyone ever had an experience like this?" demonstrate to students that the stuff of their own lives is often mirrored in the books they read. This understanding helps them experience literature as a world of possibilities inextricably intertwined with their own lives.

Connections between life and text are still at the core of children's experiences with literature, but connections among and between books are important as well. As children read and listen to stories, they begin to build their personal storehouse of literary understanding. They begin to recognize thematic connections across stories, similarities in plot structures and characterization, and distinctive styles in text and illustration. Teachers can encourage this kind of understanding by drawing on their knowledge of how literature works, and planning a literature curriculum that contains books selected specifically to help students make connections among texts, connections that result in a deeper understanding of what literature is and how it works. Understanding how authors manipulate literary elements to create outstanding texts of many genres allows teachers to plan questions and devise activities that encourage their students to explore literature more deeply. You will find examples of this kind of teaching in Chapters 13 and 14. Teaching Idea 12.1 presents some questions teachers can ask themselves that serve to heighten their awareness of literary structures and elements in the books they share with their students. This kind of teacher preparation helps children develop an understanding of the unity of all literature.

Teachers enhance their students' growing literary understandings when they structure opportunities for students to make links across books, or *intertextual* connections. Learning about the world of literature is an ongoing process as students come to recognize similarities and differences in plot structures, characters, and themes. As with connecting books to life, connecting books to other books adds dimension to future reading and responding. Wide reading (many varied books) and deep reading (many books in a particular genre, by a particular author, with a particular structure, and so on) acquaint children with the world of literature and help them learn a lot about specific aspects of that world.

Talking about characters enables students to make comparisons among characters from various stories. These comparisons can lead to generalizations about character types that children will meet as they read widely. Discussing plot results in identification of various kinds of plots and in understandings about archetypal plots that underlie literature. In a quest story, for example, a character begins at home, leaves in search of something important (an object, a person, self-knowledge), and returns home changed in

Teaching Idea 12-1

Questions to Ask Yourself While Reading

As you are rereading a book in preparation for class discussion, pay attention to what the author has done in terms of literary elements. Peterson and Eeds (1990) suggest that when teachers focus on literary elements as they read, they are better equipped to build on tentative understandings that students might advance in discussions. Think about the following:

❋ *Plot.* What are the key events? How does the author build tension? Do the events occur chronologically, or does the author use other structures, such as flashbacks?

❋ *Character.* How do characters emerge? Which are fully developed? How do the central characters grow and change? How does this connect with the events of the story? What influence do the characters have on the events? Which characters are static? Why might the author have done this?

❋ *Setting.* Are the characters and events influenced by the place and time? Do you know where and when this story is set? If so, how does the author reveal the setting?

❋ *Point of view.* Who is telling the story? How do you know this? What are the implications of this narrator? How does that influence what you, the reader, are able to know?

❋ *Theme.* What are the big ideas that unify the story? Are there symbols or extended metaphors that help build the themes?

Source: Peterson, R. & Eeds, M. (1990). *Grand conversations: Literature groups in action.* New York: Scholastic.

treat the same general theme. Readers read similar stories about particular themes in many different books.

Children who explore how literature works also learn to look at books as works of art crafted by a writer. They notice the language that the writer uses and learn to appreciate the nuances that distinguish one writer from another. Students use their knowledge about literature in their own writing, incorporating patterns, structures, themes, character types, and language that they have encountered. Books build on books, stories lean on stories, and children become knowledgeable readers and writers.

However, the *study* of literature or of any topic related to the literature should not begin until after the literature is *experienced:* Someone tells, reads, or dramatizes a story, and a fortunate child just enjoys it. When the time comes for children to look at literature analytically and to make abstractions about its forms, structures, archetypes, and patterns, they have joyful experiences on which to draw. Even with older children, enjoyment is still uppermost, and the study of literature is sensitively introduced only as it adds to their appreciation and insight. The study of literature does not replace the original literary experience; neither does study always need to follow the experience. There is a time and a place for both. As Northrop Frye (1970) explains,

> In all of our literary experience there are two kinds of response. There is the direct experience of the work itself, while we're reading a book, . . . especially for the first time. This experience is uncritical, or rather pre-critical. . . . Then there is the conscious, critical response we make after we've finished reading . . . where we compare what we've experienced with other things of the same kind, and form a judgment of value and proportion on it. This critical response, with practice, gradually makes our pre-critical responses more sensitive and accurate. . . . But behind our responses to individual works, there's a bigger response to our literary experience as a whole, as a total possession. (pp. 104–105)

Perceptive readers develop by moving from unconscious enjoyment to self-conscious appreciation to conscious delight (Early, 1960). This kind of growth is not possible without a firm foundation in experiencing joy from books. Through carefully planned encounters with particular books, teachers build on this foundation of joy as they help their students delight in the artistry and interconnections in literature.

When children discover connections among books, the excitement is palpable. This is evident in the following discussion (Anzul, 1978) by a group of sixth-grade students who had just finished reading Ursula Le Guin's *A Wizard of Earthsea* (A) and had previously read several books in **The Chronicles of Narnia** series (I), by C. S. Lewis, and two of

some way. When students read and discuss such books, they can pinpoint characters' strengths and weaknesses, identify problems that they must solve, and discover similarities and differences in the characters' quests, thus building an understanding of quest tales.

Finding similarities and differences in the underlying conflicts of stories also helps readers make connections among books. The connections build an understanding of literature. Some books revolve around several conflicts; others have only one or two central conflicts. Discussing these conflicts, or problems, helps readers notice their presence in stories and gives them another dimension along which to connect various stories.

Consideration of themes often brings about an important recognition of the various ways that different authors

Madeleine L'Engle's fantasies, *A Wrinkle in Time* (I–A) and *A Wind in the Door* (I–A).

MICHELLE: I liked **Narnia** best—it was so magicky.

JON-PAUL: Well, I liked it a lot, but not the best. For me, *A Wrinkle in Time* was best—"It," you know, the Naked Brain, and the shadowed planets, and all that.

TEACHER: There was a shadow in *A Wizard of Earthsea,* and the "black thing" caused shadowed or dark planets in *A Wrinkle in Time.* Somehow, the bad thing, the evil in several of the books we read, seems to be pictured in some way by blackness or shadows.

SARAH: Except for Narnia, and there it wasn't a black witch but a white witch. The evil spell was snow and winter.

HEDY: That's because nothing could grow or be alive then. Aslan brought the Spring.

SARAH: But still whatever it appeared like, there was a battle against the forces of evil.

TEACHER: What about *A Wizard of Earthsea?*

JON-PAUL: Well, like we read, the shadow that was following Ged was really the evil in himself, but he didn't recognize it until the end. I don't really understand that very well, but I understand it some.

TEACHER: In *A Wind in the Door* you could be "x-ed" if you weren't trying to be your real self. Again, the picture the author gives us to imagine in our own minds is rather similar: If you are "x-ed" what has happened to you?

JON-PAUL: You become annihilated. You don't exist any more. If you were a planet, where you used to be there was just a black hole of nothingness in the universe.

SARAH: And for Ged, if he didn't recognize that there *was* a bad side to his own nature, it could destroy them. He would be "x-ed" by his shadow, and he wouldn't be living any more, but just the power of evil could live in his body.

TEACHER: We talked a lot when we were reading the books by Madeleine L'Engle about the *theme* of her books—that the central idea was the battle between good and evil in the universe. What would you say is the theme of the other fantasies?

HEDY: Well, in **Narnia** it was sort of the same because Aslan was good and the White Witch was evil.

SARAH: I see it! I see it! I just finished reading Susan Cooper's **The Dark Is Rising,** and it's the same theme in that book, too. It's the light against the dark. It's good against evil. *They're all about the same thing!*

The other children sat in silence, mulling over this idea. They understood Sarah in a way. Certainly, they understood momentarily the words she was saying, though possibly they would soon forget them. They clearly would need time to read and reflect more. Listening to Sarah discover connections among the books she's read isn't the same as making those connections for themselves, but it did give them the idea that those connections are possible and exciting.

Sarah had taken one of those rare steps to a new level of understanding. As always, every book she reads can be a delightful world in itself, but from now on, Sarah can also relate each book in some way to other books. She is on that threshold where every human experience she reads about and thus makes her own experience will begin to relate somehow to all human experience, and where human experience that is transmuted into literature begins to relate to all other literature.

Teaching Idea 12-2

Connecting Stories: Considering Theme

One way to help students make connections across books is to select books for classroom study that focus on the same theme and to make an exploration of that theme an explicit activity. Throughout this textbook we have presented Teaching Ideas that explore the theme of self-knowledge, or self-discovery. Broadly put, the theme might be stated as, "Until you know yourself, you can't lead a happy or satisfying life." It's important to take the one-word theme and put it in the form of a statement. By doing so, you help make an abstract idea concrete and easier for students to grasp.

The following are some other thematic statements that you might want to explore:

✳ Maturity, or "With independence comes responsibility."

✳ Honesty, or "Being honest is sometimes difficult, but it's better in the long run."

✳ Prejudice, or "Prejudice diminishes the person who practices it."

✳ Friendship, or "A true friend provides support when you need it."

The possibilities are many. Think of a big idea and select books that explore that theme. Work with your students to write the theme as a statement. Generate several different statements and choose the one that best suits the books and your students. Then you can write response and discussion prompts and questions that ask students to explore the idea across time and books.

Frye (1970) explains it this way:

All themes and characters and stories you encounter in literature belong to one big interlocking family. . . . You keep associating your literary experiences together: you're always being reminded of some other story you read or movie you saw or character that impressed you. For most of us, most of the time, this goes on unconsciously, but the fact that it does go on suggests that perhaps in literature you don't just read one novel or poem after another, but that there's a real subject to be studied, as there is in science, and that the more you read, the more you learn about literature as a whole. (pp. 48–49)

When children link a particular work with others similar to it in some way, even at the primary school level, they begin to develop an understanding of the unity of all literature. Making connections helps children understand and appreciate literature. It is also basic to learning; some cognitive psychologists have come to define learning as the search for patterns that connect. Teaching Idea 12.2 offers suggestions for helping students connect books that explore similar themes.

• • ACTIVITIES TO HELP • •
CHILDREN CONNECT
WITH BOOKS

Research and practical experience show that most children who become involved in activities related to books read more than those who do not. As Figure 12.3 suggests, the phenomenon is cyclical—reading provides practice that makes a reader more proficient. Being a better reader leads to more pleasure and a willingness to practice more frequently.

Effective response activities allow children the time to savor and absorb books. It is important to ponder a book for a while before beginning another; students need a chance to linger in the spell cast by a good book. This may mean *doing nothing* or it may mean using creative learning activities. Response and reflection are important ingredients of a child's complete learning experience; give time for both.

In classrooms where there are many books and where students are given time to read and respond to them, children may respond in many ways without specific prompting by the teacher. In a landmark naturalistic study of response across the elementary grades, Hickman (1981, p. 346) described seven different types of responses that occurred in the classrooms she observed. They can be summarized as follows:

1. Listening behaviors, such as laughter and applause
2. Contact with books, such as browsing, intent attention
3. Acting on the impulse to share, reading together
4. Oral responses, such as storytelling, discussion
5. Actions and drama, such as dramatic play
6. Making things like pictures, games, displays
7. Writing, by using literary models, summarizing, and writing about literature

Hickman makes the point that a response doesn't have to be an activity. It can range from individual thoughtfulness, to simple sharing with another reader, to a formal activity such as a group depiction of an important scene from a book. The aesthetic nature of the reading experience requires personal involvement; therefore, the impact of the book determines the response a reader makes. Reading is both a social and a private affair that calls upon the emotions of the reader. Some books should be explored; others should be read, closed, and forever locked in the reader's heart. Although some book encounters lead naturally into concrete projects, we should avoid overdoing a good thing, for in our zeal we may be engendering boredom instead of interest.

Children can be encouraged to respond to literature in many ways. They discover the pleasure in extended activities when there are many to choose from. Many of these choices involve social interaction; sharing responses with others often enlarges one's initial response. Structured and spontaneous opportunities for students to exchange and compare ideas with their peers and to build on the responses of others help children grow as responsive readers.

Opportunities for formal book sharing are fun when they tap children's creative potential; they are valuable when they help children understand a book better by clarifying thoughts and feelings. Above all, as in the activities described in this book, the prime goal is to develop in children

Figure 12-3

The Cyclical Nature of Reading

© Lee Galda

When classrooms keep reading as a central focus, students develop into communities of readers. They read books together and talk about books they read.

an enduring love of literature; everything else is secondary and is aimed at achieving this goal. Being required to read a teacher-selected book and write a report about it has turned more children away from reading than perhaps any other activity. The traditional book reports we are force-fed—dull and uninspiring for the child who writes them, time-consuming for the teacher who reads and grades them, and boring for the children who must listen to them read aloud—subvert our main goal.

Book sharing should take children back to the book and give them a chance to reexperience the spell of a good story. Many ways of sharing books are enjoyable and meaningful to the child and valuable to the teacher who can discern from them what the child has gained from the book. Teaching Ideas 12.3 and 12.4 present some ideas for sharing books in meaningful ways.

Creative Ways to Share Books

Children can express themselves through reading, writing, listening, speaking, art, music, and movement. Some might want to respond on the computer; others won't. Remember, however, that children need choices. Some may like to put themselves in imaginative situations as they discuss books they have read; others may prefer just to talk about a book; and still others may choose to keep the reading experience personal. Be flexible. Teach them many ways to respond to

Teaching Idea 12-3

Creative Ways to Share Books

✳ Devise a television or newspaper announcement to advertise a book. Include words and pictures.

✳ Make puppet characters, write a play about a book, and put on a puppet show.

✳ Choose a character from a book and write a new story about him or her.

✳ Write an account of what you would have done or how you would have acted had you been one of the characters in a book you read.

✳ Write about the author or illustrator of a book.

✳ Write a summary of a book, telling what you especially liked or disliked about it.

✳ Compare two books about the same subject.

✳ Compare two books by the same author.

✳ Write a story about the funniest incident in a book.

Source: Adapted from Pilar, A. (1975). Individualizing book reviews. *Elementary English* (now *Language Arts*), 52, 467–469.

Teaching Idea 12-4

Book Buddies

Sharing books with other readers benefits both older and younger students. When children talk about books it increases their understanding and improves their ability to express themselves orally. Participants also gain in reading and writing achievement and in self-esteem.

Classmate Book Buddies

To implement Book Buddies in your classroom, follow this procedure:

1. Students choose partners; one reads aloud, or they both read silently.

2. After completing a book, partners go off to a quiet place to talk.

3. They discuss the book, with or without teacher prompts.

Cross-Age Book Buddies

To implement cross-age Book Buddies, ask a friend who teaches two or three grade levels higher to join you. Proceed as follows:

1. The older students come to visit and get acquainted.

2. The older students receive training in how to select books, read aloud, engage in discussion, and plan appropriate activities.

3. Book Buddies meet on a regular schedule to read together, talk about what they read, and do related activities.

what they read. Encourage them to use your ideas as a springboard for other ideas that may be more important to them. Ask yourself what a particular idea is good for; if it leads to thoughtful consideration of a book by the student or to further reading, then it has a place in your plans. Ask your students, "What do you want others to understand about your book?" and then ask "What could you do?" In a classroom that encourages many ways of responding, students will have many options for sharing books.

Oral Language

Oral language is central to many book extension activities. These range from the spontaneous recommendation of a book by its reader to structured panel discussions about books by one author. Effective oral-language response activities may be extensive or brief, but they always help children share and explore their responses to the books they read.

STORYTELLING BY CHILDREN Children's writing skills seldom match their oral language skills before the end of their elementary school years. Storytelling activities contribute to their sense of story and provide opportunities for developing and expanding language. A strong read-aloud program is vital; children will use the literary language they hear in creating their own stories.

Wordless books are an excellent stimulus to storytelling. Because the story line depends entirely on the illustrations, children become much more aware of the details in the pictures; they do not make a quick scan of them. These books provide a story structure—plot, characters, theme—as do conventional books, and so provide the framework on which to build stories. Another excellent resource for storytelling activities is the folklore collection in your classroom. These structured stories, once told orally, are perfect for classroom storytelling. Beginning with familiar tales helps children feel confident of their ability to tell a story orally, and they soon experiment with new tales.

Children can tell such stories to each other, to a group, or into an audio or video recorder. Storytelling can be done with partners. In group storytelling, children take a role, each telling the story from one character's point of view. From the experience gained, children learn how the elements of the story interconnect and build on each other.

Tape recorders are indispensable for storytelling activities. When children record their stories, these become available for other children to listen to while looking at the book. Each storyteller's version of the book will be different, adding some variety to the classroom collection. In addition to using tape recorders for recording stories based on books, children can use them to dictate original stories, make background soundtracks for stories read aloud, record choral speaking, create dialogue for puppet shows, and carry out other dramatic activities. Digital recorders expand the possibilities. Folktales for storytelling are discussed in Chapter 5.

CHORAL SPEAKING Choral speaking—people speaking together—can be adapted for any age level. For the youngest it may mean joining in as a refrain is read aloud; for older students it may involve the group reading of a poem. Young children unconsciously chime in when you read aloud passages that strike a sympathetic chord. For example, children quickly pick up and repeat the refrain when you read Bill Martin and John Archambault's *Chicka Chicka Boom Boom* (P). Rhythm and repetition in language, both of which are conducive to choral speaking, are found in abundance in literature for every age group, especially in folklore, poetry, and patterned picture storybooks.

When introducing choral speaking, read aloud two or three times the story or poem you are using so that the rhythm of the language can be absorbed by your listeners. Encourage them to follow along with hand clapping until the beat is established. Favorite poems and refrains from stories—which become unconsciously committed to memory after repeated group speaking—stay in the mind as treasures to be savored for years.

Teachers use choral speaking for warm-up routines to get students to tune in to the task at hand. When we draw students together in a group speaking activity, it not only focuses their attention but also gives them practice in using various patterns of oral language. Most often schools provide a great amount of practice in using written language but very little in using oral language. Choral speaking helps balance this inequity.

Students feel comfortable taking part in choral speaking; they are members of a group. Choral speaking supports unsure readers; they do not risk the embarrassment that comes from being singled out. Most important, the students become a community of learners. Joining together in group routines solidifies the sense of community.

As your students participate in choral speaking exercises, they can decide how they want to say certain pieces. Rhythm, stress, pitch, and tempo can be adjusted until your students feel that they are capturing the meaning of the piece. This is especially effective with poetry, as much of the meaning in poetry relates to the sound of the poem. Teaching Idea 12.5 suggests a way to explore the relation of sound and meaning in poetry through choral speaking.

DRAMA Children engage in imaginative play instinctively. They re-create what they see on television, in everyday life, and in their books. "Let's pretend" games are a natural way for children to express their thoughts and feelings in the guise of characters and roles. Informal dramatic play capitalizes on children's natural desire to pretend and can be the forerunner of numerous drama experiences. These experiences can promote dialogue among students and between students and teachers that allows children to explore their responses to literature (Edmiston, 1993). Dramatic activities provide opportunities to discuss and reflect on a book.

Many forms of drama can be explored in the classroom. Variations, often called creative dramatics, include pantomime, using body movements and expression but no words; interpreting, enacting, or re-creating a story or a scene; and improvising, extending, and extrapolating beyond a story or a poem.

Pantomime is silent. In pantomime, a story or meaning is conveyed solely through facial expressions, shrugs, frowns, gestures, and other forms of body language. The situations, stories, or characters that are pantomimed should be ones

---

Teaching Idea 12-5

Using Choral Speaking to Explore Poetry

One effective way of introducing choral speaking to your class is to put one of your favorite poems on the overhead projector and explore how different ways of reading the same poem can create different effects. Even a simple tempo or stress change alters the effect and often the meaning of the poem. Here are some ways to explore the connections between meaning and sound in poetry:

✳ Vary the tempo. Read faster or slower and discuss the effect.

✳ Experiment with stress, discussing which words might be emphasized, and why.

✳ Play with tone; some poems seem to call for a deep, somber tone, whereas others need a light tone.

✳ Try different groupings of voices. Poems can be read in many ways—in unison, with choruses, using single voices paired with other single or blended voices, or cumulatively, with voices blending to an increasingly powerful effect.

After you have worked with several poems this way, encourage your students to experiment in small groups with choral speaking as a way to explore meaning and sound in poetry. They might want to present several readings to the class or to other classes.

---

that the children are familiar with, recognize easily, or want to explore further.

Reenacting a story can immediately follow a read-aloud session. After reading aloud "The Three Billy Goats Gruff," for example, the teacher might ask, "Who wants to be the troll? . . . the big billy goat? . . . the middle billy goat? . . . the little billy goat?" Discuss with the children how the troll sounds when he asks, "Who's that tripping over my bridge?" Ask them to explain how he shows his anger and how each of the billy goats sounds as he answers the troll. As children learn to enact stories, they can do so without teacher guidance. Children who are working together in groups might decide to enact the story, or parts of the story, to explore character relationships, cause and effect, sequence, or any number of issues related to their story.

Interpretation involves an oral dramatic reading of a story that the children are interested in. This activity builds enthusiasm for reading and develops oral reading skills. It also encourages children to discuss characters, their personalities, and how they might talk given their personalities and the situations facing them in the story.

Improvisation goes beyond acting out the basic story line. It begins with a supposition, often about plot or characterization, that goes beyond the story itself. What happens after Snow White and her prince get married? What is Gilly Hopkins like after living with her grandmother for a year? Well-developed characters often inspire children to think about how those characters might behave in new situations. Improvisation can be particularly powerful as a way for older children to explore characterization.

Role playing allows students to assume a role and interact with others in roles. It is usually done with short vignettes or with specific incidents from stories. This activity allows students to explore and discuss meaningful episodes in stories, various characters' points of view, and characters' motivations. Brief role-playing episodes often become scenes in more fully developed presentations.

In *readers' theatre,* children learn a great deal about how stories work by working closely with a text to make their own scripts. Students read orally from student-generated scripts that are based on selections from literature. Performances are not formal: Lines are not memorized; there are virtually no sets, costumes, or staging; and participants do not move about the stage. A few gestures or changes in position are permitted, but the real effect must come from the readers' oral interpretation of characters and the narration. Teaching Idea 12.6 suggests steps for implementing readers' theatre.

Dramatization techniques differ depending on the students and books involved and the purposes and goals of the experience—primarily according to whether it is done as a performance for others or for the benefit of the participants themselves. A guiding rule in this area, no less than in others, is to hold the children's benefit as the highest value. This is not to say that performances for others should not be given, only that they should not be given at the cost of exploiting children as performers. Remember that the dramatic activities that students engage in begin as ways of more fully exploring the stories and poems they are reading. Keep the focus on the child, and the story and dramatic activities will be memorable learning experiences for children.

DISCUSSION Books can become a valued stimulus for discussion. Teachers and librarians develop the ability to recognize when discussion is appropriate and when it is not. No rules can be given for this; it is sensed intuitively by those who base decisions on knowledge of children in the group. Children themselves can also determine whether or not discussion is appropriate.

When discussion is warranted, the purpose of the discussion determines how the discussion is organized, who participates, and what the focus is. It may be that a group of children spontaneously comes together to talk about a book

---

Teaching Idea 12-6

How to Prepare for Readers' Theatre Performances

1. Select a story with lots of dialogue and a strong plot. The best stories have a taut plot with an "and then" quality to pique your students' interest and make them want to know what will happen next.

2. Discuss with students the number of characters needed, including one or more narrators who read the parts between the dialogue.

3. Have students adapt the story to a play script format, deleting unnecessary phrases like "he said."

4. Assign roles and allow students to practice. Students work best with a partner or a director who can advise them on whether the character is coming through in the reading.

5. For the finished production, have performers sit or stand side by side, with the narrators off to one side and slightly closer to the audience. Readers stand statue-still, holding their scripts. When not in a scene, readers may turn around or lower their heads.

Source: Based on Sloyer, S. (1982). *Readers theatre: Story dramatization in the classroom.* Urbana, IL: National Council of Teachers of English.

---

or books that they have been reading. These spontaneous sharings may occur on the playground, at the water fountain, or during independent reading or reading workshop time. Teachers who encourage spontaneous discussions of books notice that they occur frequently and serve important purposes, such as talking about good books to read, furthering understanding of the content of a book, and expanding interpretations as children talk together. All this is done without the presence of a teacher.

In their description of the "grand conversations" that fifth-grade children had in their literature study groups, Eeds and Wells (1989) demonstrate how children construct meaning together, share personal stories, question what they read, and discuss an author's style during literature discussions. Other teachers and researchers write eloquently of how children help each other become more thoughtful and discerning readers when they work together in book clubs or literature study groups (Galda, Rayburn, & Stanzi, 2000; McMahon, Raphael, Goatley, & Pardo, 1997; Short & Pierce, 1990). These groups are sometimes led by teachers, but are often led by students who have learned to work together without the presence of a teacher. Teachers demonstrate and discuss with children the kinds of questions that can be considered and the procedures that might be followed; when students are ready to work together independently, they do so. We discuss book clubs further in Chapter 14.

In many cases, teachers first need to learn new ways of talking about books. For many years educators have been concerned with the types of questions that teachers ask of their students. Unfortunately, many of these questioning sessions take the form of brief oral examinations that end with a teacher evaluation (Cazden, 1988). This type of questioning is not conducive to generating real, interesting discussion about books.

Asking good questions is one way that teachers demonstrate what might happen in literature discussion groups; good questions elicit high-level thinking from children, and poorly framed ones invite surface thinking. *Literal* questions elicit recall of factual information explicitly stated in the printed material. Such questions based on the familiar "Goldilocks and the Three Bears" might be: Where did the three bears go? What did Goldilocks do in their house?

Interpretive questions seek information inferred from text. They are best answered by reading between the lines and synthesizing information from two or more stated facts. Interpretive questions for the Goldilocks story could be: Why did Goldilocks go into the bears' house? Why did she choose to fall asleep in Baby Bear's bed? Interpretive questions have more than one right answer. They ask for educated guesses and hunches.

Critical questions intended to elicit evaluation of the book invite judgments about the quality of writing and authenticity of information (if nonfiction); they also encourage hypothesizing beyond the story. All these are tasks that require higher-level thinking. This kind of questioning is not answered fully by giving one's personal opinion; the basis for the judgment must also be given. Critical questions for Goldilocks (where two versions have been read) could include: Which version do you like best and why? What is another possible ending for the story? What did Goldilocks tell her parents when she got home? Why do you think she told them that? Does the repetition of three (three bowls of porridge, three chairs, three beds) remind you of other folktales? What other stories use the same pattern?

For many years educators thought that teachers should proceed from literal to interpretive to critical questions, assuming that being able to answer literal questions is necessary before interpretation and critical evaluation can occur. This is not the case, however, as readers can have a powerful aesthetic experience with a book and be able to evaluate it critically without getting literal details.

Other kinds of questions that teachers can demonstrate involve exploring their own understanding of and responses to the books they read. The goal of a discussion might be to clarify personal responses and extend those responses by talking with others. In this case, teachers would share their own responses and encourage children to share their responses, expand on what they have said, and react to others' comments. The discussion of fantasy novels excerpted in this chapter is an excellent example of a clarifying discussion. Hynds (1992) suggests that teachers ask real questions, questions that they don't know the answers to, in discussions about books; encourage students to respond to each other by asking them to comment on others' ideas; and try to respond to the answers students give in a positive and supportive manner. In other words, teachers respond as readers interested in discussing a book they have read with others who also have read it.

As we discussed earlier, teachers can also ask themselves questions about the books they are reading and then share these questions and answers with students during literary discussion groups. Discussion groups are wonderful opportunities for helping children learn about literature; they often present teachable moments that allow teachers to explore how literature works with interested students. Books can be explored in any number of ways. Eeds and Peterson (1990) suggest that teachers read a book twice to prepare for discussion, with the second reading focusing on structure, character, place, time, point of view, mood, and symbol as they apply to the book under consideration. Teaching Idea 12.1 presents their specific suggestions. Notes in the margins, Post-its, notebooks, book markers, and other devices help teachers record what they have noticed and allow them to get ready for an exciting dialogue with students in literature discussions.

Questions are not the only way to organize discussions. Other strategies, such as webbing, allow children to find a focus in their discussions without teacher questions. Creating a visual representation of ideas and information and their relationships can be a powerful tool for organizing and clarifying understanding. Webs can be used to explore characters, setting, artistic elements in picture books, relationships among books, plot, and just about anything that students are interested in exploring. Excellent examples of dynamic discussions appear in Chapters 13 and 14.

WRITING The values of literature extend far beyond appreciation and enjoyment, although these are primary. When they read on their own, children build a storehouse of language possibilities. The stories, poems, and nonfiction texts they read and hear, created by skilled writers, serve as models for children in their own writing. When children write, they draw on the literature they know as they select significant details, organize their thoughts, and express them with clarity. When children write, they also read differently, or, as Smith (1982) puts it, they "read like writers." They become sensitive to what other writers do, and learn to read with a fine-tuned appreciation of the author's craft (Lancia, 1997).

Writing in response to what is read helps readers discover what they are thinking and feeling, and make connections between life and text. Keeping a response journal helps children explore their own responses in a more private fashion than talking with peers. Journals are often an effective first step toward the more public response activities discussed earlier. Journals also serve as a record of what books students have read and how they felt about them, and they demonstrate how students grow as readers across time.

Keeping a journal can be an in-class or an at-home activity. Each journal entry should contain the date, the title, and the author of the book under consideration. Some teachers simply tell students to "Say whatever you want to say about the book you are reading," whereas others give students general questions to answer, such as, "What would you like to ask the author of this book?" or specific response prompts to follow (discussed in Chapter 14). Some teachers ask students to write in their journals every day, establishing a regularly scheduled journal time, whereas others ask students to write in their journals whenever they finish a book. Teachers can read and respond to journals on a regular basis, either frequently or periodically, or can merely check to see that students are writing in their journals as requested. Some teachers make journals dialogic—writing letters back and forth with their students or having students write to each other. Experiment with what works best for you and your students.

ART Art activities can be as extensive as your creativity and energy permit. Resources expand when you have access to an art specialist; in any case, your classroom should house numerous supplies and examples of children's artistic work. Art projects related to books should be used regularly, not saved for special occasions. A well-stocked art center leads to inventive projects in classrooms and libraries.

What you and your students do is not as important as how what you do fits the book that has sparked the project. Art can be a vehicle for thinking more deeply about a book. Many children express themselves better in art than in oral or written language; art becomes a way of responding, a way of exploring important aspects of the reading experience. Figure 12.4 shows an example of such a response. Children might labor painstakingly to depict an unusual and important setting, recreate a vivid scene, capture characterization in a portrait, or explore a favorite artist's technique. Like drama, art is a way for readers to discover what they know and how they feel about what they have read.

Art can also be used as a way to present books to others. Talking and writing about a book are not the only ways of sharing books; many students enjoy sharing through art. This does not mean simply drawing a picture about a story,

Figure 12-4

Student's Artistic Response

This first grader used both words and pictures to respond to the many nonfiction books he is reading about the natural world.

© Lee Galda

but using varied activities to capture the essence of a book. A wall hanging might be a perfect way to present a story with a strong episodic structure; a collage might be an effective portrayal of a character. Students need to know about and have the resources for a variety of artistic presentations. Teaching Idea 12.7 contains ideas for art projects that might be the perfect way to respond to a book. Allow your students the freedom to choose among them.

Teachers can do a great deal to help children connect with books. There are many more ideas for response activities than are presented here, and you will adapt many suggestions to suit the needs of your students. When you know your readers and the books they are reading, and when you provide a context that encourages them to explore and expand their connections with books, engaged and responsive readers flower. Reading achievement, oral language

Teaching Idea 12-7

Art Activities for Response

Encouraging children to express their response to literature through art activities invites creativity. Use the ideas here to come up with others of your own.

Collage

An arrangement of cut or torn paper or fabric. Use Ezra Jack Keats's books, such as *The Snowy Day* or *Whistle for Willie,* as models for cut-paper collages. Use Jeannie Baker's *Window* as a model for three-dimensional twig and grass collages.

Wall Hanging

Large pieces of fabric decorated with scenes from a book and suspended from a dowel rod. Use a heavy fabric, such as burlap, for the background. Cut shapes of characters from other materials; attach to the background fabric.

Mosaic

Small bits of colored paper or tiles arranged into designs. Create figures from books. Use such books as Leo Lionni's *Pezzetino* as models for mosaics.

Flannel Board

A piece of flannel cloth attached to fiberboard. Cut shapes of characters or objects from other pieces of flannel or material to move about as you tell the story. Such stories as "The Gingerbread Boy," which have few characters and a brief, straightforward plot, work well as flannel board stories.

Roller Movies

A story illustrated in scenes on a long piece of shelf paper with each end attached to a dowel rod. Use a cardboard carton to cut a TV screen; scroll the paper from one dowel to the other to show the appropriate scene as you tell the story.

Filmstrips and Slides

Pictures drawn on clear acetate film or slides to illustrate a story. Project them onto a screen as you tell the story.

Puppets

Figures made from paper bags, popsicle sticks, or plastic foam and fabric to represent characters. Shape the puppets to look like the characters and move them about as you speak the dialogue for them.

development, and writing development are related to the amount of reading students do (Galda & Cullinan, 2003). That, in turn, depends on the availability of reading materials (Krashen, 1993; Morrow, 1992). Surround students with the best books you know, and use them wisely. There are several different ways to implement literature-based instruction. When done well, as we describe in this text, it works (Morrow & Gambrell, 2000).

• • • Summary • • •

Reading is a transaction that occurs between a reader and a text: The reader actively constructs the meaning, under the guidance of a text. Students bring experiences with life and literature to any act of reading; a text guides them as they use prior understandings to construct new meaning. Readers select their purpose for reading; it may be primarily efferent, in which readers seek to gain information, or aesthetic, in which they focus on what they are experiencing as they read. Factors inherent in readers and texts influence the aesthetic experience, as do social and cultural contexts.

Teachers can help children grow as responsive readers by allowing them time to read and respond and by giving them choices about what they read, where they read, who they read with, and how they respond. Literature discussion groups, writing, informal sharing, dramatic activities, and art offer children opportunities for connecting with books.

INFOTRAC   Perry Nodelman's article, "Reading across the Border," in the May/June 2004 issue of *The Horn Book Magazine,* explores some of the differences between adult "experts" reading children's books and children reading those same books. You are probably somewhere between a naive, childlike reader and an expert, as you are just learning about the world of children's and adolescent literature. Read what Nodelman has to say and think about how you read. Do you read as a reader or as a teacher? That is, can you read to understand and appreciate a book before you think about how you might use that book? In what ways might your response to a book differ from the response of a young reader? How might you build on these differences for effective teaching?

Selected Books from Children's Choices, 2004

BEGINNING AND YOUNG READERS

Cronin, Doreen, *Diary of a Worm,* illustrated by Harry Bliss

Dodds, Dayle Ann, *Where's Pup?* illustrated by Pierce Pratt

Falconer, Ian, *Olivia . . . and the Missing Toy*

Kroll, Virginia, *Busy, Busy Mouse,* illustrated by Fumi Kosaka

Lewin, Betsy, *Cat Count*

Long, Melinda, *How I Became a Pirate,* illustrated by David Shannon

Luthardt, Kevin, *Peep!*

Nelson, Kristin, *Hunting Sharks*

Shore, Diane Z., *Bus-a-saurus Bop,* illustrated by David Clark

Spinelli, Eileen, *Moe McTooth: An Alley Cat's Tale,* illustrated by Linda Bronson

Stanley, Diane, *Goldie and the Three Bears*

Weston, Tamson, *Hey, Pancakes!* illustrated by Stephen Gammell

INTERMEDIATE READERS

Christelow, Eileen, *Vote!*

Danziger, Paula, *Amber Brown Is Green with Envy*

Erdich, Lise, *Sacagawea,* illustrated by Julie Buffalohead

Florian, Douglas, *Bow Wow Meow Meow*

Gaiman, Neil, *The Wolves in the Walls,* illustrated by Dave McKean

George, Jean Craighead, *Fire Storm,* illustrated by Wendell Minor

Goble, Paul, *Mystic Horse*

Hollyer, Brenda, *The Kingfisher Book of Family Poems,* illustrated by Holly Swain

King-Smith, Dick, *The Nine Lives of Aristotle,* illustrated by Bob Graham

Naylor, Phyllis Reynolds, *Alice in Blunderland*

Osborne, Will, and Mary Pope Osborne, *Twisters and Other Terrible Storms: A Nonfiction Companion to* Twister on Tuesday

Pinkwater, Daniel, *The Picture of Morty and Ray,* illustrated by Jack E. Davis

San Souci, Robert D., *Little Pierre: A Cajun Story from Louisiana,* illustrated by David Catrow

Smith, Charles R., Jr., *Hoop Queens*

Stevens, Janet, and Susan Stevens Crummel, *Jackalope*

Wick, Walter, *Can You See What I See? Dream Machine*

ADVANCED READERS

DuPrau, Jeanne, *City of Ember*

Griffin, Adele, *Overnight*

Koss, Amy Goldman, *The Cheat*

O'Dell, Kathleen, *Agnes Parker . . . Girl in Progress*

Oppel, Kenneth, *Firewing*

Van Draanen, Wendelin, *Sammy Keyes and the Art of Deception*

Woodson, Jacqueline, *Locomotion*

Yee, Lisa, *Millicent Min, Girl Genius*

Selected Books from Young Adult Choices, 2004

Cabot, Meg, *All-American Girl*

Crowe, Chris, *Mississippi Trial, 1955*

Farmer, Nancy, *The House of the Scorpion*

Ferris, Jean, *Once upon a Marigold*

Hiassen, Carl, *Hoot*

Korman, Gordon, *Son of the Mob*

Martin, Ann, *A Corner of the Universe*

McDonald, Janet, *Chill Wind*

McLaren, Clemence, *Aphrodite's Blessings: Love Stories from the Greek Myths*

Meyer, Carolyn, *Doomed Queen Anne*

Mikaelsen, Ben, *Red Midnight*

Rinaldi, Ann, *Taking Liberty: The Story of Oney Judge, George Washington's Runaway Slave*

Literature-Based Instruction in Preschool and Primary Grades

Brown bear, brown bear, what do you see?
I see a red bird, looking at me.

—BILL MARTIN, *Brown Bear, Brown Bear,*
What Do You See?, unpaged

EVERYWHERE YOU LOOK IN BETTY'S FIRST-GRADE CLASSROOM YOU SEE children and books intermingled. Groups of children are sitting on the floor in the book corner, where most of the books are found. Many books are displayed with their covers facing outward, inviting children in. Other children are sitting on an elevated stage area, looking through cartons of books. There's a box of alphabet books that the children have been exploring over the past few weeks, and a box of books by Donald Crews, the author they are currently studying. The children have books with them during writing time. Some use them to find out how to spell words they want to use in their writing. Some use the story patterns as models for the original stories they are writing. During center time, too, children have books in their hands so they can reenact favorite stories or recite poems that appeal to them.

Betty reads to the whole class several times a day: She does guided reading, shared reading, and choral reading with oversized books. She reads aloud to introduce new books into the classroom collection. She discusses story patterns, word choice, illustration style, authors, and illustrators. As a group the children sing songs found in book form, do choral readings of patterned stories, and repeat familiar phrases they love. They have many books on tape, such as Bill Martin's *Brown Bear, Brown Bear, What Do You See?* (N–P), so they can listen over and over again, following along in the book. Literature is a pervasive element in this classroom; children know that literature is fundamental to their lives.

A Literature-Based Literacy Curriculum

Betty's classroom practice is based on literature; learning about literature and learning through literature are essential to every school day. Teachers like Betty who implement a literature-based curriculum seek to increase their knowledge of the books available for today's children and to make these books an integral part of their teaching. They know that reading literature helps children learn to like to read; children then read more and, in the process, become better readers and better language users (Anderson, Hiebert, Scott, & Wilkinson, 1985; Fielding, Wilson, & Anderson, 1984). They know that without learning to love reading, the children in their classrooms will not ever be avid readers. Teachers who base their literacy program on literature focus on the teaching of reading and writing, while also being concerned with engagement—the affective component of reading that supports learning.

Good literature provides a strong foundation for building a literacy curriculum in the preschool and primary grades. Students need good literature to feed their minds and to practice their developing reading skills. Betty's students are wonderful examples of how far good books can take children who are learning to read and think about themselves and their world. Teachers and librarians need good literature if they are to succeed in handing down the magic—a love of reading—while also teaching children how to be fluent readers, writers, and oral language users, as well as thoughtful people.

Literature provides a rich array of resources for preschool and primary-grade teachers. There are books for emergent readers that support their initial attempts at making sense of text. There are books that support newly independent readers as they build fluency. There are transitional chapter books that provide support for those readers who are ready to move beyond picture book–length texts. These books also support children as they learn to write; children quite naturally borrow patterns and structures from what they read as they create their own stories, poems, and nonfiction material. These same books also provide opportunities for oral language experiences, such as drama, choral reading, storytelling, and discussion—opportunities for students to speak, as well as listen. Children's books provide a perfect opportunity for integrating the English language arts: reading, writing, listening, and speaking. Children's books also provide opportunities for children to develop their visual literacy skills as they learn to "read the pictures" in picture books. Teaching Idea 13.1 suggests ideas for helping children explore literature.

Books support all curriculum areas; many teachers try to integrate not just the English language arts but also science, mathematics, and social studies, as well as art and music,

Teaching Idea 13-1

Ways to Explore Literature

Exploring literature with students increases students' desire to read on their own. When the teacher reads aloud, tells stories, and gets students to talk about books, students respond by increasing the number of books they read.

* Read aloud. You are modeling what good reading is and exposing students to the high-quality literature you choose.

* Retell stories and poems. Retelling makes stories and poems a natural part of talk. Students will soon retell stories and poems to younger children and to their peers.

* Create a picture story. Tell a story in pictures as a sequence of drawings, a comic strip, collage, stylized frieze, or a story map inset with small pictures. This helps students recognize literary elements and structures, such as setting, plot, dialogue, and conclusion.

* Talk about books. Make talk about books a natural part of every day. Enthusiasm is contagious; share your enthusiasm for books.

* Recast old tales. List the basic elements of an old tale and ask your students to write their own stories using the same elements in a modern setting. Create a comparison chart with elements from their stories. Students will realize that basic stories can be retold endlessly.

* Dramatize scenes. Role-play characters confronting each other, working their way out of dilemmas. Improvisation makes literature memorable and helps students "own" it.

* Keep reading logs as a place to record books students have read.

* Identify themes, or big ideas. Encourage students to think about books that have similar themes. This helps students make connections among books and see patterns in literature.

* Organize a classroom library. Ask students to consider alternate ways to organize books. Discuss pros and cons of each way, and as a group decide which method works best.

* Draw story structures. Stories proceed in circular ways, along a straight line with rising action, or in interrelated sequences of events. Discuss how the plot "looks" and draw or graph memorable events in a shape that makes the structure understandable.

through the use of children's books. Teachers who use this approach link curriculum areas by teaching reading and writing in conjunction with a topic in a particular area. They select children's books about that area and use them as the texts through which they teach reading skills and strategies.

A print-rich environment contains numerous books that invite students to read and write. In Joanne Payne Lionetti's third-grade classroom, books are not only accessible, they are unavoidable!

There are many ways to enact a literature-based literacy curriculum. Such a curriculum varies along many dimensions, including curricular goals, learning activities, and selection of books. In a study of how literature-based programs look in various classrooms, Hiebert and Colt (1989) discovered that the programs vary along two main dimensions: the instructional format and the selection of literature. The variations are linked to the amount of teacher control in each dimension, ranging from teacher-led instruction to independent application in terms of instructional format, and from teacher-selected to student-selected material in terms of literature selection.

For example, many primary grades focus on the community in their social studies curriculum. Using that focus to develop a thematic unit around the idea of belonging to a number of different communities can allow teachers to integrate their curriculum in a way that makes it meaningful to their students' lives. The books also become resources for students as they look for information and ideas, and models as students craft their own writing. Teaching Idea 13.2 presents guidelines for building a classroom library for the primary grades.

Although you can certainly find curriculum guides and book study guides that provide step-by-step ideas for building a curriculum around literature, we encourage you to think for yourself. Think about your students—what they are interested in, what they know how to do, what they need to learn, and how they like to learn. Then think about your curriculum—what you need to teach, how much time you have to teach it, and what materials you have available. Consider how literature can help you create meaningful and effective learning experiences for your students.

Teaching Idea 13-2

Create a Primary-Grade Classroom Library

Research shows that when there is a classroom library, students read 50 percent more books than when there is not. Classroom libraries provide easy access to books, magazines, and other materials. To make sure your classroom library is attractive and inviting, follow these guidelines.

Collect books that are
* Good examples of literature
* Written about the curriculum topics being studied
* Related to the current literature focus
* Suitable for recreational reading
* About diverse people and cultures
* "Touchstone" books, enduring favorites

Organize books
* In consultation with students
* In a simple manner
* In a way that accommodates routine changes in focus
* So that book covers, not spines, are visible (when possible)

Include such support materials as
* Story props, including flannel boards and feltboard stories and figures
* Tapes, filmstrips, VHS/DVD stories, CD-ROMs
* Roller movies, puppets
* Posters, bulletin boards, dust jackets

Provide a comfortable, quiet space
* Where students can read privately or sit and relax
* That is away from vigorous activity
* That features an appealing display of books

Some programs are marked by a high degree of teacher control; teachers select the materials and lead the instruction. Other programs are marked by student selection of materials and student direction of their own learning, with less teacher intervention. All sorts of variations and combinations of student independence and teacher direction are possible. In some cases, you will want to select materials that will help students learn something they need to know in order to progress in the curriculum. In other cases, you and your students will negotiate what is to be explored, how it will be explored, and which materials will be used. Often, students will independently select books and decide what to do with them, either within parameters that you have set or entirely on their own.

Many books have been written about the ways in which teachers have enacted a literature-based curriculum. Some of the best books about this topic are listed in Figure 13.1. Such journals such as *Language Arts* and *The Reading Teacher*

Figure 13-1

Good Books about a Literature-Based Curriculum for Grades K–8

See Resources for the Poetry Teacher at the end of Chapter 4 for a list of books about teaching with poetry.

Bamford, Rosemary, and Janice Kristo, editors, *Making Facts Come Alive: Choosing Quality Nonfiction Literature K–8*

Blatt, Gloria, editor, *Once upon a Folktale: Capturing the Folklore Process with Children*

Bosma, Betty, *Fairy Tales, Fables, Legends, and Myths*

Cullinan, Bernice E., editor, *Invitation to Read: More Children's Literature in the Reading Program*

Daniels, Harvey, *Literature Circles: Voice and Choice in the Student-Centered Classroom*

Daniels, Harvey, and Nancy Steineke, *Mini-Lessons for Literature Circles*

Daniels, Harvey, and Steven Zemelman, *Subjects Matter: Every Teacher's Guide to Content-Area Reading*

Edinger, Monica, *Fantasy Literature in the Elementary Classroom: Strategies for Reading, Writing, and Responding*

Galda, Lee, Shane Rayburn, and Lisa Stanzi, *Looking through the Faraway End: Creating a Literature-Based Curriculum with Second Graders*

Hancock, Marjorie, *A Celebration of Literature and Response: Children, Books, and Teachers in K–8 Classrooms*

Hefner, Christine, and Kathryn Lewis, *Literature-Based Science: Children's Books and Activities to Enrich the K–5 Curriculum*

Hickman, Janet, and Bernice E. Cullinan, *Children's Literature in the Classroom: Weaving Charlotte's Web*

Hickman, Janet, Bernice E. Cullinan, and Susan Hepler, *Children's Literature in the Classroom: Extending Charlotte's Web*

Hill, Bonnie, Nancy Johnson, and Katherine Schlick Noe, editors, *Literature Circles and Response*

Holland, Kathleen, Rachel Hungerford, and Shirley Ernst, editors, *Journeying: Children Responding to Literature*

Jago, Carol, *Classics in the Classroom: Designing Accessible Literature Lessons*

Lattimer, Heather, *Thinking through Genre: Units of Study in Reading and Writing Workshops 4–12*

Laughlin, Mildred, and Terri Street, *Literature-Based Art and Music: Children's Books and Activities to Enrich the K–5 Curriculum*

Martinez, Miriam, and Nancy Roser, *What a Character! Character Study as a Gateway to Literary Understanding*

McMahon, Susan, and Taffy Raphael, editors, *The Book Club Connection: Literacy Learning and Classroom Talk*

Moss, Jay, *Teaching Literature in the Elementary School: A Thematic Approach* (2nd ed.)

Peterson, Ralph, and Maryann Eeds, *Grand Conversations: Literature Groups in Action*

Raphael, Taffy, Marcella Kehus, and Karen Damphousse, *Book Club for Middle School*

Reynolds, Marilyn, *I Won't Read and You Can't Make Me: Reaching Reluctant Teen Readers*

Roser, Nancy, and Miriam Martinez, editors, *Book Talk and Beyond: Children and Teachers Respond to Literature*

Samway, Katharine, and Gail Whang, *Literature Study Circles in a Multicultural Classroom*

Schlick Noe, Katherine, and Nancy Johnson, *Getting Started with Literature Circles*

Short, Kathy, *Literature as a Way of Knowing*

Short, Kathy, and Kathleen Pierce, editors, *Talking about Books: Creating Literate Communities*

Sorensen, Marilou, and Barbara Lehman, editors, *Teaching with Children's Books: Paths to Literature-Based Instruction*

Wilhelm, Jeffrey, *"You Gotta BE the Book": Teaching Engaged and Reflective Reading with Adolescents*

Wood, Karen, and Anita Moss, editors, *Exploring Literature in the Classroom: Contents and Methods*

Young, Terrell, *Happily Ever After: Sharing Folk Literature with Elementary and Middle School Students*

Zarnowski, Myra, and Arlene Gallagher, editors, *Children's Literature and Social Studies: Selecting and Using Notable Books in the Classroom* contain articles written by classroom teachers and by university researchers that inform us about the difficulties and benefits of literature-based instruction. Many language arts and reading textbooks also explain in great detail ways of structuring such a curriculum. In this chapter, we present the ways a few primary-grade teachers structured their curriculum using literature; we do the same for upper elementary and middle school in Chapter 14. As you read these chapters, think about the children and the books you know and about how you might adapt these ideas for your own classroom.

Using Literature with Emergent and Beginning Readers

Betty Shockley Bisplinghoff's class, depicted in the opening vignette, provided a good opportunity for watching many things that can happen with literature as first-grade students learn to read (Galda, Shockley, & Pellegrini, 1995). The school picture of Betty's class shows 17 children—African American, Asian American, and European American—although across the school year the number of students ranged from 16 to 22. These students varied widely in their reading ability when they entered Betty's classroom: Some were reading fairly fluently, some were at a beginning first-grade level, but most were below grade level.

There are two adults in the picture, Betty and her aide. The school itself is a medium-size K–5 school in which 74 percent of the students are eligible for free or reduced-fee lunch. Both school and classroom look like many others, but what happened in Betty's classroom was special, and the sound of children reading, writing, singing, and talking together was almost constant.

Generally, Betty organized her day around oral sharing time, writing workshop, independent reading, and whole-class reading instruction in the mornings, with afternoons devoted to math, science or social studies, and center time. Children's books were part of each segment of the day. Betty used picture books, some of which were highly patterned and thus predictable, and some of which had an oversized format; she also used transitional readers and early chapter books to support her students' developing abilities.

• • PICTURE BOOKS • •

Literally hundreds of picture books spilled from the shelves in Betty's classroom. There was a sumptuously stocked reading corner in the far right-hand corner, under some windows that looked out onto trees and grass. These books were always available for students to browse through during free time; children could also select them for their independent reading. Boxes of picture books sat on the stage. The stage was a place where Betty sat for whole-class instruction, where students sat to share their writing, and where students shared books by reading them, talking about them, telling stories, singing, and presenting dramas.

Betty read picture books aloud several times a day, for a variety of purposes. Sometimes she read a book aloud simply because it was a good book and she wanted to share it with her students. Most often, any book read aloud connected in some way to something the children were studying, whether that was frogs or patterns in writing, a particular author or illustrator, or a certain phonics pattern. Especially at the beginning of the year, the picture books that Betty selected were often patterned, predictable texts that supported the reading development of the many emergent and beginning readers in her classroom.

• • PATTERNED, PREDICTABLE TEXTS

We know that children become literate in different ways and at different rates of development; this was evident in Betty's classroom. We also know that children who have experience with literature before they come to school begin school with an advantage. They are already emergent readers, readers who have some concepts about how print works. One of the best ways that preschool and early elementary teachers can help children develop these concepts is to read to them. When the books that are read are highly patterned and thus predictable, it is easier for children to figure out how print works (Holdaway, 1979).

Children search for patterns as they learn. They like to find things that match, words that rhyme, and phrases that are repeated. Many popular books contain repeated phrases, lines that rhyme, and natural-sounding language. Texts are predictable for a variety of reasons. Bill Martin (1972) identifies patterns that appear regularly in children's books, such as repetitive sequences, cumulative sequences, rhyme and rhythm, and familiar cultural sequences. Repetitive sequences make books predictable. Many books of folklore and poetry for young children are repetitive, and many contemporary authors use repetitive structures, as Bill Martin did in *Brown Bear, Brown Bear, What Do You See?* When meaning accumulates sentence by sentence, the predictability is cumulative; the popular old favorite, Esphyr Slobodkina's *Caps for Sale,* has a cumulative sequence. Rhyme and rhythm help children predict through sound—the rhyming of words in a regular beat, or rhythm. Familiar cultural sequences, such as numbering, days of the week, or months of the year, help children predict through their reliance on these already familiar patterns.

Betty often read aloud from such stories as *Brown Bear, Brown Bear, What Do You See?* with its simple repetitive

© Lee Galda

There is no substitute for time spent being captivated by a good book.

structure and repetitive text, or from such stories as "The Little Red Hen" or "The Three Billy Goats Gruff"—folktales that are full of repetition and have an obvious structure. As Betty read, the children would chime in when they knew what was coming, saying, "Then I'll do it all by myself!" during a reading of "The Little Red Hen," or, "Trip trap, trip trap, who's that walking over my bridge?" during a reading of "The Three Billy Goats Gruff." When books like this were available in enlarged editions known as "big books," the students could actually see the text and read chorally. As they did this, they also were making connections between sounds and print, and learning about concepts of print, such as top to bottom, left to right, and the functions of capitals, periods, and white spaces.

Big books allowed Betty to use literature to teach children phonics, word patterns, and reading strategies. When the text was rhymed and the children could *see* the rhymes as well as hear them, talking about rhyming was an easy, natural thing to do. "I-n-g" words, first found in a big-book text, were soon recognized everywhere. The months of the year became sight words after spending time with a big-book version of Maurice Sendak's *Chicken Soup with Rice* (N–P). Betty had many big books, and she used them to structure meaningful phonics lessons and other reading strategy lessons throughout the year.

Patterned stories also formed the basis of rich oral language activities as students learned structures and patterns that they called upon to do storytelling and drama. In storytelling, children began by retelling familiar patterned stories. In this way, they made the language of the story their own. Most of the students loved performing and would gladly entertain their peers with their own renditions of stories the whole class knew. The storytelling was quite interac-

tive; if they forgot an important word or phrase, their peers were happy to supply it for them. Spontaneous dramatic activities also arose frequently in connection with these books. After hearing "The Three Billy Goats Gruff," a group of students dragged a bench to the stage and proceeded to enact the story, complete with narrator and, of course, help from the audience.

These stories also made their way into the students' own stories, both oral and written. Sharing time, which once had focused on brief accounts of events from the children's lives, now featured elaborated accounts of these events, with students incorporating book language and patterns into their own stories. In their writing, students often borrowed stock characters, basic plot structures, or literary phrases. These "borrowings" helped build their resources and abilities for both oral and written language production.

• • TRANSITIONAL BOOKS • • AND BEGINNING CHAPTER BOOKS

As is the case in many classrooms, Betty's students were not all at the same reading level, so her collection included picture books that were more difficult than the patterned, predictable texts we have discussed. It also included transitional books for newly fluent readers (such as the **Frog and Toad** series, by Arnold Lobel, and other titles mentioned in Chapter 3) and early chapter books, such as those mentioned in Teaching Idea 13.3. As the most advanced readers in the class grew ready for more extended text, Betty introduced the class to the **Frog and Toad** series. After Betty read aloud from one of the books, she told students that several other books were written about the same characters; she made sure students knew where they were on the shelves. As the more advanced readers began to read them, they often had an attentive audience, with two or three of their peers gathered around them. As the students in the class came to know the stories well through repeated readings, the struggling readers were able to "read" them as well, calling on their memory and the illustrations to supplement their reading skills. By the end of the year, everyone in the class had read through the series.

The more advanced readers moved from the **Frog and Toad** books to beginning chapter books. These are books that are still brief, with most being in the 40- to 60-page range, and that are arranged in a chapter book format. The illustrations, though helpful to readers trying to decode the text, are not integral to the text as they are in picture books. These books gave more advanced readers the opportunity to read extended text over time. Because the texts of these books are arranged in chapters, these students felt a sense of accomplishment—they could now read chapter books. It also gave them practice in reading stories that were a bit more complex than many of the picture books they were familiar with. No students abandoned picture books altogether—Betty's collection was so extensive that even the most fluent reader could find a picture book with a challenging text—but those who could read books with extended texts enjoyed their newly developed ability. As they became increasingly fluent, they moved on to longer versions of beginning chapter books, and eventually into novels that were episodic in structure. Books like this, such as Beverly Cleary's ever-popular **Ramona** series, have chapters that are self-contained stories yet are linked to each other to form a novel. These types of books offer children the opportunity to practice the kind of sustained reading that novels require, but their episodic structure makes comprehension less difficult.

Teaching Idea 13-3

Use Chapter Books to Support Children's Development as Readers

When children are ready for the challenge—and the thrill—of reading a chapter book, begin with something simple, such as one of the several series of transitional chapter books. Books in a series help support newly fluent readers as they learn to read extended text. The continuity of character, setting, and style allows students to anticipate what will happen, thus making it easier for them to make accurate predictions as they read. Many children begin with **Frog and Toad** or **Henry and Mudge** or the **Addie** books and then move on to savor the others. Some of the many transitional chapter book series that students enjoy include the following:

Brown, Marc, **Arthur**

Cameron, Ann, **Julian**

Conford, Ellen, **Jenny Archer**

Delton, Judy, **Pee Wee Scouts**

Giff, Patricia Reilly, **Polk Street School**

Greene, Stephanie, **Owen Foote**

Hurwitz, Johanna, **Aldo**

Joosee, Barbara, **Wild Willie**

Lobel, Arnold, **Frog and Toad**

Mills, Claudia, **Gus and Grandpa**

Park, Barbara, **Junie B. Jones**

Rylant, Cynthia, **Henry and Mudge, Mr. Putter, Poppleton Pig,** and **Cobble Street Cousins**

Robbins, Joan, **Addie and Max**

Van Leeuwen, Jean, **Amanda Pig**

• • MEDIA ADAPTATIONS • • OF CHILDREN'S BOOKS

Another way in which children can connect with books is through the media. Today's children respond delightedly to media presentations of literature. Today's teachers use media as a way of offering their students more and varied ways to connect with literature. Students can spend time listening repeatedly to a book, even if the teacher can't read it repeatedly, if the book is on tape. Rereading favorite books helps children in their attempts to read on their own, and a tape or CD-ROM recording offers unlimited practice. Many excellent audio versions of picture books are available for young readers; many teachers supplement these commercial versions with tapes they make themselves. Betty's students enjoyed listening to tapes, responding enthusiastically to an operatic version of Maurice Sendak's *Chicken Soup with Rice.* Videos also offer children the opportunity to see and hear stories they love. Some videos for young children reproduce the entire page of the book so that children can read the words as well as see the illustrations and listen to the story. Others omit the words but reproduce the illustrations, and still others recreate the story through drama or animation. CD-ROMs also offer children opportunities for exploring texts; David Macaulay's **The Way Things Work** CD-ROM, now in a second, updated version, offers children the opportunity to explore that text in an interactive fashion. Teaching Idea 13.4 offers suggestions for selecting media for the classroom.

Betty's literature-based literacy instruction offered her students the opportunity to read, write, speak, and listen for meaningful purposes. Quite often these purposes were related to the positive value these students placed on being engaged with a good book.

Using Literature to Integrate the Curriculum

On the other side of town from Betty's classroom, Karen Bliss's first-grade class was experiencing literature-based instruction of a different kind. Using the science curriculum as a basis, Karen created and maintained a single theme across the year as she and her students explored the idea of interdependence. This theme involved a study of oceans for the first seven months of the school year. Her students were so interested in what they were doing that their reading, writing, listening, and speaking activities, as well as much of their social studies and science, were linked to their exploration of the oceans of the world. They learned geography, wrote extensively about the oceans and seas and the various continents they border, read extensively from fiction, non-fiction, and poetry, and painted many beautiful pictures of the oceans and their inhabitants. Their language activities were motivated and purposeful as they read books to research and wrote to explain. One of their big projects was a group-authored book on penguins, an animal they had become intrigued with during their studies. Working together

Teaching Idea 13-4

Select Media for Your Classroom

* Set your goals. Think about why you want to use media. If you want to extend your students' time with print, then you will want material that is connected to books you have in your classroom library or those that include text. If you want to use media to help students practice visual literacy skills or to encourage them to compare across media, then you will want to find materials that suit these goals.

* Consider the literary value of the original work; a good film, tape, or video cannot improve a bad book.

* Consider if the medium is appropriate to the literary work. Does it enrich and expand the work?

* Consider the audience. Are the book and media materials appropriate for your students? Adaptations that dilute a work of art to make it accessible to a younger audience are inauthentic and misleading.

* Consider the quality of the materials. Media materials should be technically excellent; clear sound and visual reproduction are vital.

* Check the American Library Association website (www.ala.org) for their Notable Children's Recordings, Notable Children's Video, and Notable Children's Software lists.

These children are so involved in the story being read that the boy in the middle is imitating the movement of one of the characters.

© Lee Galda

and independently, they read children's books about penguins, wrote about penguins based on the models they found in the trade books they were reading, revised their writing, and published a class book about penguins. A parent made copies of the book for each student and for the classroom and school libraries. As they were learning about penguins, they were learning to read, write, speak, and listen, with fluency and effectiveness.

It was only because the children wanted to explore the rain forests, an interest that grew when they began discussing the ecology of the oceans and their endangered habitats and species, that a new theme emerged in Karen's classroom. They worked on this new theme for the remaining two months of the school year. While they were engaged in the study of these themes, the students did do other things. They pursued author studies, worked on holiday projects, and took advantage of opportunities for independent reading and writing. Karen's guided reading lessons were separate from the main thematic activity; she elected to work with the basal that the school system mandated. The day began with guided reading and math and then the class moved into the thematic study.

By structuring the content of the learning tasks within a thematic framework as Karen did, and by exploring them through quality children's literature, you build in integration and meaningfulness. Themes create opportunities for purposeful language use as children employ oral and written language strategies to find out about the theme. Excellent children's books abound for almost any theme you might choose. For example, children's books about animals, a popular topic of study in the primary grades, are readily available. There is no shortage of books about special relationships between young and old people, about friendship, or about families. There are books about weather, books about cultures and communities, and books about school.

There are also many books about writing and writers, and these can be interesting themes to explore. Fortunately, there are many fine autobiographies and biographies of writers whom children love to read. The Richard Owens series, mentioned in Chapter 9, which include such books as Patricia Polacco's *Firetalking!* or Cynthia Rylant's *Best Wishes* (both P–I), are wonderful for exploring favorite writers' lives and their craft. Teaching Idea 13.5 offers suggestions for such a study.

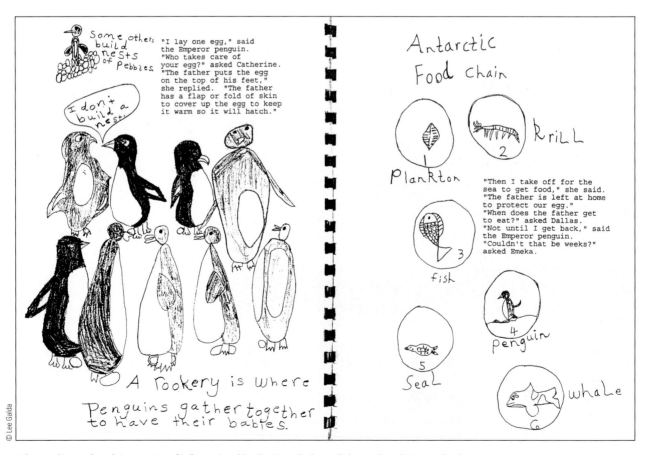

© Lee Galda

After reading and studying a series of informational books, Karen's class collaborated on their own book about penguins.

Literature provides a rich resource for any writing program. It can be used as a model for writing, providing examples of interesting language used well, and as a source for topics to write about. Karen used literature in this way. Some books illustrate unique formats: journals, letters, postcards, diaries, and autobiographies. Some books parody other forms of literature, some tell stories from different points of view, and some illustrate unique story patterns. No matter what point you want to illustrate about writing, there are books to help you make it clear.

Children who write are also interested in how writing happens in the real world—how a book gets made from beginning to end. There are many books about writing that allow primary-grade children to explore the "how" of the craft—how writers get ideas, how they work, how their books get illustrated, how they get published, and how they get to their audience. Figure 13.2 lists some books about writing, other than biographies, that primary-grade children find intriguing.

Teaching Idea 13-5

Study the Life and Work of an Author or Illustrator

Students become interested in authors' and illustrators' lives when they discover connections between writers' and artists' life experiences and their work.

1. Choose an author or illustrator whose work students like, and read as many of the person's books as possible.

2. Make some generalizations about the person's work.

3. Make a comparison chart across books.

4. Locate biographical information about the person. Look at the Richard Owens's series of autobiographies mentioned in Chapter 9, at the reference series *Something about the Author,* and on the Internet. Many children's book authors and illustrators have wonderful websites that you can find by typing their names into a search engine.

5. Read and discuss this information.

6. Make some generalizations about how the person's life influenced his or her work.

7. Compare incidents in the person's life to incidents in the books he or she has written, places where the person has lived to the settings in his or her books, and so forth.

8. Prepare a display in which students can depict the connections they found between the person's life and work.

Figure 13-2

Books about Writing and Publishing for Primary-Grade Children

Aliki, *How a Book Is Made*

Borden, Louise, *The Day Eddie Met the Author*

Christelow, Eileen, *What Do Authors Do?*

Edwards, Michelle, *Dora's Book*

Gibbons, Gail, *Deadline! From News to Newspaper*

Goffstein, M. B., *A Writer*

Gottlieb, Dale, *My Stories by Hildy Calpurnia Rose*

Joyce, William, *The World of William Joyce Scrapbook*

Kehoe, Michael, *A Book Takes Root: The Making of a Picture Book*

Leedy, Loreen, *The Furry News: How to Make a Newspaper*

_____, *Look at My Book: How Kids Can Write and Illustrate Terrific Books*

_____, *Messages in the Mailbox: How to Write a Letter*

Lester, Helen, *Author: A True Story*

Nixon, Joan Lowery, *If You Were a Writer*

Stevens, Janet, *From Pictures to Words: A Book about Making a Book*

Wong, Janet, *You Have to Write*

See also *Page by Page: Creating a Children's Book,* at www.nlc-bnc.ca/pagebypage/

Whether you link your thematic study to the science or social studies curriculum (or both), as Karen did, or to the language arts curriculum, a thematic organization offers children the opportunity to learn about language while they are learning through language.

Literature Study with Primary-Grade Readers

In yet another part of town, the children in Lisa Stanzi's second-grade reading group were learning about reading and writing, listening and speaking, as they engaged in the study of literature. Lisa's elementary school had an unusual way of organizing reading instruction: For 70 minutes each morning, students in a particular grade level were grouped according to ability, with each group receiving instruction from one teacher. Each of the two second-grade teachers worked with a group, and specialists worked with the other groups. Lisa's group consisted of five students from her class and six to seven from the other second-grade class; all were reading at or above grade level. In spite of this, the group was quite heterogeneous in many ways. Some were struggling at a second-grade reading level; others were fluent at a fourth-grade level. The students were from many parts of the world—China, India, and Africa, as well as the United States. Further, they all had varying levels of experience with books.

Lisa was in the process of moving from a basal-based reading curriculum to a more literature-based curriculum, hoping to transform her "reading" group into something that looked more like a book discussion group or literature study group. To accomplish this, she gathered hundreds of trade books that supported the six themes that appeared in the system-mandated basal reader and planned her lessons around the literature in the basal, the books she offered the children for independent reading, and those she read aloud. The books ranged from very easy to more difficult picture books, fiction, poetry, and nonfiction, and included such transitional books as the **Frog and Toad** and **Henry and Mudge** series, and easy chapter books such as John Peterson's **The Littles** series. They also included brief chapter books, such as Patricia MacLachlan's *Arthur, for the Very First Time, Sarah, Plain and Tall,* and *Skylark,* as well as James Howe's *The Celery Stalks at Midnight* and Sid Fleischman's *The Whipping Boy* (all I). When she introduced the first chapter book in November, Lisa read it aloud; by the end of the year the students were reading chapters at home in the evening in preparation for the next day's discussion. Every day for 70 minutes, her "literature group," as they called themselves, read, wrote, and talked about literature (Galda, Rayburn, & Stanzi, 2000).

Lisa taught reading through literature, using both the stories, poems, and nonfiction found in the basal and the hundreds of trade books that the children read. Oral discussion of literature was at the heart of her reading program, and she spent a significant amount of time helping her students learn to talk about books. Although Lisa worked on decoding skills and strategies with those students who needed this work, her focus was on comprehension strategies, which are directly linked to children's being able to read and respond to a book. In this way she was much like Betty, incorporating reading instruction when her students were engaged in reading children's books, and responding to students' strengths and weaknesses. She also taught her students about literature by teaching them about literary elements, about how to make connections between what they

were reading and their own lives, and about how to make connections among texts.

Lisa's students learned about what authors do by talking about the books they were reading. They studied authors and their work across the year, but they focused primarily on Patricia MacLachlan, reading three of her chapter books and all of her picture books. They began to understand how her love of the prairie infused her stories.

Lisa's second-grade readers also explored genre characteristics and conventions, trying to distinguish between fantasy and realism, historical and contemporary settings, fiction and nonfiction. They did all of this by reading widely, writing in response journals, and discussing what they read. They delighted in noticing and discussing an author's particular use of a literary element such as plot, setting, or characterization.

On one spring morning, a group of students talked about the relationships that the characters in *The Whipping Boy* have with each other; they hypothesized about characters' motives for some of their actions. Sarah commented that she thought the prince didn't want to go back to his castle. Chris added, "I think the prince likes Jemmy." Brett responded, "I think they're going to be friends." And Cameron moved the discussion to another level with his perceptive comment: "On the inside he likes him, but on the outside he's just mean." They went on to discuss the characters and their own lives as they wrestled with the idea that a person can be different on the inside from the way he or she is on the outside. Discussions like this prompted Chris to make a comment that revealed the heart of what Lisa did with books when he said, "In here we read differently. Here we think about what we read."

Lisa also helped her students develop their visual literacy skills as she taught them how to "read" the illustrations in their basal reader and in the books in the classroom. In many group discussions, the children pored over illustrations as they sought to determine a mood, defend a theme, or describe a setting or character. For example, when one boy commented that the character in Anthony Browne's *Willy and Hugh* (P) was sad, another challenged this by pointing out that the words didn't say that Willy was sad. The first child responded by showing an illustration in which Willy is walking with his shoulders slumped forward and his head down. At this point, Lisa talked about looking at illustrations for information. "Reading" illustrations is also important in determining genre, as when Lisa's students read Arthur Dorros's *Abuela* (P) and based their decision that the story was fantasy rather than realism on the illustrations. These kinds of discussions can lead to lessons about the art of illustrating, focusing on such topics as line, shape, color, white space, and media, which we discuss in Chapter 2.

Lisa's young readers spent the year honing their reading skills while engaging in often passionate discussions of the

Teaching Idea 13-6

Connecting Books: Exploring Themes

During the course of the school year, Lisa and her students considered many thematic connections. This was easy because her curriculum was thematically organized. They began the year by talking about families as portrayed in the picture books they were reading, exploring the idea, "What makes a family?" As they continued to read and talk about books, they frequently linked them by theme because that was something that Lisa did as she talked with them. You can do this with your students. If you comment that a book reminds you of another book because they are both "about the same thing" and then discuss the themes, your students will emulate your behavior.

In the late fall and early winter, Lisa's students discussed Patricia MacLachlan's *Arthur, for the Very First Time,* in which a young boy begins to understand the feelings he has about becoming a big brother. At this point these second-grade readers began to talk, just a little, about themselves in relation to the books they were reading. Many of them could connect to Arthur, as they had experienced feeling sad or angry without knowing why. As one boy put it,

"It helps when you understand how you feel." This was the beginning of a yearlong consideration of how important it is to "know thyself," a discussion that culminated with their talk about Sid Fleischman's *The Whipping Boy.* The following are tips for leading your students into a consideration of theme:

* Begin talking about themes with the picture books you read.

* Group books by theme. Allow the children to physically manipulate the books as they consider how they connect.

* Introduce brief novels by reading aloud and discussing the themes as a group.

* Ask children to think about themes through both writing and discussion prompts.

* Continue to explore thematic connections across the school year, linking books to books, and books to the children's own lives.

---

stories, poems, novels, and nonfiction books they read. They read many books, made many connections across books and with their own lives, and learned a lot about themselves and about literature. They were able to do this because their teacher, Lisa, created a literature-based reading program that was based on time, choice, and good books. Teaching Idea 13.6 describes one of the ways Lisa helped her students link the many books they were reading and connect them to their own lives.

Assessment

When literature abounds in classrooms, there is less time for traditional assessment procedures than when children are busy working on "gradable" products, such as worksheets. There is, however, more opportunity for what some teachers describe as "authentic" assessment. This type of assessment involves observing children as they are reading and responding to literature, examining the work they produce as part of their reading and responding, and talking with them about what they are doing. It also involves assessing yourself as a teacher—looking critically at your plan-

ning, at the daily life of your classroom, and at your students' literacy development to determine what is and is not effective practice. The focus is on what children can do and are doing, as teachers gather artifacts, observe student behaviors, listen to students talk, and record what goes on.

You will want to keep records that represent what your students are doing in the classroom and how they are performing. These records may include artifacts that children produce, such as reading logs or response journals. Children's response activities often involve products, such as pictures they paint or writing they produce. Save these so that you can inform yourself about students' understanding of and response to the books they are reading. Reading tests, such as informal reading inventories or standardized tests, become part of the record as well.

Notes from observation of students as they select books and as they read and respond to books provide a picture of what they are actually doing in the classroom—how they are performing the tasks that you have set for them. Watch to see if your students select books they can read and are likely to enjoy. If they are not yet reading fluently, see if they can retell the story through the illustrations. Find out how your students select books and whom they ask for suggestions. Discover whom they read with and where they like to read. Keep track of how your students respond to the books they read and examine the kinds of things they do. Notice the writing they do in response, and note how often they choose art or dramatic activities as response options. Watch students as they engage in these activities, looking for demonstrations of their engagement with and understanding of the books they read. As you observe, jot down brief notes about what you are seeing. If you use mailing labels to write on, you can affix them to a sheet of paper in each child's record. As you keep adding notes, you build a picture of each child's reading behavior.

Notes from listening to their conversations about literature provide information about students' comprehension and response, just as an analysis of their oral reading provides information about their decoding strategies. Listening to children discuss books is a good way to assess their development as readers. Note the kinds of things they talk about, whether they attend to others' ideas, and whether others' ideas enrich their own reading and responding. This helps you know what you need to focus on in your instruction. Ask individual children to read aloud to you on a regular basis and note the skills and strategies they call on as they decode unfamiliar text. This helps tell you what you need to teach.

As you engage in these assessment activities, you will find that you learn things about your students that inform the instructional decisions you make. You will find yourself teaching more effectively as you focus on students rather than on a standard curriculum. This focus is crucial to a literature-based literacy curriculum. For a more complete discussion of assessment and of literature-based instruction, see Strickland, Galda, and Cullinan, 2004.

● ● ● Summary ● ● ●

There are many ways to structure literature-based instruction for young children. Some teachers use literature to teach reading and writing, listening and speaking. They seek out patterned, predictable texts, transitional books, beginning chapter books, and media adaptations of literature to provide their students with rich literacy experiences. Other teachers use children's books to support a thematic organization that links several areas of the curriculum. The books become a resource for practicing the English language arts, and they provide learning content about a particular theme. Still other teachers teach students about literature through literature-based instruction, even as they teach them how to read, write, and respond and to discuss the books they read. There are as many ways to structure literature-based instruction as there are teachers and classrooms. In all cases, however, teachers pay careful attention to what their students are doing, assessing their progress in order to plan instruction.

Robin Smith writes about her own childhood and her life as a second-grade teacher in her article "Teaching New Readers to Love Books," in the September/October 2003 issue of *The Horn Book Magazine.* Read her article and then either write your own literary autobiography, in which you describe how you came to be a reader (or not), or compare Robin's classroom with those described in this chapter.

Chapter 14

Literature-Based Instruction in Intermediate Grades and Middle School

Dr. Death faced me across the kitchen table. He touched my hand with his long curved fingers. I caught the scent of tobacco that surrounded him. I saw the black spots on his skin. Dad was telling him the story: my disappearance in the night, my sleepwalking. I heard in his voice how scared he still was, how he thought he'd lost me. I wanted to tell him again that I was all right, everything was all right.

—DAVID ALMOND, *Skellig,* p. 122

THE STUDENTS IN GEORGE'S SIXTH-GRADE CLASS ARE SCATTERED AROUND the room in small groups, heatedly discussing David Almond's *Skellig* (1), a Michael L. Printz honor book. They have just finished the part where Michael and Mina visit Skellig in the night, and Michael's father awakes to find him gone. They are trying to decide just what or who Skellig is. Is he an angel? A vagrant? A figment of Mina and Michael's overactive imaginations? An apparition sent to comfort Michael during his newborn sister's medical crisis? Because there is so much to think and talk about, so many things to figure out, George is reading this brief novel aloud so that everyone is, quite literally, on the same page. The surreal story has gripped everyone, and students ask George to go back a few chapters to reread some of the earlier descriptions of Skellig. Many students have asked their parents to buy them their own copy of the book; others are hoping that it will be offered through the book club that their class participates in. Later, George will ask his students to talk about the genre that *Skellig* belongs in, another query that will provoke lively discussion.

Reading and talking together about books that provoke strong responses are making these sixth-grade students more avid readers. It is also helping them become better readers, because their desire to understand and be able to participate in class discussions is strong. These students are lucky to have the opportunity to engage with good books on a regular basis, to have time to talk about them with their peers, and to have opportunities to respond in journals, projects, and more formal papers. Both fluent and still struggling readers are caught up in the ideas that Almond is exploring and are actively creating meaning as they read. And they're enjoying it!

David Almond has written a powerful novel about life, death, hope, and goodwill that leaves young readers wondering.

There are many ways to make literature a central part of intermediate-grade and middle school instruction. Figure 13.1 lists many books that describe how various teachers incorporate literature in their curriculums. Here we explore different structures that allow teachers and students to read, think, and talk about books in a variety of ways and for a variety of purposes.

Reading Workshop

In the upper grades, and especially in middle and junior high schools, teachers often use the workshop as an organizing structure for reading and writing instruction. Atwell

(1998) describes how the workshop runs in her classroom. She often begins each class with a brief lesson about literature, focusing on what she has noticed her students need to learn or what in the curriculum they are ready to learn. Her students then read independently. Following the reading, they write a letter or an entry in a dialogue journal to a peer or to her. Because the recipient of the letter writes back, these letters serve the social function that is so important to reading. The partners engage in a written conversation about books. (As an alternative to the letters, students could discuss their books in pairs or small groups.)

The reading workshop integrates well with a writing workshop, as students learn to pace themselves in their reading and writing; to expect brief, explicit instruction from their teacher; and to interact with their peers in a structured manner. Teachers can allow their students to select their own

Teaching Idea 14-1

Create a Classroom Reader's Choice Award

To help your students learn to rely on one another's opinions as they select books, create a Classroom Choices Award file. Ask students to do the following:

1. Conduct a survey to determine favorite books.

2. Write the titles of books that they especially like on index cards.

3. Give book talks to promote the reading of their favorite books.

4. Create a file from the index cards for students to browse through when selecting books.

5. Rate each book read by marking the index card from 0 to 5 and adding a one-sentence comment.

6. At the end of the year, add up the ratings to determine the "best" books.

7. Share this list with students who will be in the classroom next year. It makes a great summer reading list!

---

books, or can offer students the opportunity to select from a collection that relates to the curriculum. This structure offers choice about what to read, allows time to read and respond, and provides someone to "talk" with about reading. Teaching Idea 14.1 suggests a way to get students engaged in sharing their responses to the books they are reading.

Book Club

Book Club (McMahon, Raphael, Goatley, & Pardo, 1997) was developed by classroom teachers in conjunction with university researchers. It is structured to include multiple opportunities for language use, and easily accommodates thematic studies in a language arts curriculum or links between language arts and other curricular areas.

Book Club is grounded in a sociocultural perspective on language and learning and in response theory, discussed in Chapter 12. A sociocultural perspective reflects an understanding that language first develops through social interaction and eventually becomes internalized as thought. During this interaction, learning occurs when individuals work on tasks in the company of more knowledgeable others who guide them. Through this interaction, individuals develop their own sense of self and of others and learn to use language in particular forms within particular contexts (McMahon et al., 1997). Because readers are reading and responding to literature in Book Club, this perspective includes the idea that readers read within a social context and construct their responses over time as they read and share their thinking with others. These theoretical concepts shape the structure of Book Club. This includes reading, writing, small-group discussions, whole-class interactions, and multiple opportunities for instruction.

● ● READING ● ●

If we want our students to read more, then we have to provide time for them to read during the school day. Book Club does just this. The reading in Book Club differs from independent reading in an SSR format, because the books are selected by the teacher or by teacher and students to explore a theme or curricular area. Criteria for selection include age-appropriateness, thematic connection, literary quality, and substance; the book must be sufficiently engaging and stimulating that students will want to think, write, and talk about it.

The whole class may be reading the same book, or the class may divide into small groups, or book clubs, with each book club reading a different book, all relating to the unifying theme. Reading may be done individually, in pairs (often called buddy reading), through teacher read-alouds, or with the support of audiotapes. The point is that everyone has time to read an age-appropriate book so that he

Nothing can replace time spent engaged in a good book.

or she will be able to respond to it through writing and discussion. For struggling readers, this offers the opportunity to see what reading is all about—engaging with interesting ideas and compelling language—because many struggling readers never have the opportunity to work with age-appropriate texts.

• • WRITING • •

After reading, students have the opportunity to write about what they are reading. This writing may be unstructured journal writing, but more often it will be structured by the teacher through the use of "think sheets" or questions and tasks that both support students' developing responses and offer alternative ways for students to think and talk about books. Writing helps students articulate their developing understandings about text and prepares them for an oral discussion of these texts. The writing component can also include more sustained writing activities.

• • TALKING ABOUT TEXT WITH PEERS: THE BOOK CLUB

After reading and writing, students meet in small, heterogeneous, peer-led discussion groups, or book clubs, to talk about their responses, to ask questions, and to compare ideas. These discussions offer students the opportunity to build on their personal responses within the social context of the group, to use oral language to talk about books in meaningful ways, to learn how to conduct themselves as a member of a group, and to serve as a resource for others.

• • COMMUNITY SHARE: • • WHOLE-CLASS INTERACTIONS

Both preceding and following the book club discussions, the class as a whole talks together about the book they are reading. This is called "community share." Before reading, the teacher might focus students on strategies and skills they will need as they read, write, and talk about their book. Specific literary elements might be presented to guide students in their understanding of an author's craft. Following book clubs, the teacher might bring up interesting ideas that have come up in book clubs, or raise questions that she would like the class to consider. At any time she could choose to read aloud from another book that explores the focal theme and ask students to consider their developing ideas in light of this additional experience. These brief whole-class activities serve as means to maintain a community of readers that stretches across individual book clubs. They also add to the richness and diversity of the social interaction around the target book.

• • OPPORTUNITIES • • FOR INSTRUCTION

Teachers who use Book Club have various opportunities for instruction, including the writing and thinking tasks they set for their students and the focus they provide during community share. In some classrooms, this is enough. In others, there is a need for more extensive direct instruction in reading and language arts.

Recently, a group of teachers and university researchers developed what they call Book Club Plus in response to their need to ensure enough instructional time around reading. Book Club Plus provides a structured opportunity for reading and language arts instruction in guided reading groups. The texts read in these groups are thematically related to the Book Club book, but are at students' instructional level rather than at their age level. Thus students get practice thinking and talking about books that engage their emotions and also get intensive instructional support from their teacher (Raphael, Florio-Ruane, & George, 2002).

Book Club and Book Club Plus provide a framework that is based on sound theory and research yet is flexible enough that teachers can use the framework to support the needs of their students and the demands of their curriculum. The invariant structure of time to read, time to think and write, time to talk with peers, and time to interact as a whole class, coupled with multiple opportunities for instruction, supports the literacy learning of diverse students in diverse contexts. It allows teachers to present thematically focused units of study that provide students with opportunities to learn about themselves and others and to grapple with powerful ideas, while at the same time developing their reading, writing, listening, and speaking skills and learning about how literature works.

Exploring the Civil War through Book Club

As part of her graduate work, Deb Kruse-Field, a fifth/sixth grade teacher, has developed a Book Club unit that serves as a resource for creating an instruction plan. She wants to use Book Club to link her social studies curriculum with her language arts and reading curriculum. This particular unit focuses on the Civil War, an important event in United States history. Deb has identified a variety of books and has developed whole-group lessons, individual activities, and thinking and writing prompts that she can select from as she tailors the unit to the needs and demands of a specific class. Here we present some of her ideas as an example of what a Book Club unit might look like.

• • THE BOOKS • •

Because she knows that she will have many kinds of learners in any class she teaches, Deb has selected a diverse array of books at a variety of levels. Her prime criterion is the quality of the literature, closely followed by the potential interest of her students. She has also selected literature that offers a variety of perspectives on the Civil War: female and male, Union and Confederate, immigrant and mill worker, slave and master. She has also selected diverse genres—novels, picture books, poetry, nonfiction, and biography—to add to her students' reading experiences as well as to enrich the potential activities and assignments she might select.

Deb divides the books she has selected into three types: books that might be read in common, books that might be read in small groups, and books that serve as extensions and resource material. Figure 14.1 lists the books she has selected. There are, of course, many more titles she could have chosen. Her choices reflect her resources and the needs and demands of curriculum and community.

• • WHOLE-CLASS • • LESSONS AND ACTIVITIES

After selecting the books, Deb generates a list of possibilities for whole-class lessons that focus on a particular topic but also address multiple skills. She decides to explore language; structure and time; characterization; conflict, cooperation, and change; point of view; and also the focus of Book Club itself: asking good questions in order to have smart discussions.

Regarding structure and time, Deb plans to sequence events in one or two picture storybooks (*Pink and Say* and *Nettie's Trip South*) so that students can distinguish critical events and create a synopsis of either story. She may ask

Figure **14-1**

Bibliography for a Civil War Unit

Possible Texts to Read in Common

Crist-Evans, Craig, *Moon over Tennessee: A Boy's Civil War Journal*

Fleischman, Paul, *Bull Run*

McKissack, Patricia, and Fredrick McKissack, *Christmas in the Big House, Christmas in the Quarters*

Polacco, Patricia, *Pink and Say*

Turner, Ann, *Nettie's Trip South*

Whitman, Walt, *Leaves of Grass*

_____, *Specimen Days*

Possible Small-Group Texts

Armstrong, Jennifer, *The Dreams of Mairhe Mehan*

_____, *Steal Away*

Beatty, Patricia, *Charley Skedaddle*

_____, *Turn Homeward, Hannalee*

_____, *Who Comes with Cannons?*

Paulsen, Gary, *Soldier's Heart*

Reeder, Carolyn, *Shades of Gray*

Possible Texts for Research and Extensions

Freedman, Russell, *Lincoln: A Photobiography*

Hamilton, Virginia, *Many Thousand Gone: African Americans from Slavery to Freedom*

Haskins, Jim, *Black, Blue, and Gray: African Americans in the Civil War*

_____, *Get on Board: The Story of the Underground Railroad*

Herbert, Janis, *The Civil War for Kids*

Hunt, Irene, *Across Five Aprils*

Lester, Julius, *To Be a Slave*

Marrin, Albert, *Unconditional Surrender: U. S. Grant and the Civil War*

Murphy, Jim, *The Boys' War: Confederate and Union Soldiers Talk about the Civil War* students to create a story map that reflects the unique shape of the books they are reading, and she is sure that she will ask students to create a class time line of events as they read the fiction and nonfiction she has selected.

Deb plans to help her students explore language by having them look at the beginnings and endings of the books they read, then analyze them for elements that make them "grabbers." Such books as Craig Crist-Evans's *Moon over Tennessee* are packed with metaphorical language, and she plans to explore the similes, metaphors, and imagery the authors use. Many of the books she has selected have rich dialogue that brings the time and characters to life; she can explore dialogue through both texts and real-life experiences and have students work with dialogue to create brief dramas that could be used as a final project. *Moon over Tennessee* and Paul Fleischman's *Bull Run* (both I–A) have vivid language; she may use these books as sources from which her students can create "found" poems that express an appropriate mood or feeling about the time period.

Creating character maps and listing character traits will help her students explore characterization in the books they read and will help students understand how time and place shape character. Comparing fictional characters with the actual people described in some of the nonfiction Deb has selected will help students think about an author's process of character development. Deb may also ask students to examine the characters in their books with an eye toward the difference between an author's "telling" and "showing" what a character is like.

Conflict, cooperation, and change can be explored by asking students to develop "once/now" statements about themselves and then about the characters they have met in their reading. For instance, the main character in *Charley Skedaddle* (I–A) might be characterized by this statement: "Once, Charley loved a good fight. Now, he runs away." This is a perfect opportunity to discuss the impact of the Civil War and link it to character development, as well as to explore juxtaposition, paradox, and comparison. Students might also use a graphic organizer to make note of how conflict, cooperation, and change operate in the books they read and in the actual events of the Civil War.

Point of view is an important issue in *Pink and Say* and in *Nettie's Trip South,* and Deb has deliberately selected novels that present different points of view about the war. This is a perfect opportunity to explore both literary and historical point of view and how it shapes the story being constructed. *Bull Run* is told in different points of view and lends itself to readers' theatre, which heightens the impact of various perspectives on one event in time. Finally, brief debates about central questions of the Civil War between students who have taken on the persona of characters will allow students to make intertextual connections, learn about the various perspectives on the Civil War, and hone their critical thinking and oral debating skills.

Most of these activities do double duty—they ask students to consider literary elements, structures, and processes, and they help students consider the historical period they are studying. Other activities center on the process of conducting book club discussions. Deb might ask students to distinguish between such questions as "Who won the war?"—which does not lead to an interesting discussion—and "When can war be good?"—which does.

• • WRITING PROMPTS • •

Deb has also generated a series of writing prompts for students to respond to individually in their journals or in whole-class exercises. These prompts are designed to complement the whole-class lessons that she may teach and to fit well with the particular books the students will be reading. She also has prompts that reflect more general ways to approach text, as well as some that help students focus on the historical period they are exploring. Offering students writing prompts allows Deb to focus on skills, strategies, and content that she wants them to learn; it helps students see how they can "write to learn" as well. Some of these prompts are listed in Figure 14.2.

• • CULMINATING AND • • EXTENSION ACTIVITIES

Finally, Deb has generated several ideas for culminating and extension activities. Ideas for whole-group work include writing a play or a dialogue among characters from the novels the students have read, emphasizing points of view. If time permits, students can create costumes and give performances for parents and other students. A less time-consuming adaptation would be to have students write and perform a series of monologues, using *Bull Run* as a model. Another idea would be to have a debate or trial about a Civil War issue. Possible topics could include hiding slaves or deserting during battle.

Individual and small-group projects include research, creative writing, and formal papers. These ideas are listed in Figure 14.3; Teaching Idea 14.2 describes another type of project. Deb plans to select from these ideas according to the abilities and needs of her students, and to allow them to select from this less extensive range of possibilities. As in her other lessons, activities, and writing prompts, these project ideas reflect her dual focus on the literature itself and on the historical period, or, in curriculum terms, on English language arts and social studies. Note that none of her activities ask students to read inappropriately; that is, they are not asked to read a novel for facts about the Civil War, although they may certainly pick some up as they read!

Writing Prompts

Prediction

✳ Look at the cover and read the back of the book. What will this story be about? How will it end? What will be the book's point of view?

✳ After you finish reading a chapter or a group of chapters, predict what will happen next and explain why you think this will happen.

Characterization

✳ What good attributes does your character possess? Bad attributes? Use examples from the text that show these attributes in your character.

✳ What does your character care about most? How do you know?

✳ In what ways does your character change throughout the book or in a particular chapter? Give examples of specific changes. Would you consider these changes positive or negative?

✳ Compare your main character with a character from one of our community share books or from another book of your choice.

✳ What do you like about how your character solves problems? What would you do differently?

✳ If you were the main character of your book for a day, what would you do?

✳ Draw a symbol to represent your character. Why did you choose this particular image?

Point of View

✳ Whose perspective do you most relate to in the book? Why?

✳ How do characters look at issues differently in your book?

Setting and Time Period

✳ How do you picture the setting of the story? (Draw a picture if you want to.) How does the author create these images?

✳ Would you like to experience the story's setting? Why? Why not?

✳ Does the way this author writes about setting remind you of any other authors or settings?

✳ Draw a picture of an important scene.

Language

✳ Pick out wonderful first and last lines of chapters. How do they set the story's tone? Compare these phrases with first and last lines in another book. How are they similar or different?

✳ Find literary techniques in the story that are especially effective (for example, similes, metaphors, foreshadowing, juxtaposition). How do these techniques add to the story?

✳ What kinds of sentences does the author use? Short? Long? What about punctuation? Why would the author choose to write this way? Do you like this style?

✳ Find words that are extraordinary (words that you know and that you don't know are fine). Look up words you don't know. What catches you about the words? Why would the author choose them?

✳ Pick a passage that grabs you. Divide your paper into two columns. Write the page number and at least part of the passage on one side. Write your reaction to the passage on the other.

Conflict, Cooperation, and Change

✳ What are the two best examples of conflict in your book? Why?

✳ What are the two best examples of cooperation in your book? Why?

✳ When is change good in the story? When is conflict good? What about in your own life?

Sequence and Structure

✳ Make a chain of events that happen in a chapter or over several chapters.

✳ Are there flashbacks in your book? Why would the author use them? Do you like them?

✳ How many different story lines are in your book? What are they? Do they work together?

✳ Write a synopsis of a chapter or group of chapters in five sentences or less.

Author's Purpose and Process

✳ Why do you think the author wrote this book?

✳ What kind of research would the author have to do to write this story?

Analysis, Synthesis, and Generalization

✳ How might our country be different if the Civil War had not occurred?

✳ What new ideas about the Civil War did you discover?

✳ Should the South have seceded?

✳ How else could the conflict have been solved?

✳ Should army deserters have been punished?

✳ Should blacks have been allowed to fight on either side in the war from the beginning?

✳ Should women have been allowed to fight?

✳ What was the biggest impact of the Civil War? Why do you think that?

✳ Was either the North or the South right about its cause? Why or why not?

✳ What else do you still want to know about this period?

Figure 14-3

Small-Group and Individual Project Ideas

Research

EXTENDED RESEARCH

Research one aspect of the Civil War in depth, such as camp life, a battle, women in the war, leaders, abolitionists, prisons, and so on. Write about the topic and how it relates to what you learned from your reading in class. Also keep in mind conflict, cooperation, and change and point of view. You may want to include maps or drawings if appropriate for your subject.

LINK TO CIVIL WAR WRITERS

Many writers, such as Walt Whitman, flourished during the time of the Civil War. Read some of Whitman or another Civil War writer and compare their writings to what you have learned in class. What is their point of view? How do they describe conflict, cooperation, and change? How does their writing relate to the novel you read?

Creative Writing

TWO-SIDED JOURNAL

Write Civil War journal entries from at least two different points of view: Union and Confederate soldier, mother and soldier, slave and master, and so on. Your entries should reflect different perspectives; include conflict, cooperation, and change; and be packed with "meat."

POETRY PAPER

Although it uses fewer words, poetry is not easier to write than prose. Create a series of poems that shows what you know about the Civil War. Think about your point of view in the poems, and include conflict, cooperation, and change as you express your ideas.

NEWSPAPER

Create a newspaper about a day during the Civil War. You can include editorials, cartoons, news articles, advertisements, and so forth.

PICTURE BOOK

Patricia Polacco and Ann Turner have shown what powerful information can come from picture books. Create your own fiction or nonfiction picture book about the Civil War.

NEW ENDING OR NEW CHAPTER

Rewrite the ending of your novel or write a new chapter. Make sure your writing fits with the author's style and shows an understanding of the book and Civil War issues.

Formal Papers

ANALYSIS OF BEGINNINGS AND ENDINGS

Choose several authors and explain how they effectively write beginning and ending lines of chapters. How do they grab the reader's attention? How do they tie up loose ends? Be sure to include quotations and page numbers.

ONCE/NOW ESSAY

Write a once/now essay (*Once* this character was *x,* but *now* this character is *y* because . . .). This should be about one of the characters in your book, and your ideas should be supported with examples from the text.

BOOK REVIEW

Be a book critic. Rate your book and explain how such areas as style, story structure, language, content, and message relate to your rating. What could the author have done differently? Why would this change be an improvement?

COMPARISON PAPER

Compare your book with at least one other book. Which book do you like better? Why? Think about style, point of view, story, content, structure, and characters.

Teaching Idea 14-2

The Literature Newsletter

A classroom newsletter devoted to what students are reading is a good place to publish students' writing and also artwork that was prompted by their reading. It is a wonderful way to send home news of the classroom and to make suggestions for books that can be read outside of school. The student-produced newsletter can include the following:

* Book reviews
* Editorials about issues raised in books
* Crossword puzzles using book knowledge
* An advice column directed to book characters
* Book-related cartoons
* Feature articles on authors

Connecting Literature Study and Writing

Many teachers do not have the opportunity or perhaps the desire to integrate literature into other parts of the curriculum through Book Club, but do use literature as a foundation for their language arts curriculum. They might do as Lisa Stanzi (described in Chapter 13) does and ask students to read short stories, poems, fiction, and nonfiction that complement the basal series they use, or use literature to help students develop their literary knowledge.

Many teachers also use literature as an important component of their writing program, teaching their students to appreciate the wordsmithery demonstrated by the writers, to explore structures and styles as they relate to mood and tone, or to use the books they read as models for their own writing. Students who write read differently from those who do not write. When students are learning the craft of writing, they are sensitive to what other writers do, and adopt some of the strategies as their own.

Students who read are better writers than those who do not read. The only source of knowledge sufficiently rich and reliable for learning about written language is the writing already done by others. We learn to write by reading what others have written; we enrich our repertoire of language possibilities by reading what others have said. Hearing and reading good stories, poems, and nonfiction develops vocabulary, sharpens sensitivity to language, and fine-tunes a sense of writing styles. These benefits may be especially important in regard to nonfiction. Students who read nothing but textbooks have no way of knowing just how graceful nonfiction writing can be, have no understanding of how different expository structures and techniques can support concept development or build arguments. No wonder their research papers read like encyclopedia entries!

Teachers who use literature to integrate reading and writing talk about how aspects of published writers' styles crop up in student writing, about how familiar structures are borrowed and used in new ways. Students of all ages do this—borrow from the books they read—to their great advantage. Teachers can capitalize on this by structuring lessons that focus students on exploring how language works in the books they are reading and how they can use their newfound knowledge to produce their own texts.

Students can observe how changing the point of view alters a story or the presentation of information. They can study how setting influences character and events, and how the same story can be told in a variety of ways. They can consider the words and the arrangements of those words in favorite stories, poems, and nonfiction texts. Structure can be explored in this way as well, as young readers experiment with the forms they find in the books they read. Students can notice and discuss the wide variety of topics that successful authors explore in poetry, fiction, and nonfiction, and consider the topics that they know about and are interested in exploring further through their own writing. No matter what point you might want to make about writing, there is a book to help you make it clear.

Books about writing have been written for students in intermediate grades and middle school; many are listed in Figure 14.4. These books complement those for younger students listed in Chapter 13.

Being surrounded by good models of writing helps students learn to write well in a variety of genres. Students usually receive a great deal of exposure to stories, but are often asked to write reports or poems without much experience in reading these genres. Textbooks in content areas

Figure 14-4

Good Books about the Writing Process

Bauer, Marion Dane, *Our Stories: A Fiction Workshop for Young Authors*

_____, *What's Your Story? A Young Person's Guide to Writing Fiction*

_____, *A Writer's Story: From Life to Fiction*

Esbensen, Barbara Juster, *A Celebration of Bees: Helping Children Write Poetry*

Fletcher, Ralph, *How Writers Work: Finding a Process That Works for You*

_____, *Live Writing: Breathing Life into Your Words*

_____, *Poetry Matters: Writing a Poem from the Inside Out*

_____, *A Writer's Notebook: Unlocking the Writer within You*

Graves, Donald, *Explore Fiction*

_____, *Explore Nonfiction*

_____, *Explore Poetry*

Janeczko, Paul, *How to Write Poetry*

Livingston, Myra Cohn, *I Am Writing a Poem About . . . : A Game of Poetry*

_____, *Poem-Making: Ways to Begin Writing Poetry*

Stanek, Lou Willett, *Thinking Like a Writer*

Yolen, Jane, *Take Joy: A Book for Writers*

are not always well written, and the amount of poetry that students encounter in basal reading series is simply inadequate. Susan, who teaches seventh graders, knows that she has to give students consistent and sustained opportunities to read and explore poetry before she can expect them to study it or write it. Consequently, from the beginning of the school year she makes poetry available for students to read and share. She regularly reads or recites poetry to her students, and she takes pains to find poetry that relates to other books they are reading.

This time spent with poetry is necessary because many of Susan's students begin the year afraid of poetry; it is that funny kind of writing that they find difficult to understand and that they have learned to dislike because of excessive analysis or handwriting practice. Seven years of answering literal questions about poetry take their toll. Because Susan gives her students time to enjoy poetry, however, they are ready to join her enthusiastically when she is ready to focus on poetry in her writing curriculum. Armed with many of the books on poetry that are listed in Figure 14.4, Susan devises a series of lessons that combine reading and discussing poetry, talking about form and poetic devices, and experimenting with writing various types of poetry using different poetic devices.

For six weeks, her three seventh-grade classes spend their 50 minutes a day immersed in reading and writing poetry. The boundaries between reading and writing workshops blur, and they are truly reading like writers—and writing like the readers they are. One student, an avid horse-lover, produced the following poem:

SHOW

We dance into the ring,
a flash of chestnut.
Together,
we can work miracles.
And she dances,
her hooves barely touching the ground.
At "X" we salute the judge.
She nods, and we move on.
At "C" we canter,
a rollicking gait,
and I dare not give her her head.
She, too, is strong.
When we are done
once more we salute the judge
and when we leave, there is also
a flash of blue.
Later, after the show,
I am alone with her in a yellow-green meadow.
We canter.
This time her head is free.
The wind spreads the grass afore us

like a race track.
And she is the horse
And she is winning.

Can you tell that this young woman has enjoyed reading the many books of free verse that Susan has placed in her classroom library?

Using literature to connect many areas of the curriculum helps students learn; it makes sense to them to link the various things they are learning across the day. Using literature to connect the English language arts is critical. Students learn language—reading, writing, listening, and speaking—best when they make connections among these language domains. Another way to use literature is to select books that can help alter your teaching so that it becomes a challenge to students to think about themselves, our society, and the way the world works.

Using Literature to Transform the Curriculum

Asking students to read widely about the ideas you are exploring in your classroom encourages them to discover what they are interested in and to delve deeply into that interest. This, in turn, means they are more likely to discover differing perspectives and new ways to think about things. Reading widely also provides an important opportunity for critical reading and thinking. Through wise selection, teachers can transform their curriculum, as Banks and Banks (1993) suggest, so their students come to consider knowledge as being shaped by culture, and learn to consider ideas, issues, and events within a framework that embraces diversity. One way to help students recognize how their own ideas were shaped is presented in Teaching Idea 14.3.

Teaching to transform a curriculum relies on a good collection of culturally diverse books—books from mainstream and parallel cultures that present a wide variety of perspectives on the human experience. Chapters 2 through 11 describe the books and how to build a culturally diverse collection. Here we offer yet another way to think about the books you teach with—considering them in light of the perspectives they present, the picture of the world that the author presents. The most effective books invite readers to explore alternative ways of thinking and living; they invite reader transformation and promote cross-cultural affective understanding. If you select books that do this, you will be able to teach your students to consider various perspectives and read critically.

Writing about multicultural education, Banks and Banks (1993) distinguish among the contributions approach, the additive approach, the transformation approach, and the

Teaching Idea 14-3

Exploring Personal Attitudes and Beliefs

Choose a current topic, such as homelessness, that is sure to generate some heated discussion. You might ask students to answer the following questions in writing. It's important that they write down their answers; doing so commits them to a stance.

✳ What are the characteristics of homeless people?

✳ What are the causes of homelessness?

✳ Can't homeless people just get jobs?

✳ What should the government do about homelessness?

After students have had the opportunity to think about and answer these questions, ask them to discuss them in small groups, with one person in the group being responsible for recording all of their answers on an *anonymous,* brief chart. You might want them to write on transparencies so that their ideas can be shared on the overhead projector.

Then have a whole-class discussion of the answers that students have given, categorizing them and discussing the assumptions inherent in each category. For example, do students assume that homeless people are alcoholics, lazy, all male? Then share with your students some recent articles from your local paper and discuss the assumptions that the reporters hold. Finally, read a book that presents the topic from a particular perspective. In the case of homelessness, any one of the books presented in Teaching Idea 8.4 would be a good choice. For example, in Eve Bunting's *Fly Away Home* (I), a homeless father, who has a job, and his son live in an airport because the mother has died and the father's salary is insufficient to continue to pay their rent. This book, told from the perspective of a young child, will challenge some of the assumptions of your students.

social action approach. The *contributions approach* is certainly the easiest way to incorporate culturally diverse literature into your curriculum. Using this approach, you select books that, for example, celebrate heroes and holidays from various cultures. Spending time reading about Dr. Martin Luther King in January is a common practice that falls into this category. This approach does not integrate culturally diverse books and issues into the curriculum and is not likely to promote critical reading and thinking.

The *additive approach,* in which "content, concepts, themes, and perspectives are added to the curriculum with-

out changing its basic structure" (Banks & Banks, 1993, p. 201), involves incorporating literature by and about people from diverse cultures into the mainstream curriculum, without changing the curriculum. For example, Thanksgiving might still be part of a unit on holidays, but having students read Michael Dorris's *Guests* (I), a slim novel about the first Thanksgiving, told from the perspective of Moss, a young Native American boy whose family has invited the Pilgrims to feast with them, would be "adding" cultural diversity to the traditional view of Thanksgiving. This approach, like the contributions approach, does not fundamentally transform thinking.

The *transformation approach* "changes the basic assumptions of the curriculum and enables students to view concepts, issues, themes, and problems from several ethnic perspectives and points of view" (Banks & Banks, 1993, p. 203). In this approach, the Thanksgiving unit would become a unit exploring cultural conflict. Students might read *Guests,* discuss the irony in the term *Thanksgiving,* study historical documents, and read Marcia Sewall's *People of the Breaking Day* (I). They would consider the colonization of America from the perspectives of those who were colonized as well as from the perspectives of those who came looking for a better life. This kind of experience can lead to the habit of considering ideas, issues, and events from a variety of perspectives—critical thinking. This kind of teaching is not occasional or superficial; it involves a consideration of diversity as a basic premise.

The *social action approach* adds striving for social change to the transformation approach. In this approach, students are taught to understand, question, and do something about important social issues. After reading a number of books, both fiction and nonfiction, about recent immigrants to North America, students might write letters to senators, representatives in Congress, and newspaper editors to express their opinions about some of the new immigration policies in the United States.

If you examine your own teaching, it is easy to determine where you stand in your current practice. Wherever you are now in your development as a responsive teacher, you can alter your curriculum and classroom practices to include a variety of perspectives. Judy, a fifth-grade teacher, sought to transform her curriculum by finding books that reflect the themes and issues that she explores in social studies, in which the focus is on American history.

Judy has always combined language arts and social studies instruction through children's literature, but this year she decides to do more than select books that illuminate the historical periods she is covering. First, she organizes her social studies and language arts curriculum around the theme of progress and cultural conflict, hoping to create a climate in her classroom whereby her diverse students will question what we mean by "progress" and will begin to see the history of the United States from multiple perspectives. Because the notion of progress often includes environmental issues, she decides to connect her theme to that portion of the science curriculum that covers ecology and environmental issues as well.

Judy begins the year by starting at the beginning—at least from the mainstream perspective. A study of Columbus and his "discovery" of the Americas provides an interesting introduction to the importance of perspective in interpreting historical events. Such books as Betsy Maestro's *The Discovery of the Americas* (I), Jane Yolen's *Encounter* (P–I), and Pam Conrad's *Pedro's Journal* (I) add contrast to the account of the age of exploration in the social studies text. Classic biographies of Columbus, in which he is praised as a great man, such as the d'Aulaires' *Columbus* (P–I), are compared to more recent texts, such as Vicki Liestman's *Columbus Day* (I) and Milton Meltzer's *Columbus and the World around Him* (A). These readings provide a perfect context for learning to critically assess nonfiction texts.

Simultaneously, the whole class is reading Dorris's *Morning Girl* (I), sometimes aloud, sometimes silently, and students are writing about the book and discussing it after each chapter. The fifth graders have really come to know Morning Girl and Star Boy as people, and they have begun to talk about what a gentle, peaceful life the Taino had. Then the book ends with an excerpt from Columbus's journal in which he disparages the Taino as having no language and being fit only for slavery. What a shock! This experience helps these young readers see the power of perspective and the conflict that "progress," in this case the exploration of new lands, can bring.

With this strong beginning, it is easy for students to continue to explore the idea of progress and cultural conflict through the social studies topics they study and the literature they read. Both the Civil War and the westward expansion are illuminated as historical periods when they are viewed as instances of cultural conflict, and they are made memorable through the reading and discussion of evocative books. Reading such picture books as Ann Turner's *Nettie's Trip South* (I–A) and Patricia Polacco's *Pink and Say* (I), such biographical works as Mary E. Lyons's *Letters from a Slave Girl* (I–A) and Russell Freedman's *Lincoln: A Photobiography* (I–A), and such novels as Patricia Beatty's *Who Comes with Cannons?* (I–A) becomes an important experience for these students as they discuss, from a variety of perspectives, the ideas of states' rights and secession, slavery and emancipation. The Civil War becomes not just an event in the history of their country but another example of cultural conflict and resolution.

The study of the westward expansion is given breadth and impact through the reading of such nonfiction books as Russell Freedman's *Indian Winter* (A), Leonard Everett Fisher's *The Oregon Trail* (A), and Dee Brown's *Wounded Knee: An Indian History of the American West* (A), adapted by Amy Ehrlich for young readers from Brown's original *Bury My Heart at Wounded Knee.* These books, along with such novels as Scott O'Dell and Elizabeth Hall's *Thunder Rolling in the Mountains* (A), the powerful story of the last days of the Nez Percé as a free people in 1877, help students understand not only the exhilaration of moving to a new land, taming it, and making it your own but also the agony of living through the destruction of your people, values, and way of life.

The story of immigration in America is also a story of cultural conflict and change, and Judy's class goes on to read and discuss such books as Lawrence Yep's *The Star Fisher* (I–A), which chronicles the difficulties of adjusting to a new culture. This becomes a subtheme that continues through the year and expands into family history projects.

By integrating social studies and literature within a meaningful thematic framework, Judy is able to transform her social studies curriculum from a study of history to a study of progress and cultural conflict in history. She also is able to incorporate the idea of cultural perspective in her science curriculum when the class studies ecology and the environment. Adding a Native American perspective to the discussion of the use of natural resources helps her students see that there are at least two sides to every issue. For example, although farming the prairie meant food for an expanding American population, it also meant severe loss of topsoil and destruction of the natural habitat for several species, which were also destroyed as a result. This in turn led to the starvation of Native Americans who relied on hunting the prairie to feed their people. Faced with facts like these, students find it easier to understand and admire alternative perspectives, such as the Native American attitude toward natural resources. Rather than being held up as an example of an "undeveloped" or naive cultural attitude or a quaint and amusing belief, the Native American reverence for nature becomes a prophetic lesson for all.

Judy chooses books that she hopes will provoke discussions of cultural conflict and perspective—books to engage students who read at different levels, books from a variety of genres. She provides time to read and gives students the opportunity to think, write, and talk about what they are reading. By bringing students together around meaningful books, Judy enables them to explore issues in history and science that are still important today. This in turn leads to discussions of contemporary issues, discussions that allow students to question previously held beliefs and form lasting values.

Judy has transformed her curriculum into one that not only allows her students to learn the "facts" of history and to practice their reading and comprehension skills but also offers them multiple opportunities to think critically. As they read, wrote about, and discussed the books she assigned, they learned a great deal. They learned to read with greater comprehension through her instruction in comprehension strategies and their application of those strategies to their reading assignments. They learned about the history of the United States. They learned to recognize various perspectives on the events of history. And, Judy hopes, they learned how to be more critical in their reading and thinking.

Assessment

No matter how you structure your literature-based curriculum, assessment will be an important part of what you do. It is impossible to be a responsive teacher unless you are carefully observing your students. As we state in Chapter 13, a literature-based classroom provides many opportunities for assessment, even though it uses far fewer worksheets. Teachers understand that standardized tests are part of the school year, but they also develop assessment practices that can inform them of their students' progress on a regular basis. Teaching Idea 14.4 lists some ideas that teachers can use as part of an ongoing assessment.

One such idea is a formal observation of students as they are doing what has been assigned. For example, a teacher can sit next to and formally observe a book club discussion group, evaluating the group's effectiveness based on predetermined criteria that have been shared with the students beforehand. Most teachers develop an observation form that allows them to check off or briefly describe whatever it is they are observing. Students know when and how they will be observed, and these observations take place periodically during the school year. This allows teachers to assess current progress and document individual students' growth over the course of the year.

The curriculum usually also includes gradable "products" that students generate. These too become an important component of any teacher's assessment. Students can evaluate their own success and progress by compiling a portfolio that reflects their best efforts. Asking students to look at their work and select materials that demonstrate what they have learned is a powerful step toward the practice of self-evaluation, a necessary skill for independent learners. See Strickland, Galda, and Cullinan (2004) for more extended discussion of assessment and of teaching with literature.

• • • Summary • • •

There are many ways to structure literature-based instruction in the intermediate grades and middle school. A reading and writing workshop is one structure that allows students time and choice about their reading as well as the opportunity to interact with peers during literacy events. Book Club is another structure that allows social interaction, time spent reading, and opportunities for students to think about what they have read as they respond in writing and in talking with peers. One advantage of Book Club is the many opportunities for instruction that it provides.

Teachers who don't use either of these structures might simply infuse literature into their curriculum with the goal of encouraging students to read. Many teachers combine literature study and writing, using the books students read as resources for and examples of good writing. Others work toward transforming the curriculum they teach by using literature that provides students with alternative perspectives. All these ways of incorporating literature into the curriculum are supported by assessment practices that keep teachers informed about how their students are performing.

Teaching with literature helps readers think about themselves and their world and expand their ideas about people, places, history, current events, and important issues. It helps students learn to read and think critically, considering multiple points of view. Books and the right kind of teaching can transform much more than the curriculum. They can transform lives.

INFOTRAC   In the September/October 2002 issue of *The Horn Book Magazine,* Lauren Adams writes about "disorderly fiction" for adolescents. Disorderly fiction is fiction in which the writer breaks the traditional linear narrative pattern. Read Adams's article and then find one or more of the books she cites, or some of the many "disorderly" books that are cited in this text. Read the books and think about the kinds of literary lessons you might be able to teach using them.

Teaching Idea 14-4

Things to Observe about Reading Literature

* What books are your students reading, and how long are they taking to read them? Use reading logs; observe library behavior.

* How do your students decide what books to select? Observe library behavior; ask students to describe in writing.

* How do your students feel about reading? Use a reading attitude survey.

* Are your students good conversationalists about books? Observe a group discussion; ask students to self-evaluate their group behavior.

* Do your students comprehend the books they are reading? Are they engaged by the books? Observe students' comments during discussion; use artifacts that students produce (such as journal or log entries).

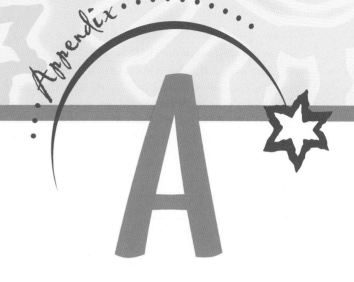

Selected Children's and Adolescent Book Awards

American Library Association Awards

• • • The John Newbery Medal • • • and Honor Books

The John Newbery Medal, established in 1922 and named for an 18th-century British publisher and bookseller, the first to publish books for children, is given annually for the most distinguished contribution to literature for children published in the United States in the preceding year. This award is administered by the Association for Library Service to Children, a division of the American Library Association.

1922

The Story of Mankind, by Hendrik Willem van Loon (Liveright)

Honor Books: *The Great Quest,* by Charles Hawes (Little, Brown); *Cedric the Forester,* by Bernard Marshall (Appleton); *The Old Tobacco Shop,* by William Bowen (Macmillan); *The Golden Fleece and the Heroes Who Lived before Achilles,* by Padraic Colum (Macmillan); *Windy Hill,* by Cornelia Meigs (Macmillan)

1923

The Voyages of Doctor Doolittle, by Hugh Lofting (HarperCollins)

Honor Books: No record

1924

The Dark Frigate, by Charles Hawes (Little, Brown)

Honor Books: No record

1925

Tales from Silver Lands, by Charles Finger (Doubleday)

Honor Books: *Nicholas,* by Anne Carroll Moore (Putnam); *Dream Coach,* by Anne Parrish (Macmillan)

1926

Shen of the Sea, by Arthur Bowie Chrisman (Dutton)

Honor Book: *Voyagers,* by Padraic Colum (Macmillan)

1927

Smoky, the Cowhorse, by Will James (Scribner's)

Honor Books: No record

1928

Gay-Neck: The Story of a Pigeon, by Dhan Gopal Mukeri (Dutton)

Honor Books: *The Wonder Smith and His Son,* by Ella Young (Longman); *Downright Dencey,* by Caroline Snedeker (Doubleday)

1929

The Trumpeter of Krakow, by Eric P. Kelly (Macmillan)

Honor Books: *Pigtail of Ah Lee Ben Loo,* by John Benett (Longman); *Millions of Cats,* by Wanda Gág (Coward-McCann); *The Boy Who Was,* by Grace Hallock (Dutton); *Clearing Weather,* by Cornelia Meigs (Little, Brown); *Runaway Papoose,* by Grace Moon (Doubleday); *Tod of the Fens,* by Elinor Whitney (Macmillan)

1930

Hitty, Her First Hundred Years, by Rachel Field (Macmillan)

HONOR BOOKS: *A Daughter of the Seine,* by Jeanette Eaton (HarperCollins); *Pran of Albania,* by Elizabeth Miller (Doubleday); *Jumping-Off Place,* by Marian Hurd McNeely (Longman); *Tangle-Coated Horse and Other Tales,* by Ella Young (Random House); *Vaino,* by Julia Davis Adams (Dutton); *Little Blacknose,* by Hildegarde Swift (Harcourt)

1931

The Cat Who Went to Heaven, by Elizabeth Coatsworth (Macmillan)

HONOR BOOKS: *Floating Island,* by Anne Parrish (Harper-Collins); *The Dark Star of Itza,* by Alida Malkus (Harcourt); *Queer Person,* by Ralph Hubbard (Doubleday); *Mountains Are Free,* by Julia Davis Adams (Dutton); *Spice and the Devil's Cave,* by Agnes Hewes (Knopf); *Meggy Macintosh,* by Elizabeth Janet Gray (Doubleday); *Garram the Hunter,* by Herbert Best (Doubleday); *Ood-Le-Uk the Wanderer,* by Alice Lide and Margaret Johansen (Little, Brown)

1932

Waterless Mountain, by Laura Adams Armer (Random House)

HONOR BOOKS: *The Fairy Circus,* by Dorothy P. Lathrop (Macmillan); *Calico Bush,* by Rachel Field (Macmillan); *Boy of the South Seas,* by Eunice Tietjens (Coward-McCann); *Out of the Flame,* by Eloise Lownsbery (Longman); *Jane's Island,* by Marjorie Allee (Houghton Mifflin); *Truce of the Wolf and Other Tales of Old Italy,* by Mary Gould Davis (Harcourt)

1933

Young Fu of the Upper Yangtze, by Elizabeth Foreman Lewis (Winston)

HONOR BOOKS: *Swift Rivers,* by Cornelia Meigs (Little, Brown); *The Railroad to Freedom,* by Hildegarde Swift (Harcourt); *Children of the Soil,* by Nora Burglon (Doubleday)

1934

Invincible Louisa, by Cornelia Meigs (Little, Brown)

HONOR BOOKS: *The Forgotten Daughter,* by Caroline Snedeker (Doubleday); *Swords of Steel,* by Elsie Singmaster (Houghton Mifflin); *ABC Bunny,* by Wanda Gág (Coward-McCann); *Winged Girl of Knossos,* by Erik Berry (Appleton); *New Land,* by Sarah Schmidt (McBride); *Big Tree of Buntahy,* by Padraic Colum (Macmillan); *Glory of the Seas,* by Agnes Hewes (Knopf); *Apprentice of Florence,* by Ann Kyle (Houghton Mifflin)

1935

Dobry, by Monica Shannon (Viking)

HONOR BOOKS: *Pageant of Chinese History,* by Elizabeth Seeger (Random House); *Davy Crockett,* by Constance Rourke (Harcourt); *A Day on Skates,* by Hilda Van Stockum (Harper-Collins)

1936

Caddie Woodlawn, by Carol Ryrie Brink (Macmillan)

HONOR BOOKS: *Honk the Moose,* by Phil Stong (Trellis); *The Good Master,* by Kate Seredy (Viking); *Young Walter Scott,* by Elizabeth Janet Gray (Viking); *All Sail Set,* by Armstrong Sperry (Winston)

1937

Roller Skates, by Ruth Sawyer (Viking)

HONOR BOOKS: *Phoebe Fairchild: Her Book,* by Lois Lenski (Stokes); *Whistler's Van,* by Idwal Jones (Viking); *Golden Basket,* by Ludwig Bemelmans (Viking); *Winterbound,* by Margery Bianco (Viking); *Audubon,* by Constance Rourke (Harcourt); *The Codfish Musket,* by Agnes Hewes (Doubleday)

1938

The White Stag, by Kate Seredy (Viking)

HONOR BOOKS: *Pecos Bill,* by James Cloyd Bowman (Little, Brown); *Bright Island,* by Mabel Robinson (Random House); *On the Banks of Plum Creek,* by Laura Ingalls Wilder (Harper-Collins)

1939

Thimble Summer, by Elizabeth Enright (Henry Holt)

HONOR BOOKS: *Nino,* by Valenti Angelo (Viking); *Mr. Popper's Penguins,* by Richard and Florence Atwater (Little, Brown); *"Hello the Boat!"* by Phyllis Crawford (Henry Holt); *Leader by Destiny: George Washington, Man and Patriot,* by Jeanette Eaton (Harcourt); *Penn,* by Elizabeth Janet Gray (Viking)

1940

Daniel Boone, by James Daugherty (Viking)

HONOR BOOKS: *The Singing Tree,* by Kate Seredy (Viking); *Runner of the Mountain Tops,* by Mabel Robinson (Random House); *By the Shores of Silver Lake,* by Laura Ingalls Wilder (HarperCollins); *Boy with a Pack,* by Stephen W. Meader (Harcourt)

1941

Call It Courage, by Armstrong Sperry (Macmillan)

HONOR BOOKS: *Blue Willow,* by Doris Gates (Viking); *Young Mac of Fort Vancouver,* by Mary Jane Carr (HarperCollins); *The Long Winter,* by Laura Ingalls Wilder (HarperCollins); *Nansen,* by Anna Gertrude Hall (Viking)

1942

The Matchlock Gun, by Walter D. Edmonds (Putnam)

HONOR BOOKS: *Little Town on the Prairie,* by Laura Ingalls Wilder (HarperCollins); *George Washington's World,* by Genevieve Foster (Scribner's); *Indian Captive: The Story of Mary Jemison,* by Lois Lenski (HarperCollins); *Down Ryton Water,* by Eva Roe Gaggin (Viking)

1943

Adam of the Road, by Elizabeth Janet Gray (Viking)

HONOR BOOKS: *The Middle Moffat,* by Eleanor Estes (Harcourt); *Have You Seen Tom Thumb?* by Mabel Leigh Hunt (Harper-Collins)

1944

Johnny Tremain, by Esther Forbes (Houghton Mifflin)

HONOR BOOKS: *These Happy Golden Years,* by Laura Ingalls Wilder (HarperCollins); *Fog Magic,* by Julia Sauer (Viking); *Rufus M.,* by Eleanor Estes (Harcourt); *Mountain Born,* by Elizabeth Yates (Coward-McCann)

1945

Rabbit Hill, by Robert Lawson (Viking)

HONOR BOOKS: *The Hundred Dresses,* by Eleanor Estes (Harcourt); *The Silver Pencil,* by Alice Dalgliesh (Scribner's); *Abraham Lincoln's World,* by Genevieve Foster (Scribner's); *Lone Journey: The Life of Roger Williams,* by Jeannette Eaton (Harcourt)

1946

Strawberry Girl, by Lois Lenski (HarperCollins)

HONOR BOOKS: *Justin Morgan Had a Horse,* by Marguerite Henry (Rand McNally); *The Moved-Outers,* by Florence Crannel Means (Houghton Mifflin); *Bhimsa, the Dancing Bear,* by Christine Weston (Scribner's); *New Found World,* by Katherine Shippen (Viking)

1947

Miss Hickory, by Carolyn Sherwin Bailey (Viking)

HONOR BOOKS: *Wonderful Year,* by Nancy Barnes (Messner); *Big Tree,* by Mary and Conrad Buff (Viking); *The Heavenly Tenants,* by William Maxwell (HarperCollins); *The Avion My Uncle Flew,* by Cyrus Fisher (Appleton); *The Hidden Treasure of Glaston,* by Eleanore Jewett (Viking)

1948

The Twenty-One Balloons, by William Pène du Bois (Viking)

HONOR BOOKS: *Pancakes-Paris,* by Claire Huchet Bishop (Viking); *Li Lun, Lad of Courage,* by Carolyn Treffinger (Abingdon); *The Quaint and Curious Quest of Johnny Longfoot,* by Catherine Besterman (Bobbs); *The Cow-Tail Switch and Other West African Stories,* by Harold Courlander (Henry Holt); *Misty of Chincoteague,* by Marguerite Henry (Rand McNally)

1949

King of the Wind, by Marguerite Henry (Rand McNally)

HONOR BOOKS: *Seabird,* by Holling C. Holling (Houghton Mifflin); *Daughter of the Mountains,* by Louise Rankin (Viking); *My Father's Dragon,* by Ruth Stiles Gannett (Random House); *Story of the Negro,* by Arna Bontemps (Knopf)

1950

The Door in the Wall, by Marguerite de Angeli (Doubleday)

HONOR BOOKS: *Tree of Freedom,* by Rebecca Caudill (Viking); *The Blue Cat of Castle Town,* by Catherine Coblentz (Random House); *Kildee House,* by Rutherford Montgomery (Doubleday); *George Washington,* by Genevieve Foster (Scribner's); *Song of the Pines,* by Walter and Marion Havighurst (Winston)

1951

Amos Fortune, Free Man, by Elizabeth Yates (Aladdin)

HONOR BOOKS: *Better Known as Johnny Appleseed,* by Mabel Leigh Hunt (HarperCollins); *Gandhi: Fighter without a Sword,* by Jeanette Eaton (Morrow); *Abraham Lincoln, Friend of the People,* by Clara Ingram Judson (Follett); *The Story of Appleby Capple,* by Anne Parrish (HarperCollins)

1952

Ginger Pye, by Eleanor Estes (Harcourt)

HONOR BOOKS: *Americans before Columbus,* by Elizabeth Baity (Viking); *Minn of the Mississippi,* by Holling C. Holling (Houghton Mifflin); *The Defender,* by Nicholas Kalashnikoff (Scribner's); *The Light at Tern Rock,* by Julia Sauer (Viking); *The Apple and the Arrow,* by Mary and Conrad Buff (Houghton Mifflin)

1953

Secret of the Andes, by Ann Nolan Clark (Viking)

HONOR BOOKS: *Charlotte's Web,* by E. B. White (HarperCollins); *Moccasin Trail,* by Eloise McGraw (Coward-McCann); *Red Sails to Capri,* by Ann Weil (Viking); *The Bears on Hemlock Mountain,* by Alice Dalgliesh (Scribner's); *Birthdays of Freedom,* Vol. 1, by Genevieve Foster (Scribner's)

1954

. . . and now Miguel, by Joseph Krumgold (HarperCollins)

HONOR BOOKS: *All Alone,* by Claire Huchet Bishop (Viking); *Shadrach,* by Meindert DeJong (HarperCollins); *Hurry Home, Candy,* by Meindert DeJong (HarperCollins); *Theodore Roosevelt, Fighting Patriot,* by Clara Ingram Judson (Follett); *Magic Maize,* by Mary and Conrad Buff (Houghton Mifflin)

1955

The Wheel on the School, by Meindert DeJong (HarperCollins)

HONOR BOOKS: *The Courage of Sarah Noble,* by Alice Dalgliesh (Scribner's); *Banner in the Sky,* by James Ullman (HarperCollins)

1956

Carry on, Mr. Bowditch, by Jean Lee Latham (Houghton Mifflin)

HONOR BOOKS: *The Secret River,* by Marjorie Kinnan Rawlings (Scribner's); *The Golden Name Day,* by Jennie Linquist (Harper-Collins); *Men, Microscopes, and Living Things,* by Katherine Shippen (Viking)

1957

Miracles on Maple Hill, by Virginia Sorensen (Harcourt)

HONOR BOOKS: *Old Yeller,* by Fred Gipson (HarperCollins); *The House of Sixty Fathers,* by Meindert DeJong (HarperCollins); *Mr. Justice Holmes,* by Clara Ingram Judson (Follett); *The Corn Grows Ripe,* by Dorothy Rhoads (Viking); *Black Fox of Lorne,* by Marguerite de Angeli (Doubleday)

1958

Rifles for Watie, by Harold Keith (Crowell)

HONOR BOOKS: *The Horsecatcher,* by Mari Sandoz (Westminster); *Gone-Away Lake,* by Elizabeth Enright (Harcourt); *The Great Wheel,* by Robert Lawson (Viking); *Tom Paine, Freedom's Apostle,* by Leo Gurko (HarperCollins)

1959

The Witch of Blackbird Pond, by Elizabeth George Speare (Houghton Mifflin)

HONOR BOOKS: *The Family under the Bridge,* by Natalie Savage Carlson (HarperCollins); *Along Came a Dog,* by Meindert DeJong (HarperCollins); *Chucaro: Wild Pony of the Pampa,* by Francis Kalnay (Harcourt); *The Perilous Road,* by William O. Steele (Harcourt)

1960

Onion John, by Joseph Krumgold (HarperCollins)

HONOR BOOKS: *My Side of the Mountain,* by Jean Craighead George (Dutton); *America Is Born,* by Gerald W. Johnson (Morrow); *The Gammage Cup,* by Carol Kendall (Harcourt)

1961

Island of the Blue Dolphins, by Scott O'Dell (Houghton Mifflin)

HONOR BOOKS: *America Moves Forward,* by Gerald W. Johnson (Morrow); *Old Ramon,* by Jack Schaefer (Houghton Mifflin); *The Cricket in Times Square,* by George Selden (Farrar, Straus & Giroux)

1962

The Bronze Bow, by Elizabeth George Speare (Houghton Mifflin)

HONOR BOOKS: *Frontier Living,* by Edwin Tunis (World); *The Golden Goblet,* by Eloise McGraw (Coward-McCann); *Belling the Tiger,* by Mary Stolz (HarperCollins)

1963

A Wrinkle in Time, by Madeleine L'Engle (Farrar, Straus & Giroux)

HONOR BOOKS: *Thistle and Thyme,* by Sorche Nic Leodhas (Henry Holt); *Men of Athens,* by Olivia Coolidge (Houghton Mifflin)

1964

It's Like This, Cat, by Emily Cheney Neville (HarperCollins)

HONOR BOOKS: *Rascal,* by Sterling North (Dutton); *The Loner,* by Ester Wier (McKay)

1965

Shadow of a Bull, by Maia Wojciechowska (Atheneum)

HONOR BOOK: *Across Five Aprils,* by Irene Hunt (Follett)

1966

I, Juan de Pareja, by Elizabeth Borton de Treviño (Farrar, Straus & Giroux)

HONOR BOOKS: *The Black Cauldron,* by Lloyd Alexander (Henry Holt); *The Animal Family,* by Randall Jarrell (Pantheon); *The Noonday Friends,* by Mary Stolz (HarperCollins)

1967

Up a Road Slowly, by Irene Hunt (Follett)

HONOR BOOKS: *The King's Fifth,* by Scott O'Dell (Houghton Mifflin); *Zlateh the Goat and Other Stories,* by Isaac Bashevis Singer (HarperCollins); *The Jazz Man,* by Mary H. Weik (Atheneum)

1968

From the Mixed-Up Files of Mrs. Basil E. Frankweiler, by E. L. Konigsburg (Atheneum)

HONOR BOOKS: *Jennifer, Hecate, Macbeth, William McKinley, and Me, Elizabeth,* by E. L. Konigsburg (Atheneum); *The Black Pearl,* by Scott O'Dell (Houghton Mifflin); *The Fearsome Inn,* by Isaac Bashevis Singer (Scribner's); *The Egypt Game,* by Zilpha Keatley Snyder (Atheneum)

1969

The High King, by Lloyd Alexander (Henry Holt)

HONOR BOOKS: *To Be a Slave,* by Julius Lester (Dial Books); *When Shlemiel Went to Warsaw and Other Stories,* by Isaac Bashevis Singer (Farrar, Straus & Giroux)

1970

Sounder, by William H. Armstrong (HarperCollins)

HONOR BOOKS: *Our Eddie,* by Sulamith Ish-Kishor (Pantheon); *The Many Ways of Seeing: An Introduction to the Pleasures of Art,* by Janet Gaylord Moore (World); *Journey Outside,* by Mary Q. Steele (Viking)

1971

Summer of the Swans, by Betsy Byars (Viking)

HONOR BOOKS: *Kneeknock Rise,* by Natalie Babbitt (Farrar, Straus & Giroux); *Enchantress from the Stars,* by Sylvia Louise Engdahl (Atheneum); *Sing Down the Moon,* by Scott O'Dell (Houghton Mifflin)

1972

Mrs. Frisby and the Rats of NIMH, by Robert C. O'Brien (Atheneum)

HONOR BOOKS: *Incident at Hawk's Hill,* by Allan W. Eckert (Little, Brown); *The Planet of Junior Brown,* by Virginia Hamilton (Macmillan); *The Tombs of Atuan,* by Ursula Le Guin (Atheneum); *Annie and the Old One,* by Miska Miles (Little, Brown); *The Headless Cupid,* by Zilpha Keatley Snyder (Atheneum)

1973

Julie of the Wolves, by Jean Craighead George (HarperCollins)

HONOR BOOKS: *Frog and Toad Together,* by Arnold Lobel (Harper Collins); *The Upstairs Room,* by Johanna Reiss (Harper-Collins); *The Witches of Worm,* by Zilpha Keatley Snyder (Atheneum)

1974

The Slave Dancer, by Paula Fox (Bradbury)

HONOR BOOK: *The Dark Is Rising,* by Susan Cooper (McElderry)

1975

M. C. Higgins, the Great, by Virginia Hamilton (Macmillan)

HONOR BOOKS: *Figgs and Phantoms,* by Ellen Raskin (Dutton); *My Brother Sam Is Dead,* by James Lincoln and Christopher Collier (Four Winds); *The Perilous Guard,* by Elizabeth Marie Pope (Houghton Mifflin); *Philip Hall Likes Me. I Reckon Maybe,* by Bette Greene (Dial Books)

1976

The Grey King, by Susan Cooper (McElderry)

HONOR BOOKS: *The Hundred Penny Box,* by Sharon Bell Mathis (Viking); *Dragonwings,* by Laurence Yep (HarperCollins)

1977

Roll of Thunder, Hear My Cry, by Mildred Taylor (Dial Books)

HONOR BOOKS: *Abel's Island,* by William Steig (Farrar, Straus & Giroux); *A String in the Harp,* by Nancy Bond (McElderry)

1978

Bridge to Terabithia, by Katherine Paterson (HarperCollins)

HONOR BOOKS: *Ramona and Her Father,* by Beverly Cleary (Morrow); *Anpao: An American Indian Odyssey,* by Jamake Highwater (HarperCollins)

1979

The Westing Game, by Ellen Raskin (Dutton)

HONOR BOOK: *The Great Gilly Hopkins,* by Katherine Paterson (HarperCollins)

1980

A Gathering of Days: A New England Girl's Journal, 1830-32, by Joan Blos (Scribner's)

HONOR BOOK: *The Road from Home: The Story of an Armenian Girl,* by David Kherdian (Greenwillow)

1981

Jacob Have I Loved, by Katherine Paterson (HarperCollins)

HONOR BOOKS: *The Fledgling,* by Jane Langton (HarperCollins); *A Ring of Endless Light,* by Madeleine L'Engle (Farrar, Straus & Giroux)

1982

A Visit to William Blake's Inn: Poems for Innocent and Experienced Travelers, by Nancy Willard (Harcourt)

HONOR BOOKS: *Ramona Quimby, Age 8,* by Beverly Cleary (Morrow); *Upon the Head of the Goat: A Childhood in Hungary, 1939-1944,* by Aranka Siegel (Farrar, Straus & Giroux)

1983

Dicey's Song, by Cynthia Voigt (Atheneum)

HONOR BOOKS: *The Blue Sword,* by Robin McKinley (Greenwillow); *Doctor De Soto,* by William Steig (Farrar, Straus & Giroux); *Graven Images,* by Paul Fleischman (Harper-Collins); *Homesick: My Own Story,* by Jean Fritz (Putnam); *Sweet Whispers, Brother Rush,* by Virginia Hamilton (Philomel)

1984

Dear Mr. Henshaw, by Beverly Cleary (Morrow)

HONOR BOOKS: *The Wish Giver: Three Tales of Coven Tree,* by Bill Brittain (HarperCollins); *A Solitary Blue,* by Cynthia Voigt (Atheneum); *The Sign of the Beaver,* by Elizabeth George Speare (Houghton Mifflin); *Sugaring Time,* by Kathryn Lasky (Macmillan)

1985

The Hero and the Crown, by Robin McKinley (Greenwillow)

HONOR BOOKS: *The Moves Make the Man,* by Bruce Brooks (HarperCollins); *One-Eyed Cat,* by Paula Fox (Bradbury); *Like Jake and Me,* by Mavis Jukes (Knopf)

1986

Sarah, Plain and Tall, by Patricia MacLachlan (HarperCollins)

HONOR BOOKS: *Commodore Perry in the Land of Shogun,* by Rhoda Blumberg (Lothrop, Lee & Shepard); *Dogsong,* by Gary Paulsen (Bradbury)

1987

The Whipping Boy, by Sid Fleischman (Greenwillow)

HONOR BOOKS: *On My Honor,* by Marion Dane Bauer (Clarion); *A Fine White Dust,* by Cynthia Rylant (Bradbury); *Volcano,* by Patricia Lauber (Bradbury)

1988

Lincoln: A Photobiography, by Russell Freedman (Clarion)

HONOR BOOKS: *Hatchet,* by Gary Paulsen (Bradbury); *After the Rain,* by Norma Fox Mazer (Morrow)

1989

Joyful Noise: Poems for Two Voices, by Paul Fleischman (HarperCollins)

HONOR BOOKS: *In the Beginning: Creation Stories from around the World,* by Virginia Hamilton (Harcourt); *Scorpions,* by Walter Dean Myers (HarperCollins)

1990

Number the Stars, by Lois Lowry (Houghton Mifflin)

HONOR BOOKS: *Afternoon of the Elves,* by Janet Taylor Lisle (Orchard Books); *Shabanu: Daughter of the Wind,* by Suzanne Fisher Staples (Knopf); *The Winter Room,* by Gary Paulsen (Orchard Books)

1991

Maniac Magee, by Jerry Spinelli (Little, Brown)

HONOR BOOK: *The True Confessions of Charlotte Doyle,* by Avi (Orchard Books)

1992

Shiloh, by Phyllis Reynolds Naylor (Atheneum)

HONOR BOOKS: *Nothing but the Truth,* by Avi (Orchard Books); *The Wright Brothers: How They Invented the Airplane,* by Russell Freedman (Holiday House)

1993

Missing May, by Cynthia Rylant (Orchard Books)

HONOR BOOKS: *What Hearts,* by Bruce Brooks (HarperCollins); *The Dark Thirty: Southern Tales of the Supernatural,* by Patricia McKissack (Knopf); *Somewhere in the Darkness,* by Walter Dean Myers (Scholastic)

1994

The Giver, by Lois Lowry (Houghton Mifflin)

HONOR BOOKS: *Crazy Lady!* by Jane Leslie Conly (Harper Collins); *Dragon's Gate,* by Laurence Yep (HarperCollins); *Eleanor Roosevelt: A Life of Discovery,* by Russell Freedman (Clarion)

1995

Walk Two Moons, by Sharon Creech (HarperCollins)

HONOR BOOKS: *Catherine, Called Birdy,* by Karen Cushman (Clarion); *The Ear, the Eye and the Arm,* by Nancy Farmer (Orchard Books)

1996

The Midwife's Apprentice, by Karen Cushman (Clarion)

HONOR BOOKS: *The Great Fire,* by Jim Murphy (Scholastic); *The Watsons Go to Birmingham—1963,* by Christopher Paul Curtis (Delacorte Press); *What Jamie Saw,* by Carolyn Coman (Front Street); *Yolanda's Genius,* by Carol Fenner (McElderry)

1997

The View from Saturday, by E. L. Konigsburg (Atheneum)

HONOR BOOKS: *A Girl Named Disaster,* by Nancy Farmer (Orchard Books); *The Moorchild,* by Eloise McGraw (McElderry); *The Thief,* by Megan Whalen Turner (Greenwillow); *Belle Prater's Boy,* by Ruth White (Farrar, Straus & Giroux)

1998

Out of the Dust, by Karen Hesse (Scholastic)

HONOR BOOKS: *Lilly's Crossing,* by Patricia Reilly Giff (Delacorte Press); *Ella Enchanted,* by Gail Carson Levine (HarperCollins); *Wringer,* by Jerry Spinelli (HarperCollins)

1999

Holes, by Louis Sachar (Farrar, Straus & Giroux)

HONOR BOOK: *A Long Way from Chicago,* by Richard Peck (Dial Books)

2000

Bud, Not Buddy, by Christopher Paul Curtis (Delacorte Press)

HONOR BOOKS: *Getting Near to Baby,* by Audrey Coloumbis (Delacorte Press); *26 Fairmount Avenue,* by Tomie dePaola (Putnam); *Our Only May Amelia,* by Jennifer L. Holm (HarperCollins)

2001

A Year Down Yonder, by Richard Peck (Dial Books)

HONOR BOOKS: *Hope Was Here,* by Joan Bauer (Putnam); *The Wanderer,* by Sharon Creech (HarperCollins); *Because of Winn-Dixie,* by Kate DiCamillo (Candlewick Press); *Joey Pigza Loses Control,* by Jack Gantos (Farrar, Straus & Giroux)

2002

A Single Shard, by Linda Sue Park (Clarion)

HONOR BOOKS: *Everything on a Waffle,* by Polly Horvath (Farrar Straus & Giroux); *Carver: A Life in Poems,* by Marilyn Nelson (Front Street)

2003

Crispin: The Cross of Lead, by Avi (Hyperion)

HONOR BOOKS: *House of the Scorpion,* by Nancy Farmer (Atheneum); *Pictures of Hollis Woods,* by Patricia Reilly Giff (Lamb Books); *Hoot,* by Carl Hiaasen (Knopf); *A Corner of the Universe,* by Ann Martin (Scholastic); *Surviving the Applewhites,* by Stephanie Tolan (HarperCollins)

2004

The Tale of Despereaux: Being the Story of a Mouse, a Princess, Some Soup, and a Spool of Thread, by Kate DiCamillo (Candlewick Press)

HONOR BOOKS: *Olive's Ocean,* by Kevin Henkes (Greenwillow); *An American Plague: The True and Terrifying Story of the Yellow Fever Epidemic of 1793,* by Jim Murphy (Clarion)

2005

Kira-Kira, by Cynthia Kadohata (Atheneum)

HONOR BOOKS: *Lizzie Bright and the Buckminster Boy,* by Gary Schmidt (Clarion); *Al Capone Does My Shirts,* by Gennifer Choldenko (Putnam); *The Voice That Challenged a Nation: Marian Anderson and the Struggle for Equal Rights,* by Russell Freedman (Clarion)

• • • The Randolph Caldecott • • • Medal and Honor Books

The Randolph Caldecott Medal, established in 1938 and named for a 19th-century British illustrator of books for children, is given annually to the illustrator of the most distinguished picture book for children published in the United States in the preceding year. This award is administered by the Association for Library Service to Children, a division of the American Library Association.

1938

Animals of the Bible, by Helen Dean Fish, illus. by Dorothy P. Lathrop (Lippincott)

HONOR BOOKS: *Seven Simeons,* by Boris Artzybasheff (Viking); *Four and Twenty Blackbirds,* by Helen Dean Fish, illus. by Robert Lawson (Stokes)

1939

Mei Li, by Thomas Handforth (Doubleday)

HONOR BOOKS: *The Forest Pool,* by Laura Adams Armer (Longman); *Wee Gillis,* by Munro Leaf, illus. by Robert Lawson (Viking); *Snow White and the Seven Dwarfs,* by Wanda Gág (Coward-McCann); *Barkis,* by Clare Newberry (HarperCollins); *Andy and the Lion,* by James Daugherty (Viking)

1940

Abraham Lincoln, by Ingri and Edgar Parin D'Aulaire (Doubleday)

HONOR BOOKS: *Cock-a-Doodle Doo...,* by Berta and Elmer Hader (Macmillan); *Madeline,* by Ludwig Bemelmans (Viking); *The Ageless Story,* by Lauren Ford (Dodd, Mead)

1941

They Were Strong and Good, by Robert Lawson (Viking)

HONOR BOOK: *April's Kittens,* by Clare Newberry (HarperCollins)

1942

Make Way for Ducklings, by Robert McCloskey (Viking)

HONOR BOOKS: *An American ABC,* by Maud and Miska Petersham (Macmillan); *In My Mother's House,* by Ann Nolan Clark, illus. by Velino Gerrera (Viking); *Paddle-to-the-Sea,* by Holling C. Holling (Houghton Mifflin); *Nothing at All,* by Wanda Gág (Coward-McCann)

1943

The Little House, by Virginia Lee Burton (Houghton Mifflin)

HONOR BOOKS: *Dash and Dart,* by Mary and Conrad Buff (Viking); *Marshmallow,* by Clare Newberry (HarperCollins)

1944

Many Moons, by James Thurber, illus. by Louis Slobodkin (Harcourt)

HONOR BOOKS: *Small Rain: Verses from the Bible* selected by Jessie Orton Jones, illus. by Elizabeth Orton Jones (Viking); *Pierre Pigeon,* by Lee Kingman, illus. by Arnold E. Bare (Houghton Mifflin); *The Mighty Hunter,* by Berta and Elmer Hader (Macmillan); *A Child's Good Night Book,* by Margaret Wise Brown, illus. by Jean Charlot (Scott); *Good Luck Horse,* by Chih-Yi Chan, illus. by Plao Chan (Whittlesey)

1945

Prayer for a Child, by Rachel Field, illus. by Elizabeth Orton Jones (Macmillan)

HONOR BOOKS: *Mother Goose,* illus. by Tasha Tudor (Walck); *In the Forest,* by Marie Hall Ets (Viking); *Yonie Wondernose,* by Marguerite de Angeli (Doubleday); *The Christmas Anna Angel,* by Ruth Sawyer, illus. by Kate Seredy (Viking)

1946

The Rooster Crows, illus. by Maud and Miska Petersham (Macmillan)

HONOR BOOKS: *Little Lost Lamb,* by Golden MacDonald, illus. by Leonard Weisgard (Doubleday); *Sing Mother Goose,* by Opal Wheeler, illus. by Marjorie Torrey (Dutton); *My Mother Is the Most Beautiful Woman in the World,* by Becky Reyher, illus. by Ruth Gannett (Lothrop, Lee & Shepard); *You Can Write Chinese,* by Kurt Weise (Viking)

1947

The Little Island, by Golden MacDonald, illus. by Leonard Weisgard (Doubleday)

HONOR BOOKS: *Rain Drop Splash,* by Alvin Tresselt, illus. by Leonard Weisgard (Lothrop, Lee & Shepard); *Boats on the River,* by Marjorie Flack, illus. by Jay Hyde Barnum (Viking); *Timothy Turtle,* by Al Graham, illus. by Tony Palazzo (Viking); *Pedro, the Angel of Olvera Street,* by Leo Politi (Scribner's); *Sing in Praise: A Collection of the Best Loved Hymns,* by Opal Wheeler, illus. by Marjorie Torrey (Dutton)

1948

White Snow, Bright Snow, by Alvin Tresselt, illus. by Roger Duvoisin (Lothrop, Lee & Shepard)

HONOR BOOKS: *Stone Soup,* by Marcia Brown (Scribner's); *McElligot's Pool,* by Dr. Seuss (Random House); *Bambino the Clown,* by George Schreiber (Viking); *Roger and the Fox,* by Lavinia Davis, illus. by Hildegard Woodward (Doubleday); *Song of Robin Hood,* ed. by Anne Malcolmson, illus. by Virginia Lee Burton (Houghton Mifflin)

1949

The Big Snow, by Berta and Elmer Hader (Macmillan)

HONOR BOOKS: *Blueberries for Sal,* by Robert McCloskey (Viking); *All Around the Town,* by Phyllis McGinley, illus. by Helen Stone (Lippincott); *Juanita,* by Leo Politi (Scribner's); *Fish in the Air,* by Kurt Wiese (Viking)

1950

Song of the Swallows, by Leo Politi (Scribner's)

HONOR BOOKS: *America's Ethan Allen,* by Stewart Holbrook, illus. by Lynd Ward (Houghton Mifflin); *The Wild Birthday Cake,* by Lavinia Davis, illus. by Hildegard Woodward (Doubleday); *The Happy Day,* by Ruth Krauss, illus. by Marc Simont (HarperCollins); *Bartholomew and the Oobleck,* by Dr. Seuss (Random House); *Henry Fisherman,* by Marcia Brown (Scribner's)

1951

The Egg Tree, by Katherine Milhous (Scribner's)

HONOR BOOKS: *Dick Whittington and His Cat,* by Marcia Brown (Scribner's); *The Two Reds,* by William Lipkind, illus. by Nicholas Mordvinoff (Harcourt); *If I Ran the Zoo,* by Dr. Seuss (Random House); *The Most Wonderful Doll in the World,* by Phyllis McGinley, illus. by Helen Stone (Lippincott); *T-Bone, the Baby Sitter,* by Clare Newberry (HarperCollins)

1952

Finders Keepers, by William Lipkind, illus. by Nicholas Mordvinoff (Harcourt)

HONOR BOOKS: *Mr. T. W. Anthony Woo,* by Marie Hall Ets (Viking); *Skipper John's Cook,* by Marcia Brown (Scribner's); *All Falling Down,* by Gene Zion, illus. by Margaret Bloy Graham (HarperCollins); *Bear Party,* by William Pène du Bois (Viking); *Feather Mountain,* by Elizabeth Olds (Houghton Mifflin)

1953

The Biggest Bear, by Lynd Ward (Houghton Mifflin)

HONOR BOOKS: *Puss in Boots,* by Charles Perrault, illus. and trans. by Marcia Brown (Scribner's); *One Morning in Maine,* by Robert McCloskey (Viking); *Ape in a Cape,* by Fritz Eichenberg (Harcourt); *The Storm Book,* by Charlotte Zolotow, illus. by Margaret Bloy Graham (HarperCollins); *Five Little Monkeys,* by Juliet Kepes (Houghton Mifflin)

1954

Madeline's Rescue, by Ludwig Bemelmans (Viking)

HONOR BOOKS: *Journey Cake, Ho!* by Ruth Sawyer, illus. by Robert McCloskey (Viking); *When Will the World Be Mine?* by Miriam Schlein, illus. by Jean Charlot (Scott); *The Steadfast Tin Soldier,* by Hans Christian Andersen, illus. by Marcia Brown (Scribner's); *A Very Special House,* by Ruth Krauss, illus. by Maurice Sendak (HarperCollins); *Green Eyes,* by A. Birnbaum (Capitol)

1955

Cinderella, or the Little Glass Slipper, by Charles Perrault, trans. and illus. by Marcia Brown (Scribner's)

HONOR BOOKS: *Books of Nursery and Mother Goose Rhymes,* illus. by Marguerite de Angeli (Doubleday); *Wheel on the Chimney,* by Margaret Wise Brown, illus. by Tibor Gergely (Lippincott); *The Thanksgiving Story,* by Alice Dalgliesh, illus. by Helen Sewell (Scribner's)

1956

Frog Went A-Courtin', ed. by John Langstaff, illus. by Feodor Rojankovsky (Harcourt)

HONOR BOOKS: *Play with Me,* by Marie Hall Ets (Viking); *Crow Boy,* by Taro Tashima (Viking)

1957

A Tree Is Nice, by Janice May Udry, illus. by Marc Simont (HarperCollins)

HONOR BOOKS: *Mr. Penny's Race Horse,* by Marie Hall Ets (Viking); *1 Is One,* by Tasha Tudor (Walck); *Anatole,* by Eve Titus, illus. by Paul Galdone (McGraw-Hill); *Gillespie and the Guards,* by Benjamin Elkin, illus. by James Daugherty (Viking); *Lion,* by William Pène du Bois (Viking)

1958

Time of Wonder, by Robert McCloskey (Viking)

HONOR BOOKS: *Fly High, Fly Low,* by Don Freeman (Viking); *Anatole and the Cat,* by Eve Titus, illus. by Paul Galdone (McGraw-Hill)

1959

Chanticleer and the Fox, adapted from Chaucer and illus. by Barbara Cooney (Crowell)

HONOR BOOKS: *The House That Jack Built,* by Antonio Frasconi (Harcourt); *What Do You Say, Dear?* by Sesyle Joslin, illus. by Maurice Sendak (Scott); *Umbrella,* by Taro Yashima (Viking)

1960

Nine Days to Christmas, by Marie Hall Ets and Aurora Labastida, illus. by Marie Hall Ets (Viking)

HONOR BOOKS: *Houses from the Sea,* by Alice E. Goudey, illus. by Adrienne Adams (Scribner's); *The Moon Jumpers,* by Janice May Udry, illus. by Maurice Sendak (HarperCollins)

1961

Baboushka and the Three Kings, by Ruth Robbins, illus. by Nicolas Sidjakov (Parnassus)

HONOR BOOK: *Inch by Inch,* by Leo Lionni (Obolensky)

1962

Once a Mouse . . ., by Marcia Brown (Scribner's)

HONOR BOOKS: *The Fox Went Out on a Chilly Night,* by Peter Spier (Doubleday); *Little Bear's Visit,* by Else Holmelund Minarik, illus. by Maurice Sendak (HarperCollins); *The Day We Saw the Sun Come Up,* by Alice E. Goudey, illus. by Adrienne Adams (Scribner's)

1963

The Snowy Day, by Ezra Jack Keats (Viking)

HONOR BOOKS: *The Sun Is a Golden Earring,* by Natalie M. Belting, illus. by Bernarda Bryson (Holt); *Mr. Rabbit and the Lovely Present,* by Charlotte Zolotow, illus. by Maurice Sendak (Harper)

1964

Where the Wild Things Are, by Maurice Sendak (Harper)

HONOR BOOKS: *Swimmy,* by Leo Lionni (Pantheon); *All in the Morning Early,* by Sorche Nic Leodhas, illus. by Evaline Ness (Holt); *Mother Goose and Nursery Rhymes,* illus. by Philip Reed (Atheneum)

1965

May I Bring a Friend? by Beatrice Schenk de Regniers, illus. by Beni Montresor (Atheneum)

HONOR BOOKS: *Rain Makes Applesauce,* by Julian Scheer, illus. by Marvin Bileck (Holiday); *The Wave,* by Margaret Hodges, illus. by Blair Lent (Houghton); *A Pocketful of Cricket,* by Rebecca Caudill, illus. by Evaline Ness (Holt)

1966

Always Room for One More, by Sorche Nic Leodhas, illus. by Nonny Hogrogian (Holt)

HONOR BOOKS: *Hide and Seek Fog,* by Alvin Tresselt, illus. by Roger Duvoisin (Lothrop); *Just Me,* by Marie Hall Ets, Viking; *Tom Tit Tot,* by Evaline Ness (Scribner's)

1967

Sam, Bangs and Moonshine, by Evaline Ness (Holt)

HONOR BOOK: *One Wide River to Cross,* by Barbara Emberley, illus. by Ed Emberley (Prentice)

1968

Drummer Hoff, by Barbara Emberley, illus. by Ed Emberley (Prentice)

HONOR BOOKS: *Frederick,* by Leo Lionni (Pantheon); *Seashore Story,* by Taro Yashima (Viking); *The Emperor and the Kite,* by Jane Yolen, illus. by Ed Young (World)

1969

The Fool of the World and the Flying Ship, by Arthur Ransome, illus. by Uri Shulevitz (Farrar, Straus and Giroux)

HONOR BOOK: *Why the Sun and the Moon Live in the Sky,* by Elphinstone Dayrell, illus. by Blair Lent (Houghton)

1970

Sylvester and the Magic Pebble, by William Steig (Windmill)

HONOR BOOKS: *Goggles!* by Ezra Jack Keats (Macmillan); *Alexander and the Wind-Up Mouse,* by Leo Lionni (Pantheon); *Pop Corn and Ma Goodness,* by Edna Mitchell Preston, illus. by Robert Andrew Parker (Viking); *Thy Friend, Obadiah,* by Brinton Turkle (Viking); *The Judge,* by Harve Zemach, illus. by Margot Zemach (Farrar, Straus and Giroux)

1971

A Story—A Story, by Gail E. Haley (Atheneum)

HONOR BOOKS: *The Angry Moon,* by William Sleator, illus. by Blair Lent (Atlantic/Little); *Frog and Toad Are Friends,* by Arnold Lobel (Harper); *In the Night Kitchen,* by Maurice Sendak (Harper)

1972

One Fine Day, by Nonny Hogrogian (Macmillan)

HONOR BOOKS: *If All the Seas Were One Sea,* by Janina Domanska (Macmillan); *Moja Means One: Swahili Counting Book,* by Muriel Feelings, illus. by Tom Feelings (Dial); *Hildidid's Night,* by Cheli Duran Ryan, illus. by Arnold Lobel (Macmillan)

1973

The Funny Little Woman, retold by Arlene Mosel, illus. by Blair Lent (Dutton)

HONOR BOOKS: *Anansi the Spider,* adapted and illus. by Gerald McDermott (Holt); *Hosie's Alphabet,* by Hosea, Tobias, and Lisa Baskin, illus. by Leonard Baskin (Viking); *Snow-White and the Seven Dwarfs,* tr. by Randall Jarrell, illus. by Nancy Ekholm Burkert (Farrar, Straus and Giroux); *When Clay Sings,* by Byrd Baylor, illus. by Tom Bahti (Scribner's)

1974

Duffy and the Devil, by Harve Zemach, illus. by Margot Zemach (Farrar, Straus and Giroux)

HONOR BOOKS: *Three Jovial Huntsmen,* by Susan Jeffers (Bradbury); *Cathedral: The Story of Its Construction,* by David Macaulay (Houghton)

1975

Arrow to the Sun, adapted and illus. by Gerald McDermott (Viking)

HONOR BOOK: *Jambo Means Hello,* by Muriel Feelings, illus. by Tom Feelings (Dial)

1976

Why Mosquitoes Buzz in People's Ears, retold by Verna Aardema, illus. by Leo and Diane Dillon (Dial Books)

HONOR BOOKS: *The Desert Is Theirs,* by Byrd Baylor, illus. by Peter Parnall (Scribner's); *Strega Nona,* retold and illus. by Tomie dePaola (Prentice Hall)

1977

Ashanti to Zulu: African Traditions, by Margaret Musgrove, illus. by Leo and Diane Dillon (Dial Books)

HONOR BOOKS: *The Amazing Bone,* by William Steig (Farrar, Straus & Giroux); *The Contest,* retold and illus. by Nonny Hogrogian (Greenwillow); *Fish for Supper,* by M. B. Goffstein (Dial Books); *The Golem,* by Beverly Brodsky McDermott (Lippincott); *Hawk, I'm Your Brother,* by Byrd Baylor, illus. by Peter Parnall (Scribner's)

1978

Noah's Ark, illus. by Peter Spier (Doubleday)

HONOR BOOKS: *Castle,* by David Macaulay (Houghton Mifflin); *It Could Always Be Worse,* retold and illus. by Margot Zemach (Farrar, Straus & Giroux)

1979

The Girl Who Loved Wild Horses, by Paul Goble (Bradbury)

HONOR BOOKS: *Freight Train,* by Donald Crews (Greenwillow); *The Way to Start a Day,* by Byrd Baylor, illus. by Peter Parnall (Scribner's)

1980

Ox-Cart Man, by Donald Hall, illus. by Barbara Cooney (Viking)

HONOR BOOKS: *Ben's Trumpet,* by Rachel Isadora (Greenwillow); *The Garden of Abdul Gasazi,* by Chris Van Allsburg (Houghton Mifflin)

1981

Fables, by Arnold Lobel (HarperCollins)

HONOR BOOKS: *The Bremen-Town Musicians,* by Ilse Plume (Doubleday); *The Grey Lady and the Strawberry Snatcher,* by Molly Bang (Four Winds); *Mice Twice,* by Joseph Low (McElderry); *Truck,* by Donald Crews (Greenwillow)

1982

Jumanji, by Chris Van Allsburg (Houghton Mifflin)

HONOR BOOKS: *Where the Buffaloes Begin,* by Olaf Baker, illus. by Stephan Gammell (Warne); *On Market Street,* by Arnold Lobel, illus. by Anita Lobel (Greenwillow); *Outside over There,* by Maurice Sendak (HarperCollins); *A Visit to William Blake's Inn,* by Nancy Willard, illus. by Alice and Martin Provensen (Harcourt)

1983

Shadow, by Blaise Cendrars, trans. and illus. by Marcia Brown (Scribner's)

HONOR BOOKS: *When I Was Young in the Mountains,* by Cynthia Rylant, illus. by Diane Goode (Dutton); *A Chair for My Mother,* by Vera B. Williams (Greenwillow)

1984

The Glorious Flight: Across the Channel with Louis Blériot, by Alice and Martin Provensen (Viking)

HONOR BOOKS: *Ten, Nine, Eight,* by Molly Bang (Greenwillow); *Little Red Riding Hood,* retold and illus. by Trina Schart Hyman (Holiday House)

1985

St. George and the Dragon, retold by Margaret Hodges, illus. by Trina Schart Hyman (Little, Brown)

HONOR BOOKS: *Hansel and Gretel,* retold by Rika Lesser, illus. by Paul O. Zelinsky (Dodd, Mead); *Have You Seen My Duckling?* by Nancy Tafuri (Greenwillow); *The Story of Jumping Mouse,* by John Steptoe (Lothrop, Lee & Shepard)

1986

The Polar Express, by Chris Van Allsburg (Houghton Mifflin)

HONOR BOOKS: *The Relatives Came,* by Cynthia Rylant, illus. by Stephen Gammell (Bradbury); *King Bidgood's in the Bathtub,* by Audrey Wood, illus. by Don Wood (Harcourt)

1987

Hey, Al, by Arthur Yorinks, illus. by Richard Egielski (Farrar, Straus & Giroux)

HONOR BOOKS: *The Village of Round and Square Houses,* by Ann Grifalconi (Little, Brown); *Alphabetics,* by Suse MacDonald (Bradbury); *Rumplestiltskin,* adapted and illus. by Paul O. Zelinsky (Dutton)

1988

Owl Moon, by Jane Yolen, illus. by John Schoenherr (Philomel)

HONOR BOOK: *Mufaro's Beautiful Daughters: An African Tale,* adapted and illus. by John Steptoe (Lothrop, Lee & Shepard)

1989

Song and Dance Man, by Karen Ackerman, illus. by Stephen Gammell (Knopf)

HONOR BOOKS: *The Boy of the Three Year Nap,* by Allen Say (Houghton Mifflin); *Free Fall,* by David Wiesner (Lothrop, Lee & Shepard); *Goldilocks and the Three Bears,* adapted and illus. by James Marshall (Dial Books); *Mirandy and Brother Wind,* by Patricia McKissack, illus. by Jerry Pinkney (Knopf)

1990

Lon Po Po: A Red Riding Hood Story from China, adapted and illus. by Ed Young (Philomel)

HONOR BOOKS: *Bill Peet: An Autobiography,* by Bill Peet (Houghton Mifflin); *Color Zoo,* by Lois Ehlert (Lippincott); *Hershel and the Hanukkah Goblins,* by Eric Kimmel, illus. by Trina Schart Hyman (Holiday House); *The Talking Eggs,* by Robert D. San Souci, illus. by Jerry Pinkney (Dial Books)

1991

Black and White, by David Macaulay (Houghton Mifflin)

HONOR BOOKS: *"More More More," Said the Baby: 3 Love Stories,* by Vera B. Williams (Greenwillow); *Puss in Boots,* by Charles Perrault, trans. by Malcolm Arthur, illus. by Fred Marcellino (Farrar, Straus & Giroux)

1992

Tuesday, by David Wiesner (Clarion)

HONOR BOOK: *Tar Beach,* by Faith Ringgold (Crown)

1993

Mirette on the High Wire, by Emily Arnold McCully (Putnam)

HONOR BOOKS: *The Stinky Cheese Man,* by Jon Scieszka and Lane Smith (Viking); *Working Cotton,* by Sherley Anne Williams, illus. by Carole Byard (Harcourt); *Seven Blind Mice,* by Ed Young (Philomel)

1994

Grandfather's Journey, by Allen Say (Houghton Mifflin)

HONOR BOOKS: *In the Small, Small Pond,* by Denise Fleming (Henry Holt); *Owen,* by Kevin Henkes (Greenwillow); *Peppe the Lamplighter,* by Elisa Bartone, illus. by Ted Lewin (Lothrop, Lee & Shepard); *Raven: A Trickster Tale from the Pacific Northwest,* by Gerald McDermott (Harcourt); *Yo! Yes?* by Chris Raschka (Orchard Books)

1995

Smoky Night, by Eve Bunting, illus. by David Diaz (Harcourt)

HONOR BOOKS: *John Henry,* by Julius Lester, illus. by Jerry Pinkney (Dial Books); *Swamp Angel,* by Anne Isaacs, illus. by Paul O. Zelinsky (Dutton); *Time Flies,* by Eric Rohmann (Crown)

1996

Officer Buckle and Gloria, by Peggy Rathmann (Putnam)

HONOR BOOKS: *Alphabet City,* by Stephen Johnson (Viking); *The Faithful Friend,* by Robert D. San Souci, illus. by Brian Pinkney (Simon & Schuster); *Tops and Bottoms,* by Janet Stevens (Harcourt); *Zin! Zin! Zin! a Violin,* by Lloyd Moss, illus. by Marjorie Priceman (Simon & Schuster)

1997

Golem, by David Wisniewski (Clarion)

HONOR BOOKS: *Hush! A Thai Lullaby,* by Minfong Ho, illus. by Holly Meade (Orchard Books); *The Graphic Alphabet,* by David Pelletier (Orchard Books); *The Paperboy,* by Dav Pilkey (Orchard Books); *Starry Messenger,* by Peter Sis (Farrar, Straus & Giroux)

1998

Rapunzel, by Paul O. Zelinsky (Dutton)

HONOR BOOKS: *Harlem,* by Walter Dean Myers, illus. by Christopher Myers (Scholastic); *The Gardener,* by Sarah Stewart, illus. by David Small (Farrar, Straus & Giroux); *There Was an Old Lady Who Swallowed a Fly,* by Simms Taback (Viking)

1999

Snowflake Bentley, by Jacqueline Briggs Martin, illus. by Mary Azarian (Houghton Mifflin)

HONOR BOOKS: *Duke Ellington,* by Andrea Davis Pinkney, illus. by Brian Pinkney (Hyperion); *No, David!* by David Shannon (Blue Sky Press); *Snow,* by Uri Shulevitz (Farrar, Straus & Giroux); *Tibet: Through the Red Box,* by Peter Sis (Farrar, Straus & Giroux)

2000

Joseph Had a Little Overcoat, by Simms Taback (Viking)

HONOR BOOKS: *The Ugly Duckling,* by Hans Christian Andersen, illus. by Jerry Pinkney (Morrow); *A Child's Calendar,* by John Updike, illus. by Trina Schart Hyman (Holiday House); *Sector 7,* by David Wiesner (Clarion); *When Sophie Gets Angry—Really, Really Angry . . . ,* by Molly Bang (Blue Sky Press)

2001

So You Want to Be President? by Judith St. George, illus. by David Small (Philomel)

HONOR BOOKS: *Casey at the Bat: A Ballad of the Republic Sung in the Year 1888,* by Ernest Lawrence Thayer, illus. by Christopher Bing (Handprint Books); *Click, Clack, Moo: Cows That Type,* by Doreen Cronin, illus. by Betsy Lewin (Simon & Schuster); *Olivia,* by Ian Falconer (Atheneum)

2002

The Three Pigs, by David Wiesner (Clarion)

HONOR BOOKS: *The Dinosaurs of Waterhouse Hawkins,* by Barbara Kerley, illus. by Brian Selznick (Scholastic); *Martin's Big Words: The Life of Dr. Martin Luther King, Jr.,* by Doreen Rappaport, illus. by Bryan Collier (Jump at the Sun); *The Stray Dog,* by Marc Simont (HarperCollins)

2003

My Friend Rabbit, by Eric Rohmann (Roaring Brook Press)

HONOR BOOKS: *The Spider and the Fly,* by Mary Howitt, illus. by Tony DiTerlizzi (Simon & Schuster); *Hondo & Fabian,* by Peter McCarty (Henry Holt); *Noah's Ark,* by Jerry Pinkney (SeaStar Books)

2004

The Man Who Walked between the Towers, by Mordicai Gerstein (Roaring Brook Press)

HONOR BOOKS: *Ella Sarah Gets Dressed,* by Margaret Chodos-Irvine (Harcourt); *What Do You Think with a Tail Like This?* by Steve Jenkins and Robin Page (Houghton Mifflin); *Don't Let the Pigeon Drive the Bus!* by Mo Willems (Hyperion)

2005

Kitten's First Full Moon, by Kevin Henkes (Greenwillow)

HONOR BOOKS: *The Red Book,* by Barbara Lehman (Houghton Mifflin); *Coming On Home Soon,* by Jacqueline Woodson, illus. by E. B. Lewis (Putnam); *Knuffle Bunny: A Cautionary Tale,* by Mo Willems (Hyperion)

• • • The Coretta Scott King • • • Awards and Honor Books

These awards, administered by the Social Responsibilities Round Table and the American Library Association, recognize an outstanding African American author and illustrator whose work commemorates and fosters the life, work, and dreams of Dr. Martin Luther King Jr. and honors the courage and determination of Coretta Scott King to continue to work for peace and world brotherhood. Prior to 1974, the Coretta Scott King Award was given to authors only.

1970

AUTHOR AWARD: *Martin Luther King, Jr.: Man of Peace,* by Lillie Patterson (Garrand)

1971

AUTHOR AWARD: *Black Troubador: Langston Hughes,* by Charlemae Rollins (Rand McNally)

1972

AUTHOR AWARD: *17 Black Artists,* by Elton C. Fax (Dodd, Mead)

1973

AUTHOR AWARD: *I Never Had It Made,* by Jackie Robinson as told to Alfred Duckett (Putnam)

1974

AUTHOR AND ILLUSTRATOR AWARDS: *Ray Charles,* by Sharon Bell Mathis, illus. by George Ford (Crowell)

1975

AUTHOR AWARD: *The Legend of Africania,* by Dorothy Robinson (Johnson)

ILLUSTRATOR AWARD: No award given

1976

AUTHOR AWARD: *Duey's Tale,* by Pearl Bailey (Harcourt)

ILLUSTRATOR AWARD: No award given

1977

AUTHOR AWARD: *The Story of Stevie Wonder,* by James Haskins (Lothrop, Lee & Shepard)

ILLUSTRATOR AWARD: No award given

1978

AUTHOR AWARD: *Africa Dream,* by Eloise Greenfield (Crowell)

AUTHOR HONOR BOOKS: *The Days When the Animals Talked: Black Folk Tales and How They Came to Be,* by William J. Faulkner (Follett); *Marvin and Tige,* by Frankcina Glass (St. Martin's Press); *Mary McCleod Bethune,* by Eloise Greenfield (Crowell); *Barbara Jordan,* by James Haskins (Dial Books); *Coretta Scott King,* by Lillie Patterson (Garrard); *Portia: The Life of Portia Washington Pittman, the Daughter of Booker T. Washington,* by Ruth Ann Steward (Doubleday)

ILLUSTRATOR AWARD: *Africa Dream,* illus. by Carole Byard, text by Eloise Greenfield (Crowell)

1979

AUTHOR AWARD: *Escape to Freedom,* by Ossie Davis (Viking)

AUTHOR HONOR BOOKS: *Benjamin Banneker,* by Lillie Patterson (Abingdon); *I Have a Sister—My Sister Is Deaf,* by Jeanne Whitehouse Peterson (HarperCollins); *Justice and Her Brothers,* by Virginia Hamilton (Greenwillow); *Skates of Uncle Richard,* by Carol Fenner (Random House)

ILLUSTRATOR AWARD: *Something on My Mind,* illus. by Tom Feelings, text by Nikki Grimes (Dial Books)

1980

AUTHOR AWARD: *The Young Landlords,* by Walter Dean Myers (Viking)

AUTHOR HONOR BOOKS: *Movin' Up,* by Berry Gordy (HarperCollins); *Childtimes: A Three-Generation Memoir,* by Eloise Greenfield and Lessie Jones Little (HarperCollins); *Andrew Young: Young Man with a Mission,* by James Haskins (Lothrop, Lee & Shepard); *James Van Der Zee: The Picture Takin' Man,* by James Haskins (Africa World Press); *Let the Lion Eat Straw,* by Ellease Southerland (Scribner's)

ILLUSTRATOR AWARD: *Cornrows,* illus. by Carole Byard, text by Camille Yarbrough (Coward-McCann)

1981

AUTHOR AWARD: *This Life,* by Sidney Poitier (Knopf)

AUTHOR HONOR BOOK: *Don't Explain: A Song of Billie Holiday,* by Alexis De Veaux (HarperCollins)

ILLUSTRATOR AWARD: *Beat the Story Drum, Pum-Pum,* by Ashley Bryan (Atheneum)

ILLUSTRATOR HONOR BOOKS: *Grandmama's Joy,* illus. by Carole Byard, text by Eloise Greenfield (Collins); *Count on Your Fingers African Style,* illus. by Jerry Pinkney, text by Claudia Zaslavsky (Crowell)

1982

AUTHOR AWARD: *Let the Circle Be Unbroken,* by Mildred Taylor (Dial Books)

AUTHOR HONOR BOOKS: *Rainbow Jordan,* by Alice Childress (Coward-McCann); *Lou in the Limelight,* by Kristin Hunter (Scribner's); *Mary: An Autobiography,* by Mary E. Mebane (Viking)

ILLUSTRATOR AWARD: *Mother Crocodile,* by John Steptoe (Delacorte Press)

ILLUSTRATOR HONOR BOOK: *Daydreamers,* illus. by Tom Feelings, text by Eloise Greenfield (Dial Books)

1983

AUTHOR AWARD: *Sweet Whispers, Brother Rush,* by Virginia Hamilton (Philomel)

AUTHOR HONOR BOOK: *This Strange New Feeling,* by Julius Lester (Dial Books)

ILLUSTRATOR AWARD: *Black Child,* by Peter Magubane (Knopf)

ILLUSTRATOR HONOR BOOKS: *All the Colors of the Race,* illus. by John Steptoe, text by Arnold Adoff (Lothrop, Lee & Shepard); *I'm Going to Sing: Black American Spirituals,* illus. by Ashley Bryan (Atheneum); *Just Us Women,* illus. by Pat Cummings, text by Jeanette Caines (HarperCollins)

1984

AUTHOR AWARD: *Everett Anderson's Goodbye,* by Lucille Clifton (Henry Holt)

SPECIAL CITATION: *The Words of Martin Luther King, Jr.,* compiled by Coretta Scott King (Newmarket Press)

AUTHOR HONOR BOOKS: *The Magical Adventures of Pretty Pearl,* by Virginia Hamilton (HarperCollins); *Lena Horne,* by James Haskins (Coward-McCann); *Bright Shadow,* by Joyce Carol Thomas (Avon); *Because We Are,* by Mildred Pitts Walter (Lothrop, Lee & Shepard)

ILLUSTRATOR AWARD: *My Mama Needs Me,* illus. by Pat Cummings, text by Mildred Pitts Walter (Lothrop, Lee & Shepard)

1985

AUTHOR AWARD: *Motown and Didi,* by Walter Dean Myers (Viking)

HONOR BOOKS: *Circle of Gold,* by Candy Dawson Boyd (Apple); *A Little Love,* by Virginia Hamilton (Philomel)

ILLUSTRATOR AWARD: No award given

1986

AUTHOR AWARD: *The People Could Fly: American Black Folktales,* by Virginia Hamilton (Knopf)

AUTHOR HONOR BOOKS: *Junius over Far,* by Virginia Hamilton (HarperCollins); *Trouble's Child,* by Mildred Pitts Walter (Lothrop, Lee & Shepard)

ILLUSTRATOR AWARD: *The Patchwork Quilt,* illus. by Jerry Pinkney, text by Valerie Flournoy (Dial Books)

ILLUSTRATOR HONOR BOOK: *The People Could Fly: American Black Folktales,* illus. by Leo and Diane Dillon, text by Virginia Hamilton (Knopf)

1987

AUTHOR AWARD: *Justin and the Best Biscuits in the World,* by Mildred Pitts Walter (Lothrop, Lee & Shepard)

AUTHOR HONOR BOOKS: *Lion and the Ostrich Chicks and Other African Folk Tales,* by Ashley Bryan (Atheneum); *Which Way Freedom,* by Joyce Hansen (Walker)

ILLUSTRATOR AWARD: *Half a Moon and One Whole Star,* illus. by Jerry Pinkney, text by Crescent Dragonwagon (Macmillan)

ILLUSTRATOR HONOR BOOKS: *Lion and the Ostrich Chicks and Other African Folk Tales,* by Ashley Bryan (Atheneum); *C.L.O.U.D.S.,* by Pat Cummings (Lothrop, Lee & Shepard)

1988

AUTHOR AWARD: *The Friendship,* by Mildred Taylor (Dial Books)

AUTHOR HONOR BOOKS: *An Enchanted Hair Tale,* by Alexis De Veaux (HarperCollins); *The Tales of Uncle Remus: The Adventures of Brer Rabbit,* by Julius Lester (Dial Books)

ILLUSTRATOR AWARD: *Mufaro's Beautiful Daughters: An African Tale,* by John Steptoe (Lothrop, Lee & Shepard)

ILLUSTRATOR HONOR BOOKS: *What a Morning! The Christmas Story in Black Spirituals,* illus. by Ashley Bryan, selected by John Langstaff (Macmillan); *The Invisible Hunters: A Legend from the Miskito Indians of Nicaragua,* illus. by Joe Sam, compiled by Harriet Rohmer, Octavio Chow, and Morris Vedaure (Children's Book Press)

1989

AUTHOR AWARD: *Fallen Angels,* by Walter Dean Myers (Scholastic)

AUTHOR HONOR BOOKS: *A Thief in the Village and Other Stories,* by James Berry (Orchard Books); *Anthony Burns: The Defeat and Triumph of a Fugitive Slave,* by Virginia Hamilton (Knopf)

ILLUSTRATOR AWARD: *Mirandy and Brother Wind,* illus. by Jerry Pinkney, text by Patricia McKissack (Knopf)

ILLUSTRATOR HONOR BOOKS: *Under the Sunday Tree,* illus. by Amos Ferguson, text by Eloise Greenfield (HarperCollins); *Storm in the Night,* illus. by Pat Cummings, text by Mary Stolz (HarperCollins)

1990

AUTHOR AWARD: *A Long Hard Journey: The Story of the Pullman Porter,* by Patricia and Fredrick McKissack (Walker)

AUTHOR HONOR BOOKS: *Nathaniel Talking,* by Eloise Greenfield, illus. by Jan Spivey Gilchrist (Black Butterfly); *The Bells of Christmas,* by Virginia Hamilton (Harcourt); *Martin Luther King, Jr., and the Freedom Movement,* by Lillie Patterson (Facts on File)

ILLUSTRATOR AWARD: *Nathaniel Talking,* illus. by Jan Gilchrist, text by Eloise Greenfield (Black Butterfly)

ILLUSTRATOR HONOR BOOKS: *The Talking Eggs,* illus. by Jerry Pinkney, text by Robert D. San Souci (Dial Books)

1991

AUTHOR AWARD: *The Road to Memphis,* by Mildred Taylor (Dial Books)

AUTHOR HONOR BOOKS: *Black Dance in America,* by James Haskins (Crowell); *When I Am Old with You,* by Angela Johnson (Orchard Books)

ILLUSTRATOR AWARD: *Aida,* illus. by Leo and Diane Dillon, told by Leontyne Price (Harcourt)

1992

AUTHOR AWARD: *Now Is Your Time! The African American Struggle for Freedom,* by Walter Dean Myers (HarperCollins)

AUTHOR HONOR BOOKS: *Night on Neighborhood Street,* by Eloise Greenfield, illus. by Jan Spivey Gilchrist (Dial Books)

ILLUSTRATOR AWARD: *Tar Beach,* by Faith Ringgold (Crown)

ILLUSTRATOR HONOR BOOKS: *All Night, All Day: A Child's First Book of African American Spirituals,* by Ashley Bryan (Atheneum); *Night on Neighborhood Street,* illus. by Jan Spivey Gilchrist, text by Eloise Greenfield (Dial Books)

1993

AUTHOR AWARD: *The Dark Thirty: Southern Tales of the Supernatural,* by Patricia McKissack (Knopf)

AUTHOR HONOR BOOKS: *Mississippi Challenge,* by Mildred Pitts Walter (Bradbury); *Sojourner Truth: Ain't I a Woman?* by Patricia and Fredrick McKissack (Scholastic); *Somewhere in the Darkness,* by Walter Dean Myers (Scholastic)

ILLUSTRATOR AWARD: *The Origin of Life on Earth: An African Creation Myth,* illus. by Kathleen Atkins Wilson, retold by David Anderson (Sights Productions)

ILLUSTRATOR HONOR BOOKS: *Little Eight John,* illus. by Wil Clay, text by Jan Wahl (Lodestar); *Sukey and the Mermaid,* illus. by Brian Pinkney, text by Robert D. San Souci (Four Winds); *Working Cotton,* illus. by Carole Byard, text by Sherley Anne Williams (Harcourt)

1994

AUTHOR AWARD: *Toning the Sweep,* by Angela Johnson (Orchard Books)

AUTHOR HONOR BOOKS: *Brown Honey in Broomwheat Tea,* by Joyce Carol Thomas, illus. by Floyd Cooper (HarperCollins); *Malcolm X: By Any Means Necessary,* by Walter Dean Myers (Scholastic); *Soul Looks Back in Wonder,* ed. by Phyllis Fogelman, illus. by Tom Feelings (Dial Books)

ILLUSTRATOR AWARD: *Soul Looks Back in Wonder,* illus. by Tom Feelings, ed. by Phyllis Fogelman (Dial Books)

ILLUSTRATOR HONOR BOOKS: *Brown Honey in Broomwheat Tea,* illus. by Floyd Cooper, by Joyce Carol Thomas (HarperCollins); *Uncle Jed's Barbershop,* illus. by James Ransome, text by Margaree King Mitchell (Simon & Schuster)

1995

AUTHOR AWARD: *Christmas in the Big House, Christmas in the Quarters,* by Patricia and Fredrick McKissack (Scholastic)

AUTHOR HONOR BOOKS: *The Captive,* by Joyce Hansen (Scholastic); *I Hadn't Meant to Tell You This,* by Jacqueline Woodson (Delacorte Press); *Black Diamond: Story of the Negro Baseball League,* by Patricia and Fredrick McKissack (Scholastic)

ILLUSTRATOR AWARD: *The Creation,* illus. by James Ransome, text by James Weldon Johnson (Holiday House)

ILLUSTRATOR HONOR BOOKS: *The Singing Man,* illus. by Terea Shaffer, text by Angela Shelf Medearis (Holiday House); *Meet Danitra Brown,* illus. by Floyd Cooper, text by Nikki Grimes (Lothrop, Lee & Shepard)

1996

AUTHOR AWARD: *Her Stories: African American Folktales, Fairy Tales, and True Tales,* by Virginia Hamilton, illus. by Leo and Diane Dillon (Blue Sky Press)

AUTHOR HONOR BOOKS: *The Watsons Go to Birmingham—1963,* by Christopher Paul Curtis (Delacorte Press); *Like Sisters on the Homefront,* by Rita Williams-Garcia (Delacorte Press); *From the Notebooks of Melanin Sun,* by Jacqueline Woodson (Scholastic)

ILLUSTRATOR AWARD: *The Middle Passage: White Ships/Black Cargo,* by Tom Feelings (Dial Books)

ILLUSTRATOR HONOR BOOKS: *Her Stories,* illus. by Leo and Diane Dillon, text by Virginia Hamilton (Blue Sky Press); *The Faithful Friend,* illus. by Brian Pinkney, text by Robert D. San Souci (Simon & Schuster)

1997

AUTHOR AWARD: *Slam,* by Walter Dean Myers (Scholastic)

AUTHOR HONOR BOOKS: *Rebels against Slavery: American Slave Revolts,* by Patricia and Fredrick McKissack (Scholastic)

ILLUSTRATOR AWARD: *Minty: A Story of Harriet Tubman,* illus. by Jerry Pinkney, text by Alan Schroeder (Dial Books)

ILLUSTRATOR HONOR BOOKS: *The Palm of My Heart: Poetry by African American Children,* illus. by Gregorie Christie, ed. by Davida Adedjouma (Lee & Low Books); *Running the Road to ABC,* illus. by Reynold Ruffins, text by Denize Lauture (Simon & Schuster); *Neeny Coming, Neeny Going,* illus. by Synthia Saint James, text by Karen English (Bridgewater Books)

1998

AUTHOR AWARD: *Forged by Fire,* by Sharon M. Draper (Atheneum)

AUTHOR HONOR BOOKS: *Bayard Rustin: Behind the Scenes of the Civil Rights Movement,* by James Haskins (Hyperion); *I Thought My Soul Would Rise and Fly: The Diary of Patsy, a Freed Girl,* by Joyce Hansen (Scholastic)

ILLUSTRATOR AWARD: *In Daddy's Arms I Am Tall: African Americans Celebrating Fathers,* illus. by Javaka Steptoe, text by Alan Schroeder (Lee & Low Books)

ILLUSTRATOR HONOR BOOKS: *Ashley Bryan's ABC of African American Poetry,* by Ashley Bryan (Atheneum); *Harlem,* illus. by Christopher Myers, text by Walter Dean Myers (Scholastic); *The Hunterman and the Crocodile,* by Baba Wague Diakite (Scholastic)

1999

AUTHOR AWARD: *Heaven,* by Angela Johnson (Simon & Schuster)

AUTHOR HONOR BOOKS: *Jazmin's Notebook,* by Nikki Grimes (Dial Books); *Breaking Ground, Breaking Silence: The Story of New York's African Burial Ground,* by Joyce Hansen and Gary McGowan (Henry Holt); *The Other Side: Shorter Poems,* by Angela Johnson (Orchard Books)

ILLUSTRATOR AWARD: *I See the Rhythm,* illus. by Michele Wood, text by Toyomi Igus (Children's Book Press)

ILLUSTRATOR HONOR BOOKS: *I Have Heard of a Land,* illus. by Floyd Cooper, text by Joyce Carol Thomas (HarperCollins); *The Bat Boy and His Violin,* illus. by E. B. Lewis, text by Gavin Curtis (Simon & Schuster); *Duke Ellington: The Piano Prince and His Orchestra,* illus. by Brian Pinkney, text by Andrea Davis Pinkney (Hyperion)

2000

AUTHOR AWARD: *Bud, Not Buddy,* by Christopher Paul Curtis (Delacorte Press)

AUTHOR HONOR BOOKS: *Francie,* by Karen English (Farrar, Straus & Giroux); *Black Hands, White Sails: The Story of African-American Whalers,* by Patricia and Fredrick McKissack (Scholastic); *Monster,* by Walter Dean Myers (HarperCollins)

ILLUSTRATOR AWARD: *In the Time of the Drums,* illus. by Brian Pinkney, text by Kim L. Siegelson (Jump at the Sun)

ILLUSTRATOR HONOR BOOKS: *My Rows and Piles of Coins,* illus. by E. B. Lewis, text by Tololwa M. Mollel (Clarion); *Black Cat,* by Christopher Myers (Scholastic)

2001

AUTHOR AWARD: *Miracle's Boys,* by Jacqueline Woodson (Putnam)

AUTHOR HONOR BOOKS: *Let It Shine! Stories of Black Women Freedom Fighters,* by Andrea Davis Pinkney, illus. by Stephen Alcorn (Harcourt)

ILLUSTRATOR AWARD: *Uptown,* by Bryan Collier (Henry Holt)

ILLUSTRATOR HONOR BOOKS: *Freedom River,* by Bryan Collier (Jump at the Sun); *Only Passing Through: The Story of Sojourner Truth,* illus. by R. Gregory Christie, text by Anne Rockwell (Random House); *Virgie Goes to School with Us Boys,* illus. by E. B. Lewis, text by Elizabeth Fitzgerald Howard (Simon & Schuster)

2002

AUTHOR AWARD: *The Land,* by Mildred Taylor (Fogelman Books)

AUTHOR HONOR BOOKS: *Money-Hungry,* by Sharon G. Flake (Jump at the Sun); *Carver: A Life in Poems,* by Marilyn Nelson (Front Street)

ILLUSTRATOR AWARD: *Goin' Someplace Special,* illus. by Jerry Pinkney, text by Patricia McKissack (Atheneum)

ILLUSTRATOR HONOR BOOKS: *Martin's Big Words,* illus. by Bryan Collier, text by Doreen Rappaport (Jump at the Sun)

2003

AUTHOR AWARD: *Bronx Masquerade,* by Nikki Grimes (Dial Books)

AUTHOR HONOR BOOKS: *The Red Rose Box,* by Brenda Woods (Putnam); *Talkin' about Bessie: The Story of Aviator Elizabeth Coleman,* by Nikki Grimes (Orchard Books)

ILLUSTRATOR AWARD: *Talkin' about Bessie: The Story of Aviator Elizabeth Coleman,* illus. by E. B. Lewis, text by Nikki Grimes (Orchard Books)

ILLUSTRATOR HONOR BOOKS: *Rap a Tap Tap: Here's Bojangles—Think of That,* illus. by Leo and Diane Dillon (Blue Sky Press); *Visiting Langston,* illus. by Bryan Collier (Henry Holt)

2004

AUTHOR AWARD: *The First Part Last,* by Angela Johnson (Simon & Schuster)

AUTHOR HONOR BOOKS: *Days of Jubilee: The End of Slavery in the United States,* by Patricia and Fredrick McKissack (Scholastic); *Locomotion,* by Jacqueline Woodson (Putnam); *The Battle of Jericho,* by Sharon M. Draper (Atheneum)

ILLUSTRATOR AWARD: *Beautiful Blackbird,* by Ashley Bryan (Atheneum)

ILLUSTRATOR HONOR BOOKS: *Almost to Freedom,* illus. by Colin Bootman, text by Vaunda Micheaux Nelson (Carolrhoda Books); *Thunder Rose,* illus. by Kadir Nelson, text by Jerdine Nolen (Silver Whistle)

2005

AUTHOR AWARD: *Remember: The Journey to Integration,* by Toni Morrison (Houghton Mifflin)

AUTHOR HONOR BOOKS: *The Legend of Buddy Bush,* by Sheila Moses (McElderry); *Who Am I without Him? Short Stories about Girls and the Boys in Their Lives,* by Sharon Flake (Hyperion); *Fortune's Bones: The Manumission Requiem,* by Marilyn Nelson (Front Street)

ILLUSTRATOR AWARD: *Ellington Was Not a Street,* illus. by Kadir Nelson, text by Ntozake Shange (Simon & Schuster)

ILLUSTRATOR HONOR BOOKS: *God Bless the Child,* illus. by Jerry Pinkney, text by Billie Holiday and Arthur Herzog Jr. (Amistad); *The People Could Fly: The Picture Book,* illus. by Leo and Diane Dillon, text by Virginia Hamilton (Knopf)

• • • The Pura Belpré Award • • •

The Pura Belpré Award, established in 1996, is presented biennially to a Latino/Latina writer and illustrator whose work best portrays, affirms, and celebrates the Latino cultural experience in an outstanding work of literature for children and youth. It is cosponsored by the Association for Library Service to Children, a division of the American Library Association, and the National Association to Promote Library Services to the Spanish Speaking, an ALA affiliate. the award is named in honor of Pura Belpré, the first Latina librarian in the New York Public Library. As children's librarian, storyteller, and author, she enriched the lives of Puerto Rican children in the United States through her pioneering work of preserving and disseminating Puerto Rican folklore.

1996

NARRATIVE WINNER: *An Island Like You: Stories of the Barrio,* by Judith Ortiz Cofer (Orchard Books, 1995)

HONOR BOOKS FOR NARRATIVE: *The Bossy Gallito/El Gallo de Bodas: A Traditional Cuban Folktale,* by Lucía González, illus. by Lulu Delacre (Scholastic, 1994); *Baseball in April and Other Stories,* by Gary Soto (Harcourt, 1994)

ILLUSTRATION WINNER: *Chato's Kitchen,* illus. by Susan Guevara, text by Gary Soto (Putnam, 1995)

HONOR BOOKS FOR ILLUSTRATION: *Pablo Remembers: The Fiesta of the Day of the Dead,* by George Ancona (Lothrop, Lee & Shepard, 1993) (also available in a Spanish-language edition: *Pablo Recuerda: La Fiesta de Día de los Muertos*); *The Bossy Gallito/El Gallo de Bodas: A Traditional Cuban Folktale,* illus. by Lulu Delacre, by Lucía González (Scholastic, 1994); *Family Pictures/Cuadros de Familia,* by Carmen Lomas Garza, Spanish text by Rosalma Zubizarreta (Children's Book Press, 1990)

1998

NARRATIVE WINNER: *Parrot in the Oven: Mi Vida,* by Victor Martinez (HarperCollins, 1996)

HONOR BOOKS FOR NARRATIVE: *Laughing Tomatoes and Other Spring Poems/Jitomates Risuenos y Otros Poemas de Primavera,* by Francisco X. Alarcón, illus. by Maya Christina Gonzalez (Children's Book Press, 1997); *Spirits of the High Mesa,* by Floyd Martinez (Arte Público Press, 1997)

ILLUSTRATION WINNER: *Snapshots from the Wedding,* illus. by Stephanie Garcia, text by Gary Soto (Putnam, 1997)

HONOR BOOKS FOR ILLUSTRATION: *In My Family/En Mi Familia,* by Carmen Lomas Garza (Children's Book Press, 1996); *The Golden Flower: A Taino Myth from Puerto Rico,* illus. by Enrique O. Sánchez, text by Nina Jaffe (Simon & Schuster, 1996); *Gathering the Sun: An Alphabet in Spanish and English,* illus. by Simon Silva, text by Alma Flor Ada, English trans. by Rosa Zubizarreta (Lothrop, Lee & Shepard, 1997)

2000

NARRATIVE WINNER: *Under the Royal Palms: A Childhood in Cuba,* by Alma Flor Ada (Atheneum, 1998)

HONOR BOOKS FOR NARRATIVE: *From the Bellybutton of the Moon and Other Summer Poems/Del Ombligo de la Luna y Otros Poemas de Verano,* by Francisco X. Alarcón, illus. by Maya Christina Gonzalez (Children's Book Press, 1998); *Laughing Out Loud, I Fly: Poems in English and Spanish,* by Juan Felipe Herrera, illus. by Karen Barbour (HarperCollins, 1998)

ILLUSTRATION WINNER: *Magic Windows,* by Carmen Lomas Garza (Children's Book Press, 1999)

HONOR BOOKS FOR ILLUSTRATION: *Barrio: Jose's Neighborhood,* by George Ancona (Harcourt, 1998); *The Secret Stars,* illus. by Felipe Dávalos, text by Joseph Slate (Cavendish, 1998); *Mama and Papa Have a Store,* by Amelia Lau Carling (Dial Books, 1998)

2002

NARRATIVE WINNER: *Esperanza Rising,* by Pam Muñoz Ryan (Scholastic, 2000)

HONOR BOOKS FOR NARRATIVE: *Breaking Through,* by Francisco Jiménez (Houghton Mifflin, 2001); *Iguanas in the Snow,* by Francisco X. Alarcón, illus. by Maya Christina Gonzalez (Children's Book Press, 2001)

ILLUSTRATION WINNER: *Chato and the Party Animals,* illus. by Susan Guevara, text by Gary Soto (Putnam, 2000)

HONOR BOOKS FOR ILLUSTRATION: *Juan Bobo Goes to Work,* illus. by Joe Cepeda, retold by Marisa Montes (HarperCollins, 2000)

2004

NARRATIVE WINNER: *Before We Were Free,* by Julia Alvarez (Knopf, 2002)

HONOR BOOKS FOR NARRATIVE: *Cuba 15,* by Nancy Osa (Delacorte Press, 2003); *My Diary from Here to There/Mi Diario de Aquí Hasta Allá,* by Amada Irma Pérez (Children's Book Press, 2002)

ILLUSTRATION WINNER: *Just a Minute: A Trickster Tale and Counting Book,* by Yuyi Morales (Chronicle Books, 2003)

HONOR BOOKS FOR ILLUSTRATION: *First Day in Grapes,* illus. by Robert Casilla, text by L. King Pérez (Lee & Low Books, 2002); *The Pot That Juan Built,* illus. by David Diaz, text by Nancy Andrews-Goebel (Lee & Low Books, 2002); *Harvesting Hope: The Story of Cesar Chavez,* illus. by Yuyi Morales, text by Kathleen Krull (Harcourt, 2003)

• • • The Robert F. Sibert Award • • •

The Robert F. Sibert Award, established in 2001, is sponsored by Bound to Stay Bound Books, Inc., in honor of its longtime president, Robert F. Sibert. It is administered by the Association of Library Service to Children, a division of the American Library Association, and seeks outstanding informational books written and illustrated to present, organize, and interpret verifiable, factual material for children.

2001

Sir Walter Raleigh and the Quest for El Dorado, by Marc Aronson (Clarion)

HONOR BOOKS: *The Longitude Prize,* by Joan Dash, illus. by Susan Petricic (Farrar, Straus & Giroux); *Blizzard,* by Jim Murphy (Scholastic); *My Season with Penguins: An Antarctic Journal,* by Sophie Webb (Houghton Mifflin); *Pedro and Me: Friendship, Loss, and What I Learned,* by Judd Winick (Henry Holt)

2002

Black Potatoes: The Story of the Great Irish Famine, 1845-1850, by Susan Campbell Bartoletti (Houghton Mifflin)

HONOR BOOKS: *Surviving Hitler: A Boy in the Nazi Death Camps,* by Andrea Warren (HarperCollins); *Vincent van Gogh,* by Jan Greenberg and Sandra Jordan (Delacorte Press); *Brooklyn Bridge,* by Lynn Curlee (Atheneum)

2003

The Life and Death of Adolf Hitler, by James Cross Giblin (Clarion)

HONOR BOOKS: *Six Days in October: The Stock Market Crash of 1929,* by Karen Blumenthal (Atheneum); *Hole in My Life,* by Jack Gantos (Farrar, Straus & Giroux); *Action Jackson,* by Jan Greenberg and Sandra Jordan, illus. by Robert Andrew Parker (Roaring Brook Press); *When Marian Sang,* by Pam Muñoz Ryan, illus. by Brian Selznick (Scholastic)

2004

An American Plague: The True and Terrifying Story of the Yellow Fever Epidemic of 1793, by Jim Murphy (Clarion)

HONOR BOOKS: *I Face the Wind,* by Vicki Cobb, illus. by Julia Gorton (HarperCollins)

2005

The Voice That Challenged a Nation: Marian Anderson and the Struggle for Equal Rights, by Russell Freedman (Clarion)

HONOR BOOKS: *Sequoyah: The Cherokee Man Who Gave His People Writing,* by James Rumford (Houghton Mifflin); *The Tarantula Scientist,* by Sy Montgomery, illus. by Nic Bishop (Houghton Mifflin); *Walt Whitman: Words for America,* by Barbara Kerley, illus. by Brian Selznick (Scholastic)

• • • The Laura Ingalls Wilder Medal • • •

The Laura Ingalls Wilder Medal, established in 1954 and named for its first winner, the author of the **Little House** books, is given to an author or illustrator whose books, published in the United States, have made a substantial and lasting contribution to literature for children. Until 1980, the award was given every five years; currently it is awarded every three years. This award is administered by the Association for Library Service to Children, a division of the American Library Association.

1954	Laura Ingalls Wilder	1989	Elizabeth George Speare
1960	Clara Ingram Judson	1992	Marcia Brown
1965	Ruth Sawyer	1995	Virginia Hamilton
1970	E. B. White	1998	Russell Freedman
1975	Beverly Cleary	2001	Milton Meltzer
1980	Theodor S. Geisel (Dr. Seuss)	2003	Eric Carle
1983	Maurice Sendak	2005	Laurence Yep
1986	Jean Fritz		

• • • The Margaret A. Edwards Award • • •

The Margaret A. Edwards Award, established in 1988, honors an author's lifetime achievement for writing books that have been popular over a period of time. The annual award is administered by the Young Adult Library Services Association, a division of the American Library Association, and sponsored by *School Library Journal.* It recognizes an author's work in helping adolescents become aware of themselves and addressing questions about their role and importance in relationships, society, and in the world.

1988	S. E. Hinton	1998	Madeleine L'Engle
1990	Richard Peck	1999	Anne McCaffrey
1991	Robert Cormier	2000	Chris Crutcher
1992	Lois Duncan	2001	Robert Lipsyte
1993	M. E. Kerr	2002	Paul Zindel
1994	Walter Dean Myers	2003	Nancy Garden
1995	Cynthia Voigt	2004	Ursula Le Guin
1996	Judy Blume	2005	Francesca Lia Block
1997	Gary Paulsen		

• • • The Michael L. Printz Award • • •

The Michael L. Printz Award, established in 2000, is administered by the Young Adult Library Services Association, a division of the American Library Association. The award honors the author of an outstanding young adult book.

2000

Monster, by Walter Dean Myers (HarperCollins)

HONOR BOOKS: *Skellig,* by David Almond (Delacorte Press); *Speak,* by Laurie Halse Anderson (Farrar, Straus & Giroux); *Hard Love,* by Ellen Wittlinger (Simon & Schuster)

2001

Kit's Wilderness, by David Almond (Delacorte Press)

HONOR BOOKS: *Many Stones,* by Carolyn Coman (Front Street); *The Body of Christopher Creed,* by Carol Plum-Ucci (Harcourt); *Angus, Thongs, and Full-Frontal Snogging,* by Louise Rennison (HarperCollins); *Stuck in Neutral,* by Terry Trueman (HarperCollins)

2002

Step from Heaven, by An Na (Front Street)

HONOR BOOKS: *The Ropemaker,* by Peter Dickinson (Delacorte Press); *Heart to Heart: New Poems Inspired by Twentieth-Century American Art,* by Jan Greenberg (Abrams); *Freewill,* by Chris Lynch (HarperCollins); *True Believer,* by Virginia Euwer Wolff (Atheneum)

2003

Postcards from No Man's Land, by Aidan Chambers (Dutton)

HONOR BOOKS: *The House of the Scorpion,* by Nancy Farmer (Atheneum); *My Heartbeat,* by Garret Freymann-Weyr (Houghton Mifflin); *Hole in My Life,* by Jack Gantos (Farrar, Straus & Giroux)

2004

The First Part Last, by Angela Johnson (Simon & Schuster)

HONOR BOOKS: *A Northern Light,* by Jennifer Donnelly (Harcourt); *Keesha's House,* by Helen Frost (Farrar, Straus & Giroux); *Fat Kid Rules the World,* by K. L. Going (Putnam); *The Earth, My Butt and Other Big Round Things,* by Carolyn Mackler (Candlewick Press).

2005

How I Live Now, by Meg Rosoff (Random House)

HONOR BOOKS: *Airborn,* by Kenneth Oppel (EOS); *Chanda's Secrets,* by Allan Stratton (Annick); *Lizzie Bright and the Buckminster Boy,* by Gary Schmidt (Clarion)

National Council of Teachers of English Awards

• • • The Award for Excellence in Poetry for Children • • •

The NCTE Award for Excellence in Poetry for Children, established in memory of Jonathan Cullinan (1969-1975), is given to a living American poet in recognition of an outstanding body of poetry for children. The award is administered by the National Council of Teachers of English and was given annually from 1977 to 1982; currently, the award is presented every three years. The poet receives a citation. A medallion designed by Karla Kuskin is available for use on dust jackets of all the poet's books. An archival collection of the poets' books is housed at the Children's Literature Research Center, Andersen Library, at the University of Minnesota. Another collection is housed at Boston Public Library in the David McCord Room.

1977	David McCord
1978	Aileen Fisher
1979	Karla Kuskin
1980	Myra Cohn Livingston
1981	Eve Merriam
1982	John Ciardi
1985	Lilian Moore
1988	Arnold Adoff
1991	Valerie Worth
1994	Barbara Esbensen
1997	Eloise Greenfield
2000	X. J. Kennedy
2003	Mary Ann Hoberman

• • • The Orbis Pictus Award and Honor Books • • •

The Orbis Pictus Award, established in 1990, is administered by the National Council of Teachers of English and honors the author of an outstanding nonfiction book.

1990

The Great Little Madison, by Jean Fritz (Putnam)

HONOR BOOKS: *The Great American Gold Rush,* by Rhoda Blumberg (Bradbury Press); *The News about Dinosaurs,* by Patricia Lauber (Bradbury Press)

1991

Franklin Delano Roosevelt, by Russell Freedman (Clarion)

HONOR BOOKS: *Arctic Memories,* by Normee Ekoomiak (Henry Holt); *Seeing Earth from Space,* by Patricia Lauber (Orchard Books)

1992

Flight: The Journey of Charles Lindbergh, by Robert Burleigh and Mike Wimmer (Philomel)

HONOR BOOKS: *Now Is Your Time! The African American Struggle for Freedom,* by Walter Dean Myers (HarperCollins); *Prairie Vision: The Life and Times of Solomon Butcher,* by Pam Conrad (HarperCollins)

1993

Children of the Dust Bowl: The True Story of the School at Weedpatch Camp, by Jerry Stanley (Crown)

HONOR BOOKS: *Talking with Artists,* by Pat Cummins (Bradbury Press); *Come Back, Salmon,* by Molly Cone (Sierra Club Books)

1994

Across America on an Emigrant Train, by Jim Murphy (Clarion)

HONOR BOOKS: *To the Top of the World: Adventures with Arctic Wolves,* by Jim Brandenburg (Walker); *Making Sense: Animal Perception and Communication,* by Bruce Brooks (Farrar, Straus & Giroux)

1995

Safari beneath the Sea: The Wonder of the North Pacific Coast, by Diane Swanson (Sierra Club Books)

HONOR BOOKS: *Wildlife Rescue: The Work of Dr. Kathleen Ramsay,* by Jennifer Owings Dewey (Boyds Mills Press); *Kids at Work: Lewis Hine and the Crusade against Child Labor,* by Russell Freedman (Clarion); *Christmas in the Big House, Christmas in the Quarters,* by Patricia McKissack and Fredrick McKissack (Scholastic)

1996

The Great Fire, by Jim Murphy (Scholastic)

HONOR BOOKS: *Dolphin Man: Exploring the World of Dolphins,* by Laurence Pringle, photos by Randall S. Wells (Atheneum); *Rosie the Riveter: Women Working on the Home Front in World War II,* by Penny Colman (Crown)

1997

Leonardo da Vinci, by Diane Stanley (Morrow Junior Books)

HONOR BOOKS: *Full Steam Ahead: The Race to Build a Transcontinental Railroad,* by Rhoda Blumberg (National Geographic Society); *The Life and Death of Crazy Horse,* by Russell Freedman (Holiday House); *One World, Many Religions: The Way We Worship,* by Mary Pope Osborne (Knopf)

1998

An Extraordinary Life: The Story of a Monarch Butterfly, by Laurence Pringle, illus. by Bob Marstall (Orchard Books)

HONOR BOOKS: *A Drop of Water: A Book of Science and Wonder,* by Walter Wick (Scholastic); *A Tree Is Growing,* by Arthur Dorros, illus. by S. D. Schindler (Scholastic); *Charles A. Lindbergh: A Human Hero,* by James Cross Giblin (Clarion); *Kennedy Assassinated! The World Mourns: A Reporter's Story,* by Wilborn

Hampton (Candlewick Press); *Digger: The Tragic Fate of the California Indians from the Missions to the Gold Rush,* by Jerry Stanley (Crown)

1999

Shipwreck at the Bottom of the World: The Extraordinary True Story of Shackleton and the Endurance, by Jennifer Armstrong (Crown)

HONOR BOOKS: *Black Whiteness: Admiral Byrd Alone in the Antarctic,* by Robert Burleigh, illus. by Walter Lyon Krudop (Atheneum); *Fossil Feud: The Rivalry of the First American Dinosaur Hunters,* by Thom Holmes (Messner); *Hottest, Coldest, Highest, Deepest,* by Steve Jenkins (Houghton Mifflin); *No Pretty Pictures: A Child of War,* by Anita Lobel (Greenwillow)

2000

Through My Eyes, by Ruby Bridges and Margo Lundell (Scholastic)

HONOR BOOKS: *At Her Majesty's Request: An African Princess in Victorian England,* by Walter Dean Myers (Scholastic); *Clara Schumann: Piano Virtuoso,* by Susanna Reich (Clarion); *Mapping the World,* by Sylvia Johnson (Atheneum); *The Snake Scientist,* by Sy Montgomery, illus. by Nic Bishop (Houghton Mifflin); *The Top of the World: Climbing Mount Everest,* by Steve Jenkins (Houghton Mifflin)

2001

Hurry Freedom: African Americans in Gold Rush California, by Jerry Stanley (Crown)

HONOR BOOKS: *The Amazing Life of Benjamin Franklin,* by James Cross Giblin, illus. by Michael Dooling (Scholastic); *America's Champion Swimmer: Gertrude Ederle,* by David Adler, illus. by Terry Widener (Harcourt); *Michelangelo,* by Diane Stanley (HarperCollins); *Osceola: Memories of a Sharecropper's Daughter,* by Alan Govenar, illus. by Shane W. Evans (Jump at the Sun); *Wild and Swampy,* by Jim Arnosky (HarperCollins)

2002

Black Potatoes: The Story of the Great Irish Famine, 1845-1850, by Susan Campbell Bartoletti (Houghton Mifflin)

HONOR BOOKS: *The Cod's Tale,* by Mark Kurlansky, illus. by S. D. Schindler (Putnam); *The Dinosaurs of Waterhouse Hawkins: An Illuminating History of Mr. Waterhouse Hawkins, Artist and Lecturer,* by Barbara Kerley, illus. by Brian Selznick (Scholastic); *Martin's Big Words: The Life of Dr. Martin Luther King, Jr.,* by Doreen Rappaport, illus. by Bryan Collier (Hyperion)

2003

When Marian Sang: The True Recital of Marian Anderson: The Voice of a Century, by Pam Muñoz Ryan, illus. by Brian Selznick (Scholastic)

HONOR BOOKS: *Confucius: The Golden Rule,* by Russell Freedman, illus. by Frederic Clement (Levine Books); *Emperor's Silent Army: Terracotta Warriors of Ancient China,* by Jane O'Connor (Viking); *Phineas Gage: A Gruesome but True Story about Brain Science,* by John Fleischman (Houghton Mifflin); *Tenement: Immigrant Life on the Lower East Side,* by Raymond Bial (Houghton Mifflin); *To Fly: The Story of the Wright Brothers,* by Wendie Old, illus. by Robert Andrew Parker (Clarion)

2004

An American Plague: The True and Terrifying Story of the Yellow Fever Epidemic of 1793, by Jim Murphy (Clarion)

HONOR BOOKS: *Empire State Building: When New York Reached for the Skies,* by Elizabeth Mann, illus. by Alan Witschonke (Mikaya Press); *In Defense of Liberty: The Story of America's Bill of Rights,* by Russell Freedman (Holiday House); *Leonardo: Beautiful Dreamer,* by Robert Byrd (Dutton); *The Man Who Made Time Travel,* by Kathryn Lasky, illus. by Kevin Hawkes (Farrar, Straus & Giroux); *Shutting Out the Sky: Life in the Tenements of New York, 1880-1924,* by Deborah Hopkinson (Orchard Books)

International Reading Association Awards

• • • The IRA Children's Book Award • • •

The IRA Children's Book Award, established in 1975, sponsored by the Institute for Reading Research and administrated by the International Reading Association, is presented for a children's book published in the preceding year by an author who shows unusual promise. Since 1987, the award has been presented for both picture books and novels. Currently, the award is given for both fiction and nonfiction in each of three categories: primary, intermediate, and young adult. Books originating in any country are eligible. For books written in a language other than English, the IRA committee first determines if the book warrants an English translation and, if so, extends to it an additional year of eligibility.

1975
Transport 7-41-R, by T. Degens (Viking)

1976
Dragonwings, by Laurence Yep (HarperCollins)

1977
A String in the Harp, by Nancy Bond (McElderry)

1978

A Summer to Die, by Lois Lowry (Houghton Mifflin)

1979

Reserved for Mark Anthony Crowder, by Alison Smith (Dutton)

1980

Words by Heart, by Ouida Sebestyen (Little, Brown)

1981

My Own Private Sky, by Delores Beckman (Dutton)

1982

Good Night, Mr. Tom, by Michelle Magorian (Kestrel/Penguin, Great Britain; HarperCollins, USA)

1983

The Darkangel, by Meredith Ann Pierce (Little, Brown)

1984

Ratha's Creature, by Clare Bell (Atheneum)

1985

Badger on the Barge, by Janni Howker (Greenwillow)

1986

Prairie Songs, by Pam Conrad (HarperCollins)

1987

PICTURE BOOK: *The Line Up Book,* by Marisabina Russo (Greenwillow)

NOVEL: *After the Dancing Days,* by Margaret Rostkowski (HarperCollins)

1988

PICTURE BOOK: *Third Story Cat,* by Leslie Baker (Little, Brown)

NOVEL: *The Ruby in the Smoke,* by Philip Pullman (Knopf)

1989

PICTURE BOOK: *Rechenka's Eggs,* by Patricia Polacco (Philomel)

NOVEL: *Probably Still Nick Swansen,* by Virginia Euwer Wolff (Henry Holt)

1990

PICTURE BOOK: *No Star Nights,* by Anna Egan Smucker (Knopf)

NOVEL: *Children of the River,* by Linda Crew (Delacorte Press)

1991

PICTURE BOOK: *Is This a House for Hermit Crab?* by Megan McDonald (Orchard Books)

NOVEL: *Under the Hawthorn Tree,* by Marita Conlon-McKenna (O'Brien Press)

1992

PICTURE BOOK: *Ten Little Rabbits,* by Virginia Grossman (Chronicle Books)

NOVEL: *Rescue Josh McGuire,* by Ben Mikaelsen (Hyperion)

1993

PICTURE BOOK: *Old Turtle,* by Douglas Wood (Pfeiffer-Hamilton)

NOVEL: *Letters from Rifka,* by Karen Hesse (Henry Holt)

1994

PICTURE BOOK: *Sweet Clara and the Freedom Quilt,* by Deborah Hopkinson, illus. by James Ransome (Knopf)

NOVEL: *Behind the Secret Window: A Memoir of a Hidden Childhood,* by Nelly Toll (Dutton)

1995

PICTURE BOOK: *The Ledgerbook of Thomas Blue Eagle,* by Gay Matthaei and Jewel Grutman, illus. by Adam Cvijanovic (Thomasson-Grant)

NOVEL: *Spite Fences,* by Trudy Krisher (Bantam)

NONFICTION: *Stranded at Plimoth Plantation 1626,* by Gary Bowen (HarperCollins)

1996

PICTURE BOOK: *More Than Anything Else,* by Marie Bradby and Chris Soentpiet (Orchard Books)

NOVEL: *The King's Shadow,* by Elizabeth Adler (Farrar, Straus & Giroux)

NONFICTION: *The Case of the Mummified Pigs and Other Mysteries in Nature,* by Susan Quinlan (Boyds Mills Press)

1997

PICTURE BOOK: *The Fabulous Flying Fandinis,* by Ingrid Slyder (Cobblehill Books)

NOVEL: *Don't You Dare Read This, Mrs. Dunphrey,* by Margaret Peterson Haddix (Simon & Schuster)

NONFICTION: *The Brooklyn Bridge,* by Elizabeth Mann (Mikaya Press)

1998

YOUNGER READER: *Nim and the War Effort,* by Milly Lee and Yangsook Choi (Farrar, Straus & Giroux)

OLDER READER: *Moving Mama to Town,* by Ronder Thomas Young (Orchard Books)

NONFICTION: *Just What the Doctor Ordered: The History of American Medicine,* by Brandon Marie Miller (Lerner)

1999

YOUNGER READER: *My Freedom Trip: A Child's Escape from North Korea,* by Frances and Ginger Park (Boyds Mills Press)

OLDER READER: *Choosing Up Sides,* by John Ritter (Philomel)

NONFICTION: *First in the Field: Baseball Hero Jackie Robinson,* by Derek Dingle (Hyperion)

2000

YOUNGER READER: *The Snake Scientist,* by Sy Montgomery (Houghton Mifflin)

OLDER READER: *Bud, Not Buddy,* by Christopher Paul Curtis (Delacorte Press); *Eleanor's Story: An American Girl in Hitler's Germany,* by Eleanor Ramrath Garner (Peachtree)

NONFICTION: *Molly Bannaky,* by Alice McGill (Houghton Mifflin)

2001

YOUNGER READER: *Stranger in the Woods,* by Carl R. Sams II and Jean Stoick (Carl R. Sams II Photography)

OLDER READER: *Jake's Orphan,* by Peggy Brooke (DK Publishing); *Girls Think of Everything,* by Catherine Thimmesh (Houghton Mifflin)

NONFICTION: *My Season with Penguins,* by Sophie Webb (Houghton Mifflin)

2002

PRIMARY-FICTION: *Silver Seeds,* by Paul Paolilli and Dan Brewer (Viking)

PRIMARY-NONFICTION: *Aero and Officer Mike,* by Joan Plummer Russell (Boyds Mills Press)

INTERMEDIATE-FICTION: *Coolies,* by Yin (Philomel)

INTERMEDIATE-NONFICTION: *Pearl Harbor Warriors,* by Dorinda Makanaonalani Nicholson and Larry Nicholson (Woodson House)

YOUNG ADULT-FICTION: *A Step from Heaven,* by An Na (Front Street)

YOUNG ADULT-NONFICTION: *A Race against Nuclear Disaster at Three Mile Island,* by Wilborn Hampton (Candlewick Press)

2003

PRIMARY-FICTION: *One Leaf Rides the Wind,* by Celeste Davidson Mannis (Viking)

PRIMARY-NONFICTION: *The Pot That Juan Built,* by Nancy Andrews-Goebel (Lee & Low Books)

INTERMEDIATE-FICTION: *Who Will Tell My Brother?* by Marlene Carvell (Hyperion)

INTERMEDIATE-NONFICTION: *If the World Were a Village: A Book about the World's People,* by David Smith (Kids Can Press)

YOUNG ADULT-FICTION: *Mississippi Trial, 1955,* by Chris Crowe (Fogelman Books)

YOUNG ADULT-NONFICTION: *Headin' for Better Times: The Arts of the Great Depression,* by Duane Damon (Lerner)

2004

PRIMARY-FICTION: *Mary Smith,* by Andrea U'ren (Farrar, Straus & Giroux)

PRIMARY-NONFICTION: *Uncle Andy's: A Faabbbulous Visit with Andy Warhol,* by James Warhola (Penguin Books)

INTERMEDIATE-FICTION: *Sahara Special,* by Esmé Raji Codell (Hyperion)

INTERMEDIATE-NONFICTION: *Carl Sandburg: Adventures of a Poet,* by Penelope Niven (Harcourt)

YOUNG ADULT-FICTION: *Buddha Boy,* by Kathe Koja (Farrar, Straus & Giroux)

YOUNG ADULT-NONFICTION: *At the End of Words: A Daughter's Memoir,* by Miriam Stone (Candlewick Press)

• • • The Lee Bennett Hopkins • • • Promising Poet Award

The Lee Bennett Hopkins Promising Poet Award, established in 1995 and administered by the International Reading Association, is presented every three years. The award is given to an American living poet who has had one book, but not more than two, published. The award consists of an engraved trophy and a $500 honorarium.

1995	Deborah Chandra
1998	Kristine O'Connell George
2001	Craig Crist-Evans
2004	Lindsay Lee Johnson

International Awards

• • • The Library Association Carnegie Medal • • •

Instituted in 1936 to mark the centenary of the birth of Andrew Carnegie, philanthropist and benefactor of libraries, the Library Association Carnegie Medal is awarded annually for an outstanding book for children written in English receiving its first publication in the United Kingdom during the preceding year.

1936	Arthur Ransome, *Pigeon Post*
1937	Eve Garnet, *The Family from One End Street*
1938	Noel Streatfeild, *The Circus Is Coming*
1939	Eleanor Doorly, *The Radium Woman* (biography of Marie Curie)
1940	Kitty Barne, *Visitors from London*
1941	Mary Treadgold, *We Couldn't Leave Dinah*
1942	"B.B." (D. J. Watkins-Pitchford), *The Little Grey Men*
1943	No award
1944	Eric Linklater, *The Wind on the Moon*
1945	No award

1946   Elizabeth Goudge, *The Little White Horse*

1947   Walter de la Mare, *Collected Stories for Children*

1948   Richard Armstrong, *Sea Change*

1949   Agnes Allen, *The Story of Your Home* (nonfiction)

1950   Elfrida Vipont, *The Lark on the Wing*

1951   Cynthia Harnett, *The Wool-Pack*

1952   Mary Norton, *The Borrowers*

1953   Edward Osmond, *A Valley Grows Up* (nonfiction)

1954   Ronald Welch, *Knight Crusaders*

1955   Eleanor Farjeon, *The Little Bookroom*

1956   C. S. Lewis, *The Last Battle*

1957   William Mayne, *A Grass Rope*

1958   Philippa Pearce, *Tom's Midnight Garden*

1959   Rosemary Sutcliff, *The Lantern Bearers*

1960   Ian W. Cornwall and Howard M. Maitland, *The Making of Man* (nonfiction)

1961   Lucy M. Boston, *A Stranger at Green Knowe*

1962   Pauline Clark, *The Twelve and the Genii*

1963   Hester Burton, *Time of Trial*

1964   Sheena Porter, *Nordy Bank*

1965   Philip Turner, *The Grange at High Force*

1966   No award

1967   Alan Garner, *The Owl Service*

1968   Rosemary Harris, *The Moon in the Cloud*

1969   K. M. Peyton, *The Edge of the Cloud*

1970   Edward Blishen and Leon Garfield, *The God beneath the Sea*

1971   Ivan Southall, *Josh*

1972   Richard Adams, *Watership Down*

1973   Penelope Lively, *The Ghost of Thomas Kempe*

1974   Mollie Hunter, *The Stronghold*

1975   Robert Westall, *The Machine Gunners*

1976   Jan Mark, *Thunder and Lightnings*

1977   Gene Kemp, *The Turbulent Term of Tyke Tyler*

1978   David Rees, *The Exeter Blitz*

1979   Peter Dickinson, *Tulku*

1980   Peter Dickinson, *City of Gold*

1981   Robert Westall, *The Scarecrows*

1982   Margaret Mahy, *The Haunting*

1983   Jan Mark, *Handles*

1984   Margaret Mahy, *The Changeover*

1985   Kevin Crossley-Holland, *Storm*

1986   Berlie Doherty, *Granny Was a Buffer Girl*

1987   Susan Price, *The Ghost Drum*

1988   Geraldine McCaughrean, *A Pack of Lies*

1989   Anne Fine, *Goggle-Eyes*

1990   Gillian Cross, *Wolf*

1991   Berlie Doherty, *Dear Nobody*

1992   Anne Fine, *Flour Babies*

1993   Robert Swindells, *Stone Cold*

1994   Theresa Breslin, *Whispers in the Graveyard*

1995   Philip Pullman, *Northern Lights*

1996   Melvin Burgess, *Junk*

1997   Tim Bowler, *River Boy*

1998   David Almond, *Skellig*

1999   Aiden Chambers, *Postcards from No Man's Land*

2000   Beverly Naidoo, *The Other Side of Truth*

2001   Terry Pratchett, *The Amazing Maurice and His Educated Rodents*

2002   Sharon Creech, *Ruby Holler*

2003   Jennifer Donnelly, *A Gathering Light*

• • • The Hans Christian Andersen Award • • •

The Hans Christian Andersen Award, established in 1956, is given biennially and administered by the International Board on Books for Young People. It is given to one author and, since 1966, to one illustrator in recognition of his or her entire body of work. A medal is presented to the recipient.

1956

Eleanor Farjeon, Great Britain

1958

Astrid Lindgren, Sweden

1960

Erich Kästner, Germany

1962

Meindert DeJong, USA

1964

René Guillot, France

1966

AUTHOR: Tove Jansson, Finland

ILLUSTRATOR: Alois Carigiet, Switzerland

1968

AUTHORS: James Krüss, Germany, and José Maria Sanchez-Silva, Spain

ILLUSTRATOR: Jiri Trnka, Czechoslovakia

1970

AUTHOR: Gianni Rodari, Italy

ILLUSTRATOR: Maurice Sendak, USA

1972

AUTHOR: Scott O'Dell, USA

ILLUSTRATOR: Ib Spang Olsen, Denmark

1974

AUTHOR: Maria Gripe, Sweden

ILLUSTRATOR: Farshid Mesghali, Iran

1976

AUTHOR: Cecil Bodker, Denmark

ILLUSTRATOR: Tatjana Mawrina, USSR

1978

AUTHOR: Paula Fox, USA

ILLUSTRATOR: Otto S. Svend, Denmark

1980

AUTHOR: Bohumil R'ha, Czechoslovakia

ILLUSTRATOR: Suekichi Akaba, Japan

1982

AUTHOR: Lygia Bojunga Nunes, Brazil

ILLUSTRATOR: Zbigniew Rychlicki, Poland

1984

AUTHOR: Christine Nöstlinger, Austria

ILLUSTRATOR: Mitsumasa Anno, Japan

1986

AUTHOR: Patricia Wrightson, Australia

ILLUSTRATOR: Robert Ingpen, Australia

1988

AUTHOR: Annie M. G. Schmidt, Holland

ILLUSTRATOR: Dusan Kallay, Czechoslovakia

1990

AUTHOR: Tormod Haugen, Norway

ILLUSTRATOR: Lisbeth Zwerger, Austria

1992

AUTHOR: Virginia Hamilton, USA

ILLUSTRATOR: Kveta Pacovská, Czechoslovakia

1994

AUTHOR: Michio Mado, Japan

ILLUSTRATOR: Jörg Müller, Switzerland

1996

AUTHOR: Uri Orlev, Israel

ILLUSTRATOR: Klaus Ensikat, Germany

1998

AUTHOR: Katherine Paterson, USA

ILLUSTRATOR: Tomi Ungerer, France

2000

AUTHOR: Ana Maria Machado, Brazil

ILLUSTRATOR: Anthony Browne, United Kingdom

2002

AUTHOR: Aidan Chambers, United Kingdom

ILLUSTRATOR: Quentin Blake, United Kingdom

2004

AUTHOR: Martin Waddell, Ireland

ILLUSTRATOR: Max Velthuijs, The Netherlands

• • • The Mildred L. Batchelder Awards • • •

The Mildred L. Batchelder Award, established in 1966, is given by the Association of Library Service to Children of the American Library Association to the publisher of the most outstanding book of the year that is a translation, published in the United States, of a book that was first published in another country. In 1990, honor books were added to this award. The original country of publication is given here.

1968

The Little Man, by Erich Kastner, trans. by James Kirkup, illus. by Rick Schreiter (Knopf), Germany

1969

Don't Take Teddy, by Babbis Friis-Baastad, trans. by Lise Somme McKinnon (Scribner's), Norway

1970

Wildcat under Glass, by Alki Zei, trans. by Edward Fenton (Henry Holt), Greece

1971

In the Land of Ur, by Hans Baumann, trans. by Stella Humphries (Pantheon), Germany

1972

Friedrich, by Hans Peter Richter, trans. by Edite Kroll (Henry Holt), Germany

1973

Pulga, by S. R. Van Iterson, trans. by Alison and Alexander Gode (Morrow), Netherlands

1974

Petros' War, by Alki Zei, trans. by Edward Fenton (Dutton), Greece

1975

An Old Tale Carved out of Stone, by A. Linevsky, trans. by Maria Polushkin (Crown), Russia

1976

The Cat and Mouse Who Shared a House, by Ruth Hurlimann, trans. by Anthea Bell, illus. by the author (Walck), Germany

1977

The Leopard, by Cecil Bødker, trans. by Gunnar Poulsen (Atheneum), Denmark

1978

Konrad, by Christine Nostlinger, illus. by Carol Nicklaus (Watts), Germany

1979

Rabbit Island, by Jörg Steiner, trans. by Ann Conrad Lammers, illus. by Jörg Müller (Harcourt), Germany

1980

The Sound of the Dragon's Feet, by Alki Zei, trans. by Edward Fenton (Dutton), Greece

1981

The Winter When Time Was Frozen, by Els Pelgrom, trans. by Maryka and Rafael Rudnik (Morrow), Netherlands

1982

The Battle Horse, by Harry Kullman, trans. by George Blecher and Lone Thygesen-Blecher (Bradbury), Sweden

1983

Hiroshima No Pika, by Toshi Maruki (Lothrop, Lee & Shepard), Japan

1984

Ronia, the Robber's Daughter, by Astrid Lindgren, trans. by Patricia Crampton (Viking), Sweden

1985

The Island on Bird Street, by Uri Orlev, trans. by Hillel Halkin (Houghton Mifflin), Israel

1986

Rose Blanche, by Christophe Gallaz and Roberto Innocenti, trans. by Martha Coventry and Richard Graglia (Creative Education), Italy

1987

No Hero for the Kaiser, by Rudolf Frank, trans. by Patricia Crampton (Lothrop, Lee & Shepard), Germany

1988

If You Didn't Have Me, by Ulf Nilsson, trans. by Lone Tygesen-Blecher and George Blecher, illus. by Eva Eriksson (McElderry), Sweden

1989

Crutches, by Peter Hatling, trans. by Elizabeth D. Crawford (Lothrop, Lee & Shepard), Germany

1990

Buster's World, by Bjarne Reuter, trans. by Anthea Bell (Dutton), Denmark

1991

Two Long and One Short, by Nina Ring Aamundsen (Houghton Mifflin), Norway

1992

The Man from the Other Side by Uri Orlev, trans. by Hillel Halkin (Houghton Mifflin), Israel

1993

No award

1994

The Apprentice, by Molina Llorente, trans. by Robin Longshaw (Farrar, Straus & Giroux), Spain

1995

The Boys from St. Petri, by Bjarne Reuter, trans. by Anthea Bell (Dutton), Denmark

1996

The Lady with the Hat, by Uri Orlev, trans. by Hillel Halkin (Houghton Mifflin), Israel

1997

The Friends, by Kazumi Yumoto, trans. by Cathy Hirano (Farrar, Straus & Giroux), Japan

1998

The Robber and Me, by Josef Holub, ed. by Mark Aronson, trans. by Elizabeth Crawford (Henry Holt), Germany

1999

Thanks to My Mother, by Schoschana Rabinovici, trans. by James Skofield (Dial Books), Lithuania

2000

The Baboon King, by Anton Quintana, trans. by John Nieuwenhuizen (Walker), Holland

2001

Samir and Yonatan, by Daniella Carmi, trans. by Arthur A. Levine (Scholastic), Israel

2002

How I Became an American, by Karin Gündisch (Cricket Books), Austria-Hungary

2003

The Thief Lord, by Cornelia Funke, trans. by Oliver Latsch (Scholastic), Venice

2004

Run, Boy, Run, by Uri Orlev (Houghton Mifflin), Poland

2005

The Shadows of Ghadames, by Joëlle Stolz (Delacorte Press), France

Other Awards

• • • The Ezra Jack Keats Awards • • •

This award, first presented in 1985, is administered by the Ezra Jack Keats Foundation and the New York Public Library. The award was originally given biennially to a promising new writer. Beginning in the year 2001, the award has been given annually to an illustrator as well as to a writer. The award honors work done in the tradition of Ezra Jack Keats, using the criteria of appeal to young children, storytelling quality, relation between text and illustration, positive reflection of families, and the multicultural nature of the world. The award is presented at the Early Childhood Resource and Information Center of the New York Public Library. Funded by the Ezra Jack Keats Foundation, the award consists of a monetary gift and a medallion.

1985

The Patchwork Quilt, by Valerie Flournoy, illus. by Jerry Pinkney (Dial Books)

1987

Jamaica's Find, by Juanita Havill, illus. by Anne Sibley O'Brien (Houghton Mifflin)

1989

Anna's Special Present, by Yoriko Tsutsui, illus. by Akiko Hayashi (Viking)

1991

Tell Me a Story, Mama, by Angela Johnson, illus. by David Soman (Orchard Books)

1993

Tar Beach, by Faith Ringgold (Crown)

1995

Taxi! Taxi! by Cari Best, illus. by Dale Gottlieb (Little, Brown)

1997

Calling the Doves, by Juan Felipe Herrera, illus. by Elly Simmons (Children's Book Press)

1999

Dear Juno, by Soyung Park, illus. by Susan Kathleen Hartung (Viking)

2001

WRITER: *Henry Hikes to Fitchburg,* by D. B. Johnson (Houghton Mifflin)

ILLUSTRATOR: *Uptown,* by Bryan Collier (Henry Holt)

2002

WRITER AND ILLUSTRATOR: *Freedom Summer,* by Deborah Wiles; illus. by Jerome Lagarrigue (Atheneum)

2003

WRITER AND ILLUSTRATOR: *Ruby's Wish,* by Shirin Yim Bridges, illus. by Sophie Blackall (Chronicle Books)

2004

WRITER: *Yesterday I Had the Blues,* by Jeron Ashford Frame (Ten Speed Press)

ILLUSTRATOR: *My Name Is Yoon,* illus. by Gabi Swiatkowska (Farrar, Straus & Giroux)

• • • The Boston Globe–Horn Book Awards • • •

The Boston Globe-Horn Book Awards have been presented annually since 1967 by the *Boston Globe* newspaper and *The Horn Book Magazine.* Through 1975, two awards were given, one for outstanding fiction and one for outstanding picture book. In 1976, the award categories were changed to fiction or poetry, nonfiction, and picture book. A monetary gift is awarded to the winner in each category.

1967

FICTION: *The Little Fishes,* by Erik Christian Haugaard (Houghton Mifflin)

PICTURE BOOK: *London Bridge Is Falling Down!* illus. by Peter Spier (Doubleday)

1968

FICTION: *The Spring Rider,* by John Lawson (Crowell)

FICTION HONORS: *Young Mark,* by E. M. Almedingen (Farrar); *Dark Venture,* by Audrey White Beyer (Knopf); *Smith,* by Leon Garfield (Pantheon); *The Endless Steppe,* by Esther Hautzig (Crowell)

PICTURE BOOK: *Tikki Tikki Tembo,* by Arlene Mosel, illus. by Blair Lent (Henry Holt)

PICTURE BOOK HONORS: *Gilgamesh: Man's First Story,* retold and illus. by Bernarda Bryson (Henry Holt); *Rosie's Walk,* by Pat Hutchins (Macmillan); *Jorinda and Joringel,* text by Jacob and Wilhelm Grimm, illus. by Adrienne Adams (Scribner's); *All in Free but Janey,* text by Elizabeth Johnson, illus. by Trina Schart Hyman (Little, Brown)

1969

FICTION: *A Wizard of Earthsea,* by Ursula Le Guin (Houghton Mifflin)

FICTION HONORS: *Flambards,* by K. M. Peyton (World); *Turi's Poppa,* by Elizabeth Borton de Treviño (Farrar, Straus & Giroux); *The Pigman,* by Paul Zindel (HarperCollins)

PICTURE BOOK: *The Adventures of Paddy Pork,* by John S. Goodall (Harcourt)

PICTURE BOOK HONORS: *New Moon Cove,* by Ann Atwood (Scribner's); *Monkey in the Jungle,* text by Edna Mitchell Preston, illus. by Clement Hurd (Viking); *Thy Friend, Obadiah,* by Brinton Turkle (Viking)

1970

FICTION: *The Intruder,* by John Rowe Townsend (Lippincott)

FICTION HONOR: *Where the Lilies Bloom,* by Vera and Bill Cleaver (Lippincott)

PICTURE BOOK: *Hi, Cat!* by Ezra Jack Keats (Macmillan)

PICTURE BOOK HONOR: *A Story, a Story,* by Gail Haley (Atheneum)

1971

FICTION: *A Room Made of Windows,* by Eleanor Cameron (Little, Brown)

FICTION HONORS: *Beyond the Weir Bridge,* by Hester Burton (Crowell); *Come by Here,* by Olivia Coolidge (Houghton Mifflin); *Mrs. Frisby and the Rats of NIMH,* by Robert C. O'Brien (Atheneum)

PICTURE BOOK: *If I Built a Village,* by Kazue Mizumura (HarperCollins)

PICTURE BOOK HONORS: *If All the Seas Were One Sea,* by Janina Domanska (Macmillan); *The Angry Moon,* retold by William Sleator, illus. by Blair Lent (Little, Brown); *A Firefly Named Torchy,* by Bernard Waber (Houghton Mifflin)

1972

FICTION: *Tristan and Iseult,* by Rosemary Sutcliff (Dutton)

PICTURE BOOK: *Mr. Gumpy's Outing,* by John Burningham (Henry Holt)

1973

FICTION: *The Dark Is Rising,* by Susan Cooper (McElderry)

FICTION HONORS: *The Cat Who Wished to Be a Man,* by Lloyd Alexander (Dutton); *An Island in a Green Sea,* by Mabel Esther Allan (Atheneum); *No Way of Telling,* by Emma Smith (McElderry)

PICTURE BOOK: *King Stork,* by Trina Schart Hyman (Little, Brown)

PICTURE BOOK HONORS: *The Magic Tree,* by Gerald McDermott (Henry Holt); *Who, Said Sue, Said Whoo?* by Ellen Raskin (Atheneum); *The Silver Pony,* by Lynd Ward (Houghton Mifflin)

1974

FICTION: *M. C. Higgins, the Great,* by Virginia Hamilton (Macmillan)

FICTION HONORS: *And Then What Happened, Paul Revere?* by Jean Fritz (Coward-McCann); *The Summer after the Funeral,* by Jane Gardam (Macmillan); *Tough Chauncey,* by Doris Buchanan Smith (Morrow)

PICTURE BOOK: *Jambo Means Hello,* by Muriel Feelings, illus. by Tom Feelings (Dial Books)

PICTURE BOOK HONORS: *All Butterflies,* by Marcia Brown (Scribner's); *Herman the Helper,* text by Robert Kraus, illus. by Jose Aruego and Ariane Dewey (Windmill); *A Prairie Boy's Winter,* by William Kurelek (Houghton Mifflin)

1975

FICTION: *Transport 7-41-R,* by T. Degens (Viking)

FICTION HONOR: *The Hundred Penny Box,* text by Sharon Bell Mathis, illus. by Leo and Diane Dillon (Viking)

PICTURE BOOK: *Anno's Alphabet,* by Mitsumasa Anno (HarperCollins)

PICTURE BOOK HONORS: *She Come Bringing Me That Little Baby Girl,* text by Eloise Greenfield, illus. by John Steptoe (Lippincott); *Scram, Kid!* text by Ann McGovern, illus. by Nola Langner (Viking); *The Bear's Bicycle,* text by Emilie Warren McLeod, illus. by David McPhail (Little, Brown)

1976

FICTION: *Unleaving,* by Jill Paton Walsh (Farrar, Straus & Giroux)

FICTION HONORS: *A String in the Harp,* by Nancy Bond (McElderry); *A Stranger Came Ashore,* by Mollie Hunter (HarperCollins); *Dragonwings,* by Laurence Yep (HarperCollins)

NONFICTION: *Voyaging to Cathay: Americans in the China Trade,* by Alfred Tamarin and Shirley Glubok (Viking)

NONFICTION HONORS: *Will You Sign Here, John Hancock?* text by Jean Fritz, illus. by Trina Schart Hyman (Coward-McCann); *Never to Forget: The Jews of the Holocaust,* by Milton Meltzer (HarperCollins); *Pyramid,* by David Macaulay (Houghton Mifflin)

PICTURE BOOK: *Thirteen,* by Remy Charlip and Jerry Joyner (Four Winds Press)

PICTURE BOOK HONORS: *The Desert Is Theirs,* text by Byrd Baylor, illus. by Peter Parnall (Scribner's); *Six Little Ducks,* by Chris Conover (Crowell); *Song of the Boat,* text by Lorenz Graham, illus. by Leo and Diane Dillon (Crowell)

1977

FICTION: *Child of the Owl,* by Laurence Yep (HarperCollins)

FICTION HONORS: *Blood Feud,* by Rosemary Sutcliff (Dutton); *Roll of Thunder, Hear My Cry,* by Mildred Taylor (Dial Books); *The Machine Gunners,* by Robert Westall (Greenwillow)

NONFICTION: *Chance, Luck and Destiny,* by Peter Dickinson (Little, Brown)

NONFICTION HONORS: *Watching the Wild Apes,* by Betty Ann Kevles (Dutton); *The Colonial Cookbook,* by Lucille Recht Penner (Hastings); *From Slave to Abolitionist,* by Lucille Schulberg Warner (Dial Books)

PICTURE BOOK: *Grandfa' Grig Had a Pig and Other Rhymes without Reason from Mother Goose,* by Wallace Tripp (Little, Brown)

PICTURE BOOK HONORS: *Anno's Counting Book,* by Mitsumasa Anno (Crowell); *Ashanti to Zulu: African Traditions,* text by Margaret Musgrove, illus. by Leo and Diane Dillon (Dial Books); *The Amazing Bone,* by William Steig (Farrar, Straus & Giroux)

SPECIAL CITATION: *The Changing City and the Changing Countryside,* by Jörg Müller (McElderry)

1978

FICTION: *The Westing Game,* by Ellen Raskin (Dutton)

FICTION HONORS: *Ramona and Her Father,* by Beverly Cleary (Morrow); *Anpao: An American Indian Odyssey,* by Jamake Highwater (Lippincott); *Alan and Naomi,* by Myron Levoy (HarperCollins)

NONFICTION HONORS: *Settlers and Strangers: Native Americans of the Desert Southwest and History as They Saw It,* by Betty Baker (Macmillan); *Castle,* by David Macaulay (Houghton Mifflin)

NONFICTION: *Mischling, Second Degree: My Childhood in Nazi Germany,* by Ilse Koehn (Greenwillow)

PICTURE BOOK: *Anno's Journey,* by Mitsumasa Anno (Philomel)

PICTURE BOOK HONORS: *The Story of Edward,* by Philippe Dumas (Parents); *On to Widecombe Fair,* text by Patricia Lee Gauch, illus. by Trina Schart Hyman (Putnam); *What Do You Feed Your Donkey On? Rhymes from a Belfast Childhood,* collected by Collette O'Hare, illus. by Jenny Rodwell (Collins)

1979

FICTION: *Humbug Mountain,* by Sid Fleischman (Little, Brown)

FICTION HONORS: *All Together Now,* by Sue Ellen Bridgers (Knopf); *Silas and Ben-Godik,* by Cecil Bodker (Delacorte Press)

NONFICTION: *The Road from Home: The Story of an Armenian Girl,* by David Kherdian (Greenwillow)

NONFICTION HONORS: *The Iron Road: A Portrait of American Railroading,* text by Richard Snow, photos by David Plowden (Four Winds); *Self-Portrait: Margot Zemach,* by Margot Zemach (Addison-Wesley); *The Story of American Photography: An Illustrated History for Young People,* by Martin Sandler (Little, Brown)

PICTURE BOOK: *The Snowman,* by Raymond Briggs (Random House)

PICTURE BOOK HONORS: *Cross-Country Cat,* text by Mary Calhoun, illus. by Erik Ingraham (Morrow); *Ben's Trumpet,* by Rachel Isadora (Greenwillow)

1980

FICTION: *Conrad's War,* by Andrew Davies (Crown)

FICTION HONORS: *The Night Swimmers,* by Betsy Byars (Delacorte Press); *Me and My Million,* by Clive King (Crowell); *The Alfred Summer,* by Jan Slepian (Macmillan)

NONFICTION: *Building the Fight against Gravity,* text by Mario Salvadori, illus. by Saralinda Hooker and Christopher Ragus (McElderry)

NONFICTION HONORS: *Childtimes: A Three-Generation Memoir,* text by Eloise Greenfield, illus. by Jerry Pinkney, and with photos (Crowell); *Stonewall,* text by Jean Fritz, illus. by Stephen Gammell (Putnam); *How the Forest Grew,* text by William Jaspersohn, illus. by Chuck Eckart (Greenwillow)

PICTURE BOOK: *The Garden of Abdul Gasazi,* by Chris Van Allsburg (Houghton Mifflin)

PICTURE BOOK HONORS: *The Gray Lady and the Strawberry Snatcher,* by Molly Bang (Greenwillow); *Why the Tides Ebb and Flow,* text by John Chase Bowden, illus. by Marc Brown (Houghton Mifflin)

SPECIAL CITATION: *Graham Oakley's Magical Changes,* by Graham Oakley (Atheneum)

1981

FICTION: *The Leaving,* by Lynn Hall (Scribner's)

FICTION HONORS: *Ida Early Comes over the Mountain,* by Robert Burch (Viking); *Flight of the Sparrow,* by Julia Cunningham (Pantheon); *Footsteps,* by Leon Garfield (Delacorte Press)

NONFICTION: *The Weaver's Gift,* text by Kathyrn Lasky, photos by Christopher Knight (Warne)

NONFICTION HONORS: *You Can't Be Timid with a Trumpet: Notes from the Orchestra,* by Betty English (Lothrop, Lee & Shepard); *The Hospital Book,* text by James Howe, photos by Mal Warshaw (Crown); *Junk Food, Fast Food, Health Food: What America Eats and Why,* by Lila Perl (Clarion)

PICTURE BOOK: *Outside over There,* by Maurice Sendak (HarperCollins)

PICTURE BOOK HONORS: *Where the Buffaloes Begin,* text by Olaf Baker, illus. by Stephen Gammell (Warne); *On Market Street,* text by Arnold Lobel, illus. by Anita Lobel (Greenwillow); *Jumanji,* by Chris Van Allsburg (Houghton Mifflin)

1982

FICTION: *Playing Beatie Bow,* by Ruth Park (Atheneum)

FICTION HONORS: *The Voyage Begun,* by Nancy Bond (Atheneum); *Ask Me No Questions,* by Ann Schlee (Henry Holt); *The Scarecrows,* by Robert Westall (Greenwillow)

NONFICTION: *Upon the Head of the Goat: A Childhood in Hungary, 1939-1944,* by Aranka Siegal (Farrar, Straus & Giroux)

NONFICTION HONORS: *Lobo of the Tasaday,* by John Nance (Pantheon); *Dinosaurs of North America,* text by Helen Roney Sattler, illus. by Anthony Rao (Lothrop, Lee & Shepard)

PICTURE BOOK: *A Visit to William Blake's Inn: Poems for Innocent and Experienced Travelers,* by Nancy Willard, illus. by Alice and Martin Provensen (Harcourt)

PICTURE BOOK HONOR: *The Friendly Beasts: An Old English Christmas Carol,* by Tomie dePaola (Putnam)

1983

FICTION: *Sweet Whisper, Brother Rush,* by Virginia Hamilton (Philomel)

FICTION HONORS: *Homesick: My Own Story,* by Jean Fritz (Putnam); *The Road to Camlann,* by Rosemary Sutcliff (Dutton); *Dicey's Song,* by Cynthia Voigt (Atheneum)

NONFICTION: *Behind Barbed Wire: The Imprisonment of Japanese Americans during World War II,* by Daniel Davis (Dutton)

NONFICTION HONORS: *Hiroshima No Pika,* by Toshi Maruki (Lothrop, Lee & Shepard); *The Jewish Americans: A History in Their Own Words: 1650-1950,* by Milton Meltzer (Crowell)

PICTURE BOOK: *A Chair for My Mother,* by Vera B. Williams (Greenwillow)

PICTURE BOOK HONORS: *Friends,* by Helme Heine (McElderry); *Yeh-Shen: A Cinderella Story from China,* text by Ai-Ling Louie, illus. by Ed Young (Philomel); *Doctor De Soto,* by William Steig (Farrar, Straus & Giroux)

1984

FICTION: *A Little Fear,* by Patricia Wrighton (McElderry)

FICTION HONORS: *Archer's Goon,* by Diana Wynne Jones (Greenwillow); *Unclaimed Treasures,* by Patricia MacLachlan (HarperCollins); *A Solitary Blue,* by Cynthia Voigt (Atheneum)

NONFICTION: *The Double Life of Pocahontas,* by Jean Fritz (Putnam)

NONFICTION HONORS: *Queen Eleanor: Independent Spirit of the Medieval World: A Biography of Eleanor of Aquitaine,* by Polly Schoyer Brooks (Lippincott); *Children of the Wild West,* by Russell Freedman (Clarion); *The Tipi: A Center of Native American Life,* by David and Charlotte Yue (Knopf)

PICTURE BOOK: *Jonah and the Great Fish,* by Warwick Hutton (McElderry)

PICTURE BOOK HONORS: *Dawn,* by Molly Bang (Morrow); *The Guinea Pig ABC,* by Kate Duke (Dutton); *The Rose in My Garden,* text by Arnold Lobel, illus. by Anita Lobel (Greenwillow)

1985

FICTION: *The Moves Make the Man,* by Bruce Brooks (Harper-Collins)

FICTION HONORS: *Babe: The Gallant Pig,* by Dick King-Smith (Crown); *The Changeover: A Supernatural Romance,* by Margaret Mahy (McElderry)

NONFICTION: *Commodore Perry in the Land of the Shogun,* by Rhoda Blumberg (Lothrop, Lee & Shepard)

NONFICTION HONORS: *Boy,* by Roald Dahl (Farrar, Straus & Giroux); *1812: The War Nobody Won,* by Albert Marrin (Atheneum)

PICTURE BOOK: *Mama Don't Allow,* by Thacher Hurd (HarperCollins)

PICTURE BOOK HONORS: *Like Jake and Me,* text by Mavis Jukes, illus. by Lloyd Bloom (Knopf); *How Much Is a Million?* text by David M. Schwartz, illus. by Stephen Kellogg (Lothrop, Lee &

Shepard); *The Mysteries of Harris Burdick,* by Chris Van Allsburg (Houghton Mifflin)

SPECIAL CITATION: *1, 2, 3,* by Tana Hoban (Greenwillow)

1986

FICTION: *In Summer Light,* by Zibby Oneal (Viking)

FICTION HONORS: *Prairie Songs,* by Pam Conrad (Harper-Collins); *Howl's Moving Castle,* by Diana Wynne Jones (Greenwillow)

NONFICTION: *Auks, Rocks, and the Odd Dinosaur: Inside Stories from the Smithsonian's Museum of Natural History,* by Peggy Thomson (Crowell)

NONFICTION HONORS: *Dark Harvest: Migrant Farmworkers in America,* text by Brent Ashabranner, photos by Paul Conklin (Dodd, Mead); *The Truth about Santa Claus,* by James Cross Giblin (Crowell)

PICTURE BOOK: *The Paper Crane,* by Molly Bang (Greenwillow)

PICTURE BOOK HONORS: *Gorilla,* by Anthony Browne (Knopf); *The Trek,* by Ann Jonas (Greenwillow); *The Polar Express,* by Chris Van Allsburg (Houghton Mifflin)

1987

FICTION: *Rabble Starkey,* by Lois Lowry (Houghton Mifflin)

FICTION HONORS: *Georgia Music,* by Helen V. Griffith (Greenwillow); *Isaac Campion,* by Janni Howker (Greenwillow)

NONFICTION: *The Pilgrims of Plimoth,* by Marcia Sewall (Atheneum)

NONFICTION HONORS: *Being Born,* text by Sheila Kitzinger, photos by Lennart Nilsson (Grosset & Dunlap); *The Magic Schoolbus at the Waterworks,* text by Joanna Cole, illus. by Bruce Degen (Scholastic); *Steamboat in a Cornfield,* by John Hartford (Crown)

PICTURE BOOK: *Mufaro's Beautiful Daughters,* by John Steptoe (Lothrop, Lee & Shepard)

PICTURE BOOK HONORS: *In Coal Country,* text by Judith Hendershot, illus. by Thomas B. Allen (Knopf); *Cherries and Cherry Pits,* by Vera B. Williams (Greenwillow); *Old Henry,* text by Joan Blos, illus. by Stephen Gammell (Morrow)

1988

FICTION: *The Friendship,* by Mildred Taylor (Dial Books)

FICTION HONORS: *Granny Was a Buffer Girl,* by Berlie Doherty (Orchard Books); *Joyful Noise: Poems for Two Voices,* by Paul Fleischman (HarperCollins); *Memory,* by Margaret Mahy (McElderry)

NONFICTION: *Anthony Burns: The Defeat and Triumph of a Fugitive Slave,* by Virginia Hamilton (Knopf)

NONFICTION HONORS: *African Journey,* by John Chiasson (Bradbury); *Little by Little: A Writer's Education,* by Jean Little (Viking)

PICTURE BOOK: *The Boy of the Three-Year Nap,* text by Diane Snyder, illus. by Allen Say (Houghton Mifflin)

PICTURE BOOK HONORS: *Where the Forest Meets the Sea,* by Jeannie Baker (Greenwillow); *Stringbean's Trip to the Shining Sea,* text by Vera B. Williams, illus. by Jennifer and Vera B. Williams (Greenwillow)

1989

FICTION: *The Village by the Sea,* by Paula Fox (Orchard Books)

FICTION HONORS: *Eva,* by Peter Dickinson (Delacorte Press); *Gideon Ahoy!* by William Mayne (Delacorte Press)

NONFICTION: *The Way Things Work,* by David Macaulay (Houghton Mifflin)

NONFICTION HONORS: *The Rainbow People,* by Laurence Yep (HarperCollins); *Round Buildings, Square Buildings, and Buildings That Wiggle Like a Fish,* by Philip M. Isaacson (Knopf)

PICTURE BOOK: *Shy Charles,* by Rosemary Wells (Dial Books)

PICTURE BOOK HONORS: *Island Boy,* by Barbara Cooney (Viking); *The Nativity,* illus. by Julie Vivas (Harcourt)

1990

FICTION: *Maniac Magee,* by Jerry Spinelli (Little, Brown)

FICTION HONORS: *Saturnalia,* by Paul Fleischman (HarperCollins); *Stonewords,* by Pam Conrad (HarperCollins)

NONFICTION: *The Great Little Madison,* by Jean Fritz (Putnam)

NONFICTION HONOR: *Insect Metamorphosis: From Egg to Adult,* text by Ron and Nancy Goor, photos by Ron Goor (Atheneum)

PICTURE BOOK: *Lon Po Po: A Red Riding Hood Story from China,* by Ed Young (Philomel)

PICTURE BOOK HONOR: *Chicka Chicka Boom Boom,* text by Bill Martin Jr. and John Archambault, illus. by Lois Ehlert (Simon & Schuster)

SPECIAL CITATION: *Valentine and Orson,* by Nancy Ekholm Burkert (Farrar, Straus & Giroux)

1991

FICTION: *The True Confessions of Charlotte Doyle,* by Avi (Orchard Books)

FICTION HONORS: *Paradise Cafe and Other Stories,* by Martha Brooks (Joy Street); *Judy Scuppernong,* by Brenda Seabrooke (Cobblehill Books)

NONFICTION: *Appalachia: The Voices of Sleeping Birds,* text by Cynthia Rylant, illus. by Barry Moser (Harcourt)

NONFICTION HONORS: *The Wright Brothers: How They Invented the Airplane,* by Russell Freedman (Holiday House); *Good Queen Bess: The Story of Elizabeth I of England,* text by Diane Stanley and Peter Vennema, illus. by Diane Stanley (Four Winds)

PICTURE BOOK: *The Tale of the Mandarin Ducks,* by Katherine Paterson, illus. by Leo and Diane Dillon (Dutton)

PICTURE BOOK HONORS: *Aardvarks, Disembark!* by Ann Jonas (Greenwillow); *Sophie and Lou,* by Petra Mathers (HarperCollins)

1992

FICTION: *Missing May,* by Cynthia Rylant (Orchard Books)

FICTION HONORS: *Nothing but the Truth,* by Avi (Orchard Books); *Somewhere in the Darkness,* by Walter Dean Myers (Scholastic)

NONFICTION: *Talking with Artists,* by Pat Cummings (Bradbury)

NONFICTION HONORS: *Red Leaf, Yellow Leaf,* by Lois Ehlert (Harcourt); *The Handmade Alphabet,* by Laura Rankin (Dial Books)

PICTURE BOOK: *Seven Blind Mice,* by Ed Young (Philomel)

PICTURE BOOK HONOR: *In the Tall, Tall Grass,* by Denise Fleming (Henry Holt)

1993

FICTION: *Ajeemah and His Son,* by James Berry (HarperCollins)

FICTION HONOR: *The Giver,* by Lois Lowry (Houghton Mifflin)

NONFICTION: *Sojourner Truth: Ain't I a Woman?* by Patricia and Fredrick McKissack (Scholastic)

NONFICTION HONOR: *Lives of the Musicians: Good Times, Bad Times (and What the Neighbors Thought),* text by Kathleen Krull, illus. by Kathryn Hewitt (Harcourt)

PICTURE BOOK: *The Fortune Tellers,* by Lloyd Alexander, illus. by Trina Schart Hyman (Dutton)

PICTURE BOOK HONORS: *Komodo!* by Peter Sis (Greenwillow); *Raven: A Trickster Tale from the Pacific Northwest,* by Gerald McDermott (Harcourt)

1994

FICTION: *Scooter,* by Vera B. Williams (Greenwillow)

FICTION HONORS: *Flour Babies,* by Anne Fine (Little, Brown); *Western Wind,* by Paula Fox (Orchard Books)

NONFICTION: *Eleanor Roosevelt: A Life of Discovery,* by Russell Freedman (Clarion)

NONFICTION HONORS: *Unconditional Surrender: U. S. Grant and the Civil War,* by Albert Marrin (Atheneum); *A Tree Place and Other Poems,* text by Constance Levy, illus. by Robert Sabuda (McElderry)

PICTURE BOOK: *Grandfather's Journey,* by Allen Say (Houghton Mifflin)

PICTURE BOOK HONORS: *Owen,* by Kevin Henkes (Greenwillow); *A Small Tall Tale from the Far Far North,* by Peter Sis (Knopf)

1995

FICTION: *Some of the Kinder Planets,* by Tim Wynne-Jones (Orchard Books)

FICTION HONORS: *Jericho,* by Janet Hickman (Greenwillow); *Earthshine,* by Theresa Nelson (Orchard Books)

NONFICTION: *Abigail Adams, Witness to a Revolution,* by Natalie Bober (Atheneum)

NONFICTION HONORS: *It's Perfectly Normal: Changing Bodies, Growing Up, Sex, and Sexual Health,* text by Robie H. Harris, illus. by Michael Emberley (Candlewick Press); *The Great Fire,* by Jim Murphy (Scholastic)

PICTURE BOOK: *John Henry,* by Julius Lester, illus. by Jerry Pinkney (Dial Books)

PICTURE BOOK HONOR: *Swamp Angel,* text by Anne Isaacs, illus. by Paul O. Zelinsky (Dutton)

1996

FICTION: *Poppy,* by Avi, illus. by Brian Floca (Orchard Books)

FICTION HONORS: *The Moorchild,* by Eloise McGraw (McElderry); *Belle Prater's Boy,* by Ruth White (Farrar, Straus & Giroux)

NONFICTION: *Orphan Train Rider: One Boy's True Story,* by Andrea Warren (Houghton Mifflin)

NONFICTION HONORS: *The Boy Who Lived with the Bears: And Other Iroquois Stories,* text by Joseph Bruchac, illus. by Murv Jacob (HarperCollins); *Haystack,* text by Bonnie and Arthur Geisert, illus. by Arthur Geisert (Houghton Mifflin)

PICTURE BOOK: *In the Rain with Baby Duck,* text by Amy Hest, illus. by Jill Barton (Candlewick Press)

PICTURE BOOK HONORS: *Fanny's Dream,* text by Caralyn Buehner, illus. by Mark Buehner (Dial Books); *Home Lovely,* by Lynne Rae Perkins (Greenwillow)

1997

FICTION AND POETRY: *The Friends,* by Kazumi Yumoto, trans. by Cathy Hirano (Farrar, Straus & Giroux)

FICTION AND POETRY HONORS: *Lily's Crossing,* by Patricia Reilly Giff (Delacorte Press); *Harlem,* by Walter Dean Myers, illus. by Christopher Myers (Scholastic)

NONFICTION: *A Drop of Water: A Book of Science and Wonder,* by Walter Wick (Scholastic)

NONFICTION HONORS: *Lou Gehrig: The Luckiest Man,* by David Adler, illus. by Terry Widener (Harcourt); *Leonardo da Vinci,* by Diane Stanley (Morrow)

PICTURE BOOK: *The Adventures of Sparrowboy,* by Brian Pinkney (Simon & Schuster)

PICTURE BOOK HONORS: *Home on the Bayou: A Cowboy's Story,* by G. Brian Karas (Simon & Schuster); *Potato: A Tale from the Great Depression,* by Kate Lied, illus. by Lisa Campbell Ernst (National Geographic Society)

1998

FICTION AND POETRY: *The Circuit: Stories from the Life of a Migrant Child,* by Francisco Jiménez (University of New Mexico Press)

FICTION AND POETRY HONORS: *While No One Was Watching,* by Jane Leslie Conly (Henry Holt); *My Louisiana Sky,* by Kimberly Willis Holt (Henry Holt)

NONFICTION: *Leon's Story,* by Leon Walter Tillage, illus. by Susan L. Roth (Farrar, Straus & Giroux)

NONFICTION HONORS: *Martha Graham: A Dancer's Life,* by Russell Freedman (Clarion); *Chuck Close up Close,* by Jan Greenberg and Sandra Jordan (DK Publishing)

PICTURE BOOK: *And If the Moon Could Talk,* by Kate Banks, illus. by Georg Hallensleben (Farrar, Straus & Giroux)

PICTURE BOOK HONORS: *Seven Brave Women,* by Betsy Hearne, illus. by Bethanne Andersen (Greenwillow); *Popcorn: Poems,* by James Stevenson (Greenwillow)

1999

FICTION: *Holes,* by Louis Sachar (Farrar, Straus & Giroux)

FICTION HONORS: *The Trolls,* by Polly Horvath (Farrar, Straus & Giroux); *Monster,* by Walter Dean Myers, illus. by Christopher Myers (HarperCollins)

NONFICTION: *The Top of the World: Climbing Mount Everest,* by Steve Jenkins (Houghton Mifflin)

NONFICTION HONORS: *Shipwreck at the Bottom of the World: The Extraordinary True Story of Shackleton and the* Endurance, by Jennifer Armstrong (Crown); *William Shakespeare and the Globe,* by Aliki (HarperCollins)

PICTURE BOOK: *Red-Eyed Tree Frog,* by Joy Cowley, illus. by Nic Bishop (Scholastic)

PICTURE BOOK HONORS: *Dance,* by Bill T. Jones and Susan Kuklin, illus. by Susan Kuklin (Hyperion); *The Owl and the Pussycat,* by Edward Lear, illus. by James Marshall (HarperCollins)

SPECIAL CITATION: *Tibet: Through the Red Box,* by Peter Sis (Farrar, Straus & Giroux)

2000

FICTION: *The Folk Keeper,* by Franny Billingsley (Atheneum)

FICTION HONORS: *King of Shadows,* by Susan Cooper (McElderry); *145th Street: Short Stories,* by Walter Dean Myers (Delacorte Press)

NONFICTION: *Sir Walter Raleigh and the Quest for El Dorado,* by Marc Aronson (Clarion)

NONFICTION HONORS: *Osceola: Memories of a Sharecropper's Daughter,* collected and ed. by Alan Govenar, illus. by Shane W. Evans (Jump at the Sun); *Sitting Bull and His World,* by Albert Marrin (Dutton)

PICTURE BOOK: *Henry Hikes to Fitchburg,* by D. B. Johnson (Houghton Mifflin)

PICTURE BOOK HONORS: *Buttons,* by Brock Cole (Farrar, Straus & Giroux); *A Day, a Dog,* by Gabrielle Vincent (Front Street)

2001

FICTION AND POETRY: *Carver: A Life in Poems,* by Marilyn Nelson (Front Street)

FICTION AND POETRY HONORS: *Everything on a Waffle,* by Polly Horvath (Farrar, Straus & Giroux); *Troy,* by Adèle Geras (Harcourt)

NONFICTION: *The Longitude Prize,* by Joan Dash, illus. by Dusan Petricic (Farrar, Straus & Giroux)

NONFICTION HONORS: *Rocks in His Head,* by Carol Otis Hurst, illus. by James Stevenson (Greenwillow); *Uncommon Traveler: Mary Kingsley in Africa,* by Don Brown (Houghton Mifflin)

PICTURE BOOK: *Cold Feet,* by Cynthia DeFelice, illus. by Robert Andrew Parker (DK Publishing)

PICTURE BOOK HONORS: *Five Creatures,* by Emily Jenkins, illus. by Tomek Bogacki (Farrar, Straus & Giroux); *The Stray Dog,* retold and illus. by Marc Simont (HarperCollins)

2002

FICTION AND POETRY: *Lord of the Deep,* by Graham Salisbury (Delacorte Press)

FICTION AND POETRY HONORS: *Amber Was Brave, Essie Was Smart,* by Vera B. Williams (Greenwillow); *Saffy's Angel,* by Hilary McKay (McElderry)

NONFICTION: *This Land Was Made for You and Me: The Life and Songs of Woody Guthrie,* by Elizabeth Partridge (Viking)

NONFICTION HONORS: *Handel, Who Knew What He Liked,* by M. T. Anderson, illus. by Kevin Hawkes (Candlewick Press); *Woody Guthrie: Poet of the People,* by Bonnie Christensen (Knopf)

PICTURE BOOK: *"Let's Get a Pup!" Said Kate,* by Bob Graham (Candlewick Press)

PICTURE BOOK HONORS: *I Stink!* by Kate McMullan, illus. by Jim McMullan (HarperCollins); *Little Rat Sets Sail,* by Monika Bang-Campbell, illus. by Molly Bang (Harcourt)

2003

FICTION AND POETRY: *The Jamie and Angus Stories,* by Anne Fine, illus. by Penny Dale (Candlewick Press)

FICTION AND POETRY HONORS: *Feed,* by M. T. Anderson (Candlewick Press); *Locomotion,* by Jacqueline Woodson (Putnam)

NONFICTION: *Fireboat: The Heroic Adventures of the* **John J. Harvey,** by Maira Kalman (Putnam)

NONFICTION HONORS: *To Fly: The Story of the Wright Brothers,* by Wendie C. Old, illus. by Robert Andrew Parker (Clarion); *Revenge of the Whale: The True Story of the Whaleship* **Essex,** by Nathaniel Philbrick (Putnam)

PICTURE BOOK: *Big Momma Makes the World,* by Phyllis Root, illus. by Helen Oxenbury (Candlewick Press)

PICTURE BOOK HONORS: *Dahlia,* by Barbara McClintock (Farrar, Straus & Giroux); *blues journey,* by Walter Dean Myers, illus. by Christopher Myers (Holiday House)

2004

FICTION AND POETRY: *The Fire Eaters,* by David Almond (Delacorte Press)

FICTION AND POETRY HONORS: *God Went to Beauty School,* by Cynthia Rylant (HarperTempest); *The Amulet of Samarkand: The Bartimaeus Trilogy, Book One,* by Jonathan Stroud (Hyperion)

NONFICTION: *An American Plague: The True and Terrifying Story of the Yellow Fever Epidemic of 1793,* by Jim Murphy (Clarion)

NONFICTION HONORS: *Surprising Sharks,* by Nicola Davies, illus. by James Croft (Candlewick Press); *The Man Who Went to the Far Side of the Moon: The Story of* **Apollo 11** *Astronaut Michael Collins,* by Bea Uusma Schyffert (Chronicle Books)

PICTURE BOOK: *The Man Who Walked between the Towers,* by Mordicai Gerstein (Roaring Brook Press)

PICTURE BOOK HONORS: *The Shape Game,* by Anthony Browne (Farrar, Straus & Giroux); *Snow Music,* by Lynne Rae Perkins (Greenwillow)

• • • The Lee Bennett Hopkins Poetry Award • • •

The Lee Bennett Hopkins Poetry Award, established in 1993 and administered by Penn State University, is given annually to a living American poet for a volume of poetry, either an original collection or an anthology. In 1999, the Penn State University group decided to choose honor books for the award.

1993
Sing to the Sun, by Ashley Bryan (McElderry)

1994
Spirit Walker, by Nancy Wood (Doubleday)

1995
Beast Feast, by Douglas Florian (Greenwillow)

1996
Dance with Me, by Barbara Juster Esbensen (HarperCollins)

1997
Voices from the Wild, by David Bouchard (Chronicle Books)

1998
The Great Frog Race, by Kristine O'Connell George (Clarion)

1999
The Other Side: Shorter Poems, by Angela Johnson (Orchard Books)

HONOR BOOK: *A Crack in the Clouds,* by Constance Levy (McElderry)

2000
What Have You Lost? ed. by Naomi Shihab Nye (Greenwillow)

HONOR BOOKS: *An Old Shell,* by Tony Johnston (Farrar, Straus & Giroux); *The Rainbow Hand,* by Janet S. Wong (McElderry)

2001
Light Gathering Poems, ed. by Liz Rosenberg (Henry Holt)

HONOR BOOK: *Stone Bench in an Empty Park,* ed. by Paul Janeczko (Orchard Books)

2002

Pieces: A Year in Poems and Quilts, by Anna Grossnickle Hines (Greenwillow)

Honor Books: *A Humble Life: Plain Poems,* by Linda Oatman High, illus. by Bill Farnsworth (Eerdmans); *A Poke in the I: A Collection of Concrete Poems,* by Paul Janeczko, illus. by Chris Raschka (Candlewick Press); *Short Takes: Fast-Break Basketball Poetry,* by Charles R. Smith Jr. (Dutton)

2003

Splash! Poems of Our Watery World, by Constance Levy, illus. by David Soman (Orchard Books)

Honor Books: *Girl Coming in for a Landing: A Novel in Poems,* by April Halprin Wayland, illus. by Elaine Clayton (Knopf); *Becoming Joe DiMaggio,* by Maria Testa (Candlewick Press); *The Song Shoots out of My Mouth,* by Jaime Adoff, illus. by Martin French (Dutton)

2004

The Wishing Bone and Other Poems, by Stephen Mitchell, illus. by Tom Pohrt (Candlewick Press)

Honor Books: *Animal Sense,* by Diane Ackerman, illus. by Peter Sis (Knopf); *blues journey,* by Walter Dean Myers, illus. by Christopher Myers (Holiday House); *The Pond God and Other Stories,* by Samuel Jay Keyser, illus. by Robert Shetterly (Front Street); *The Way a Door Closes,* by Hope Anita Smith, illus. by Shane W. Evans (Henry Holt)

• • • How to Update Current Listings • • • and Find Other Awards

There are about 150 to 200 different awards given for children's and adolescent books; each has its own unique selection process and criteria. Some awards are chosen by adults, some by children, and some by young adults; some are international, some state or regional; some are for a lifetime of work, some for one book. We used the comprehensive listing of various award winners in *Children's Books: Awards and Prizes,* published by the Children's Book Council. This publication is updated periodically. We also used websites of professional organizations for the most up-to-date information: www.ala.org, www.reading.org, and www.ncte.org, among others.

B

Resources

• • • Book Selection Aids • • •

Adventuring with Books: Grades Pre-K–6 (13th ed.), edited by Amy A. McClure and Janice V. Kristo (National Council of Teachers of English, 2002). A comprehensive list of books selected for their merit and potential use in the classroom. Approximately 2,000 new books are annotated with several hundred from previous editions listed by genre. New editions are prepared periodically.

Best Science and Technology Reference Books for Young People, edited by H. Robert Malinowsky (Greenwood, 1991). Reviews science and technology resources and recommends grade levels for sci-tech reference books.

Books to Help Children Cope with Separation and Loss (4th ed.), compiled by Masha Kabakow Rudman, Kathleen Dunne Gagne, and Joanne E. Bernstein (Bowker, 1993). 514 pages. Discussion of bibliotherapy with annotated lists of books grouped by category, such as adoption, divorce, and disabilities.

Children's Books: Awards and Prizes, compiled and edited by the Children's Book Council (1996). 497 pages. A comprehensive list of honors awarded to children's books. Awards chosen by adults and children are grouped by state, national, and international designations.

Children's Books in Print (Bowker, annual). A comprehensive index of all children's books in print at time of publication. Author, title, and illustrator indexes give pertinent publishing information. A directory of publishers and addresses is included.

Children's Catalog (Wilson, annual). A comprehensive catalog classified by Dewey decimal system, with nonfiction, fiction, short stories, and easy books. Five-year cumulations and annual supplements available.

Children's Literature Review (Gale Research). Since 1976, new volumes have been added periodically. Articles about authors and topics of interest with excerpts from reviews of the works of each author.

Continuum Encyclopedia of Children's Literature, edited by Bernice E. Cullinan and Diane G. Person (Giniger/Continuum International, 2003). A comprehensive collection of author and illustrator biographies, and topic and genre entries about children's literature in the major English-speaking countries.

Elementary School Library Collection (25th ed.), edited by Linda Homa (Bro-Dart, 2000). A comprehensive bibliography of print and nonprint materials for school media collections. Dewey decimal subject classification, age level, and brief annotations.

For Reading Out Loud! by Elizabeth Segel and Margaret Mary Kimmel (Bantam Dell, 1991). A guide to selecting books for sharing with young people and techniques for sharing them. Subject, title, and author index.

Hey! Listen to This: Stories to Read Aloud, edited by Jim Trelease (Penguin, 1992). Selections from literature to read to primary-grade children. Trelease adds intriguing background information about each excerpt.

Jewish Children's Books: How to Choose Them, How to Use Them, by Marcia Posner (Hadassah, 1986). 48 pages. Summaries, themes, discussion guides, questions and activities, and further resources are given for more than 30 books.

Kaleidoscope: A Multicultural Booklist for Grades K–8 (4th ed.), edited by Nancy Hansen-Krening, Elaine M. Aoki, Donald T. Mizokawa (National Council of Teachers of English, 2003). Hundreds of fiction and nonfiction texts for elementary and middle school students, featuring culturally diverse populations.

Library Services for Hispanic Children: A Guide for Public and School Librarians, edited by Adela Artola Allen (Oryx Press, 1987). 201 pages. Articles on professional issues related to library service for Hispanic children. Annotated bibliographies of children's books in English about Hispanics, recent noteworthy children's books in Spanish, computer software, and resources about Hispanic culture for librarians.

The New Read-Aloud Handbook (5th ed.), by Jim Trelease (Penguin, 2001). An enthusiastic argument for why we should read to children, techniques for reading aloud, and a treasury of more than a thousand books that work well as read-alouds.

Newbery and Caldecott Medal Books: 1986–2000: A Comprehensive Guide to the Winner (Horn Book/Association for Library Service to Children, 2001). A continuing collaboration features book summaries, selected excerpts, reviews, acceptance speeches, and biographical essays about the winners.

Pass the Poetry, Please (3rd ed.), by Lee Bennett Hopkins (HarperCollins, 1998). A well-informed author describes engaging interviews with outstanding poets. Hopkins includes comments from interviews and insights into the poets' work, and suggests ways to use poetry with children.

Read to Me: Raising Kids Who Love to Read (2nd ed.), by Bernice E. Cullinan (Scholastic, 2000). A book that encourages parents to make reading a central part of children's lives and shows them how to do it.

Selected Jewish Children's Books, compiled by Marcia Posner (Jewish Book Council, 1991). Annotated list of books containing Jewish content and values, categorized by topic and age levels.

Subject Guide to Children's Books in Print (Bowker, annual). Approximately 140,000 titles are grouped under 7,000 subject categories. This indispensable reference helps you find books on specific topics.

Subject Index to Poetry for Children and Young People, compiled by Violet Sell (Core Collection Books, 1982). 1,035 pages. An index of poetry organized by subject with a code for title and author.

With Women's Eyes: Visitors to the New World, 1775–1918, edited by Marion Tinling (Shoe String Press, 1993). 204 pages. Twenty-seven European women who visited America between 1775 and 1918 tell about their experiences.

• • • Reference Books about Authors • • • and Illustrators

The Art of Leo and Diane Dillon, edited by Byron Preiss (Ballantine Books, 1981). Introductory critical essay with 120 illustrations, including 8 color plates of the Dillons' art. The Dillons comment on the meaning, context, and techniques used in each painting.

The Art of Nancy Ekholm Burkert, edited by David Larkin (HarperCollins, 1977). 50 pages. Full-page color spreads of 40 Burkert paintings with an interpretive essay by Michael Danoff.

Author Talk: Conversations with Judy Blume, Bruce Brooks, Karen Cushman, Russell Freedman, Lee Bennett Hopkins, James Howe, Johanna Hurwitz, E. L. Konigsburg, Lois Lowry, Ann M. Martin, Nicholasa Mohr, Gary Paulsen, Jon Scieszka, Seymour Simon, and Laurence Yep, by Leonard S. Marcus (Simon & Schuster, 2000). Interviews with well-known children's writers.

Awakened by the Moon: Margaret Wise Brown, by Leonard Marcus (Beacon Press, 1992). A literary study of an outstanding author who helped establish modern picture books.

Boy: Tales of Childhood, by Roald Dahl (Viking, 1984). 176 pages. An autobiography that describes the origins of one author's ideas.

Carl Larsson, by the Brooklyn Museum and the National Museum in Stockholm, with the support of the Swedish Institute in Stockholm (Brooklyn Museum, 1982). 96 pages. A catalog of Carl Larsson's paintings with commentary by critics. Chronology and selected bibliography.

Caldecott Medal Books: 1938–1957, by Bertha Mahony Miller and Elinor Whitney Field (Horn Book, 1958). Artists' acceptance speeches and biographical articles of the Caldecott Medal winners.

Celebrating Children's Books, edited by Betsy Hearne and Marilyn Kaye (Lothrop, Lee & Shepard, 1981). Articles about their craft by the foremost authors writing for children today. The essays in this collection appear in honor of Zena Sutherland.

Children's Book Illustration and Design (Vol. 1, 1992; Vol. 2, 1998), edited by Julie Cummins (PBC International). Each book is a showcase for the work of about 80 illustrators of children's books selected by a knowledgeable critic.

From Writers to Students: The Pleasures and Pains of Writing, edited by Jerry Weiss (International Reading Association, 1979). 113 pages. Interviews with 19 noted authors who reveal the inside story on their writing, including Judy Blume, Mollie Hunter, Milton Meltzer, Mary Rodgers, and Laurence Yep.

Illustrators of Children's Books: 1744–1945, edited by Bertha E. Mahony, Louise Payson Latimer, and Beulah Folmsbee (Horn Book, 1947). 527 pages. *Illustrators of Children's Books: 1946–1956,* edited by Bertha Mahony Miller, Ruth Hill Viguers, and Marcia Dalphin (Horn Book, 1958). 229 pages. *Illustrators of Children's Books: 1957–1966,* edited by Lee Kingman, Joanna Foster, and Ruth Giles Lontoft (Horn Book, 1968). 295 pages. *Illustrators of Children's Books: 1967–1976,* edited by Lee Kingman, Grace Allen Hogarth, and Harriet Quimby (Horn Book, 1978). 290 pages. *Illustrators of Children's Books: 1977–1986,* edited by Lee Kingman (Horn Book, 1987). Biographical sketches and discussion of artists' techniques.

Little by Little: A Writer's Education, by Jean Little (Viking, 1987). 233 pages. *Stars Come Out Within,* by Jean Little (Viking, 1992). A two-part autobiography by Canadian writer Jean Little.

Meet the Authors and Illustrators, by Deborah Kovacs and James Preller (Scholastic, 1991). Sixty creators of favorite children's books talk about their work.

Meet the Author Series (Richard C. Owen Publishers). Autobiographies by Verna Aardema, Frank Asch, Eve Bunting, Lois Ehlert, Jean Fritz, Paul Goble, Ruth Heller, Lee Bennett Hopkins, James Howe, Karla Kuskin, George Ella Lyon, Margaret Mahy, Rafe Martin, Patricia McKissack, Patricia Polacco, Laurence Pringle, Cynthia Rylant, Jane Yolen, and others. A continuing series suitable for students in primary and intermediate grades.

Newbery and Caldecott Medal Books: 1956–1965, edited by Lee Kingman (Horn Book, 1965). 300 pages. *Newbery and Caldecott Medal Books: 1966–1975,* edited by Lee Kingman (Horn Book, 1975). *Newbery and Caldecott Medal Books: 1976–1985,* edited by Lee Kingman (Horn Book, 1987). *Newbery Medal Books: 1922–1955,* edited by Bertha Mahony Miller and Elinor Whitney Field (Horn Book, 1955). Acceptance speeches and biographical sketches about the winners.

Oxford Companion to Children's Literature, compiled by Humphrey Carpenter and Mari Prichard (Oxford University Press, 1984). Includes nearly 2,000 entries, more than 900 of which are biographical sketches of authors, illustrators, printers, and publishers. Other entries cover topic and genre issues and plot summaries of major works.

Pauses: Autobiographical Reflections of 101 Creators of Children's Books, by Lee Bennett Hopkins (HarperCollins, 1995). Biographical information and excerpts from interviews with authors and illustrators.

Secret Gardens, by Humphrey Carpenter (Houghton Mifflin, 1985). A book about the authors who wrote during the years called the golden age of children's literature in the late nineteenth and early twentieth centuries.

Self-Portrait: Erik Blegvad, by Erik Blegvad (Addison-Wesley, 1979). 32 pages. Blegvad discusses himself, his life, and his work.

Self-Portrait: Trina Schart Hyman, by Trina Schart Hyman (Addison-Wesley, 1981). 32 pages. Hyman describes her life, friends, and family and their reflections in her painting.

Self-Portrait: Margot Zemach, by Margot Zemach (Addison-Wesley, 1978). 32 pages. Zemach talks about her life, her family, and her work.

Something about the Author (Gale Research). In 120 volumes, extensive biographical information, photographs, publication records, awards received, and quotations about thousands of authors and illustrators of children's books.

Speaking for Ourselves: Autobiographical Sketches by Notable Authors of Books for Young Adults, edited by Donald R. Gallo (National Council of Teachers of English, 1990). Includes brief first-person statements from writers about writing and a bibliography for each writer.

Speaking for Ourselves, Too, edited by Donald R. Gallo (National Council of Teachers of English, 1993). More autobiographical sketches by notable authors of books for adolescents. Also includes brief first-person statements from writers about writing and a bibliography for each writer.

Speaking of Poets: Interviews with Poets Who Write for Children and Young Adults, edited by Jeffrey S. Copeland (National Council of Teachers of English, 1993). *Speaking of Poets: Interviews with Poets Who Write for Children and Young Adults 2,* edited by Jeffrey S. and Vicki L. Copeland (National Council of Teachers of English, 1994). Brief biographies and substantial interviews, followed by individual bibliographies.

Starting from Home: A Writer's Beginnings, by Milton Meltzer (Viking, 1988). Meltzer's life story.

Talking with Artists (Vol. 1, 1992, Vol. 2, 1995, Vol. 3, 1999), edited by Pat Cummings (Bradbury). Children's book illustrators talk about their work.

• • • Periodicals about Children's Literature • • •

Bookbird: A Journal of International Children's Literature A refereed journal published quarterly by the International Board on Books for Young People, Nonnenweg 12 Postfach, CH-4004 Basel, Switzerland. Editors Siobhán Parkinson and Valerie Coghlan. Past editor-in-chief Meena G. Khorana. The journal provides a forum to exchange experience and information among readers and writers in 50 nations of the world. Includes analyses of children's literature in particular regions—for example, children's literature of Latin America.

Book Links: Connecting Books, Libraries, and Classrooms Editor Laura Tillotson, American Library Association, published six times a year. Features booklists, interviews, teaching guides, and theme-related bibliographies to help teachers and librarians bring literature to children in ways that make connections across the curriculum.

Booklist Editor Bill Ott, American Library Association, published biweekly September through August, once each in July and August. Reviews children's, adolescent, and adult books and nonprint materials. Periodic bibliographies on a specific subject, reference tools, and commentary on issues are invaluable.

Bulletin of the Center for Children's Books Graduate School of Library and Information Science of the University of Illinois at Urbana–Champaign, distributed by the University of Illinois Press, published monthly, except August. A review journal now edited by Deborah Stevenson that was initiated by Zena Sutherland and edited by Betsy Hearne. One of the few journals to include critical starred reviews of books rated as * (books of special distinction), R (recommended), Ad (additional), M (marginal), NR (not recommended), SpC (special collection), SpR (special reader). Curriculum use and developmental values are assigned when appropriate.

CBC Features Children's Book Council, published semi-annually. A newsletter about current issues and events, free and inexpensive materials, materials for Children's Book Week, topical bibliographies, and essays by publishers and authors or illustrators.

Children and Libraries: The Journal of the Association for Library Service to Children Articles of interest to teachers and librarians on current issues, specialized bibliographies, acceptance speeches by the Newbery and Caldecott Award winners, conference proceedings, and organizational news.

Children's Literature Association Quarterly   Children's Literature Association. Book reviews and articles on British and American children's literature, research, teaching children's literature, theater, and conference proceedings. Special sections on current topics of interest, poetry, censorship, awards, and announcements.

The Horn Book Magazine   Editor Roger Sutton, Horn Book, published bimonthly. A review journal with intelligent commentary by the editor and invited writers, and articles by creators of children's books, publishers, critics, teachers, and librarians. Ratings include starred reviews for outstanding books and comprehensive reviews of recommended books. Also includes Newbery and Caldecott acceptance speeches, biographical sketches of winners, and Boston Globe–Horn Book Award winners. Announces children's literature conferences and events. Two cumulative indexes with ratings for all books published appear in *The Horn Book Guide*.

Scholastic Instructor   Editor Terry Cooper, Scholastic, published eight times a year. Teachers and librarians write feature articles about trends, new books, and authors and illustrators of note. Bernice E. Cullinan is editor of the primary-grade poetry column; Paul Janeczko is editor of the intermediate-grade poetry column. Conducts an annual poetry writing contest for children.

School Library Media Research: Refereed Research Journal of the American Association of School Librarians   Published online at www.ala.org/aasl/SLMR. Includes research articles on censorship, using books in the classroom, research, library services, and current issues.

Language Arts   A journal published monthly from September through May by the National Council of Teachers of English. A book review column reviews current recommended books for children. Profiles on authors and illustrators; articles on using books in the classroom, response to literature, and writing as an outgrowth of reading literature.

The New York Times Book Review   Includes occasional column of reviews written by authors, illustrators, or reviewers. Special section in spring and fall features children's books; annual list of the 10 best illustrated books of the year.

Publishers Weekly   Published by Reed Elsvier with a spring and fall special edition on children's books. Diane Roback is senior children's book editor, Jennifer M. Brown is forecasts editor, and Joy Bean is associate editor. Both positive and negative reviews of books and news articles of interest to publishers, teachers, librarians, and authors. Interviews with authors, illustrators, and publishers are regular features.

The Reading Teacher   Coeditors Priscilla L. Griffith and Carol Lynch Brown, International Reading Association, published nine times a year. A column of reviews of current children's books is a regular feature. Articles appear on the use of books in the classroom, special bibliographies, cross-cultural studies, and research using children's books in reading programs.

School Library Journal   Editor-in-chief Julie Cummins, Cahners, published 11 times a year. Includes articles on current issues and reviews of children's books written by practicing librarians. Information is given about conferences and library services. Also includes an annual "Best Books of the Year" column and a cumulative index of starred reviews.

Science and Children   Published eight times per year by the National Science Teachers Association. Monthly column of reviews of informational books on science topics, plus an annual list of recommended books chosen by NSTA/Children's Book Council Liaison Committee.

Young Adult Library Services: The Journal of the Young Adult Library Services Association   Articles of interest to teachers and librarians on current issues, specialized bibliographies, acceptance speeches by the Printz award winner, conference proceedings, and organizational news.

Note: Each professional organization and journal publisher has a website. Check the Internet for listings of current events and features.

Publishers' Addresses

Abrams Books for Young Readers
100 Fifth Avenue
New York, NY 10011
www.abramsbooks.com

Addison-Wesley and Benjamin Cummings
75 Arlington Street
Suite 300
Boston, MA 02116
www.aw-bc.com

Africa World Press and The Red Sea Press
541 West Ingham Avenue Suite B
Trenton, NJ 08638
E-mail: awprsp@africanworld.com
www.africanworld.com

Arte Público Press
University of Houston
452 Cullen Performance Hall
Houston, TX 77204-2004
www.arte.uh.edu

Atheneum (*see* Simon & Schuster)

Avon Books (*see* HarperCollins)

Bantam Doubleday Dell Books for Young
Readers (*see* Random House)

Black Classic Press
PO Box 13414
Baltimore, MD 21203
E-mail: bcp@charm.net
www.blackclassic.com

Blue Sky Press (*see* Scholastic)

Boyds Mills Press
815 Church Street
Honesdale, PA 18431
www.boydsmillspress.com

Bradbury Press (*see* Simon & Schuster)

Candlewick Press
2067 Massachusetts Avenue
Cambridge, MA 02140
www.candlewick.com

Carolrhoda Books (*see* Lerner)

Cavendish Children's Books
Marshall Cavendish
99 White Plains Road
Tarrytown, NY 10591-9001
www.marshallcavendish.com

Children's Book Press (*see* Scholastic)

Clarion (*see* Houghton Mifflin)

Cricket Books
Division of Carus Publishing
315 Fifth Street
Peru, IL 61354
www.cricketmag.com

Crown (*see* Random House)

Delacorte Press (*see* Random House)

Dell (*see* Random House)

Dial Books for Young Readers (*see* Penguin
Putnam)

Disney Books
Division of Walt Disney Co.
500 S. Buena Vista Street
Burbank, CA 91521
www.disney.go.com/disneybooks/index
.html

DK Publishing
Subsidiary of Dorling Kindersley Ltd.
375 Hudson Street
New York, NY 10014
www.dk.com

Doubleday (*see* Random House)

Dutton (*see* Penguin Putnam)

Wm. B. Eerdmans Publishing
255 Jefferson Ave. SE
Grand Rapids, MI 49503
E-mail: youngreaders@eerdmans.com
www.eerdmans.com/youngreaders

Farrar, Straus & Giroux
19 Union Square West
New York, NY 10003
www.fsgbooks.com

Phyllis Fogelman Books (*see* Penguin
Putnam)

Four Winds Press (*see* Simon & Schuster)

Front Street Books
862 Haywood Road
Asheville, NC 28806
www.frontstreetbooks.com

David R. Godine Publisher
9 Hamilton Place
Boston, MA 02108-4715
www.godine.com

Golden Books Children's Publishing
Group (*see* Random House)

Greenwillow (*see* HarperCollins)

Grolier Publishing (*see* Scholastic)

Grosset & Dunlap (*see* Penguin Putnam)

Groundwood Books
720 Bathurst Street
Suite 500
Toronto, Ontario
M5S 2R4 Canada
www.groundwoodbooks.com

Harcourt Trade Publishers
525 B Street, Suite 1900
San Diego, CA 92101
www.harcourtbooks.com

HarperCollins Children's Books
1350 Avenue of the Americas
New York, NY 10019
www.harperchildrens.com

HarperTempest (*see* HarperCollins)

Holiday House
425 Madison Avenue
New York, NY 10017
www.holidayhouse.com

Henry Holt & Co.
115 West 18th Street
New York, NY 10011
www.henryholt.com

Houghton Mifflin
222 Berkeley Street
Boston, MA 02116
www.hmco.com

Hyperion Books for Children
114 Fifth Avenue
New York, NY 10010-5690
www.hyperionbooksforchildren.com

Jewish Publication Society
2100 Arch Street, 2nd floor
Philadelphia, PA 19103
www.jewishpub.org

Jump at the Sun (*see* Hyperion)

Just Us Books
356 Glenwood Avenue, 3rd floor
East Orange, NJ 07017
www.justusbooks.com

The Kane Press
240 West 35th Street, Suite 300
New York, NY 10001
www.kanepress.com

Kane/Miller Book Publishers
PO Box 8515
La Jolla, CA 92038
www.kanemiller.com

Kids Can Press Ltd.
2250 Military Road
Tonawanda, NY 14150
www.kidscanpress.com

Alfred A. Knopf (*see* Random House)

Lee & Low Books
95 Madison Avenue, Suite 606
New York, NY 10016
www.leeandlow.com

Lerner Publications
241 First Avenue North, Suite 1
Minneapolis, MN 55401
www.lernerbooks.com

Lippincott (*see* HarperCollins)

Little, Brown and Company
Div. of Time Warner Trade Publishing
1271 Avenue of the Americas
New York, NY 10020
www.twbookmark.com

Lothrop, Lee & Shepard
(*see* HarperCollins)

Margaret McElderry Books (*see* Simon
& Schuster)

The Millbrook Press (*see* Lerner
Publications Co.)

Mondo Publishing
980 Avenue of the Americas
New York, NY 10018
www.mondopub.com

Morrow (*see* HarperCollins)

North-South Books
875 Sixth Avenue, Suite 1901
New York, NY 10001
www.northsouth.com

Orchard Books (*see* Scholastic)

Richard C. Owen Publishers
Box 585
Katonah, NY 10536
www.rcowen.com

Oxford University Press
198 Madison Avenue
New York, NY 10016
www.oup.com/us

Pantheon (*see* Random House)

Peachtree Publishers Ltd.
1700 Chattahoochee Avenue
Atlanta, GA 30318-2112
www.peachtree-online.com

Penguin Putnam
375 Hudson Street
New York, NY 10014
www.penguinputnam.com

Philomel Books (*see* Penguin Putnam)

Piñata Books (*see* Arte Público Press)

Pleasant Company Publications
PO Box 620991
Middleton, WI 53562-0991
www.pleasantcopublications.com

Rand McNally
Educational Publishing
8255 N. Central Park Avenue
Skokie, IL 60076
www.randmcnally.com

Random House
1745 Broadway
New York, NY 10019
www.randomhouse.com

Rizzoli/Universe International
Publications
300 Park Avenue South, 3rd floor
New York, NY 10010
www.rizzoliusa.com

Scholastic
557 Broadway
New York, NY 10012
www.scholastic.com

Sierra Club Books
85 Second Street, 2nd floor
San Francisco, CA 94105
www.sierraclub.org/books

Silver Moon Press
160 Fifth Avenue
New York, NY 10010
www.silvermoonpress.com

Simon & Schuster
1230 Avenue of the Americas
New York, NY 10020
www.simonsays.com

Third World Press
7822 S. Dobson Ave.
PO Box 19730
Chicago, IL 60619
www.thirdworldpressinc.com

Tristan Publishing
(formerly Waldman House Press)
2300 Louisiana Avenue North, Suite B
Golden Valley, MN 55427

Viking (*see* Penguin Putnam)

Walker & Co.
104 Fifth Avenue
New York, NY 10011
www.walkerbooks.com

Frederick Warne (*see* Penguin Putnam)

Franklin Watts Inc.
The Watts Publishing Group
96 Leonard Street
London, EC2A 4XD
www.wattspub.co.uk

Albert Whitman & Co.
6340 Oakton Street
Morton Grove, IL 60053-2723
www.awhitmanco.com

Winston-Derek Publishers Group
PO Box 90883
Nashville, TN 37203

Wordsong (*see* Boyds Mills Press)

• • • Paperback Book Clubs • • •

Scholastic Book Clubs
557 Broadway
New York, NY 10012
www.scholastic.com

TrollCarnival Book Clubs (*see* Scholastic)
www.trollcarnival.com

Trumpet Book Club (*see* Scholastic)

• • • Professional • • • Organizations

American Library Association
50 East Huron Street
Chicago, IL 60611
www.ala.org

Children's Book Council
12 West 37th Street, 2nd floor
New York, NY 10018-7480
www.cbcbooks.org

International Reading Association
800 Barksdale Road
Newark, DE 19714-8139
www.reading.org

National Council of Teachers of English
1111 Kenyon Road
Urbana, IL 61801-1096
www.ncte.org

Children's Magazines and Newspapers

Chickadee

Age range: 6–9. Introduces the world of science, nature, and technology to young children through engaging stories and well-developed illustrations. Chickadee Magazine, The OWL Group, 49 Front Street, #200, Toronto, ON Canada M53 1B3. www.owlkids.com/chickadee.

Cicada

Age range: 9–18. A literary magazine for teenagers with fiction and poetry written by adults and teens. Cicada Magazine, Carus Publishing Company, 315 Fifth Street, Peru, IL 61345. www.cricketmag.com.

Click: Opening Windows for Young Minds

Age range: 3–7. Published 10 times a year by the publishers of *Cricket Magazine* and *Smithsonian Magazine,* and contains 36 pages that visualize a child's world. Click Magazine, Carus Publishing Company, 315 Fifth Street, Peru, IL 61345. www.cricketmag.com.

Cobblestone

Age range: 8–14. This is a magazine of American history containing stories of the past for middle school students. Cobblestone Publishing, 30 Grove Street, Suite C, Peterborough, NH 03458. www.cobblestonepub.com.

Creative Kids

Age range: 8–14. Games, art, stories, poetry, and opinion by and for kids. Creative Kids Magazine, Prufrock Press, 5926 Balcones Dr., Suite 220, Austin, TX 78731.

Cricket

Age range: 8–14. Contains quality literature in folktales, fantasy, science fiction, history, biographies, poems, science, and sports stories. Cricket Magazine, Carus Publishing Company, 315 Fifth Street, Peru, IL 61345. www.cricketmag.com.

Current Events

Age range: 11–16. Contains articles on current events that students in social studies classes in middle, junior, and early senior high schools can understand. WRC Media Inc., 512 Seventh Avenue, New York, NY 10018. www.weeklyreader.com.

Current Science

Age range: 11–16. Filled with current science discoveries and issues that students in middle, junior, and early senior high schools can understand. WRC Media Inc., 512 Seventh Avenue, New York, NY 10018. www.weeklyreader.com.

Dream/Girl

Age range: 8–18. Established in 1997 to provide girls with arts and literary information. Dream/Girl Magazine, PO Box 51867, Durham, NC 27717. www.dgarts.com.

Faces

Age range: 8–14. Anthropologists of the American Museum of Natural History advise editors about the lifestyles, beliefs, and customs of cultures throughout the world. Faces Magazine, Cobblestone Publishing, 30 Grove Street, Suite C, Peterborough, NH 03458. www.cobblestonepub.com.

Highlights for Children

Age range: 2–12. The flagship general-interest magazine that combines learning and fun in 42 pages filled with stories, poems, information, hidden pictures, cartoons, and crafts. Highlights for Children, 1800 Watermark Drive, Box 269, Columbus, OH 43216-0269. www.highlights.com.

Junior Scholastic

Age range: Grades 6–8. A classroom magazine published 18 times during the school year that features social studies events and issues. Scholastic Inc., PO Box 3725, Jefferson City, MO 65102-3725. www.scholastic.com.

Ladybug

Age range: 2–6. Contains a collection of stories, poems, songs, and games for young children. A parent's companion suggests additional activities, crafts, and books. Ladybug Magazine, Carus Publishing Company, 315 Fifth Street, Peru, IL 61345. www.cricketmag.com.

Merlyn's Pen: The National Magazine of Student Writing

Age range: Grades 6–9. Published four times a year, the magazine contains stories, poems, and expository pieces written by teens in the United States. The Merlyn's Pen Foundation, PO Box 2550, Providence, RI 02906. www.merlynspen.org.

The Mini Page

Age range: 5–12. A four-page educational newspaper inserted in 500 newspapers, often part of Newspaper in Education Week programs. Universal Press Syndicate, 4520 Main Street, Kansas City, MO 64111-7701.

National Geographic World

Age Range: 8–14. Contains natural history, science, diverse cultural groups, and outdoor adventure captured in excellent photographs and engaging writing. National Geographic Society, 1145 17th St. NW, Washington, DC 20036-4688. www.nationalgeographic.com.

Odyssey

Age range: 10–16. Features current events about space exploration and astronomy in each 48-page, fully illustrated, theme-related issue. Odyssey Magazine, Cobblestone Publishing, 30 Grove St., Suite C, Peterborough, NH 03458. www.odysseymagazine.com.

Owl: The Discovery Magazine for Kids

Age range: 8 and up. Each 32-page issue contains nature, science, animals, technology, games, puzzles, pull-out poster, and a comic strip. Owl Magazine, The OWL Group, 49 Front Street, #200, Toronto, ON Canada M53 1B3. www.owlkids.com.

Ranger Rick

Age range: 6–12. Each 48-page issue contains nature stories, information, poems, animal life histories, natural history, riddles, crafts, and activities in well-illustrated pages. Animal lovers are regular readers. National Wildlife Federation, 11100 Wildlife Center Drive, Reston, VA 20190-5362. www.nwf.org.

Science World

Age range: Grades 7–10. This 24-page news magazine is published biweekly during the school year. It features current research in life, earth, astronomy, space, physical, and health sciences. Scholastic Inc., PO Box 3725, Jefferson City, MO 65102-3725. www.scholastic.com.

Sesame Street

Age range: 2–6. This appealing magazine features stories, games, and activities to introduce the alphabet, numbers, and problem solving. Its stories reinforce social skills using characters from the television program (free with *Parenting* magazine). Sesame Street Magazine, Box 52000, Boulder, CO 80321-2000.

Skipping Stones

Age range: 8–18. Published bimonthly, this nonprofit children's magazine celebrates cultural richness with stories, articles, and photos from all over the world. Skipping Stones Magazine, PO Box 3939, Eugene, OR 97403. www.skippingstones.org.

Spider

Age range: 6–9. Intended for independent readers, the magazine contains stories, poems, informational articles, multicultural tales, activities, and well-illustrated pages that appeal to primary-grade readers. Spider Magazine, Carus Publishing Company, 315 Fifth Street, Peru, IL 61345. www.cricketmag.com.

Spire Magazine

Age range: 8–18. A biannual magazine dedicated to publishing traditionally marginalized and young writers and artists. Spire Press, 532 LaGuardia Place, Suite 298, New York, NY 10012. www.spirepress.org.

Sports Illustrated for Kids

Age range: 8–14. This magazine, modeled on its adult predecessor, introduces young readers to professional and amateur sports events and sports heroes. Time Life, Inc., Direct Holdings Inc., Virginia Beach, VA 23479-1003. www.sikids.com.

Stone Soup: The Magazine by Young Writers and Artists

Age range: 6–14. This magazine publishes poems, stories, art, and expository pieces written by children. Stone Soup, PO Box 83, Santa Cruz, CA 95063. www.stonesoup.com.

Storyworks Magazine

Age range: Grades 3–5. Good stories, poems, plays, nonfiction, word games, author interviews, news briefs about books, and student-written book reviews excite readers and teachers. Scholastic, Inc., PO Box 3725, Jefferson City, MO 65102-3725. www.scholastic.com.

Teen Voices

Age range: 13–18. Written by and about teenage and young adult women. Women Express, Inc., PO Box 120-027, Boston, MA 02112-0027. www.teenvoices.com.

Time for Kids

Age range: Grades 4–6. This weekly classroom news magazine presents current events in language that intermediate-grade students can understand. A teacher's edition suggests ways to extend the learning. Time for Kids, 1271 6th Avenue, 22nd floor, New York, NY 10020. www.timeforkids.com.

U*S* Kids

Age range: 6–11. Stories, articles, and activities in this 42-page full-color magazine interest children in their world and the people who live in it. Games, interactive activities, and puzzles with a historical focus combine learning and pleasure. Children's Better Health Institute, 1100 Waterway Blvd, Indianapolis, IN 46202. www.cbhi.org/cbhi/magazines.

Weekly Reader

Age range: Grades K–6. This graded series of classroom newspapers contains current news, activities, and recreational reading. WRC Media Inc., 512 Seventh Avenue, New York, NY 10018. www.weeklyreader.com.

Your Big Backyard

Age range: 8–12. Outstanding photography and illustrations attract readers to this nature and conservation magazine. National Wildlife Federation, 11100 Wildlife Center Drive, Reston, VA 20190-5362. www.nwf.org.

Zillions: The Consumer Report for Kids

Age range: 8–14. The place kids learn how to determine when a bargain is a bargain; they become wise consumers (online only). Consumer Reports for Kids Online, 101 Truman Ave., Yonkers, NY 10703-1057. www.zillions.org.

Reference

Magazines for Kids and Teens: A Resource for Teachers, Parents, Librarians, and Kids. Editor Don Stoll. Foreword by Jim Trelease. Published by International Reading Association and EdPress Association, 1997.

The History of Children's Literature

The Evolution of Childhood

Children's books, produced as early as four hundred years ago, have changed dramatically across time. Literature never grows in a vacuum; it grows as a part of the surrounding world of thought, economics, and customs. Children's literature is no exception. The prevailing concept of childhood and what children should be taught determines the kinds of books published for them. Therefore, we find in children's books a record of the ideals and standards each generation wants to teach their young.

Historically, Europeans viewed children as miniature adults and made few concessions for their differences. In the seventeenth and eighteenth centuries, adults were concerned about saving children's souls and guaranteeing their entrance into heaven. Books praised pious children. Beginning in the nineteenth century and evolving in the twentieth century, the idea grew that children are developmentally distinct from adults; they have different needs and abilities. This vision of childhood led to a demand for books unique to children's needs and interests; thereafter, children's book publishing flourished.

Fifteenth- and Sixteenth-Century Children's Literature

THE ORAL TRADITION

During the 1500s and 1600s, literature for children was primarily oral folktales, fables, and Bible stories told in family circles, or ballads and epics told by wandering performers. Life was harsh. Everyone, including children, worked long hours. During dark winter months, light to read by was a luxury.

Fables, brief allegorical narratives that illustrate a moral or satirize human behavior, were widely told. The oldest known fables are those from the Sanskrit collection *Pachatantra,* but many fables are attributed to the Greek Aesop. Very little is known about Aesop, but one legend says he was a slave of Samos in the sixth century B.C. He is associated with wild adventures. Aesop's fables were preserved mainly through Babrius, a Greek fabulist; Phaedrus, a first-century Latin writer; and Planudes Maximus, a Byzantine scholar circa 1260–1330.

Canterbury became the spiritual center of England when St. Augustine arrived from Rome to convert people to Christianity in 597. He founded an abbey at Canterbury and became the first archbishop of Canterbury. The early cathedral was burned and rebuilt several times (in 1011, 1067, and 1174). After the murder of Thomas Becket in 1170 and the penance of Henry II, Canterbury became famous as the object of a pilgrimage. Chaucer's *Canterbury Tales* are based on stories of the travelers.

Stories of King Arthur and the Knights of the Round Table were told from the sixth century onward. The origins of the tales are lost in antiquity; origins are irrelevant, however, for the tales serve as symbols of courage, goodness, and gallantry today. Over the years additions include the exploits of Tristram, Gawaine, Lancelot, and Merlin as well as the quest for the Holy Grail—the cup used by Christ at the Last Supper. The stories still enjoy an enthusiastic audience today.

THE INVENTION OF PRINTING

A German, Johann Gutenberg (1397–1468), is believed to be the first European to print with movable type cast in molds. Similar printing had been done earlier in China but there is no evidence that this printing was known in Europe in Gutenberg's time. Gutenberg's name does not appear on any printing attributed to him and details of his life are cloudy. Gutenberg lived in Strasbourg and there is some evidence that in 1436 or 1437 he made his great invention there. He returned to his birthplace, Mainz near Frankfort, where the printing attributed to him was produced. The masterpiece from his printing press was known as the *Gutenberg Bible.* In order to produce the Bible he borrowed money that he was unable to repay. He lost his press and types. The Gutenberg Museum in Mainz has examples of his work but not of his features; these are unknown.

William Caxton, an English businessman, went to Cologne, Germany, to learn the printing trade. Caxton set up his first printing press in England around 1476 and published *A Book of Curtesey* (1477), *The Historye of Reynart the Foxe* (1481), and *Aesop's Fables* (1484). Caxton published Thomas Malory's version of the Arthurian legends, *Le Morte d'Arthur,* in 1485.

HORNBOOKS   *Hornbooks* are small wooden paddles with attached lesson sheets covered by transparent cow's horn (like very heavy plastic) tacked down with brass strips. They were first used around 1550 to teach children the alphabet, syllables, vowels, the Lord's Prayer, and short verses. The verses had a religious message, such as "In Adam's fall, we sinned all" used to illustrate the letter 'A.' The ultimate goal of learning was religious salvation.

CHAPBOOKS   *Chapbooks,* crudely printed little books or pamphlets sold by itinerant peddlers (chapmen), first appeared in the late 1500s but became widely popular in the seventeenth and eighteenth centuries. Chapbooks containing fairy tales, nursery rhymes, and retold stories were usually anonymous and undated. Despite their cheap quality, they circulated widely, created a readership, and preserved the tales and rhymes for later publication.

Seventeenth- and Eighteenth-Century Children's Literature

MORAL LESSONS

Bookmaking in America was a slow, costly process. Not many colonists owned books. If they did own one, it was likely the Bible or another religious book. Books for pleasure reading were virtually nonexistent; there was little distinction between books for children and books for adults. The primary purpose of books was to lead readers toward religious salvation. The few books available to children were moralistic, didactic, and riddled with sanctions. Through books of catechism and lists of duties, children were instructed to live spiritual lives, to obey their parents, to prepare for death, and to avoid incurring the wrath of God. Books glorified saintly lives and pious deaths. Images of fire and brimstone burned brightly in books for children.

John Cotton (1584–1652), an outspoken Puritan clergyman in England, was summoned to appear before the High Court of Commission (1632) for his nonconformist statements. Instead of appearing, he resigned and fled with his parishioners to the Massachusetts Bay Colony in 1633. He was a firm believer in the minister's right to dictate to the congregation. His *Milk for Babes* (1646),

Figure 1

Landmarks of the Colonial Period and the Seventeenth and Eighteenth Centuries

Colonial Period

1484	*Aesop's Fables*
1550	Hornbooks (small wooden paddle with lesson sheet attached)
1636	*Youth's Behavior*
1646	John Cotton, *Milk for Babes, drawn out of the breasts of both Testaments, chiefly for the spiritual nourishment of Boston babes in either England, but may be of like use for any children*

Seventeenth Century

1658	John Amos Comenius, *Orbis Sensualium Pictus*
1665	Henry Winstanly, *All the Principal Nations of the World*
1672	James Janeway, *A Token for Children*
1678	John Bunyan, *Pilgrim's Progress*
1697	Charles Perrault, *Contes de ma Mere l'Oye (Tales of Mother Goose)*
1679	Benjamin Harris, *The New England Primer*

Eighteenth Century

1702	Cotton Mather, *A Token for the Children of New England, or some examples of children in whom the fear of God was remarkably budding before they died*
1715	Isaac Watts, *Divine and Moral Songs for Children*
1719	Daniel Defoe, *Robinson Crusoe*
1740	Chapbooks
1744	John Newbery, *A Little Pretty Pocket-Book: Intended for the Instruction and Amusement of Little Master Tommy and Pretty Miss Polly*
1765	Oliver Goldsmith, *The History of Little Goody Two Shoes*
1769	Battledores
1778	Anna Laetitia Barbauld, *Lessons for Children*
1786	Sarah Trimmer, *Fabulous Histories, History of the Robins*
1783	Noah Webster, *Webster's Blue-Backed Speller*

a well-known catechism for children, asked questions such as "How did God make you?" to be answered, "I was conceived in sin and born in iniquity."

John Bunyan (1628–1688), an English author, son of a tinsmith, read chapbooks as a child but as he grew older and more religious he turned to the Bible and its teachings. His fiery sermons caused him to be locked up for unlicensed preaching and nonconformity to practices of the Church of England. While in jail, he wrote about Christian and Christiana, troubled souls who make a pilgrimage from the City of Destruction to everlasting life in Celestial City, in *Pilgrim's Progress* (Part I, 1678; Part II, 1684). Bunyan's early experiences reading fairy tales influenced his storytelling so that the pilgrimages read like fairy-tale heroes fighting enemies with symbolic names, such as Giant Despair. The books, written for adults, contained a great deal of theology, but children were attracted to the good stories underlying the preaching.

BOOKS FOR FORMAL INSTRUCTION

Children attended "dame schools" conducted in private homes while the teacher carried on her household duties. Neighborhood children sat at the kitchen table to read and recite their lessons while the teacher (dame) continued to bake bread and prepare meals. The curriculum included reading, writing, spelling, arithmetic, prayers, hymns, and catechism read from hornbooks, the Bible, and a few other books.

Battledores, made from folded heavy paper, had a cover embellished with crude woodcuts of animals, while the inside was filled with alphabets, numerals, and simple reading lessons. They were intended to instruct and amuse and contained only vague references to religion. Battledores were popular in England and North America from the mid-1700s well into the 1800s.

The New England Primer provided religious education in language children could understand. First published in London as *The Protestant Tutor,* its author, Benjamin Harris, was sent to the pillory in 1681 for printing the book, one of the first to omit the traditional religious catechism. Harris escaped to Boston where he reissued the book in 1690. *The New England Primer* was illustrated with crude woodcuts and gruesome accounts of hangings and burnings. *The New England Primer* was published in several editions, all containing the alphabet, couplets advising virtuous and mannerly behavior, the catechism, and various hymns and prayers. Children were expected to study it until they memorized it word-for-word.

CHANGING IDEAS OF EDUCATION

While the colonists were learning to live in an untamed land, educators in Europe were moving away from stern Puritan morality. John Amos Comenius (1592–1670), John Locke (1632–1704), and Jean-Jacques Rousseau (1712–1778) directed educational thought toward a child-centered view.

John Amos Comenius wrote a compendium of the information he believed every child should know in *Orbis Sensualium Pictus (Illustrated World of the Senses).* Comenius, a Moravian churchman, advocated relating education to everyday life by emphasizing contact with objects in the environment and systematizing all knowledge. Teaching was to be done in the vernacular (language or dialect native to a region) instead of Latin and language was to be learned in a conversational method, not through rote repetition. His book, *Orbis Pictus,* was the first book in which pictures were as important as the text. (See Appendix A: The Orbis Pictus Award.)

John Locke held the view that a child is born as a *tabula rasa,* a blank slate ready to have life experiences written on it.

Jean-Jacques Rousseau believed that a child is born with an innate sense of right and wrong and, left to his own natural impulses, the "noble savage" would grow into a superior adult. Rousseau set forth his ideas in *Emile* (1762), giving rise to the image of a mentor and student sitting on a log as the ideal teaching/learning situation.

BEGINNINGS OF CHILDREN'S BOOK PUBLISHING

In 1744, a London merchant, John Newbery (1713–1767), opened a shop called The Bible and Sun (originally called The Bible and Crown) near St. Paul's churchyard. Newbery offered for sale, along with medicines, the first book specifically designed to entertain as well as to instruct children. *A Little Pretty Pocket-Book: Intended for the Instruction and Amusement of Little Master Tommy and Pretty Miss Polly* was the first attempt to teach children the alphabet by way of diversion. John Newbery earned a spot in history because of his notable act of selling children's books. The Newbery Medal, named in his honor, is given annually for the most distinguished contribution to literature for children published in the United States. (See Appendix A.) Later, in 1765, Newbery published *The History of Little Goody Two Shoes,* a book attributed to Oliver Goldsmith and one that established the image of a pious, virtuous child.

MOVING BEYOND RELIGION: ENTERTAINMENT AND DIDACTICISM

Once started, the movement toward publishing books for children's pleasure began. The "teachy-preachy" books with virtuous, religious characters gradually gave way to fanciful stories, poetry, and picture books for entertainment. Despite the desire for pure pleasure in stories, authors tucked lessons underneath a thin plot line. For example, children would ask questions such as "Pray Papa, what is a camel?" and adults would respond with an uninterrupted barrage of factual information.

At the end of the eighteenth century, children in books were polite, diligent, dutiful, and prudent. Well-behaved boys and girls searched relentlessly for information. Parents, teachers, ministers, and librarians were unquestioned as sources of information and translators of God's prescription for behavior.

In an attempt to expand the bookselling market started by John Newbery, some publishers commissioned people to write expressly for children. Most of the writers were women; among them, Mrs. Sarah Kirby Trimmer (1741–1810), Mrs. Laetitia Aiken Barbauld (1743–1825), and Maria Edgeworth (1767–1849). Mrs. Trimmer, mother of twelve, wrote about a family of robins to teach moralistic lessons. Mrs. Barbauld created stories for her adopted son to express her belief that there was a proper, rigid, respectful order for parents and children to follow. Maria Edgeworth, the eldest daughter in a large Irish family, learned firsthand what children liked and disliked. Maria's mother died a few years after her birth; her father remarried three times and fathered 21 children, 18 of whom survived infancy. Maria wrote stories to entertain the ever-expanding brood. She wrote the stories, tried them out on her siblings, revised them, and copied them over in ink (Goldstone, 1984, p. 48). One of Maria Edgeworth's stories, *The Purple Jar* (1796), illustrates the subtle message of obeying elders.

After the American Revolution (1775–1781), Americans struggled to unite their nation and were eager to show that they no longer belonged to England. Writers praised their new land to develop a sense of national pride. Many books claimed that Americans were more fortunate than people from other lands; others were pitied because they could not live in America. Books for children featured adventure stories of travel on the American frontier and courageous battles with the Indians. The books were as didactic as the earlier "teachy-preachy" books, but they added history and geography lessons to the new American ethic of "work hard and make good."

Nineteenth-Century Children's Literature

Early in the nineteenth century, righteous teachings still prevailed in children's books, but they were made a little more palatable under the guise of entertainment. Mary Poppins's rule "A little bit of sugar makes the medicine go down" worked for books as well as

discipline. During the early 1800s, stories written expressly for children's enjoyment grew.

Children sought adventure in books such as *Robinson Crusoe, Gulliver's Travels,* and *The Swiss Family Robinson,* originally written for adults but taken over by children. Books written specifically for children slowly made their way to America although a stern work ethic condemned frivolity. Fairy tales collected by Charles Perrault, *Histoires ou Contes du Temps Passé avec Moralités (Stories or Tales of Times Past with Morals)* and *Contes de ma Mere l'Oye (Tales of Mother Goose),* which included "Sleeping Beauty," "Little Red Riding Hood," "Blue Beard," "Puss in Boots," "Cinderella," and "Tom Thumb," were considered silly fluff. Puritanical adults did not want children to waste time on them because they thought they were a dangerous corrupting influence. Good behavior and knowledge were highly valued.

Between 1825 and 1850, Samuel Goodrich, who believed books could guide children along the right path, collaborated with other writers, such as Nathaniel Hawthorne, to produce the **Peter Parley** series. Peter Parley is a distinguished elderly gentleman who answers children's questions about history, science, and geography in *Tales of Peter Parley about America* (1827) and in more than a hundred titles that followed. Although some Peter Parley books were designed as textbooks, most were intended for out-of-school reading and called "toy books." They were simple, well illustrated, clearly printed, and inexpensive. Despite wide approval of the information and codes of conduct, the books were criticized because people believed they made children imaginative and indolent (Perkinson, 1978). Nevertheless, the Peter Parley books were forerunners of a type of literature popular with children—series books.

Once begun, series books flourished. Children read them avidly as alternatives to textbooks. Jacob Abbott's series is about a boy who learns all that he can about the world while remaining

Figure 2

Landmark Books of the Nineteenth Century

1801	Maria Edgeworth, *Early Lessons*		1858	Jacob Abbott, *Rollo in Rome*
1801	Maria Edgeworth, *Moral Tales*		1858	Jacob Abbott, *Rollo's Tour in Europe*
1812	Johann Wyss, *The Swiss Family Robinson*		1865	Lewis Carroll, *Alice's Adventures in Wonderland*
1822	Samuel and Charles Goodrich, *Peter Parley's History of the United States*		1867	Martha Farquharson Finley, *Elsie Dinsmore*
1826	James Fenimore Cooper, *The Last of the Mohicans*		1868	Louisa May Alcott, *Little Women*
1827	Samuel and Charles Goodrich, *Tales of Peter Parley about America*		1868	Horatio Alger, *Ragged Dick*
1834	Jacob Abbott, *Rollo Learning to Talk*		1876	Mark Twain, *The Adventures of Tom Sawyer*
1834	*McGuffy's Eclectic Readers*		1880	Margaret Sidney, *The Five Little Peppers and How They Grew*
1843	Charles Dickens, *A Christmas Carol*		1883	Robert Lewis Stevenson, *Treasure Island*
			1891	C. Collodi, *Pinocchio*

aware of his supposedly superior American heritage. The series, **Rollo's Tour in Europe,** reads like a travelogue, with wise Uncle George serving as mentor to young Rollo. Rollo eventually returns to America satisfied that he hails "from a land superior to those inhabited by foreigners" (Jordan, 1983, pp. 48–49). Authors felt obliged to tell readers they were lucky to live in the budding democracy of America.

BOOKS FOR FORMAL INSTRUCTION

The New England Primer continued to be a popular textbook for children during the first half of the 1800s. It was revised several times to reflect changing American values. For example, immediately following the American Revolution, textbook authors tried to develop a pure American education and get rid of any reference to England. Books stressed practicality and loyalty. Noah Webster led the way with his spelling book, *Webster's Blue-Backed Speller,* a standard used to judge an educated person.

The United States was 60 years old when the first system of public education was established in Massachusetts under the leadership of Horace Mann. The young nation expanded westward but organized public education was slow to follow. Decades passed before all children had access to public schools. Textbooks were the primary resource for education. School attendance was sporadic because children worked; children most often learned their lessons at home. Textbooks were the one constant in a pupil's education. Students reported their progress by telling how far they had read in textbooks: They had completed the Primer or were halfway through Webster. The method of study was always the same: Students memorized the lessons and recited them to the teacher.

McGuffey's Eclectic Readers, first appearing in 1834, were a series of books of increasing difficulty filled with stories, poems, and information written by many authors—America's first basal readers. They provided a national literature and a national curriculum for people who wanted to unify Americans by giving them common experiences.

THE NEED FOR FANTASY

Children had little time to be children in the mid-nineteenth century. Social and economic conditions dictated that many young people work, often in horrendous circumstances. The Industrial Revolution created the need for a plentiful supply of cheap labor. Women, children, and immigrants were enticed to cities to live lives filled with unremitting drudgery and a considerable amount of danger. Women and children worked in the mills 12 hours a day, 6 days a week where gruesome accidents were common (Holland, 1970; Paterson, *Lyddie* [I–A], 1991).

The society that tolerated grim conditions for children developed a literature that provided a fantasy escape from the harsh workaday world while still giving a justification for the work ethic. Much of the fanciful literature came from England but hardworking American children welcomed it with open arms.

Alice's Adventures in Wonderland (1865) and *Through the Looking Glass* (1871) by Charles Dodgson are the first significant works of fantasy for children. Dodgson, a clergyman and scholarly math professor at Oxford, chose a pen name (Lewis Carroll) to avoid being identified with the books for children—the very reason he is remembered today. The legend says that Dodgson often told stories to the three Liddell girls, daughters of a minister friend. One afternoon, Alice asked for a story with nonsense. The story she heard that day became the world-famous one. He wrote it down for her the following Christmas.

The complicated nonsense and word play Alice Liddell loved intrigue readers, who become "curiouser and curiouser" as Alice follows a white rabbit down a hole. The story of memorable madness, read by generations of children and adults alike, is filled with subtleties that poke fun at English social customs. Some of the satire eludes modern readers, but the cleverness of the story and the word play still charms them.

THE DEVELOPMENT OF POETRY

Mother Goose verses were the earliest poetic forms to delight the ear and tickle the tongue and imagination of children. Doggerel, sentimental lines, riddles, and traditional rhymes were plentiful. Poetry written especially for children began to show up around the middle of the 1800s.

Some truly great works, though written for adults, preceded the flowering of poetry written for children. For example, the English poet William Blake (1757–1827) captured the spirit of childhood in verse. Barely noticed in his lifetime, his *Songs of Innocence* (1789) and *Songs of Experience* (1794) live on. The poems in *Songs of Innocence* portray the human mind with a childlike quality. In the introduction, Blake begins:

> *Piping down the valleys wild,*
> *Piping songs of pleasant glee,*
> *On a cloud I saw a child,*
> *And he laughing said to me.*
> *Pipe a song about a Lamb.*

PUBLIC DOMAIN,
REPRINTED 1925, P. 65

Blake's poems show the child as refreshingly curious and responding intuitively to unfathomable beauty. They are a benchmark for subsequent poetry for children.

Ann Taylor (1782–1866) and Jane Taylor (1783–1824) began writing verses quite young. When Ann was 22 and Jane 21, they published *Original Poems for Infant Minds by Several Young Persons* (1804). Their verses reflected a childlike spirit despite subtle lessons. "Twinkle, twinkle, little star" by Jane Taylor is a song that children sing today. This and other early poems, such as "Mary had a little lamb" (1830) by Sarah Josepha Hale and "'Will you walk into my parlor?' said the Spider to the Fly" in *Fireside Verses* by Mary Howitt (1799–1888), were spread so widely it is difficult to remember they are not folklore.

Most nineteenth-century poets still had a strong desire to teach lessons, but some went beyond preachy moralistic verses. A few early English poets portrayed life from a child's point of view and sang the pleasures of childhood as children saw them. The tradition begun by William Blake led to poetic conventions we draw upon today. Early poets include William Roscoe, *The Butterfly's Ball* (1806); Edward Lear, *A Book of Nonsense* (1846); William Allingham, *In Fairyland* (1870); Robert Louis Stevenson, *A Child's Garden of Verses* (1885); and A. A. Milne, *When We Were Very Young* (1924) and *Now We Are Six* (1927).

An American, Clement C. Moore, wrote *A Visit from St. Nicholas* (1823), a poem that keeps the magic of Christmas alive even today. Written for his own children, it appeared anonymously in the Troy (N.Y.) *Sentinel* on December 23, 1823. It is a rarity completely free from the didactic teachings of the time. Children's delight in the imaginative vision that Clement C. Moore's words created caused them to take the poem for their own and, as an owner's right, to rename it "The Night Before Christmas," which it shall forever remain. The words by Moore inviting us "To the top of the porch, to the top of the wall! Now, dash away, dash away, dash away all!" (Public Domain, 1823; 1971) may have been a signal to move toward the boundless visions future poets would paint. Moore could never have predicted the growth of poetry from a slender branch into the center of the school curriculum: not as an add-on, but as the basic material for children learning to read, to write, to speak, and to listen.

THE DEVELOPMENT OF BOOK ILLUSTRATION

The illustration of picture books has developed into a fine art through the growth of publishing. Picture book art is the first and perhaps the only art children ever see; it has a lasting effect on their developing taste. Today's children need to understand pictures because we are surrounded by visual information texts using pictures and symbols as well as words. Visual texts are accessible to a wider range of readers than word texts.

Children's book illustration developed rapidly after 1850, although bright spots appeared earlier. Illustrated books actually began with artless, anonymous woodcuts used on catechism pages. Printers used any woodcuts they happened to have lying about the shop, not necessarily pictures connected to the text they were printing.

George Cruikshank (1792–1878), an early outstanding artist, illustrated *Grimm's Fairy Tales* in 1823. His unforgettable, luxuriant but delicate, art for the tenacious tales extended the fancy and became the standard by which other art was judged. Cruikshank's distinctive style appears in the four volumes of *George Cruikshank's Fairy Library* (1853–54).

Prior to 1850, artists merely decorated a text with designs or occasional illustrations to fill gaps in a page or to emphasize crucial moments in a story. Because of technical limitations they seldom achieved a perfect match between picture images and literary images. In the 1860s, Edmund Evans, a talented printer and bookmaker, began to make vast improvements in picture books by perfecting color printing. Evans joined artist Walter Crane, the son of a portrait painter, in criticizing the poor quality of art in children's books. They worked together to implement the use of color. The pair brought out Walter Crane's first alphabet books, *Railroad Alphabet* and *Farm Yard Alphabet* in 1865. Nursery song picture books—*Sing a Song of Sixpence, The House That Jack Built, Dame Trot and Her Comical Cat,* and *The History of Cock Robin and Jenny Wren*—followed in 1867 and 1869, establishing Crane's productive career. Walter Crane's toy book, *Sleeping Beauty,* illustrates the fairy tales that followed.

Improved photo-engraving processes in the 1880s freed artists from the tyranny of the hand-engraved (and distorted) translations of their art. Full-fledged color illustrations by Walter Crane, Kate Greenaway, and Randolph Caldecott, and skillfully crafted black-and-white art by John Tenniel flourished. Artists became partners in storytelling. The combination of an increasing literacy and improvements in printing lowered the cost of books. This led to wider distribution of books toward the end of the century.

Randolph Caldecott (1846–1886) contributed sketches to magazines in England and America, but the turning point in his career came in *The Diverting History of John Gilpin* (1878). His art showed vitality, movement, and humor; it immortalized Caldecott in the field of children's literature. The Caldecott Medal for outstanding illustration is named in his honor; the medal carries a scene from *John Gilpin* (see Appendix A).

Kate Greenaway (1846–1901) made a living decorating greeting cards with prim, well-groomed children playing in flower gardens. She turned her considerable talent to books in *Under the Window* (1878), her first picture book. Greenaway's distinguished career merited having the Greenaway Medal—the award for the most distinguished illustrated book in England—named in her honor (see Appendix A).

John Tenniel left his artistic mark on Lewis Carroll's *Alice's Adventures in Wonderland* (1865) and *Through the Looking Glass* (1871). His vision of Alice is so distinctive that we find it difficult to think of her without Tenniel's art.

THE GROWTH OF REALISM

The desire to indoctrinate children in the American work ethic was evident in a series begun by Horatio Alger in 1868. Alger created characters who worked hard but were well paid for their efforts. Horatio Alger wrote more than 100 stories in which male characters acquired power and wealth through great effort, courage, and impeccable morality. The stories were dramatic: Alger's hero would snatch a baby from a burning building or rescue a damsel from the heels of a runaway horse. Children read the books avidly. Alger set *Ragged Dick* (1868) in a New York slum rather than in the usual rural surroundings. Subtitled "Street Life in New York with the Boot Blacks," *Ragged Dick,* like other books in the series, traces a poor boy's progress from poverty to wealth and respectability. The author's name, Horatio Alger, invokes the same work ethic today. A contemporary Horatio Alger Award is given to honor a person who works hard and succeeds.

Books for boys differed from books for girls. Boys' books were filled with adventure, travel, and the desire to succeed, but girls' books had characters who practiced the genteel arts of homemaking, caring for others, and piety. Martha Farquharson (Finley) described female behavior melodramatically in the **Elsie Dinsmore** series, wherein tears, fainting spells, and prayers were called forth regularly. Elsie Dinsmore is a link in the chain of tearful, saintly girls that includes *Little Goody Two Shoes* and Rosamond (of *The Purple Jar*).

Gradually a new type of literature appeared in which characters were portrayed more realistically. Priggishness gave way to devilment as boys—but not yet girls—acted more like real children. Thomas Bailey Aldrich's autobiographical *The Story of a Bad Boy* (1870) acknowledges tricks, pranks, and mischievous behavior in a "boys will be boys" spirit. The book began an era of "bad-boy literature" that peaked in Mark Twain's *The Adventures of Huckleberry Finn* (1884). The trend continues today.

Girls were given an alternative to Elsie Dinsmore's overly dramatic fainting spells when Louisa May Alcott wrote *Little Women* in 1868. Alcott began her career by writing and selling potboilers to magazines to support her family. Although considered too worldly by fundamentalist leaders at the time, *Little Women* has been called the century's most significant piece of fiction. Alcott's substantial work focused on the homespun virtues of a wholesome American family. We are still finding some of her long-lost fiction, for example *A Long Fatal Love Chase*.

Girls took pleasure in a series of family stories by Margaret Sidney (pseudonym of Harriet M. Lothrop). *The Five Little Peppers and How They Grew* (1880) begins a sentimental series about a widowed mother's brave struggle to raise her five children. Generosity, humility, and proper manners are rewarded in the stories of a family with little money but lots of love.

The last half of the nineteenth century brought forth a surfeit of inexpensive, aesthetically weak, mass-produced series written to formula. The series books, printed on poor-quality paper, had little literary distinction to recommend them, but children devoured them with the same enthusiasm as readers of today's series books. The Immortal Four—Finley, Alger, Adams, and Fosdick—all used a variety of pseudonyms under which they ground out hundreds of books. This wave of fast-paced, cheap, and extremely popular books provoked adult objections, but they were popular entertainment for children.

Writers built on the success of the Horatio Alger and Elsie Dinsmore series by producing other fast-moving adventure stories. One entrepreneur, Edward Stratemeyer, developed a syndicate of hack writers to produce millions of cheap juvenile books—some still available today. Mass marketing made it possible for children to obtain books without adult supervision; inexpensive production made books disposable.

Edward Stratemeyer wrote for pulp magazines and, shortly after the Spanish-American War, wrote *Under Dewey at Manila.* He enjoyed writing war stories and wrote several series with America's wars as background. As his sales increased, Stratemeyer outlined plots and hired hack writers to produce the **Colonial Boys** series, the **Mexican War** series, and **Pan American** series. He developed other series, including the **Rover Boys,** the **Motor Boys, Tom Swift,** the **Hardy Boys,** and the **Bobbsey Twins**—using the pseudonyms Arthur Winfield, Clarence Young, Victor Appleton, Franklin W. Dixon, and Laura Lee Hope, respectively. Stratemeyer produced 68 different series under 46 pseudonyms. After his death in 1935, his daughter, Harriet Stratemeyer Adams, took over the massive operation that still produces books including the **Nancy Drew** series under the pseudonym Carolyn Keene. Harriet Stratemeyer died at age 89 in 1982 but the series continues to be published under the editorial direction of Simon and Schuster.

Eventually Americans could envision a world beyond native shores; provincialism waned and authors wrote about children in other lands. For example, Mary Mapes Dodge's *Hans Brinker; or The Silver Skates* (1865) popularized a story about a Dutch boy who saved Holland by putting his finger in a hole in a dike, a levee built to prevent the sea from flooding the land. Johanna Spyri wrote *Heidi* (1884) as a glimpse of life in Switzerland, but children loved it for its portrayal of a girl's relationship with her grandfather.

EARLY MAGAZINES

Many magazines for children began as Sunday School periodicals. *The Encourager* (Methodist), *The Children's Magazine* (Episcopal), *The Juvenile Instructor* (Mormon), and *Catholic Youth's Magazine* contained religious stories and Biblical verse. Secular magazines such as *Frank Leslie's Chatterbox* (1879–1886) advertised that they could "improve the mind, diffuse knowledge," and provide healthy, interesting literature for the young. Sketches conveyed morals or useful information in purified language.

St. Nicholas (1873–1943), a high-quality journal for children that survived for 70 years, was a breath of fresh air due to its good stories and warm, informal tone communicated by editor Mary Mapes Dodge. Dodge sought excellent writers; she included work by Louisa May Alcott, Frances Hodgson Burnett, Joel Chandler Harris, Rudyard Kipling, Howard Pyle, Laura Richards, Mark Twain, and Frank Stockton, who became associate editor. Many of the magazine's short stories were reprinted as books or in anthologies; some of the serialized novels remain classics today. Frances Hodgson Burnett's *Sara Crewe* (1888), Frank Stockton's *America's Birthday Party* (1876), Susan Coolidge's *What Katy Did* (1872), Louisa May Alcott's *Jo's Boys* (1873), *An Old-Fashioned Girl* (1870), and *Eight Cousins* (1875), Rudyard Kipling's *The Jungle Book* (1894), and Lucretia P. Hale's *The Peterkin Papers* (1880) first appeared in the pages of *St. Nicholas.*

The Youth's Companion (1827–1929) was published for 102 years, longer than any other children's magazine in America. In 1929, it merged with *The American Boy,* which ceased publication in 1941. Editorial policy demanded that its content remain seemly; parents could give the magazine to children without fear of introducing them to any untoward subject. A distinguished list of contributors—Sarah Orne Jewett, Jack London, Theodore Roosevelt, Henry Wadsworth Longfellow, Alfred Lord Tennyson, James M.

Barrie, H. G. Wells, and Oliver Wendell Holmes—wrote for the magazine.

The first children's magazine published in America, *The Juvenile Miscellany* (1826–1834), edited by Lydia Maria Child, became an immediate success. Lydia Maria Child, a former teacher, wanted children to learn to read with material they could enjoy, but found very little to fulfill this requirement. She filled the void with *The Juvenile Miscellany*. When she spoke out vehemently against slavery, however, sales dropped so drastically that the magazine was forced to stop publication in 1834. Sarah Josepha Hale's "Mary Had a Little Lamb" first appeared in this magazine.

Twentieth-Century Children's Literature

The new century brought forth new stories for children. Moral overtones were not forgotten, but most books contained humor, adventure, spirit, imagination, and enough rough-and-tumble to satisfy readers who liked real live action.

1900–1920: FANTASY AND REALISM

Boys read adventure stories: George Grinnell's *Jack Among the Indians* (1900) and George Henty's *With Kitchener in the Soudan* (1903). Girls read quiet home and family stories: Kate Douglas Wiggin's *Rebecca of Sunnybrook Farm* (1903), Lucy M. Montgomery's *Anne of Green Gables* (1908), Frances Hodgson Burnett's *The Secret Garden* (1911). One story, *Pollyanna* (1912), by Eleanor Porter, became so well loved that the character's name continues to symbolize her joyful optimistic disposition. Fantasy continued to flourish; the classic story-play *Peter Pan* (1904) by J. M. Barrie is still loved by adults and children everywhere.

Picture books as we know them today flourished around the turn of the century, when many of today's classics were published. Arthur Rackham illustrated Barrie's *Peter Pan in Kensington Gardens* (1906) and Beatrix Potter created *The Tale of Peter Rabbit* (1902). W. W. Denslow drew pictures for Frank Baum's *Wizard of Oz* (1900) and L. Leslie Brooke illustrated *The Golden Goose Book* (1905). The works earned the artists a place beside Cruikshank, Crane, Tenniel, Greenaway, and Caldecott as outstanding illustrators of early children's books.

1920–1940: PICTURE BOOKS

The American school of illustration developed during the 1920s and 1930s. Prior to 1920 most picture books originated in England. Wanda Gág's *Millions of Cats* (P), published in 1928, showed the work of an artist who used sophisticated printing technology to produce her unique vision (Meigs, Eaton, Nesbitt, & Viguers, 1969).

Public libraries opened children's rooms and children flocked to them. *The Horn Book Magazine,* a review journal of children's books, appeared in 1924. Publishers created children's departments and inaugurated promotional activities such as Children's Book Week. The demand for children's books grew. During these decades Laura Ingalls Wilder began her **Little House** (I) series, and J.R.R. Tolkien wrote *The Hobbit* (I–A) (1938).

During the Holocaust and World War II, talented artists and authors escaped from Europe to live and work in America. American children's literature was enriched by the work of Ingri and Edgar Parin d'Aulaire (**Abraham Lincoln,** 1939) (P), Ludwig Bemelmans (**Madeline,** 1939) (P), and Roger Duvoisin (**White Snow, Bright Snow** by Alvin Tresselt, 1947) (P).

1940–1960: QUALITY FICTION

During the 1940s and 1950s, children's books became an important part of libraries, schools, homes, and publishing houses. Books published during this period, such as Robert McCloskey's **Make Way for Ducklings** (1941) (P), Eleanor Estes's *The Moffats* (1941) (I), *Johnny Tremain* (1943) (I–A) by Esther Forbes, *Charlotte's Web* (1952) (I) by E. B. White, *My Side of the Mountain* (1959) (I) by Jean George, and the **Chronicles of Narnia** (1950) (I–A) series by C. S. Lewis remain popular today.

1960–1980: GOVERNMENT FUNDING

The 1960s and 1970s were a time of growth in children's literature. Congress passed the National Defense Education Act of 1958 with Title II to provide federal funds for the purchase of children's science and mathematics books. The Elementary and Secondary School Education Act of 1965 brought another wave of federal funds for non-textbook purchases. Teachers used children's books in the classroom to enrich the curriculum and to encourage students to read. School and public librarians guided students to books for information and books for pleasure. Public librarians served more—and younger—children in story hours, summer reading programs, after-school programs, and author visits. Literacy organizations held conferences and established journals to study literature and to promote reading. High fantasy, such as Susan Cooper's *The Dark Is Rising* (1966) (A) and Lloyd Alexander's *The Book of Three* (1964) (I–A) enriched the field. Outstanding picture books such as Ezra Jack Keats's *Snowy Day* (1962) (P), Leo Lionni's *Swimmy* (1963) (P), and Maurice Sendak's *Where the Wild Things Are* (1963) (P) enjoyed great popularity. Authors and illustrators from minority groups made major contributions, such as Virginia Hamilton's *M. C. Higgins, the Great* (1974) (I–A) and Laurence Yep's *Dragonwings* (1975) (I–A). Television programs based on children's books—*Reading Rainbow* and *After School Specials*—attracted children to reading.

1980–2000: NEW MARKETS

Children's-only bookstores mushroomed in the 1980s, while large chain supermarket stores opened in the 1990s. Barnes & Noble, Borders, and Little Professor chains, for example, devote an unprecedented amount of floor space to children's books. Enthusiasm for children's books runs high and sales of children's books hold steady.

Multimedia products—CD-ROMs and interactive game adaptations of stories and informational books—are sold everywhere. David Macaulay published *The Way Things Work* (1988) (I–A) as an informational book but it soon became available on CD-ROM. Students can enter a museum and step back 250 million years to search for buried dinosaur bones in *Dinosaur Hunter,* an Eyewitness Virtual Reality CD-ROM. It seems miraculous to obtain a 30-volume set encyclopedia that shows such things as volcanoes erupting and mushrooms growing right before our eyes on one CD-ROM!

Poetry received a vote of confidence when the 1982 Newbery Medal was awarded to *A Visit to William Blake's Inn* (1982) (I–A) by Nancy Willard and the 1989 Newbery Medal was awarded to *Joyful Noise: Poems for Two Voices* by Paul Fleischman.

Literature-based programs became a driving force in shifting teaching practice away from isolated skill instruction toward integrated reading, writing, listening, and speaking. Library materials are no longer used primarily as supplementary material; they have become central to teaching and learning. Now teachers and librarians work together to develop thematic units, to introduce concepts across content areas, and to make connections among subject areas. In fact, the role of the school media specialist evolved into that of a literature and curriculum consultant. Literature-based instruction engages students in active inquiry where they not only develop research skills, but develop the library habit. Students ask for flexible scheduling so they can have free access to libraries and their resources. Teacher–librarians recognize the need for books and collaborative planning as critical; they often spend their own money on books when public funds are not available.

Enthusiasm for children's books has created new markets; new markets have led to increased production. Whereas approximately 2,000 children's books were published each year in the 1960s, in the 1990s more than 5,000 were published annually. In addition to teachers and librarians who spend money on children's books, parents are discovering their role in children's reading. Parents understand that children of any age learn when adults read to them. As a result, publishers produce books for children at every developmental stage—from infants and toddlers to young adults. Marketing departments create products to accompany children's books—dolls, stuffed animals, jewelry, clothing, toys, and memorabilia. Children's books mean business—big business—for writers, illustrators, publishers, booksellers, and literary agents.

Illustrated folklore, fantasy, realism, and poetry marked the beginning of the twentieth century. Toy books, picture books, series books, science fiction, biography, historical fiction, and nonfiction and an increasing paperback market set the tone for the twenty-first century. The genres change across time. As the world changes, so, too, does literature for children. The ease of world travel and communication has turned children's books into a global industry. International book fairs lead to co-publishing among many nations. Children's books truly have universal appeal.

Glossary of Literary Terms

Alliteration Repetition of initial consonant sound.

Allusion A reference to a literary work, character, or setting contained in another literary work, also called literary allusion.

Antagonist Character directly opposed to the protagonist or hero.

Anthropomorphism Attribution of human qualities to animals or objects.

Character A personality in literature.

Characterization Means by which an author establishes the credibility of a person or creature created by words, for example, physical description, or character's actions, words, thoughts, and feelings.

Chronological order Events related in temporal order of occurrence.

Classic Literary work from a past generation that retains popularity over time.

Cliché Expression used so often that it loses its freshness and clarity. Overused term that loses meaning.

Cliffhanger Suspenseful plot structure.

Climax Peak of action that brings about resolution of conflict.

Conflict Central problem or struggle—person against self, person against person, person against society, person against nature.

Connotation Emotional meaning of a word.

Convention Standard formulas and elements, often found in folklore.

Denotation Dictionary meaning of a word.

Denouement Closing action after climax and resolution.

Didactic Preachy, moralistic.

End papers Insides of front and back covers.

Episodic plot Problem, action, climax, and resolution appear in individual chapters.

Flashback Earlier scene out of sequence.

Folklore Myths, legends, proverbs, nursery rhymes, and stories handed down by word of mouth from generations past.

Folk song Song of unknown authorship preserved and transmitted by oral tradition.

Folktale Short narrative handed down through oral tradition.

Foreshadowing Hints of things to come.

Format Physical makeup of a book, including page size, typeface, margins, paper, and binding.

Genre Category of literature.

Hyperbole Exaggeration and overstatement, usually for the sake of humor.

Imagery Words that appeal to the senses.

Jacket Dust jacket; paper cover on a hardbound book.

Language style Choice and arrangement of words to tell a story or poem that express the individuality, the ideas, and the intent of the author.

Metaphor Implied comparison of unlike things.

Motif Recurring element in literature; a conventional situation, device, or incident; prevailing idea or design.

Narrative A story; the recounting of events in temporal order.

Omniscient narrator All-knowing narrator tells the story in third person.

Onomatopoeia Words sound like their meaning, for example, "Boom!"

Parody Composition designed to ridicule in humorous fashion another piece of work or its author. Burlesque or humorous imitation of a work.

Pattern Repeated structure or device, for example, use of three.

Personification Human traits given to inanimate objects.

Plot Sequence and relationship of events.

Plot structure Way a story is organized, the arrangements of the incidents, the ordering of events, the sequence, the story pattern. Types of plots: episodic, cumulative, flashback, chronological, cyclical.

Point of view Perspective from which an author tells a story or a poet speaks: first person, third person, omniscient narrator.

Protagonist Central character; hero.

Resolution Action following climax; solution of the central problem.

Rhythm Recurring flow of strong and weak beats in the language of prose or poetry.

Setting Time and place of the story events.

Simile Stated comparison.

Symbol Element with figurative and literal meaning.

Tall tale Humorous tale of the American frontier that recounts extravagantly impossible happenings.

Theme Central or dominating idea. In nonfiction, it may be the topic; in poetry, fiction, and drama, it is an abstract concept that is made vivid through character, plot, and image.

Unity Coordination of text and illustration.

Unity of character and action Mutual influence of character on events and events on character development.

Variant Different version of the same folktale.

Verisimilitude Appearance or semblance of truth.

Verse Unit of poetry; a metrical composition.

Professional References

Alexander, L. (1970). Identifications and identities. *Wilson Library Bulletin, 45*(2), 144–148.

Alexander, L. (1981). The grammar of story. In B. Hearne & M. Kaye (Eds.), *Celebrating children's books* (pp. 3–13). New York: Lothrop, Lee & Shepard.

Anderson, R. C., Hiebert, E. H., Scott, J. A., & Wilkinson, I.A.G. (1985). *Becoming a nation of readers: The report of the commission on reading.* Washington, DC: National Institute of Education.

Anzul, M. (1988). Exploring literature with children within a transactional framework. *Dissertation Abstracts International, 49*(08), 2132A.

Applebee, A. N. (1978). *The child's concept of story.* Chicago: University of Chicago Press.

Applebee, A. N. (1979). Children and stories: Learning the rules of the game. *Language Arts, 56,* 645.

Atwell, N. (1998). *In the middle: New understandings about writing, reading, and learning.* Portsmouth, NH: Heinemann.

Babbitt, N. (1990). Protecting children's literature. *The Horn Book Magazine, 66,* 696–703.

Bader, B. (1976). *American picture books from Noah's ark to the beast within.* Old Tappan, NJ: Macmillan.

Bader, B. (2002, November/December). How the little house gave ground: The beginnings of multiculturalism in a new, black children's literature. *The Horn Book Magazine, 78,* 657–673.

Bader, B. (2003a, March/April). Multiculturalism takes root. *The Horn Book Magazine, 79,* 143–162.

Bader, B. (2003b, May/June). Multiculturalism in the mainstream. *The Horn Book Magazine, 79,* 265–291.

Bang, M. (2000). *Picture this: How pictures work.* New York: SeaStar Books.

Banks, J. A., & Banks, C.A.M. (1993). *Multicultural education: Issues and perspectives* (3rd ed.). Boston: Allyn & Bacon.

Benton, M. (1984). The methodology vacuum in teaching literature. *Language Arts, 61,* 265–275.

Bishop, R. S. (1992). Multicultural literature for children: Making informed choices. In V. J. Harris (Ed.), *Teaching multicultural literature in grades K–8* (pp. 37–54). Norwood, MA: Christopher-Gordon.

Bishop, R. S. (Ed.). (1994). *Kaleidoscope: A multicultural booklist for grades K–8.* Urbana, IL: National Council of Teachers of English.

Bishop, R. S. (1997). Selecting literature for a multicultural curriculum. In V. J. Harris (Ed.), *Using multiethnic literature in the K–8 classroom* (pp. 1–20). Norwood, MA: Christopher-Gordon.

Blos, J. (1992). Perspectives on historical fiction. In R. Ammon & M. Tunnell (Eds.), *The story of ourselves: Teaching history through children's literature* (pp. 11–17). Portsmouth, NH: Heinemann.

Botkin, B. A. (1944). *A treasury of American folklore.* New York: Crown.

Britton, J. (1970). *Language and learning.* London: Penguin.

Bruner, J. S. (1987). *Actual minds, possible worlds.* Cambridge, MA: Harvard University Press.

Cameron, E. (1969). *The green and burning tree.* New York: Little, Brown.

Campbell, P. (2004). Vetting the verse novel. *The Horn Book Magazine, 80,* 611–616.

Cazden, C. (1988). *Classroom discourse.* Portsmouth, NH: Heinemann.

Chukovsky, K. (1963). *From two to five* (M. Morton, Ed. & Trans.). Berkeley: University of California Press.

Cianciolo, P. J. (1976). *Illustrations in children's books.* Dubuque, IA: Brown.

Cianciolo, P. J. (1997). *Picture books for children* (4th ed.). Chicago: American Library Association.

Clark, M. M. (1976). *Young fluent readers.* London: Heinemann.

Cochran-Smith, M. (1984). *The making of a reader.* Norwood, NJ: Ablex.

Cooper, S. (1981). Escaping into ourselves. In B. Hearne & M. Kaye (Eds.), *Celebrating children's books* (pp. 14–23). New York: Lothrop, Lee & Shepard.

Cooper, S. (1996). Fantasy in the real world. In *Dreams and wishes: Essays on writing for children* (pp. 57–71). New York: Simon & Schuster.

Corso, G. (1983). Comment. In Paul Janeczko (Ed.), *Poetspeak* (p. 11). New York: Bradbury.

Cox, M. R. (1893). *Cinderella: Three hundred and forty-five variants.* New York: David Nutt/Folklore Society.

Cullinan, B. E. (1982). *Literature and the child.* San Diego: Harcourt.

Cullinan, B. E., Harwood, K., & Galda, L. (1983). The reader and the story: Comprehension and response. *Journal of Research and Development in Education, 16*(3), 29–38.

Cummins, J. (2004). Accessing the international children's digital library. *The Horn Book Magazine, 80,* 145–151.

de la Mare, W. (1942). *Peacock pie.* London: Faber & Faber.

de la Mare, W. (1962). Cited in W. S. Baring-Gould & C. Baring-Gould, *The annotated Mother Goose.* New York: Bramhall.

Durkin, D. (1966). *Children who read early.* New York: Teachers College Press.

Early, M. J. (1960). Stages of growth in literary appreciation. *English Journal, 49,* 161–167.

Edmiston, B. (1993). Going up the beanstalk: Discovering giant possibilities for responding to literature through drama. In K. E. Holland, R. A. Hungerford, & S. B. Ernst (Eds.), *Journeying: Children responding to literature* (pp. 250–266). Portsmouth, NH: Heinemann.

Eeds, M., & Peterson, R. (1991). Teacher as curator: Learning to talk about literature. *Reading Teacher, 45,* 118–126.

Eeds, M., & Wells, D. (1989). Grand conversations: An exploration of meaning construction in literature study groups. *Research in the Teaching of English, 23,* 4–29.

Egoff, S. A. (1981). *Thursday's child: Trends and patterns in contemporary children's literature.* Chicago: American Library Association.

Farmer, P. (1979). *Beginnings: Creation myths of the world.* New York: Atheneum.

Favat, F. A. (1977). *Child and tale: The origins of interest.* Urbana, IL: National Council of Teachers of English.

Feitelsen, D., Kita, B., & Goldstein, Z. (1986). Effects of listening to series stories on first graders' comprehension and use of language. *Research in the Teaching of English, 20,* 339–356.

Fielding, L., Wilson, P. T., & Anderson, R. (1986). A new focus on free reading: The role of trade books in reading instruction. In T. E. Raphael & R. E. Reynolds (Eds.), *The contexts of school-based literacy* (pp. 149–160). New York: Random House.

Fisher, C. J., & Natarella, M. A. (1982). Young children's preferences in poetry: A national survey of first-, second-, and third-graders. *Research in the Teaching of English, 16*(4), 339–354.

Fletcher, R. (2000). *Poetry matters: Writing a poem from the inside out.* New York: HarperCollins.

Fox, D., & Short, K. (Eds.). (2003). *Stories matter: The complexity of cultural authenticity in children's literature.* Urbana, IL: National Council of Teachers of English.

Frye, N. (1963). *The well-tempered critic.* Bloomington: Indiana University Press.

Frye, N. (1970). *The educated imagination.* Bloomington: Indiana University Press.

Galda, L. (1980). *Three children reading stories: Response to literature in preadolescents.* Unpublished doctoral dissertation, New York University.

Galda, L. (1982). Assuming the spectator stance: An examination of the responses of three young readers. *Research in the Teaching of English, 16,* 1–20.

Galda, L. (1988). Readers, texts, and contexts: A response-based view of literature. *New Advocate, 1,* 92–102.

Galda, L. (1990). A longitudinal study of the spectator stance as a function of age and genre. *Research in the Teaching of English, 24,* 261–278.

Galda, L. (1992). Evaluation as a spectator: Changes across time and genre. In J. Many & C. Cox (Eds.), *Reader stance and literary understanding: Exploring the theories, research, and practice* (pp. 127–142). Norwood, NJ: Ablex.

Galda, L. (1993). How preferences and expectations influence evaluative responses to literature. In K. E. Holland, R. Hungerford, & S. Ernst (Eds.), *Journeying: Children responding to literature* (pp. 302–315). Portsmouth, NH: Heinemann.

Galda, L. (1998). Mirrors and windows: Reading as transformation. In T. E. Raphael & K. H. Au (Eds.), *Literature-based instruction: Reshaping the curriculum* (pp. 1–12). Norwood, MA: Christopher-Gordon.

Galda, L. (2001). [Review of the book *The land*]. *Riverbank Review, 4*(4), 36–37.

Galda, L. (2002). [Review of *The house of the scorpion*]. *Riverbank Review, 5*(3), 38–40.

Galda, L. (2003). [Review of the book *Pictures of Hollis Woods*]. *Riverbank Review, 6*(3), 42.

Galda, L., Ash, G. E., & Cullinan, B. E. (2000). Children's literature. In M. L. Kamil, P. B. Mosenthal, P. D. Pearson, & R. Barr (Eds.), *Handbook of reading research* (Vol. 3, pp. 361–379). Mahway, NJ: Erlbaum.

Galda, L., & Beach, R. (2004). Response to literature as a cultural activity. In R. B. Ruddell & N. J. Unrau (Eds.), *Theoretical models and processes of reading* (5th ed., pp. 852–869). Newark, DE: International Reading Association.

Galda, L., & Cullinan, B. E. (2003). Literature for literacy: What research says about the benefits of using trade books in the classroom. In J. Flood, D. Lapp, J. R. Squire, & J. M. Jensen (Eds.), *Handbook of research on teaching the English language arts* (2nd ed., pp. 640–648). Old Tappan, NJ: Macmillan.

Galda, L., & Liang, L. A. (2003). Literature as experience or looking for facts: Stance in the classroom. *Reading Research Quarterly, 38,* 268–275.

Galda, L., Rayburn, J. S., & Stanzi, L. C. (2000). *Looking through the faraway end: Creating a literature-based reading curriculum with 2nd graders.* Newark, DE: International Reading Association.

Galda, L., Shockley, B. S., & Pellegrini, A. D. (1995). Sharing lives: Reading, writing, talking, and living in a first grade classroom. *Language Arts, 72,* 334–339.

Goodman, K. S. (1985). Transactional psycholinguistics model: Unity in reading. In H. Singer & R. B. Ruddell (Eds.), *Theoretical models and processes of reading* (3rd ed., pp. 813–840). Newark, DE: International Reading Association.

Greenberg, J., & Jordan, S. (1991). *The painter's eye: Learning to look at contemporary American art.* New York: Delacorte Press.

Greenberg, J., & Jordan, S. (1993). *The sculptor's eye: Looking at contemporary American art.* New York: Delacorte Press.

Greenberg, J., & Jordan, S. (1995). *The American eye: Eleven artists of the twentieth century.* New York: Delacorte Press.

Grimal, P. (1965). *Larousse world mythology.* Secaucus, NJ: Chartwell.

Hall, S. T. (2001). *Using picture storybooks to teach literary devices: Recommended books for children and young adults* (Vol. 3). Westport, CT: Greenwood.

Halliday, M.A.K. (1982). Three aspects of children's language development: Learning language, learning through language, and learning about language. In Y. Goodman, M. Huassle, & D. S. Strickland (Eds.), *Oral and written language development research: Impact on the schools* (pp. 7–19). Urbana, IL: National Council of Teachers of English.

Hamilton, V. (1993). Everything of value: Moral realism in the literature for children. *Journal of Youth Services in Libraries, 6,* 364–377.

Hansen, S. (2004). *Fourth and fifth graders' poetry preferences before and after classroom poetry experiences: A case study.*

(Plan B project submitted to the faculty of the Graduate School of the University of Minnesota in partial fulfillment of the requirements for the degree of master of arts).

Hansen-Krening, N., Aoki, E. M., & Mizokawa, D. T. (Eds.). (2003). *Kaleidoscope: A multicultural booklist for grades K–8* (4th ed.). Urbana, IL: National Council of Teachers of English.

Hardy, B. (1978). Towards a poetics of fiction: An approach through narrative. In M. Meek, A. Warlow, & G. Barton (Eds.), *The cool web* (pp. 12–23). New York: Atheneum.

Harrison, D., & Cullinan, B. E. (2003). *Easy poetry lessons that dazzle and delight.* New York: Scholastic.

Hazard, P. (1967). *Books, children, and men.* Boston: Horn Book.

Heath, S. B. (1982). What no bedtime story means: Narrative skills at home and school. *Language and Society, 11,* 49–75.

Heath, S. B. (1983). *Ways with words: Language, life, and work in communities and classrooms.* New York: Cambridge University Press.

Heinlein, R. A. (1953, July). Ray guns and rocket ships. *Library Journal, 78,* 1188.

Herman, G. B. (1978). "Footprints in the sands of time": Biography for children. *Children's Literature in Education, 9*(2), 85–94.

Hickman, J. (1981). A new perspective on response to literature: Research in an elementary school setting. *Research in the Teaching of English, 15,* 343–354.

Hiebert, E. H., & Colt, J. (1989). Patterns of literature-based reading instruction. *The Reading Teacher, 43,* 14–20.

Holdaway, D. (1979). *The foundations of literacy.* Sydney: Ashton Scholastic.

Hynds, S. (1992). Challenging questions in the teaching of literature. In J. A. Langer (Ed.), *Literature instruction: A focus on student response* (pp. 78–100). Urbana, IL: National Council of Teachers of English.

Jackson, J. (1992, October). [Paper presented at the Holmes-Hunter Lecture]. University of Georgia, Athens.

Jung, C. G. (1976). *Psychology of the unconscious.* Princeton, NJ: Princeton University Press. (Original work published 1916).

Kamil, M., Mosenthal, P. B., Pearson, P. D., & Barr, R. (2000). *Handbook of reading research* (Vol. 3). Mahwah, NJ: Erlbaum.

Kiefer, B. Z. (1986). The child and the picture book: Creating live circuits. *Children's Literature Association Quarterly, 11,* 63–68.

Krashen, S. (1993). *The power of reading: Insights from the research.* Littleton, CO: Libraries Unlimited.

Lancia, P. J. (1997). Literary borrowing: The effects of literature on children's writing. *Reading Teacher, 50,* 470–475.

Lang, A. (1893). Foreword. In M. R. Cox, *Cinderella: Three hundred and forty-five variants.* New York: David Nutt/Folklore Society.

Langer, J. A. (1990). The process of understanding: Reading for literary and informative purposes. *Research in the Teaching of English, 24,* 229–260.

Langer, J. A. (1995). *Envisioning literature: Literary understanding and literature instruction.* New York: Teachers College Press.

Lehman, B. (1989). Child reader and literary work: Children's literature merges two perspectives. *Children's Literature Association Quarterly, 14,* 123–128.

Lehr, S. S. (1991). *The child's developing sense of theme: Responses to literature.* New York: Teacher's College Press.

Lester, J. (2004). *On writing for children and other people.* New York: Dial Books.

Lunge-Larsen, L. (2004, October). *Folklore for today's children.* Speech given for Book Week at the University of Minnesota, Minneapolis.

Luthi, M. (1970). *Once upon a time: On the nature of fairy tales.* New York: Unger.

MacDonald, M. R., & Sturm, B. W. (2001). *The storytellers sourcebook: A subject, title, and motif index to folklore collections for children, 1983–1999.* Detroit: Gale.

MacLean, M., Bryant, P. E., & Bradley, L. (1987). Rhymes, nursery rhymes and reading in early childhood. *Merrill-Palmer Quarterly, 33,* 225–281.

Many, J. E., & Wiseman, D. L. (1992). The effect of teaching approach on third grade students' response to literature. *Journal of Reading Behavior, 24,* 265–287.

Martin, Bill, Jr. (1972). *Sounds of laughter* (Teacher's Edition). Austin, TX: Holt, Reinhart and Winston.

May, J. (1984). Judy Blume as Archie Bunker. *Children's Literature Association Quarterly, 9*(1), 2.

McClure, A. (1985). *Children's responses to poetry in a supportive literary context.* Unpublished doctoral dissertation, Ohio State University.

McGinley, W., & Kamberelis, G. (1996). *Maniac Magee* and *Ragtime Tumpie:* Children negotiating self and world through reading and writing. *Research in the Teaching of English, 30,* 75–113.

McMahon, S., Raphael, T. E., Goatley, V. J., & Pardo, L. S. (1997). *The book club connection: Literacy learning and classroom talk.* New York: Teachers College Press.

Meltzer, M. (1976). Where do all the prizes go? The case for nonfiction. *The Horn Book Magazine, 52*(1), 21–22.

Meltzer, M. (1989). The social responsibility of the writer. *The New Advocate, 2*(3), 155–157.

Michaels, J. (2004). Pulp fiction. *The Horn Book Magazine, 80,* 299–306.

Mills, C. (2002, September/October). The portrayal of mental disability in children's literature: An ethical appraisal. *The Horn Book Magazine, 78,* 531–542.

Moll, L. C. (1994). Literacy research in community and classrooms: A sociocultural approach. In R. B. Ruddell, M. R. Ruddell, & H. Singer (Eds.), *Theoretical models and processes of reading* (4th ed., pp. 179–207). Newark, DE: International Reading Association.

Morrow, L. M. (1992). The impact of a literature-based program on the literacy achievement, use of literature, and attitudes of children from minority backgrounds. *Reading Research Quarterly, 27,* 251–275.

Morrow, L. M., & Gambrell, L. B. (2000). Literature-based reading instruction. In M. L. Kamil, P. B. Mosenthal, P. D. Pearson, & R. Barr (Eds.), *Handbook of reading research* (Vol. 3, pp. 563–586). Mahwah, NJ: Erlbaum.

National Council of Teachers of English. (1983). Statement on censorship and professional guidelines. *The Bulletin, 9*(1–2), 17–18.

Nieto, S. (2002). *Language, culture, and teaching: Critical perspectives for a new century.* Mahwah, NJ: Erlbaum.

One hundred books that shaped the century. (2000). *School Library Journal, 46*(1), 50–58.

Opie, I., & Opie, P. (1951). *The Oxford dictionary of nursery rhymes.* London: Oxford University Press.

Opie, I., & Opie, P. (1974). *Classic fairy tales.* London: Oxford University Press.

Pellowski, A. (1984). *The story vine: A source book of unusual and easy-to-tell tales from around the world.* Old Tappan, NJ: Macmillan.

Pillar, A. M. (1983). Aspects of moral judgment in response to fables. *Journal of Research and Development in Education, 16*(3), 37–46.

Pressley, M., Dolezal, S. E., Raphael, L. M., Mohan, L., Roehrig, A. D., & and Bogner, K. (2003). *Motivating primary grade students.* New York: Guilford Press.

Pringle, L. (1986, July). *Science writing.* Presentation at the 2nd annual Highlights Foundation Writer's Workshop, Chautauqua, NY.

Purves, A. C., Rogers, T., & Soter, A. D. (1990). *How porcupines make love II: Teaching a response-centered literature curriculum.* New York: Longmans.

Raphael, T. E., Florio-Ruane, S., & George, M. (2001). Book Club *Plus:* A conceptual framework to organize literacy instruction. *Language Arts, 79,* 159–168.

Rosen, C., & Rosen, H. (1973). *The language of primary school children.* London: Penguin.

Rosenblatt, L. M. (1976). *Literature as exploration.* New York: Noble & Noble. (Original work published 1938).

Rosenblatt, L. M. (1978). *The reader, the text, the poem: The transactional theory of the literary work.* Carbondale: Southern Illinois University Press.

Rosenblatt, L. M. (1991). Literature—S.O.S! *Language Arts, 68,* 444–448.

Saul, W. (1986, October). Living proof: Children's biographies of Marie Curie. *School Library Journal, 33,* 103–108.

Sawyer, R. (1962). *The way of the storyteller.* New York: Viking.

Sebesta, S. L., & Monson, D. L. (2003). Reading preferences. In J. Flood, D. Lapp, J. R. Squire, & J. M. Jensen (Eds.), *Handbook of research on teaching the English language arts* (2nd ed., pp. 835–847). Old Tappan, NJ: Macmillan.

Short, K. G., & Pierce, K. M. (1990). *Talking about books: Creating literate communities.* Portsmouth, NH: Heinemann.

Silvey, A. (2004). *100 best books for children.* Boston: Houghton Mifflin.

Sipe, L. R. (1998). Individual literary response styles of first and second graders. In T. Shanahan & F. V. Rodriguez-Brown (Eds.), *National Reading Conference yearbook* (Vol. 47, pp. 76–89). Chicago: National Reading Conference.

Sipe, L. R. (1999). Children's response to literature: Author, text, reader, context. *Theory into Practice, 38,* 120–129.

Slapin, B., & Seale, D. (Eds.). (1998). *Through Indian eyes: The Native experience in books for children.* Berkeley: University of California American Studies Center.

Smith, F. (1978). *Understanding reading* (2nd ed.). New York: Henry Holt.

Smith, F. (1982). *Writing and the writer.* New York: Henry Holt.

Stan, S. (Ed.). (2002). *The world through children's books.* Lanham, MD: Scarecrow.

Strickland, D. L., Galda, L., & Cullinan, B. E. (2004). *Language arts: Learning and teaching.* Belmont, CA: Wadsworth.

Sutcliff, R. (1973). History is people. In V. Haviland (Ed.), *Children and literature: Views and reviews* (pp. 307–308). Glenview, IL: Scott, Foresman.

Sutherland, Z. (Ed.). (1983). *The Scott, Foresman anthology of children's literature.* Glenview, IL: Scott, Foresman.

Taxel, J. (1984). The American Revolution in children's fiction: An analysis of historical meaning and narrative structure. *Curriculum Inquiry, 14*(1), 7–55.

Taylor, B. M., Frye, B., & Maruyama, G. (1990). Time spent reading and reading growth. *American Educational Research Journal, 27,* 351–362.

A tenth anniversary celebration of multicultural publishing. (2003). New York: Lee & Low Books.

Terry, A. (1974). *Children's poetry preferences: A national survey of upper elementary grades.* Urbana, IL: National Council of Teachers of English.

Thompson, S. (1955–1958). *Motif-index of folk-literature* (Vols. 1–5). Bloomington: Indiana University Press.

Tomlinson, C. (Ed.). (1998). *Children's books from other countries.* Lanham, MD: Scarecrow.

Tomlinson, C. (2002). An overview of international children's literature. In S. Stan (Ed.), *The world through children's books* (pp. 3–26). Lanham, MD: Scarecrow.

Townsend, J. R. (1987). *Written for children.* Philadelphia: Lippincott.

Varley, P. (2002). As good as reading? Kids and the audiobook revolution. *The Horn Book Magazine, 78,* 251–262.

Vygotsky, L. S. (1962). *Thought and language.* Cambridge, MA: Harvard University Press.

Vygotsky, L. S. (1978). *Mind in society.* Cambridge, MA: Harvard University Press.

Wells, G. (1986). *The meaning makers.* Portsmouth, NH: Heinemann.

West, R., Stanovich, K., & Mitchell, H. (1993). Reading in the real world and its correlates. *Reading Research Quarterly, 28,* 34–50.

Wolf, S. A., & Heath, S. B. (1992). *The braid of literature: Children's worlds of reading.* Cambridge, MA: Harvard University Press.

Wynne-Jones, T. (2004). Tigers and poodles and birds, oh my! *The Horn Book Magazine, 80,* 265–284.

Yolen, J. (2000). *Touch magic: Fantasy, faerie and folklore in the literature of childhood.* Little Rock, AR: August House.

Zipes, J. (1979; rev. ed., 2002). *Breaking the magic spell: Radical theories of folk and fairy tales.* Lexington: University Press of Kentucky.

Children's Literature References

Aardema, Verna. (1975). *Why Mosquitoes Buzz in People's Ears: A West African Tale.* Illus. Leo and Diane Dillon. New York: Dial Books.

Aaseng, Nathan. (1997). *Black Inventors.* New York: Facts on File.

Ackerman, Diane. (2003). *Animal Sense.* Illus. Peter Sis. New York: Knopf.

Ada, Alma Flor. (1994). *Where the Flame Trees Bloom.* New York: Atheneum.

Ada, Alma Flor. (1998). *Under the Royal Palms: A Childhood in Cuba.* New York: Atheneum.

Ada, Alma Flor, and Isabel Campoy. (2003). *¡Pio Peep! Traditional Spanish Nursery Rhymes.* New York: HarperCollins.

Adams, Richard. (1974). *Watership Down.* Old Tappan, NJ: Macmillan.

Addams, Charles. (2002). *The Charles Addams Mother Goose.* New York: Simon & Schuster.

Adler, David. (1990). *A Picture Book of Benjamin Franklin.* New York: Holiday House.

Adoff, Arnold. (1973). *Black Is Brown Is Tan.* Illus. Emily A. McCully. New York: HarperCollins.

Adoff, Arnold. (1979). *Eats: Poems.* Illus. Susan Russo. New York: Lothrop, Lee & Shepard.

Adoff, Arnold. (1991). *In for Winter, Out for Spring.* Illus. Jerry Pinkney. San Diego: Harcourt.

Adoff, Jamie. (2004). *Names Will Never Hurt Me.* New York: Dutton's Children's Books.

Agee, Jon. (2000). *Elvis Lives! and Other Anagrams.* New York: Farrar, Straus & Giroux.

Agee, Jon. (2003). *Z Goes Home.* New York: Hyperion.

Ahlberg, Allan. (2004). *The Improbable Cat.* New York: Delacorte Press.

Ajmera, Maya, and John Ivanko. (2004). *Be My Neighbor.* Watertown, MA: Charlesbridge.

Alcott, Louisa May. (1968). *Little Women.* Illus. Jessie Willcox Smith. New York: Little, Brown. (Original work published 1868)

Alexander, Lloyd. (1999). *The Book of Three* (**The Prydain Chronicles**). New York: Henry Holt. (Original work published 1969)

Aliki. (1998). *Marianthe's Story: Painted Words/Spoken Memories.* New York: Greenwillow.

Aliki. (1999). *William Shakespeare and the Globe.* New York: HarperCollins.

Aliki. (2002). *Ah, Music.* New York: HarperCollins.

Almond, David. (1999). *Skellig.* New York: Delacorte Press.

Almond, David. (2004). *The Fire-Eaters.* New York: Random House.

al-Windawi, Thura. (2004). *Thura's Diary: My Life in Wartime Iraq.* Trans. Robin Bray. New York: Viking.

Ambrose, Stephen. (2003). *This Vast Land.* New York: Simon & Schuster.

Anderson, Laurie Halse. (1999). *Speak.* New York: Farrar, Straus & Giroux.

Anderson, Laurie Halse. (2000). *Fever 1793.* New York: Simon & Schuster Books for Young Readers.

Anderson, M. T. (2002). *Feed.* Cambridge, MA: Candlewick Press.

Anno, Mitsumasa. (1977). *Anno's Counting Book.* New York: HarperCollins.

Ardley, Neil. (2004). *Music: An Eyewitness Book.* New York: DK Publishing.

Armstrong, Jennifer. (1998). *Shipwreck at the Bottom of the World: The Extraordinary True Story of Shackleton and the Endurance.* New York: Crown.

Arnosky, Jim. (2002). *Field Trips: Bug Hunting, Animal Tracking, Bird-Watching, and Shore Walking with Jim Arnosky.* New York: HarperCollins.

Aronson, Marc. (1999). *Sir Walter Raleigh and the Quest for El Dorado.* New York: Clarion.

Aronson, Marc. (2004). *John Winthrop, Oliver Cromwell, and the Land of Promise.* New York: Clarion.

Arrington, Frances. (2003). *Prairie Whispers.* New York: Philomel.

Ashman, Linda. (2001). *Castles, Caves, and Honeycombs.* Illus. Lauren Stringer. San Diego: Harcourt.

Asimov, Isaac. (1961). *Words from the Myths.* Illus. William Barss. Boston: Houghton Mifflin.

Avi. (1991). *Nothing but the Truth.* New York: Orchard Books.

Avi. (1992). *Who Was That Masked Man Anyway?* New York: Orchard Books.

Avi. (1997). *Poppy.* Illus. Brian Floca. New York: Orchard Books.

Avi. (1999). *Poppy and Rye.* Illus. Brian Floca. New York: Camelot.

Avi. (2000). *Ereth's Birthday.* Illus. Brian Floca. New York: HarperCollins.

Avi. (2000). *Ragweed: A Tale for Dimwood Forest.* Illus. Brian Floca. New York: HarperCollins.

Avi. (2002). *Crispin: The Cross of Lead.* New York: Hyperion.

Avi. (2002). *Silent Movie.* Illus. C. B. Mordan. New York: Atheneum.

Azarian, Mary. (2000). *A Gardener's Alphabet.* Boston: Houghton Mifflin.

Babbitt, Natalie. (1975). *Tuck Everlasting.* New York: Farrar, Straus & Giroux.

Baker, Jeanne. (1991). *Window.* New York: Greenwillow.

Baker, Jeanne. (2004). *Home.* New York: Greenwillow.

Balliett, Blue. (2004). *Chasing Vermeer.* New York: Scholastic.

Bang, Molly. (1983). *Ten, Nine, Eight.* New York: Greenwillow.

Bang, Molly. (1999). *When Sophie Gets Angry—Really, Really Angry . . .* New York: Blue Sky Press.

Bania, Michael. (2004). *Kumak's Fish: A Tall Tale from the Far North.* Portland, OR: Alaska Northwest Books.

Banks, Kate. (2003). *The Cat Who Walked across France.* Illus. Georg Hallensleben. New York: Foster Books.

Barrett, Tracy. (1999). *Anna of Byzantium.* New York: Delacorte Press.

Barron, T. A. (2004). *The Great Tree of Avalon: Child of the Dark Prophecy.* New York: Philomel.

Beatty, Patricia. (1987). *Charley Skedaddle.* New York: Morrow.

Beatty, Patricia. (1992). *Who Comes with Cannons?* New York: Morrow.

Begay, Shonto. (1992). *Ma'ii and Cousin Horned Toad: A Traditional Navajo Story.* New York: Scholastic.

Begay, Shonto. (1995). *Navajo: Visions and Voices across the Mesa.* New York: Scholastic.

Bemelmans, Ludwig. (1962). *Madeline.* New York: Viking. (Original work published 1939)

Best, Cari. (1999). *Three Cheers for Catherine the Great!* Illus. Giselle Potter. New York: DK Publishing.

Best, Cari. (2003). *When Catherine the Great and I Were Eight!* Illus. Giselle Potter. New York: Farrar, Straus & Giroux.

Bierhorst, John. (1984). *The Hungry Woman: Myths and Legends of the Aztecs.* New York: Morrow.

Billingsley, Franny. (1999). *The Folk Keeper.* New York: Atheneum.

Billout, Guy. (2002). *Something's Not Quite Right.* Boston: Godine.

Bishop, Nic. (2000). *Digging for Bird-Dinosaurs: An Expedition to Madagascar.* Boston: Houghton Mifflin.

Bjork, Christina. (1999). *Vendela in Venice.* Illus. Inga-Karin Eriksson. New York: R & S Books.

Blackwood, Alan. (1993). *Orchestra: An Introduction to the World of Classical Music.* Brookfield, CT: Millbrook.

Blizzard, Gladys. (1992). *Come Look with Me: Animals in Art.* Charlottesville, VA: Thomasson-Grant.

Bolden, Tonya. (1996). *The Book of African American Women: 150 Crusaders, Creators, and Uplifters.* Holbrook, MA: Adams Media.

Bolden, Tonya. (2001). *Tell All the Children Our Story: Memories and Mementos of Being Young and Black in America.* New York: Abrams.

Bolden, Tonya. (2004). *The Champ: The Story of Muhammad Ali.* Illus. Gregory Christie. New York: Knopf.

Bolden, Tonya. (2004). *Wake Up Our Souls: A Celebration of Black American Artists.* New York: Abrams.

Borden, Louise. (2004). *The Greatest Skating Race: A World War II Story from the Netherlands.* Illus. Niki Daly. New York: McElderry Books.

Bottner, Barbara. (2003). *The Scaredy Cats.* Illus. Victoria Chess. New York: Simon & Schuster.

Bowler, Tim. (2001). *Storm Catchers.* New York: McElderry Books.

Bray, Rosemary. (1995). *Martin Luther King.* Illus. Malcah Zeldis. New York: Greenwillow.

Brett, Jan. (1994). *Town Mouse, Country Mouse.* New York: Putnam.

Bridges, Ruby. (1999). *Through My Eyes.* New York: Scholastic.

Briggs, Raymond. (1970). *Jim and the Beanstalk.* New York: Coward-McCann.

Brooklyn Public Library Staff. (2000). *Brooklyn Pops Up: A Moveable Book of Brooklyn.* New York: Simon & Schuster.

Brooks, Martha. (2003). *True Confessions of a Heartless Girl.* New York: Farrar, Straus & Giroux.

Brown, Dee. (1993). *Wounded Knee: An Indian History of the American West.* Adapted by Amy Ehrlich. New York: Henry Holt.

Brown, Don. (2004). *Odd Boy Out: Young Albert Einstein.* Boston: Houghton Mifflin.

Brown, Jackie. (2004). *Little Cricket.* New York: Hyperion.

Brown, Marcia. (1961). *Once a Mouse.* New York: Scribner.

Brown, Margaret Wise. (1947). *Goodnight Moon.* Illus. Clement Hurd. New York: HarperCollins.

Browne, Anthony. (1986). *Piggybook.* New York: Knopf.

Browne, Anthony. (1991). *Willy and Hugh.* New York: Knopf.

Browne, Anthony. (2003). *The Shape Game.* New York: Farrar, Straus, & Giroux.

Bruchac, Joseph. (1993). *The First Strawberries.* New York: Dial Books.

Bruchac, Joseph. (1994). *A Boy Called Slow: The True Story of Sitting Bull.* New York: Philomel.

Bruchac, Joseph. (1996). *Between Earth and Sky: Legends of Native American Sacred Places.* San Diego: Harcourt.

Bruchac, Joseph. (1996). *Four Ancestors: Stories, Songs, and Poems from Native North America.* Illus. S. S. Burrus, Murv Jacob, Jeffrey Chapman, and Duke Sine. Mahwah, NJ: Bridge-Water Books.

Bruchac, Joseph. (1997). *Bowman's Store: A Journey to Myself.* New York: Dial Books.

Bruchac, Joseph. (1997). *Eagle Song.* New York: Dial Books.

Bruchac, Joseph. (1998). *The Arrow over the Door.* New York: Dial Books.

Bruchac, Joseph. (2000). *Sacajawea.* San Diego: Silver Whistle.

Bruchac, Joseph. (2001). *The Heart of a Chief.* New York: Penguin Putnam.

Bruchac, Joseph. (2001). *How Chipmunk Got His Stripes: A Tale of Bragging and Teasing.* New York: Dial Books.

Bruchac, Joseph. (2002). *The Winter People.* New York: Dial Books.

Bruchac, Joseph. (2003). *Pocahontas.* San Diego: Silver Whistle.

Bruchac, Joseph. (2004). *The Dark Pond.* New York: HarperCollins.

Bruchac, Joseph. (2004). *Hidden Roots.* New York: Scholastic.

Bruchac, Joseph, and Jonathan London. (1992). *Thirteen Moons on Turtle's Back: A Native American Year of Moons.* Illus. Thomas Locker. New York: Philomel.

Bryan, Ashley. (1992). *Sing to the Sun.* New York: HarperCollins.

Bryan, Ashley. (2003). *Beautiful Blackbird.* New York: Atheneum.

Bryant, Jen. (2004). *The Trial: A Novel.* New York: Knopf.

Bunting, Eve. (1990). *The Wall.* New York: Clarion.

Bunting, Eve. (1994). *Smoky Night.* Illus. David Diaz. San Diego: Harcourt.

Burchard, Peter. (2003). *Frederick Douglass: For the Great Family of Man.* New York: Atheneum.

Burgess, Melvin. (1996). *Smack.* New York: Henry Holt.

Burgess, Melvin. (2004). *Doing It.* New York: Henry Holt.

Burks, Brian. (1998). *Walks Alone.* San Diego: Harcourt.

Burleigh, Robert. (2004). *Langston's Train Ride.* Illus. Leonard Jenkins. New York: Orchard Books.

Burnett, Frances Hodgson. (1962). *The Secret Garden.* New York: HarperCollins.

Byars, Betsy. (1970). *The Summer of the Swans.* New York: Viking.

Cadnum, Michael. (2003). *Ship of Fire.* New York: Viking.

Cadnum, Michael. (2004). *Blood Gold.* New York: Viking.

Cadnum, Michael. (2004). *Starfall: Phaeton and the Chariot of the Sun.* New York: Orchard Books.

Calvert, Patricia. (1997). *Great Lives: The American Frontier.* New York: Atheneum.

Cameron, Ann. (2003). *Colibri.* New York: Farrar, Straus & Giroux.

Carle, Eric. (1989). *The Very Busy Spider.* New York: Philomel.

Carlson, Lori. (Ed.). (1994). *American Eyes: New Asian-American Short Stories for Young Adults.* New York: Henry Holt.

Carmi, Daniella. (2000). *Samir and Yonatan.* New York: Levine Books.

Carroll, Lewis. (1977). *Through the Looking Glass.* Illus. John Tenniel. New York: St. Martin's Press. (Original work published 1871)

Carroll, Lewis. (1992). *Alice's Adventures in Wonderland.* New York: Morrow. (Original work published 1865)

Cart, Michael. (Ed.). (2002). *911: The Book of Help.* New York: Cricket Books.

Cart, Michael. (Ed.). (2003). *Necessary Noise: Stories about Our Families as They Really Are.* New York: HarperCollins.

Carter, David, and James Diaz. (1999). *The Elements of Pop-Up.* New York: Simon & Schuster.

Casanova, Mary. (1995). *Moose Tracks.* New York: Hyperion.

Casanova, Mary. (1996). *Wolf Shadows.* New York: Hyperion.

Cassedy, Sylvia. (Ed.). (1996). *Red Dragonfly on My Shoulder.* New York: HarperCollins.

Cauley, Lorinda Bryan. (1983). *Jack and the Beanstalk.* New York: Putnam.

Cazet, Denys. (2003). *Minnie and Moo: Will You Be My Valentine?* New York: HarperCollins.

Cendrars, Blaise. (1982). *Shadow.* New York: Scribner.

Chalk, Gary. (1993). *Yankee Doodle.* New York: DK Publishing.

Chambers, Aidan. (1999). *Postcards from No Man's Land.* London: Bodley Head.

Chandra, Deborah, and Madeleine Comora. (2003). *George Washington's Teeth.* Illus. Brock Cole. New York: Farrar, Straus, & Giroux.

Chase, Richard. (Ed.). (1943). *Jack Tales.* Boston: Houghton Mifflin.

Chen, Chih-Yuan. (2004). *Guji Guji.* La Jolla, CA: Kane/Miller.

Cheng, Andrea. (2004). *Honeysuckle House.* Asheville, NC: Front Street.

Chodos-Irvine, Margaret. (2003). *Ella Sarah Gets Dressed.* San Diego: Harcourt.

Choldenko, Gennifer. (2004). *Al Capone Does My Shirts.* New York: Putnam.

Christensen, Bonnie. (2001). *Woody Guthrie: Poet of the People.* New York: Knopf.

Christopher, John. (1967). *The City of Gold and Lead.* Old Tappan, NJ: Macmillan.

Christopher, John. (1967). *The White Mountains.* Old Tappan, NJ: Macmillan.

Christopher, John. (1970). *The Pool of Fire.* Old Tappan, NJ: Macmillan.

Ciardi, John. (1987). *You Read to Me, I'll Read to You.* New York: HarperCollins.

Ciardi, John. (2002). *Someone Could Win a Polar Bear.* Illus. Edward Gorey. Honesdale, PA: Boyds Mills.

Cisneros, Sandra. (1991). *The House on Mango Street.* New York: Vintage.

Cleary, Brian. (2000). *Hairy, Scary, Ordinary: What Is an Adjective?* Minneapolis: Carolrhoda Books.

Clements, Andrew. (2002). *Things Not Seen.* New York: Philomel.

Clifton, Lucille. (1980). *My Friend Jacob.* Illus. Thomas Di Grazia. New York: Dutton.

Climo, Shirley. (1995). *Atalanta's Race: A Greek Myth.* Illus. Alexander Koshkin. New York: Clarion.

Cline-Ransome, Lesa. (2000). *Satchel Paige.* Illus. James Ransome. New York: Simon & Schuster.

Codell, Esme Raji. (2003). *Sahara Special.* New York: Hyperion.

Codell, Esme Raji. (2004). *Sing a Song of Tuna Fish: Hard-to-Swallow Stories from Fifth Grade.* New York: Hyperion.

Cofer, Judith Ortiz. (1995). *An Island Like You: Stories of the Barrio.* New York: Orchard Books.

Cofer, Judith Ortiz. (2004). *Call Me Maria.* New York: Orchard Books.

Cole, Joanna. (1987). *Evolution.* Illus. Aliki. New York: Harper-Collins.

Collier, James Lincoln, and Christopher Collier. (1974). *My Brother Sam Is Dead.* Old Tappan, NJ: Macmillan.

Collodi, Carlo. (1993). *Pinocchio.* Illus. Lorenzo Mattotti. New York: Lothrop, Lee & Shepard. (Original work published 1883)

Colum, Padraic. (1984). *The Children of Odin: The Book of Northern Myths.* Old Tappan, NJ: Macmillan.

Conrad, Pam. (1991). *Pedro's Journal.* Honesdale, PA: Caroline House.

Cooper, Susan. (1966). *Over Sea, under Stone.* San Diego: Harcourt.

Cooper, Susan. (1973). *Greenwitch.* New York: McElderry Books.

Cooper, Susan. (1973). *The Dark Is Rising.* Illus. Alan E. Cober. New York: Atheneum.

Cooper, Susan. (1974). *The Grey King.* New York: McElderry Books.

Cooper, Susan. (1977). *Silver on the Tree.* New York: McElderry Books.

Cormier, Robert. (2003). *The Rag and Bone Shop.* New York: Bantam Doubleday Dell.

Cornelissen, Cornelia. (1998). *Soft Rain: A Story of the Cherokee Trail of Tears.* New York: Delacorte Press.

Coville, Bruce. (1991). *Jeremy Thatcher, Dragon Hatcher.* San Diego: Harcourt.

Coville, Bruce. (1992). *Jennifer Murdley's Toad.* Illus. Gary Lippincott. San Diego: Harcourt.

Creech, Sharon. (1994). *Walk Two Moons.* New York: Harper-Collins.

Creech, Sharon. (2000). *The Wanderer.* New York: Harper-Collins.

Creech, Sharon. (2001). *Love That Dog.* New York: Harper-Collins.

Creech, Sharon. (2003). *Granny Torrelli Makes Soup.* New York: Colter Books.

Creech, Sharon. (2004). *Heartbeat.* New York: HarperCollins.

Crews, Donald. (1978). *Inside Freight Train.* New York: Greenwillow.

Crews, Nina. (2004). *The Neighborhood Mother Goose.* New York: Greenwillow.

Crist-Evans, Craig. (1999). *Moon over Tennessee: A Boy's Civil War Journal.* Boston: Houghton Mifflin.

Crossley-Holland, Kevin. (1998). *The World of King Arthur and His Court: People, Places, Legend and Lore.* Illus. Peter Malone. New York: Dutton.

Crossley-Holland, Kevin. (2001). *The Seeing Stone.* New York: Levine Books.

Crossley-Holland, Kevin. (2002). *At the Crossing Places.* New York: Levine Books.

Crossley-Holland, Kevin. (2004). *King of the Middle March.* New York: Levine Books.

Crowe, Chris. (2003). *Getting Away with Murder: The True Story of the Emmett Till Case.* New York: Fogelman Books.

Crutcher, Chris. (2001). *Whale Talk.* New York: Greenwillow.

Crutcher, Chris. (2003). *King of the Mild Frontier: An Ill-Advised Biography.* New York: Greenwillow.

Cullinan, Bernice. (Ed.). (1996). *A Jar of Tiny Stars: Poems by NCTE Award-Winning Poets.* Honesdale, PA: Boyds Mills.

Cullinan, Bernice. (Ed.). (2001). *Sing of the Earth and Sky: Poems about Our Planet and the Wonders Beyond.* Illus. Karmen Thompson. Honesdale, PA: Boyds Mills.

Curtis, Christopher Paul. (1995). *The Watsons Go to Birmingham—1963.* New York: Delacorte Press.

Curtis, Christopher Paul. (1999). *Bud, Not Buddy.* New York: Delacorte Press.

Curtis, Christopher Paul. (2004). *Bucking the Sarge.* New York: Lamb Books.

Cushman, Karen. (1994). *Catherine, Called Birdy.* New York: Clarion.

Cushman, Karen. (1995). *The Midwife's Apprentice.* New York: Clarion.

Cushman, Karen. (2000). *Matilda Bone.* New York: Clarion.

D'Adamo, Francesco. (2003). *Iqbal.* New York: Atheneum.

d'Aulaire, Ingri, and Edgar Parin d'Aulaire. (1955). *Columbus.* Sandwich Village, MA: Beautiful Feet Books.

d'Aulaire, Ingri, and Edgar Parin d'Aulaire. (1969). *East of the Sun and West of the Moon.* New York: Viking.

d'Aulaire, Ingri, and Edgar Parin d'Aulaire. (1986). *Norse Gods and Giants.* New York: Doubleday.

Danticat, Edwidge. (2004). *Behind the Mountains.* New York: Scholastic.

Dasent, George Webbe. (Trans.). (1992). *East o' the Sun, West o' the Moon.* Illus. P. J. Lynch. New York: Candlewick Press.

Dash, Joan. (2000). *The Longitude Prize.* Illus. Dusan Petricic. New York: Farrar, Straus & Giroux.

Davies, Nicola. (2003). *Surprising Sharks.* Illus. James Croft. Cambridge, MA: Candlewick Press.

Davot, Marguerite. (1997). *The Paper Dragon.* Illus. Robert Sabuda. New York: Atheneum.

Debon, Nicolas. (2003). *Four Pictures by Emily Carr.* Toronto: Groundwood Books.

DeFelice, Cynthia. (1999). *Nowhere to Call Home.* New York: Farrar, Straus & Giroux.

Delacre, Lulu. (1989). *Arroz con Leche: Popular Songs and Rhymes from Latin America.* New York: Scholastic.

Dematons, Charlotte. (2003). *The Yellow Balloon.* Asheville, NC: Front Street.

Demi. (2004). *The Hungry Coat: A Tale from Turkey.* New York: McElderry Books.

dePaola, Tomie. (1975). *Strega Nona.* New York: Simon & Schuster.

dePaola, Tomie. (1999). *26 Fairmount Avenue.* New York: Putnam.

dePaola, Tomie. (2000). *Here We All Are.* New York: Putnam.

dePaola, Tomie. (2001). *On My Way.* New York: Putnam.

dePaola, Tomie. (2002). *What a Year.* New York: Putnam.

Dessen, Sarah. (2004). *The Truth about Forever.* New York: Penguin Books.

DiCamillo, Kate. (2000). *Because of Winn-Dixie.* Cambridge, MA: Candlewick Press.

DiCamillo, Kate. (2003). *The Tale of Despereaux.* Illus. Timothy Basil Ering. Cambridge, MA: Candlewick Press.

Dickinson, Peter. (1998). *Noli's Story.* New York: Grosset & Dunlap.

Dickinson, Peter. (1998). *Po's Story.* New York: Grosset & Dunlap.

Dickinson, Peter. (1998). *Suth's Story.* New York: Grosset & Dunlap.

Dickinson, Peter. (1999). *Mana's Story.* New York: Grosset & Dunlap.

Dodds, Dayle Ann. (2003). *Where's Pup?* Illus. Pierre Pratt. New York: Dial Books.

Donnelly, Jennifer. (2003). *A Northern Light.* San Diego: Harcourt.

Dorris, Michael. (1992). *Morning Girl.* New York: Hyperion.

Dorris, Michael. (1994). *Guests.* New York: Hyperion.

Dorris, Michael. (1996). *Sees Behind Trees.* New York: Hyperion.

Dorris, Michael. (1997). *The Window.* New York: Hyperion.

Dorros, Arthur. (1991). *Abuela.* New York: Dutton.

Dorros, Arthur. (2004). *Under the Sun.* New York: Abrams/Amulet.

Doyle, Malachy. (2004). *One, Two, Three O'Leary.* Illus. Will Hillenbrand. New York: McElderry Books.

Draper, Sharon. (2003). *The Battle of Jericho.* New York: Atheneum.

Duffey, Betsy. (1999). *Alien for Rent.* New York: Delacorte Press.

Dunrea, Olivier. (2002). *Gossie.* Boston: Houghton Mifflin.

Dunrea, Olivier. (2002). *Gossie and Gertie.* Boston: Houghton Mifflin.

Dunrea, Olivier. (2003). *Ollie.* New York: Houghton Mifflin.

Edwards, Pamela Duncan. (2001). *Boston Tea Party.* Illus. Henry Cole. New York: Putnam.

Edwards, Pamela Duncan. (2003). *The Wright Brothers.* Illus. Henry Cole. New York: Hyperion.

Ehlert, Lois. (1989). *Color Zoo.* Philadelphia: Lippincott.

Ehlert, Lois. (2004). *Pie in the Sky.* San Diego: Harcourt.

Ellis, Deborah. (2000). *The Breadwinner.* Toronto: Douglas & McIntyre.

Ellis, Deborah. (2001). *Parvanna's Journey.* Toronto: Groundwood.

Ellsworth, Loretta. (2002). *The Shrouding Woman.* New York: Henry Holt.

English, Karen. (1999). *Francie.* New York: Farrar, Straus & Giroux.

English, Karen. (2004). *Hot Day on Abbott Avenue.* Illus. Javaka Steptoe. New York: Clarion.

Erdrich, Louise. (1996). *Grandmother's Pigeon.* Illus. Jim LaMarche. New York: Hyperion.

Erdrich, Louise. (1999). *The Birchbark House.* New York: Hyperion.

Erdrich, Louise. (2005). *The Game of Silence.* New York: HarperCollins.

Ernst, Lisa Campbell. (2004). *The Turn-Around, Upside-Down Alphabet Book.* New York: Simon & Schuster.

Esbensen, Barbara Juster. (1986). *Words with Wrinkled Knees: Animal Poems.* Illus. John Stadler. New York: HarperCollins.

Esbensen, Barbara Juster. (2000). *The Night Rainbow.* New York: Scholastic.

Farjeon, Eleanor. (1951). *Poems for Children.* Philadelphia: Lippincott.

Farjeon, Eleanor. (1986). *The Children's Bells.* New York: Watts.

Farmer, Nancy. (1994). *The Ear, the Eye, and the Arm.* New York: Scholastic.

Farmer, Nancy. (2002). *The House of the Scorpion.* New York: Atheneum.

Farmer, Nancy. (2004). *The Sea of Trolls.* New York: Atheneum.

Farris, Christine King. (2003). *My Brother Martin.* New York: Simon & Schuster.

Feelings, Tom. (1995). *Middle Passage: White Ships/Black Cargo.* New York: Dial Books.

Fisher, Leonard Everett. (1984). *Olympians: Great Gods and Goddesses of Ancient Greece.* New York: Holiday House.

Fisher, Leonard Everett. (1990). *The Oregon Trail.* New York: Holiday House.

Flake, Sharon. (2004). *Who Am I without Him? Short Stories about Girls and the Boys in Their Lives.* New York: Hyperion.

Fleischman, Paul. (1986). *I Am Phoenix.* Illus. Ken Nut (Eric Beddows). New York: HarperCollins.

Fleischman, Paul. (1988). *Joyful Noise: Poems for Two Voices.* New York: HarperCollins.

Fleischman, Paul. (1993). *Bull Run.* New York: HarperCollins.

Fleischman, Paul. (1996). *Dateline: Troy.* Cambridge, MA: Candlewick Press.

Fleischman, Paul. (1997). *Seedfolks.* New York: HarperCollins.

Fleischman, Paul. (2000). *Big Talk: Poems for Four Voices.* Illus. Beppe Giacoppe. Cambridge, MA: Candlewick Press.

Fleischman, Paul. (2001). *Seek.* Chicago: Cricket Books.

Fleischman, Paul, and Kevin Hawkes. (2004). *Sidewalk Circus.* Cambridge, MA: Candlewick Press.

Fleischman, Sid. (1986). *The Whipping Boy.* New York: Greenwillow.

Fleming, Candace. (2003). *Ben Franklin's Almanac: Being a True Account of the Good Gentleman's Life.* New York: Atheneum.

Fleming, Denise. (1992). *Lunch.* New York: Henry Holt.

Fleming, Denise. (1993). *In the Small, Small Pond.* New York: Henry Holt.

Fleming, Denise. (1994). *Barnyard Banter.* New York: Henry Holt.

Fleming, Denise. (1996). *Where Once There Was a Wood.* New York: Henry Holt.

Fleming, Denise. (2000). *The Everything Book.* New York: Henry Holt.

Fletcher, Susan. (1998). *Shadow Spinner.* New York: Atheneum.

Floca, Brian. (2003). *The Racecar Alphabet.* New York: Atheneum.

Florian, Douglas. (1997). *In the Swim.* San Diego: Harcourt.

Florian, Douglas. (2000). *Mammalabilia.* San Diego: Harcourt.

Forbes, Esther. (1969). *Johnny Tremain.* Illus. Lynd Ward. New York: Dell.

Foreman, Michael. (2003). *Wonder Goal!* New York: Farrar, Straus & Giroux.

Fox, Mem. (1983). *Possum Magic.* Nashville: Abingdon.

Fox, Mem. (1997). *Whoever You Are.* San Diego: Harcourt.

Fox, Mem. (2004). *Where Is the Green Sheep?* Illus. Judy Horacek. San Diego: Harcourt.

Frank, E. R. (2000). *Life Is Funny.* New York: DK Publishing.

Franklin, Kris. (2003). *The Grape Thief.* Cambridge, MA: Candlewick Press.

Frasier, Debra. (1991). *On the Day You Were Born.* San Diego: Harcourt.

Frasier, Debra. (2000). *Miss Alaineus: A Vocabulary Disaster.* San Diego: Harcourt.

Frasier, Debra. (2004). *The Incredible Water Show.* San Diego: Harcourt.

Frazee, Marla. (2003). *Roller Coaster.* San Diego: Harcourt.

Frazee, Marla. (2004). *New Baby Train.* New York: Little, Brown.

Freedman, Russell. (1989). *Lincoln: A Photobiography.* New York: Clarion.

Freedman, Russell. (1991). *The Wright Brothers: How They Invented the Airplane.* New York: Holiday House.

Freedman, Russell. (1992). *An Indian Winter.* New York: Holiday House.

Freedman, Russell. (1993). *Eleanor Roosevelt: A Life of Discovery.* New York: Clarion.

Freedman, Russell. (2000). *Give Me Liberty! The Story of the Declaration of Independence.* New York: Holiday House.

Freedman, Russell. (2002). *Confucius: The Golden Rule.* New York: Levine Books.

Freedman, Russell. (2003). *In Defense of Liberty: The Story of America's Bill of Rights.* New York: Holiday House.

Freedman, Russell. (2004). *The Voice That Challenged a Nation: Marian Anderson and the Struggle for Equal Rights.* New York: Clarion.

French, Simon. (2003). *Where in the World.* Atlanta: Peachtree.

French, Vivian. (2004). *T. Rex.* Cambridge, MA: Candlewick Press.

Fukuda, Hanako. (1970). *Wind in My Hand: The Story of Issa, Japanese Haiku Poet.* San Carlos, CA: Golden Gate.

Funke, Cornelia. (2003). *Inkheart.* New York: Scholastic.

Furlong, Monica. (2004). *Colman.* New York: Random House.

Furlong, Monica. (2004). *Juniper.* New York: Random House.

Furlong, Monica. (2004). *Wise Child.* New York: Random House.

Fyleman, Rose. (2004). *Mary Middling and Other Silly Folk: Nursery Rhymes and Nonsense Poems.* Illus. Katja Bandlow. New York: Clarion.

Gag, Wanda. (Trans.). (1936). *Tales from Grimm.* New York: Coward-McCann.

Gag, Wanda. (Trans.). (1947). *More Tales from Grimm.* New York: Coward-McCann.

Galdone, Paul. (1982). *Jack and the Beanstalk.* Boston: Houghton Mifflin.

Gantos, Jack. (2000). *Joey Pigza Loses Control.* New York: Farrar, Straus & Giroux.

Gantos, Jack. (2002). *Hole in My Life.* New York: Farrar, Straus & Giroux.

Geisert, Bonnie. (2002). *Prairie Summer.* Illus. Arthur Geisert. Boston: Houghton Mifflin.

Geisert, Bonnie, and Arthur Geisert. (2001). *Desert Town.* Boston: Houghton Mifflin.

Gelman, Rita Golden. (2004). *Doodler Doodling.* Illus. Paul Zelinsky. New York: Greenwillow.

George, Jean Craighead. (1993). *Dear Rebecca, Winter Is Here.* New York: HarperCollins.

George, Kristine O'Connell. (2001). *Toasting Marshmallows.* Illus. Kate Kiesler. New York: Clarion.

George, Kristine O'Connell. (2002). *Swimming Upstream: Middle School Poems.* Illus. Debbie Tilley. New York: Clarion.

George, Kristine O'Connell. (2004). *Hummingbird Nest: A Journal of Poems.* Illus. Barry Moser. San Diego: Harcourt.

George, Kristine O'Connell. (2005). *Fold Me a Poem.* Illus. Lauren Stringer. San Diego: Harcourt.

Geras, Adele. (2001). *Troy.* San Diego: Harcourt.

Gerson, Mary-Joan. (1992). *Why the Sky Is Far Away: A Nigerian Folktale.* Illus. Carla Golembe. New York: Little, Brown.

Gerstein, Mordicai. (2003). *The Man Who Walked between the Towers.* Brookfield, CT: Roaring Brook Press.

Gibbs, May. (1918). *Snugglepot and Cuddlepie.* Sydney: Ingres & Robertson.

Giblin, James Cross. (2000). *The Amazing Life of Benjamin Franklin.* New York: Scholastic.

Giblin, James Cross. (2002). *The Life and Death of Adolf Hitler.* New York: Clarion.

Giff, Patricia Reilly. (2000). *Nory Ryan's Song.* New York: Delacorte Press.

Giff, Patricia Reilly. (2002). *Pictures of Hollis Woods.* New York: Lamb Books.

Giff, Patricia Reilly. (2003). *Maggie's Door.* New York: Lamb Books.

Giff, Patricia Reilly. (2004). *A House of Tailors.* New York: Lamb Books.

Goble, Paul. (1980). *The Gift of the Sacred Dog.* New York: Bradbury.

Gold, Alison Leslie. (2000). *A Special Fate: Chiune Sugihara: Hero of the Holocaust.* New York: Scholastic.

Goldstein, Bobbye. (Ed.). (1992). *Inner Chimes: Poems on Poetry.* Illus. Jane Breskin Zalben. Honesdale, PA: Boyds Mills.

Goodman, Susan. (2004). *Skyscraper: From the Ground Up.* Illus. Michael Doolittle. New York: Knopf.

Graham, Joan Bransfield. (1994). *Splish Splash.* Illus. Steve Scott. New York: Ticknor & Fields.

Grahame, Kenneth. (1961). *Wind in the Willows.* New York: Scribner. (Original work published 1908)

Gralley, Jean. (2004). *The Moon Came Down on Milk Street.* New York: Henry Holt.

Graves, Bonnie. (2002). *Taking Care of Trouble.* New York: Dutton.

Gray, Dianne. (2000). *Holding Up the Earth.* Boston: Houghton Mifflin.

Gray, Dianne. (2002). *Together Apart.* Boston: Houghton Mifflin.

Greenberg, Jan, and Sandra Jordan. (1991). *The Painter's Eye: Learning to Look at Contemporary American Art.* New York: Delacorte Press.

Greenberg, Jan, and Sandra Jordan. (1993). *The Sculptor's Eye: Looking at Contemporary American Art.* New York: Delacorte Press.

Greenfield, Eloise. (1978). *Honey, I Love and Other Love Poems.* Illus. Leo and Diane Dillon. New York: HarperCollins.

Greenfield, Eloise. (1991). *Night on Neighborhood Street.* Illus. Jan Spivey Gilchrist. New York: Dial Books.

Grimes, Nikki. (1996). *Come Sunday.* Illus. Michael Bryant. Grand Rapids, MI: Eerdmans.

Grimes, Nikki. (1999). *My Man Blue.* Illus. Jerome Lagarrigue. New York: Dial Books.

Grimes, Nikki. (2001). *A Pocketful of Poems.* Illus. Javaka Steptoe. New York: Clarion.

Grimes, Nikki. (2001). *Stepping Out with Grandma Mac.* Illus. Angelo. New York: Orchard Books.

Grimes, Nikki. (2002). *Talkin' about Bessie: The Story of Aviator Elizabeth Coleman.* Illus. E. B. Lewis. New York: Orchard Books.

Grimes, Nikki. (2003). *Bronx Masquerade.* New York: Puffin.

Grimm, Jacob, and Wilhelm Grimm. (1972). *Snow White and the Seven Dwarfs.* Trans. Randall Jarrell. Illus. Nancy Ekholm Burkert. New York: Farrar, Straus & Giroux.

Grimm, Jacob, and Wilhelm Grimm. (1979). *Hansel and Gretel.* Illus. Lisbeth Zwerger. New York: Morrow.

Grimm, Jacob, and Wilhelm Grimm. (1981). *Cinderella.* Illus. Nonny Hogrogian. New York: Greenwillow.

Grimm, Jacob, and Wilhelm Grimm. (2004). *The Annotated Brothers Grimm.* Trans. and ed. Maria Tatar. New York: Norton.

Grovenar, Alan. (2000). *Osceola: Memories of a Sharecropper's Daughter.* New York: Hyperion.

Gunning, Monica. (1993). *Not a Copper Penny in Me House.* Illus. Frané Lessac. Honesdale, PA: Woodsong.

Haddix, Margaret Peterson. (1998). *Among the Hidden.* New York: Simon & Schuster.

Haddix, Margaret Peterson. (2001). *Among the Imposters.* New York: Simon & Schuster.

Haddix, Margaret Peterson. (2002). *Among the Betrayed.* New York: Simon & Schuster.

Haddix, Margaret Peterson. (2003). *Among the Barons.* New York: Simon & Schuster.

Haddon, Mark. (2003). *The Curious Incident of the Dog in the Night-Time.* New York: Doubleday.

Haley, Gail E. (1986). *Jack and the Bean Tree.* New York: Crown.

Haley, Gail E. (1992). *Mountain Jack Tales.* New York: Dutton.

Hall, Bruce Edward. (2004). *Henry and the Kite Dragon.* Illus. William Low. New York: Philomel.

Hall, Donald. (1979). *Ox-Cart Man.* Illus. Barbara Cooney. New York: Viking.

Hamilton, Virginia. (1985). *The People Could Fly: American Black Folktales.* Illus. Leo and Diane Dillon. New York: Random House.

Hamilton, Virginia. (1988). *In the Beginning: Creation Stories from around the World.* Illus. Barry Moser. San Diego: Harcourt.

Hamilton, Virginia. (2000). *The Girl Who Spun Gold.* Illus. Leo and Diane Dillon. New York: Blue Sky Press.

Hamilton, Virginia. (2003). *Bruh Rabbit and the Tar Baby Girl.* Illus. James Ransome. New York: Blue Sky Press.

Hamilton, Virginia. (2004). *The People Could Fly: The Picture Book.* Illus. Leo and Diane Dillon. New York: Random House.

Hamilton, Virginia. (2004). *Wee Winnie Witch's Skinny: An Original African American Scare Tale.* Illus. Barry Moser. New York: Blue Sky Press.

Hampton, Wilborn. (2003). *September 11, 2001: Attack on New York City.* Cambridge, MA: Candlewick Press.

Hannigan, Katherine. (2004). *Ida B.* New York: Greenwillow.

Hansen, Joyce. (1998). *Women of Hope: African Americans Who Made a Difference.* New York: Scholastic.

Harel, Nira. (2003). *The Key to My Heart.* Illus. Yossi Abulafia. La Jolla, CA: Kane/Miller.

Harley, Avis. (2000). *Fly with Poetry: An ABC of Poetry.* Honesdale, PA: Boyds Mills.

Harrington, Janice. (2004). *Going North.* Illus. Jerome Lagarrigue. New York: Farrar, Straus, & Giroux.

Harrison, David, and Bernice Cullinan. (2003). *Easy Poetry Lessons That Dazzle and Delight.* New York: Scholastic.

Hart, Jane. (Compiler). (1982). *Singing Bee! A Collection of Favorite Children's Songs.* Illus. Anita Lobel. New York: Lothrop, Lee & Shepard.

Hartinger, Brent. (2003). *Geography Club.* New York: Harper-Collins.

Hautman, Pete. (2004). *Godless.* New York: Simon & Schuster.

Hawthorne, Nathaniel. (1893). *A Wonder Book for Boys and Girls.* Boston: Houghton Mifflin. (Original work published 1851)

Hayes, Joe. (2004). *La Llorona/The Weeping Woman: An Hispanic Legend Told in Spanish and English.* Illus. Vicki Trego Hill and Mona Pennypacker. El Paso, TX: Cinco Puntos Press.

Heard, Georgia. (1992). *Creatures of Earth, Sea, and Sky.* Honesdale, PA: Boyds Mills.

Heller, Ruth. (1997). *Mine, All Mine: A Book about Pronouns.* New York: Grosset & Dunlap.

Henderson, Douglas. (2000). *Asteroid Impact.* New York: Dial Books.

Henkes, Kevin. (1991). *Chrysanthemum.* New York: Greenwillow.

Henkes, Kevin. (2000). *Wemberly Worried.* New York: Greenwillow.

Henkes, Kevin. (2003). *Olive's Ocean.* New York: Greenwillow.

Henkes, Kevin. (2004). *Kitten's First Full Moon.* New York: Greenwillow.

Hesse, Karen. (1997). *Out of the Dust.* New York: Scholastic.

Hesse, Karen. (2003). *Witness.* New York: Scholastic.

Hesse, Karen. (2004). *The Cats in Krasinski Square.* Illus. Wendy Watson. New York: Scholastic.

Hiaasen, Carl. (2002). *Hoot.* New York: Knopf.

Hickman, Janet. (1994). *Jericho.* New York: Greenwillow.

Hiçyilmaz, Gaye. (2000). *Smiling for Strangers.* New York: Farrar, Straus & Giroux.

Hirsch, Odo. (2004). *Yoss.* New York: Random House.

Ho, Minfong. (1990). *Rice without Rain.* New York: Lothrop, Lee & Shepard.

Ho, Minfong. (1991). *The Clay Marble.* New York: Farrar, Straus & Giroux.

Ho, Minfong. (1996). *Hush! A Thai Lullaby.* Illus. Holly Meade. New York: Orchard Books.

Ho, Minfong. (2003). *Gathering the Dew.* New York: Orchard Books.

Ho, Minfong, and Saphan Nos. (1997). *Brother Rabbit: A Cambodian Tale.* Illus. Jennifer Hewitson. New York: Lothrop, Lee & Shepard.

Hoban, Russell. (1986). *Bread and Jam for Frances.* Illus. Lillian Hoban. New York: HarperCollins. (Original work published 1964)

Hoban, Tana. (2003). *Cubes, Cones, Cylinders, and Spheres.* New York: Greenwillow.

Hobbs, Will. (1999). *Jason's Gold.* New York: Morrow.

Hoberman, Mary Ann. (1991). *Fathers, Mothers, Sisters, Brothers.* Illus. Marilyn Hafner. New York: Little, Brown.

Hodges, Margaret. (2004). *Merlin and the Making of the King.* Illus. Trina Schart Hyman. New York: Holiday House.

Holt, Kimberly Willis. (1999). *When Zachary Beaver Came to Town.* New York: Henry Holt.

Holt, Kimberly Willis. (2003). *Keeper of the Night.* New York: Henry Holt.

Hoose, Phillip. (2002). *It's Our World, Too! Young People Who Are Making a Difference (How They Do It—How You Can, Too!).* New York: Farrar, Straus & Giroux.

Hoose, Phillip. (2004). *The Race to Save the Lord God Bird.* New York: Farrar, Straus & Giroux.

Hopkins, Lee Bennett. (1983). *A Song in Stone: City Poems.* Illus. Anna Held Audette. New York: Crowell.

Hopkins, Lee Bennett. (1988). *Side by Side: Poems to Read Together.* New York: Simon & Schuster.

Hopkins, Lee Bennett. (Ed.). (1990). *Good Books, Good Times!* Illus. Harvey Stevensen. New York: HarperCollins.

Hopkins, Lee Bennett. (Ed.). (1994). *Hand in Hand: An American History through Poetry.* New York: Simon & Schuster.

Hopkins, Lee Bennett. (1995). *Small Talk: A Book of Short Poems.* Illus. Susan Gaber. San Diego: Harcourt.

Hopkins, Lee Bennett. (Ed.). (2000). *My America: A Poetry Atlas of the United States.* New York: Simon & Schuster.

Hopkins, Lee Bennett. (Ed.). (2002). *Home to Me: Poems across America.* Illus. Stephen Elkhorn. New York: Scholastic.

Hopkins, Lee Bennett. (Ed.). (2002). *Hoofbeats, Claws, and Rippled Fins: Creature Poems.* Illus. Stephen Elkhorn. New York: HarperCollins.

Hopkinson, Deborah. (2003). *Shutting Out the Sky: Life in the Tenements of New York, 1880–1924.* New York: Orchard Books.

Hort, Lenny. (2000). *The Seals on the Bus.* Illus. G. Brian Karas. New York: Henry Holt.

Horvath, Polly. (1999). *The Trolls.* New York: Farrar, Straus & Giroux.

Horvath, Polly. (2003). *The Canning Season.* New York: Farrar, Straus & Giroux.

Horvath, Polly. (2004). *The Pepins and Their Problems.* New York: Farrar, Straus & Giroux.

Howe, James. (1983). *The Celery Stalks at Midnight.* New York: Atheneum.

Huck, Charlotte. (1996). *Toads and Diamonds.* Illus. Anita Lobel. New York: Greenwillow.

Hudson, Wade. (2004). *Powerful Words: More Than 200 Years of Extraordinary Writing by African Americans.* New York: Scholastic.

Hunt, Irene. (1964). *Across Five Aprils.* Chicago: Follett.

Hunter, Mollie. (1998). *The King's Swift Rider.* New York: HarperCollins.

Hutchins, Pat. (1986). *The Doorbell Rang.* New York: Greenwillow.

Hutchins, Pat. (1990). *What Game Shall We Play?* New York: Greenwillow.

Hyman, Trina Schart. (1977). *The Sleeping Beauty.* New York: Little, Brown.

Isadora, Rachel. (2000). *ABC Pop!* New York: Viking.

Isadora, Rachel. (2000). *1 2 3 Pop!* New York: Viking.

Issa. (1969). *Don't Tell the Scarecrow.* New York: Simon & Schuster.

Jacobs, Joseph. (1923). *English Fairy Tales.* New York: Putnam.

Jacobs, Joseph. (1965). *Tom Tit Tot.* Illus. Evaline Ness. New York: Scribner.

Jacques, Brian. (2002). *Triss.* New York: Philomel.

Jacques, Brian. (2003). *Loamhedge.* New York: Philomel.

Jagendorf, M. A. (1957). *Noodlehead Stories from around the World.* New York: Vanguard.

Janeczko, Paul. (Ed.). (1983). *Poetspeak: In Their Work, about Their Work.* New York: Atheneum.

Janeczko, Paul. (1989). *Brickyard Summer.* Illus. Ken Rush. New York: Scholastic.

Janeczko, Paul. (1990). *The Place My Words Are Looking For: What Poets Say about and through Their Work.* New York: Bradbury.

Janeczko, Paul. (1993). *Stardust Otel.* New York: Scholastic.

Janeczko, Paul. (1995). *Poetry from A to Z: A Guide for Young Writers.* New York: Bradbury.

Janeczko, Paul. (1995). *Wherever Home Begins: 100 Contemporary Poems.* New York: Scholastic.

Janeczko, Paul. (1998). *The Music of What Happens: Poems That Tell Stories.* New York: Scholastic.

Janeczko, Paul. (1998). *That Sweet Diamond: Baseball Poems.* New York: Atheneum.

Janeczko, Paul. (Ed.). (2000). *Stone Bench in an Empty Park.* Photo: Henri Silberman. New York: Orchard Books.

Janeczko, Paul. (Ed.). (2001). *A Poke in the I: A Collection of Concrete Poems.* Illus. Chris Raschka. Cambridge, MA: Candlewick Press.

Janeczko, Paul, and Naomi Shihab Nye. (Eds.). (1996). *I Feel a Little Jumpy around You.* New York: Simon & Schuster.

Jenkins, Steve. (1995). *Biggest, Strongest, Fastest.* New York: Ticknor & Fields Books.

Jenkins, Steve. (2004). *Actual Size.* Boston: Houghton Mifflin.

Jenkins, Steve, and Robin Page. (2003). *What Do You Do with a Tail Like This?* Boston: Houghton Mifflin.

Jiménez, Francisco. (1997). *The Circuit: Stories from the Life of a Migrant Child.* Boston: Houghton Mifflin.

Jiménez, Francisco. (1998). *La Mariposa.* Boston: Houghton Mifflin.

Jiménez, Francisco. (2001). *Breaking Through.* Boston: Houghton Mifflin.

Johnson, Angela. (1990). *Do Like Kyla.* New York: Orchard Books.

Johnson, Angela. (1990). *When I Am Old with You.* New York: Orchard Books.

Johnson, Angela. (1991). *Do You Love Me, Mama?* Illus. Barbara Lavallee. San Francisco: Chronicle Books.

Johnson, Angela. (2003). *The First Part Last.* New York: Simon & Schuster.

Johnson, D. B. (2000). *Henry Hikes to Fitchburg.* Boston: Houghton Mifflin.

Johnson, Dinah. (2000). *Quinnie Blue.* New York: Henry Holt.

Johnson, James Weldon. (1994). *The Creation.* Illus. James Ransome. New York: Holiday House.

Johnson, Lindsay Lee. (2002). *Soul Moon Soup.* Asheville, NC: Front Street.

Johnson, Stephen. (1996). *Alphabet City.* New York: Viking.

Johnson, Stephen. (2002). *As the City Sleeps.* New York: Viking.

Johnson, Stephen. (2003). *City by Numbers.* New York: Viking.

Johnson, Sylvia. (1999). *Mapping the World.* New York: Atheneum.

Jones, Bill T., and Susan Kuklin. (1998). *Dance.* New York: Hyperion.

Jones, Hettie. (1971). *The Trees Stand Shining: Poetry of the North American Indians.* Illus. Robert Andrew Parker. New York: Dial Books.

Jones, Rebecca C. (1991). *Matthew and Tilly.* Illus. Beth Peck. New York: Dutton.

Kadohata, Cynthia. (2004). *Kira-Kira.* New York: Atheneum.

Kalman, Maira. (2002). *Fireboat: The Heroic Adventures of the John J. Harvey.* New York: Putnam.

Kashmira, Sheth. (2002). *Blue Jasmine.* New York: Hyperion.

Kasza, Keiko. (2003). *My Lucky Day.* New York: Putnam.

Keenan, Sheila. (2000). *Gods, Goddesses and Monsters: A Book of World Mythology.* New York: Scholastic.

Kellogg, Steven. (1988). *Johnny Appleseed.* New York: Morrow.

Kendall, Carol. (1959). *The Gammage Cup.* San Diego: Harcourt.

Kendall, Carol. (2000). *The Whisper of Glocken: A Novel of the Minnipins.* Illus. Imero Gobotto. New York: Odyssey.

Kennedy, X. J. (2002). *Exploding Gravy: Poems to Make You Laugh.* Illus. Joy Allen. New York: Little, Brown.

Kennedy, X. J., and Dorothy Kennedy. (1992). *Talking Like the Rain: A First Book of Poems.* Illus. Jane Dyer. New York: Little, Brown.

Kennedy, X. J., and Dorothy Kennedy. (1999). *Knock at a Star: A Child's Introduction to Poetry.* (Rev. ed.) New York: Little, Brown.

Kerley, Barbara. (2001). *The Dinosaurs of Waterhouse Hawkins.* Illus. Brian Selznick. New York: Scholastic.

Kimmel, Eric. (1988). *Anansi and the Moss-Covered Rock.* Illus. Janet Stevens. New York: Holiday House.

Kimmel, Eric. (1993). *Anansi Goes Fishing.* Illus. Janet Stevens. New York: Holiday House.

Kimmel, Eric. (2004). *Cactus Soup.* Illus. Phil Huling. New York: Cavendish.

Kingsley, Charles. (1995). *The Water Babies.* New York: Puffin. (Original work published 1863)

King-Smith, Dick. (1985). *Babe, the Gallant Pig.* New York: Crown.

King-Smith, Dick. (1988). *Martin's Mice.* New York: Crown.

Koertge, Ron. (2003). *Shakespeare Bats Cleanup.* Cambridge, MA: Candlewick Press.

Koja, Kathe. (2003). *Buddha Boy.* New York: Foster Books.

Konigsburg, E. L. (2000). *Silent to the Bone.* New York: Atheneum.

Krauss, Ruth. (1981). *A Very Special House.* New York: Harper-Collins.

Krishnaswami, Uma. (2004). *Naming Maya.* New York: Farrar, Straus & Giroux.

Krull, Kathleen. (1996). *Wilma Unlimited: How Wilma Rudolph Became the World's Fastest Woman.* Illus. David Diaz. San Diego: Harcourt.

Kunhardt, Dorothy. (1940). *Pat the Bunny.* Racine, WI: Western.

Kurtz, Jane. (1998). *The Storyteller's Beads.* San Diego: Harcourt.

Kurtz, Jane. (2001). *Jakarta Missing.* New York: Greenwillow.

Kurtz, Jane. (2003). *Saba: Under the Hyena's Foot.* Middleton, WI: Pleasant Company.

Kurtz, Jane. (2004). *Memories of Sun: Stories of Africa and America.* New York: Greenwillow.

Kuskin, Karla. (1980). *Dogs and Dragons, Trees and Dreams.* New York: HarperCollins.

Kuskin, Karla. (2004). *Under My Hood I Have a Hat.* Illus. Fumi Kosaka. New York: Geringer Books.

La Fontaine, Jean de. (1987). *The Hare and the Tortoise.* Illus. Brian Wildsmith. New York: Oxford University Press.

Lagerlof, Selma. (1991). *The Wonderful Adventures of Nils.* Minneapolis, MN: Skandisk.

Lang, Andrew. (1994). *The Blue Fairy Book.* New York: Fine Communications.

Lasky, Kathryn. (1996). *Beyond the Burning Time.* New York: Scholastic.

Lasky, Kathryn. (1999). *Elizabeth I: Red Rose of the House of Tudor.* New York: Scholastic.

Lasky, Kathryn. (2003). *The Man Who Made Time Travel.* Illus. Kevin Hawkes. New York: Kroups Books.

Lawrence, Iain. (2001). *Lord of the Nutcracker Men.* New York: Delacorte Press.

Lawrence, Louise. (2002). *Children of the Dust.* London: Random House.

Lee, Marie G. (1996). *Necessary Roughness.* New York: Harper-Collins.

Leedy, Loreen, and Pat Street. (2003). *There's a Frog in My Throat! 440 Animal Sayings a Little Bird Told Me.* New York: Holiday House.

Le Guin, Ursula. (1968). *A Wizard of Earthsea.* Illus. Ruth Robbins. Boston: Houghton Mifflin.

Lehman, Barbara. (2004). *The Red Book.* Boston: Houghton Mifflin.

Leiner, Katherine. (2001). *Mama Does the Mambo.* Illus. Edel Rodriguez. New York: Hyperion.

L'Engle, Madeleine. (1962). *A Wrinkle in Time.* New York: Farrar, Straus & Giroux.

L'Engle, Madeleine. (1973). *A Wind in the Door.* New York: Farrar, Straus & Giroux.

L'Engle, Madeleine. (1978). *A Swiftly Tilting Planet.* New York: Farrar, Straus & Giroux.

Lessie, Pat. (1999). *Fablesauce: Aesop Reinterpreted in Rhymed Couplets.* Illus. Karen Gaudette. London: Haley's.

Lester, Julius. (1987). *The Tales of Uncle Remus: The Adventures of Brer Rabbit.* Illus. Jerry Pinkney. New York: Dial Books.

Lester, Julius. (1988). *More Tales of Uncle Remus: Further Adventures of Brer Rabbit, His Friends, Enemies, and Others.* Illus. Jerry Pinkney. New York: Dial Books.

Lester, Julius. (1990). *Further Tales of Uncle Remus: The Misadventures of Brer Rabbit, Brer Fox, Brer Wolf, the Doodang, and Other Creatures.* Illus. Jerry Pinkney. New York: Dial Books.

Lester, Julius. (1994). *John Henry.* Illus. Jerry Pinkney. New York: Dial Books.

Lester, Julius. (1999). *Uncle Remus: The Complete Tales.* Illus. Jerry Pinkney. New York: Fogelman Books.

Lester, Julius. (2000). *Pharaoh's Daughter: A Novel of Ancient Egypt.* San Diego: Harcourt.

Levine, Anna. (1999). *Running on Eggs.* New York: Cricket Books.

Levine, Gail Carson. (1997). *Ella Enchanted.* New York: Harper-Collins.

Levithan, David. (2003). *Boy Meets Boy.* New York: Knopf.

Levy, Constance. (2002). *Splash! Poems of Our Watery World.* Illus. David Soman. New York: Scholastic.

Lewis, C. S. (1994). *The Lion, the Witch, and the Wardrobe.* Illus. Pauline Baynes. New York: HarperCollins.

Lewis, J. Patrick. (1998). *Doodle Dandies: Poems That Take Shape.* Illus. Lisa Desimini. New York: Atheneum.

Lewis, J. Patrick. (1998). *Riddle-Lightful: Oodles of Little Riddle Poems.* Illus. Debbie Tilley. New York: Knopf.

Lewis, J. Patrick. (2002). *A World of Wonders: Geographic Travels in Verse and Rhyme.* Illus. Alison Jay. New York: Dial Books.

Lewis, J. Patrick. (2004). *Scien-Trickery: Riddles in Science.* San Diego: Silver Whistle.

Lewis, Richard. (1991). *All of You Was Singing.* Illus. Ed Young. New York: Atheneum.

Lewis, Rose. (2000). *I Love You like Crazy Cakes.* New York: Little, Brown.

Liestman, Vicki. (1991). *Columbus Day.* Minneapolis: Carolrhoda Books.

Lindbergh, Reeve. (1990). *Johnny Appleseed: A Poem.* Illus. Kathy Jacobsen. New York: Little, Brown.

Lisle, Janet Taylor. (2000). *The Art of Keeping Cool.* New York: Atheneum.

Livingston, Myra Cohn. (1991). *Lots of Limericks.* New York: McElderry Books.

Livingston, Myra Cohn. (1993). *Abraham Lincoln: A Man for All the People.* New York: Holiday House.

Livingston, Myra Cohn. (1994). *Keep on Singing: A Ballad of Marion Anderson.* New York: McElderry Books.

Llorente, Pilar Molina. (1994). *The Apprentice.* Trans. Robin Longshaw. Illus. Juan Ramon Alonso. New York: Farrar, Straus & Giroux.

Lobel, Anita. (2002). *One Lighthouse, One Moon.* New York: HarperCollins.

Lobel, Arnold. (1970). *Frog and Toad Are Friends.* New York: HarperCollins.

Lobel, Arnold. (1983). *The Book of Pigericks.* New York: Harper-Collins.

Lobel, Arnold. (1986). *The Random House Book of Mother Goose.* New York: Random House.

Longfellow, Henry Wadsworth. (2001). *The Midnight Ride of Paul Revere.* Illus. Chistopher Bing. New York: Handprint Books.

Look, Lenore. (1999). *Love as Strong as Ginger.* Illus. Stephen Johnson. New York: Atheneum.

Louie, Ai-Ling. (1982). *Yeh-Shen: A Cinderella Story from China.* Illus. Ed Young. New York: Philomel.

Lowry, Lois. (1989). *Number the Stars.* Boston: Houghton Mifflin.

Lowry, Lois. (1993). *The Giver.* Boston: Houghton Mifflin.

Lowry, Lois. (1999). *Zooman Sam.* Boston: Houghton Mifflin.

Lowry, Lois. (2000). *Gathering Blue.* Boston: Houghton Mifflin.

Lowry, Lois. (2003). *The Silent Boy.* Boston: Houghton Mifflin.

Lowry, Lois. (2004). *Messenger.* Boston: Houghton Mifflin.

Luján, Jorge. (2004). *Rooster/Gallo.* Trans. Elisa Amado. Illus. Manuel Monroy. Toronto: Groundwood Books.

Lunge-Larsen, Lise. (1999). *The Troll with No Heart in His Body.* Illus. Betsy Bowen. Boston: Houghton Mifflin.

Lunge-Larsen, Lise. (2004). *The Hidden Folk: Stories of Fairies, Dwarves, Selkies, and Other Secret Beings.* Illus. Beth Krommes. Boston: Houghton Mifflin.

Lunn, Janet. (2000). *The Hollow Tree.* New York: Viking.

Lyon, George Ella. (2004). *Weaving the Rainbow.* Illus. Stephanie Anderson. New York: Atheneum.

Lyons, Mary E. (1992). *Letters from a Slave Girl.* New York: Scribner.

Lyons, Mary E. (1995). *The Butter Tree: Tales of Bruh Rabbit.* Illus. Mireille Vautier. New York: Henry Holt.

Macaulay, David. (2003). *Mosque.* Boston: Houghton Mifflin.

MacDonald, George. (1989). *At the Back of the North Wind.* New York: Morrow. (Original work published 1871)

MacDonald, Ross. (2003). *Achoo! Bang! Crash! The Noisy Alphabet.* Brookfield, CT: Roaring Brook Press.

MacLachlan, Patricia. (1980). *Arthur, for the Very First Time.* New York: HarperCollins.

MacLachlan, Patricia. (1985). *Sarah, Plain and Tall.* New York: HarperCollins.

MacLachlan, Patricia. (1994). *Skylark.* New York: HarperCollins.

Maestro, Betsy. (1991). *The Discovery of the Americas.* New York: Lothrop, Lee & Shepard.

Mah, Adeline Yen. (1998). *Falling Leaves: The True Story of an Unwanted Chinese Daughter.* New York: Wiley.

Major, Kevin. (2004). *Ann and Seamus.* Illus. David Blackwood. Toronto: Groundwood Books.

Malory, Sir Thomas. (1988). *Le Morte d'Arthur.* New York: Random House. (Original work published 1485)

Manning, Maurie. (2003). *The Aunts Go Marching.* Honesdale, PA: Boyds Mills.

Mannis, Celeste. (2003). *The Queen's Progress: An Elizabethan Alphabet.* Illus. Bagram Ibatoulline. New York: Viking.

Marcus, Leonard. (2000). *Author Talk: Conversations with Judy Blume, Bruce Brooks, Karen Cushman, Russell Freedman, Lee Bennett Hopkins, James Howe, Johanna Hurwitz, E. L. Konigsburg, Lois Lowry, Ann M. Martin, Nicholasa Mohr, Gary Paulsen, Jon Scieszka, Seymour Simon, and Laurence Yep.* New York: Simon & Schuster.

Marcus, Leonard. (2001). *Side by Side: Five Favorite Picture-Book Teams Go to Work.* New York: Walker.

Mark, Jan. (2004). *Useful Idiots.* Oxford: David Fickling.

Markle, Sandra. (2000). *Outside and inside Dinosaurs.* New York: Atheneum.

Marrin, Albert. (2002). *Dr. Jenner and the Speckled Monster: The Search for the Smallpox Vaccine.* New York: Dutton.

Marsden, John. (1995). *Tomorrow, When the War Began.* Boston: Houghton Mifflin.

Marshall, James. (1988). *Goldilocks and the Three Bears.* New York: Dial Books.

Marshall, James. (2003). *Pocketful of Nonsense.* New York: Houghton Mifflin.

Martel, Yann. (2001). *The Life of Pi.* San Diego: Harcourt.

Martin, Ann. (2002). *A Corner of the Universe.* New York: Scholastic.

Martin, Ann. (2004). *Here Today.* New York: Scholastic.

Martin, Bill, Jr. (1992). *Brown Bear, Brown Bear, What Do You See?* New York: Henry Holt.

Martin, Bill, Jr., and John Archambault. (1989). *Chicka Chicka Boom Boom.* Illus. Lois Ehlert. New York: Simon & Schuster.

Martin, Jacqueline Briggs. (1998). *Snowflake Bentley.* Illus. Mary Azarian. Boston: Houghton Mifflin.

Martin, Rafe. (1985). *Foolish Rabbit's Big Mistake.* Illus. Ed Young. New York: Putnam.

Martin, Rafe. (1992). *The Rough-Face Girl.* Illus. David Shannon. New York: Putnam.

Martinez, Victor. (1996). *Parrot in the Oven: Mi Vida.* New York: HarperCollins.

Martini, Clem. (2004). *The Mob: Feather and Bone Chronicles.* Toronto: Kids Can Press.

Marx, Trish. (2000). *One Boy from Kosovo.* New York: HarperCollins.

Mathis, Sharon Bell. (1975). *The Hundred Penny Box.* Illus. Leo and Diane Dillon. New York: Viking.

Mbitu, Ngangur, and Ranchor Prime. (1997). *Essential African Mythology.* New York: Thorsons/Element.

McCaughrean, Geraldine. (2002). *Gilgamesh the Hero.* Illus. David Parkins. Grand Rapids, MI: Eerdmans.

McCaughrean, Geraldine. (2002). *My Grandmother's Clock.* Illus. Stephen Lambert. New York: Clarion.

McClintock, Barbara. (2002). *Dahlia.* New York: Farrar, Straus & Giroux.

McCloskey, Robert. (1941). *Make Way for Ducklings.* New York: Viking.

McCord, David. (1986). *One at a Time.* New York: Little, Brown. (Original work published 1977)

McCully, Emily Arnold. (1984). *Picnic.* New York: HarperCollins.

McCully, Emily Arnold. (1987). *School.* New York: HarperCollins.

McCully, Emily Arnold. (1988). *New Baby.* New York: HarperCollins.

McCully, Emily Arnold. (1992). *Mirette on the High Wire.* New York: Putnam.

McCully, Emily Arnold. (2004). *First Snow.* New York: HarperCollins.

McCully, Emily Arnold. (2004). *Squirrel and John Muir.* New York: Farrar, Straus, & Giroux.

McDermott, Gerald. (1994). *Coyote.* San Diego: Harcourt.

McDermott, Gerald. (2001). *Jabuti the Tortoise.* San Diego: Harcourt.

McDermott, Gerald. (2003). *Creation.* New York: Dutton.

McKay, Hilary. (1992). *The Exiles.* New York: McElderry Books.

McKay, Hilary. (1994). *The Exiles at Home.* New York: McElderry Books.

McKay, Hilary. (1998). *Exiles in Love.* New York: McElderry Books.

McKinley, Robin. (1997). *Rose Daughter.* New York: Greenwillow.

McKinley, Robin. (1999). *Beauty.* New York: HarperCollins.

McKinley, Robin. (2000). *Spindle's End.* New York: Putnam.

McKissack, Patricia. (1998). *Mirandy and Brother Wind.* Illus. Jerry Pinkney. New York: Knopf.

McKissack, Patricia, and Fredrick McKissack. (1994). *Christmas in the Big House, Christmas in the Quarters.* New York: Scholastic.

McKissack, Patricia, and Onawumi Jean Moss. (2004). *Precious and the Boo Hag.* Illus. Kyrsten Brooker. New York: Atheneum.

McMillan, Bruce. (1991). *Eating Fractions.* New York: Scholastic.

McMullan, Kate. (2004). *My Travels with Capts. Lewis and Clark by George Shannon.* New York: Colter Books.

Meltzer, Milton. (1990). *Columbus and the World around Him.* New York: Watts.

Meltzer, Milton. (1993). *Lincoln: In His Own Words.* San Diego: Harcourt.

Meltzer, Milton. (1995). *Frederick Douglass: In His Own Words.* San Diego: Harcourt.

Meyer, L. A. (2002). *Bloody Jack: Being an Account of the Curious Adventures of Mary "Jacky" Faber, Ship's Boy.* San Diego: Harcourt.

Meyer, L. A. (2004). *Curse of the Blue Tattoo: Being an Account of the Misadventures of Jacky Faber, Midshipman and Fine Lady.* San Diego: Harcourt.

Mikaelsen, Ben. (2002). *Red Midnight.* New York: HarperCollins.

Milnes, Gerald. (1990). *Granny Will Your Dog Bite and Other Mountain Rhymes.* Illus. Kimberly Bulcken Root. Little Rock, AR: August House.

Miranda, Anne. (1997). *To Market, to Market.* Illus. Janet Stevens. San Diego: Harcourt.

Mochizuki, Ken. (1993). *Baseball Saved Us.* Illus. Dom Lee. New York: Lee & Low Books.

Mohr, Nicholasa. (1979). *Felita.* New York: Dial Books.

Mohr, Nicholasa. (1985). *Nilda.* Houston, TX: Arte Público Press.

Mohr, Nicholasa. (1986). *Going Home.* New York: Dial Books.

Mohr, Nicholasa. (1988). *In Nueva York.* Houston, TX: Arte Público Press.

Mohr, Nicholasa. (1995). *The Magic Shell.* New York: Scholastic.

Mohr, Nicholasa. (1996). *Old Letivia and the Mountain of Sorrows.* Illus. Rudy Gutierrez. New York: Viking.

Montgomery, Sy. (1999). *The Snake Scientist.* Boston: Houghton Mifflin.

Montgomery, Sy. (2004). *The Tarantula Scientist.* Boston: Houghton Mifflin.

Moore, Lilian. (1969). *I Thought I Heard the City.* New York: Atheneum.

Moore, Lilian. (1996). *Something New Begins.* New York: Simon & Schuster.

Mora, Pat. (1992). *A Birthday Basket for Tía.* Illus. Cecily Lang. New York: Simon & Schuster.

Mora, Pat. (1994). *The Desert Is My Mother/El Desierto Es Mi Madre.* Illus. Daniel Lechón. Houston, TX: Piñata Books.

Mora, Pat. (1996). *Confetti: Poems for Children.* Illus. Enrique O. Sanchez. New York: Lee & Low Books.

Mori, Kyoki. (1993). *Shizuko's Daughter.* New York: Henry Holt.

Mori, Kyoki. (1995). *One Bird.* New York: Henry Holt.

Morley, Jacqueline. (1999). *Egyptian Myths.* Illus. Giovanni Caselli. Grand Rapids, MI: School Specialty Children's Publishing.

Morpurgo, Michael. (2003). *Kensuke's Kingdom.* New York: Scholastic.

Morpurgo, Michael. (2004). *Private Peaceful.* New York: Scholastic.

Morpurgo, Michael. (2004). *Sir Gawain and the Green Knight.* Cambridge, MA: Candlewick Press.

Morris, Gerald. (2003). *The Ballad of Sir Dinadan.* Boston: Houghton Mifflin.

Morris, Gerald. (2004). *The Prince, the Crone, and the Dung-Cart Knight.* Boston: Houghton Mifflin.

Morrison, Lillian. (1992). *Whistling the Morning In.* Illus. Joel Cook. Honesdale, PA: Boyds Mills.

Mosher, Richard. (2001). *Zazoo.* New York: Clarion.

Moss, Lloyd. (1995). *Zin! Zin! Zin! a Violin.* Illus. Marjorie Priceman. New York: Simon & Schuster.

Munsch, Robert. (1985). *The Paper Bag Princess.* Toronto: Annick Press.

Murphy, Jim. (2003). *An American Plague: The True and Terrifying Story of the Yellow Fever Epidemic of 1793.* New York: Clarion.

Murray, Martine. (2002). *The Slightly True Story of Cedar B. Hartley (Who Planned to Live an Unusual Life).* New York: Levine Books.

Muth, Jon. (2003). *Stone Soup.* New York: Scholastic.

Myers, Christopher. (2000). *Wings.* New York: Scholastic.

Myers, Walter Dean. (1988). *Fallen Angels.* New York: Scholastic.

Myers, Walter Dean. (1994). *The Glory Field.* New York: Scholastic.

Myers, Walter Dean. (1996). *Slam!* New York: Scholastic.

Myers, Walter Dean. (1997). *Harlem.* Illus. Christopher Myers. New York: Scholastic.

Myers, Walter Dean. (1999). *Monster.* New York: HarperCollins.

Myers, Walter Dean. (2000). *145th Street Stories.* New York: Delacorte Press.

Myers, Walter Dean. (2001). *Bad Boy.* New York: HarperCollins.

Myers, Walter Dean. (2003). *The Beast.* New York: Scholastic.

Myers, Walter Dean. (2003). *blues journey.* Illus. Christopher Myers. New York: Holiday House.

Myers, Walter Dean. (2004). *Here in Harlem.* New York: Holiday House.

Myers, Walter Dean. (2004). *Shooter.* New York: HarperCollins.

Na, An. (2001). *A Step from Heaven.* Asheville, NC: Front Street.

Naidoo, Beverly. (2003). *Out of Bounds: Seven Stories of Conflict and Hope.* New York: HarperCollins.

Namioka, Lensey. (1992). *Yang the Youngest and His Terrible Ear.* Boston: Joy Street Books.

Namioka, Lensey. (1994). *April and the Dragon Lady.* San Diego: Browndeer Press.

Namioka, Lensey. (1995). *Yang the Third and Her Impossible Family.* New York: Little, Brown.

Namioka, Lensey. (1998). *Yang the Second and Her Secret Admirers.* New York: Little, Brown.

Napoli, Donna Jo. (1993). *The Magic Circle.* New York: Dutton.

Napoli, Donna Jo. (1996). *Zel.* New York: Dutton.

Napoli, Donna Jo. (1999). *Crazy Jack.* New York: Delacorte Press.

Napoli, Donna Jo. (1999). *Spinners.* New York: Dutton.

Napoli, Donna Jo. (2000). *Beast.* New York: Atheneum.

Naylor, Phyllis Reynolds. (1991). *Shiloh.* New York: Simon & Schuster.

Neil, Philip. (1994). *King Midas.* Illus. Isabelle Brent. New York: Little, Brown.

Neil, Philip. (1995). *Songs Are Thoughts: Poems of the Inuit.* New York: Orchard Books.

Nelson, Marilyn. (2001). *Carver: A Life in Poems.* Asheville, NC: Front Street.

Nelson, Marilyn. (2005). *A Wreath for Emmett Till.* New York: Houghton Mifflin.

Newbery, John. (1765). *The Renowned History of Little Goody Two Shoes.* London: John Newbery.

Newbery, John. (1967). *A Little Pretty Pocket-Book: Intended for the Instruction and Amusement of Little Master Tommy and Pretty Miss Polly.* San Diego: Harcourt. (Original work published 1744)

Newth, Mette. (2000). *The Transformation.* New York: Farrar, Straus & Giroux.

Norton, Mary. (1953). *The Borrowers.* Illus. Beth and Joe Krush. San Diego: Harcourt.

Nye, Naomi Shihab. (Ed.). (1992). *This Same Sky: A Collection of Poems from around the World.* New York: Simon & Schuster.

Nye, Naomi Shihab. (1994). *Sitti's Secrets.* New York: Four Winds Press.

Nye, Naomi Shihab. (1997). *Habibi.* New York: Simon & Schuster.

Nye, Naomi Shihab. (1999). *What Have You Lost?* New York: HarperCollins.

Nye, Naomi Shihab. (Ed.). (2000). *Salting the Ocean: 100 Poems by Young Poets.* Illus. Ashley Bryan. New York: HarperCollins.

Nye, Naomi Shihab. (2002). *19 Varieties of Gazelle.* New York: Greenwillow.

O'Connell, Rebecca. (2003). *The Baby Goes Beep.* Illus. Ken Wilson-Max. Brookfield, CT: Roaring Brook Press.

O'Dell, Kathleen. (2004). *Ophie out of Oz.* New York: Dial Books.

O'Dell, Scott, and Elizabeth Hall. (1992). *Thunder Rolling in the Mountains.* Boston: Houghton Mifflin.

Olaleye, Isaac. (1995). *The Distant Talking Drum.* Honesdale, PA: Boyds Mills.

Olaleye, Isaac. (2000). *In the Rainfield: Who Is the Greatest?* Illus. Ann Grifalconi. New York: Scholastic.

Onyefulu, Ifeoma. (2001). *Saying Good-Bye: A Special Farewell to Mama Nkwelle.* Brookfield, CT: Millbrook Press.

Onyefulu, Ifeoma. (2002). *Here Comes Our Bride! An African Wedding.* New York: Pub Group West.

Opie, Iona. (1996). *My Very First Mother Goose.* Illus. Rosemary Wells. Cambridge, MA: Candlewick Press.

Opie, Iona. (1999). *Here Comes Mother Goose.* Illus. Rosemary Wells. Cambridge, MA: Candlewick Press.

Opie, Iona, and Peter Opie. (1951). *The Oxford Dictionary of Nursery Rhymes.* New York: Oxford University.

Opie, Iona, and Peter Opie. (1955). *The Oxford Nursery Rhyme Book.* New York: Oxford University.

Opie, Iona, and Peter Opie. (1988). *Tail Feathers from Mother Goose: The Opie Rhyme Book.* Illus. various artists. Boston: Houghton Mifflin.

Opie, Iona, and Peter Opie. (1992). *I Saw Esau: The Schoolchild's Pocket Book.* Illus. Maurice Sendak. Cambridge, MA: Candlewick Press.

Orgel, Doris. (2004). *The Bremen Town Musicians: And Other Animal Tales from Grimm.* Illus. Bert Kitchen. Brookfield, CT: Roaring Brook Press.

Orozco, Jose-Luis. (1994). *De Colores and Other Latin American Folk Songs for Children.* Illus. Elisa Kleven. New York: Dutton.

Osa, Nancy. (2003). *Cuba 15.* New York: Delacorte Press.

Osborne, Mary Pope. (1996). *Favorite Norse Myths.* New York: Scholastic.

Osborne, Mary Pope. (2000). *Kate and the Beanstalk.* Illus. Giselle Potter. New York: Atheneum.

Osborne, Mary Pope. (2002). *The Land of the Dead.* New York: Hyperion.

Osborne, Mary Pope. (2002). *The One-Eyed Giant.* New York: Hyperion.

Osborne, Mary Pope. (2003). *The Gray-Eyed Goddess.* New York: Hyperion.

Osborne, Mary Pope. (2003). *Sirens and Sea Monsters.* New York: Hyperion.

Osborne, Mary Pope. (2004). *Return to Ithaca.* New York: Hyperion.

Oswald, Nancy. (2004). *Nothing Here But Stones.* New York: Henry Holt.

Oxenbury, Helen. (1972). *ABC of Things.* New York: Delacorte Press.

Pak, Soyung. (2003). *Sumi's First Day of School Ever.* Illus. Joung Un Kim. New York: Viking.

Park, Linda Sue. (2000). *The Kite Fighters.* Illus. Eung Won Park. Boston: Houghton Mifflin.

Park, Linda Sue. (2001). *A Single Shard.* New York: Clarion.

Park, Linda Sue. (2002). *When My Name Was Keoko.* New York: Clarion.

Park, Van Dyke. (1987). *Jump Again! More Adventures of Brer Rabbit.* Illus. Barry Moser. San Diego: Harcourt.

Park, Van Dyke. (1989). *Jump on Over! The Adventures of Brer Rabbit and His Family.* Illus. Barry Moser. San Diego: Harcourt.

Park, Van Dyke, and Malcom Jones. (1986). *Jump! The Adventures of Brer Rabbit.* Illus. Barry Moser. San Diego: Harcourt.

Parkinson, Siobhan. (2003). *Kathleen: The Celtic Knot.* Illus. Troy Howell. Middleton, WI: Pleasant Company.

Parks, Rosa. (1992). *Rosa Parks: My Story.* New York: Dial Books.

Partridge, Elizabeth. (2000). *This Land Was Made for You and Me: The Life and Songs of Woody Guthrie.* New York: Viking.

Paterson, Katherine. (1976). *Bridge to Terabithia.* Illus. Donna Diamond. New York: HarperCollins.

Paterson, Katherine. (1994). *Flip-Flop Girl.* New York: Dutton.

Paterson, Katherine. (1999). *Preacher's Boy.* New York: Clarion.

Paulsen, Gary. (1987). *Hatchet.* New York: Atheneum.

Paulsen, Gary. (1996). *Brian's Winter.* New York: Delacorte Press.

Paulsen, Gary. (1999). *Brian's Return.* New York: Delacorte Press.

Pearce, Philippa. (1958). *Tom's Midnight Garden.* Philadelphia: Lippincott.

Pearson, Kit. (1990). *The Sky Is Falling.* New York: Viking.

Peck, Richard. (1998). *A Long Way from Chicago: A Novel in Stories.* New York: Dial Books.

Peck, Richard. (2000). *A Year down Yonder.* New York: Dial Books.

Peck, Richard. (2003). *The River between Us.* New York: Dial Books.

Perkins, Lynne Rae. (2002). *The Broken Cat.* New York: Greenwillow.

Perkins, Lynne Rae. (2003). *Snow Music.* New York: Greenwillow.

Perrault, Charles. (1954). *Cinderella.* New York: Scribner.

Peters, Lisa Westberg. (1988). *The Sun, the Wind and the Rain.* New York: Henry Holt.

Peters, Lisa Westberg. (2000). *Cold Little Duck, Duck, Duck.* Illus. Sam Williams. New York: Greenwillow.

Peters, Lisa Westberg. (2003). *Our Family Tree: An Evolution Story.* Illus. Lauren Stringer. San Diego: Harcourt.

Peterson, John Lawrence. (1967). *The Littles.* New York: Scholastic.

Pfeffer, Wendy. (2003). *Dolphin Talk: Whistles, Clicks, and Clapping Jaws.* New York: HarperCollins.

Pfeffer, Wendy. (2003). *Wiggling Worms at Work.* New York: HarperCollins.

Philbrick, Nathaniel. (2001). *In the Heart of the Sea: The Tragedy of the Whaleship* Essex. New York: Penguin Books.

Philbrick, Nathaniel. (2002). *Revenge of the Whale: The True Story of the Whaleship* Essex. New York: Putnam.

Pinkney, Andrea Davis. (1993). *Alvin Ailey.* Illus. Brian Pinkney. New York: Hyperion.

Pinkney, Jerry. (2000). *Aesop's Fables.* New York: North-South.

Plum-Ucci, Carol. (2000). *The Body of Christopher Creed.* San Diego: Harcourt.

Polacco, Patricia. (1994). *Firetalking!* Katonah, NY: Owen.

Polacco, Patricia. (1994). *Pink and Say.* New York: Philomel.

Polacco, Patricia. (1995). *Babushka's Mother Goose.* New York: Philomel.

Pollock, Penny. (1996). *The Turkey Girl: A Zuni Cinderella Story.* Illus. Ed Young. New York: Little, Brown.

Potter, Beatrix. (1902). *The Tale of Peter Rabbit.* New York: Warne.

Pratchett, Terry. (2003). *The Wee Free Men.* New York: HarperCollins.

Pratt, Kristin Joy. (1992). *A Walk in the Rain Forest.* Nevada City, CA: Dawn.

Pratt, Kristin Joy. (1994). *A Swim through the Sea.* Nevada City, CA: Dawn.

Prelutsky, Jack. (1974). *Circus.* Old Tappan, NJ: Macmillan.

Prelutsky, Jack. (1980). *The Headless Horseman Rides Tonight.* Illus. Arnold Lobel. New York: Greenwillow.

Prelutsky, Jack. (2003). *The Frogs Wore Red Suspenders.* Illus. Petra Mathers. New York: Greenwillow.

Prelutsky, Jack. (2004). *Scranimals.* Illus. Peter Sis. New York: Greenwillow.

Pressler, Mirjam. (1998). *Halinka.* Trans. Elizabeth D. Crawford. New York: Henry Holt.

Pressler, Mirjam. (2002). *Malka.* Trans. Brian Murdoch. New York: Philomel.

Price, Susan. (2000). *The Sterkarm Handshake.* New York: HarperCollins.

Price, Susan. (2004). *A Sterkarm Kiss.* New York: HarperCollins.

Pringle, Laurence. (1997). *Everybody Has a Belly Button.* Honesdale, PA: Boyds Mills Press.

Pringle, Laurence. (1997). *An Extraordinary Life: The Story of a Monarch Butterfly.* New York: Orchard Books.

Proddow, Penelope. (1979). *Art Tells a Story: Greek and Roman Myths.* New York: Doubleday.

Provensen, Alice. (1990). *The Buck Stops Here: The Presidents of the United States.* New York: HarperCollins.

Provensen, Alice, and Martin Provensen. (1976). *The Mother Goose Book.* New York: Random House.

Pullman, Philip. (1995). *The Golden Compass.* New York: Knopf.

Pullman, Philip. (1997). *The Subtle Knife.* New York: Knopf.

Pullman, Philip. (2000). *The Amber Spyglass.* New York: Knopf.

Pulver, Robin. (2003). *Punctuation Takes a Vacation.* New York: Holiday House.

Pyle, Howard. (1913). *Pepper and Salt.* New York: HarperCollins. (Original work published 1886)

Pyle, Howard. (2003). *The Wonder Clock.* New York: Doherty. (Original work published 1888)

Rappaport, Doreen. (2001). *Martin's Big Words: The Life of Dr. Martin Luther King.* Illus. Bryan Collier. New York: Hyperion.

Raschka, Chris. (2002). *John Coltrane's Giant Steps.* New York: Atheneum.

Rascol, Sabina. (2004). *The Impudent Rooster.* Illus. Holly Berry. New York: Dutton.

Rash, Andy. (2004). *Agent A to Agent Z.* New York: Levine Books.

Rathman, Peggy. (1995). *Officer Buckle and Gloria.* New York: Putnam.

Rathman, Peggy. (2003). *The Day the Babies Crawled Away.* New York: Putnam.

Ray, Deborah Kogan. (2004). *The Flower Hunter: William Bartram, America's First Naturalist.* New York: Farrar, Straus & Giroux.

Rayner, Mary. (1976). *Mr. and Mrs. Pig's Evening Out.* New York: Atheneum.

Recorvitz, Helen. (2003). *My Name Is Yoon.* Ill. Gabe Swiatkowska. New York: Farrar, Straus & Giroux.

Reiser, Lynn. (2003). *Ten Puppies.* New York: Greenwillow.

Ride, Sally, and Tam O'Shaughnessy. (2003). *Exploring Our Solar System.* New York: Crown.

Rinaldi, Ann. (1999). *My Heart Is on the Ground: The Diary of Nannie Little Rose, a Sioux Girl, Carlisle Indian School, PA 1880.* New York: Scholastic.

Roalf, Peggy. (1993). *Children.* New York: Hyperion.

Roalf, Peggy. (1993). *Flowers.* New York: Hyperion.

Robberecht, Thierry. (2004). *Angry Dragon.* Illus. Philippe Goossens. New York: Clarion.

Robbins, Ken. (1991). *Bridges.* New York: Dial Books.

Robbins, Ken. (2005). *Seeds.* New York: Atheneum.

Robinson, Sharon. (2004). *Promises to Keep: How Jackie Robinson Changed America.* New York: Scholastic.

Rockwood, Joyce. (2003). *To Spoil the Sun.* New York: Henry Holt. (Original work published 1976)

Rodowsky, Colby. (2003). *Not Quite a Stranger.* New York: Farrar, Straus & Giroux.

Rogers, Gregory. (2004). *The Boy, the Bear, the Baron, the Bard.* Brookfield, CT: Roaring Brook Press.

Rohmann, Eric. (2002). *My Friend Rabbit.* Brookfield, CT: Roaring Brook Press.

Root, Phyllis. (2002). *Big Momma Makes the World.* Illus. Helen Oxenbury. Cambridge, MA: Candlewick Press.

Rosenberg, Liz. (Ed.). (2001). *Roots and Flowers: Poets and Poems on Family.* New York: Henry Holt.

Rosenberg, Liz. (2002). *17: A Novel in Prose Poems.* Chicago: Cricket Books.

Rosenberry, Vera. (2004). *Vera Rides a Bike.* New York: Henry Holt.

Rosoff, Meg. (2004). *How I Live Now.* New York: Lamb Books.

Roth, Susan. (2004). *Hard Hat Area.* New York: Bloomsbury Children's Books.

Rounds, Glen. (1976). *Ol' Paul the Mighty Logger.* New York: Holiday House.

Rowling, J. K. (1998). *Harry Potter and the Sorcerer's Stone.* Illus. Mary Grandpré. New York: Scholastic.

Rowling, J. K. (1999). *Harry Potter and the Chamber of Secrets.* Illus. Mary Grandpré. New York: Scholastic.

Rowling, J. K. (1999). *Harry Potter and the Prisoner of Azkaban.* Illus. Mary Grandpré. New York: Scholastic.

Rowling, J. K. (2000). *Harry Potter and the Goblet of Fire.* Illus. Mary Grandpré. New York: Scholastic.

Rowling, J. K. (2003). *Harry Potter and the Order of the Phoenix.* Illus. Mary Grandpré. New York: Scholastic.

Rumford, James. (2004). *Sequoyah: The Cherokee Man Who Gave His People Writing.* Translated into Cherokee by Anna Sixkiller Huckaby. Boston: Houghton Mifflin.

Rupert, Janet. (1994). *The African Mask.* Boston: Houghton Mifflin.

Ryan, Pam Muñoz. (2002). *When Marian Sang: The True Recital of Marian Anderson, the Voice of a Century.* Illus. Brian Selznick. New York: Scholastic.

Ryder, Joanne. (1982). *The Snail's Spell.* New York: Warne.

Rylant, Cynthia. (1992). *Best Wishes.* Illus. Carlo Ontal. Katonah, NY: Owen.

Rylant, Cynthia. (1992). *Missing May.* New York: Orchard Books.

Sabuda, Robert. (1995). *Arthur and the Sword.* New York: Atheneum.

Sabuda, Robert. (2003). *Alice's Adventures in Wonderland: A Pop-Up Adaptation.* New York: Simon & Schuster.

Sachar, Louis. (1987). *There's a Boy in the Girls' Bathroom.* New York: Knopf.

Sachar, Louis. (1998). *Holes.* New York: Farrar, Straus & Giroux.

Sachar, Louis. (1999). *Marvin Redpost: A Flying Birthday Cake?* New York: Random House.

Saint-Exupéry, Antoine de. (1943). *The Little Prince.* San Diego: Harcourt.

San Souci, Robert D. (1989). *The Talking Eggs.* Illus. Jerry Pinkney. New York: Dial Books.

San Souci, Robert D. (1993). *Cut from the Same Cloth: American Women of Myth, Legend, and Tall Tale.* New York: Philomel.

Sanchez, Alex. (2001). *Rainbow Boys.* New York: Simon & Schuster.

Sanchez, Alex. (2003). *Rainbow High.* New York: Simon & Schuster.

Sandburg, Carl. (1990). *The American Songbag.* San Diego: Harcourt.

Say, Allen. (1991). *Tree of Cranes.* Boston: Houghton Mifflin.

Say, Allen. (1993). *Grandfather's Journey.* Boston: Houghton Mifflin.

Say, Allen. (1999). *Tea with Milk.* Boston: Houghton Mifflin.

Schmidt, Gary. (2001). *Mara's Stories: Glimmers in the Darkness.* New York: Henry Holt.

Schmidt, Gary. (2004). *Lizzie Bright and the Buckminster Boy.* New York: Clarion.

Schories, Pat. (2004). *Breakfast for Jack.* Asheville, NC: Front Street.

Schories, Pat. (2004). *Jack and the Missing Piece.* Asheville, NC: Front Street.

Schumacher, Julie. (2004). *Grass Angel.* New York: Delacorte Press.

Schwartz, Alvin. (1973). *Witcracks: Jokes and Jests from American Folklore.* Illus. John O'Brien. New York: HarperCollins.

Schwartz, Alvin. (1980). *Flapdoodle: Pure Nonsense from American Folklore.* New York: HarperCollins.

Schwartz, Alvin. (1990). *Whoppers: Tall Tales and Other Lies.* New York: HarperCollins.

Schwartz, Alvin. (1992). *And the Green Grass Grew All Around.* Illus. Sue Truesdell. New York: HarperCollins.

Schwartz, Amy. (2003). *What James Likes Best.* New York: Atheneum.

Schwartz, David M. (1998). *G Is for Googol: A Math Alphabet Book.* Berkeley, CA: Tricycle Press.

Schwartz, David M. (2001). *Q Is for Quark: A Science Alphabet Book.* Berkeley, CA: Tricycle Press.

Schwartz, David M. (2003). *Millions to Measure.* New York: HarperCollins.

Scieszka, Jon. (1989). *The True Story of the Three Little Pigs.* Illus. Lane Smith. New York: Viking.

Scieszka, Jon. (1992). *The Stinky Cheese Man and Other Fairly Stupid Tales.* Illus. Lane Smith. New York: Viking.

Scieszka, Jon. (1995). *Math Curse.* Illus. Lane Smith. New York: Viking.

Scieszka, Jon. (1999). *It's All Greek to Me.* New York: Viking.

Scieszka, Jon. (2004). *Science Verse.* Illus. Lane Smith. New York: Viking.

Segal, Lore, and Randall Jarrell. (Trans.). (1973). *The Juniper Tree and Other Tales from Grimm.* 2 vols. Illus. Maurice Sendak. New York: Farrar, Straus & Giroux.

Seidler, Tor. (2002). *Brothers below Zero.* New York: Geringer Books.

Sendak, Maurice. (1962). *Chicken Soup with Rice: A Book of Months.* New York: HarperCollins.

Sendak, Maurice. (1963). *Where the Wild Things Are.* New York: HarperCollins.

Sendak, Maurice. (1981). *Outside over There.* New York: HarperCollins.

Sewall, Marcia. (1990). *People of the Breaking Day.* New York: Atheneum.

Sfar, Joann. (2003). *Little Vampire Goes to School.* New York: Simon & Schuster.

Shange, Ntozake. (2004). *Ellington Was Not a Street.* Illus. Kadir Nelson. New York: Simon & Schuster.

Shannon, David. (1998). *No, David!* New York: Blue Sky Press.

Shannon, David. (1999). *David Goes to School.* New York: Blue Sky Press.

Shannon, David. (2002). *David Gets in Trouble.* New York: Blue Sky Press.

Shea, Pegi Dietz. (1995). *The Whispering Cloth.* Illus. Anita Riggio. Honesdale, PA: Caroline House.

Shea, Pegi Dietz. (2003). *Tangled Threads.* New York: Clarion.

Sherlock, Patti. (2004). *Letters from Wolfie.* New York: Viking.

Sheth, Kashmira. (2004). *Blue Jasmine.* New York: Hyperion.

Shyer, Marlene Fanta. (1978). *Welcome Home, Jellybean.* New York: Scribner.

Sidman, Joyce. (2003). *The World According to Dog: Poems and Teen Voices.* Photo. Doug Mindell. Boston: Houghton Mifflin.

Sierra, Judy. (1996). *Nursery Tales around the World.* New York: Clarion.

Simon, Seymour. (1992). *Mercury.* New York: Morrow.

Simon, Seymour. (1992). *Venus.* New York: Morrow.

Simon, Seymour. (1993). *Wolves.* New York: HarperCollins.

Simon, Seymour. (2000). *Destination: Mars.* New York: Harper-Collins. (Revised edition of *Mars,* originally published 1987)

Simon, Seymour. (2000). *Gorillas.* New York: HarperCollins.

Simon, Seymour. (2003). *The Moon.* New York: Simon & Schuster. (Original work published 1984)

Simon, Seymour. (2003). *Our Planet in Space.* New York: Simon & Schuster. (Original work published 1984)

Singer, Isaac Bashevis. (1968). *When Shlemiel Went to Warsaw and Other Stories.* Illus. Margot Zemach. New York: Farrar, Straus & Giroux.

Singer, Isaac Bashevis. (1976). *Naftali the Storyteller and His Horse, Sus.* Illus. Margot Zemach. New York: Farrar, Straus & Giroux.

Sis, Peter. (1994). *The Three Golden Keys.* New York: Doubleday.

Sis, Peter. (1996). *Starry Messenger: Galileo Galilei.* New York: Farrar, Straus & Giroux.

Sis, Peter. (2000). *Madlenka.* New York: Farrar, Straus & Giroux.

Sis, Peter. (2002). *Madlenka's Dog.* New York: Farrar, Straus, & Giroux.

Sis, Peter. (2003). *The Tree of Life: A Book Depicting the Life of Charles Darwin, Naturalist, Geologist and Thinker.* New York: Farrar, Straus & Giroux.

Sis, Peter. (2004). *The Train of States.* New York: Greenwillow.

Slobodkina, Esphyr. (1968). *Caps for Sale: The Tale of a Peddler, Some Monkeys, and Their Monkey Business.* Reading, MA: Young Scott Books.

Smith, Cynthia Leitich. (2000). *Jingle Dancer.* New York: Morrow.

Smith, Cynthia Leitich. (2001). *Rain Is Not My Indian Name.* New York: HarperCollins.

Smith, Cynthia Leitich. (2002). *Indian Shoes.* New York: Harper-Collins.

Snell, Gordon. (Ed.). (2001). *Thicker Than Water: Coming-of-Age Stories by Irish and Irish American Writers.* New York: Delacorte Press.

Sneve, Virginia Driving Hawk. (1972). *High Elk's Treasure.* Illus. Oren Lyons. New York: Holiday House.

Sneve, Virginia Driving Hawk. (1989). *Dancing Teepees: Poems of American Indian Youth.* Illus. Stephen Gammell. New York: Holiday House.

Sneve, Virginia Driving Hawk. (1994). *The Seminoles.* New York: Holiday House.

So, Meilo. (2004). *Gobble, Gobble, Slip, Slop: A Tale of a Very Greedy Cat.* New York: Knopf.

Soto, Gary. (1990). *Baseball in April and Other Stories.* San Diego: Harcourt.

Soto, Gary. (1990). *Fire in My Hands.* Illus. James M. Cardillo. New York: Scholastic.

Soto, Gary. (1992). *Neighborhood Odes.* Illus. David Diaz. San Diego: Harcourt.

Soto, Gary. (1993). *Local News.* San Diego: Harcourt.

Soto, Gary. (1995). *Canto Familiar.* San Diego: Harcourt.

Soto, Gary. (1995). *Chato's Kitchen.* Illus. Susan Guevara. New York: Putnam.

Soto, Gary. (1997). *Buried Onions.* San Diego: Harcourt.

Soto, Gary. (2003). *The Afterlife.* San Diego: Harcourt.

Souhami, Jessica. (2000). *No Dinner! The Story of the Old Woman and the Pumpkin.* New York: Cavendish.

Speare, Elizabeth George. (1958). *The Witch of Blackbird Pond.* Boston: Houghton Mifflin.

Speare, Elizabeth George. (1983). *Sign of the Beaver.* Boston: Houghton Mifflin.

Spiegelman, Art. (1986). *Maus: A Survivor's Tale. I: My Father Bleeds History.* New York: Pantheon.

Spinelli, Jerry. (2003). *Milkweed.* New York: Knopf.

Spires, Elizabeth. (1999). *Riddle Road: Puzzles in Poems and Pictures.* Illus. Erik Blegvad. New York: McElderry Books.

Spyri, Johanna. (1945). *Heidi.* New York: Grosset & Dunlap.

Stanley, Diane. (1992). *Bard of Avon: The Story of William Shakespeare.* New York: Morrow.

Stanley, Diane. (2002). *Saladin: Noble Prince of Islam.* New York: HarperCollins.

Staples, Suzanne Fisher. (1989). *Shabanu.* New York: Knopf.

Staples, Suzanne Fisher. (1993). *Haveli.* New York: Knopf.

Steig, Jeanne. (1998). *A Handful of Beans: Six Fairy Tales.* Illus. William Steig. New York: HarperCollins.

Steig, Jeanne. (2001). *A Gift from Zeus: Sixteen Favorite Myths.* Illus. William Steig. New York: HarperCollins.

Steig, Jeanne. (2004). *Tales from Gizzard's Grill.* Illus. Sandy Turner. New York: HarperCollins.

Steig, William. (1969). *Sylvester and the Magic Pebble.* New York: Windmill Books.

Steptoe, John. (1987). *Mufaro's Beautiful Daughters.* New York: Lothrop, Lee & Shepard.

Stevenson, James. (2003). *Corn Chowder.* New York: Greenwillow.

Stevenson, Robert Louis. (1905). *A Child's Garden of Verses.* Illus. Jessie Willcox Smith. Old Tappan, NJ: Macmillan.

Stewart, Sarah. (2004). *The Friend.* Illus. David Small. New York: Farrar, Straus, & Giroux.

St. George, Judith. (2000). *So You Want to Be President?* Illus. David Small. New York: Philomel.

Still, James. (1997). *Jack and the Wonder Beans.* New York: Putnam.

Strete, Craig Kee. (1974). *The Bleeding Man and Other Science Fiction Stories.* New York: Greenwillow.

Strete, Craig Kee. (1979). *When Grandfather Journeys into Winter.* Illus. Hal Frenck. New York: Greenwillow.

Strete, Craig Kee. (1990). *Big Thunder Magic.* New York: Greenwillow.

Strete, Craig Kee. (1995). *The World in Grandfather's Hands.* New York: Clarion.

Stuve-Bodeen, Stephanie. (1998). *Elizabeti's Doll.* Illus. Christy Hale. New York: Lee & Low Books.

Stuve-Bodeen, Stephanie. (2000). *Mama Elizabeti.* Illus. Christy Hale. New York: Lee & Low Books.

Sutcliff, Rosemary. (1992). *The Shining Company.* New York: Farrar, Straus & Giroux.

Sutcliff, Rosemary. (1993). *The Eagle of the Ninth.* New York: Farrar, Straus & Giroux.

Sutcliff, Rosemary. (1994). *The Lantern Bearers.* New York: Farrar, Straus & Giroux.

Swinburne, Stephen. (2002). *The Woods Scientist.* Boston: Houghton Mifflin.

Taback, Simms. (1999). *Joseph Had a Little Overcoat.* New York: Viking.

Taylor, Mildred. (1976). *Roll of Thunder, Hear My Cry.* New York: Dial Books.

Taylor, Mildred. (1981). *Let the Circle Be Unbroken.* New York: Dial Books.

Taylor, Mildred. (1985). *The Song of the Trees.* New York: Dial Books.

Taylor, Mildred. (1987). *The Friendship.* New York: Dial Books.

Taylor, Mildred. (1990). *Mississippi Bridge.* New York: Dial Books.

Taylor, Mildred. (1995). *The Well: David's Story.* New York: Dial Books.

Taylor, Mildred. (2001). *The Land.* New York: Fogelman Books.

Tchana, Katrin. (2002). *Sense Pass King: A Story from Cameroon.* Illus. Trina Schart Hyman. New York: Holiday House.

Temple, Frances. (1996). *The Beduin's Gazelle.* New York: Scholastic.

Terban, Marvin. (1988). *Guppies in Tuxedos: Funny Eponyms.* Illus. Giulio Maestro. Boston: Houghton Mifflin.

Thayer, Ernest Lawrence. (2000). *Casey at the Bat.* Illus. Christopher Bing. Brooklyn, NY: Handprint Books.

Thesman, Jean. (2004). *Singer.* New York: Viking.

Thimmesh, Catherine. (2004). *Madam President: The Extraordinary, True (and Evolving) Story of Women in Politics.* Boston: Houghton Mifflin.

Thomas, Joyce Carol. (1993). *Brown Honey in Broomwheat Tea.* Illus. Floyd Cooper. New York: HarperCollins.

Thomas, Joyce Carol. (1995). *Gingerbread Days: Poems.* New York: HarperCollins.

Thomas, Joyce Carol. (1998). *I Have Heard of a Land.* Illus. Floyd Cooper. New York: HarperCollins.

Thomas, Joyce Carol. (2000). *Hush Songs: African American Lullabies.* Illus. Brenda Joysmith. New York: Jump at the Sun.

Tillage, Leon Walter. (1997). *Leon's Story.* Illus. Susan L. Roth. New York: Farrar, Straus & Giroux.

Tolan, Stephanie. (2002). *Surviving the Applewhites.* New York: HarperCollins.

Townley, Roderick. (2001). *The Great Good Thing.* New York: Atheneum.

Townley, Roderick. (2002). *Into the Labyrinth.* New York: Atheneum.

Traill, Catharine Parr. (1985). *Canadian Crusoes: A Tale of the Rice Lake Plains.* Ontario: Carleton University Press. (Original work published 1852)

Trueman, Terry. (2000). *Stuck in Neutral.* New York: HarperCollins.

Trueman, Terry. (2004). *Cruise Control.* New York: HarperTempest.

Trueman, Terry. (2004). *Inside Out.* New York: HarperTempest.

Tucker, Jean. (1994). *Come Look with Me: Discovering Photographs with Children.* Charlottesville, VA: Thomasson-Grant.

Turner, Ann. (1987). *Nettie's Trip South.* Illus. Ronald Himler. Old Tappan, NJ: Macmillan.

Turner, Ann. (1990). *Through Moon and Stars and Night Skies.* New York: HarperCollins.

Turner, Ethel. (2004). *Seven Little Australians.* Available on the Web through Project Gutenberg, www.gutenberg.org/catalog. (Original work published 1894)

Uchida, Yoshiko. (1971). *Journey to Topaz.* New York: Scribner.

Uchida, Yoshiko. (1978). *Journey Home.* New York: Atheneum.

Ungerer, Tomi. (1991). *The Moon Man.* New York: Delacorte Press.

Van Allsburg, Chris. (1981). *Jumanji.* Boston: Houghton Mifflin.

Van Allsburg, Chris. (1984). *The Mysteries of Harris Burdick.* Boston: Houghton Mifflin.

Van Allsburg, Chris. (1985). *The Polar Express.* Boston: Houghton Mifflin.

Van Draanen, Wendelin. (2004). *Sammy Keyes and the Psycho Kitty Queen.* New York: Knopf.

Van Laan, Nancy. (1995). *Sleep, Sleep, Sleep: A Lullaby for Little Ones around the World.* Illus. Holly Meade. New York: Little, Brown.

Vecchione, Patrice. (2004). *Revenge and Forgiveness: An Anthology of Poems.* New York: Henry Holt.

Veciana-Suarez, Ana. (2002). *Flight to Freedom.* New York: Orchard Books.

Vincent, Gabrielle. (1999). *A Day, a Dog.* Asheville, NC: Front Street.

Voigt, Cynthia. (1981). *Homecoming.* New York: Atheneum.

Waddell, Martin. (2003). *Hi, Harry!* Illus. Barbara Firth. Cambridge, MA: Candlewick Press.

Waddell, Martin. (2004). *Tiny's Big Adventure.* Illus. John Lawrence. Cambridge, MA: Candlewick Press.

Wall, Dorothy. (1990). *Blinky Bill.* Sydney: Ingres & Robertson. (Original work published 1933)

Wallace, Rich. (1996). *Wrestling Sturbridge.* New York: Knopf.

Wallace, Rich. (1997). *Shots on Goal.* New York: Knopf.

Wallace, Rich. (2000). *Playing without the Ball.* New York: Knopf.

Wallace, Rich. (2003). *Losing Is Not an Option.* New York: Knopf.

Walsh, Ellen Stoll. (1989). *Mouse Paint.* San Diego: Harcourt.

Walsh, Jill Paton. (1986). *The Green Book.* New York: Farrar, Straus & Giroux.

Walsh, Jill Paton. (2004). *The Emperor's Winding Sheet.* Asheville, NC: Front Street.

Ward, Helen. (2004). *Unwitting Wisdom: An Anthology of Aesop's Fables.* San Francisco: Chronicle Books.

Warhola, James. (2003). *Uncle Andy's.* New York: Putnam.

Watkins, Yoko Kawashima. (1986). *So Far from the Bamboo Grove.* New York: Lothrop, Lee & Shepard.

Watkins, Yoko Kawashima. (1994). *My Brother, My Sister, and I.* New York: Bradbury.

Webb, Sophie. (2000). *My Season with Penguins: An Antarctic Journal.* Boston: Houghton Mifflin.

Webb, Sophie. (2004). *Looking for Seabirds: Journal from an Alaskan Voyage.* Boston: Houghton Mifflin.

Weeks, Sarah. (2004). *So B. It.* New York: Geringer Books.

Wein, Elizabeth. (1993). *The Winter Prince.* New York: Atheneum.

Wein, Elizabeth. (2003). *A Coalition of Lions.* New York: Viking.

Wein, Elizabeth. (2004). *The Sunbird.* New York: Viking.

Weitzman, Jacqueline Preiss, and Robin Preiss Glasser. (2000). *You Can't Take a Balloon into the National Gallery.* New York: Putnam.

Wells, Rosemary. (1979). *Max's First Word. Max's New Suit. Max's Ride.* (Boxed set of board books). New York: Dial Books.

Wells, Rosemary. (1991). *Max's Dragon Shirt.* New York: Dial Books.

Wells, Rosemary. (1995). *Lassie Come-Home: Eric Knight's Original 1938 Classic.* Illus. Susan Jeffers. New York: Henry Holt.

Wells, Rosemary. (2004). *My Kindergarten.* New York: Hyperion.

Whelan, Gloria. (2000). *Homeless Bird.* New York: HarperCollins.

White, E. B. (1952). *Charlotte's Web.* Illus. Garth Williams. New York: HarperCollins.

White, Ruth. (2000). *Memories of Summer.* New York: Farrar, Straus & Giroux.

White, Ruth. (2004). *Buttermilk Hill.* New York: Farrar, Straus & Giroux.

White, T. H. (1958). *The Once and Future King.* New York: Putnam.

Wiesner, David. (1991). *Tuesday.* New York: Clarion.

Wiesner, David. (1999). *Sector 7.* Boston: Houghton Mifflin.

Wiesner, David. (2001). *The Three Pigs.* New York: Clarion.

Willard, Nancy. (1989). *East of the Sun and West of the Moon.* Illus. Barry Moser. San Diego: Harcourt.

Willems, Mo. (2003). *Don't Let the Pigeon Drive the Bus!* New York: Hyperion.

Willems, Mo. (2004). *Knuffle Bunny: A Cautionary Tale.* New York: Hyperion.

Willems, Mo. (2004). *The Pigeon Finds a Hot Dog!* New York: Hyperion.

Willey, Margaret. (2001). *Clever Beatrice.* Illus. Heather M. Solomon. New York: Atheneum.

Willey, Margaret. (2004). *Clever Beatrice and the Best Little Pony.* Illus. Heather M. Solomon. New York: Atheneum.

Williams, Marcia. (2000). *Bravo, Mr. William Shakespeare!* Cambridge, MA: Candlewick Press.

Williams, Marcia. (2004). *Tales from Shakespeare.* Cambridge, MA: Candlewick Press.

Williams, Margery. (1991). *The Velveteen Rabbit.* Illus. William Nicholson. New York: Doubleday. (Original work published 1922)

Williams, Vera B. (2001). *Amber Was Brave, Essie Was Smart.* New York: Greenwillow.

Winter, Jeanette. (2000). *The House That Jack Built.* New York: Dial Books.

Winter, Jeanette. (2003). *Beatrix: Various Episodes from the Life of Beatrix Potter.* New York: Farrar, Straus & Giroux.

Winter, Jeanette. (2003). *Nino's Mask.* New York: Dial Books.

Winter, Jeanette. (2004). *September Roses.* New York: Farrar, Straus & Giroux.

Winter, Jeanette. (2005). *The Librarian of Basra: A True Story from Iraq.* San Diego: Harcourt.

Wisniewski, David. (1989). *The Warrior and the Wiseman.* New York: Lothrop, Lee & Shepard.

Wittlinger, Ellen. (2000). *What's in a Name?* New York: Simon & Schuster.

Wolf, Allan. (2004). *New Found Land: Lewis and Clark's Voyage of Discovery.* Cambridge, MA: Candlewick Press.

Wolff, Virginia Euwer. (1993). *Make Lemonade.* New York: Henry Holt.

Wolff, Virginia Euwer. (1998). *Bat 6.* New York: Scholastic.

Wolff, Virginia Euwer. (2001). *True Believer.* New York: Atheneum.

Wong, Janet. (1994). *Good Luck Gold: And Other Poems.* New York: McElderry Books.

Wong, Janet. (1996). *A Suitcase of Seaweed: And Other Poems.* New York: McElderry Books.

Wong, Janet. (2000). *Night Garden: Poems from the World of Dreams.* Illus. Julie Paschkis. New York: McElderry Books.

Woodson, Jacqueline. (1995). *From the Notebooks of Melanin Sun.* New York: Scholastic.

Woodson, Jacqueline. (1997). *The House You Pass on the Way.* New York: Delacorte Press.

Woodson, Jacqueline. (2000). *Miracle's Boys.* New York: Putnam.

Woodson, Jacqueline. (2001). *The Other Side.* Illus. E. B. Lewis. New York: Putnam.

Woodson, Jacqueline. (2004). *Coming on Home Soon.* Illus. E. B. Lewis. New York: Putnam.

Woodson, Jacqueline. (2004). *Locomotion.* New York: Puffin.

Worth, Valerie. (1987). *All the Small Poems and Fourteen More.* Illus. Natalie Babbitt. New York: Farrar, Straus & Giroux.

Worth, Valerie. (2002). *Peacock and Other Poems.* Illus. Natalie Babbitt. New York: Farrar, Straus & Giroux.

Wright, Blanche Fisher. (1916). *The Real Mother Goose.* New York: Rand/Checkerboard.

Wyndham, Robert. (Ed.). (1968). *Chinese Mother Goose Rhymes.* Illus. Ed Young. New York: Philomel.

Yang, Belle. (2004). *Hannah Is My Name.* Cambridge, MA: Candlewick Press.

Yates, Philip. (2003). *Ten Little Mummies: An Egyptian Counting Book.* Illus. G. Brian Karas. New York: Viking.

Yee, Lisa. (2003). *Millicent Min, Girl Genius.* New York: Levine Books.

Yee, Paul. (2004). *A Song for Ba.* Illus. Jan Peng Wang. Toronto: Groundwood Books.

Yenawine, Philip. (1991). *Lines.* New York: Museum of Modern Art.

Yep, Laurence. (1991). *The Star Fisher.* New York: Morrow.

Yep, Laurence. (1993). *Dragon's Gate.* New York: HarperCollins.

Yep, Laurence. (1995). *Thief of Hearts.* New York: HarperCollins.

Yep, Laurence. (1998). *The Case of the Lion Dance.* New York: HarperCollins.

Yep, Laurence. (1998). *The Cook's Family.* New York: Putnam.

Yep, Laurence. (2000). *Dream Soul.* New York: HarperCollins.

Yep, Laurence. (2003). *The Traitor: 1885.* New York: HarperCollins.

Yolen, Jane. (1980). *Commander Toad in Space.* New York: Putnam.

Yolen, Jane. (1987). *Owl Moon.* Illus. John Schoenherr. New York: Philomel.

Yolen, Jane. (1988). *The Devil's Arithmetic.* New York: Viking.

Yolen, Jane. (1991). *Wings.* San Diego: Harcourt.

Yolen, Jane. (1992). *Encounter.* Illus. David Shannon. San Diego: Harcourt.

Yolen, Jane. (1993). *Sleep Rhymes around the World.* Illus. native artists. Honesdale, PA: Boyds Mills.

Yolen, Jane. (1993). *Weather Report.* Illus. Annie Gusman. Honesdale, PA: Boyds Mills.

Yolen, Jane. (1995). *Alphabestiary.* Honesdale, PA: Boyds Mills.

Yolen, Jane. (1995). *Water Music.* Illus. Jason Stemple. Honesdale, PA: Boyds Mills.

Yolen, Jane. (1996). *Sky Scrape/City Scape.* Honesdale, PA: Boyds Mills.

Yolen, Jane. (1997). *Once upon Ice and Other Frozen Poems.* Photo. Jason Stemple. Honesdale, PA: Boyds Mills.

Yolen, Jane. (1998). *Snow, Snow: Winter Poems for Children.* Illus. Jason Stemple. Honesdale, PA: Boyds Mills.

Yolen, Jane. (2000). *Color Me a Rhyme: Nature Poems for Young People.* Illus. Jason Stemple. Honesdale, PA: Boyds Mills.

Yolen, Jane. (2000). *Not One Damsel in Distress: World Folktales for Strong Girls.* Illus. Susan Guevara. San Diego: Harcourt.

Yolen, Jane. (2003). *How Do Dinosaurs Say Goodnight?* Illus. Mark Teague. New York: Scholastic.

Yolen, Jane. (2003). *Sword of the Rightful King: A Novel of King Arthur.* San Diego: Harcourt.

Yolen, Jane. (2004). *Fine Feathered Friends.* Photo. Jason Stemple. Honesdale, PA: Boyds Mills.

Yolen, Jane. (Ed.). (1995). *Mother Earth Father Sky.* Illus. Jennifer Hewitson. Honesdale, PA: Boyds Mills.

Yolen, Jane, and Robert Harris. (2000). *The Queen's Own Fool: A Novel of Mary Queen of Scots.* Illus. Cynthia Von Buhler. New York: Philomel.

Yolen, Jane, and Robert Harris. (2002). *Girl in a Cage.* New York: Philomel.

Yolen, Jane, and Robert Harris. (2004). *Prince across the Water.* New York: Philomel.

Yorinks, Arthur. (1999). *The Alphabet Atlas.* Illus. Adrienne Yorinks. Delray Beach, FL: Winslow Press.

Young, Ed. (1989). *Lon Po Po: A Red Riding Hood Story from China.* New York: Philomel.

Young, Ed. (1992). *Seven Blind Mice.* New York: Philomel.

Young, Ed. (2004). *The Sons of the Dragon King: A Chinese Legend.* New York: Atheneum.

Zelinsky, Paul. (Reteller). (1986). *Rumpelstiltskin.* New York: Dutton.

Zelinsky, Paul. (1997). *Rapunzel.* New York: Dutton.

Zemach, Harve. (1973). *Duffy and the Devil: A Cornish Tale.* Illus. Margot Zemach. New York: Farrar, Straus & Giroux.

Zusak, Marcus. (2003). *Getting the Girl.* New York: Levine Books.

Text Credits

This page constitutes an extension of the copyright page. We have made every effort to trace the ownership of all copyrighted material and to secure permission from copyright holders. In the event of any question arising as to the use of any material, we will be pleased to make the necessary corrections in future printings. Thanks are due to the following authors, publishers, and agents for permission to use the material indicated.

CHAPTER 4

86: Paul Fleischman, *Joyful Noise: Poems for Two Voices.* Text copyright 1988 by Paul Fleischman. Used by permission of HarperCollins Publishers. **88:** "What Is Poetry?" by Eleanor Farjeon from *Poems for Children.* Copyright © 1936 by Eleanor Farjeon, renewed 1966 by Gervase Farjeon. **88:** Text copyright © 1970 by John Ciardi from *Someone Could Win a Polar Bear* by John Ciardi. Published by Boyds Mills Press, Inc. Reprinted by permission. **88:** "The Aardvarks" From *Mammalabilia,* copyright © 2000 by Douglas Florian, reproduced by permission of Harcourt, Inc. **89:** Text copyright © 1992 by Georgia Heard from *Creatures of Earth, Sea and Sky* by Georgia Heard. Published by Boyds Mills Press, Inc. Reprinted with permission. **89:** From *Fathers, Mothers, Sisters, Brothers* by Mary Ann Hoberman. Copyright © 1991 by Marilyn Hafner (illustrations). By permission of Little, Brown and Company (Inc.). **96:** Paul Fleischman, *Joyful Noise: Poems for Two Voices.* Text copyright 1988 by Paul Fleischman. Used by permission of HarperCollins Publishers. **99:** Copyright © 1996 by Jane Yolen. First appeared in *Sky Scrape/City Scape,* published by Boyds Mills Press. Reprinted by permission of Curtis Brown, Ltd. **100:** From *One at a Time* by David McCord. Copyright © 1925, 1929, 1931, 1941, 1949, 1952, 1961, 1962, 1965, 1966, 1968, 1970, 1971, 1972, 1973, 1974 by David McCord. By permission of Little, Brown and Company (Inc.). **100:** Reprinted with permission of David Harrison. **101:** From *One at a Time* by David McCord. Copyright © 1925, 1929, 1931, 1941, 1949, 1952, 1961, 1962, 1965, 1966, 1968, 1970, 1971, 1972, 1973, 1974 by David McCord. By permission of Little, Brown and Company (Inc.). **101:** Copyright © 1962, 1980 by Karla Kuskin. Reprinted by permission of Scott Treimel, NY. **102:** "Galoshes" from *Stories to Begin On* by Rhoda W. Bacmeister, illustrated by Tom Maley, copyright 1940 by E. P. Dutton, renewed © 1968 by Rhoda W. Bacmeister. Used by permission of Dutton Children's Books, a division of Penguin Putnam Books for Young Readers Group, a member of Penguin Group (USA) Inc., 345 Hudson Street, New York, NY 10014. All rights reserved. **102:** Reprinted with the permission of Simon & Schuster Books for Young Readers, an imprint of Simon & Schuster Children's Publishing Division from *Circus* by Jack Prelutsky. Copyright © 1974 Jack Prelutsky. **102:** Reprinted with the permission of Simon and Schuster Books for Young Readers, an imprint of Simon and Schuster Children's Publishing Division from *A Child's Garden of Verses* by Robert Louis Stevenson (NY, 1999). **103:** From *It Doesn't Always Have to Rhyme* by Eve Merriam. Copyright © 1964, 1992 Eve Merriam. Used by permission of Marian Reiner. **103:** Text copyright © 1992 by Lillian Morrison from *Whistling the Morning In* by Lillian Morrison. Pub-

lished by Boyds Mills Press, Inc. Reprinted by permission. **103:** From *I Thought I Heard the City* by Lilian Moore. Copyright © 1969, 1997 Lilian Moore. Used by permission of Marian Reiner for the author. **104:** "Dandelion" from *All the Small Poems and Fourteen More* by Valerie Worth. Copyright © 1987, 1994 by Valerie Worth. Used by permission of Farrar, Straus, and Giroux, LLC. **104:** Text copyright © 1986 by Barbara Juster Esbensen from *Words with Wrinkled Knees* by Barbara Juster Esbensen. Published by Boyds Mills Press, Inc. Reprinted by permission. **104–105:** Text copyright © 1992 by Georgia Heard, Illustrations Copyright © 1992 by Jennifer Owings Dewey, from *Creatures of the Earth, Sea, and Sky.* Published by Wordsong, Boyds Mills Press, Inc. Reprinted by permission. **107–108:** Reprinted by Harold Ober Associates Incorporated. Copyright © 1957 by Eleanor Farjeon. From *The Children's Bells.* **109:** "Possibilities" and "Pond" from *Fold Me a Poem,* text copyright © 2005 by Kristine O'Connell George, reprinted by permission of Harcourt, Inc. **111:** Copyright © 2000 by Jane Yolen. First appeared in *Stone Bench in an Empty Park,* published by Scholastic, Inc. Reprinted by permission of Curtis Brown, Ltd. **111:** Copyright © 2000 by Anita Wintz. Used by permission of Marian Reiner for the author. **111:** From *One at a Time* by David McCord. Copyright © 1925, 1929, 1931, 1941, 1949, 1952, 1961, 1962, 1965, 1966, 1968, 1970, 1971, 1972, 1973, 1974 by David McCord. By permission of Little, Brown and Company (Inc.). **111:** Kobayashi Issa, *Don't Tell the Scarecrow.* **112:** *A Poke in the I,* by Joan Bransfield Graham from *Splish Splash.* Copyright © 1994 Houghton Mifflin Co. **113:** James Marshall, *Pocketful of Nonsense.* Copyright © 2003 Houghton Mifflin Co.

CHAPTER 5

135: Published with permission of Rafe Martin. **22:** "Tougher Tank Armor Developed by Pentagon" by George C. Willson. *The Washington Post,* March 15, 1988. © 1988, The Washington Post. Reprinted with permission.

CHAPTER 6

168: From DiCamillo, K. (2002). "Look, Listen, Lie." *A View from the Loft,* 25(8), 4–5. Reprinted with permission.

CHAPTER 7

192: Published with permission of Patricia Reilly Giff.

CHAPTER 8

207: Published with permission of Avi Wortis.

CHAPTER 10

267: Published with permission of Lisa Westberg Peters. **268:** Published with permission of Lauren Stringer.

Illustration and Photo Credits

Penguin Putnam, Inc. **70:** From *Vera Rides a Bike* by Vera Rosenberry, copyright © 2004. Used by permission of Henry Holt and Company. **71:** *Elizabeth's Doll*, text copyright © 1998 by Stephanie Stuve-Bodeen. Illustrations © 1998 by Christy Hale. Permission arranged with Lee & Low Books, Inc., New York, NY 10016. **74, 75 top/bottom, 76:** *The Tale of Peter Rabbit* by Beatrix Potter. Copyright © Frederick Warne & Co., 1902, 1987. Reproduced by kind permission of Frederick Warne.

CHAPTER 4

88: Illustration from *Mammalabilia*, copyright © 2000 by Douglas Florian, reproduced by permission of Harcourt, Inc. **89:** Illustration copyright © 1993 by Jennifer Owings Dewey from *Creatures of Earth, Sea and Sky* by Georgia Heard. Published by Wordsong/BoydsMills Press, Inc. Reprinted by permission. **90:** Cover from *Carver, A Life in Poems* by Marilyn Nelson, copyright © 2001 by Marilyn Nelson. Used by permission of Front Street Books. **92 bottom:** Cover from *A Jar of Tiny Stars*, edited by Bernice E. Cullinan, copyright © 1996 Boyds Mills Press and NCTE. Used by permission of Boyds Mills Press and NCTE. **92 top:** National Council of Teachers of English. **93 center:** © Thomas V. Crowell. **93 left:** Courtesy Little, Brown and Company. **93 right:** Courtesy HarperCollins Publishers. **95 center:** Bachrach. **95 left:** Marilyn Sanders. **95 right:** Courtesy Houghton Mifflin Company. **97:** Cover from *Joyful Noise* by Paul Fleischman, cover illustration copyright © 1988 by Eric Beddows. Used by permission of Harper-Collins Publishers. **98 center:** Courtesy HarperCollins Publishers. **98 left:** Courtesy HarperCollins Publishers. **98 right:** © Temple Studios. **101:** Text copyright © 1996 by Jane Yolen. Illustrations copyright © 1996 by Ken Condon from *Sky Scrape City Scrape* by Jane Yolen. Published by Wordsong/Boyds Mills Press, Inc. Reprinted by permission. **104:** Illustration copyright © 1993 by Jennifer Owings Dewey from *Creatures of Earth, Sea and Sky* by Georgia Heard. Published by Wordsong/BoydsMills Press, Inc. Reprinted by permission. **106 left:** Courtesy HarperCollins Publishers. **106 right:** Courtesy HarperCollins Publishers. **107 left:** Courtesy Curtis Brown, Ltd. **107 right:** © Photo by Helen Neafsey. **108:** Cover from *Here in Harlem: Poems in Many Voices* by Walter Dean Meyers, copyright © 2004 by Walter Dean Myers. All rights reserved. Reprinted by permission of Holiday House, Inc. **109:** "Possibilities," "Pond," and illustrations that accompany the poems from *Fold Me a Poem*, text copyright © 2005 by Kristine O'Connell George, illustrations copyright © 2005. Reprinted by permission of Harcourt Inc. **111:** From *Stone Bench in an Empty Park* by Paul B. Janeczko, photographs by Henri Silberman. Published by Orchard Books, an imprint of Scholastic, Inc. Text copyright © 2000 by Paul B. Janeczko, photographs copyright © 2000 by Henri Silberman. **112:** *A Poke in the I*. Illustrations, copyright © 2001 Chris Raschka. This collection copyright © 2001 Paul B. Janeczko. Reproduced by permission of the publisher, Candlewick Press, Cambridge, MA. **113:** "Old Man of Peru" by James Marshall from *Pocketful of Nonsense* copyright © 1993 by James Marshall. Illustrations © 1992 by James Marshall. Reprinted by permission of Houghton Mifflin Company. All rights reserved.

CHAPTER 5

132: Illustration from *The Rough-Face Girl* by Rafe Martin and David Shannon, text copyright © 1992 by Rafe Martin, illustrations copyright © 1992 by David Shannon. Reprinted by permission of A PaperStar Book, Penguin Putnam Books for Young Readers. **133:** Courtesy Scholastic. **134:** Illustration from *The Rough-Face Girl* by Rafe Martin and David Shannon, text copyright © 1992 by Rafe Martin, illustrations copyright © 1992 by David Shannon. Reprinted by permission of A PaperStar Book, Penguin Putnam Books for Young Readers. **138:** Illustrations copyright © 1994 by Boyds Mills Press from *Sleep Rhymes around the World* edited by Jane Yolen. Published by Wordsong/Boyds Mills Press, Inc. Reprinted by permission. **139:** From *Clever Beatrice and the Best Little Pony* by Margaret Willey. Illustration copyright © 2001 by Heather Solomon. Used with per-

mission of Atheneum Books for Young Readers, an imprint of Simon & Schuster Children's Publishing. **141:** Cover from *The Hidden Folk: Stories of Fairies, Dwarves, Selkies and Other Secret Beings* by Lise Lunge-Larsen. Illustrated by Beth Krommes. Jacket art copyright © 2004 by Beth Krommes. Reprinted by permission of Houghton Mifflin Company. All rights reserved. **143:** Illustration from *Mufaro's Beautiful Daughters* by John Steptoe, copyright © 1987. Used by permission of Harper & Row Junior Books, an imprint of HarperCollins Publishers. **144:** Illustration by Leo and Diane Dillon from *The Girl Who Spun Gold* by Virginia Hamilton. Published by the Blue Sky Press, an imprint of Scholastic, Inc. Illustration copyright © 2000 by Leo & Diane Dillon. Reprinted with permission. **145:** From *Unwitting Wisdom* by Helen Ward, copyright © 2005 Helen Ward. Used with permission from Chronicle Books LLC, San Francisco. Please visit www.ChronicleBooks.com. **147:** Illustration from *A Gift from Zeus* by William Steig. Illustration copyright © 2001 by Jeanne Steig. Used by permission of HarperCollins Publishers. **148:** From the book *Dateline: Troy* by Paul Fleischman. Illustrations copyright © 1996 by Gwen Frankfeldt & Glenn Morrow. Reprinted by permission of the publisher Candlewick Press, Cambridge, MA. **150:** Cover from *The Sons of the Dragon King* by Ed Young. Illustration copyright © 2004 by Ed Young. Used with permission of Atheneum Books for Young Readers, an imprint of Simon & Schuster Children's Publishing. **151:** From *Wings* by Christopher Myers. Published by Scholastic Press, a division of Scholastic, Inc. Copyright © 2000 by Christopher Myers. Reprinted with permission.

CHAPTER 6

165: Reprinted with permission of Margaret K. McElderry Books, an imprint of Simon & Schuster Children's Publishing Division, from *The Dark Is Rising* by Susan Cooper. Illustrated by Alan E. Cober. Illustrations copyright © Alan E. Cober. **167:** Cover from *The Tale of Despereaux* by Kate DiCamillo, illustrations copyright © 2003 by Timothy Basil Ering. Used by permission of Candlewick Press, Inc. **168:** Courtesy Candlewick Press, Cambridge, MA. **170:** © Harold Farmer. Photo of Nancy Farmer used with permission of Simon & Schuster, Inc. **172:** Cover from *The House of the Scorpion* by Nancy Farmer. Copyright © 2002. Used with permission of Richard Jackson Books/Atheneum Books for Young Readers, an imprint of Simon & Schuster Children's Publishing. **174:** Illustration from *The Wee Free Men: A Story of Discworld* by Terry Pratchett. Illustrations copyright © 2003 by Chris Gall. Used by permission of HarperCollins Publishers. **175:** Jacket illustration from *Tuck Everlasting* by Natalie Babbitt. Jacket illustration copyright © 1975 by Natalie Babbit. Used by permission of Farrar, Straus & Giroux, LLC. All rights reserved. **176:** Cover from *The Great Good Thing* by Roderick Townley, illustration copyright © 2001 Stephanie Anderson. Used with permission of Atheneum Books for Young Readers, an imprint of Simon & Schuster Children's Publishing. **179:** Cover from *The Giver* by Lois Lowry. Copyright © 1993 by Lois Lowry. Reprinted by permission of Houghton Mifflin Company. All rights reserved.

CHAPTER 7

191: Cover from *Pictures of Hollis Woods* by Patricia Reilly Giff, copyright © 2002 by Patricia Reilly Giff. Used by permission of Random House, Inc. **192:** © Tim Keating. **194:** From *Owl Moon* by Jane Yolen, illustrated by John Schoenherr, copyright © 1987 by John Schoenherr. Used with permission of Philomel Books, an imprint of Penguin Putnam Books for Young Readers, a division of Penguin Putnam, Inc. **197:** Cover from *Shiloh* by Phyllis Reynolds Naylor. Jacket illustration by Lynne Dennis. Copyright © 1991 Lynne Dennis. Reprinted with permission of Dilys Evans Fine Illustration. **199:** Cover illustration from *Olive's Ocean* by Kevin Henkes. Illustrations copyright © 2003. Used by permission of HarperCollins Publishers. **200:** Cover from *Buddha Boy* by Kathe Koja, illustration copyright © 2003 by Rick Lieder. Used by permission of Farrar, Straus and Giroux.

Author and Title Index

Note: Titles of books are listed in italic and boldface type.

Subject Index